Painting and Photography

Translated from the French
by David Radzinowicz
Design: Amélie Boutry
Copyediting: Penelope Isaac
Typesetting: Gravemaker+Scott
Proofreading: Chrisoula Petridis
Color Separation: Bussière Arts Graphiques, Paris
Printed in Portugal by Printer Portuguesa

Simultaneously published in French as
Peinture & Photographie. Les enjeux d'une rencontre, 1839–1914

English-language edition

editions.flammarion.com

12 13 14 3 2 1

ISBN: 978-2-08-020132-4

Dépôt légal: 10/2012

Dominique de Font-Réaulx

Painting and Photography

1839–1914

Flammarion

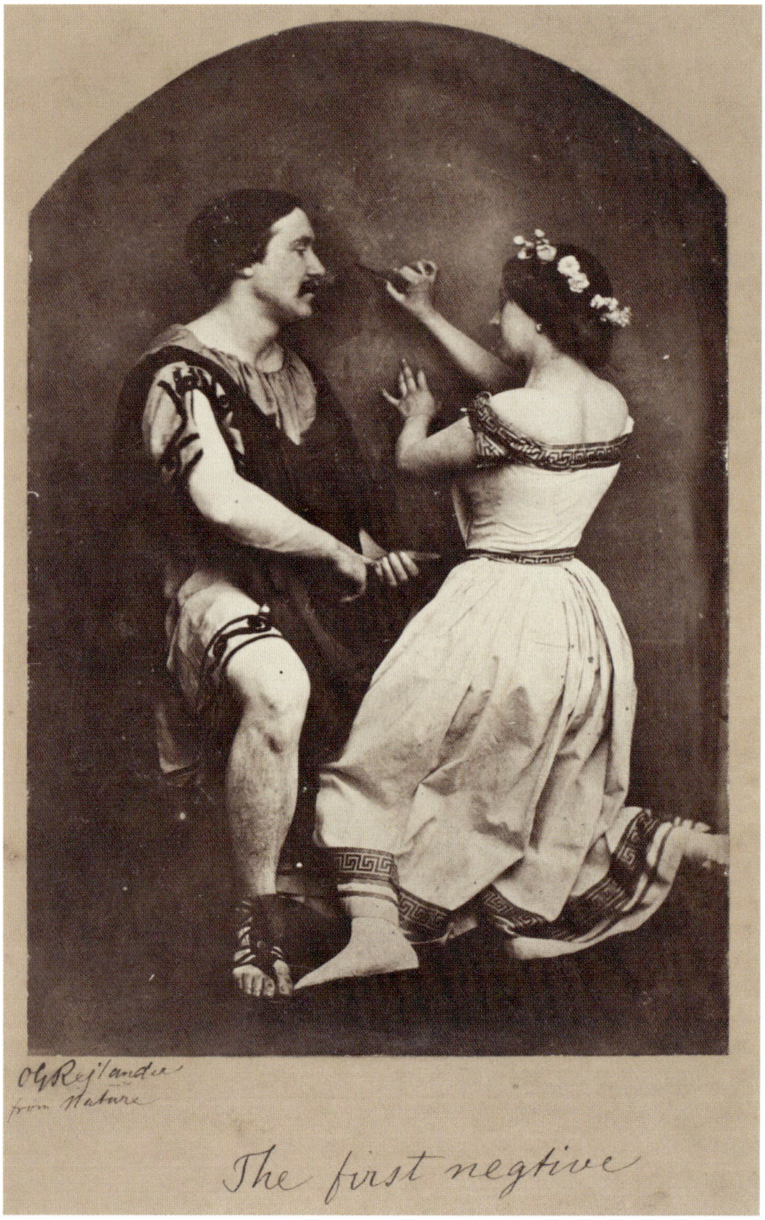

Oscar Gustav Rejlander, "The First Negative," 1857, albumen print, Musée d'Orsay, Paris.

CONTENTS

INTRODUCTION

"Initially hailed with enthusiasm, photography, like all inventions, has since stirred up a storm of criticism. Undoubtedly with the best intentions, certain minds see this admirable discovery as posing a danger for art; they were afraid lest the human hand might forget its skill, knowing that a machine exists that can do its work. As we will presently show this fear is without foundation. Besides, photography is not—as has too readily been believed—a simply chemical operation. All that man touches receives his imprint; the soul transpires in every ray: in an exhibition comprised of heliographic prints from various countries, each nationality can be recognized easily." [1]

Published in 1857, Théophile Gautier's article began by imagining the astonishment a man born in 1800 would have felt if "marooned at the age of fifteen on some Pacific island, and then brought back by chance aboard ship into the midst of our civilization." How absolutely amazed this Robinson would be, Gautier suggests, to have witnessed the inventions that had come into being since his shipwreck: the steam engine, the telegraph, and, particularly, photography, which made it possible "to purloin and fix images produced by the sun." Announced in 1839 in France by François Arago, in scarcely twenty years the new process had evolved beyond recognition. By introducing a new method of representing reality, in the field of art it occasioned as much enthusiasm and aspiration as apprehension. To allot this new arrival a position with respect to painting was no easy task, and the artistic ambition of many early photographers struggled long and hard against the ancillary role to which others thought it should be confined.

The present work is not a history of photography in the nineteenth century; neither does it purport to examine every issue surrounding its invention. Several studies of quality already provide readers with well-judged, sometimes brilliant analyses.[2] Beyond establishing parallels between certain painted works and photographs, our desire has been to outline exactly what the encounter between pictorial art in the nineteenth century and the invention of photography entailed. Our project has no intention of being encyclopedic; anyway, the number of prints and negatives rediscovered in recent years, and the countless studies to which they have given rise, would render such an ambition unrealistic. Neither is our analysis intended to vouchsafe the last word on the subject. The discipline is very much alive and its corpus constantly expanding; it is no less crucial to pave the way for more thorough investigations that might enrich or expand its scope. Interdisciplinary, the history of the links between painting and photography has also been nourished—as well as marred—by the diverse appreciations of the photographic invention. In France, in particular, the acceptance of photography in painting circles (in schools and museums, and by the Academy) was a painfully slow and far from linear process. Up to relatively recent times, many art historians ignored—indeed, sometimes obfuscated—the place and role played by photography in the creative processes of many painters. They skirted around, or even refused to examine, the contribution made by images created by photographic techniques to aesthetic representation. Work in this field is, however, far from being a recent development; as early as the 1930s, a number of historians of photography—Georges Potonniée in particular—as well as several French collectors—notably, Gabriel Cromer—sought to bring out the artistic quality of the new process. The conspectus organized in 1936 in the Pavillon de Marsan at the Louvre testified to their desire to obtain recognition for the invention.[3] Though in the United States Alfred H. Barr's Museum of Modern Art was already allotting a distinguished place to photography, the confused presentation of the Paris event, its sheer scale, as well as the difficult circumstances at the time meant that it failed to meet with the hoped-for success. In fact it was in libraries rather than in museums that groundbreaking advances in the field took place. The role of Jean Adhémar, curator in the Prints Department of the Bibliothèque Nationale, proved crucial; in 1955, in the ambit of the Biennale de l'Image, it was Adhémar who conceived the first significant exhibition at which paintings and photographs hung side by side. Under the evocative title of *A Century of the New Vision* it presented works by Gustave Courbet, Édouard Manet, Claude Monet, and Edgar Degas, cheek by jowl with photographs by Gustave Le Gray, Julien de Vallou de Villeneuve, Félix-Jacques Moulin, and Nadar. Adhémar's influence, as André Jammes has recalled, proved determinant for collectors and historians alike.[4] By creating two curator posts in his department—by then known as the Department of Prints and Photographs—and by embarking on the classification by author of the library's enormous holdings (more than one million images entered through copyright registration from 1852 and were formerly classified in thematic series established by the institution), Adhémar thus drew up the parameters for subsequent working methods. Although he is mentioned only cursorily in the bibliography, Aaron Schaaf's *Art and Photography*, published in London in 1968, also owes a great deal to Adhémar. He was also the spur behind the opening of photography departments in two flagship French museums either tabled or under construction in the 1970s: the Musée National d'Art Moderne, in its new home in Beaubourg in 1977, and the Musée d'Orsay, founded in 1979. In the Musée d'Orsay, the constitution of the collection by Philippe Néagu and Françoise Heilbrun, its active exhibitions policy (in particular the splendid and subtle *Invention d'un Regard* show of 1989, curated in collaboration with Bernard Marbot), and its many publications concerning photography enshrined the art as a museological entity.

This book thus offers due homage to Jean Adhémar, and also to his successors at the head of the Department of Prints and Photography, in particular to Laure Beaumont-Maillet and Sylvie Aubenas. It is they who, by receiving me into the institution and by proposing I should assist in the 1997 exhibition *L'Art du nu au XIXe siècle, le photographe et son modèle* (The Art of the Nude in the Nineteenth Century: The Photographer and his Model),[5] one of the first events held in the new building on quai François Mauriac—provided me with the initial impetus to explore some of the links between painting and photography.

The present volume has an agenda: it concentrates less on immediate links between a photo and a given work of painting or drawing, than on the manner in which photography gave rise to a paradigm of representation at once original yet familiar. The heart of the matter concerns how the creation of new images could spawn a whole new repertory of art. Proceeding by pictorial genre clearly brings out just how the artistic ambitions of photographers made them respectful of the genre divide. It also highlights how their work could navigate these barriers, transgress them even, and thus transform the whole visual art tradition. Naturally, in subsequent studies, it may well prove advisable to loosen this approach. While it is not the intent of this book to serve as a history of nineteenth-century painting, it is nonetheless designed—in the manner of Peter Galassi at the Museum of Modern Art in the early 1980s—to focus on what in the evolution of painting early in the century rendered the invention and diffusion of photography conceivable.[6]

The magnetism exerted by Paris on artists throughout Europe and indeed the Western world in the nineteenth century, as well as the significant developments by the French in the field of photography during this period, have led me to focus the present study predominantly on events in France. The subject is, however, an international one, and the references to Great Britain, to the United States, and, occasionally, to Germany and Italy could, of course, be further developed and extended to other Western countries.

Above and beyond the connections between photography and painting, there also transpires a less obvious relationship with the theater. Like painting, drama and stagecraft underwent major upheavals in the first half of the nineteenth century. These relate as much to questions of genre—the shift from classical tragedy to romantic drama—as to acting style, the realism of the sets, and the implication of the playwright. Nascent photography was also closely linked to the ambitions of contemporary theater, and to the search for emotional response and illusionistic virtuosity that underlay both arts. Louis Jacques Mandé Daguerre, for instance, one of the inventors of photography, played an important part in the revival of the theater. As Stephen Pinson's long-awaited publication has recently demonstrated, Daguerre's determination to control lighting effects had repercussions on all his endeavors, from opera and stage design to the diorama and the daguerreotype. It was his striving for a method of conserving the images made by light that led Daguerre to his polished, gleaming, and strange surface where magic is fused with reality.[7] Thanks to its unique relationship with the theater, photography qua image derived from a "staged" process: far from simply reproducing some preexistent reality, it recomposes it, sometimes even inventing or creating it. As Michel Poivert has recently underlined, a photograph is a "performed image."[8] In spite of its supposed exactitude, photography remains an art of subterfuge, by which an image unifies the disparate, sometimes antagonistic, elements entering into its conception. It is thus inscribed into the passing of time; not only because it records a forever vanished moment—as, with nostalgic poignancy, Roland Barthes so masterfully put it, noting the absolute "*it was*" constitutive of every photographic image[9]—but also with respect to the time it took to prepare the natural or human scene shown frozen in the photograph. The interest in photography evinced by so many nineteenth-century painters—from Jean-Léon Gérôme to Edgar Degas and Édouard Vuillard—was nurtured by this entanglement with the course of time, with this temporal extension that preempts the taking of the photograph, and which thus places it fundamentally in the same category as narrative and fiction. The study of the diorama and other optical devices as they relate to the painting of the era and to the invention of photography remains something for the future, though recent investigations around the Romantic theater and painting during the French Restoration and in the early part of the July Monarchy, however, brings with it the hope that we do not have long to wait, and that we will soon understand just how, in the fruitful years 1815–40, a dialogue was established between the arts of the stage and those of the easel—and later of the camera—in what is an effervescent—if today often neglected—period.

Inevitably the present volume stands on the shoulders of its predecessors and was written in the wake of a mass of research undertaken in cultural institutions, museums, and libraries, as well as in universities. During the last thirty years, thanks to the impetus of the Musée d'Orsay among other things, studies on photographic collections related to painting have greatly increased in number. Beyond their particular analyses, they have cast light on new collections and thus widened the corpus. Especially outstanding are two pioneering efforts from Germany: one by Erika Billeter (who sadly passed away recently), and the other—a paragon of subtlety and intelligence dating from 2005—by Ulrich Pohlmann.[10] The reappearance of a number of collections (the larger than expected oeuvre of Joseph Philibert Girault de Prangey; the photographic holdings of the painter Edmond Lebel; the very recent rediscovery of a group of daguerreotypes linked to Auguste Mestral or Gustave Le Gray, to mention only a few) gratifyingly demonstrates the vigor and ever growing scope of the discipline.[11] If the present volume thus risks quickly becoming outdated and surpassed, we nonetheless entertain the hope that the synthesis it attempts will prove beneficial for future studies.

This work could never have seen the light of day without the many encounters that fostered and encouraged it. To complete such a study, hovering as it does between painting and photography, between literature and the theater, I drew on many resources and many concepts. I would hereby like to offer my warmest thanks to all those who introduced me to new ideas and materials.

First and foremost, to Laure Beaumont-Maillet and Sylvie Aubenas, as well as to Bernard Marbot, whose thorough and methodical interest in the photographic image exercised my eye and developed my patience; then—and I hope I am not forgetting anyone—to Sylviane de Decker-Heftler, Catherine Mathon, and Hélène Pinet, who, together with Sylvie Aubenas, showed rare generosity in inviting me to join them on the adventure of the *L'Art du nu au* XIXe *siècle*; to Paul-Louis Roubert, Clément Chéroux, Michel Poivert, André Gunthert, and Thierry Gervais, who share my interest in the invention of photography and whose efforts within the Société Française de Photographie and on its journal, *Études photographiques,* remain inestimable; to Sébastien Allard, Marie-Claude Chaudonneret, Vincent Pomarède, Gary Tinterow, Laurence des Cars, Marie-Pierre Salé, Christophe Leribault, Michel Hilaire, Anne Roquebert, Anne Distel, Sylvie Patry, Barthélémy Jobert, Yves Sarfati, Cécile Debray, Jean-Claude Yon, Linda Nochlin, James Rubin, Christopher Riopelle, and Philippe Comar, whose knowledge of painting and range of taste strengthened my own; to Pierre Glaudes, Philippe Kaenel, Robert Kopp, and Daniel Couty, who shared their enthusiasm and erudition with me, thereby opening up some uncharted fields of interest; to Guy Cogeval, whose lessons at the École du Louvre fortified and reinforced my fondness for the nineteenth century and who was of such help to me at the outset of my career; to Dominique Ponnau, Philippe Durey, Claire Barbillon, and Sophie Mouquin, who provide me in turn with an opportunity to transmit what I have learnt; to Malcolm Daniel, Roger Taylor, Ulrich Pohlmann, Hans P. Kraus, Anne Lacoste, Sarah Greenough, Stephen Pinson, Sarah Kennel, Guillaume Le Gall, Denis Canguilhem, Françoise Heilbrun, Thomas Galifot, Gérard Lévy, Pierre-Lin Renié, Anne Cartier-Bresson, Françoise Reynaud, and Serge Plantureux, all of whom were and remain valuable colleagues in photography; to Jean-Gabriel Bouchaud, Astrid Thérond, and Dietmar Siegert, who allowed me access to their collections and offered me the possibility of reproducing illustrations from them.

I should like to express my heartfelt thanks to Henri Loyrette at the Musée du Louvre for the trust he shows in me and for the missions he has confided to me which have opened my research to new discoveries and enlarged my centers of interest. Finally, I should like to make clear my gratitude to all those without whose help the present volume could never have been published: to Sophy Thompson, whose invaluable backing has never wavered; to Claire Archer, who oversaw the first chapters, and to Alexandre Curnier, for his patience and attentive reading; to Katia de Azevedo, for her unfailing precision; to Amélie Boutry, who designed the volume with such talent; to Mélanie Puchault, as well as to all those who contributed to the realization of this publication at Flammarion. And finally, I should like to thank for their friendship and stimulating presence by my side, most especially, Thierry Dombreval, Édouard Papet, Laurent Le Bon, Adrien Goetz, Frédéric and Véronique Milande, Bruno Syrmen, Olivier Quennesson, Jean-Philippe Rossignol, Jean-Christophe Claude, Nathalie Bazoche, and Quentin Bajac, without whom this adventure in photography would have been unthinkable.

This book is dedicated to my children, Victoire, Constance, Stanislas, and Théophile.

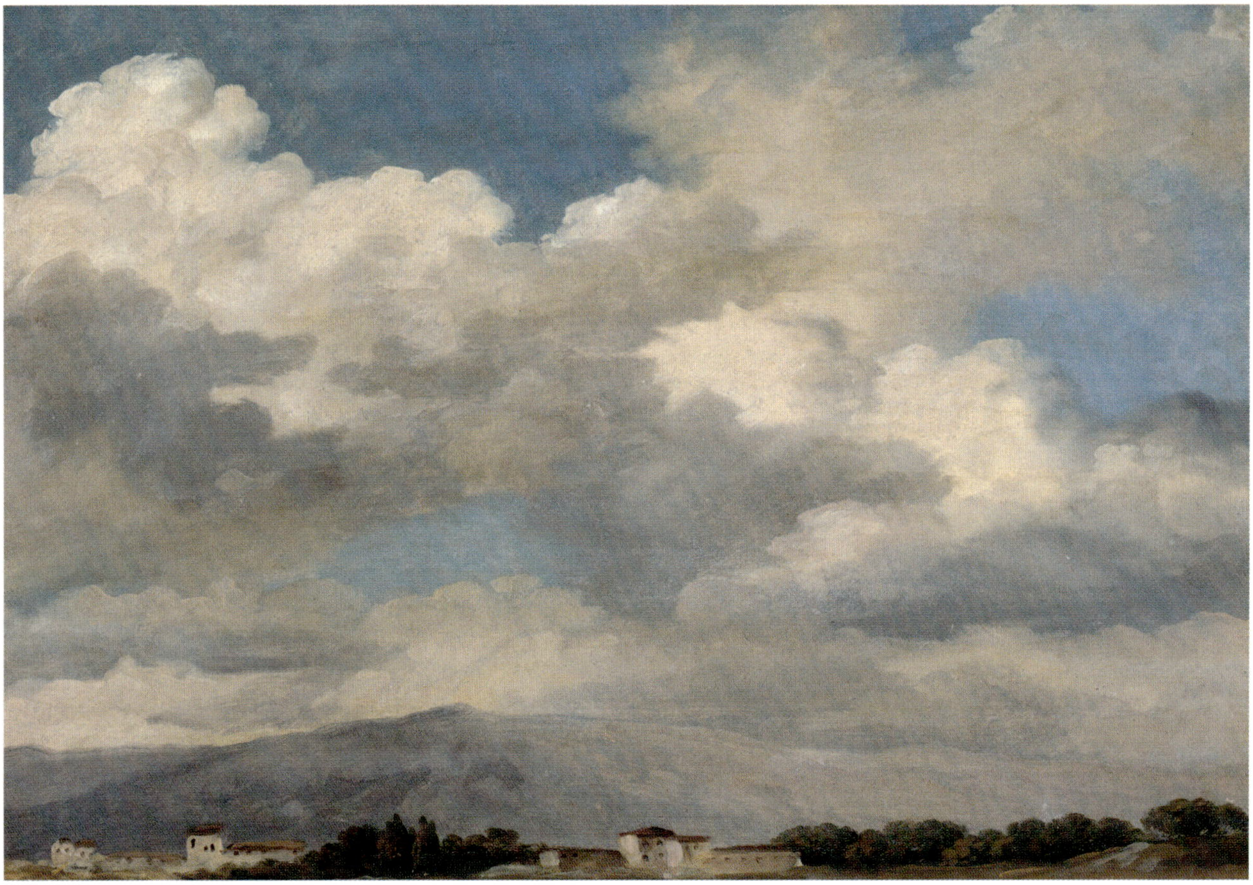

"We stand on the brink
of a revolution in the fine arts."

BEFORE PHOTOGRAPHY

Stendhal's observation, a reflection of his literary aspirations, was made in a review of the 1824 Salon, and also reads like an invitation. The aforementioned "revolution" had long been expected—yearned for, even—by an entire generation of artists, critics, and politicians, who, as the poet Alfred de Musset famously declared, had been born "too late in too old a world."[1] This was the generation that had "missed" the great revolution of 1789. As a demonstration of how the world could indeed be changed, and despite the subsequent tidal wave of political upheaval (1824 saw France's fifth political regime in thirty-five years), the French could look back on this event with nostalgia. The atrocities of the Terror and the subsequent setbacks for liberty were far from stifling the clarion call to heroism that had resounded during its iconic political and military battles.

The unveiling of Théodore Géricault's *The Raft of the Medusa* at the Salon of 1819, then the promising first stirrings of romanticism at the 1822 Salon, and the still more fiery debates between partisans of neoclassicism and romanticism on the occasion of the 1824 edition, presented further evidence of the advent of a generation determined to blaze a new path for the creative arts and shake themselves free from the influence of Jacques-Louis David and his disciples. Already the author of a book about that very Revolution, a youthful Adolphe Thiers forcefully expressed the hopes raised by the artistic turmoil of that year's Salon: "This exhibition provides a splendid revelation of the movement that burst upon the scene ten years ago and the extraordinary impetus that minds—frozen for a time during the Empire—have enjoyed since the overthrow of the military regime. For fifteen years, only one direction seemed open to literature, to the arts, to the sciences; but today the French spirit, untrammeled, can indulge all its inclinations, all its hopes, and everywhere seeks out the path to truth and beauty."[2] Clearly, this incipient

1. **Facing page:** Pierre-Henri de Valenciennes, *Study of the Sky over the Quirinal*, c. 1780, oil on paper, Musée du Louvre, Paris.

revolution was to have, as its hero, not the soldier or the politician, but the artist.

To begin a volume concerning the links between painting and photography in the nineteenth century by addressing the situation in the 1820s—that is, nearly twenty years before François Arago's official announcement of Nicéphore Niépce and Louis Jacques Mandé Daguerre's invention—might seem anachronistic, perverse even. Yet to our eyes an analysis of the profound changes initiated by and affecting the pictorial arts during the Restoration in fact throws much-needed light on the conditions subtending the invention of photography. For, historically speaking, Niépce's earliest experiments date back to 1816, and Daguerre's in all probability to 1824, while their association was enshrined only in December 1829 (see below). More crucially, such an approach can partially explain the complex nature of the artistic reception of photography in France from 1839.[3] The following brief analysis will focus on France, since it was in the ambit of the Paris Salons that the artistic maelstrom brewed and continued to rage until the end of the nineteenth century. And if (with due respect to Arago and his energetic commitment to ensuring the new invention was recognized as "French") photography was not born in France alone, it was in that nation that the arguments relating to its nature, function, and use were most amply rehearsed. As is well known, those debates were fuelled by important influences in the philosophical and aesthetic sphere that from the late eighteenth century were imported from Germany—the impact of Immanuel Kant's texts on the judgment of the taste, in particular—and from England, with the performance of *Othello* in July 1822 and the presentation at the 1824 Salon of three works by John Constable,[4] for instance.

The idea of photography

Two seminal texts have already been devoted to the study of the period "before photography." In 1980 at the Museum of Modern Art, New York, Peter Galassi presented an exhibition entitled precisely *Before Photography*, which, with the aid of a judicious selection of paintings and drawings, analyzed criteria of representation and style that hitherto had appeared inherent in photography alone, which in fact appeared before the invention of the technique: a closely mimetic depiction of reality (a taste originating in the trompe l'oeil painting of the French and German schools in the eighteenth century and taken up by the Americans); the choice of ephemeral and vernacular subjects drawn from daily life (genre scenes and cityscapes, for example); painting before the motif (as in the sketches of the sky by Pierre-Henri de Valenciennes (ills. 1–2) and the earliest Roman pictures by Camille Corot, in particular. The exhibition and its catalog defend the idea of a "photographic" style

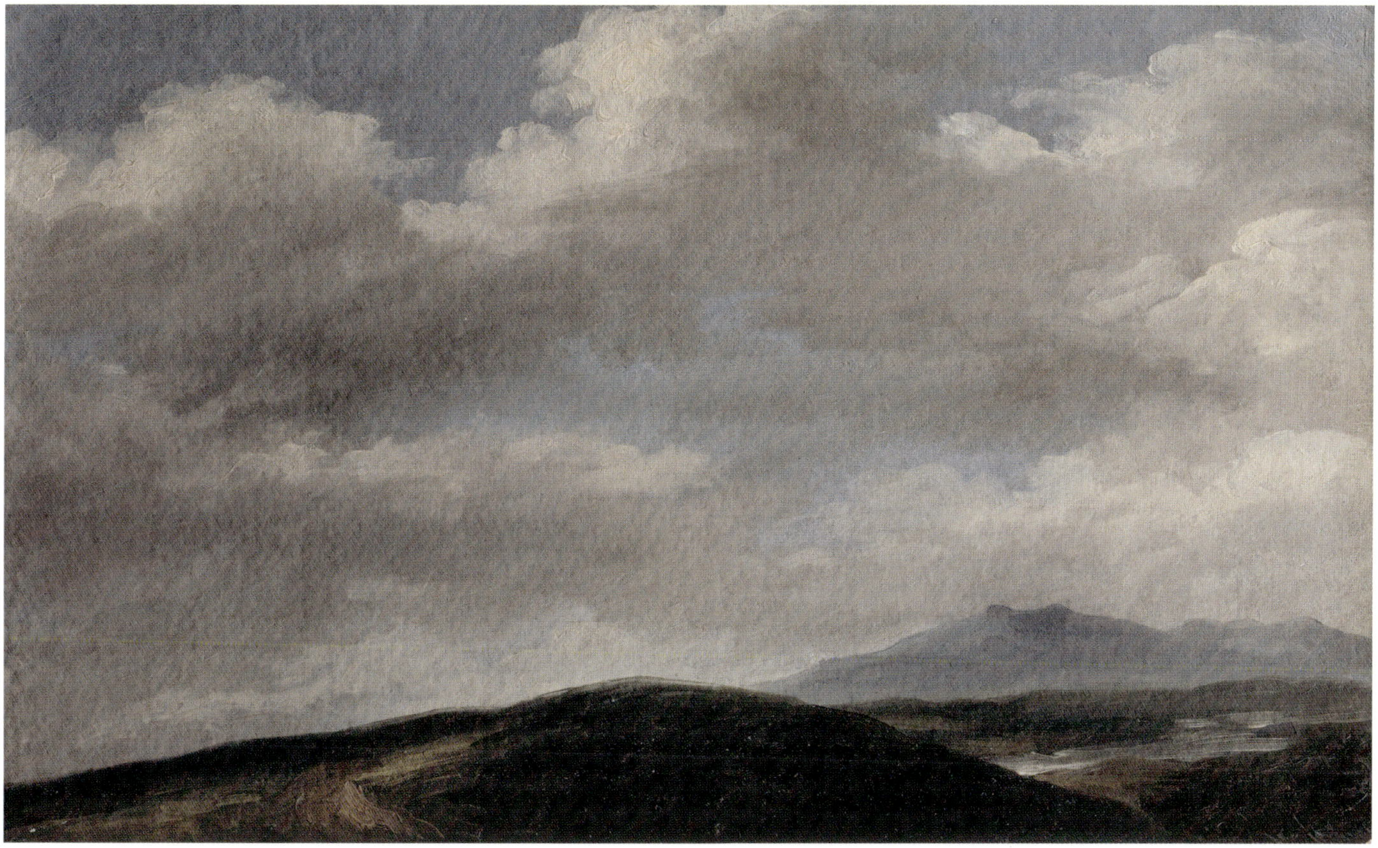

2. Pierre-Henri de Valenciennes, *At the Villa Borghese, White Clouds*, late eighteenth century, oil on paper glue-mounted on cardboard, Musée du Louvre, Paris.

and taste dating from "before photography," factors that fed into the ideas behind the new invention and determined the nature of the images its practitioners created. Up to a point, this comparison will be taken up in the following chapters, in particular in the section concerned with the landscape in painting and photography.

A remarkable volume by François Brunet, entitled *La Naissance de l'idée de photographie* (The Birth of the Idea of Photography) and published in 2000, rightly underlines the fact that, above and beyond the technical and chemical contingencies accompanying its invention,[5] an *idea* of photography as a means of reproducing and exploring the world and reality had already been gaining ground for some time. This "idea of photography" facilitated Arago's task of having the "discovery" of photography acknowledged as wholly French in the scientific and political community for political reasons; 1839 was also the year of the fiftieth anniversary of the Revolution. The employment of the terms "discovery" and "invention" willy-nilly by Arago and his peers shows how, for them as for so many of their contemporaries, the photographic process seemed to have always existed, if latently, like an uncharted continent or unexploited mine, and required "discovering" as least much as "inventing."[6]

Debates in the art world in the 1820s tended to be vociferous affairs. Stendhal opened his account of the 1824 Salon with a reference to the pitched battle between Étienne Delécluze, upholding neoclassicism and the school of David, and Adolphe Thiers, set on slaying the dragon of academic sterility. "This year, among the people who take it upon themselves to judge the Salon, it appears that two violently opposing parties have sprung up. War has already broken out."[7] The fracas was not just dust thrown up in anger in some high society scuffle; during the nineteenth century, the aesthetic arguments of the Restoration and the July Monarchy continued to feed into the arts and into drama, and their echoes can still be heard in one or other of the many "scandals" that beset the world of art until the twentieth century.

The postulate of exactitude: proof by detail

Although marked by political backsliding (a backward movement that critics such as Thiers rejected vigorously as regards the fine arts, pleading instead that the necessary and already remarkable course of evolution should if anything be accelerated), the Restoration, though politically and socially reactionary, remained a daughter of the Enlightenment. Intellectual discussion thus advanced on two fronts: the knowledge and classification of visible reality (the same drive that had motivated the originators of the *Encyclopédie*) was coupled to the apprehension of the sensual, emotional world that Rousseau had explored in *The Confessions*. The universe was thus viewed from the point of view of Man, as one who not only discovered, studied, and represented it, but also infused it with life. The scientific notions of the nineteenth century centered on classification, comprehension, and explanation: founded on the positivist spirit, scientific research was predicated on ever-finer gradations of exactitude. Thus, in the field of archaeology and the search for the vestiges of the past, for example, the rather haphazard if romantic discoveries of yesteryear were being replaced by prolonged, organized, and systematic excavations, as the foundation of the French School at Athens in 1847 demonstrates. Similarly, history was beginning to present itself as an autonomous discipline, underpinned by the description of established facts, the amassing of incontrovertible evidence, and the identification of authentic artifacts from past ages. This postulate of exactitude spawned the desire to get the details "right"—for "local color," as Thiers himself expressed it. To the observer of a work of science or art, exactitude in terms of minor factors appeared to guarantee accuracy in the whole. The biological theories of Georges Cuvier, who, basing his findings on the belief in the unity of the animal body, claimed to be able to reconstruct whole skeletons from a single vertebra, exerted a considerable influence on every field, including the arts. By

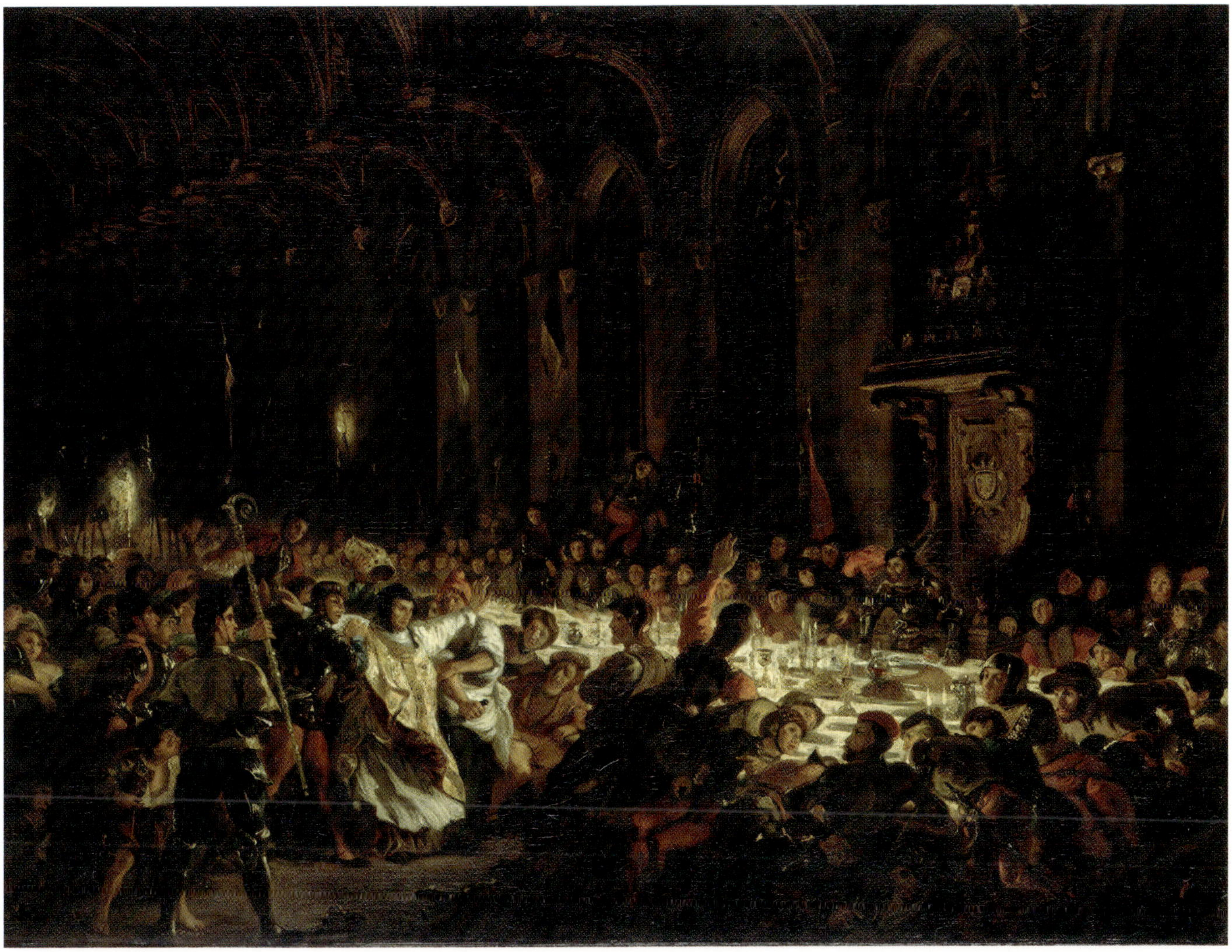

3. Eugène Delacroix, *The Assassination of the Bishop of Liège*, 1829, oil on canvas, Musée du Louvre, Paris.

analogy, Eugène-Emmanuel Viollet-le-Duc claimed he could "read" an entire Gothic cathedral from a capital. In painting, Paul Delaroche underwrote the accuracy of his historical scenes by precise details in decor and furnishings. "He [Delaroche] has taken on the task of moving us by the reality of his historical chronicles, by their faithful commentary ... he placed the insistence on *proofs*, on the accessories of his subjects—with a single detail he conjures up the passage he wishes to depict."[8]

Not without reason did Kierkegaard see the nineteenth century as the century of metonymy—that rhetorical figure by which the sign encapsulates the object signified.

The spell of the marvelous

The "postulate of exactitude" was intimately if paradoxically bound up with a desire to stimulate a reaction, especially of wonderment. A materialist epoch, the nineteenth century

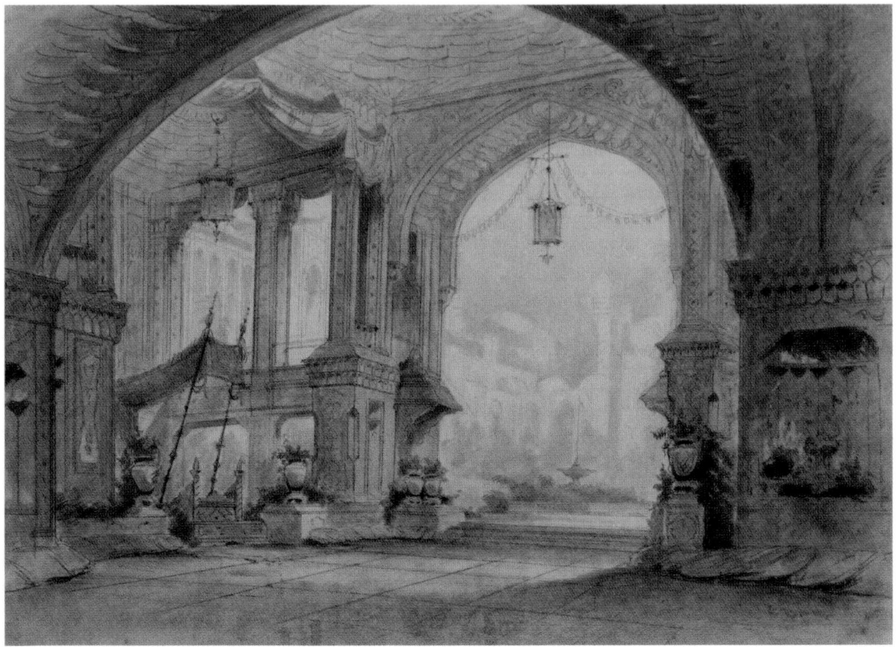

4. Louis Jacques Mandé Daguerre, *Aladdin and the Magic Lamp*, sketch for a set for Act III, 1822, charcoal on gray paper with occasional gray highlights, Bibliothèque-Musée de l'Opéra, Paris.

was also deeply marked by its quest for the marvelous, for an enchantment based on diachronic narratives that brought to museum and exhibition visitors, readers, theater goers, and opera audiences alike the allurement of action and the involvement of emotion. The era could not get enough of optical entertainments; first the panorama, invented in 1797 by Robert Barker in Scotland, but enjoying its heyday in Paris; then Daguerre's brainchild, the diorama, that opened in June 1822 in Place du Château-d'Eau (on the site of what is today Place de la République). Poking fun at what had become a voguish fashion among his contemporaries, Balzac, in *Le Père Goriot*, had the occupants of the Pension Vauquer employ the suffix "-rama" (as in "panorama," etc.) at every turn.

The theater was also being profoundly overhauled; lighting could create new and striking effects of surprise—as audiences at the Opera in 1822 saw for themselves when, for the first time, Daguerre and Pierre-Louis Cicéri used gas lanterns in a fairy opera appropriately entitled *Aladdin and the Magic Lamp* (ill. 4). While the French premiere of a play by Shakespeare in July of the same year was booed off the stage, the arrival of the English drama in the nation's theaters nonetheless proved an enduring influence on the dramatic arts. In his affecting appeal on behalf of the Elizabethan playwright, *Racine et Shakespeare*, published in 1823 and again in 1825, Stendhal takes up the gauntlet for the "*drame*" as against French classical tragedy. A few years later, in the foreword to his play *Cromwell*, Victor Hugo was to pen a veritable profession of faith in favor of a new aesthetics in which the search for emotional response would hold pride of place. The pursuit of truth

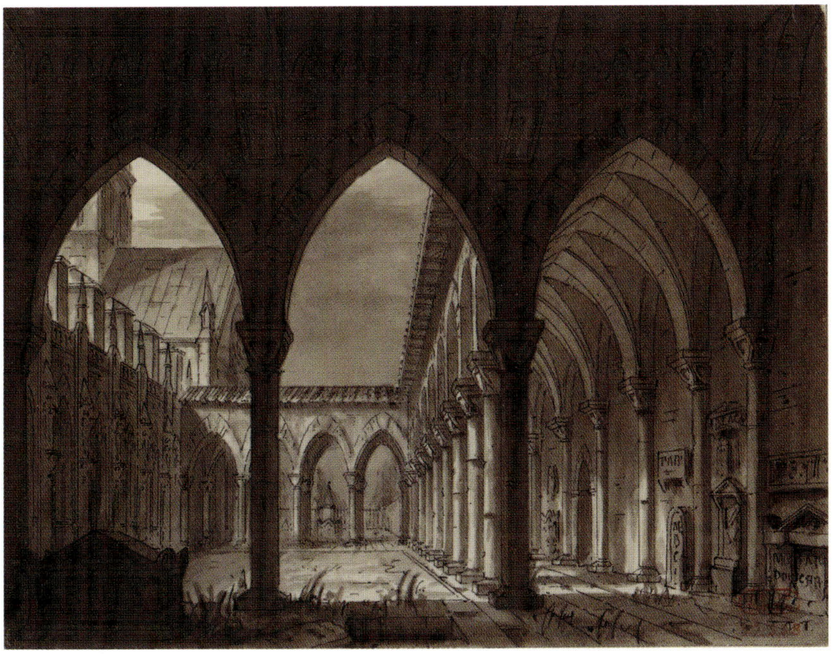

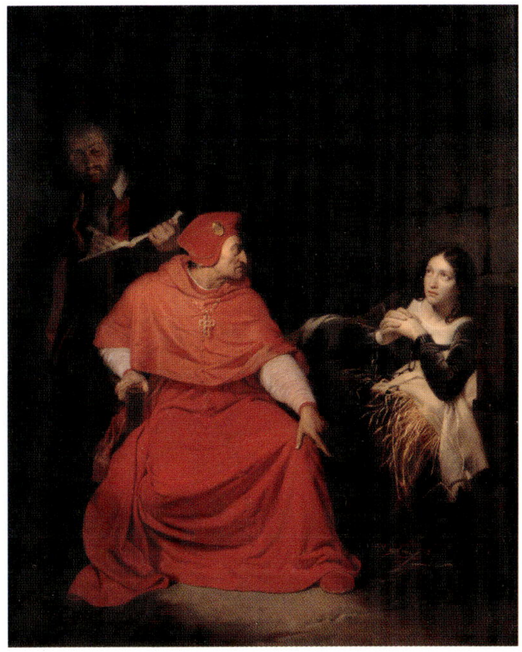

5. **Above, left:** Pierre-Luc Cicéri, "The Cloister," second set for *Robert le Diable*, 1831, color lithograph, Bibliothèque-Musée de l'Opéra, Paris.

6. **Above, right:** Paul Delaroche, *A Sick Joan of Arc Interrogated by the Cardinal of Winchester*, 1824, oil on canvas, Musée des Beaux-Arts, Rouen.

must draw on emotional as well as material resources, Hugo declared. Yet, though the drama is a painting from life, and as such characterized by the veracity of its depictions, "the truth of art can never be, as some have said, *absolute* reality."[9]

Even the writing of history could not remain immune from this drive for the subjective and the immediate. Augustin Thierry, in *Les Lettres sur l'histoire de France*, if he could hardly forget factual exactitude, nonetheless drew parallels between emotion and historical truth. Similarly, the narrative sagas of Walter Scott, translated into French from 1818, made a profound impact on the theater (around half the sets in Daguerre and Bouton's dioramas from 1822 to 1830 owe at least something to the darkly thrilling world of the author of the *Waverley* novels), as well as on the pictorial arts (Delacroix's fondness for the work of the Scottish writer is well documented): they even nourished an approach to history that binds fact to storyline to form a single gripping narrative (ill. 3). The enormous success of *Robert le Diable*, an opera by Meyerbeer set to a libretto by Scribe, which premiered in Paris in 1831 and was reprised throughout the century, presents a prime example of the period's taste for historical reconstructions mixing history and passion, light and shade (ill. 5).

Well-versed in Thierry's works, in his Salons of 1822 and 1824, the young Thiers readily indulged this taste for narrative, devoting page after page to the story of Orestes and Electra by Picou (1824, deposited in Auxerre in 1872), and to the fragile Joan of Arc depicted by Paul Delaroche—a trembling girl terrorized by the terrible Winchester, quite unlike the heroic military virgin (ill. 6). This toing and froing between objective and

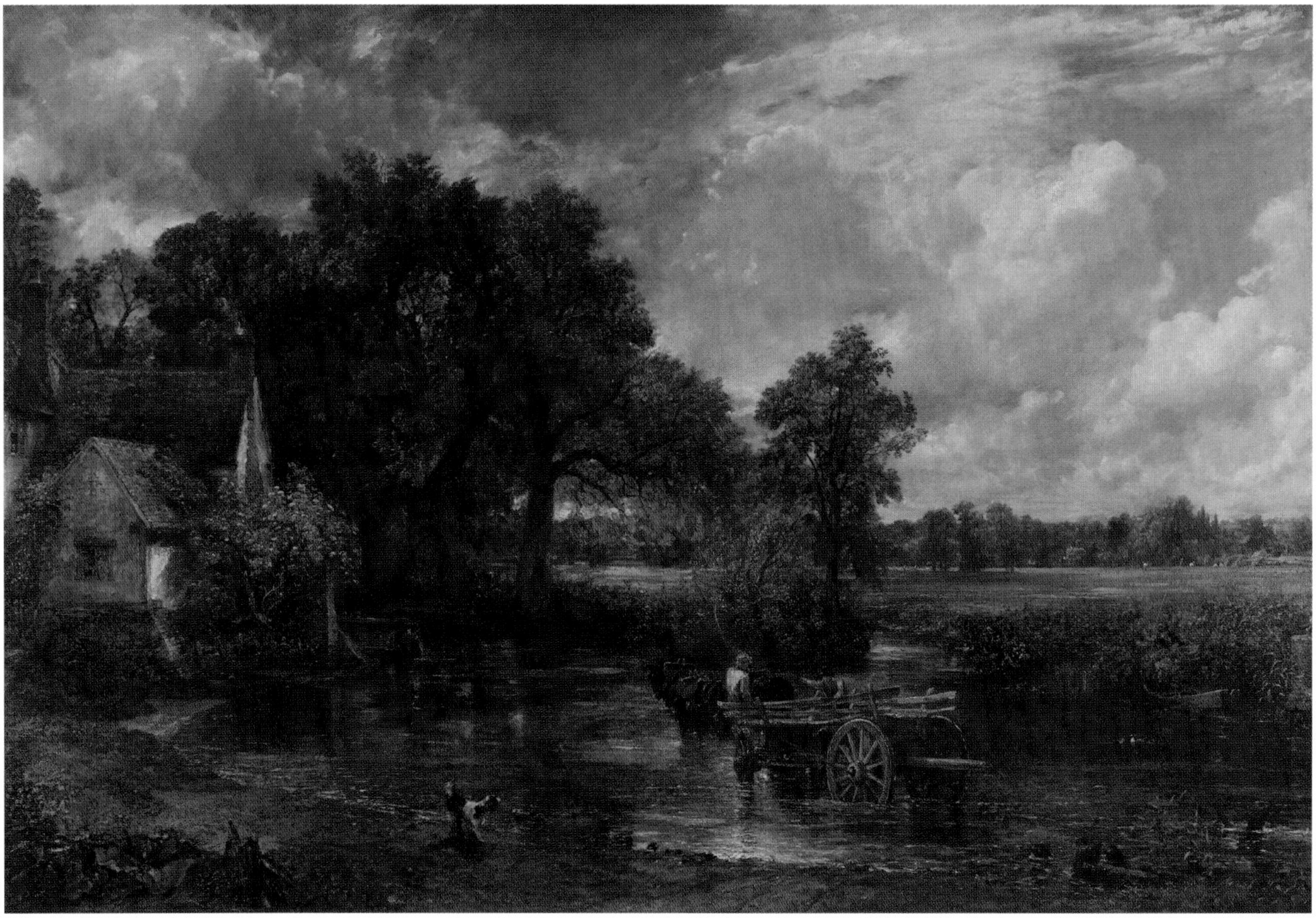

7. John Constable, *The Hay Wain*, 1821, oil on canvas, National Gallery, London.

emotional truth with respect to the representation of reality lies at the heart of both artistic creation and reception in the nineteenth century; in the eyes of both camps, a want of truth became, above and beyond a faux pas in taste, a moral stain.

Of the faculty of judgment and the diversity of the beautiful

This involved relationship with the truth of representation was further complicated by changes in attitudes to beauty. In France particularly, the end of the eighteenth century was characterized by a return to Platonic ideals that brought in its wake references to Greco-Roman Antiquity as much as to the classical tradition of seventeenth-century art and Louis XIV. Under the dual patronage of André Félibien and Winckelmann, the art of David and the French neoclassicists afforded a new lease of life to art in the country, endowing it with a moral tone. The 1820s, with the arrival of the ideas of Immanuel Kant in particular, witnessed a steady stream of works advocating subjectivity in the beautiful, some even going so far as to affirm with

Victor Hugo that, if the beautiful was unique and conventional, its contrary was manifold: "The beautiful comes in only one type; the ugly comes in a thousand." [10] Appearing in German in 1790, Kant's *Critique of the Faculty of Judgment* made an immense impact in France. The *Observations on the Beautiful and the Sublime* that derived from that section of the *Critique* appeared in French in 1796; as soon as they were digested, Kant's propositions sparked a debate as to their universality. On one side, centered around Charles de Villers, there were those who traced them back to the French Cartesian tradition, while others, such as Wilhelm von Humboldt, denied that French thinkers could hope to understand Kant.[11] It is probable that very few of the critics and artists who referred—if not always explicitly—to the German philosopher had actually read his books. In the French artistic sphere, the idea of a subjective judgment on the beautiful, of the possibility of relating reason and sensibility, reinforced the primacy of the figure of the creative artist, demiurge and sovereign over his creation. Thiers, in the introduction to his *Salon* of 1822, reviewed the arguments being bandied about at the time: "Arguments over the beautiful are no less fierce than those that arise concerning the good. People become passionate about their impressions; everyone wants to be certain that the pleasures they enjoy are the only true ones." [12] Though reactions to the concept of subjective beauty varied (the publication in 1825 of Quatremère de Quincy's book on imitation demonstrated that the neoclassical party still had its supporters), this new-found independence nurtured the burgeoning of different styles within one and the same Salon.[13] The choice of subjects taken from modern history and literature, the appearance of compositions at odds with classical equilibrium, the desire of artists to arouse emotions in the viewer, furthered an unprecedented relationship to the imitation of nature more in keeping with the age. As Stendhal asked: "What does the modern bas-relief [as a model] do for me? Let us try to do good, modern painting." He went on to affirm: "Nature must be always the artist's first guide and the point to which he must constantly return."

Salons in the 1820s were piloted by the then director of museums, the open-minded Auguste de Forbin, a painter himself, and onetime pupil of David. They found room for many new trends in art. A vast showcase, the Salon welcomed fledgling artists (when Eugène Delacroix exhibited *The Barque of Dante*, aka *Dante and Virgil in Hell* [Musée du Louvre, Paris], at the 1822 event, he was only twenty-four years old), while diverse styles, genres, and generations rubbed along in its hothouse atmosphere. Forbin kept faith with what he had perceived in 1819 at the unveiling at the Salon of *The Raft of the Medusa*: "What distinguishes the current age is the sense of freedom one finds in the finest productions of our school." [14] With a remarkable lack of prejudice, in the same Salon one could find hanging, side by side, works by pupils of David and those of younger turks eager for change. In 1824, Thiers hailed this diversity as a harbinger of the upcoming generation and a new style: "In the current exhibition, one cannot but confess that every taste has its place, every style has found an audience, and that, if no genre is followed to the exclusion of all others, none has been entirely abandoned either."[15] Contrariwise, Étienne Delécluze complained how painters had been left free to indulge their own personal idiom: "Strictly speaking, there is no school since every artist blindly follows a manner he has created for himself, either based on his own sensations, or else—as is more commonly the case—on imitating the manner of those masters he prefers."[16] The growing interest in Dutch painting encouraged many painters to try their hand at genre scenes and the exact reproduction of minute details. Small in size, painstaking in brushwork, such pictures were snapped up by collectors.

The presentation—at the same Salon in 1824—of three canvases by the English painter, John Constable, provided an impressive counterpoint. His unpretentious, rustic subjects based on landscapes in the Stour Valley, his curious manner of applying paint in delicate little touches, the care lavished upon capturing every fleeting change in meteorological conditions beguiled many artists and art lovers (ill. 7).[17]

The artist as hero

The real hero of this revolution was then to be the artist. By placing the creator at the core of his creation, French and German philosophy in the second half of the eighteenth century endowed him with a new attitude. As the sensitive soul par excellence, the poet, musician, or painter was—as he had already been with Rousseau and was later with Goethe—the preeminent mediator between his emotions and those of the beholders of or listeners to his works. The requirement that an artwork should extol—in the service of God or king—was gradually being overlaid by a desire to communicate feelings and effects. The artist is an exceptional individual, better equipped than others to plumb and convey the passions of humankind. Romantic though it was, this theory was shared by upholders of extreme conservatism. As Ingres wrote, "It is he [the artist] who is right; it is from him that come lessons in and examples of taste" (ill. 8).[18] The opening in 1818 of the Musée du Luxembourg, designed to display works by living artists (the Louvre was reserved for those of the past), brings out the importance that the restored royal power accorded contemporary creators.

In December 1824, a short pamphlet appeared that signals a key stage in the conception of the role and status of the artist, in particular from the social point of view. As the title *L'Artiste, le savant et l'industriel* (The Artist, the Scientist, and the Industrialist) suggests, in it Claude-Henri de Rouvroy,

8. **Facing page:** Jean-Auguste-Dominique Ingres, *Self-Portrait*, 1804, oil on canvas, Musée Condé, Chantilly.

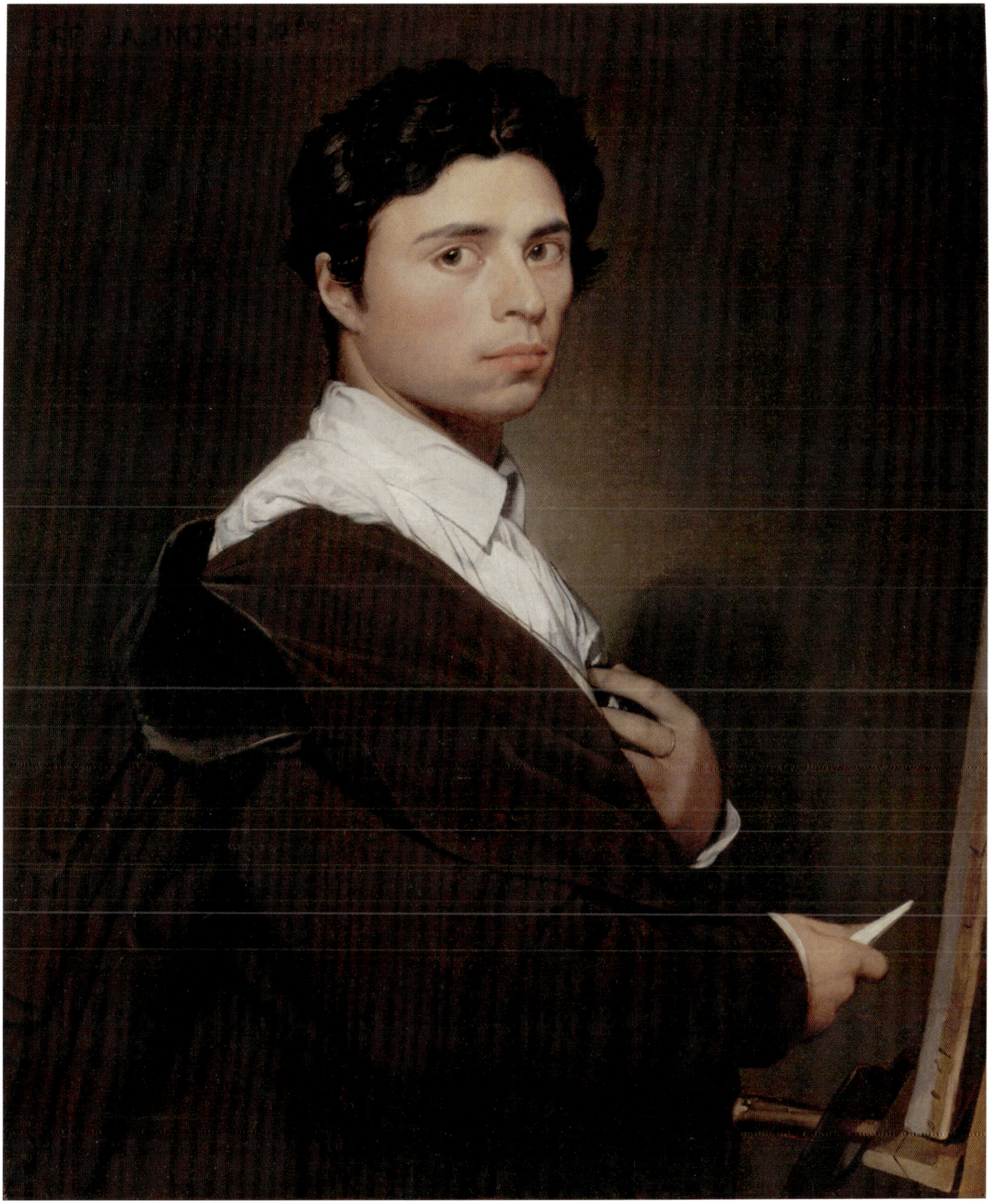

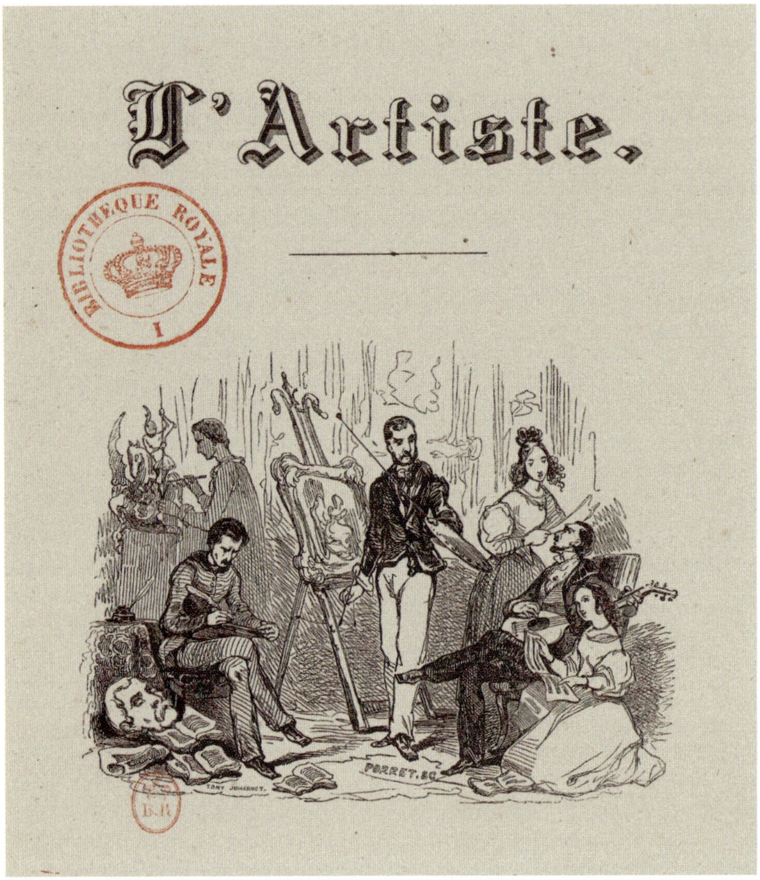

9. Tony Johannot, frontispiece for *L'Artiste*, 1831, lithograph. Bibliothèque Nationale de France, Paris.

Count Saint-Simon, describes the three leading classes of society in the future: the artist, scientist, and industrialist, with the former at the forefront. Identifying himself with this new aristocracy, he writes: "It is us, we artists, who will be in your vanguard; for the power of the arts is the swiftest and most immediate.... We address ourselves to the imagination and to the feelings of man ... and if our role today appears null or, at least, secondary, it is because hitherto the arts lacked something essential to their energy and their success—a shared impulse, an overarching idea."[19]

The role of the artist takes on a new, social dimension. Saint-Simon's utopian writings exerted an unquestioned influence on thinking in the 1830s and 1840s, though already in the 1820s the artist had become regarded as a special kind of man, not only through his creative works, but also due to his attitude, his whole way of being. In this he was sharply distinguished from the bourgeoisie—that hard-working, cheeseparing middle class, whose growing size and role is the hallmark of the nineteenth century. The artist embodied instead a sensitive, tormented outsider, who could nevertheless also be elegant, cynical, remote, at once garret-living art student and drawing-room dandy. As the lexicologist Georges Matoré has demonstrated, on entering everyday parlance, words relating to art and artistic creativity often took on unexpected connotations.[20]

Founded in 1831 by Achille Ricourt, *L'Artiste, journal de la littérature et des beaux-arts*, a review devoted to the criticism of the visual arts and the theater, as well as social questions, enshrined the new situation. The journal was instrumental in both publicizing and promoting art, its engraved illustrations making the works cited widely known. The colophon on the frontispiece shows a drawing room in which a musician, a writer, and a sculptor are all busy at work, the focus being provided by a painter standing before his easel, brush in hand (ill. 9).[21]

From the point of view of the artist: a vision of the world

The recognition of the artist as creator and social actor completely transformed the relationship to the artwork. Whereas for centuries the dominant figure had been the patron—king,

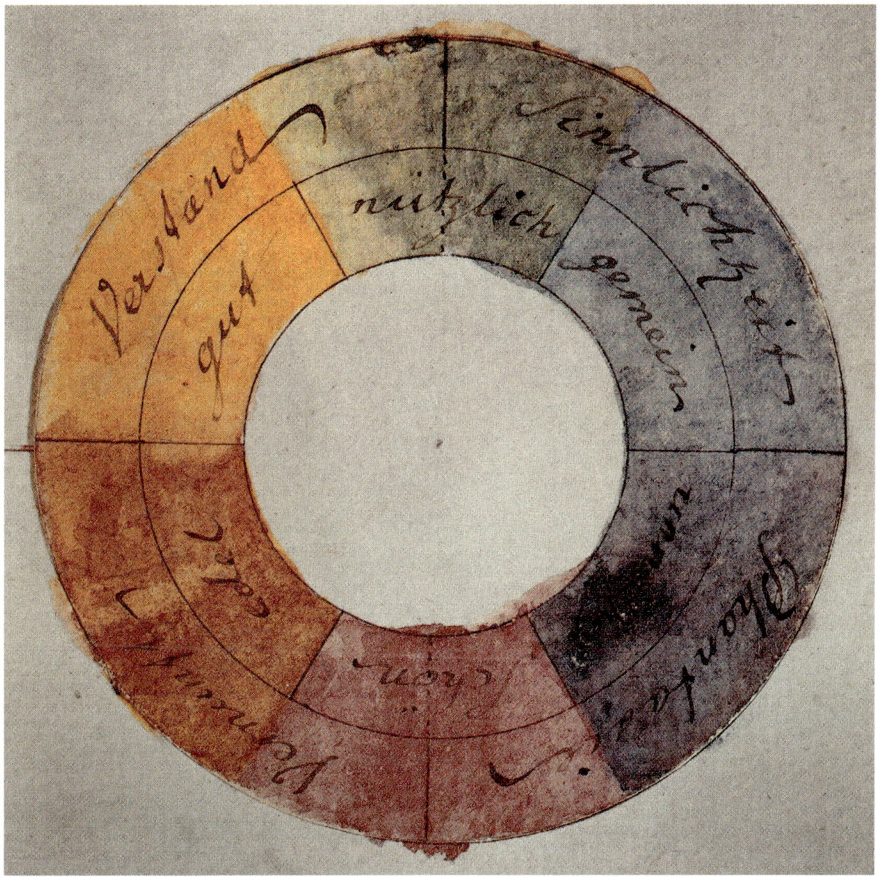

10. Johann Wolfgang von Goethe, *Color Wheel Symbolizing the Spirit of Man and the Life of the Soul*, 1809, watercolor, Goethe-Museum, Frankfurt.

overlord, religious order, and so on—as the one who determined the use, purpose, and subject of the work (an ultimate judge who could reject the art if it displeased him), now the artist asserted his role as a free agent, though inevitably subjected to the constraints of the market if he wanted to make a living from his toil. The creation of art was envisaged from the vantage point of the artist; it was his personal vision of the world that brought the work into being. The subject mattered less than the unique prism of his vision. The mirror held out by the artist to the world and to nature became a common metaphor to designate a process of creation in new genres predicated on reality, such as the novel and the drama. As an epigraph to a chapter in his novel *Le Rouge et le noir* (The Red and the Black, 1830), Stendhal added the following definition by César de Saint-Réal: "A novel is a mirror borne along a path."[22] Meanwhile, Hugo, in the foreword to his *Cromwell*, deployed a similar analogy: "A play is a mirror that reflects nature." But, as the poet added, it is a mirror which, thanks to its author, goes beyond mere reflection: "The drama must be a mirror that concentrates, and which, far from weakening [color and light], collects those tinted rays that turn a glimmer into a light and a light into a flame. Only then can the drama foster the arts."[23]

The brilliant analysis of the realist novel undertaken by Roland Barthes in the last century redeploys the metaphor of the mirror and the frame erected by an author—Balzac in this case—before the reality he describes: "Realism (so badly named) consists, not in copying the real, but in copying a (depicted) copy of reality," in placing "the empty frame that the realist author always carries about with him (more important than his easel) before a collection or continuum of objects which cannot be put into words without this obsessive operation."[24] The *specular* approach to the representation of reality thus subtly exploits the double-edged expectation of an age that required representation to be both a reflection *and* an unveiling of reality: the desire for exact formal imitation, coupled with an inner truth derived from the senses, was wedded to a demand for immediacy and revelation.

The analogical use of studio paraphernalia such as the "frame" and the "mirror" (closely followed by those of the photographer) underscores the influence on writers of new theories of perception developed, for instance, by Goethe at the beginning of the nineteenth century. Closely connecting the body of the beholder to the object appearing to the eyes, they abolished the frontier between "interior" and "exterior" by associating color vision to reactions of the soul (ill. 10). The optical shows of which Stendhal, Hugo, and Balzac—like Forbin, François Marius Granet, and Delacroix—were so fond were based on an illusory recreation of reality, as with the shift from stormy to fine weather in the diorama, for example, all the while making audiences (to those in the know, at least) sensitive to the optic processes involved: lighting, chromatic effect, afterimage, etc.[25] Easel painting inspired by optical contraptions made much of the contrast between light and shade, while the architecture depicted became the frame for a performance of exacerbated dramatic effect (ill. 23).

The artist's new role, together with the fact that some, such as Eugène Delacroix, had already freed themselves from the straitjacket of the Academy and the Prix de Rome and sought recognition among the public (that is, at the Salon), had immense repercussions on the rules governing the distinction between genres and subjects. The early nineteenth century witnessed a seismic shift in the hierarchy of genre as it had been conceived in the seventeenth century by the Académie des Beaux-Arts. Due to its evident ontological submission to reality, greater importance was now accorded landscape, a genre once considered negligible. In a text written in 1795 but published nearly thirty years later, François-René de Chateaubriand exhorted landscape painters to look for fresh subjects and a new manner by painting directly from nature.[26] Studies executed by Pierre-Henri de Valenciennes in Rome show how this aspiration was shared even in institutional circles. Of course, at that time, such pieces were preparatory

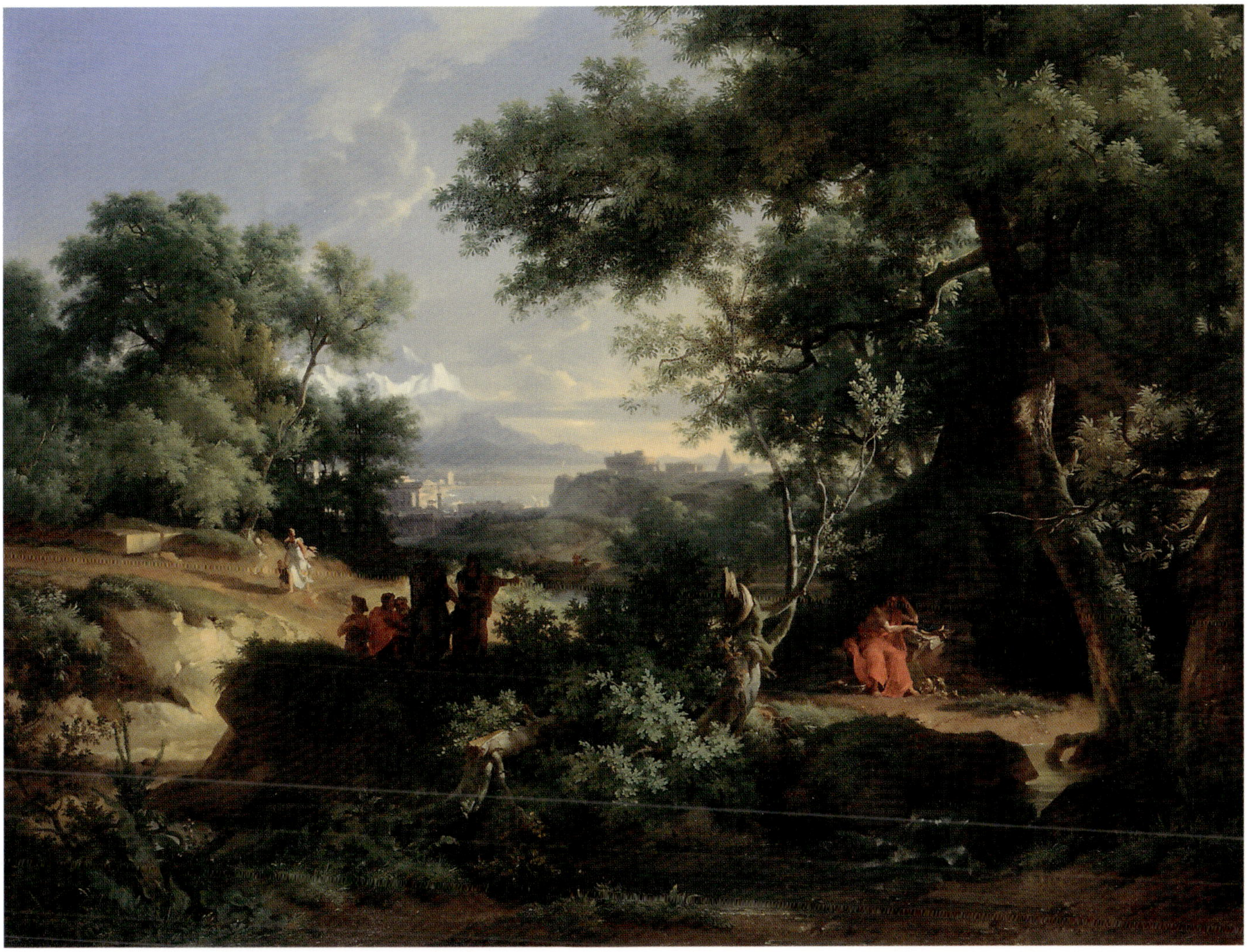

11. Achille-Etna Michallon, *Democritus and the Abderites*, 1817, oil on canvas, École Nationale Supérieure des Beaux-Arts, Paris.

sketches for large-scale pictures amalgamating landscape and history. Although seemingly rather late in the day, the creation by the Academy of a *grand prix* for Historical Landscape in 1817, a prize awarded every four years until 1863 (the *grand prix historique* was decreed annually), demonstrates the renewed appreciation of landscape as genre (ill. 11).[27] The presentation at the 1824 Salon of works by Constable and Richard Bonington provided fresh impetus to the French artists' quest for new subjects drawn straight from the countryside without any historical or mythological pretext, and based on work before the subject—that is, on first-hand observation. Not long before, the serialized publication from 1820 of *Les Voyages pittoresques et romantiques dans l'Ancienne France* (Picturesque and Romantic Journeys in Ancient France), initiated by Baron Taylor and the writer Charles Nodier and modeled on similar English collections, had already vouchsafed a new vision of landscape that associated dramatic effects and ruins

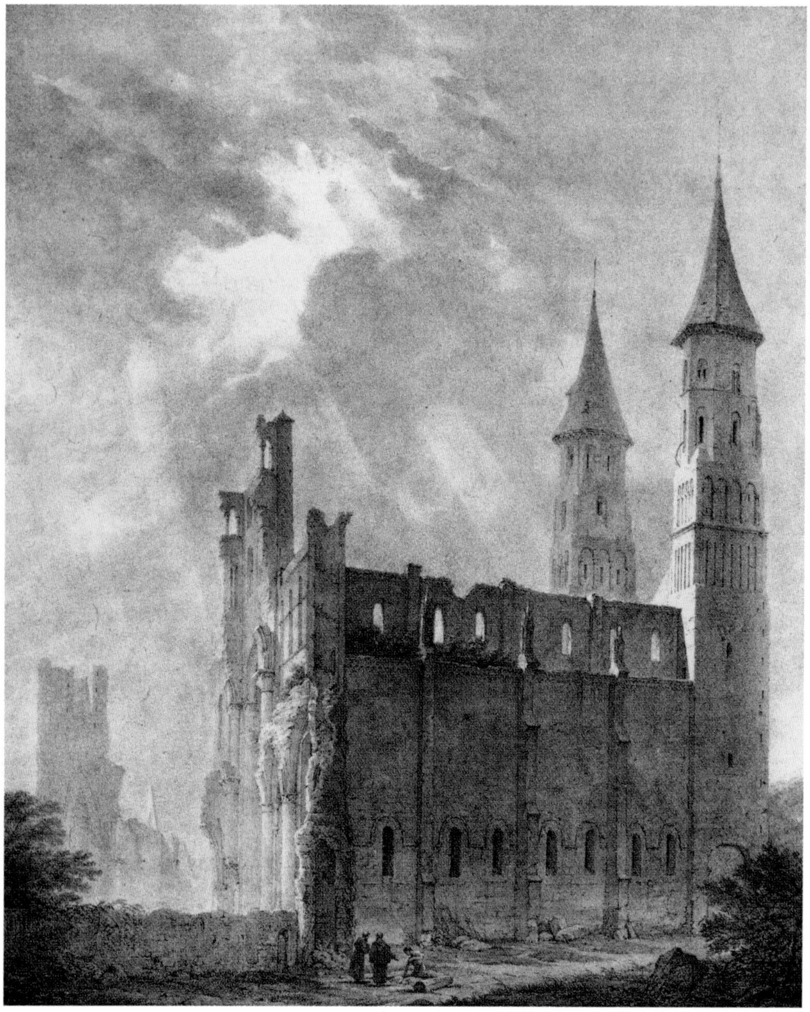

12. Louis Jacques Mandé Daguerre, "Ruins of the Abbey at Jumièges," plate 12 of *Les Voyages pittoresques et romantiques dans l'Ancienne France*, 1820, lithograph, Bibliothèque Nationale de France, Paris.

in a single, unified quest for beauty in landscape and architecture. The use of lithography, then a novel printing technique that had been invented in the late eighteenth century by Aloys Senefelder, disseminated pictures from *Les Voyages pittoresques* far and wide (ill. 12), and also furthered a renaissance of interest in the French architectural heritage, and of the medieval period in particular, which had burgeoned in the Musée des Monuments Français founded by Alexandre Lenoir in 1793. They also fixed new canons of representation, at once architectural and theatrical, that were to persist later in photography. Lithography was showcased at the Salon as an art in its own right, distinct from other techniques of reproduction such as etching and engraving, for the first time in 1824. The previous year, Adolphe Thiers had demonstrated his interest in this modern process by illustrating his Salon of 1822 with lithographs reproducing some of the works described.

History painting and genre painting

One of the more notable upheavals in the ranking of genre—certainly one of those that aroused the most comment at the time—concerned the position of the noblest form, history painting. Called upon to exalt the mind of the beholder, by promoting great historical deeds or mythological feats of gods and heroes as exempla, history painting had, from the 1770s on, undergone a revival initiated by the monarch and his representatives. A further aim of this resurgence, in which David was one of the major players from 1780, was to raise the moral status of art, something lost—as many critics saw it—in the bright colors and dainty sparkle of scenes of the loves of the gods painted by the likes of François Boucher and Louis Lagrenée. From the late eighteenth century, alongside religious, mythological, and historical material, painters, with David in the forefront, started turning to subjects drawn from contemporary history; in this way the Revolution, and then the Consulate and the Empire, spawned modern heroes.

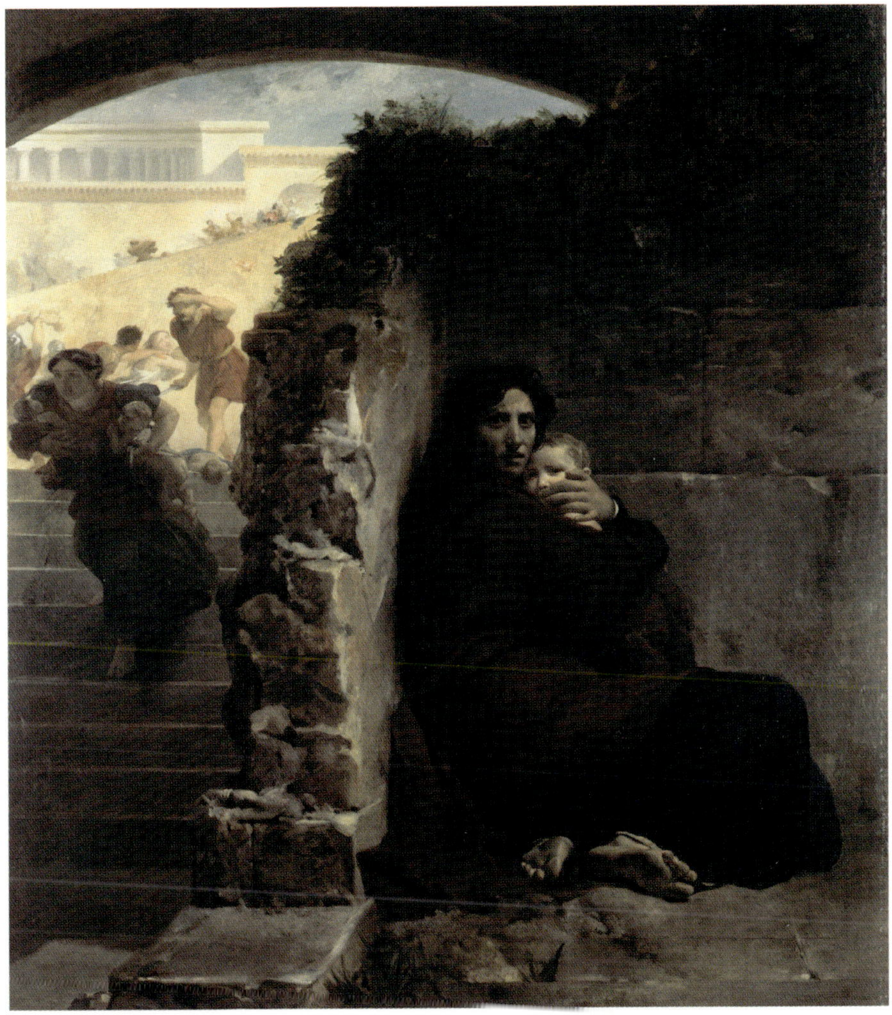

13. Léon Cogniet, *The Massacre of the Innocents*, 1824, oil on canvas, Musée des Beaux-Arts, Rennes.

Artists also delved into ancient and recent literature, not only Shakespeare and Dante, but also James Macpherson ("Ossian"), Byron, and Chateaubriand, filling their canvases with scenes and characters never before seen.

Above and beyond the subjects treated, the way history was conceived also altered. The faithful description of an action—in accordance with the narrative procedures dealt with above—replaced the *exemplum virtutis*. A search for light effects, the introduction of continuity, and suspense originating in theatrical devices—the two planes of *The Massacre of the Innocents* by Léon Cogniet (ill. 13), the executioner's raised arm in Paul Delaroche's *Joan of Arc* (1824, Musée des Beaux-Arts, Rouen), the tortured body of the patrician rolling to the bottom of the staircase in Delacroix's *Execution of the Doge Marino Faliero* (ill. 14)—emphasized anecdotal details rather than historic grandeur. Seeking to move rather than to edify, such artifices, close to those then current on the stage, were not immune from theatricality.[28] The celebration of history was being ousted, already, by its illustration, and, even before photography, the dissemination of painting through engravings made such images widely available.

Thiers, who, like many of his contemporaries, confessed to a weakness for genre scenes, emphasized the increasingly prevalent confusion between artistic categories: "Genre pictures. By arranging them under this heading," he wrote in 1824, "I am perhaps being insulting to a host of pictures with a claim, sometimes a deserving claim, to historical merit. But this title of 'genre,' the object of such heated discussion, has not yet been fully circumscribed.... And besides, it doesn't matter to what class a picture belongs; the essential thing is that it be good."[29] The difference between genre and history often boiled down to a question of size: large pictures went into museums and formed part of official decorations; small pictures furnished middle-class interiors, at whose modest dimensions Stendhal was to poke fun in the second article of his *Salon de 1824*: "A week ago," it begins, "I went to rue Godot-de-Mauroy to look for an apartment. I was struck by how cramped the rooms were; and, as this was precisely the day I had been requested to write on painting in the *Journal de Paris* ... I took a note I had made on the height and width of the most popular canvases out of my pocketbook and compared the dimensions of the pictures with those of the tiny bedrooms through which the owner led me: 'The age of painting is over ... now only engraving can hope to survive.'"[30]

This taste for cabinet pieces—genre scenes, portraits, still lifes—and their reproduction in engraving was indeed thriving, and was fostered by the many galleries selling pictures and engravings that opened at the turn of the nineteenth century. In the footsteps of Jean-Baptiste Lebrun, dealers such as John Arrowsmith, Claude Schroth, the Susse Brothers, and Alphonse Giroux also played a key role in the diffusion of seventeenth-century Dutch painting and contemporary English art, encouraging the uptake of new models. From 1821, the Girouxs not only exhibited and sold paintings, but also hired them out, making it easier for young artists to copy examples of art.[31] Variety in style, instability of genre, diversity of subject, and the profusion of canvases of modest size all converged in the establishment of the July Monarchy Salon, which, if it had become annual by 1831, was subjected to the diktats of an Academy jury less kindly disposed than during the Restoration under Auguste de Forbin. The phenomenon also sometimes seemed to turn the event into little better than a hotchpotch of works of all stripes. Balzac begins *Pierre Grassou* with an evocation of the 1839 Salon: "The Salon should have remained a delimited, restricted place of inflexible proportions, where each genre might display its own masterpieces. An experience of ten years has proved the benevolence of the old institution. Instead of a tournament, you now have a riot; instead of a glorious exhibition, you have a tumultuous bazaar; instead of choice, you have totality. And what happens? In it, the great artist gets lost."[32]

Revival and resistance

If the Restoration did not witness the birth of a revolution in art, at least not to the extent hoped for by Stendhal, it did, as Thiers in 1822 ventured it might, usher in a new generation who bridged the gap between classicism and romanticism. The revival in painting from 1819 to 1827 sparked by the Salon, accompanied by an increasingly influential body of critics, buoyed up by an ever-expanding art market, and fuelled by new ideas and doctrines, carried within it the germ of the artistic transformations to come. The increased importance allotted to the artist, the valorization of his point of view and his style, a newfound freedom as to choice of subject, the evident impossibility of ever reverting to a single, univocal aesthetic standard, new templates imported from the Netherlands, England, or Germany, the fondness for dramatic storylines, the complex nature of a reality perceived through the dual prism of a commitment to inner truth as well as to exactitude—all these together constituted a fertile breeding ground for the adumbration of a wholly new mode of representation. The invention of lithography, and with it the development of new techniques of diffusion, also altered attitudes to the artwork: the image, already, was replacing the picture; a century of illustration was dawning.

The overlap between technical research, aesthetic and philosophical theory, and pictorial and theatrical creativity, in an age where positivist confidence in technological progress blended with a weakness for the marvelous and the unworldly, brought in its wake new experiments and novel processes (studies of visual perception, Eugène Chevreul's work on color, an interest in the phenomena of light and its reproduction, etc.) that were very soon taken up by artists. The establishment of the diorama in June 1822 signaled a turning point in these developments. As Daguerre's debut invention, the diorama, closely allied by its subject matter to the romantic painting and literature of the period, proved inseparable, as shall be shown, from the invention of photography and the development of the daguerreotype.[33]

The enduring—strengthened, even—position of academic institutions as the driving force behind the art world as a whole (for pupils of David, too), as well as the source of the rules governing not only the subjects represented and the manners deployed, but also the training of young artists, forestalled the uniform, continuous acceptance of the changes afoot. The role of the Salon jury as a censor (its members were all selected from the coterie around the Académie des Beaux-Arts) placed a significant brake on developments. The Salon was still the place where a young artist had to jostle for recognition, where he had to make his name if he hoped to make a living from his works. In fact, gaining in influence due to the arrival of a middle-class clientele, its doors remained closed, or practically, to all those who refused to follow the rules and models imposed by the despots on the jury. Even Delacroix fell victim to the edicts of the Salon judges. Stendhal, in stigmatizing the juries of the competitive exhibitions (*concours*) under the Restoration, in particular those for the Prix de Rome, highlighted how perverse their judgments could be: "Everywhere during these competitive exhibitions, I see aged artists gravely occupied at gauging whether young men imitate their own manner of painting closely enough."[34] The description seems clairvoyant in the light of the rigid decisions of juries during the July Monarchy, who based their accolades on the artist's fidelity to their precepts and who rejected innovation out of hand.

The artistic revival thus looked to have petered out, not only in so far as it affected taste, but morality as well; artistic judgment was at the time inextricably associated with moral judgment, a situation that made the stance of adepts of the new manner appear still more radical. If, as luck would have it, this state of affairs did not completely extinguish the artistic flame lit in the early nineteenth century, it did nevertheless have far-reaching consequences: the sclerosis of aesthetic thought in the Academy as it retrenched behind its long-cherished preconceptions; the appearance of groups of artists independent from official circles and venues; the increasingly influential role of critics, who took up the cudgels to defend their favorite artists in the numerous and diverse organs of the press. The absence, owing to the diversity of the subjects and styles even in the academic ambit (the much vaunted "happy medium" now took up the romantic manner and its subjects) of a unique, objective aesthetic rule book, led juries to base their judgments on the processes deployed rather than on the result obtained.[35] Visible brushwork, not only impasto but also any recourse to technical procedures, was likewise decried.

Thus, the upheavals affecting the art world in the early nineteenth century and its links with contemporary revivals in the theater and literature, as well as the closer relationship between art, science, and philosophy, offered a context conducive to a new type of creation. Hence the preconditions (as will be seen below) for the invention of photography were in place, even though the academic reaction of the July Monarchy—lacking grandeur, but still powerful thanks to the sledgehammer wielded by the Salon jury—sabotaged all possibility of establishing a viable aesthetic theory. The situation surrounding the reception of photography in France, and more generally the debates concerning the artistic nature of the invention, can only be appreciated in the light of this situation.

14. **Facing page:** Eugène Delacroix, *The Execution of the Doge Marino Faliero*, 1827, oil on canvas, Wallace Collection, London.

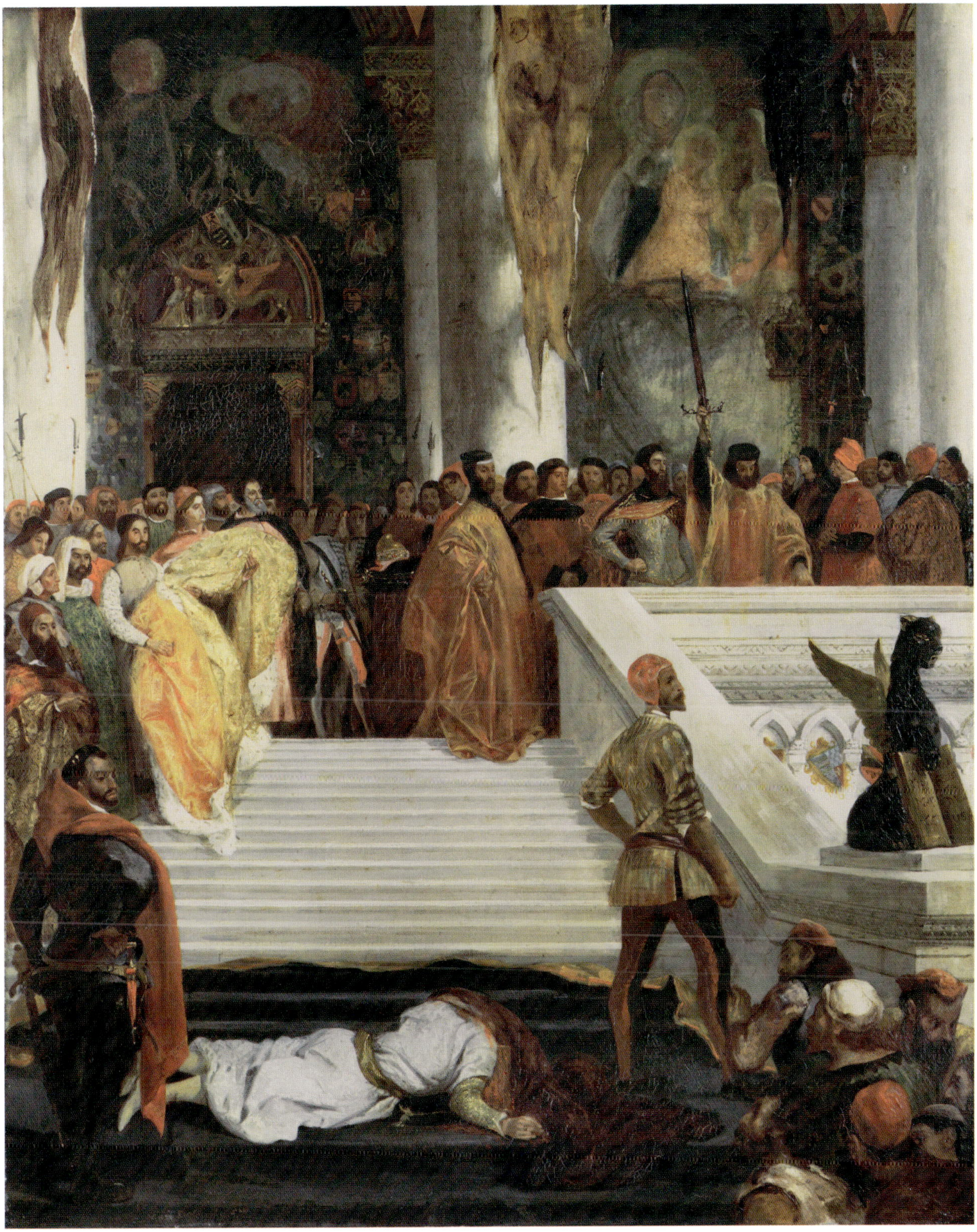

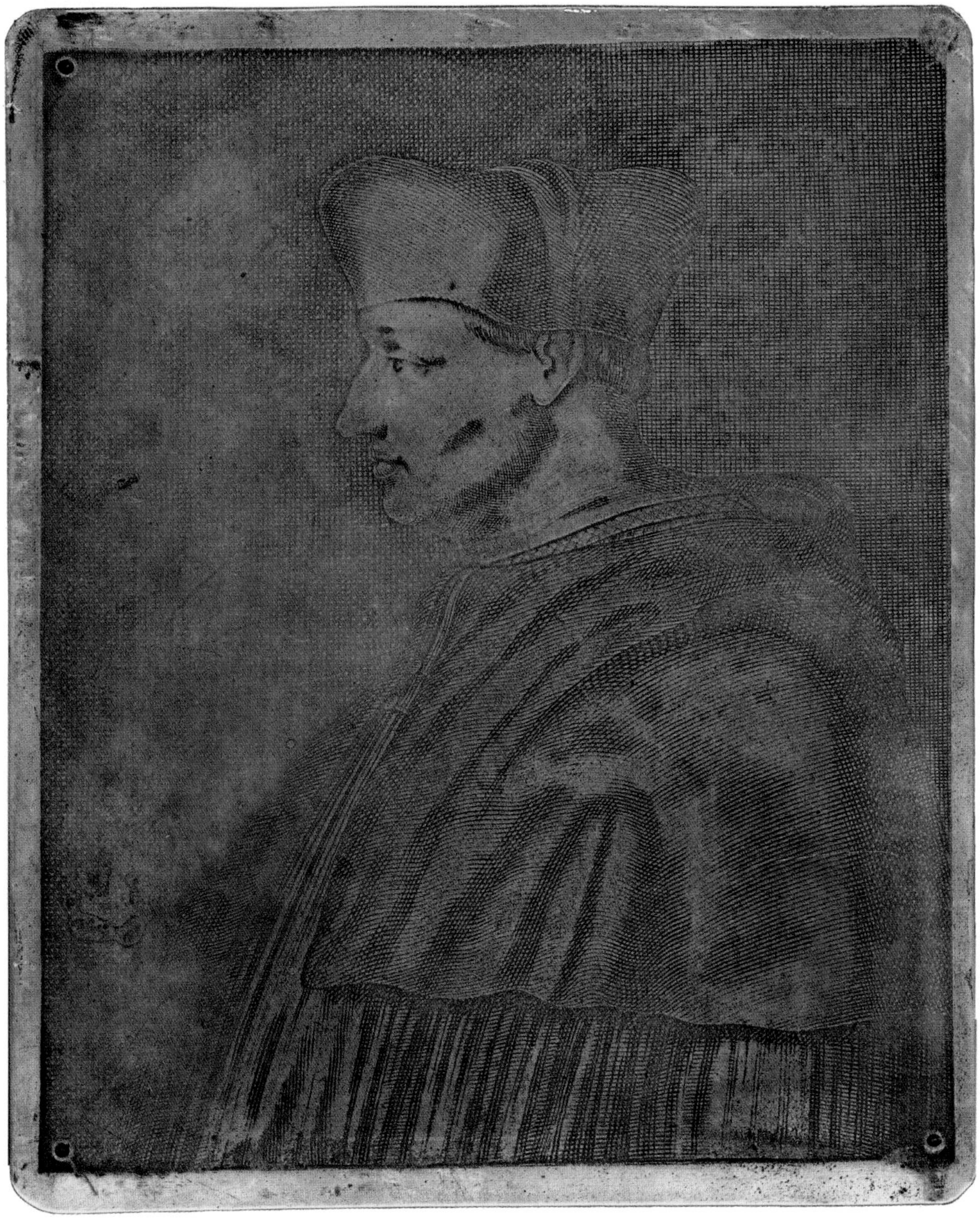

"In short, Monsieur Daguerre's admirable discovery has rendered an immense service to the arts." [1]

THE BIRTH OF PHOTOGRAPHY

CONCEPTION, ANNOUNCEMENT, AND RECEPTION

A partisan affair, the history of the invention of photography is far from being straightforward. There can be no question here of reviewing in detail the emergence of the technique, and recent scholarly works on the subject abound.[2] The ambition of this chapter is rather to outline how the announcement of its invention influenced the manner in which it was received, particularly in artistic circles. Historians have made much of the time-lapse between the idea behind the process and its revelation to the world, thus distinguishing two separate periods. Above and beyond the inevitable vagaries of research and the difficulties of unearthing the relevant historical information, this division—first shadow, then light; first secret, then public—seems inherent in the nature of the process itself. Ever since the works of Louis Figuier, Adrien Mentienne, Gaston Tissandier, and Georges Potonniée, diligently mined by twentieth-century historians, descriptions of the emergence of the invention unfold in the manner of an analogy, and seem dominated by a metaphorical use of the invention concerned.[3] Thus first comes an obscure, early period, that of the invention's conception—the mimetic double of the mystery of the photographic apparatus and the mysterious darkroom (an alchemist's den where silver and mercury mix); this is followed after Arago's announcement by a second stage taking place in broad daylight—a revelation of the process analogous to the new apprehension of reality vouchsafed by Daguerre's earliest photographs. As François Brunet and André Gunthert have noted, seldom can historiography, as it analyzes the creation or development of a process, have adhered so closely to the manner in which it is perceived.[4]

1839: The French announcement

Enshrined in dictionaries and by official celebrations, the year 1839 saw the announcement in France of a process elaborated by Daguerre and based on research undertaken during his association with Nicéphore Niépce in 1829. Many historians of

15. **Facing page:** Nicéphore Niépce, after an engraving by Isaac Briot, "The Cardinal of Amboise," 1826, photograph on acid-etched tin, heliograph by contact, Musée Niépce, Chalon-sur-Saône.

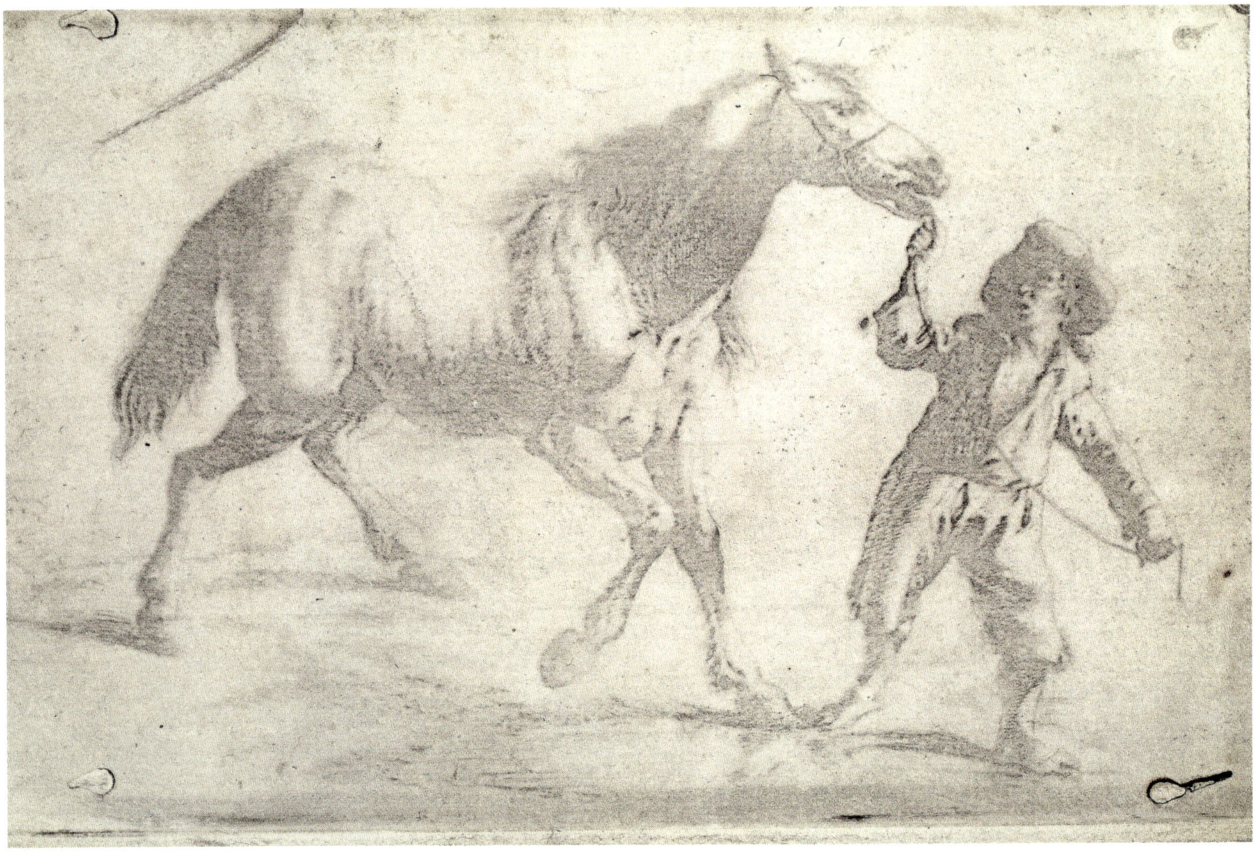

16. Nicéphore Niépce, after Dirck Van der Scoop, "Horse Led by Its Boy," 1825, heliographic engraving, print on paper from a copper plate, Bibliothèque Nationale de France, Paris.

photography, however, dispute the preeminence of this date. And in point of fact, it does not correspond to the year in which the first photographs were obtained by exposure to sunlight—in the literal sense, *photo-graphs*; or, as Niépce dubbed his own device, *hélio-graphie* ("writing by the sun")—since it appears that the Burgundian inventor had obtained some images as early as 1816. "It is as yet a quite imperfect trial," he wrote to his brother, Claude, at the time, "the image of the objects is extremely small. The possibility of painting by this process seems to me to be practically incontrovertible."[5] Niépce had in mind the model of engraving; he carried out several attempts at replicating this variant of printmaking by contact using the action of the sun on silver iodide (ills. 15–16). The oldest surviving example, considered since its discovery by Helmut Gernsheim in 1952 as the "first photograph," dates from 1826; taken by Niépce from a window in his property at Le Gras near Chalon-sur-Saône, it shows the courtyard of the house (ill. 17).[6] In the course of a text retracing the thrilling circumstances surrounding its discovery in England, Gernsheim argued that the invention should be regarded as dating from 1826.

Politically opportune (the fiftieth anniversary of the French Revolution was on everybody's lips), this "French" date of 1839 was intended to enshrine the primacy of French inventiveness over any eventual English claim. Its announcement was brilliantly

17. Nicéphore Niépce, "View from the Window at Le Gras," 1826, heliograph on tin plate, University of Texas, Austin.

orchestrated by a man of great talent, François Arago, a physicist and astronomer as well as member of parliament for his native region, the Pyrénées Orientales.[7] Doubtless it was his work on optics and the perception of light that lay behind his growing interest in Daguerre's process when the latter solicited Arago's aid in 1838. The inventor had thought of launching a subscription to fund the development of his process, the famous daguerreotype, which, if contemporary witnesses are to be believed, he had developed by 1835.[8] Daguerre had shown plates to several influential personalities in Paris, but Arago had already got wind of similar efforts being undertaken by William Fox Talbot in England, and thus thought it essential, for political and economic, as well as for scientific reasons, for the invention of photography to be announced in France without delay. Like his colleagues in the Académie des Sciences (Jean-Baptiste Dumas, Jean-Baptiste Biot, Alexander von Humboldt, among others), he was also won over by the quality of the images presented by Daguerre; their precision and clarity, in particular, revealed a control over light that captivated him (ill. 18).

Arago's announcement was stage-managed in the most remarkable fashion. Daguerre's process was first proclaimed before the French Academy of Sciences at the beginning of 1839, on January 7. On announcing the invention of a new process using a camera obscura that obtained images, exact and perfect representations

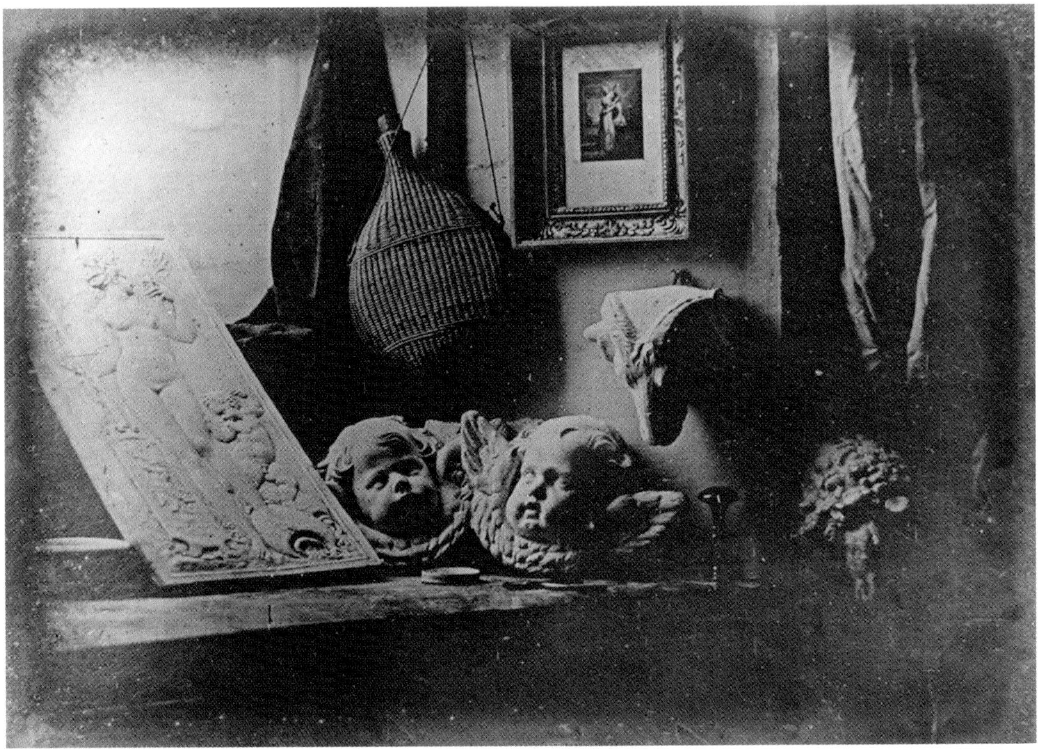

18. Louis Jacques Mandé Daguerre, "Interior of a Cabinet of Curiosities," 1837, daguerreotype, Société Française de Photographie, Paris.

of objects and places, Arago did not actually show the plates, nor did he describe the methods used. This deliberate cliffhanger proved singularly effective. The French and foreign press alike immediately reported the event, thereby sparking interest from Daguerre's competitors; it was indeed after reading reports in the British newspapers that Talbot—probably more precipitously than he would otherwise have wished—risked unveiling his "photogenic drawings" in London (ill. 19).[9] Governments likewise pricked up their ears: several European heads of state, alarmed or merely curious to learn more about this new process in which France took such pride, sent emissaries—half-spies, half-scientists—to investigate the question more closely. One such was Czar Nicolas I, who dispatched Joseph Hamel to France with a mission to get to the bottom of the invention.[10]

A law for photography

To accelerate the uptake of the new process, Arago now campaigned for a law on photography to be passed that would, through the award of an annuity to Daguerre and Isidore Niépce (Nicéphore's son, who had taken on the association after the death of his father, though without joining forces with Daguerre), render the invention of the apparatus rights-free, and thus make it accessible to all. Anticipating the technical and economic consequences of the development of the invention, the scientist expressed his hope that France would "give photography to the world." The presentation in

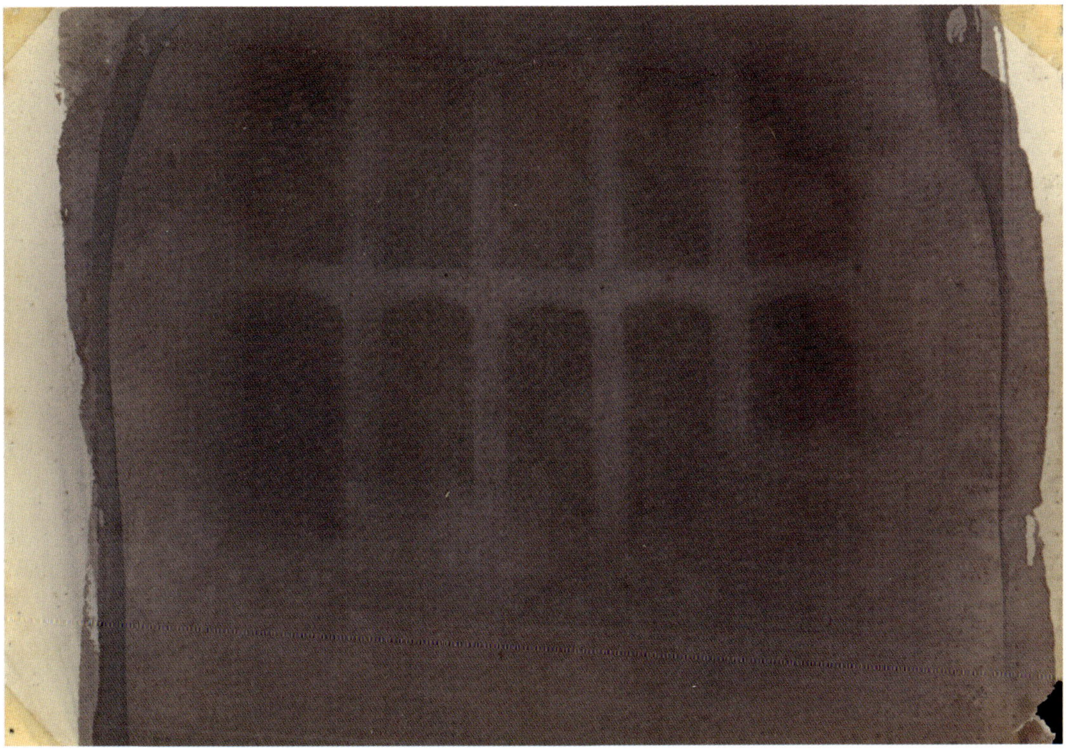

19. William Henry Fox Talbot, "Oriel Window, South Gallery, Lacock Abbey," 1835 or 1838, negative photogenic drawing, The Metropolitan Museum of Art, New York.

the Chamber of Deputies took place in July 1839; couched in somewhat utopian language, his speech amounted to a heartfelt entreaty in favor of Daguerre's invention. This time, if plates were on display, there were still no details on hand concerning the process. "The idea of photography" was thus let out of bag before the technique, audiences being left to wonder and speculate until the next episode.[11] All was made clear on August 19, 1839, the day the daguerreotype device was unveiled at the Institute in the presence of members of the Académie des Sciences, joined by a few of their colleagues from the Beaux-Arts; in September, Daguerre demonstrated the use of his process at the Conservatoire des Arts et Métiers.

The consecration of the inventor

As will be seen below, though it clearly played a decisive role at the time as well as subsequently, arguments raged as to the influence of the 1839 French announcement on the way in which photography was received; similarly, the paramount role Arago attributed to Daguerre has been the source of much controversy. Arago celebrated in Daguerre the figure of the genial inventor, honored for his inherent qualities. Although he had probably met the inventor on Daguerre's prompting only a matter of months previously,[12] the physicist sang the inventor's praises in a lyrical vein that bordered on romantic outpouring. If, as the conclusion of his lecture recalled, France was able to adopt "this discovery ... and ... [take] pride in liberally presenting it to the world at large,"[13] it could only do so thanks to Daguerre's intelligence and his many other talents (the elder Niépce had died and unfortunately his son Isidore was not possessed of the inventiveness required to take up the baton). Beyond the question of who, there was also the what? Arago carefully distinguished the daguerreotype from the other "photographic" print processes on paper that preceded it, that of Niépce included. He stressed its originality, its staggering visual impact, thereby initiating the aesthetics of clarity and precision that remains, even today, the ideal of the photographic image: "Paper impregnated with chloride or silver nitrate was in point of fact the first substance chosen by Daguerre; but its lack of sensitivity, the blurring of the image, the unpredictable results ... could not but discourage so adroit an artist. If he had persisted along that path, perhaps his photographic drawings would have appeared in collections as the product of some curious experiment in physics, but undoubtedly the Chambers would not been convened to bother with them."[14] Arago thus scorned paper-on-paper processes, trials that then seemed to him at once hazardous and imperfect. He had likewise neglected the early prints of Hippolyte Bayard when their inventor tried to show him in spring 1839, just as he attached scant importance to those created by Herschel, even though he was both Arago's colleague and a famous astronomer (ill. 20).

As early as 1839, voices were heard denouncing the academician's interest in Daguerre's brainchild; Arago was portrayed as offering barely veiled support for a showman who had recently lost his money and the secret of his inventions in a fire at the diorama. It can, however, hardly be doubted that the preference the scientist accorded the daguerreotype as against paper processes was motivated above all by the intrinsic qualities of Daguerre's plates: the exactness of the image and also the method by which it captured light. This neglect of Niépce, in spite of the pension awarded to his son Isidore, which matched the one given to Daguerre, quickly sparked other reactions. In 1841, Isidore Niépce himself brought out a brief text in defense of his father, willfully and wrongfully forgotten in his eyes. The title speaks volumes: *Histoire de la découverte improprement appelée daguerréotype, précédé d'une notice sur son véritable inventeur, Nicéphore Niépce* (A History of the Discovery Improperly Called the Daguerreotype, Preceded by a Note on Its True Inventor, Nicéphore Niépce).[15] Since then, tension between the partisans of the one or the other has scarcely abated, and most historiography in the area has focused on defending the "true" inventor and on toppling Daguerre, "the usurper," from the pedestal on which Arago placed him. The ousting from 1855 onward of the daguerreotype by paper processes close to those of Niépce, Bayard, and even more so by the method perfected by Talbot, thus fathered a counter-history of the invention that centers on photography on paper to the exclusion of the daguerreotype, henceforth viewed as an outdated and unsatisfactory dead-end.

The notion of one sole inventor—a point of view in keeping with the romanticism of the era and placed at the center of

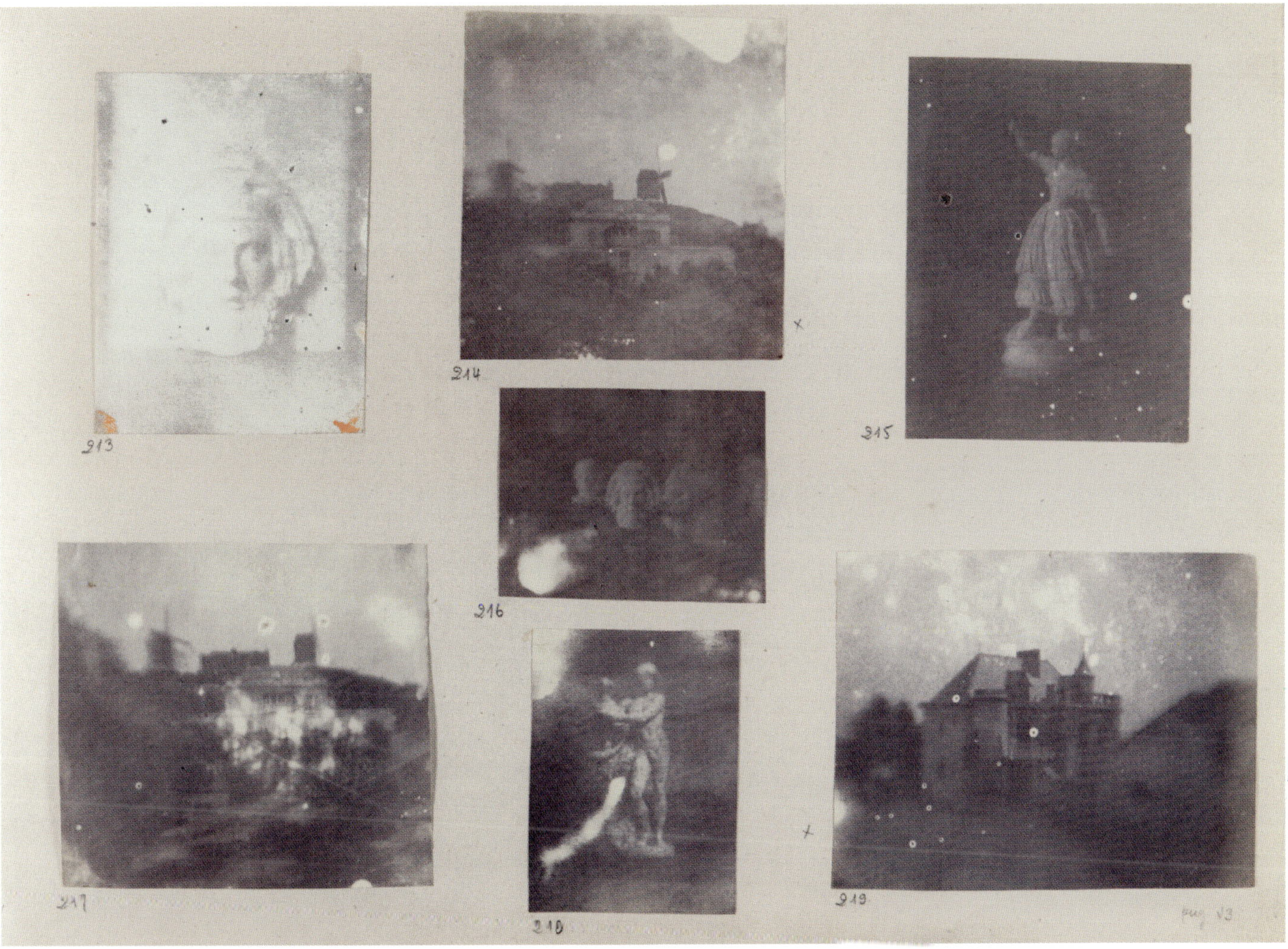

20. Hippolyte Bayard, sheet from an album of the author's trial photographs, 1839, seven direct positives, Société Française de Photographie, Paris.

the debate by Arago—is probably a mirage anyhow. In the early decades of the nineteenth century, the quest for a process able to preserve the image formed in the camera obscura was the concern of many different individuals in France and in England, but also in the United States (with Samuel Morse) and Brazil (with Hercule Florence). History has still probably not yet unearthed the names of all those who played a part; the serious-looking young man, who haunted the shop of the optician Chevalier and is mentioned by Tissandier, remains a little-known if appealing figure.[16] Furthermore other recent studies, like that by Paul-Louis Roubert on Alphonse Eugène Hubert, demonstrate that much remains to be unearthed concerning the identity and precise role of all these photographic pioneers.[17] In a nutshell, seldom can so many individuals have lent a hand in the creation of so famous an invention.

In spite of some important improvements in optics during the early nineteenth century, photography relied on a venerable device, the camera obscura, invented in the late fifteenth in Italy and commonly used by architectural painters to obtain

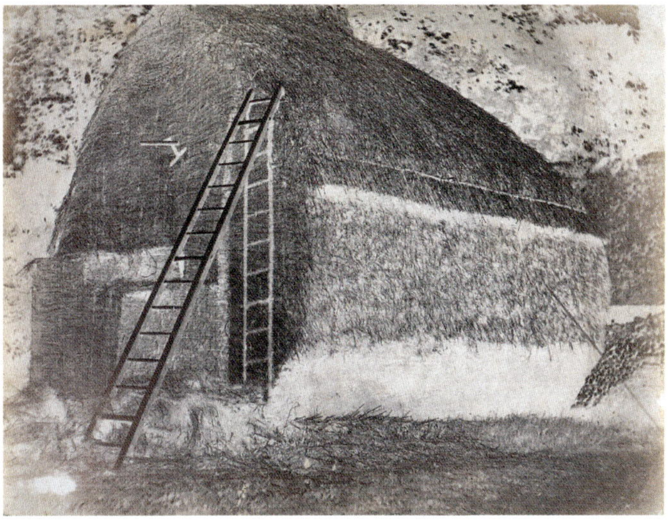

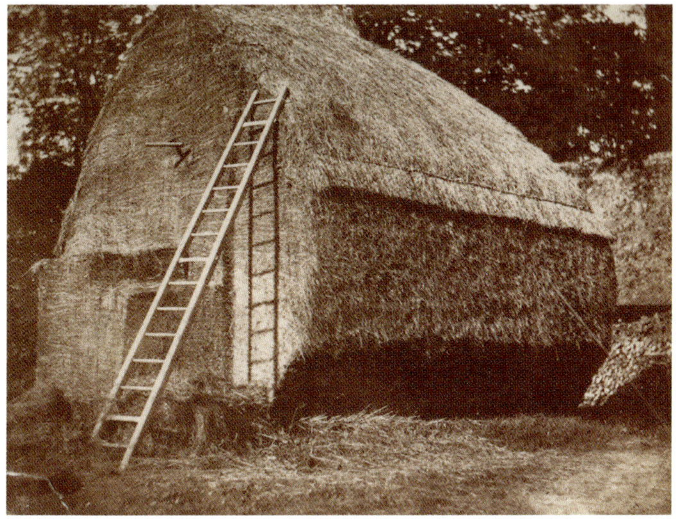

21–22. William Henry Fox Talbot, "The Haystack," 1842, negative on paper and calotype, National Media Museum, Bradford.

correct perspective views. The invention and development of the panorama, at the end of the eighteenth century, gave fresh impetus to the use of such devices. However, if the apparatus used was hardly novel, the desire to preserve and reproduce the images it permitted was. "How charming it would be if it were possible to cause these natural images to imprint themselves durably, and to remain fixed upon the paper," wrote William Henry Fox Talbot, recalling the circumstances behind the invention (ills. 21–22).[18] The desire to capture the evanescent traces left by images in a dark chamber, originated in two different ideas shared by a number of researchers at the time: first, capturing the lines and contours of an image with the utmost possible exactitude; second, reproducing the pictures obtained in the device. Tributary of both representation and imitation, these twin impulses reinforced the ontological links that the new process—by dint of its use of the camera obscura—possessed, with the art of painting. Designed to facilitate the application of the rules of Albertian perspective, from the start the deployment of the camera obscura placed photography on a par with painting; photographic representation was thus framed by the old pictorial analogy of a window open to the world. Implicitly, it valorized the eye of the operator who determined the limits—the frame—of the representation in a further illustration of the mirror metaphor established by Stendhal and Hugo for romantic art. Attempts to seize accurately the features and outlines of objects and people had already spawned mechanisms that combined technical processes and parlor games, such as Philibert Chasles's silhouettes and the "*physionotrace*." The idea of reproducing, and thus disseminating, the image was also key to the approaches both of Niépce in France and Talbot in England. The model to which they both referred was gravure, a notion doubtless reinforced by the new potential afforded by lithography, in particular in respect of the reproduction of paintings.

Its announcement by a notable scientist in the hugely prestigious forum of the Académie des Sciences in Paris naturally had major repercussions on the perception and nature of the invention. In spite of Daguerre's background (he was a painter and man of the theater who moved in artistic circles), and despite its relatively simple technical resources, from the outset photography was viewed as having to do with science and mechanics. Remarks by the originator himself bolstered this "technical" view; determined to make his arguments watertight and have his process taken up, in the descriptive note published in 1838, Daguerre had simplified its methods and skated over the role of the operator. Reading it, one would think that the hand of man had been entirely ousted by the machine: thanks to a chance, if controlled, encounter with the sun's rays, the daguerreotype allowed "the spontaneous reproduction of natural images received in the camera obscura."[19] Thus it sounded as though the desire to imitate—the foundation of pictorial representation—could at last be realized without defects, without risks, by dint of a single mechanical process. Arago went on to imagine the role of the daguerreotype had it been invented in 1799, in time for Napoleon's Egyptian campaign: "Provide the Institute with two or three of M. Daguerre's apparatuses and ... vast swathes of real hieroglyphs will replace all the fictitious or purely conventional ones."[20]

If the results proved appealing, magical almost, the manner of attaining them—seemingly dispensing with the hand and mind of man—could only arouse suspicion in a century in which academe exerted an iron grip over artistic education. In stressing the simplicity of the daguerreotype (in fact, as the testimony of the earliest photographers show, it turned out to be a far more thorny affair), its creator sought to promote a technique which at the time remained the only contemporary photographic process capable of being described in a detailed and comprehensible manner, and so repeated by an operator other than its inventor. At this juncture, neither Talbot's nor Bayard's process could have been explained so clearly.[21] Arago founded a substantial proportion of his argument on the transparency of the concept behind the new process: "The daguerreotype does not call for a single piece of information beyond the grasp of the common man.... By sticking to the letter of a very few, eminently simple stipulations, everyone should be able to succeed as surely and as satisfactorily as M. Daguerre himself."[22]

An experienced businessman with an acute nose for publicity, Daguerre quickly grasped the fact that daguerreotype could never gather the funds necessary for its development from commercial outlets alone. As he wrote to Isidore Niépce, he felt that only the portrait (then impracticable due to the long exposure times required—from three to five minutes) might create the conditions for its financial success: "If I could manage to do portraits ... I wouldn't bother to try to sell it [the photographic process that

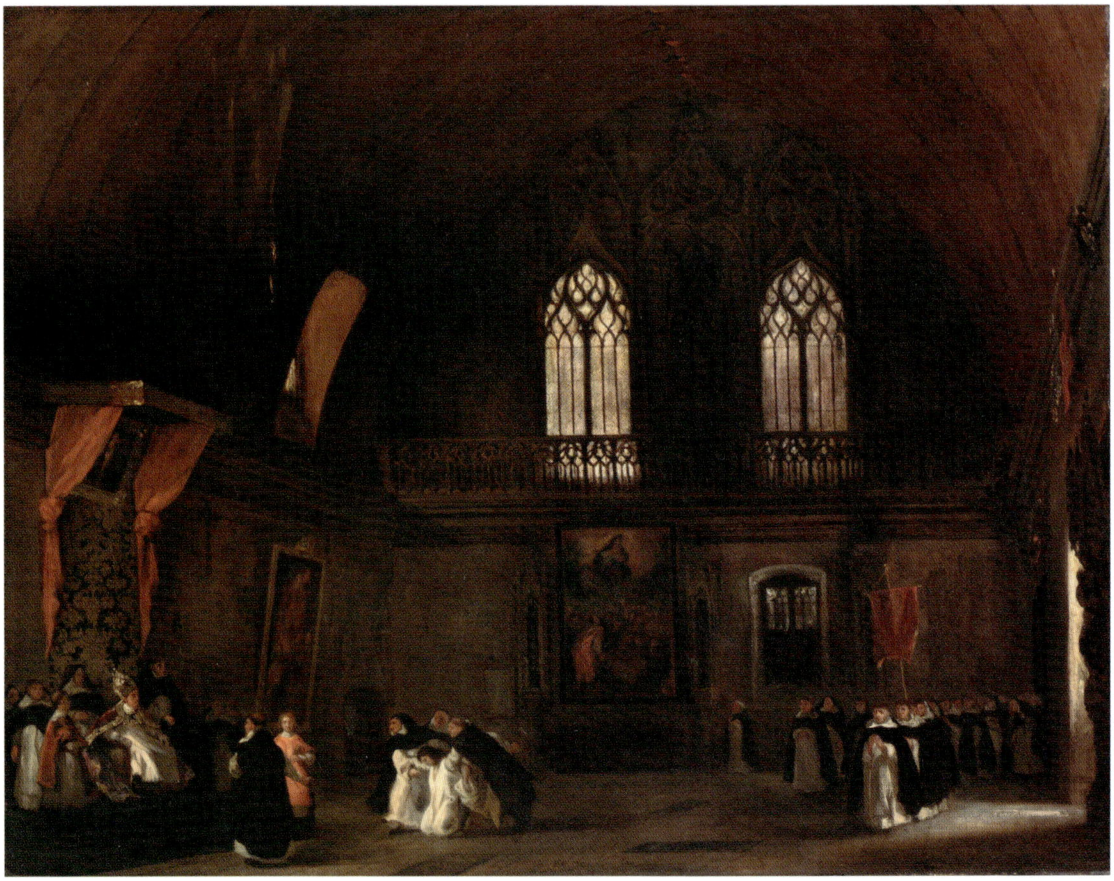

23. Eugène Delacroix, *Interior of a Dominican Convent in Madrid*, 1831, oil on canvas, Philadelphia Museum of Art, Philadelphia.

became the daguerreotype] anymore; we'd be able to exploit it ourselves."[23] Since that route was closed off, Daguerre had come up with another means—a subscription—and it was this that led him to solicit assistance from personalities in the scientific and artistic communities. Arago's eagerness and commitment to promoting the daguerreotype thus opened another door, political and official this time, that Daguerre had probably never previously envisaged. Arago thus rescued Daguerre's invention, temporarily at least, from the pitfalls of a purely commercial success that might prove transitory and belittling. By throwing his considerable weight behind the invention (something that apparently cost him dear in the Académie des Sciences, where he was accused of peddling "scientific toys"), Arago couched the description of what might have seemed a laboratory curiosity, a drawing-room amusement even, in the requisite scientific terms.

Belief in a new world

Eventually Arago's rhetorical gifts, borne along by rare conviction and aided and abetted by his unflagging commitment, paid dividends, and the battle for the recognition of the invention was won. His vision was impressive, even if it verged on the utopian;

the physicist invested much of his own belief in a new world, one in which science would enrich knowledge and serve the homeland by *discovering* a hitherto hidden process. Arago deliberately employed the terms "discovery" and "invention" without distinction, and both were taken up by commentators. Placing the daguerreotype in a historical continuum that started in the Renaissance with the revelation of images in the camera obscura of Della Porta and led finally, more than four centuries later, to their capture in Daguerre's apparatus, the academician filled in the teleological back-story to the invention. In speaking of images obtained by a process that remained for the moment unverified, he cast a veil of mystery over the invention that was all the more impenetrable since, in the clarity of their lines and the precision of their detail, the pictures seemed to contain a secret world, one formerly invisible to the naked eye. Thus, although admitted to and lauded in that temple of rationality, the Académie des Sciences, something supernatural or marvelous seemed to adhere to the daguerreotype—a reflection of the period's taste for amusements based on optical illusion, such as the magic lantern shows popular in middle-class drawing rooms of the time. Portrayed in Arago's exposition as an entity midway between rationality and enchantment, the new invention seemed to encapsulate the nineteenth-century's fusion of positivist faith and a fondness for the bizarre.

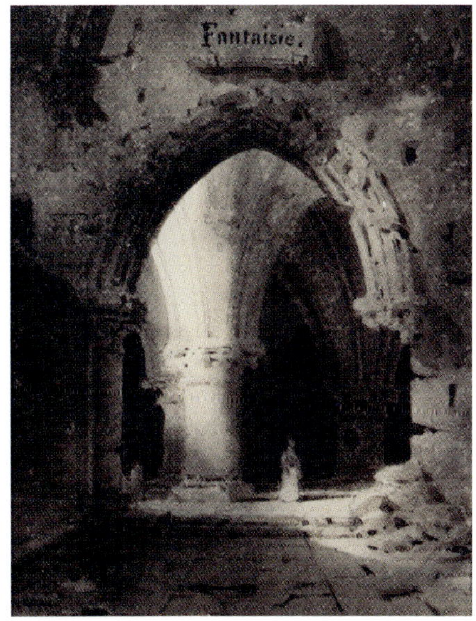

24. Louis Jacques Mandé Daguerre, *Ruins of a Church with Pointed Arches*, c. 1827, *dessin fumée*, Musée Baron-Martin, Gray.

Daguerre's decisive role

Consecrated by Arago as the inventor, and vilified by others who disapproved of his craving for recognition or who envied his skill, Daguerre thus played a key role in the emergence of the new process, even if he was not the author of the very first photographic images. It was he, surely, who rendered the announcement of the invention possible through the improvements he brought, and who paved the way for its acceptance. He had probably first tried to fix the images of the camera obscura he had been using for several years as a painter of panoramas (first at Prévost's and then in his own "diorama") in about 1824, claiming that the earliest results dated from the end of 1825. He had heard talk of Niépce's work at Chevalier, the optician's in Paris where he was a regular customer. It is conceivable, as Gernsheim advances, that Daguerre managed to earn the confidence of Niépce (a man unlikely to have been eager to work with an individual whose renown and wheeling and dealing would, if anything, have put him off), not by showing him a *héliographe*, but instead a sepia engraving reproducing one of his own drawings. It was surely his proven ability to improve Niépce's process that opened the door to their association in December 1829 (ill. 24).[24]

Niépce praised Daguerre's mastery over light in a letter to Isidore, written after a visit to the creator of the diorama: "His process and mine are completely different. There is something marvelous about his, and its swiftness can be compared to that of

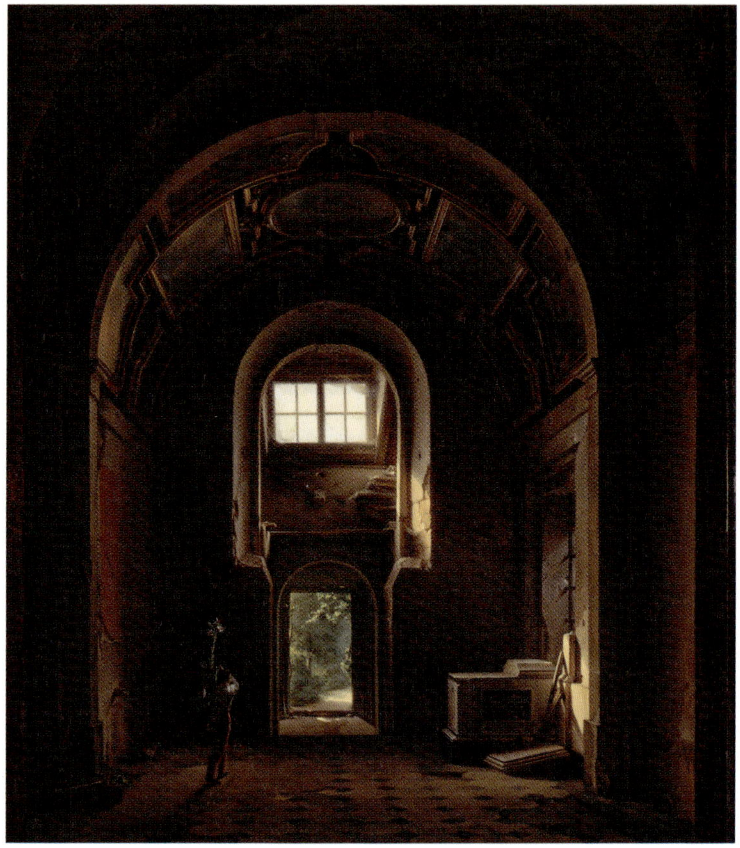

25. Louis Jacques Mandé Daguerre, *Interior of a Chapel in the Church of the Feuillants*, 1814, oil on canvas, Musée du Louvre, Paris.

26. **Facing page:** Louis Jacques Mandé Daguerre, *Interior of Rosslyn Chapel*, 1824, oil on canvas, Musée des Beaux-Arts, Rouen.

the electric fluid. M. Daguerre has managed to fix some of the light rays of the spectrum to a chemical substance."[25] Niépce pays due homage to Daguerre's skill in two essential respects: its speed (or at least the relatively short exposure time, one of the principal disadvantages of Niépce's process being that it required nearly three days' exposure to the sun), and the exactitude of the reflections, and thus of the images. Whatever one might say about Daguerre's veneer of amateurism, following his association with Niépce he devoted himself diligently to the new invention; moreover, after the closure of his diorama (it only reopened in 1836), he was left with much more leisure time. As Charles Chevalier reported, "Suddenly, Daguerre was nowhere to be seen! Cooped up in a laboratory that he had installed in the premises of the Diorama where he then resided, he set to work with new ardor, studied chemistry, and for about two years, lived almost continuously in the company of textbooks, flasks, retorts, and crucibles. I stole a glimpse of that mysterious laboratory, but I, no more than anyone else, was never permitted to enter it."[26] The analogy with the alchemist's den, and allusions to the marvelous generally, were taken up by the protagonists themselves in their accounts. Long after the invention of photography, the reference to magic endured in memories of the time.[27]

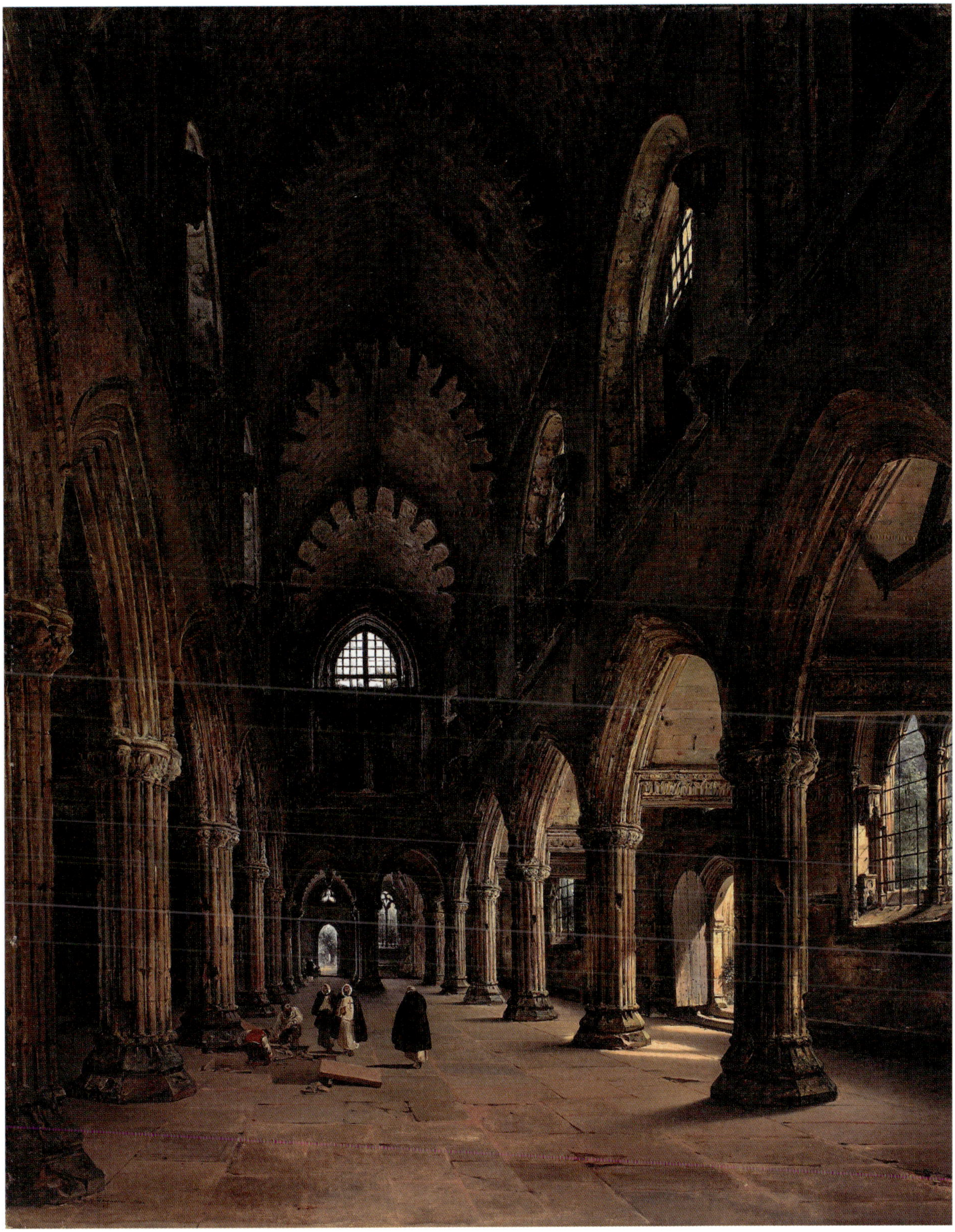

A magician with light

Daguerre now placed all his talent as a set designer, painter, and showman in the service of his new brainchild, the daguerreotype. As Jean Adhémar put it in a memorable phrase in 1961, "Throughout his professional life Daguerre had been a *perspectivist*, that is, an artist specializing in backdrops, in the distant prospects of a landscape or scene. In this, by deploying effects of shade and light that relied on his recollections of the flats and uprights on which he had also worked, he was supreme."[28] Indeed, at the very beginning of the nineteenth century, the inventor of the diorama and the daguerreotype had worked as painter of panoramas for Pierre Prévost (a French painter who exploited Robert Barker's invention in Paris), while, as an easel painter, Daguerre exhibited at the Salon for the first time in 1814 (ill. 25). Étienne Delécluze, in penning a tribute to his teacher entitled the *Histoire de l'atelier de David* in 1853, even mentions Daguerre and Charles Bouton, his associate at the diorama, as pupils of the master.[29] If this information is not, apparently, borne out by other sources, it is not without interest to see how the old painter, by then a critic on the *Journal des débats,* a review poorly disposed to photography at beginning of the 1850s, had no objection to associating its inventor with the most exalted circle to which he himself belonged—that is, with the students of David. In 1824, Daguerre was awarded the Legion of Honor for *Ruins of Holyrood Abbey* (Walker Art Gallery, Liverpool); his canvases, close in subject to a stage set, take their cue from the contemporary taste for medieval architecture, indulging in the kind of chiaroscuro effects dear to François Marius Granet and Auguste de Forbin (ill. 26). By 1816, thanks to the lighting tricks in which he excelled, Daguerre had already risen to become one of the most celebrated theatrical decorators of the time.

Daguerre was thus closely involved in the art world of his age, abreast of ongoing developments in painting and drama, aware of the new approach to the representation of history, and receptive to the taste for contemporary English painting and Dutch eighteenth-century art. His brother-in-law, John Arrowsmith, was, together with Claude Schroth, one of Constable's French dealers, while Daguerre himself was close to the firm of Giroux, founded in the early nineteenth century and with premises on Rue du Coq-Saint-Honoré, near the Louvre, since 1802. The company's activities were many and varied, combining picture dealing and restoration, as well as a trade in artists' materials; from 1822, they also rented out to painters and art lovers old masters and contemporary works in their possession, thereby securing an income less irregular than with sales. A catalog published in 1827 lists more than nine hundred numbers. By allowing works in their stock to circulate in this fashion, the Girouxs at once propagated the standard models and diffused the new aesthetics. Designated as the putative successor, their son André Giroux was a recognized landscape painter, and winner in 1827 of the *grand prix* for historical landscape; showing considerable talent, he devoted himself to photography from the early 1850s.[30] It was with the Giroux house that Daguerre designed and marketed the first daguerreotype apparatus in 1839. His contributions to the *Voyages pittoresques et romantiques dans l'Ancienne France* by Taylor and Nodier (it was he who created the large plate of the Abbey of Jumièges, in the first volume of the collection devoted to Normandy) (ill. 12) had surely provided him with the opportunity to meet Alphonse de Cailleux, an associate during the conception of the work. In 1838, Cailleux was appointed to the vital post of secretary-general to the Royal Museums; at the end of the same year, Daguerre sent to him, as he did to Arago, one of his first plates, today in the headquarters of the Société Française de Photographie.

Opening in June 1822, the diorama proved an ideal venue for putting his mastery of light effects to good use. In collaboration with the painter Charles Bouton, he staged shows that featured light flitting over a pair of extremely large canvases, some 46 feet by 65 ½ feet (14 meters by 20 meters), deploying all the resources of lighting, refraction, and reflection to conjure up views that shifted from storm to sunlight or from day to night. The invention built on the trend for miniature landscape sets used for optical entertainments, which had first appeared in the eighteenth century. Thanks to the qualities of Daguerre's machine, which drew on optical research on color perception by both Goethe and Chevreul, Parisian audiences adored the diorama. Painters, novelists, and poets were amazed by shows whose subjects, drawing their inspiration from the universe of Walter Scott, were perfectly attuned to the taste of the time.[31]

The daguerreotype as heir to the diorama

Acclaimed for its marvelous, magical effects, the diorama involved a process of diachrony, and hence of narrative. Standing stockstill, spectators watched spellbound as the picture changed before their very eyes, amazed as light first materialized, then disappeared. The implicit postulate behind the theater as fiction was transcended; the perfect illusion offered by the diorama replaced the real world entirely, deceiving the senses and arousing the emotions. As has often been stated, its true heir was to arrive on the scene more than sixty years later in the shape of the cinematograph. Photography too, as Daguerre conceived it with the daguerreotype, draws much from the illusion and artifice of the diorama. The manner in which their creator associated the two devices—signing the first announcement in 1838 as "Daguerre, painter, inventor and director of the diorama," and publishing in 1839 an *Historique et description des procédés du daguerréotype et du diorama* (A Historical and Descriptive Account of the Various Processes of the Daguerreotype and the Diorama)[32]—shows how eager he was for them to be conceived of together. The double title was not only intended to foreground his inventive skill;

it also recalls how the two processes, so unlike in their outcomes, revolved around similar postulates: the manipulation of light in order to render an object plainly visible (thereby creating an illusion and thus an emotional response), as well as to attain a clarity and precision in a type of representation in which Daguerre's image becomes an ersatz for reality. At its conception, then, the daguerreotype appeared intimately bound up with the set design and the dramaturgy of the era.

In March 1839, Jules Janin became one of the first critics to write about the process, in a substantial article published in *L'Artiste* under the title "*Daguereotype* [*sic*]." A man of the theater, Janin was well acquainted with Daguerre's earlier forays, and a few years previously had dedicated several pages to the diorama in the same review. This initial account centered on the conceptual similarity between the two inventions: "By the sheer power of this art [the diorama] that he improved still further, Daguerre draws us deep into pictures that, prior to his efforts, were just surface.... Presented with such novel spectacles, the public stood dumbfounded in amazed and confused admiration. And the painters said to each other: what a pity that Daguerre, that great painter, now busies himself making pictures more beautiful than any painting! Daguerre answered admiration and reproach alike with a smile, for only he knew what he was aiming for.... At the cost of a great deal of study, this celebrated painter has managed to become a great chemist."

Janin hailed the inventor as a lighting genius, a magician of effects: "Moreover, he knew, as we all know, about the action of the sun and light on color. Thus, with the indomitable perseverance characteristic of genius, he took up the gauntlet [... and] forced the sun, the eye of the world, to be no more than an ingenious workman toiling under the orders of a taskmaster!"[33] Thus did the daguerreotype bring image-making into the realms of performance (ill. 27). And, in its very nature, Daguerre's image also relates to passing time; it refers back to a history forever lost—though not as its copy, but as its representation. Photography, such as Daguerre conceived of it, thus combines narrative and spectacle.[34]

The exact perfection of a unique image

To attain utter perfection in one unique image, Daguerre was obliged to give up the reproducibility both Niépce and Talbot had sought. The daguerreotype, unlike processes on paper, was a one-off object, not a matrix from which multiple copies could be run off. Daguerre thus substituted the model of engraving with that of painting. The logic of the frame on the wall replaced the portfolio: the daguerreotype was intended to be hung in a gallery, like a canvas; its final destination was clearly an exhibition. If the inventor laid such store by the precision of line, it was less for scientific reasons than to conform to the precepts of exactitude and

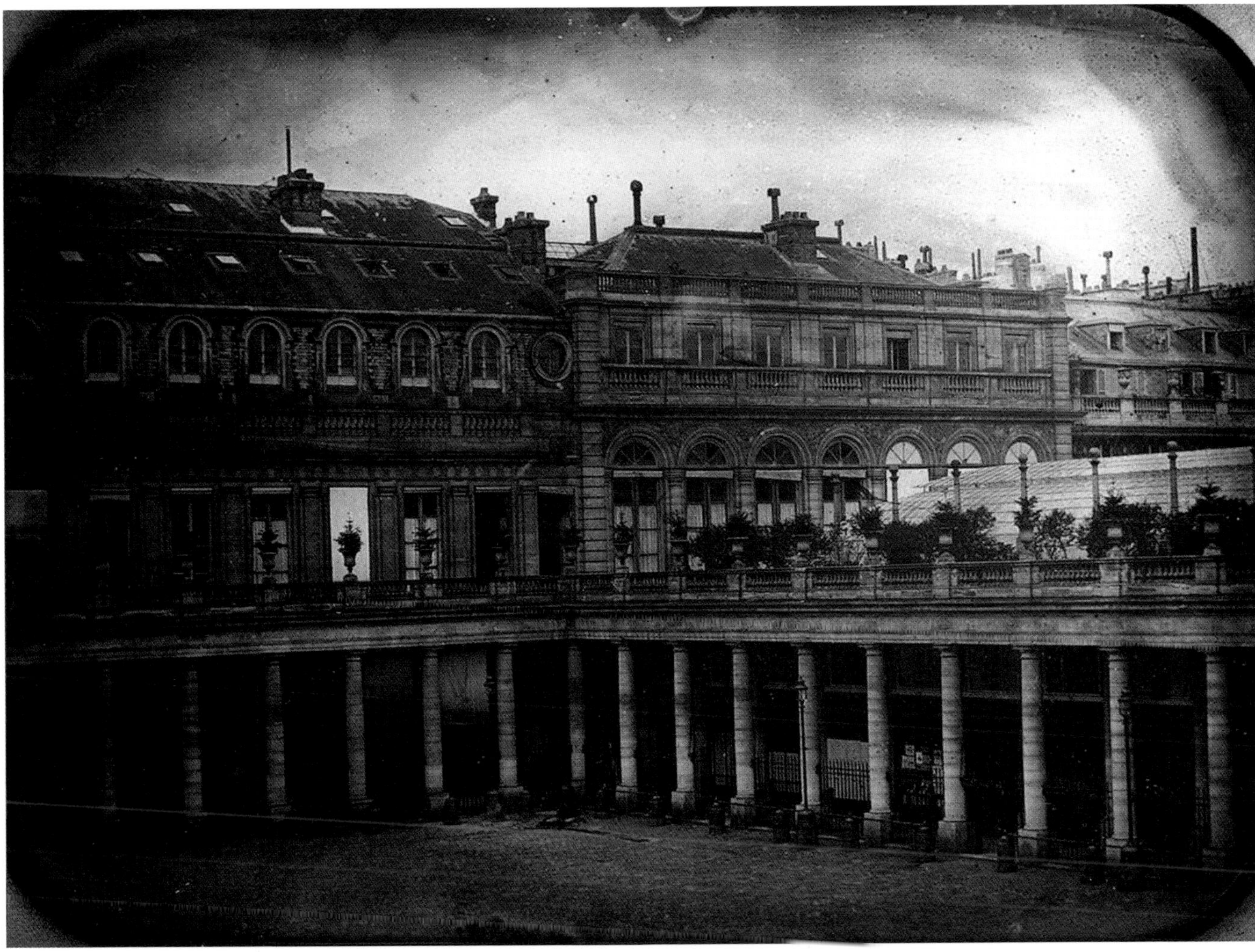

clarity in representation, as revealed in the legibility of detail. Keeping uppermost in mind what he had learned at Prévost's with the camera obscura, Daguerre paid scrupulous attention to focusing, so as to attain the finest possible exactness of line.

Ousted by photographic processes on paper during the 1850s, the daguerreotype nonetheless did much to establish canons of photographic representation founded on linear precision, clarity, balanced composition, control of light, and a feeling for the moment. Photography was then heir to the theatrical and pictorial aesthetics of the early nineteenth century, built on the dual and ambivalent pillars of rationalism and wonder. The future reception of the new invention can thus be understood only with reference to Arago's announcement. Its exceptional conditions were spatial (it took place in the most prestigious scientific institution of its time), temporal (as in the suspense built up between the discourse and the revelation of the actual process), and political (the promulgation of a law on photography involved the French nation as a whole). It must also be seen in the context of the

27. Louis Jacques Mandé Daguerre, "View of the Palais-Royal," 1838, daguerreotype, Národní Technické Muzeum, Prague.

contemporary perception of Daguerre's earlier creations, celebrated for their unique ability to summon up enchanting magic worlds. Already mitigated by the irritation inevitably occasioned by his successes, the inventor's entrepreneurship and foible for self-promotion left a sour aftertaste to some of the plaudits he received, further exacerbated by the award of a state annuity. Finally, it has to be seen, of course, in the light of developments in the use of the invention itself, as well as of the role it played in the society of the 1840s. Naturally enough, the core of its reception in artistic milieus coalesced around the potential position of photography with respect to painting.

The art world reserves its opinion

Despite his critics, Arago nonetheless managed to ensure a positive response to photography within his own circles, the Académie des Sciences and the Chambre des Députés (Chamber of Deputies). He was much more circumspect in his relations with the Académie des Beaux-Arts, preferring to give it a wide berth. He was especially wary of the irritability and narrow-mindedness of the Academy's permanent secretary, the archaeologist Désiré Raoul-Rochette, elected the previous year, perhaps as a sweetener for having lost his post as director of the cabinet of medals in the royal library after some unpleasant business concerning a theft. Stung to the quick by this unfortunate incident, and anxious to steer clear of any further mishap, throughout his mandate Raoul-Rochette adopted the unbending attitude of a guardian to the temple. He thus appeared as the last person in the world likely to welcome with open arms a dubious gadget in which science and technology seemed to take precedence over artistic creativity. Perhaps, in his speech to the chamber, even while acknowledging the utopian nature of this new time machine, when Arago conjured up the services the daguerreotype might have rendered during the archaeological campaign to Egypt, he was already thinking of Raoul-Rochette and of his work.[35]

The recognition, if not the gratitude, of the art world was, however, to be essential. With this in mind, and hoping as well to take the wind out of the objectors' sails, Arago turned to Paul Delaroche. As an academician since 1832 (when he had been elected as the youngest member of the institution), a professor at the École des Beaux-Arts since 1833, the head of the one of the most important studios of the time, son-in-law of Horace Vernet, director of the French Academy in Rome, Delaroche was one of the most highly regarded artists of the era. Still relatively young, scarcely more than forty, and a onetime pupil of Antoine-Jean Gros, having made his name at the Salons of 1824 and 1827, Delaroche possessed the added advantage of embodying, with respect to older colleagues and former pupils of David, a new taste, romantic in its choice of subject and its stagey compositions, but sufficiently placid in style, smooth and precise, to remain acceptable. The painter's fondness for precision in details and his meticulous attention to their veracity seemed likely to make him receptive to the precision of line in Daguerre's plates, as well as to their capacity to record elements invisible to the naked eye. Arago thus avoided the potential ambush represented by personally presenting the official unveiling of the process before the learned Académie des Beaux-Arts.

A finish of unimaginable finesse

Delaroche's opinion proved positive: "The finish, of unimaginable finesse, in no way disturbs the stillness of the masses, in no way mars the overall effect.... In these drawings by M. Daguerre the accuracy of the lines, the precision of the forms is as total as it could be, and one notes therein at once the broad, energetic modeling and a whole as rich in tone as in effect."[36] Like the smooth, unruffled appearance of the surface of the daguerreotype plate, the drive for legibility that had motivated the improvements made by the inventor paralleled Delaroche's pictorial aspirations. Obsessed with providing an utterly faithful depiction of an historical scene, and highlighting every detail that might signify its period, Delaroche would surely have shared the enthusiasm of Alexander von Humboldt—a member of the Académie des Sciences close to Arago—for the invention's ability to show elements invisible to the naked eye. As he averred in a letter sent in March 1839 to his friend, the painter Carl Gustav Carus: "He [Arago] handed me a magnifying glass and I saw strands of straw at all the windows ... it was possible to discern from the image that in one attic window—what a trifle this is!!—a pane of glass had been broken and the window stopped up with paper."[37]

If Delaroche makes much of the attractions and innovative nature of the contraption, as well as of its tastefulness (such as he saw it, at least), in spite of the terms employed by both the painter and Arago drawn from artistic parlance (drawings, paintings), his observations are entirely unambiguous. The only role the daguerreotype might have in the creation of art would be as a source of studies for a painting: "The painter will find in this process a rapid method for amassing a collection of studies that he could obtain otherwise only with much time and toil, and much less perfectly, however great his talent."[38] Neglecting to expound on the precise character of these studies, Delaroche mentioned neither their subject, nor their exact role. Following Arago, he placed the emphasis on the speed of execution (as it transpired, something more theoretical than real when the technical complexity of its operation became apparent), and, if he stressed its "perfect manner," and certainly paid due homage to the clarity of Daguerre's plates, he expressed himself in generalities and ignored its aesthetic applications.

In spite of this positive opinion, the Académie des Beaux-Arts kept Daguerre's invention at arm's length. When the process was

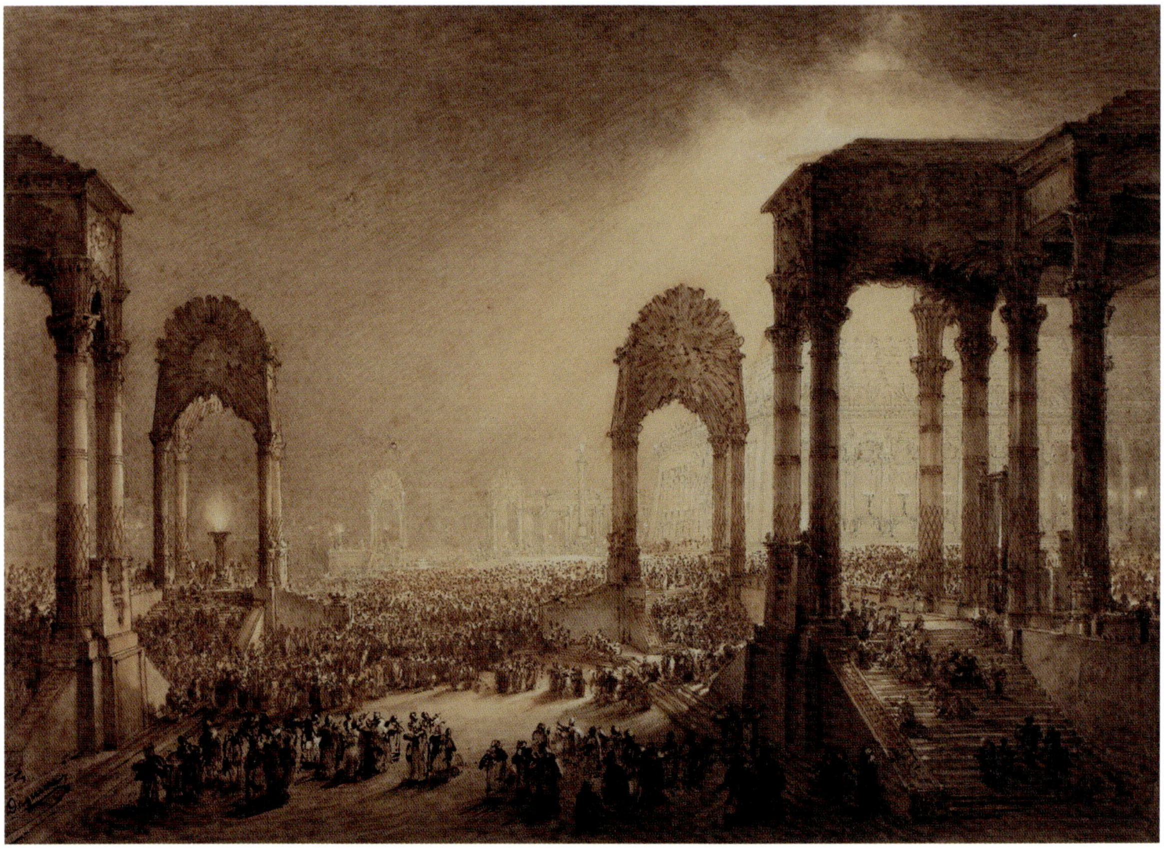

28. Louis Jacques Mandé Daguerre, *The Inauguration of the Temple of Solomon*, c. 1839, brown ink and wash, George Eastman House, Rochester, NY.

unveiled at the Institut de France on August 19, 1839, very few academicians from the Beaux-Arts were even present. The permanent secretary, Raoul-Rochette, preferred Bayard's process to Daguerre's, perceiving in photographic prints on paper "the mildly time-worn appearance of an old master drawing; they look just like them, and possess all their quality."[39] To Raoul-Rochette, the medium—paper—like the process, seemed to leave more room for the hand of the artist, who might rework or retouch the image created by the camera obscura. The very perfection of the daguerreotype, its unmodulated, gleaming image, seemed to be the product of a machine, the outcome of mechanical action. Without mentioning it by name, the archeologist was surely thinking of the new invention when, in a *Rapport sur les ouvrages envoyés de Rome par les pensionnaires de l'Académie royale de France, pour l'année 1839* (a report from 1839 on the works sent by the recipients of the Prix de Rome who were staying at the Académie Royale de France in Rome) he recalled the Academy's commitment to hard work and its distrust of all mechanical processes whose results were too rapid to seem entirely honest: "Time sanctifies only what she has produced; talent cannot do without study; modern genius is nothing without work."[40]

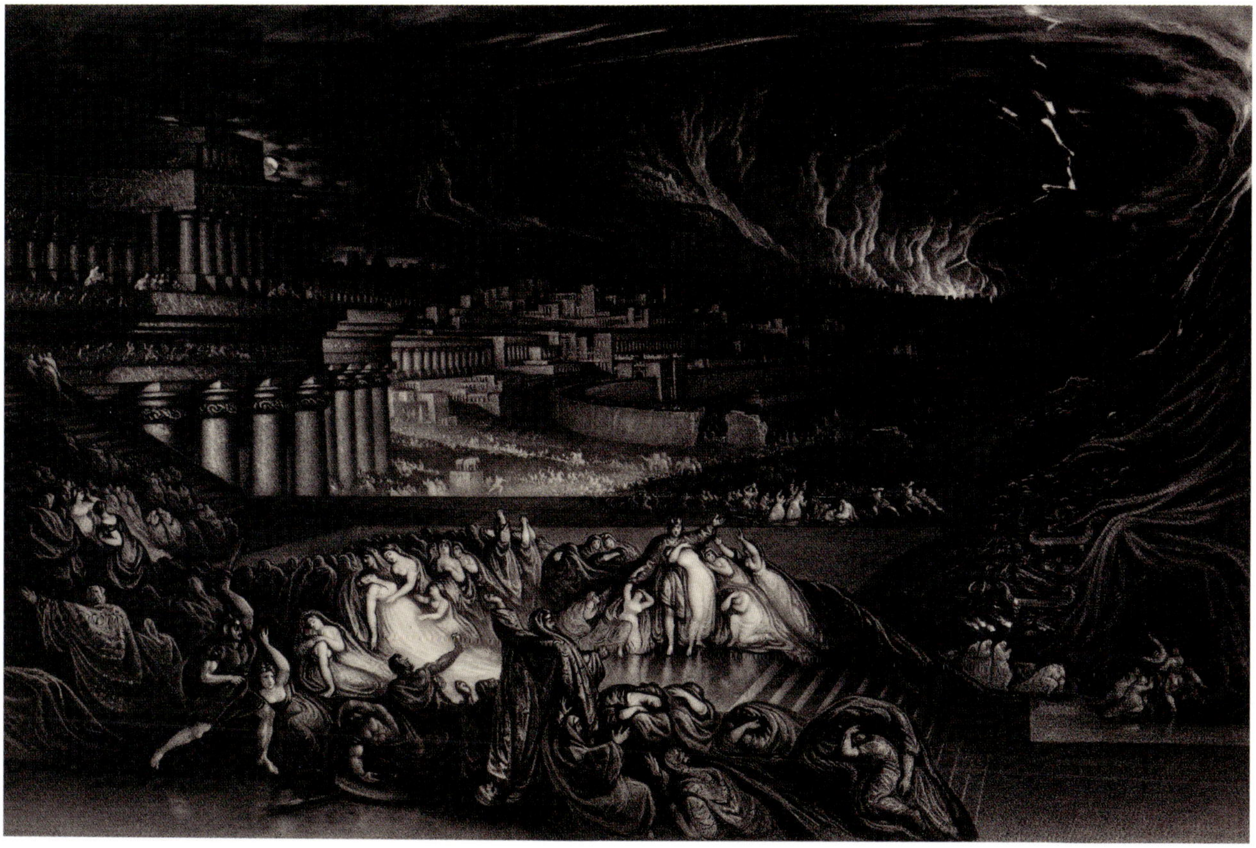

29. John Martin, *The Fall of Nineveh,* 1829–30, etching and mezzotint, The British Museum, London.

A genuine marvel

Contrariwise, it was the magical perfection of the daguerreotype that bedazzled critics who, like Jules Janin in 1839, seemed beside themselves with enthusiasm for Daguerre's novel creation: "And finally, we were able to see with our own eyes, touch with our own hands Daguerre's incredible and admirable invention."[41] Utopian in flavor, such zeal paralleled Arago's words in his first discourse before the Académie des Sciences: "The marvel occurs in an instant, as swift as thought, as fast as the sunbeam that strikes the far-off arid mountain or the scarcely budding flower." Adding, in an effort to win over a readership whose skepticism would have been deep-rooted: "What we are telling you here must sound rather strange; but nothing is as incredible as certain truths.... People will have to believe in the *Daguereotype* [*sic*]; because no human hand can draw like the sun; no human eye can penetrate so deep into a flood of light, into a darkness so complete."[42] Placing the new invention squarely in the artistic camp, he pointed to Daguerre's earlier innovations in painting, the theater, and the diorama: "Art can have no argument with this new rival." Distinguishing this type of photography from other "crude mechanical inventions," Arago highlights the importance of human intervention in obtaining its results: "and note that man

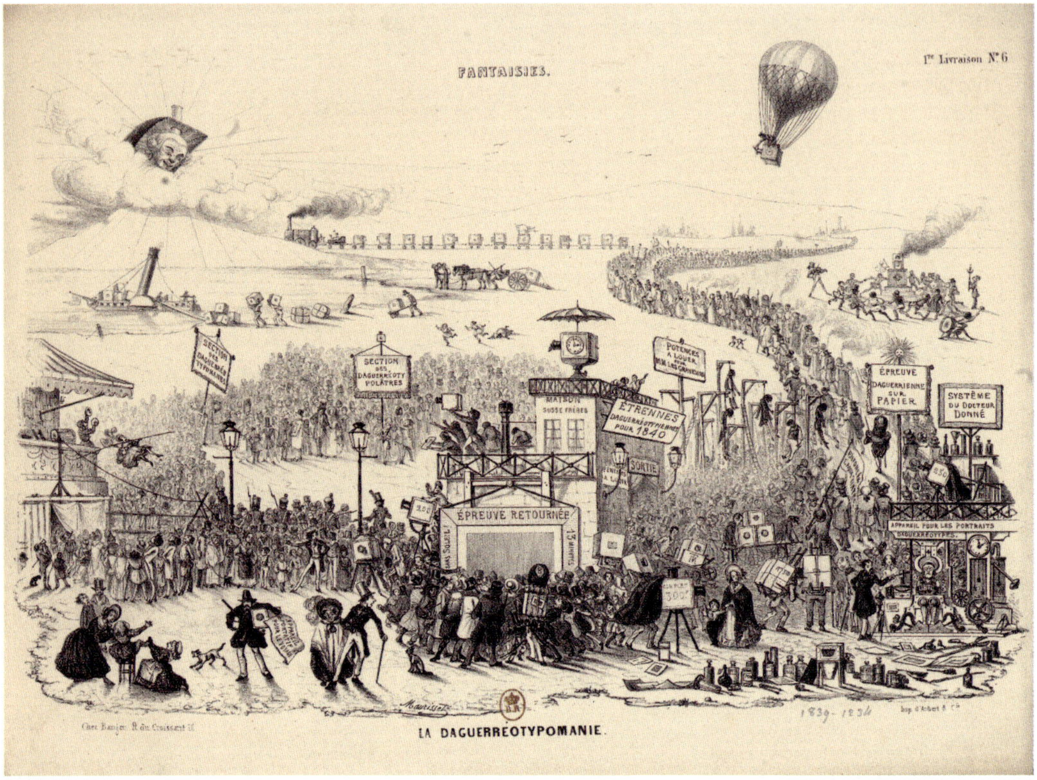

30. Théodore Maurisset, "La Daguerréotypomanie," December 8, 1839, lithograph, Bibliothèque Nationale de France, Paris.

yet remains the master, even over the light he allows to act. One second more or less devoted to this work counts for much. Do you put more store by details than by masses? In two minutes you can have a drawing like one of Martinn's [*sic*][43]; a poetic disarray, as if under a veil, in which the eye guesses at more than it sees."[44] Janin here has in mind the sets of the diorama, whose crowd effects, chiaroscuro, and dramatic opposition between light and shade are indeed redolent of the apocalyptic canvases of the English painter John Martin (ills. 28–29).

Daguerreotypemania

Following its disclosure, for more than eight months after the announcement of the process at the Institute on August 19, 1839, the daguerreotype was all the rage. The daguerreotypist Marc Gaudin recounts in his memoirs, probably with a measure of exaggeration, how he immediately rushed off to test the technique for himself. An engraving by Maurisset lampoons the veritable *daguerréotypomanie* that gripped his contemporaries in 1839. Many wealthy patrons (equipment remained expensive) tried their hand at the technique, with varying degrees of success (ill. 30), for, despite Daguerre's soothing words, the camera obscura was not child's play. Capturing an image required a steady source of external light, while exposure times meant that the subject had to be chosen beforehand and immobilized before the plate could be taken; the operations by which the image was developed called for great dexterity and there could be no qualms about handling chemical substances such as iodine, mercury, and soda.

Frédéric Goupil-Fesquet, who accompanied his uncle, the painter Horace Vernet, to Egypt in September 1839 with a Daguerre chamber lent him by the optician Lerebours, lamented the difficulties he encountered. "It seemed to me somewhat humiliating," he wrote, "to return to Cairo without bringing back a single souvenir of the most famous monuments in the world, despite the denigrations of my companions, who threatened to throw the daguerreotype into the Nile as excess luggage."[45] The first of these daguerreotypists belonged, like Goupil-Fesquet, to a well-off milieu, with links to artistic and scientific circles. Their works—at least those that have come down to us—betray both the time and dogged effort the enterprise required.[46]

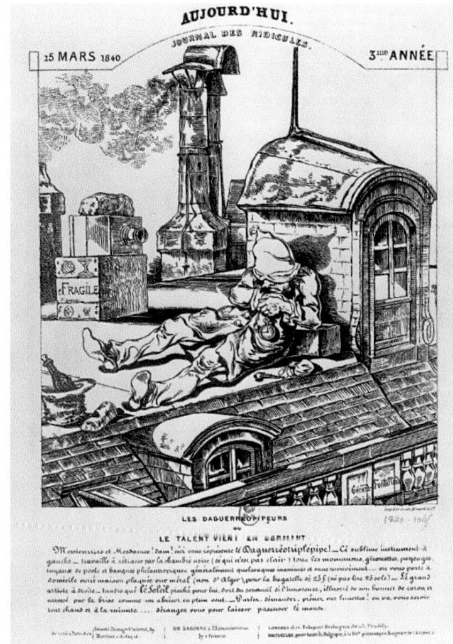

31. Henri Gérard-Fontallard, "Les Daguerréopipeurs," 1840, lithograph, Bibliothèque Nationale de France, Paris.

Countless caricatures waxed ironic about the ease of use of the daguerreotype as proclaimed by its originators (ill. 31). Showing the daguerreotypist lounging about in the sun while the light did all the work, they jeered at the indolence of the adepts of the camera obscura. A children's game -*Le Daguerréotype de la jeunesse* by Charles Letaillé—likewise scoffed at the (supposed) facility with which pictures could be obtained.[47] Other cartoons referred to the magical effect of the daguerreotype which, by capturing the image of a person, might entrap the sitter himself. A brief essay, published as "Paris daguerréotypé par Méphistophélès" (Paris Daguerreotyped by Mephistopheles), imagined the devil using the process to make off with the French capital.[48] The term "daguerreotype" also appeared figuratively in the literature to designate a method of recording as exact a representation of an event as possible. In *Le Daguerréotype des reines, histoire universelle de tous les peuples civilizes* (The Daguerreotype of Queens: A Universal History of All the Civilized Peoples), A. M. Reybert writes, "Lastly, if I chose the word *daguerreotype* in my title, it is because an essentially novel expression was required to provide an adequate idea of the goal I fixed myself."[49] Balzac opted for a similar analogy in the foreword to *Splendeurs et misères des courtisanes* (*The Splendors and Miseries of Courtesans*, or *A Harlot High and Low*), writing that his wish was to *daguerréotyper* society—that is, to produce a faithful image of it.

Compared to 1839, which was so rich in events and comments concerning the invention, succeeding years seemed relatively quiet. Publications referring to photography tended to be less well publicized, being addressed primarily to those already working with the process, and concerning possible adjustments and improvements. Research centered on the thorny question of how best to reduce exposure times.[50] In fact, the very last expository article published on the daguerreotype was to appear in *L'Artiste* in 1841.[51]

Art is not photography

In 1840, the Swiss painter and engraver Rodolphe Töpffer published an essay entitled "De la plaque Daguerre à propos des Excursions daguerriennes," which reviewed the first series of a compendium illustrated with engravings made after daguerreotypes published in fascicules by the optician Lerebours.[52] Denouncing its implicit tendency to reduce artistic creation to no more than the imitation of nature, he was wary of the reaction of middle-class audiences bewitched by the mere aping of reality but unable to distinguish beauty. "In the arts of imitation, imitation is not the goal, but the means of art," he thundered.[53] A painting is not "a well-polished and impeccably silvered looking-glass." He reminded readers that painting should keep faith with the processes of imitation characteristic of it and not become confused, he pointed out, with the *identical* imitation of objects afforded by the "Daguerre machine."[54] He laid the stress on the shortcomings of the invention, more grievous than its supposed advantages. Criticizing the tools used to obtain daguerreotype plate, he lambasted the mechanical aspects of the process. The "Daguerre machine" acts alone; really there is no operator, still less a creator. "But what is missing from Daguerre's plates, something that places with an insuperable barrier forever between the marvels of this process and the spontaneous products of the intelligent mind—that something is the hallmark of human, of individual thought. It is the soul as it spreads out on the canvas, a poetic intention expressed through some style or other, it is ... it is Art!"[55] As Töppfer saw it, the Daguerre process lacked something essential: the expressiveness of the painter: "What, then, is left? What remains? ... process without making; i.e., a body, in all its forms, with all its folds, all its veins, its tissues, its pores, but a body without a soul" (ills. 32–33).

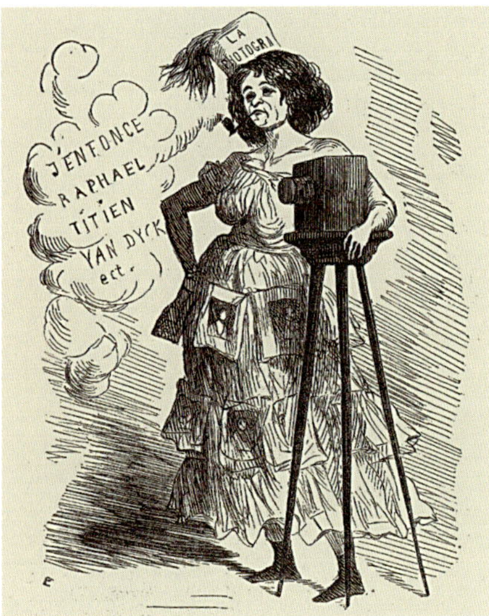

32. Émile Marcelin, "Photography: Stuff Raphael, Titian, Van Dyck, etc.," *Le Journal amusant*, 1856, lithograph, Bibliothèque Nationale de France, Paris.

The fear appeared all the more justified since, for many artists of the period, laborious craft had already won out over subject matter. It was a painting's finish that prevailed over intellectual elevation, while backbreaking attention to infinitesimal detail outweighed historical sweep. It was then incumbent upon critics to defend painting against this new rival with all the more vigor, since so many contemporary works seemed motivated precisely by the desire to imitate exactly, a task the new paragon of photography accomplished to perfection. In an analysis of a picture by François Bouchot, *The Rest on the Flight into Egypt*, in his review of the Salon of 1842, Étienne Delécluze affirms: "What really brings out the quality of this work by our late artist, what affords it such value and such charm, is the idea he brought to bear in it, it is the profound feeling that occupied the painter when his hand steered the brush. This is something that the daguerreotype, however perfect it becomes, can never vouchsafe; this is something an artist alone can produce."[56]

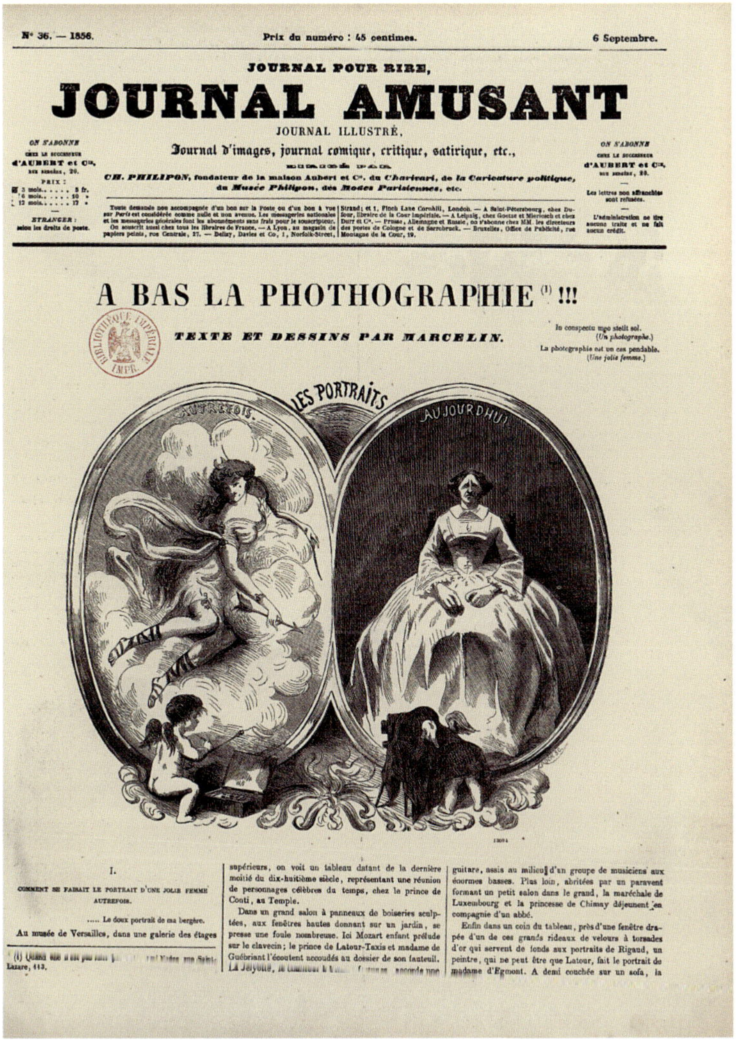

Nº 36. — 1856. Prix du numéro : 45 centimes. 6 Septembre.

JOURNAL POUR RIRE,

JOURNAL AMUSANT

JOURNAL ILLUSTRÉ,

Journal d'images, journal comique, critique, satirique, etc.,

CH. PHILIPON, fondateur de la maison Aubert et Cie. du *Charivari*, de *la Caricature politique*, du *Musée Philipon*, des *Modes Parisiennes*, etc.

ON S'ABONNE chez le successeur d'AUBERT et Cie, rue Bergère, 20.

PRIX : 3 mois. . . . . 5 fr. 6 mois. . . . . 10 » 12 mois. . . . . 17 »

ÉTRANGER : selon les droits de poste.

Les lettres non affranchies sont refusées.

L'administration ne tire aucune traite et ne fait aucun crédit.

A BAS LA PHOTHOGRAPHIE (1) !!!

TEXTE ET DESSINS PAR MARCELIN.

In conspectu meo stetit sol.
(*Un photographe.*)
La photographie est un cas pendable.
(*Une jolie femme.*)

I.

COMMENT SE FAISAIT LE PORTRAIT D'UNE JOLIE FEMME AUTREFOIS.

..... Le doux portrait de ma bergère.

Au musée de Versailles, dans une galerie des étages supérieurs, on voit un tableau datant de la dernière moitié du dix-huitième siècle, représentant une réunion de personnages célèbres du temps, chez le prince de Conti, au Temple.

Dans un grand salon à panneaux de boiseries sculptées, aux fenêtres hautes donnant sur un jardin, se presse une foule nombreuse. Ici Mozart enfant prélude sur le clavecin; le prince de Latour-Taxis et madame de Guébriant l'écoutent accoudés au dossier de son fauteuil. La Jelyotte, le chanteur à ... accorde une guitare, assis au milieu d'un groupe de musiciens aux énormes basses. Plus loin, abritées par un paravent formant un petit salon dans le grand, la maréchale de Luxembourg et la princesse de Chimay déjeunent en compagnie d'un abbé.

Enfin dans un coin du tableau, près d'une fenêtre drapée d'un de ces grands rideaux de velours à torsades d'or qui servent de fonds aux portraits de Rigaud, un peintre, qui ne peut être que Latour, fait le portrait de madame d'Egmont. A demi couchée sur un sofa, la

33. Émile Marcelin, "Down with photography!," *Le Journal amusant,* September 6, 1856, lithograph, Bibliothèque Nationale de France, Paris.

A fatal and passive mirror

Romantic criticism also mounted a stalwart defense of artistic style and of the temperament of the artist. In his *Salon* of 1844, Théophile Thoré writes appreciatively of Théodore Rousseau's unique vision as it transpires in his *Avenue of Chestnut Trees*: "I am not saying that such a thought does not exist in nature; it is just that one has to be able to feel it, express it. The artist is not merely an eye, like the daguerreotype, a fatal and passive mirror that physically reproduces the image presented to it; he is a moving and creative force who, in his turn, fertilizes external creation." [57]

In their turn, Henri Delaborde in 1856 and Charles Baudelaire in 1859 denounced, like Töpffer before them, less photography itself than the risk it carried of causing art to be relegated to slavish imitation. Delaborde, in a lengthy article in favor of the art of engraving, mocked the much-vaunted fidelity of photography, that guarantor of exact reproduction, noting how it lacked one

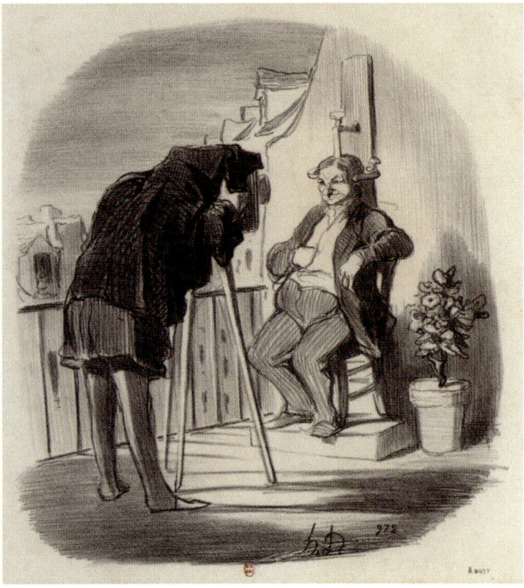

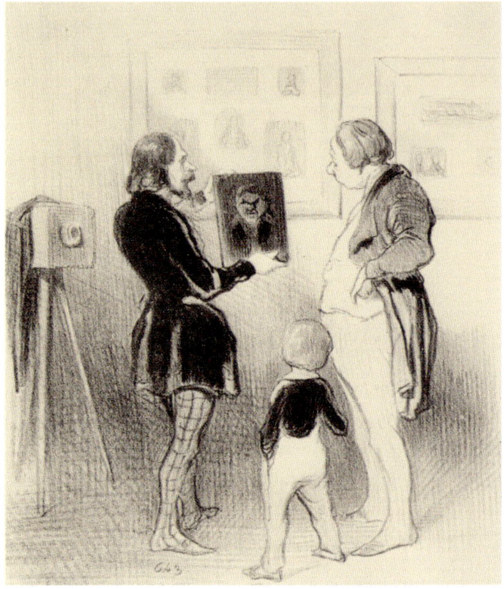

34. **Above, left:** Honoré Daumier, "The reputedly most comfortable position to ensure a pretty daguerreotype portrait," 1847, lithograph, Bibliothèque Nationale de France, Paris.

35. **Above, right:** Honoré Daumier, "The Daguerreotype Portrait," 1844, lithograph, Bibliothèque Nationale de France, Paris.

telling advantage of the talented engraver: the ability to interpret. In his review of the Salon of 1859, Baudelaire—a close friend of Nadar's, who photographed the poet with rare sensitivity on several occasions—did not deny the artistic claims of photography, but he too recoiled from the notion of equating art with bland imitation. Lambasting lowbrow bourgeois taste, and having as little truck with the academic postulate of imitation as with the quest for realism in its narrowest sense, the poet put in the mouths of the proponents of the mindless reproduction of nature the following fearsomely conclusive syllogism: "Thus an industry able to produce a result identical to nature would be the absolute art." The poet of *Les Fleurs du mal* (*The Flowers of Evil*) goes on to stigmatize the absurdity represented by the confusion between art and exactitude: "A vengeful God has granted the wishes of the multitude, Daguerre was his Messiah." Then, letting the "multitude" speak for itself, he concludes: "Since photography provides us with all the sought-after guarantees of exactitude [*that's what they think, the fools*! Baudelaire notes in an aside], art is photography." Although writing in 1859, at a time when photographic processes on paper had won out against the daguerreotype, Baudelaire was still thinking of the precision portended by the announcement of the daguerreotype, even mentioning Daguerre and referring to "the commonplace image on metal."[58] Even once the process had fallen out of favor, the advantages claimed for it in Arago's lecture lived on.

A relatively significant branch of industry

The reactions of Delaborde and Baudelaire have also to be understood in the light of the commercial development of the daguerreotype. Daguerre had not been mistaken; the diffusion of the process and its financial success stemmed from the portrait, eventually made possible by reducing exposure time to a matter of seconds. Camille Dolard had opened the first daguerreotype studio in Lyon, in 1841. By 1845, there were a dozen such studios in Paris, Charles Chevalier proclaiming that "the success of the daguerreotype is growing and photography has even become a relatively significant branch of industry."[59] By 1847, fifty-six were listed and they were sprouting up in every large French city (ill. 34). In his jury report for the Exhibition of the Products of Industry of 1849, Léon de Laborde stressed the scale of daguerreotype production that he estimated—"portraits and views" taken together—at more than 100,000 plates a year. Preindustrial in nature (the workshops remained family affairs, with very few declaring more than one employee), this commercial boom had repercussions on the perception of the fledging technique. In a society founded on the opposition between the artist and the bourgeois, moneymaking was seen as incompatible with artistic aspirations. In several caricatures, Honoré Daumier took pleasure in mocking artists who adopted the notoriously facile expedient of the daguerreotype to get rich quick (ill. 35). The soaring increase in the number of daguerreotypes produced inevitably went hand in hand with the appearance of plates of reduced size, crudely polished and/or poorly composed. The price of small-size plates—an eighth of a plate; that is, approximately 2 ¼ × 3 ¼ in. (6 × 8 cm)—made having their portrait taken available to a large number of people, while the equivalent in paint was still the preserve of the wealthy. It was a development that sounded the death knell for the art of the miniature, almost immediately ushered out by the daguerreotype.

Its success as a business and its rapid uptake by society nonetheless led some to take a dim view of the new invention. Associated with trade rather than with art, it permitted the reproduction of any sitter's features (attractive and plain, distinguished and lowly alike), a flaw compounded by the sale of plates of inferior quality. Some were equally wary of the knock-on effects of its success: today it was the miniaturists who had gone to the wall; and tomorrow, who knows, the engravers, even the painters? Did painting die the day photography was invented, as—in the words of an apocryphal tradition—Paul Delaroche himself alleged?

"The result of a poorly printed daguerreotype"

The undiscriminating reproduction by the daguerreotype of the features of all and sundry soon became a hackneyed euphemism for a world of ugliness. From the 1850s on, words from the vocabulary of photography were marshaled in negative reviews of realist painting, which labored—as some had hastily concluded the daguerreotype did—under a doubly pejorative association with the unsightliness of actuality. More than any other artist, at the beginning of the 1850s it was Gustave Courbet who was most often besmirched by critics for the supposed proximity of his works to a daguerreotype. Speaking of *A Burial at Ornans*, critic A. Desplaces snarled, "The innovation, however, does not lie in the quirk of inflating scenes of everyday life to such vast proportions. The intention of the work, here perfectly realized, is to reproduce, as if by means of a gigantic color daguerreotype, the entire cortege in its most literal vulgarity" (ill. 36).[60] Delécluze meanwhile rammed the point home: "In this scene that could pass for the result of a poorly printed daguerreotype, there is the rough naturalness that is invariably the outcome whenever nature is seized on the wing and reproduced as it appears."[61] The equivalence set up between Courbet's vast canvas and a daguerreotype might sound implausible, but it stemmed not from the size, nor from the manner, but from the presumed intention of the two endeavors. By expanding a genre scene to the dimensions of a history painting, by rejecting all idyllic idealization of the French countryside and abolishing the distance between art and humanity, here represented without concessions to the demands of painterly aesthetics, the painter found himself on a collision course with the artistic hierarchy. By depicting the inhabitants of Ornans as they actually were, by refusing to distinguish between the beautiful and the ugly, Courbet, like the daguerreotype, seemed on the face of it to be reproducing a commonplace reality: "It's called 'energy'; it is brutal and violent: it is even less reality than mere triviality; and even if it were reality?—Reality is not art; it is the opposite of art."[62] Courbet, with his clamorous entrance into the Salon in 1850–51 ("it was," wrote Jules Castagnary in 1882, "as if the blast of a waterspout rushed through the exhibition room"),[63] crystallized the complex relationship between painting and photography, little more than twelve years after Arago had presented Daguerre's invention. The vehemence of critics who made pejorative use of the photographic model in deprecating a painting that shocked them but to whose qualities they could not remain indifferent shows that, in some eyes, in just a few years and in spite of the paucity of scholarly attention devoted to it, photography had already acquired (or threatened to acquire) the status of a touchstone for art and for its perception. The invention was thus further muddying the already turbulent waters of the pictorial arts.

Photography is no longer just daguerreotype

In 1847, probably in a clandestine fashion, a printer in Lille called Louis-Desiré Blanquart-Évrard brought Talbot's calotype to France. Improved and widely taken up, after 1849 this paved the way for the development of the paper process. Promotion of the calotype stressed its distinction from a Daguerre process sullied by commercial successes. Photography was no longer just the daguerreotype. In drawing up the lines of demarcation, defenders of processes on paper made much of a semantic shift: for "photography" they substituted the words "heliography." Furthermore they changed allegiance: now it was Niépce, not Daguerre,

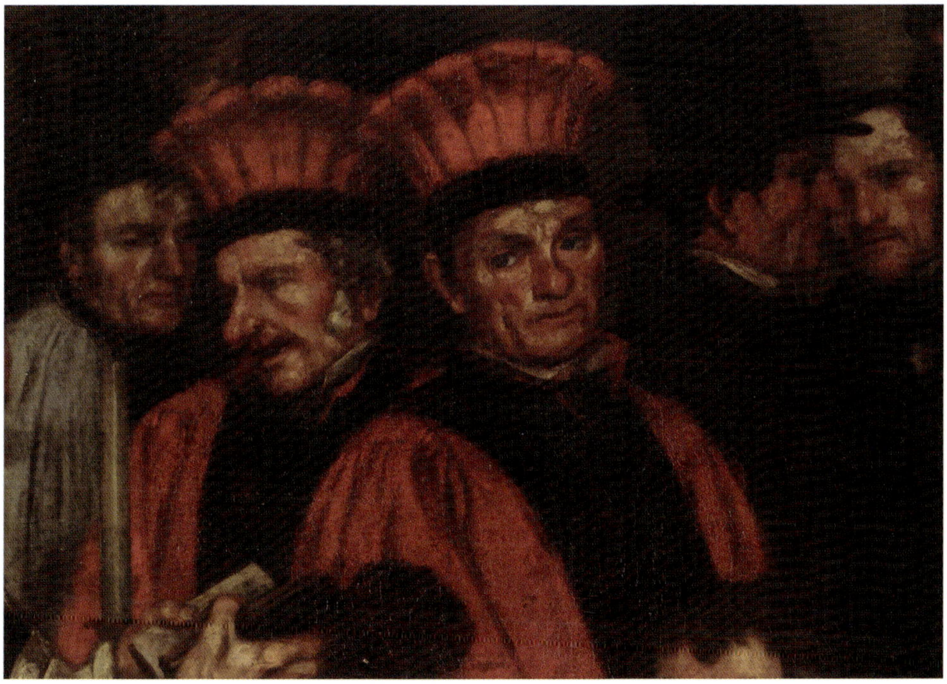

36. Gustave Courbet, *A Burial at Ornans* (detail showing the two vergers), 1850, oil on canvas, Musée d'Orsay, Paris.

who was acknowledged as the true inventor of the photographic process. Moreover, success in retail was to take a backseat with respect to artistic ambition. Established in February 1851, the French Société Héliographique (an august assembly, not only of photographers but also of painters and critics) launched a program to demonstrate how "heliography" ("process engraving"), just like the daguerreotype, might be employed successfully on any subject, an ambition materialized in albums gathering together various modes of expression.[64] The publication of a weekly, *La Lumière*, ensured sufficient press coverage for their experiments and works. The artistic ambition of the paper processes, seen as a definitive break with the daguerreotype, is underscored by author and art critic Francis Wey: "M. Nègre's 'Chiffonnier' is no longer a photograph; it is a deliberate, pondered composition, executed with all qualities alien to the daguerreotype, and asserting only those" (ill. 37).[65]

Gustave Le Gray, a painter and former pupil of Paul Delaroche, was one of the most talented photographers of his time. In 1851, he brought out a *Nouveau Traité sur la photographie sur papier et sur verre* (New Treatise on Photography on Paper and Glass), that exalted the artistic character of photography on paper: "The immense influence that the new art of photography is destined to exert on the fine arts makes it the duty of all, scholars, amateurs, and exponents alike, to accelerate its progress."[66] From the point of view of photography, the 1850s were thus marked by a twofold desire: to distinguish the new paper process and to gain artistic recognition. The best mode of presentation to attain this dual aim appeared to be the exhibition. As will be seen, throughout the

Second Empire, the issue of the organization and site of exhibitions of photography—the paramount ambition being to mimic those of painting—remained high up on the agenda.

An aesthetic standard for photography

In spite of the self-proclaimed divorce between *héliographistes* and *calotypistes*, it was essentially the daguerreotype, although it became extinct after 1865, that fixed the aesthetic template of photography.[67] The fusion of the marvelous and the positivistic endured; and the idea of an exact reproduction of nature, conjoined to the revelation of worlds invisible to the naked eye or long-since passed, persisted. From the first arose the simultaneously utopian and unattainable drive to imitate reality as exactly as possible, while in the second subsisted the close links with stage effects that had presided over its conception. The daguerreotype thus durably enshrined the basic components of an aesthetic standard for photography, whose unique qualities were stated time and again in an effort to undercut negative criticism: the notion of a one-off image, essentially distinct from what it reproduced, introducing representation into the sphere of the spectacular through placing it in a narrative sequence by evoking a moment that had disappeared for ever; the valorization of image clarity, subordinated to the exact delineation of the object's outlines and revealing details hitherto unseen by the human eye; the implementation of a new standard of representation, thanks to the photometric fidelity of an image that seemed to underwrite the peerless exactitude of its representation.[68] Thus did photography spawn a new relationship to reality, an admixture of subservience and revelation.

The conditions governing its invention, its announcement and reception, as briefly outlined above, did not, however, fully resolve the question of the definition of photography, and it continued to switch from magical discovery and glorious invention, to scientific plaything, mechanical process, commercial product, and artistic instrument. The success it enjoyed—its industrial and commercial applications, its adoption by every social echelon—further complicated the nature of an invention that shuttled between these various facets. Its relation to painting also remained unclear: preparatory study and faithfully exact reproduction or noxious corruption; peerless, unique creation or lethal model. Its links to painting, though ontologically defensible with regard to the use of the camera obscura and the shared impulse to represent the world, remained fraught. The fear that painting might simply be usurped—at least in its purely imitative function—made photography something of a pariah, a dangerously literal rival that needed watching. Looked at another way, the existence of such a (supposed) paragon might liberate the painter from his narrow submission to resemblance, further divorcing pictorial truth from exactitude.

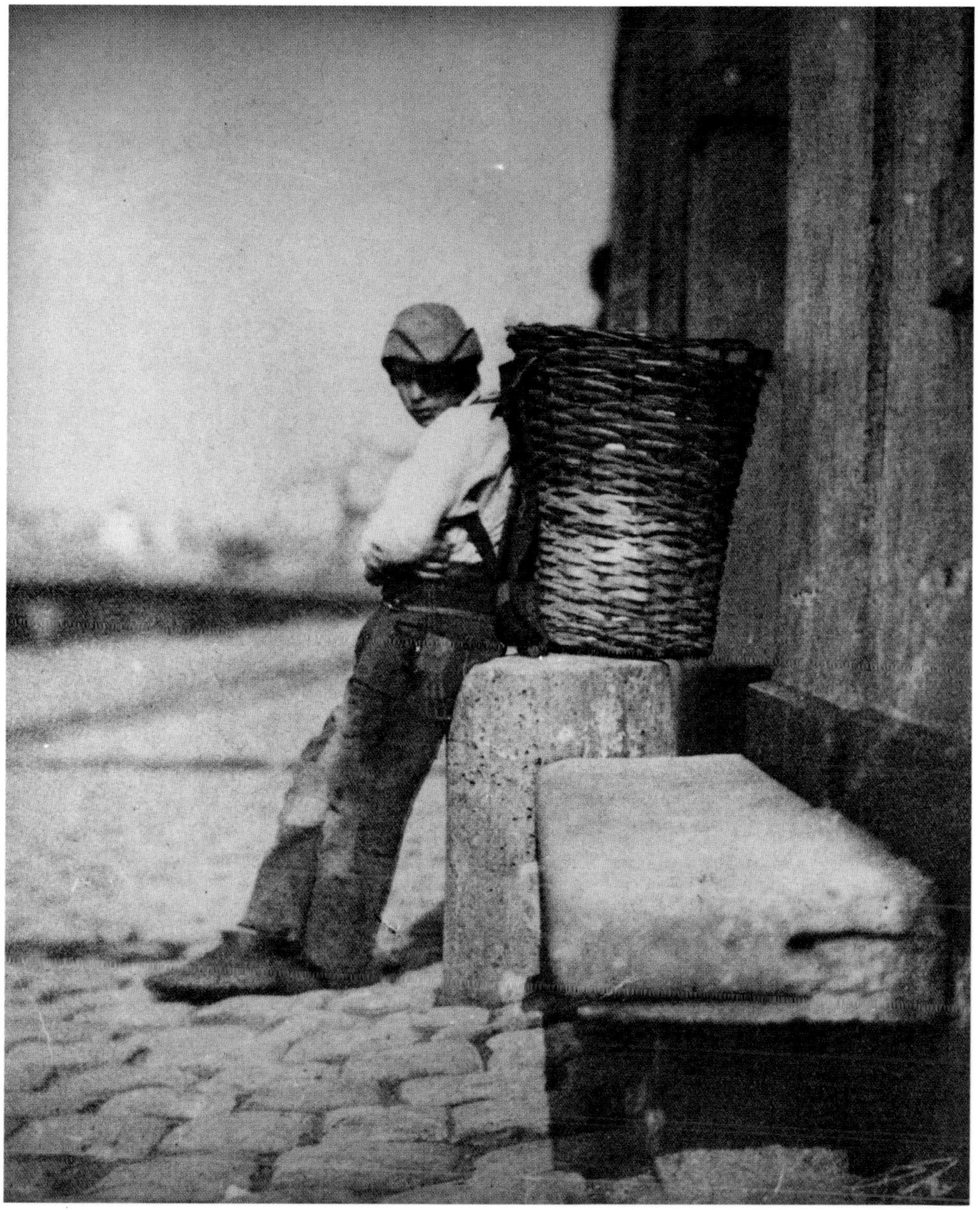

37. Charles Nègre, "Little Ragman Leaning Against the Milestone in front of 21, quai de Bourbon," 1851, negative on wax paper, Musée d'Orsay, Paris.

Intimately linked to painting, through its choice of subject matter, its representational idiom, but also through the multiplication of the image brought by its dissemination, photography gave rise to a new relationship to reality and its representation, which then boomeranged on its elder sister. An integral component in the development of an unseen universe of imagery, it forged, in collaboration with or in opposition to painting, a new art, a new way of seeing, original and yet heir to the past and to tradition. As a famous scientist and friend of Arago's elegantly put it in reference to the announcement of the daguerreotype, "photography was a new art in the midst of an old civilization." [69]

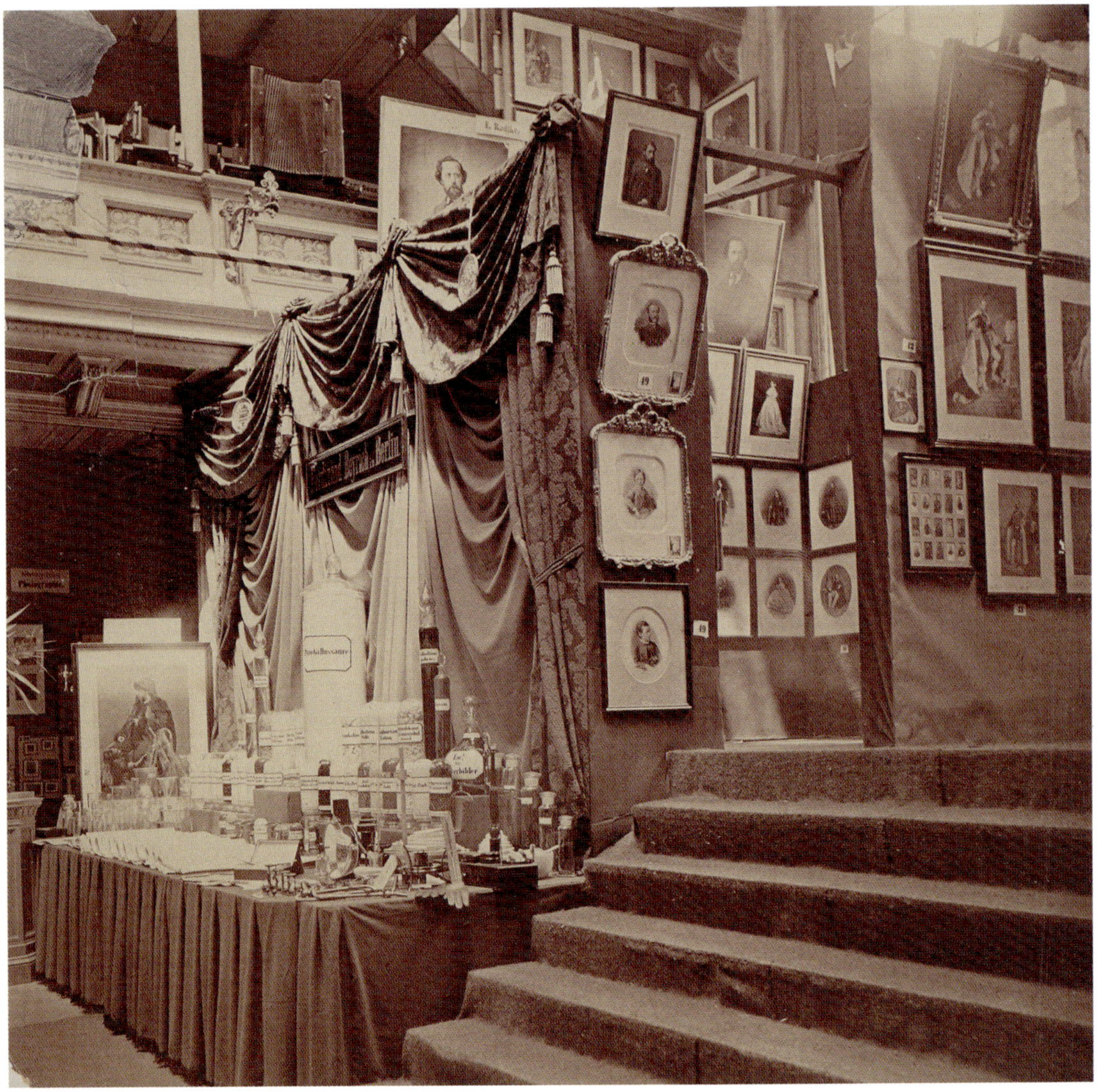

"An intelligent administration ought to seize the initiative and hold an exhibition of photography." [1]

EXHIBITING PHOTOGRAPHY

As soon as the new process became publicly known, it became important for people to see photographs exhibited. This recognition, in the first instance, concerned the reality of the invention itself. It was, after all, news of Arago's statement to the Académie des Sciences in January 1839 that had urged William Fox Talbot—afraid lest the advent of the daguerreotype eclipse his own process—to show his "photogenic drawings" at London's Royal Institution.[2] Several months later, having made fruitless attempts to enlist Arago's support, Hippolyte Bayard also opted to show his early prints on paper, this time at an exhibition organized to collect money for the victims of an earthquake that had rocked the island of Martinique some months previously. Opening on July 14, 1839, the event was primarily devoted to painting and included old masters and modern canvases lent for the occasion by private collectors. Bayard's prints on paper thus hung next to a Francisco de Zurbarán from the Aguado Collection, an Andrea del Sarto from the Magnoncourt Collection, a portrait by Girodet, and another by Gérard, as well as several canvases by Horace Vernet and a work by Géricault. If the exhibition did nothing to stem the tide of "daguerreotypomania" unleashed by Arago, it did not go wholly unnoticed. A review in *Le Constitutionnel* confessed: "But what excites the greatest enthusiasm are the photogenic drawings that their creator, M. Bayard, modestly entitles trials, obtained employing a new process distinct from M. Daguerre's.... The results achieved by M. Bayard are exquisitely fine, steady, with a mild glow that painting can never hope to attain. Nothing can be more charming than these little figures bathed in the imperceptible half-tones of Nature's chiaroscuro."[3] It was surely eulogies such as these that drew Raoul-Rochette to Bayard's process, examples of which were examined for the first time at a meeting on November 2, 1839. Apparently the academicians of the Beaux-Arts, less receptive to the aesthetics of precision

38. **Facing page:** Anonymous, "The Stand of the Ferdinand Beyrich Company at the Berlin International Photography Exhibition in 1865," 1865, albumen print, Museum Ludwig, Cologne.

conveyed by the daguerreotype, appreciated more the velvety feel of these early French photographs on paper, finding in them some of "the charm of Old Master drawings."[4] The presence of photographs in an art exhibition was only possible because the funding event to help the victims of Martinique was a private concern[5]: official institutions took far longer to accept works of this kind. Such presentations, however, provided a forum in which the question of photography's essence as art or science, work of the mind or of machine was hotly debated.

The exhibitions of the "Products of Industry"

The first exhibition of photographs in France in an official setting took place at the Exposition des Produits de l'Industrie, in Paris.[6] Initiated in 1798 and continuing until 1849, these exhibitions provided a venue in which craftsmen and manufacturers displayed their finest pieces. To catch the eye of the jury they vied with each other in virtuosity, the resulting masterpieces being subsequently used as prototypes for everyday articles. As has often been observed, such showcases for the products of cabinetmaking, bronze-founding, and gilding played a significant role in the development and promotion of the decorative arts in France. The quality and lasting impact of the Parisian exhibitions of the "Products of Industry" prefigure the great World's Fairs, such as that held with such notable success at the Crystal Palace, London, in 1851. Their aesthetic impact, in promoting the uptake of the applied arts in industry, is no less incontrovertible. Though these exhibitions presented pattern drawings, engravings, and then lithographs, the frontier with the Salons de Beaux-Arts (since 1831 an annual event, at which paintings, sculptures, drawings, and engravings were shown) remained watertight, enshrining the unbridgeable divide between creations of the mind and pieces which, despite their quality, could not be dissociated from their time-honored associations with handicraft.

An appreciable impact on the arts and on industry

In 1844, Daguerre's photographs were admitted to Section VII, that is, "Lithographs, manikins, and brushes,"—that is, as tools and instruments for making art. The jury rapporteur, Picot, highlighted the potential usefulness of the new invention: "If photography were able to guarantee satisfactory results and a ready method of producing them, it would render the greatest service."[7] By the last of these exhibitions of industry, in 1849, photography was thought worthy of more exposure (ill. 39): once again photographic creations were admitted to the Ninth Commission (one of those for the Fine Arts), with a jury featuring, among others, a sculptor (Antoine Barye), a silversmith

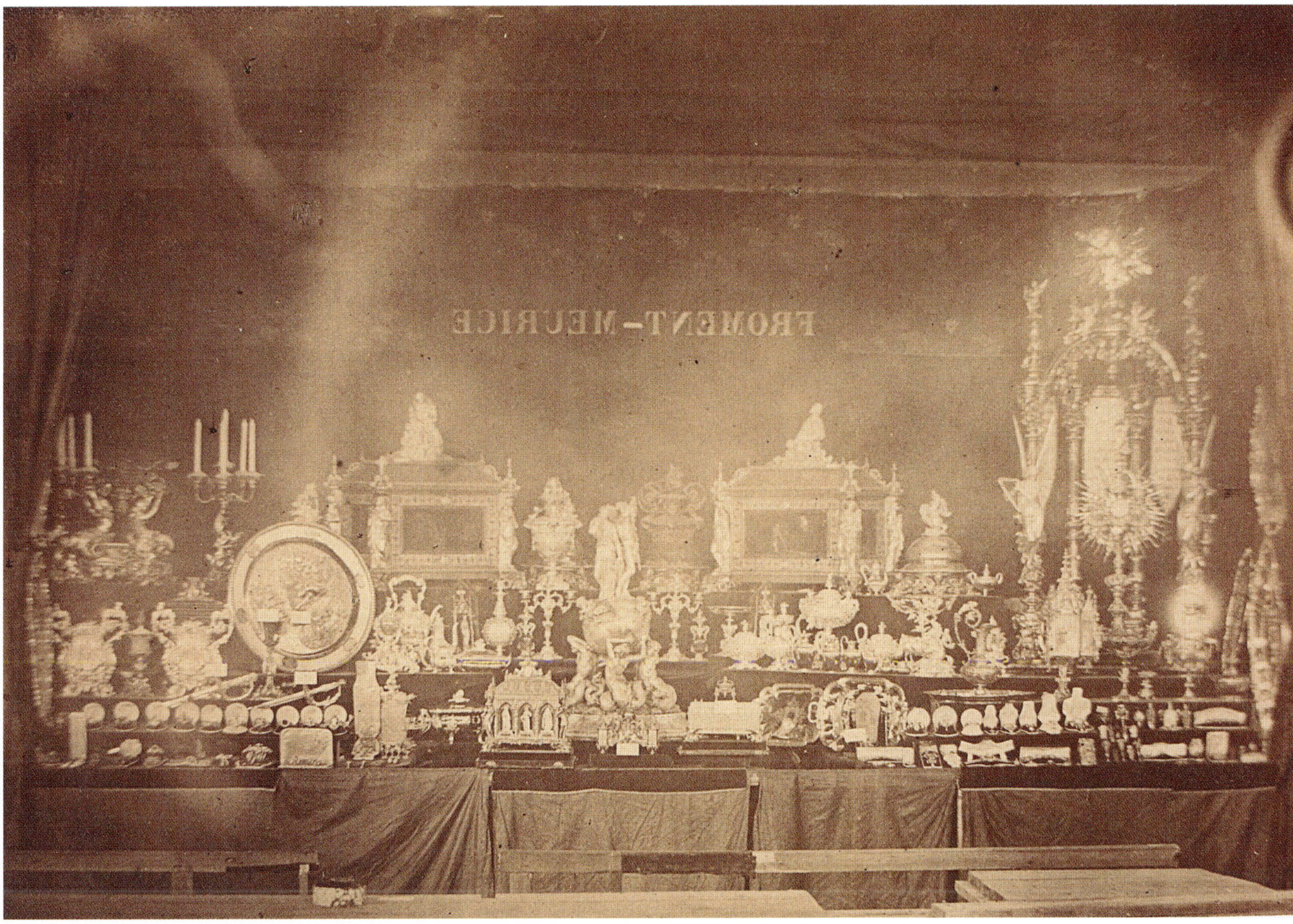

39. Pierre-Ambroise Richebourg, "Presentation of Works by Froment-Meurice at the Exposition des Produits de l'Industrie of 1849," 1849, salt print, Musée d'Orsay, Paris.

(Jean-Jacques Feuchère), and a printer (Firmin Didot). This time the rapporteur for the commission was Léon de Laborde—archivist, archaeologist, and conservator at the Louvre. His interest in photography was already well documented, and he had indeed been one of Gustave Le Gray's pupils in his workshop at the Barrière de Clichy. Ten years after the announcement of Daguerre's invention, daguerreotypes and prints on paper together lined the walls of the exhibition hall. Laborde, though, brought out the difference between the prints on paper and a daguerreotype plate: "[The new processes on paper] transform into an art a practice hitherto the sole prerogative of those with a certain financial standing. They thus place a marvelous resource within the reach of all." In designating both techniques as *héliographies*, and thus taking up the term chosen by Niépce and not by Daguerre, he reiterated the commitment he had undertaken on the publication of the report to establish the Société Héliographique.[8] He was especially keen to highlight the impressive advances the invention had made since it became publicly known. His remarks aimed at convincing readers that a new age was dawning, one that promised photographers genuine recognition in the artistic field: "Such is the situation which the jury found, and in which it leaves, this art: with heliography on plates having attained utter perfection in its results and extraordinary ease of use; with heliography on paper having made immense strides, and now on the brink of reaching a perfection that would leave no more to be desired." In conclusion he justified his general position: "The jury afforded considerable attention to this invention whose influence on the arts and industry is already appreciable and in the future will prove immense."[9]

The turning point: the 1851 Great Exhibition in London

Laborde was once again the rapporteur at the London World's Fair of 1851, which took place in the glass and metal emporium of Joseph Paxton's Crystal Palace (ill. 40). His report on the fine arts ran to more than a thousand pages and proposed an analysis of the links between the arts and industry, and between development and popularization.[10] "Today, photography, or the mechanical arts in their ideal perfection, has introduced the world to the beauties of divine and human creation."[11] The place allocated to photography in the London exhibition reflected an organization in which the host nation, Great Britain, had carved out the lion's share for itself. British productions, especially of industry (the organizers voicing the opinion that, thanks to the annual exhibitions at the Royal Academy, painting and sculpture disposed of sufficient exhibition venues), alone occupied thirty classes in the exhibition. Guest countries had, on the other hand, to display the totality of their exhibits—both artistic and technical—in a single space. Nonetheless, if the machine hall of a rapidly industrializing Great Britain left visitors spellbound, the French section devoted to photography allowed exhibitors to show off the qualities of both daguerreotypes and prints on paper—a process invented, ironically enough, by the Englishman Talbot. This was not, however, the first time French photographs had been presented in Britain; in 1839, a Daguerre plate representing the Tuileries had been shown in Edinburgh.[12] In 1841, the Royal Scottish Academy even assembled an exhibition including several daguerreotypes in its rooms. But the nuances attained in the works of Gustave Le Gray, Henri Secq, and Hippolyte Bayard, in particular, seemed to outstrip those of the inventor and his disciples. The 1851 exhibition gave a considerable fillip to photography in Great Britain as well as in France, and was the spur to an exhibition at the Royal Society of Arts, London, in 1852, which presented nearly eight hundred British, American, and French examples.[13] Its success also spawned the creation of the Photographic Society of London, founded in April 1851: "The science of Photography gradually progressing for several years seems to have advanced at a more rapid pace during and since the Exhibition of 1851."[14] "The object proposed is not only to form

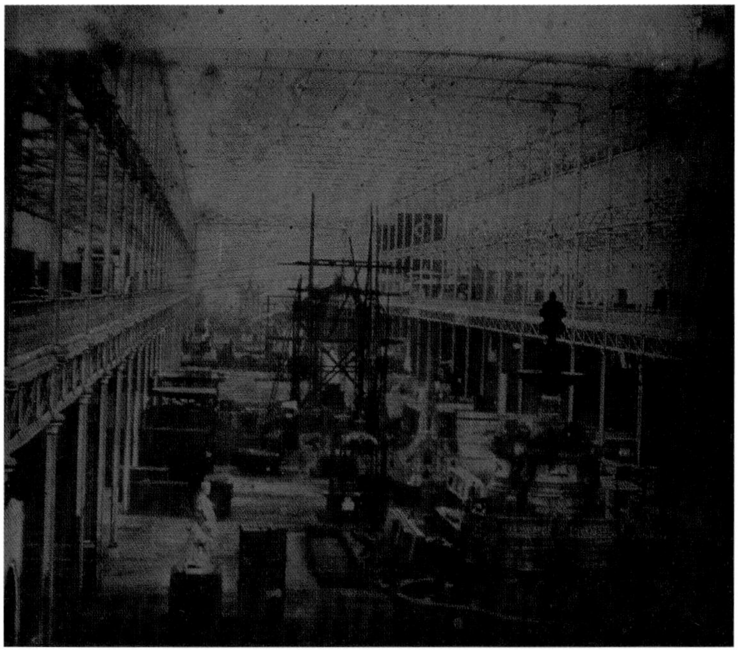

40. Jules Duboscq, "Interior View of the Nave of the Crystal Palace during the Mounting of the Great Exhibition" (detail), 1851, stereoscopic daguerreotype, Musée d'Orsay, Paris.

a pleasant and convenient Photographic Club, but a society that shall be as advantageous for the art as is the Geographic Society to the advancement of knowledge in its department."[15] In 1858, the Photographic Society organized an annual exhibition at the South Kensington Museum (now the Victoria and Albert Museum, the V&A); this marked the first occasion on which photographs were ever presented in a museum.[16]

Correlations between photography and painting

In France the Société Héliographique—with Hippolyte Bayard and Gustave Le Gray as its instigators, and comprising critics, photographers, and painters—had been created at the beginning of the year 1851. The two founders brought with them some eminent pupils: Bayard brought the painter Jules Ziegler, and Le Gray brought Léon de Laborde and Henri Le Secq. Boasting the names of Eugène Delacroix and Champfleury, the roster of members was published in the first number of *La Lumière*, the journal the association established for itself.[17] Skillful exponents of photography on paper, the founders' choice of the name "Heliographic Society" was designed to affirm the qualities of paper as against metal and thus of the heliograph over the daguerreotype. Asserting the invention's artistic nature, their review fostered dialogue between the arts with the publication (in addition to descriptions of photographic processes and their improvements) of accounts of the annual Salons and great exhibitions.[18] "We are sufficiently persuaded," wrote the poet Henri de Lacretelle, responsible for these art reviews from 1851, "of the correlation that exists, and which will exist more each day, between photography and painting, not to deal respectfully with all the facts and all the questions arising in every field of the arts."[19]

In the long expository article to *La Lumière*, "De l'influence de l'héliographie sur les beaux-arts" (On the influence of heliography on fine arts), the critic and poet Francis Wey, the review's first editor in chief, insisted upon the artistic nature of photography on paper (heliography), bolstering his argument by referring to Gustave Le Gray's unfortunate experience when he sent several works to the jury of the 1850 Salon for appraisal[20]: "Some two months ago, one of the most skilful experts in the new photographic process, M. Le Gray, sent to the jury of the 1850 exhibition nine drawings on paper representing landscapes and portraits both from the life and after pictures. Once the astonishing perfection of the results had been duly admired came the awkward task of classifying pieces worthy of being set side by side with the most accomplished works of art, but which were attained by a purely theoretical process, not related in any direct way to the practice of drawing. Arranged among the lithographs, the works of the skilful heliographer were referred to under this heading in the booklet to the current exhibition. But a sub-commission then intervened, which, considering the question from a different point of view, had M. Le Gray's drawings withdrawn." Wey went on to stress how the presence or otherwise of photographic works at the annual Salon would enshrine their status, above and beyond the personality of their creator—albeit a trained painter and sometime student of one of the most respected masters on the academic jury, Paul Delaroche: "The first judges had regarded them [Le Gray's drawings] as works of art; the second classified them among the products of science," he wrote. Then comes the sentence that articulates the critic's essential argument: "Evidently, heliography derives from chemistry and physics; but, no less evidently, this discovery, improved as it is on a daily basis, is bound to have an immediate and profound impact on the domain of art."[21] The vocabulary chosen by Wey—"drawings," "works"—embodies the artistic aspirations of photography on paper, without quite dispelling the ambiguity that surrounded its conception. Still, if he preferred the use of the word "theoretical" above, so as to avoid "technical" or "mechanical" (all terms that would have steered him in the same direction the Salon subcommission had steered photography), he made no attempt to finesse the physical origin of a new process "not related in any direct way to the practice of drawing."

"The serious missions of this new art"

Ten years after it was publicized, the definition of an invention whose processes were founded on techniques using optical devices and chemical compositions but whose products—or "works"—could readily vie with drawing and painting, remained a thorny subject. Its defenders sought to distance themselves from the aesthetics of clarity and exactitude of the Daguerre plate by emphasizing the radical distinction between photography on paper and the rival process. They also sought to distinguish heliographers—artists—from daguerreotypists, who, owing to the burgeoning number of portrait studios, were seen increasingly as hardly better than salespeople. The justification of photography as an art was based in addition on the existence of a creative impulse on the part of the operator, in choice of subject, model, composition, lighting, etc., as well as the tasks incumbent upon him once he put the camera down, on the negative or at the printing stage.

In 1852, in a "photographic review" published in *La Lumière*, Henri de Lacretelle restated his erstwhile misgivings about photography before going on to demolish them: "At the time we were kindly solicited to write in this journal ... we too had to combat our prejudices against photography. We today freely acknowledge that such qualms no longer exist in our mind: we believed then that what constitutes the soul of a picture was not the just model copied, or the color applied, but that parcel of his feelings that the painter, so to speak, detaches from his own individuality.... We did not forgive the mirror for replacing this vision, [the daguerreotype's] geometrical precision appearing odious in our eyes and at odds with the vagueness and boundlessness of thought." He went on in tones more gratifying to photographers: "But once we saw that photography had been taken up by eminent painters, who choose from among the lines of a landscape drawn by God, as they choose among the ideal lines of their reverie, and who have even managed to compose and harmonize subjects taken from reality ... and that the artist's mind also illumines the camera obscura, we could but applaud this admirable science."[22] His lengthy article then passes in review all the photography workshops he had visited, starting with the one belonging to the painter Jules Ziegler, whom he knew well. This survey enabled him to dispel "all his doubts as to the serious missions of this new art." A creator is defined by his creative intention: in highlighting the personal manner of each photographer, defenders of the technique were making a case for its inclusion in art exhibitions, beginning with the annual Salon. Photographs could thus be judged, not only on their technical proficiency, but also on their aesthetic qualities: "To provide it [photography] with a room in the Louvre would be an act of justice, courtesy, and farsightedness."[23] The Société Héliographique sunk without trace: its disappearance was all the less noticed since *La Lumière*, albeit with a new owner and editor in chief, continued publishing until 1862. Still, debates around the recognition of photography as an art nonetheless rumbled on throughout the 1850s.

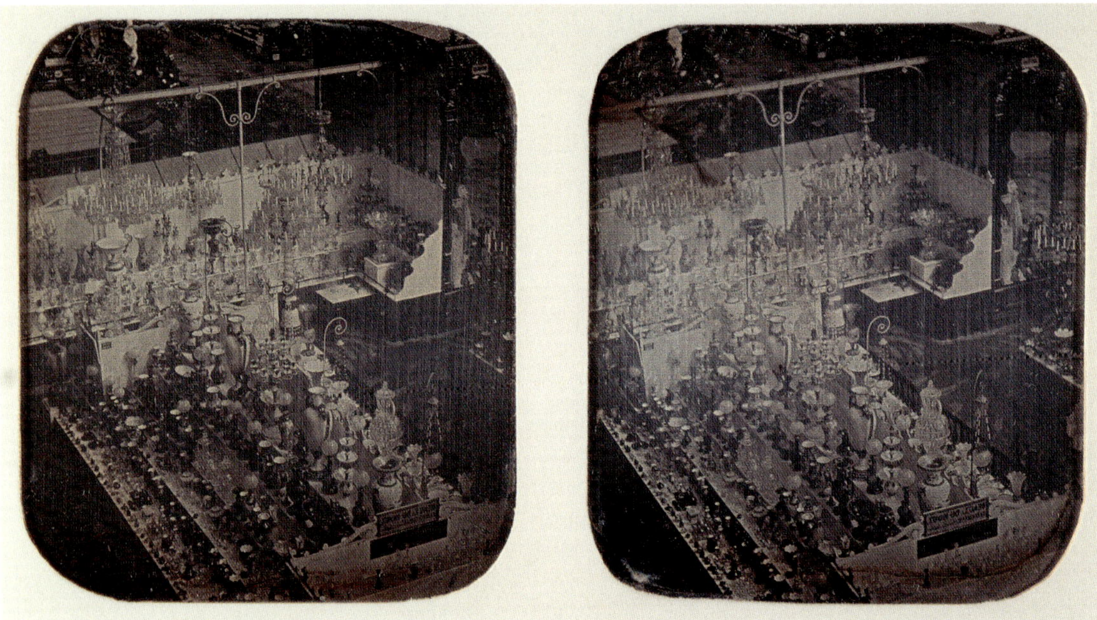

41. Anonymous, "Universal Exhibition of 1855, Porcelain and Glassware Stand," 1855, stereoscopic daguerreotype, Musée d'Orsay, Paris.

The 1855 Paris World's Fair: a landmark

It is in the light of these long-held aspirations, reiterated time and again between 1851 and 1855, that Paul Périer's virulent and passionate protest against presenting photography in the Palais de l'Industrie rather than in the Palais des Beaux-Arts at the Paris Exposition Universelle in 1855 ought to be understood (ill. 41). The stakes were all the higher since the World's Fair was envisaged by Napoleon III, the French government, and the City of Paris as an opportunity to show, in response to the success of the London Great Exhibition of 1851, that France was, among all the nations of the world, the true mother of the arts. Standing on Avenue Montaigne, the Palais des Beaux-Arts featured contemporary painting and old masters, and paid tribute to three great living artists, Jean-Auguste-Dominique Ingres, Eugène Delacroix, and Horace Vernet (ill. 42). As Périer wrote: "On entering the Palais de l'Industrie by the main gate, in one of the first corridors to the left one comes across four or five compartments, cubbyholes or cabins, on the four sides of which huddle some of the most accomplished specimens of

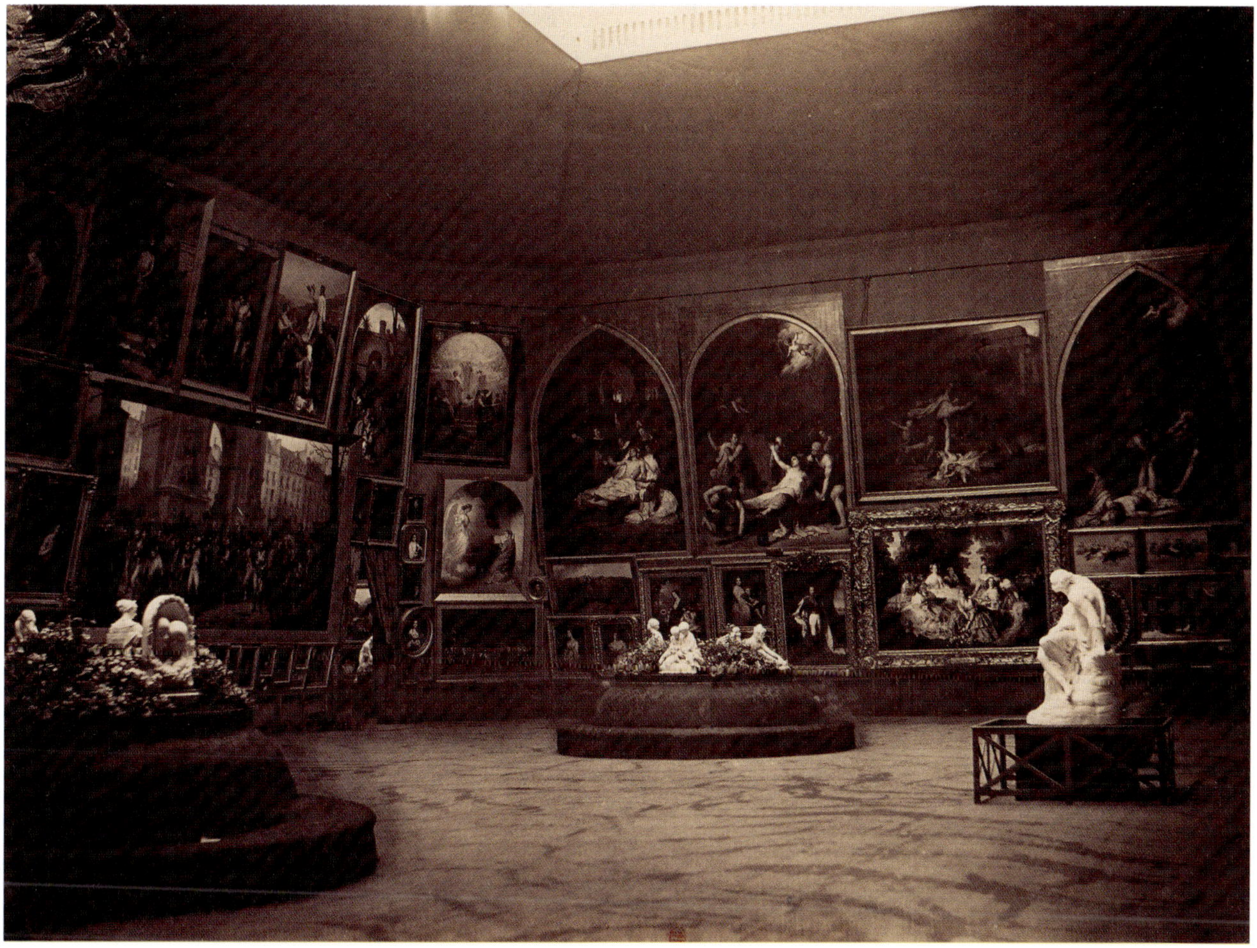

French photography.... [This exhibition] reminds one rather too forcibly of the 'catacombs' of the Louvre—too ghastly to recall—where so many painters have lived to see their works buried alive. Already many of us hardly felt at home amidst the products, wondrous though they are, of cosmopolitan industry. The glorious and fruitful results of a discovery that surpasses and threatens in their very existence lithography, engraving, and even certain types of painting seemed to [us] worthy of a place in the sanctuary of the arts."[24]

42. Attributed to André-Adolphe-Eugène Disdéri, "Grand Salon Carré, Universal Exhibition of 1855, Palais des Beaux-Arts," 1855, albumen print, Bibliothèque Nationale de France, Paris.

The photographs were arranged by nation. As the critic noted, regretfully but fairly, the English section was more intelligently hung than the French: "Our friends and neighbors the English did better in this respect: they placed Photography in galleries on the first floor where the glorious daylight illumines all impartially, allowing visitors to examine admirable works without tiring or having to wait for a break in the capricious clouds."[25] This exhibition, in particular as regards French and British photographers, and likewise in the two major sections, appears as a watershed for the photographic techniques it showed. Indeed, critics pointed out how all, French and

British alike, now mastered every method, adapting them simply according to purpose: "For the rest," wrote Périer, "paper, collodion, albumen are three strings of the same instrument, all the more remarkable since, in the hands of a skilful musician, each seems able to summon up the most surprising effects."[26] The talent of English photographers in manipulating the collodion process was particularly lauded. Turning to the landscapes of Roger Fenton, Périer conceded: "We [French photographers] have to admit defeat ... in particular in respect of the collodion landscape. This photographic method, of inimitable poise and delicate sophistication, is splendidly personified in England by the name of Roger Fenton."

"An artistic sensitivity is far from irrelevant for a successful work of photography"

The question of national characteristics, in particular in French and British photography, did not stop with technique alone, or with the potential repercussions of the attribution of awards and distinctions. More profoundly, this issue constituted the nub of a debate around the artistic nature of photography. To identify a photograph as "French" or "English" classified it ipso facto within a national aesthetic continuum and, more especially, placed the accent on the essential contribution of the operator. "Thus, whether we like it or not, we are brought by invincible logic to observe that the photographer, to produce worthwhile results otherwise than by happenstance, must be able to appreciate works of art similar to his—in other words, all works of art; his experienced eye must be able to discern, with a single swift and confident glance, the best picture ... the most beautiful engraving ... the most powerful etching—in a word, he has to be like a juror qualified (that rare thing) to judge any artistic competition."[27] In his report on the exhibition of 1855, Jules Ziegler went a step further: "An artistic sensibility is far from irrelevant for a successful photograph. To choose a precise viewpoint, to know the exact hour at which this point of view is most advantageously lit, to pose a living model, to calculate the shadows falling on a statue all demand the eye and the sense of an artist, and one can easily pick out photographs taken by a man who has practiced the fine arts or who is endowed with a natural disposition."[28]

It was the poet and critic Théophile Gautier who best articulated this national aesthetics of photography in a text published in *L'Artiste* in 1857. Gautier's attitude was in point of fact ambivalent with regard to the invention and, like a number of his contemporaries, he rejected the apparently mechanical aspect of the process. In this extended text, however, he hails photography as "a discovery with which the human mind concurs with surprising facility." He proceeds to an exhaustive if sometimes trite comparative analysis of various national schools of photography, the English and French in particular, the model for which, lifted from pictorial criticism, restates many of the arguments of the time. "English photography, for example, resembles pictures and engravings of British origin; it has the air of a *keepseake* [*sic*] or a book of beauties; in it, nature acquires something neat, natty, glossy, silky, elegant, and modish that strikes even the least attentive eye. You see animals and you'd think them made after Landseer; the landscapes remind one of Constable, Turner, Callow, and William Wyld; the familiar scenes are Mulreadys, the portraits, Lawrences."[29] Gautier describes works by French photographers in this way: "Among the French individuality reigns supreme; each acts according to his own personal conception: the same diversity of genre appears at the photographic exhibition as in the Salon—strange to say, but true nonetheless, there are draftsmen and colorists among the French photographers: the former lean into the contours, cut crisply round the outlines, admit only shades of white or gray; the latter wash out the edges of their subjects, concentrate their tones, soften the blacks, and, by 'fouling,' know how to make the sun do their work for them—like the stumping in an old Rembrandt etching on yellow paper."

Acknowledging the creators and understanding photography

Photographers began to make a point of signing their work like painters and engravers. The recognition afforded by affixing a name or a pseudonym was of prime importance, as the lawsuit between Félix Tournachon and his brother Adrien for the use of the pseudonym "Nadar" made all too clear. In winning his suit on appeal in 1857, Félix contrasted mere technical training in photography—it is easy enough, he argued, for "anyone to call themselves a photographer overnight"—with the qualities essential to the conception of a veritable photographic work. "What cannot be learned," he wrote, "is a sense of light ... the application of such or such an effect according to nature of these features, which, as an artist, you are called upon to reproduce. What can still less be taught, is the moral understanding of your subject ... the psychological side of photography."[30] These general remarks take on a deeper meaning in the context of the disagreement between the two brothers concerning a series of Pierrots they had presented at the 1855 Exposition Universelle. These exceptionally fine photographs, for which Charles Deburau, son of the famous mime artist, Baptiste Deburau, posed as Pierrot, won a gold medal. However, this was awarded solely to Adrien, who purloined his elder brother's pseudonym by calling himself "Nadar Jeune." Photographic and theatrical variations on the "expressive head" (*tête d'expression*), an academic exercise widely employed in art teaching, these images highlighted the ability

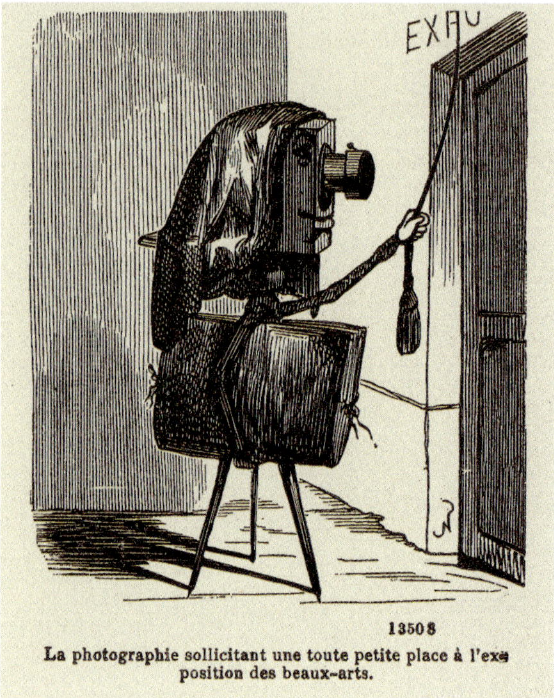

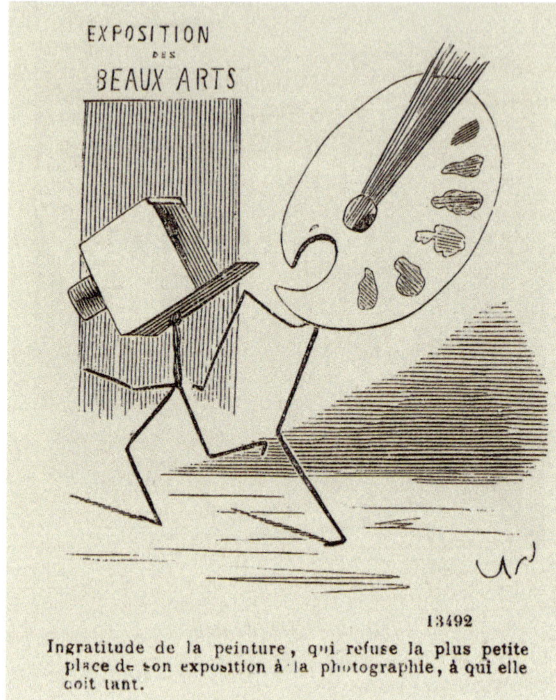

43. **Above, left:** Félix Tournachon (also called Nadar), "Photography Pleading for a Tiny Little Place...," *Le Journal amusant*, January 17, 1857, lithograph, Bibliothèque Nationale de France, Paris.

44. **Above, right:** Félix Tournachon (also called Nadar), "Ingratitude of Painting...," *Le Journal amusant*, April 16, 1859, lithograph, Bibliothèque Nationale de France, Paris.

of photography to capture, beyond mere resemblance, a subtle range of expressions conveying the sitter's emotional state.

In Paris, photography only earned the right to grace the annual Salon next to painting and sculpture in 1859; in the port of Le Havre, which had implemented a policy promoting the arts, and organized a series of ambitious exhibitions that attracted artists of nationwide reputation,[31] such events were opened to the technique in 1852, with daguerreotypes by the Macaire brothers showing the city's pier.[32] Works by Macaire-Warnod were again shown in the "drawing" section in 1858, designated as, "No. 650, Macaire-Warnod, Harbor, northern pier, instantaneous portraits and seascapes, not retouched (photographs)."[33]

Photography at the 1859 Salon

The exhibition of photographs for the World's Fair of 1855 had been organized by the Société Française de Photographie. In 1857 it staged a new exhibition, in the salons of Gustave Le Gray on Boulevard des Capucines; it was under his aegis that, for the first time, photographs were to be presented on the Champs-Élysées, paradoxically in what had been the Palais de l'Industrie of 1855, and now the venue for the annual Salon. Philippe Burty saluted the initiative in an early number of *La Gazette des beaux-arts:* "This year, finally, the Société succeeded in obtaining from the government a space in the Palais des Champs-Elysées, distinct it is true from the Beaux-Arts,

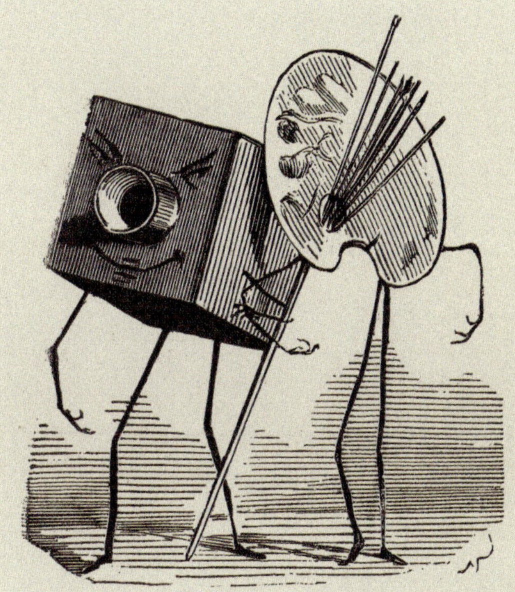

15989

La Peinture offrant à la Photographie une toute petite place à l'exposition des beaux-arts. Enfin!...

45. Félix Tournachon (also called Nadar), "Painting Offering Photography a Tiny Little Place...," *Le Journal amusant*, April 16, 1859, lithograph, Bibliothèque Nationale de France, Paris.

but which, due to its proximity, will earn in the eyes of the public a significance verging on rehabilitation" (ills. 43–45).[34]

The exhibition, boasting 1,295 exhibits presented by 148 exhibitors, enjoyed a relative measure of success; if Burty is to be believed, it attracted more than 30,000 visitors. Like the annual Salon, it also provided the opportunity for compendious written appraisals. As Louis Figuier wrote: "In consequence, and for the first time, daily newspapers feature reviews of the Photography Salon, just as for the Salon of Painting and Sculpture. The pages that follow are especially interesting in that they represent the first review of the kind occasioned by photography since it came into being."[35] A pharmacist and historian of science, Figuier was close to Francis Wey, the first editor in chief of *La Lumière*, and his column seemed to fulfill the hopes entertained by Lacretelle in 1852.[36] Upholding the specific character of each photographer, Burty took pleasure in equating the selection made by the office of the French Society of Photography with the strict exigencies of the jury at the annual Salon, the better to emphasize the right of photography to be considered as an art: "We would like to add that the individuality of each *photographiste* [*sic*] always remains perceptible in his work. Have the same natural site reproduced by various operators, request a portrait of the same person from several artists, and, though they reproduce an identical model, none of these works will resemble any other; in each of them, you will be able to identify the manner, or rather, the sensibility, of he who carried out it.... If then the *photographiste* preserves in his works

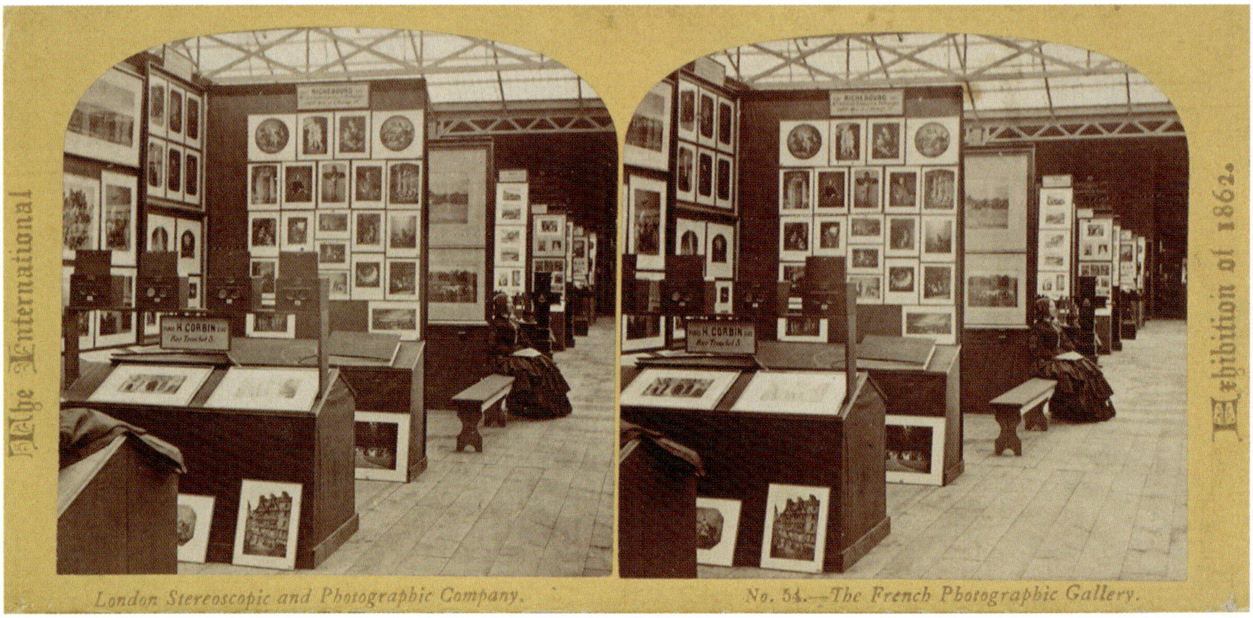

46. London Stereoscopic Company (publisher), "The French Photographic Gallery at the Great Exhibition in London in 1862," 1862, stereoscopic albumen print, Museum Ludwig, Cologne.

his individuality, personal manner, and sensibility that distinguishes and animates him, one is forced to acknowledge that photography does indeed form part of the domain of the fine arts.... The exhibition jury in its selection and rejection of the photographs subjected to its examination seems to have been animated by this thought [i.e., emphasizing the artistic aspect], and they should be congratulated for it. It [the jury] has driven the merchants from the temple; thus we enter it certain to find works solely by artists."[37] Again, in 1861 and 1865, exhibitions by the Société Française de Photographie were held within the ambit of the annual Salon. In his appraisal of that of 1865, Burty, although he situated his analysis in light of the links "between Art and something not entirely Art," devoted a significant proportion of his appraisal to the new techniques, greeting inter alia the invention of carbon printing, a permanent process that enabled photographic images to be preserved (ill. 46).

A remarkable development

In 1867, on the occasion of the second World's Fair in Paris, photography was not presented in conjunction with painting and sculpture; it was consigned to Class Nine, with the "materials and applications of the liberal arts."[38] Alphonse Davanne, president of the Société Française de Photographie, proffered no complaint though. In a lengthy account of the exposition published in three numbers of *Le Bulletin de la Société française de Photographie*, he expressed satisfaction in the quality of the pieces exhibited, warned against the pitfalls of slipshod amateurism, but concentrated chiefly on technical advances: "If one examines the photographs in themselves," he wrote, "one notes the admirable strides made since earlier exhibitions ... the jury's task would have been arduous indeed had it based its judgment solely on the beauty of the photographs presented to it; but, noting the progress made, it had to aim higher and discover what had caused it. Such excellent results had been arrived at thanks to judicious modifications in both the processes and the cameras."[39] In 1878, photography was presented in the same class, with works by many exponents of the technique. As with all the classes at the Exposition Universelle, ample room was set aside for foreign exhibitors, since the Third Republic, following its lengthy and painful gestation, was keen to invite every nation of the world to the capital. For the first time, photography is not just referred to by the jury as a section in the exhibition. In a development that demonstrates how widespread the technique had become, a substantial proportion of their recommendations, and then their analysis, related less to the display of photography than to the regulations applying to photographers wishing to take pictures of the exhibition spaces or of the works and produce presented in the various pavilions and at the Palace of the Trocadéro, laying down ground rules and fixing royalties. In 1889, and later in 1900, photography was shown in the same classes: "Materials and processes of the liberal arts," and then, "Processes of letters, the sciences, and the arts."

In 1900, Léon Vidal, rapporteur for both exhibitions, retraced the invention of photography and its development. His account makes claims for the artistic status of photography, but insists especially on its paramount role as an instrument of dissemination and illustration: "Photography is certainly a graphic art, an art of copying, with the help of which the special arts of lithography and engraving are perfected and simplified, and which has replaced the art of the miniaturists for portraits on paper and enamel, an art for illustrating books that allows for vignettes recalling the subject to feature in various texts that will constitute in the future the most exact, and consequently the most authentic, recollections of reality.... It is this state of affairs that explains why, in spite of the significant role played by photography as a helpmeet to the fine arts, it can by no means be seen as one of them. Not that it cannot lead to personal work, but because it can achieve this solely by means and processes that exclude unmediated action."[40]

The commitment of photographers and critics in the Société Héliographique and especially in the columns of *La Lumière* to obtain artistic recognition appeared, in spite of Vidal's defense of the rights of photographers, far from being able to protect their works in law. This obstacle was of course an inevitable consequence of the commercial success of the process. Accelerated by remarkable technical advances ("instantaneous" photography, and soon color and the invention of the cinematograph), sixty years after its announcement Niépce and Daguerre's invention had penetrated into every field, and first and foremost into those of art and its reproduction. In the minds of many historians of photography and of many photographers too, sustained by an ambition to affirm their practice as an artistic one, the 1850s was thought of as a golden age, owing in particular to the prevalence of paper negatives. The historiography of photography has thus been adumbrated from the point of view of these pioneering years and of the links between painting and photography.[41]

Pictorialist exhibitions

Rejecting more recent techniques, some photographers asserted an artistic and elitist conception of photography, pictorial in their approach to the subject as much as in the use of personal methods often based on idiosyncratic concoctions that allowed the negative and/or print to be altered by hand. Born in England, the pictorialist movement developed in every European country and in the United States, and betrays evident connections with the symbolist painting of the period. Often hobbyists, the pictorialists left the photographic societies and founded new associations; thus, for example, Constant Puyo, Robert Demachy, and Paul Le Bègue quit the Société Française de Photographie in 1894 and set up the Paris Photo-Club. Once again, just as at the start of the 1850s, they sought to have their talent and individual character recognized through exhibitions. The first of these pictorialist Salons was organized in Vienna in 1891, with a selective jury conceived after the model of the painting Salons. In 1893, a major German museum, the Hamburg Kunsthalle, hosted an exhibition featuring several hundred pictorialist photographs (ill. 47). Five years later, Alfred Stieglitz assembled an international exhibition of photography in Philadelphia. Then, in 1905, he opened his own galleries in New York, The Little Galleries of Photo-Secession, where works by American pictorialists were shown together with French and British exponents, and even prints by early disciples of Talbot—the Scots Hill and Adamson, and by Julia Margaret Cameron (ills. 48–49). In 1903, Stieglitz had founded a journal, *Camera Work*, in which reproductions of his own photographs and those of his close associates appear side by side with others of paintings and drawings. The latter arts gained ground over the years when his New York gallery, renamed "291," opened its doors to modern European art; he started showing works by Auguste Rodin and Henri Matisse, for instance, in 1908. In 1911, Stieglitz also became the first to exhibit works by Pablo Picasso in the United States.[42] Once again, photography and painting were jostling for position in the same space, just as they had in the pages of *La Lumière*. Despite the talent of its adherents and the attractiveness of their photographs, pictorialism proved short-lived, and the

47. **Facing page:** Alfred Stieglitz, "The Jubilee Photographic Exhibition, Berlin," 1889, silver print, Museum Ludwig, Cologne.

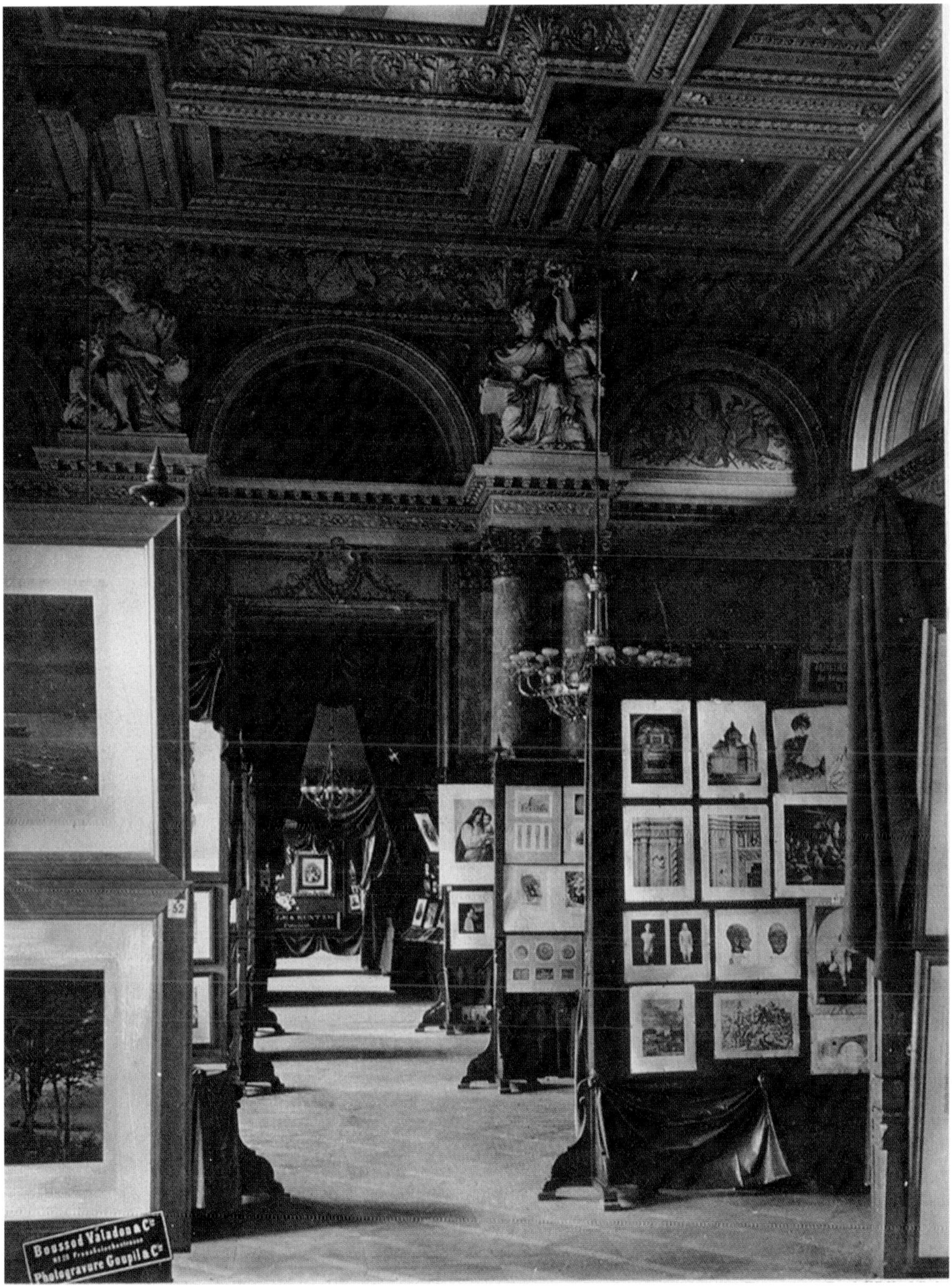
Boussod Valadon & Cie
Photogravure Goupil & Cie

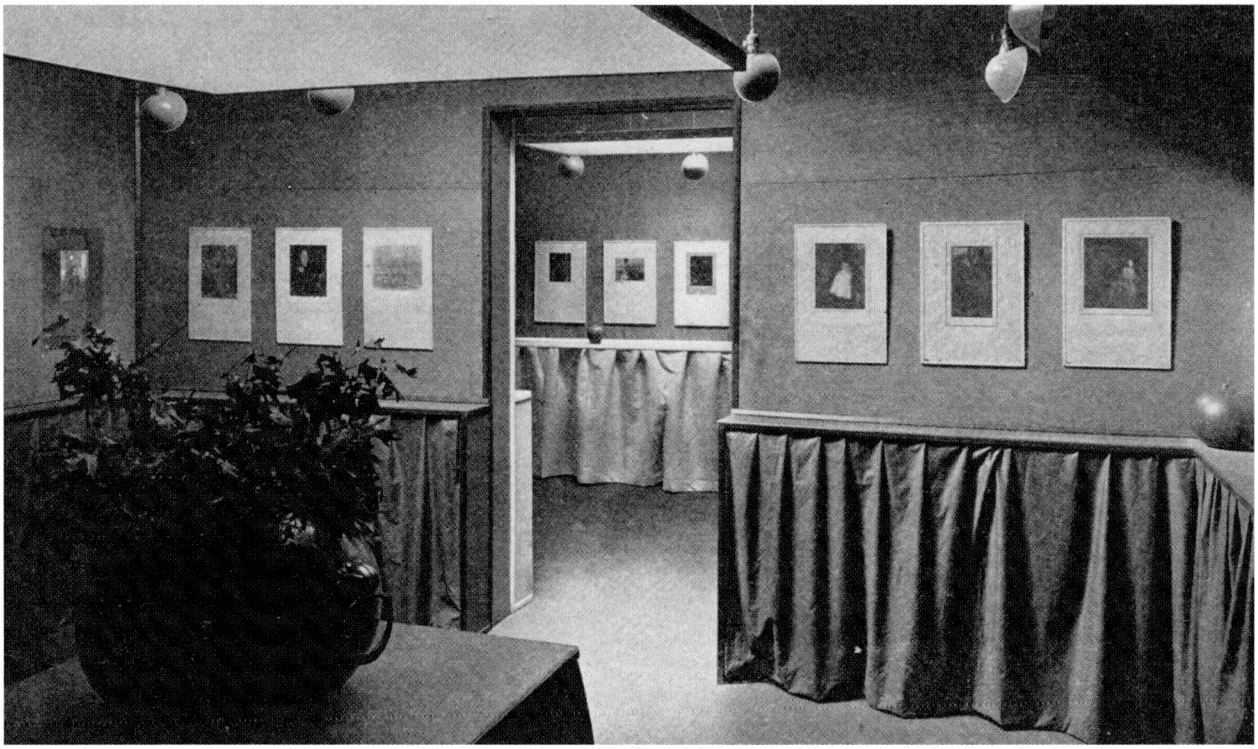

practice—by nature elitist and amateur in the fullest sense of the term—was motivated by a reactionary approach that rejected recent techniques.

Arising as soon as the invention was publicized, the debate surrounding the claim of photography to exist as an art on an equal footing with painting had since become clouded by many aesthetic, philosophical, and commercial contradictions. The first paradox: the aporia between an image—admirable in itself—and a means of obtaining it, marked by its indisputably technical nature, whatever manual interventions were involved before and/or after the act. The second inevitable clash: the legitimate aspiration of photographers to have their creations recognized through exhibitions and to defend their copyright against the misgivings of those, who, like Baudelaire in 1859, feared that photography, in its faithfulness to reality, might impose a unique model on painting and so jeopardize inventiveness and imagination. And finally, there was the distrust of the commercial, and soon industrial, rise of an invention that, leaving artistic intention far behind, was so widely distributed—through channels as varied as the book, the poster, the postcard, and packaging—that its presence had become not only universal but banal. Such developments resulted in confusion between photographs created from a strictly artistic point of view and those which, as early as the end of the 1880s, started invading daily life. But the impossibility, for its detractors as for its advocates, of a viable definition of photography,

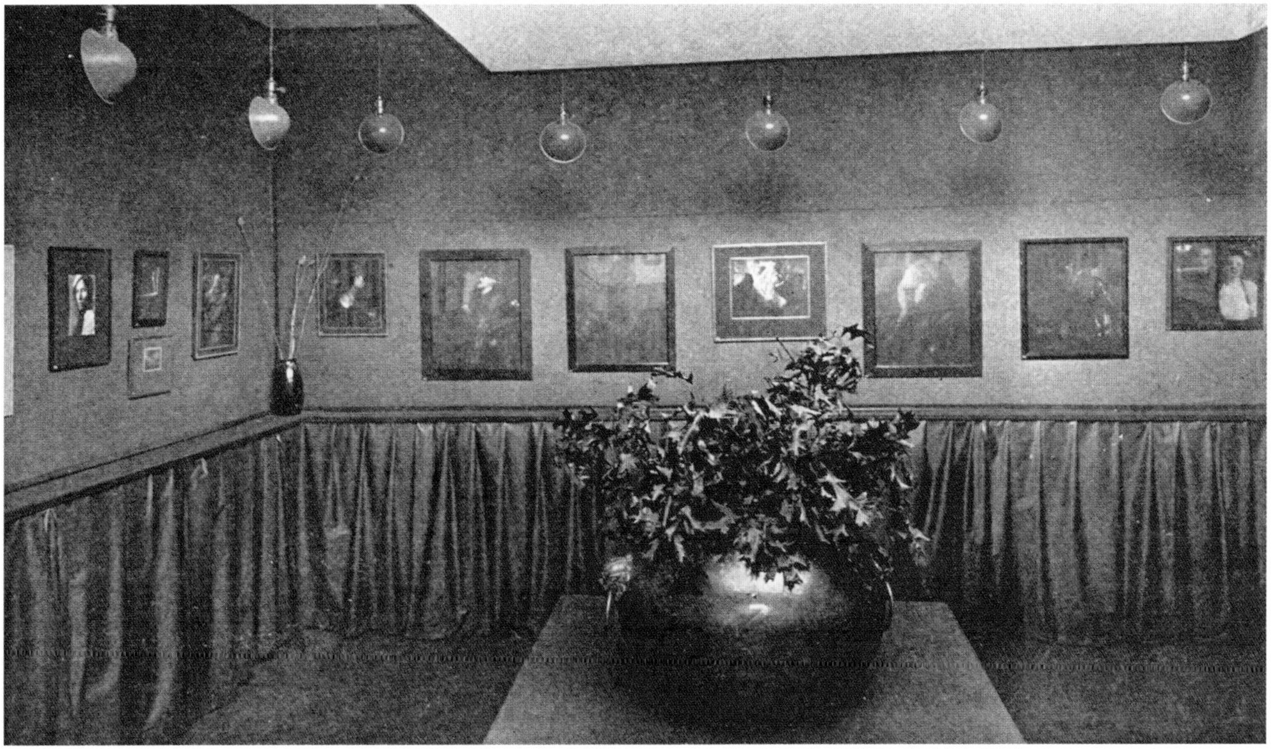

48–49. Alfred Stieglitz, "The Little Galleries of Photo-Secession," 1906, photomechanical print, Musée d'Orsay, Paris.

or of classifying it within or without the artistic domain, did not prevent the rapid development of close links between pictorial and photographic creation founded on the interchange of models, but, more especially, freighted by the advent of new images that reconfigured the codes of the representation of reality and renewed the practice of painting as both art and process. It is these interconnections that will be analyzed in the chapters to come, starting with a genre in which photography was destined to excel, to the point that its effects have become virtually transparent: the reproduction of works of painting.

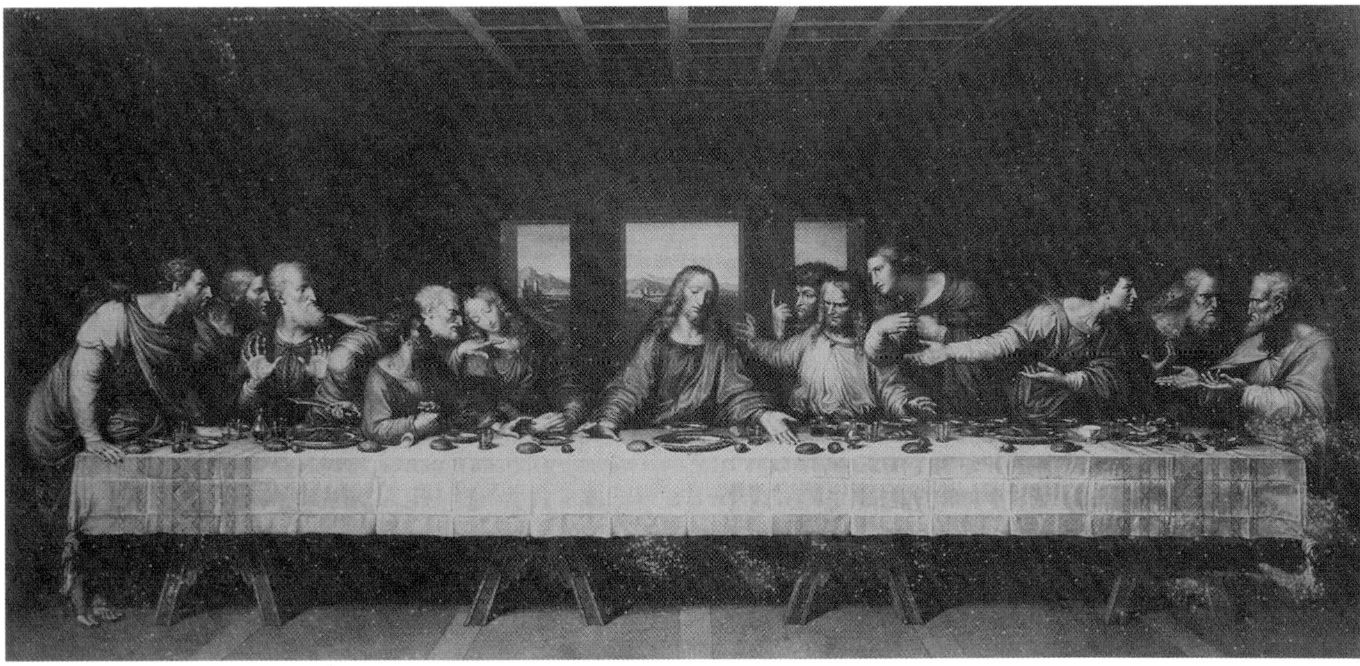

"The painter will find in this process a tool for rapidly amassing a collection of studies." [1]

REPRODUCING PAINTINGS

The reproduction of works of art lay at the heart of the invention of photography. From the 1820s, Nicéphore Niépce had tried to reproduce engravings by contact with a paper sensitized by silver iodide (ill. 15). William Fox Talbot included twenty-four reproductions of works of art—paintings, sculptures, engravings, and objets d'art—in his *Pencil of Nature*, and, in 1839, had tried to photograph one of the pictures in his family home. For a long time, however, historians of photography tended to neglect the study of the reproduction of works of art.[2] This deliberate omission is understandable, though; striving legitimately to elevate the object of their discipline to the rank of a genuine art, they preferred to keep at a safe distance a side of photography which by its very nature seemed to reduce it to the ancillary role of "very humble maidservant," which Charles Baudelaire had already scoffed at in his report of the 1859 Salon, and to circumscribe the use of photographic work, as against painting, into the category of document. In so doing, however, they skated over the technical virtuosity and aesthetic invention attained by early photographers in their efforts to reproduce artworks.

Historians of painting too took little heed; the aesthetic and philosophical primacy after World War II of the concept of the original work of art, of its unique "aura," was not favorable to the study of the nineteenth-century art of the copy (engraving, photography, and casting), at that time fundamental to the creation of art and a linchpin in art education.[3] All analysis that turned its back not only on artworks of this kind but also on the means deployed, particularly widespread after 1945, necessarily obscured the historical context of their production.

As soon as Daguerre's invention was announced in 1839, embryonic photography appeared a likely panacea to the needs of an artist requiring a copy of an artwork. As Jules Janin enthusiastically, and a mite disingenuously, exclaimed in his article published in *L'Artiste*: "The *daguerotype* [*sic*] is destined

50. **Facing page:** François Alphonse Fortier, after Leonardo da Vinci, "The Last Supper," 1851, salt print from a glass negative, Bibliothèque Municipale, Lille.

to reproduce the most beautiful features of nature and art ... that is, the ceaseless, spontaneous, tireless representation of the hundred thousand masterpieces that time has laid low or built up on the surface of the globe.... It is destined to make available, in our homes and at low cost, the most beautiful works of art of which today we can have only expensive and inaccurate copies; before long, and if one has no wish to act as one's own engraver, one will pack off one's offspring to the museum, telling him: 'You've got three hours to fetch me a picture by Murillo or Raphael.'"[4]

The onset of aesthetic acceptance

For photographers from the end of the 1840s, copying paintings constituted, above all others, a genre on which the aesthetic recognition of their practice might be based. The fidelity to the original that photography seemed to promise provided its exponents with a way into the sphere of art, after the fashion of the recent revival of reproductive engraving. During the Exposition des Produits de l'Industrie in 1849, Gustave Le Gray's commendation from the jury stemmed in particular from the quality of his reproductions of paintings: "This young painter has applied his efforts to the subjects that formed part of his early studies; to the portrait and to the reproduction of paintings and objets d'art ... the pictures he copied, the objets d'art he reproduced are masterpieces with a wonderful finish and of flattering fidelity." Once more, in the wake of Paul Delaroche, Léon de Laborde underlined the valuable contribution of photography: "Artists will discover a great resource in its ability to reproduce all the materials they find necessary and that constitute as it were the tools of their endeavor."[5] In a long inaugural article in *La Lumière*, Francis Wey underscored the unique and astonishing qualities of photography founded on representational accuracy: "It is to be understood that *heliography*, as applied to a plane surface like the canvas of a picture, reproduces the image and its appearance with mathematical accuracy. This is a precious resource for obtaining excellent reductions for the use of the engraver; the very superiority of its results condemns to oblivion every other type of copying limited to mere imitation, undertaken without the cooperation of thought through which an individual mind might elevate the translation of a model."[6] A few weeks later, Wey was articulating his ideas still more forcefully: "If the painter-copyist or engraver is knowledgeable and skilful, he will change the character of the model; and, if not, he will be unable to copy it. The only solution to these difficulties is heliography and it is on this terrain that it is destined to perform miracles."[7]

The wonders of heliography

Wey was enchanted by the splendor of a photographic reproduction of Leonardo's *Last Supper* by François Alphonse Fortier (1807–82), presented early in the year 1851 to the members of the Société Héliographique: "This minor masterpiece obtained from a far larger engraving produced something of a stir among artists; because it combines the firmness of the graver with the gentleness of mezzotint, and conveys, with greatly accentuated relief, details that the most experienced hand would be helpless to bring out. Heads the size of a chick-pea are expressive and eloquent; the overall effect loses nothing in terms of tranquility, the whole value of the original is concentrated in this miniature" (ill. 50).[8] If photography was thus able to render faithfully the creative mind of the greatest genius of the Renaissance, it became hard for its detractors to argue against the artistic qualities of its products and the talent of its exponents.

The debate around reproductive photography was all the fiercer since it flared up at a time when the art of gravure found itself confronted with a new situation thanks to the appearance of the technique of lithography, but also because of a swelling market for reproduced artworks in the wake of the increasing number of art journals, as well as the desire to illustrate articles reviewing the Salon. Invented by Aloys Senefelder in 1795 in Germany, and introduced in France at the end of the 1810s, lithography allowed artists to draw directly on the stone, a technique rather easier to acquire than line-engraving or etching, which both called for a long apprenticeship and great manual dexterity. Lithography was destined to become an independent means of expression, painters and draftsmen could practice it themselves, without having to use the intermediary of a printmaker. The perfectly even surface of the image, realized thanks to a technique of application rather than intaglio or relief, already vaguely recalled the planarity of a photograph.

"Between two machines, the most accurate, the fastest, the least expensive, will be necessarily preferred"

In the minds of critics and informed sectors of the public, the increasing number of pictures reproduced in reviews and newspapers established a distinction between two types of reproductive engraving: an artistic, interpretative engraving, in which the creator strove to produce his own version of the master's work—that is, engraving intended to hang on the walls of the annual Salon or gathered in a connoisseur's portfolio; and then a type based on close resemblance to the work copied, whose qualities were to be judged solely in that light.[9] As Wey made clear, it was only to the latter that photography

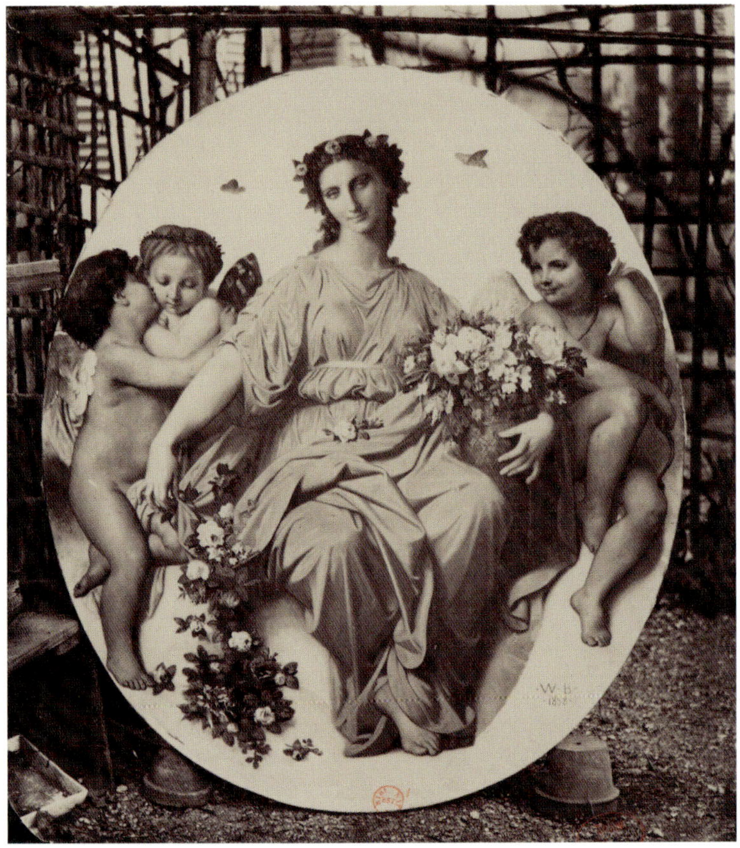

51. Anonymous, after William Bouguereau, "Spring" (preparatory cartoon for the decoration in Émile Pereire's Salon), c. 1858, albumen print, Bibliothèque Nationale de France, Paris.

could be advantageously compared: "A portrait engraved by Nanteuil or Drevet, after a Mignard or a Rigault, lives again, breathes with new life.... Heliography cannot go beyond its model: it is a faithful helpmeet, not an intellect. But we sense that this material process, invincible in the limits of its field, practically eliminates all imitation reduced to mere imitation and nothing more. Any draftsman, any lithographer, or any engraver deprived of artistic inspiration is thus likely to see himself supplanted and, between two machines, the most accurate, the fastest, the least expensive, will be necessarily preferred."[10] Turning on its head an argument often marshaled by detractors of photography (if it was a mere mechanical procedure, at least it produced realistic images of high quality, unlike other processes), Wey's contention was taken up by many critics favorable to the invention.

To the defense of engraving

This view was developed in 1857 by Paul Périer in a response to a lengthy and heartfelt plea by Henri Delaborde, curator at the department of prints in the imperial library, in favor of engraving and engravers, whose trade seemed to him to be under serious threat from the new invention: "Photography disposes of enough partisans, and enthusiastic partisans at that, for a defense of the opposing cause to appear neither superfluous nor irrelevant. While the burin often lays idle, cameras are hard at work, steadily increasing their productive power, an acceleration in activity aided and abetted by fashion."[11] Delaborde lambasted photographic copies of paintings that resulted in "slavishly faithful images, incomplete representations that do nothing but counterfeit the appearance of the pictures." He further added: "Engraving is then faced by a dual task. It must at one and the same time copy and elucidate the painting.... Photography, on the contrary, proceeding only from the fact, starts and finishes with the fact. It can go no further than blind fidelity. Apart from such excessive semblance, it simply does not exist." But in quoting this vehement tirade, Périer insisted that it was only pertinent in the context of a defense of engraving: "Engraving, which, alone, possesses the right and capacity to produce a complete imitation, will be consigned to oblivion."[12] The assertion sounded like a counsel of despair, as Périer was quick to point out: "There exist photographic copies of pictures clearly preferable to reproductions from the burin of very famous artists.... The triumph of photography is all the more remarkable and telling since it carried the day on a most unfavorable field, in a battle with colors that it has not as yet been able to master completely."[13]

A unique technical and artistic challenge

The least one can say is that this was a euphemism: photographic reproduction of color only truly developed in the early twentieth century, thanks to the Lumière brothers' autochrome plate patented in 1907. Still, the desire of photographers to have their pictorial reproductions accepted was all the stronger as they remained so difficult to produce. The imperative of relatively bright and steady light, which often meant a picture needed to be transported outdoors (ill. 51), was compounded by the limits of the camera (particularly noticeable for pictures of large dimensions that remained difficult to reproduce in their entirety and without reflections), and of the photographic emulsion that presented difficulties not only with color but also with tonal value and contrast. It was factors like these that were stressed in 1859 by Louis Figuier in praising the exceptional results obtained by certain photographers, Robert Bingham[14] in particular: "Although photography was created and given to the world to record and reproduce all that is visible to our eyes, the copying of works of art long presented insuperable difficulties. We speak of neither sculpture, nor engraving, which presented little problem to photography from its earliest beginnings; but the heliographic copy of pictures, of old masters especially, long appeared simply impossible."[15] The same year, Philippe Burty detailed the stumbling blocks

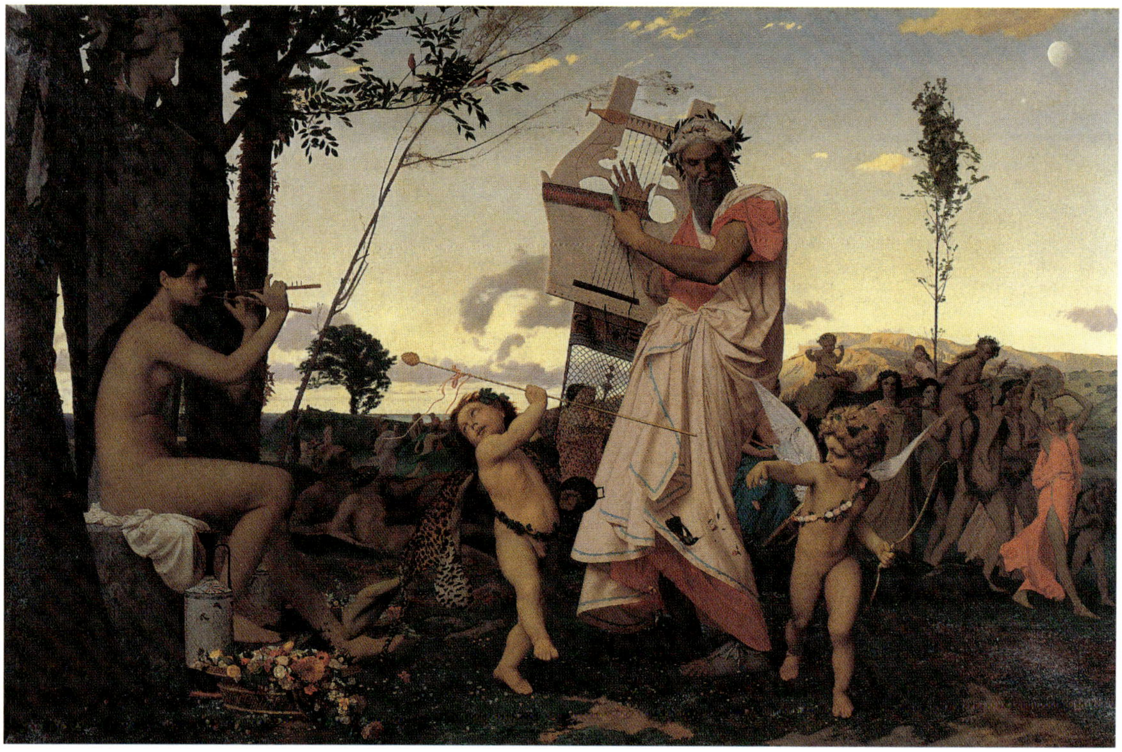

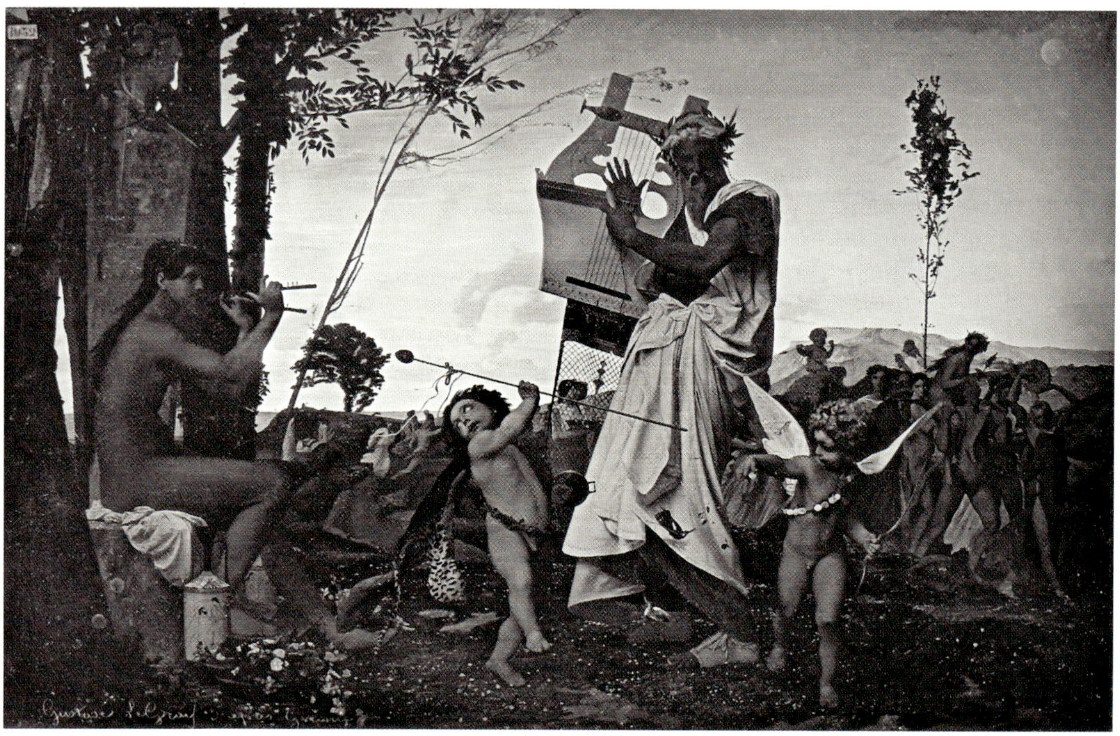
Gustave Le Gray

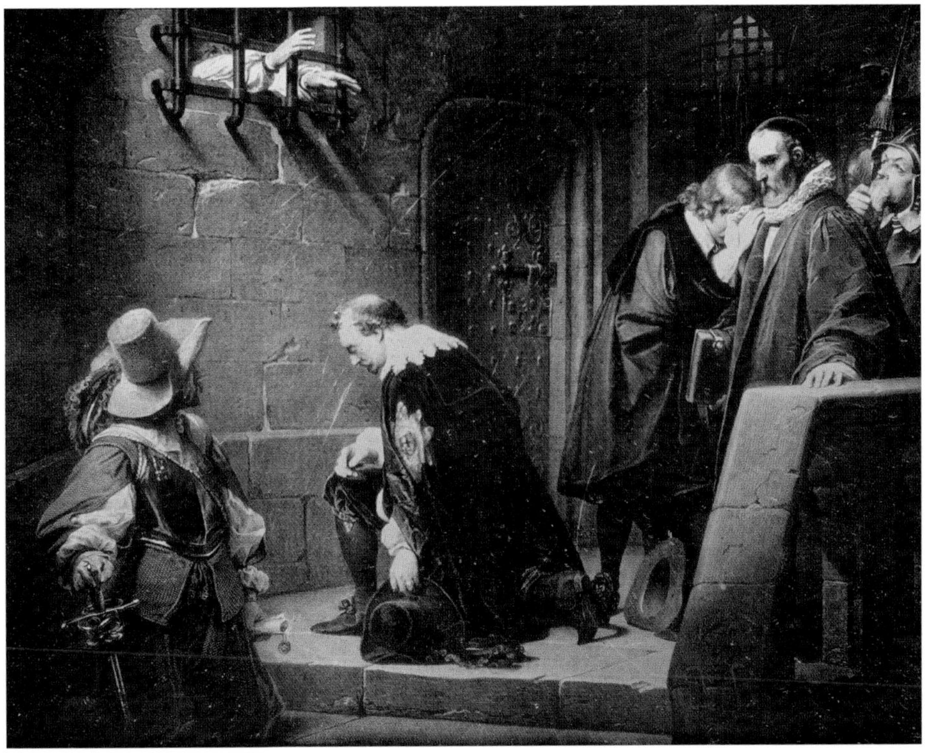

photographers encountered when tackling this kind of subject: "If the light rakes down on a painting on panel towards which the lens is directed, the grain of the oak will create a moiré effect on the photograph; if it falls on a broadly brushed painting, the bright points clinging to peaks in the impasto will result in tiny white dots.... Moreover, as light does not impress upon the chemical substances on which it acts the same proportions of tone as when it strikes our eyes, yellow veers to black, as does green; red, on the contrary, and blue, appear whiteish." [16]

Such complaints about photographic obstacles betray the extent to which the enthusiasm of the early critics had been fanned by the utopian ideal of recording and classifying everything, betraying an idealism that failed to take into account the limits of the new invention. They do nonetheless speaks volumes as to virtuosity aspired to by some photographers in taking up the gauntlet of reproducing painted canvases. One of the most masterly examples was the realization by Gustave Le Gray of a full-plate daguerreotype reproduction of Jean-Léon Gérôme's *Anacreon, Bacchus, and Cupid* in 1848, the very year it was unveiled at the Salon (latterly purchased by the state for the Musée des Augustins in Toulouse, where it still hangs). In spite of the size of the piece—9 feet 11 ¼ inches × 4 feet (3.03 × 1.24 meters)—and despite its subtle, light colors, laid on as a glaze, the photographer manages to capture perfectly its strange allure (Le Gray and Gérôme had both been students at

52. **Facing page, top:** Jean-Léon Gérôme, *Anacreon, Bacchus, and Cupid*, 1848, oil on canvas, Musée des Augustins, Toulouse.

53. **Facing page, bottom:** Gustave Le Gray, after Jean-Léon Gérôme, "Anacreon, Bacchus, and Cupid," 1848, daguerreotype, Alain and Audrey Flamand Collection.

54. **Above:** Louis-Adolphe Humbert de Molard, after an engraving by Louis-Pierre Henriquel-Dupont taken from Paul Delaroche's *Lord Strafford on his Way to the Scaffold*, 1846, daguerreotype, Musée Gatien-Bonnet, Lagny-sur-Marne.

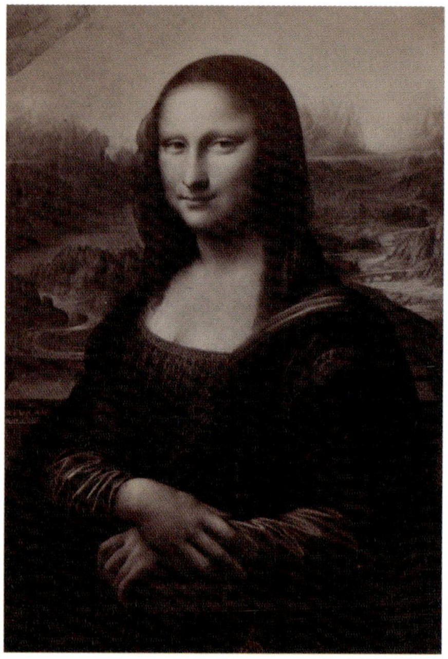

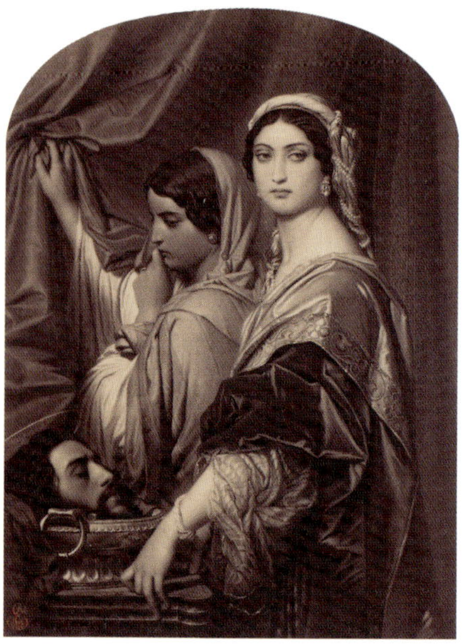

55. **Above, top:** Gustave Le Gray, after a drawing by Aimé Millet taken from Leonardo da Vinci's *Mona Lisa*, 1854–55, albumen print, Bibliothèque Nationale de France, Paris.

56. **Above, bottom:** Robert Jefferson Bingham, after Paul Delaroche, *Herodias with the Head of Saint John the Baptist*, 1858, albumen print, Musée d'Orsay, Paris.

Paul Delaroche's studio). The words "Gustave Le Gray after J.-L. Gérôme," incised in the bottom left-hand corner of the plate, express the mutual recognition sought in this early example of photographic reproduction, highlighting the talent of the painter no less than that of the photographer (ills. 52–53). For its photograph, the picture probably had to be carried out into the courtyard of the studio on Rue de Fleurus, which Gérôme shared with other artists. Le Gray took some photographs on paper of the place the same year, showing them in 1857 on the occasion of the second exhibition of the Société Française de Photographie. To obviate the difficulties presented by taking pictures of paintings, photographers often opted to reproduce, not the canvas itself, but an engraving taken from it. In 1846, Humbert de Molard made several daguerreotype copies of artworks; one of them reproduces an engraving by Henriquel-Dupont of Paul Delaroche's *Lord Strafford*; the precision of the daguerreotype plate brings out the exactitude of line in the print and enhances the blacks. With considerable dexterity, the photographer has captured all the theatricality of the scene painted. In an act that shows how seriously he took these daguerreotypes, Molard exhibited them at the first exhibition of the Société Française de Photographie at the World's Fair of 1855 in Paris (ill. 54). Likewise, in 1854, in order to produce a photograph of *The Mona Lisa*, Gustave Le Gray made recourse to a drawing of it by Aimé Millet (ill. 55).

"So exact when dealing with nature, faced with a painting photography behaves oddly"

In 1857, the publisher Adolphe Goupil commissioned Robert Bingham to produce a complete photographic record of the works of Paul Delaroche, who had died a short while previously. Each reproduction was to be accompanied by a note; issued in a portfolio, they constituted the first catalogue raisonné of a contemporary artist to be illustrated with photographs. Published in 1858, and presented at the exhibition of 1859, the quality of the work earned gasps of admiration from the critics. Hailing the interpretative skill of the photographer, who, in his eyes, brilliantly served the dramatic art of Delaroche by amplifying the narrative aspect of his painting, the poet and critic Théophile Gautier enthused: "When tackling a painting, photography, in spite of the bourgeois sentiments one imputes to it, becomes an artist and interprets the canvas placed before its lens in its own manner. Its somber tone does away with unwarranted or over conspicuous details, reserving the correct light for the figure with which it is concerned." In conclusion, Gautier refutes the idea that photography is bound to be a mere slave when copying pictorial works: "So exact when dealing with nature, faced with paintings photography behaves oddly, extinguishing some and illuminating others as it likes."[17] In taking scarcely a year over an order that ran to eighty-six issued prints, Bingham sometimes reproduced the pictures themselves (taking advantage of the posthumous exhibition organized at the École des Beaux-Arts in 1857), at others their engravings, an easy task in this case since his publisher Goupil also employed Henriquel-Dupont. The photographer managed to unify his style to such a degree that the critics of the time were hoodwinked, making no distinction between copies made directly after the canvases and those based on reproductions. Bingham's photographer thus contradicted those who lambasted photography for its incapacity to be other than mechanical, prey to the happenstances of its technique, with no place for individual manner (ill. 57).

The hopes of historians and critics

From the very onset of the 1850s, the photographic reproduction of works of art gave rise to great hopes among art historians, who admired the quality that the most experienced and expeditious photographers were by then attaining. The process seemed to them to hold the promise, at least, of an efficient form of dissemination, faster and less expensive than engraving, which would nonetheless respect the nature of work reproduced. The awards handed out during the Paris World's Fair in 1855 echoed these aspirations: more than ten of the first-class medals consigned were presented to photographers for reproductions of works of art, either entirely (Baldus, the Bisson brothers, Robert J. Bingham, Blanquart-Évrard, Adolphe Braun, and Thurston Thompson) or in part (Charles Nègre and Henri Le Secq). In his review of the exhibit, Ernest Lacan expressed sheer wonder at the quality of Le Secq's reproductions: "As for his copies of pictures, they can be listed among the most remarkable photographs of this kind. The difficulties inherent in this type of work are notorious. The triumphant manner in which M. Le Secq has overcome them is worthy of praise."[18] At the same exhibition, Benjamin Delessert presented photographs of engravings by Marcantonio Raimondi published by Goupil in 1853. To show the quality of his photographs, he placed the original engraving and the reproduction side by side in a single frame together with an indication of their price. "This shows," wrote Lacan, "without possible refutation, the importance of photography from the dual point of view of art and industry. What the artist seeks in a master engraving is the beauty of its forms, the skillfulness of its composition, the simplicity of its process; in short, everything that speaks of the genius of its creator" (ill. 57).[19]

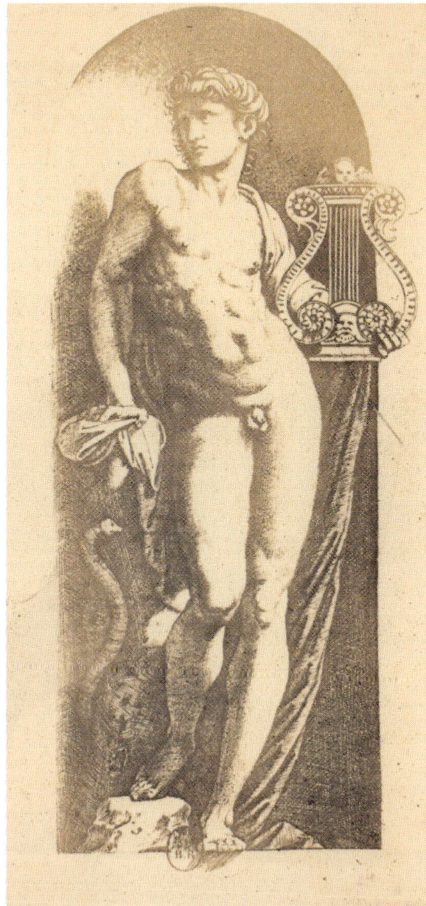

57. Benjamin Delessert after Marcantonio Raimondi's engraving of a drawing by Raphael Sanzio, "Apollo," c. 1852, salt print, Musée d'Orsay, Paris.

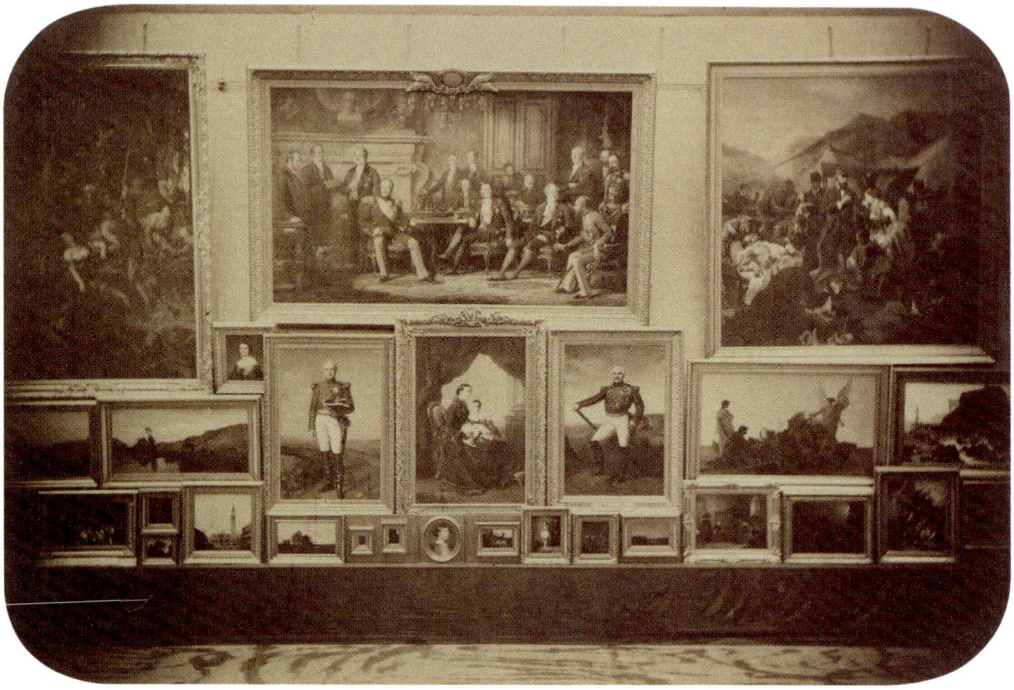

58. Pierre Ambroise Richebourg, "Salon of 1857," 1857, albumen print, Musée d'Orsay, Paris.

The utopia of a photographic museum

Beguiled by the photographic reproductions that Le Gray presented at the Exposition des Produits de l'Industrie in 1849, the following year Laborde presented the Minister for State Education with a futuristic project: a general photographic inventory of every collection in public hands, to start with the ten thousand objects then housed in the Louvre. In 1851, Francis Wey was similarly suggesting a presentation of photographic reproductions on paper of pictures absent from the national collections that might be hung in one of the rooms in the Louvre: "Photography thus offers us an inexpensive, sure, and mathematical means of acquiring, to the great benefit of scholarship and critical history, valuable information concerning masters by whom France does not possess a single picture."[20] Thus, with attention drawn to the value of pictorial reproduction, the idea of a "photographic museum" was now on the cards. In 1854, the Mayer brothers launched the idea of a national subscription for the creation of a state-owned historical museum of photography: "The third section [of this museum] would be devoted to the photographic reproduction of art objects sold, often abroad, by their creators themselves, work that the genius of the workman or the artist often cannot replicate and of which the museum would thus house a faithful copy, such as paintings, statues, important marbles, bronzework, silverwork."[21]

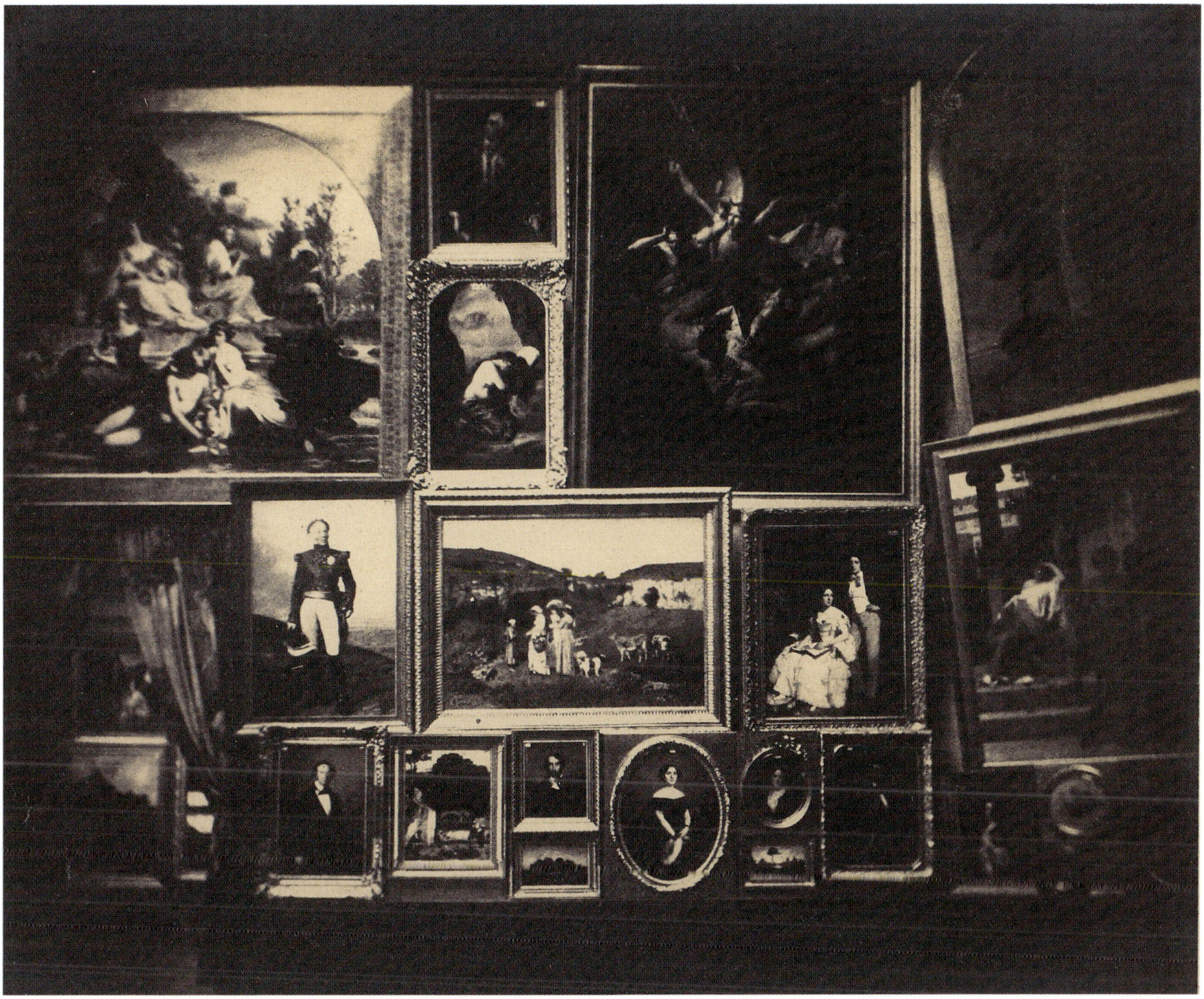

59. Gustave Le Gray, "Salon of 1852, North Wall," 1852, salt print, Musée d'Orsay, Paris.

Photographing Salons and World Fairs

These ideas must have influenced Philippe de Chennevières, who commissioned from Gustave Le Gray photographs of the showrooms at the 1852 Salon; the results were gathered together in an album that also included a remarkable early print of the Salon of 1850–51. In the 1851 pictures, Le Gray—so as to circumvent the problems of taking photographs in such a poorly lit space, where it was difficult to stand back and see the works clearly—chose to capture the depth and rhythm of the gallery where sculptures and paintings were presented together. In 1852, overhead lighting (shadows appear on the photograph) made it possible for him to reproduce the canvases hung side by side on the exhibition room walls, as was then the practice.

Reproduced in all its glory, Gustave Courbet's *Village Damsels*, a picture purchased by the Duke of Morny, appears in the place of honor it earned due to the distinguished station of its owner (ill. 59).[22] Le Gray went on to photograph the rooms of the 1853 Salon, perhaps this time on his own initiative, since no trace of an official commission has come to light. In 1857, the photographer Pierre Ambroise Richebourg, who had already produced daguerreotypes of two architectural plans presented at the Salon in 1847, took several pictures of the immense nave and galleries of the Palais de l'Industrie, where the yearly show was held for the first time. Since Richebourg gravitated around the centers of imperial power (he photographed in particular the empress's Chinese Salon at Fontainebleau), it is possible that the emperor ordered these photographs; from the early 1850s, the idea had been gaining ground that a record of the Salon in photography or engraving should be kept (ill. 58).

Richebourg again photographed the Salon galleries in 1861, anthologizing the results obtained in an album that offers "the principal pictures exhibited in the Salon of 1861"; the works were reproduced as they "had been grouped according to the panels on which [they had] hung." The Archives Nationales contain information from which it can be seen that he intended to sell the 1861 Salon album to the department of the Beaux-Arts.[23] A memo highlights the interest the state might have in "preserving the memory of the painting exhibition." On the directors' advice, the minister ordered the purchase of ten albums for a total of 1,800 francs, earmarked from the commercial profit turned by the Salon. In his report, the head of the Beaux-Arts division, H. Courmont, underlined the interest of an album "liable to be consulted by the Administration and which would prove highly useful [to it] in many circumstances."

In 1864, for the first time, the imperial government commanded photographer Charles Michelez to compile an album comprising photographs of works bought by the state. Unlike the views presented by Le Gray or Richebourg, in which the works were shown as they had appeared during the exhibition, Michelez's pictures reproduce exclusively the pieces actually acquired. The arrangement of the works, the classification of the photographic plates in the album, and the captions for each work became the responsibility of Frédéric Buon, inspector of the Beaux-Arts in charge of organizing the Salons. The administration was thus equipped—above and beyond the "souvenir albums" proposed by Richebourg—with an instrument to keep track of all State acquisitions. Civil servants in the administration of the Beaux-Arts were to refer to it on receiving a request from an artist eager to sell his works; some of the plates in albums preserved in the Archives Nationales bear handwritten notes as to their purchase price (ill. 60). These "Albums du Salon" continued to be compiled until 1880, for as long as the state remained responsible for organizing the annual Salon,

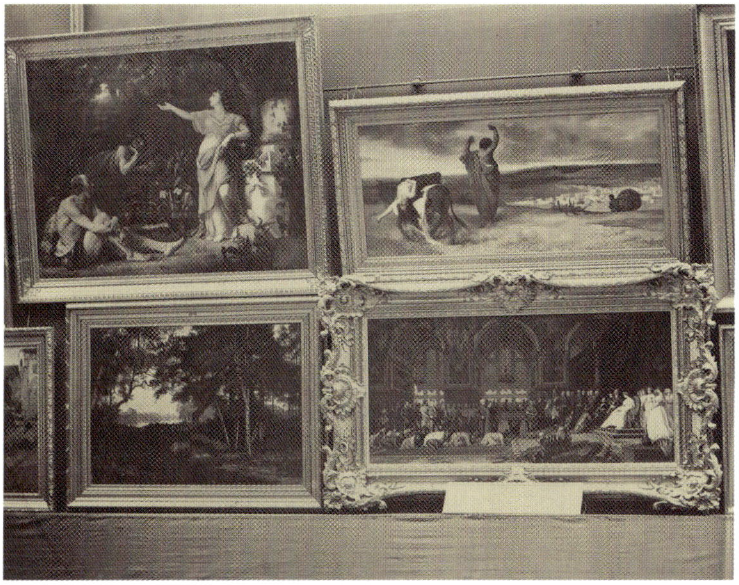

60. Charles Michelez (publisher) after Jean-Léon Gérôme, *The Reception of the Ambassadors in Siam*; Paul Lanteuil, *Amyntas*; Eugène-Romain Thirion, *The Levite of Ephraim*; and Hector Hanteau, *Un coin de parc dans le Nivernais*, 1865, albumen print, Archives Nationales, Paris.

that is. A precious testimony of the history of taste during a time of radical upheaval and the break between official art and the avant-garde, they also reveal the pitfalls of photography in such conditions: some plates betray evidence of the trestles and picture rails rigged up for the occasion.

Painters' rights vs. photographers' rights

From the time of London's Great Exhibition, photography made its way as a precious tool for the reproduction of the artworks and materials presented, and for documenting jury reports.[24] At publication, these reports were illustrated with photographs by Hugh Owen and Claude-Marie Ferrier showing the vast glazed space of the Crystal Palace and the vast accumulation of objects presented on the various stands. Whereas painting and sculpture had been little in evidence in 1851, the emperor ordained that they should be the focus of the exhibition of 1855.[25] The Palais des Beaux-Arts on Avenue Montaigne was one of the major venues of the Exposition Universelle; in preparation, the administration cancelled the 1854 Salon, arousing howls of disappointment among the artists. The views by André Adolphe Eugene Disdéri of the showrooms—later collected into an album, and covering (in addition to canvases by painters from various nations) three single-artist retrospectives dedicated to Ingres, Delacroix, and Horace Vernet (ill. 42)—were probably the outcome of a specific commission. Oddly, the photographs in this album are not signed; indeed, the name of their author is known only due to the disagreement that flared up between the photographer and two artists who complained that his work reproduced and disseminated their art without their agreement: Henry Schlesinger for

The Butterfly Hunt and Charles Louis Müller for *Long Live the Emperor*. The court condemned Disdéri to pay damages of 500 francs to Schlesinger, but Müller's suit was thrown out. These two legal claims reveal the importance already accorded to the reproduction of their works and their diffusion by artists. As the court's findings stressed: "The commercial court of the Seine has also had to judge on a dispute between painting and photography. M. Disdéri, having reproduced in photographs a picture by M. Schlesinger, *The Butterfly Hunt*, had put some of the photographs on sale with Susse, Giroux, and Goupil. Negotiators at the commercial court judge that this *infringed the painter's property rights* and has condemned M. Disdéri to pay a fine of 500 francs." If they hardly went easy on the photographer, comments by a journalist in *La Revue universelle des arts* ipso facto conceded that the technique might reproduce artworks, even the most prestigious: "This will teach photographers to reproduce masterpieces by the old masters, who, thank God, are in the public domain, instead of replicating compositions by these owner-artists who have their vulgar images defended by lawyers and bailiffs."[26] Only in 1878 would regulations governing the World's Fair enshrine a right to take photographs in its venues.

Photography in the art studio

Artists took an early interest in the possibilities of reproduction offered by photography. Already at the beginning of the 1850s, Ingres asked the photographer Désiré Millet to take daguerreotypes of several of his works. These pictures were probably intended for private use; one of the plates reproduced, leaning against an easel, shows a large picture of a nude posed for by the painter's first wife, Madeleine Chapelle, who had died prematurely in 1849. The picture has since vanished; it was in all probability destroyed at the request of Ingres's second wife. As the picture was taken in the studio (the portrait of Madame Moitessier [1851, National Gallery of Art, Washington] can be glimpsed in the background), this daguerreotype presents an important facet of the life of the painter, who, though hostile in some of his remarks to photography, wanted to preserve the memory of a canvas he had long cherished (ill. 61). Photography also presented an ideal way for artists to keep track of their paintings as they progressed; another daguerreotype by Millet reproducing the *Virgin Adoring the Host* (1854, Musée d'Orsay, Paris) shows a state slightly different from the final canvas, as betrayed in the folds of the mantle and the rays of light falling on the chalice. For the photographer, reproducing a painter's works allowed unprecedented access to their workshops.

In 1855, Gustave Courbet, wanting to illustrate the catalog of his solo exhibition, which was written by his friend the critic Champfleury, decided to have photographs taken of all the

61. **Facing page:** Désiré Millet, after Jean-Auguste-Dominique Ingres, *Reclining Nude*, c. 1851, daguerreotype, Musée Ingres, Montauban.

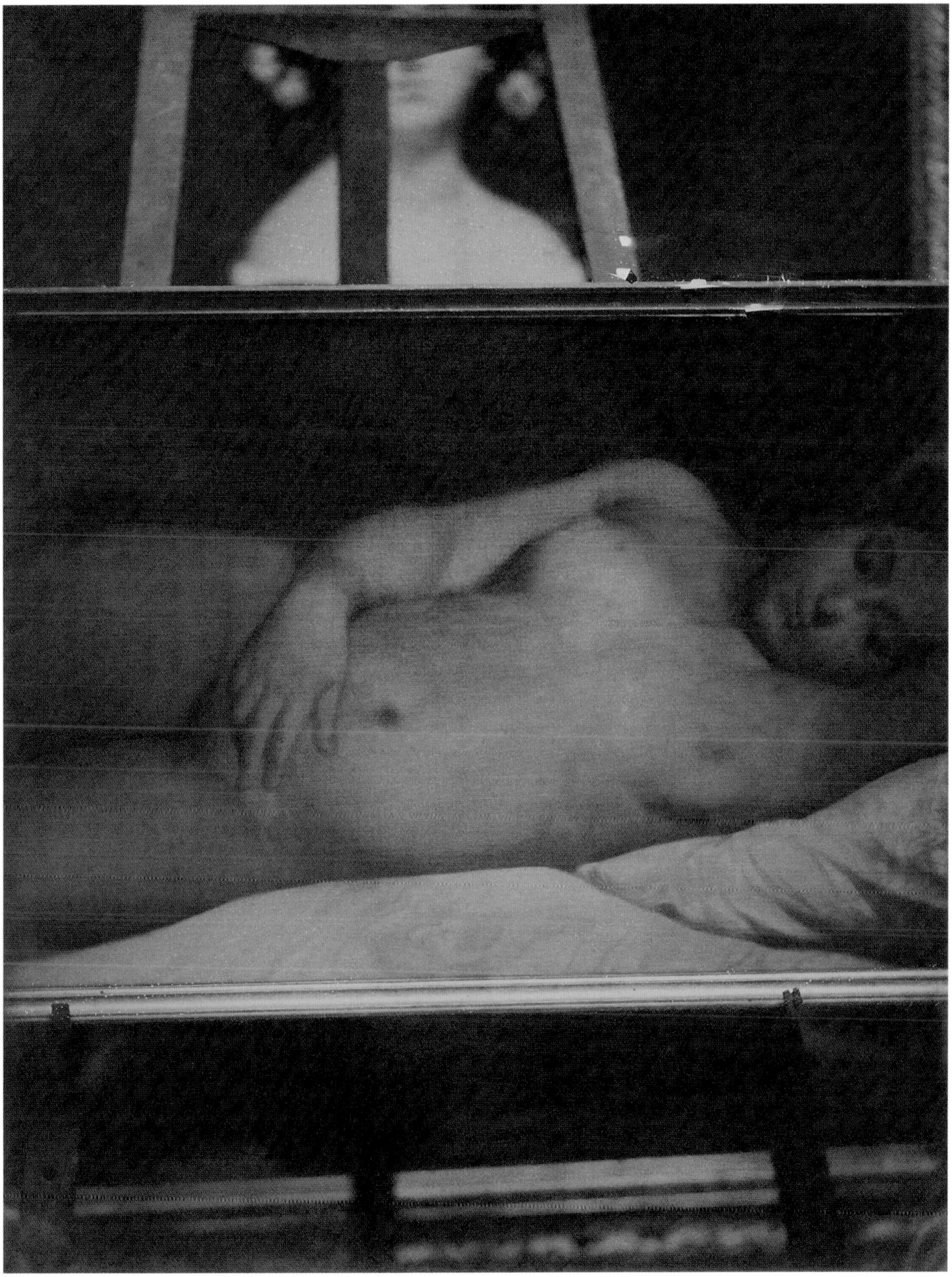

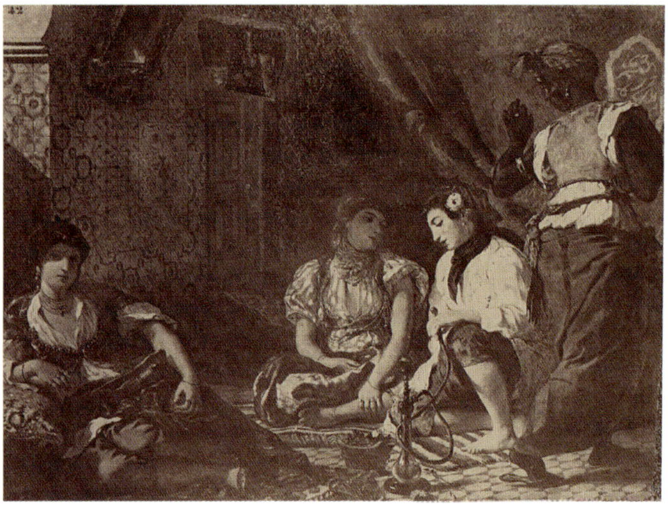

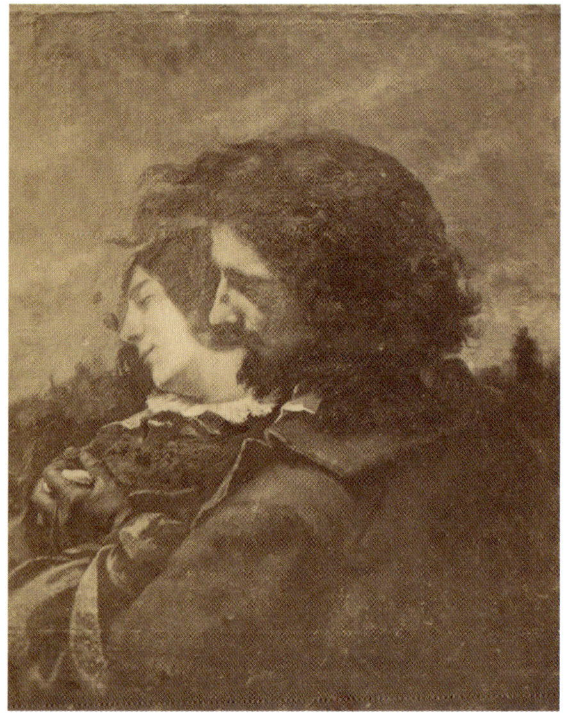

62. **Above, left:** Édouard Baldus after Eugène Delacroix, *Women of Algiers in their Apartment*, 1853, salt print, taken from Théophile Silvestre, *Histoire des Artistes vivants*, Bibliothèque Nationale de France, Paris.

63. **Above, right:** Pierre Ambroise Richebourg after Gustave Courbet, *Lovers in the Countryside*, 1855, albumen print, Bibliothèque Nationale de France, Paris.

paintings he was to show in his Pavillon du Réalisme, erected on the fringes of the Exposition Universelle. It was probably through the young Théophile Silvestre—a onetime student at the École des Chartes, who took part in the Revolution of 1848 and then served the short-lived Second Republic—that the painter was confronted for the first time with the photographic reproduction of his works. Silvestre's plan to publish an illustrated history of living artists was ambitious and innovative. His idea was to issue, in installments, biographical notes and photographic portraits of French and foreign contemporary artists, together with reproductions of their works. "*L'Histoire des Artistes vivants* has the advantage of presenting a series of studies, after the living model, stated frankly, simply, without bitterness, without weakness, or bias.... Each personality is there *imprinted*, so to speak, just as his real image is fixed on the daguerreotype plate."

Les Artistes vivants

For the time, the idea of photography illustrating such a compendium was almost unprecedented.[27] A similar desire for veracity and exactitude lay behind Silvestre's desire to undertake interviews with both the artists and people in their entourage. The editor felt that any judgment on the artists and their works should be based on a faithful portrait and on reproduction of their works. Barbey d'Aurevilly underlines how strongly the desire for truth imbued Silvestre's work: "His

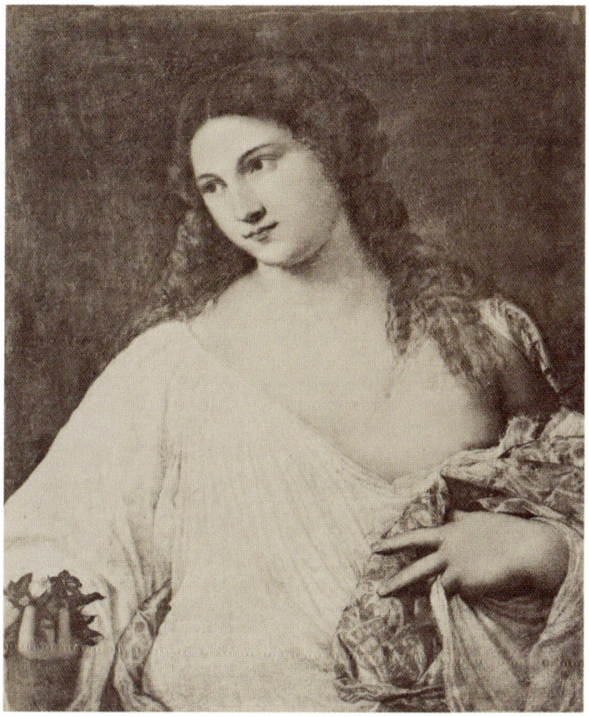

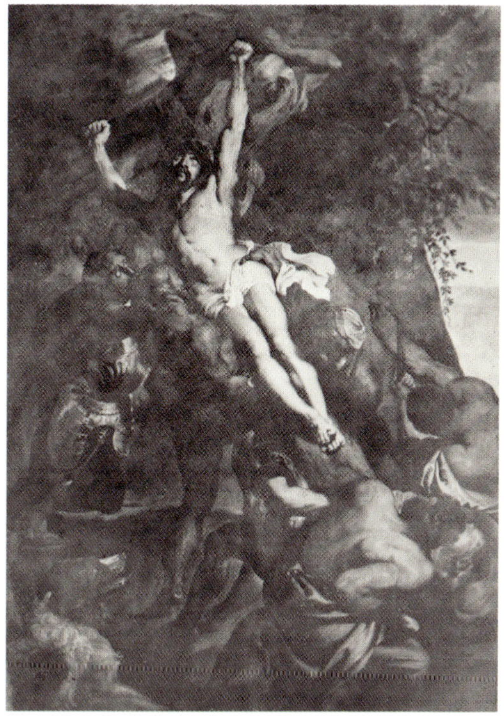

64. **Above, left:** Alinari brothers, after Titian, *Flora*, c. 1855, albumen print, Musée d'Orsay, Paris.

65. **Above, right:** Eugène Desplanques, after Peter Paul Rubens, *The Raising of the Cross*, 1853, salt print, Bibliothèque Nationale de France, Paris.

biographies blaze with color and light; the sense of reality they produce is so powerful that even the mind least sympathetic to his person and his ideas must accept his portraits as lifelike and the picture [reproduced] as virtually identical."[28] Silvestre's plans for *Les Artistes vivants* never saw the light of day in the form he intended, however. Indeed, only the portfolio devoted to Camille Corot appeared as it had been announced. Although Silvestre placed orders with several talented photographers (Victor Laisné and his colleague Émile Defonds for the portraits, Edouard Baldus, Henri Le Secq, and the Bisson brothers for the reproductions), in the work as it finally came out in 1856, photographs are replaced by engravings (ill. 62).[29] Silvestre Laisné carried out a portrait of Courbet of which the artist felt very proud. In 1853, he also photographed *The Bathers* and *The Wrestlers*, then unveiled at the Salon. At his solo exhibition of 1855, the painter saw reproductions of his works as a complementary source of income, writing to his parents: "I have had photographs taken of my pictures to be sold at the Palais de l'Industrie."[30] His plan is clearer still in a letter to his patron and friend Alfred Bruyas: "Champfleury will write me an annotated booklet to be put on sale ... and I'll sell the photographs I'm having taken by M. Laisné at that time." No trace of these photographs and no mention of any such marketing ploy appears in comments concerning the Pavillon du Réalisme at the time. A letter to Bruyas asking him to take another photograph of *The Bathers*, and Richebourg's deposit in the Imperial Library in 1855 of a photographic

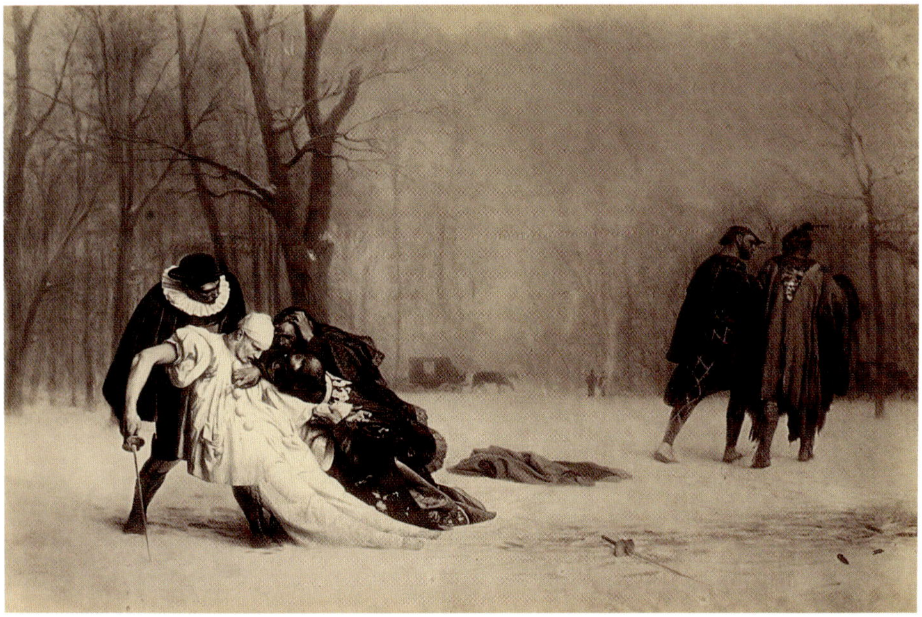

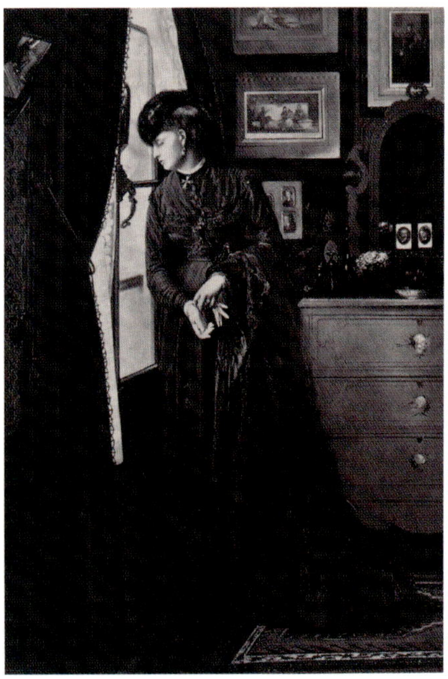

66. **Above, top:** Adolphe Goupil (publisher), after Jean-Léon Gérôme, *The Duel after the Ball*, 1867–68, albumen print, Musée Goupil, Bordeaux.

67. **Above, bottom:** Adolphe Goupil (publisher), after Jules-Émile Saintin, *Indecision*, 1871, albumen print, Musée Goupil, Bordeaux.

reproduction of *The Lovers in the Countryside* (also known as *Feelings of Youth*; Musée des Beaux-Arts, Lyon, 1845), a picture exhibited by the artist, demonstrate Courbet's determination and personal implication in this singular project (ill. 63).[31]

Photography publishing

The choice of the works to be reproduced raised the essential issue of taste and the diffusion of models. In 1851, Wey invited a number of photographers to copy examples of Flemish and Dutch primitivism, which was neglected at that time compared to Italian and French painting, and which he thought engraving failed to capture accurately. He hailed the initiative of Louis-Desiré Blanquart-Évrard, who had been the first to sell prints taken from paper negatives and gathered into portfolios. Issued in 1851, his *Album photographique de l'artiste et de l'amateur* combined photographic reproductions of architecture, painting, and sculpture. He published several albums of great quality including reproductions of artworks and travel photographs (for example, the photos taken by Maxime du Camp in Egypt), offering customers original prints of the photographs (ill. 65). These publications attracted considerable interest from critics; but, forestalled by financial setbacks (printing on paper was a costly undertaking) and technical hitches (the prints, lacking stability, often faded and lost density), in 1856 Blanquart-Évrard's photographic printing works had to close down. Disadvantages over the stability of photographs moreover encouraged the Duke of Luynes, a member of the Société Française de Photographie, as well as an enlightened collector and art lover, to launch a contest in two parts in July 1856: one prize was offered for the best photomechanical reproduction method and another for a technique for stabilizing photographs.[32] Both prizes were eventually awarded in 1867 to Alphonse Poitevin, whose work on carbon printing had also been the inspiration for all his competitors.

In 1852 in Florence, Leopoldo Alinari, together with his brothers Giuseppe and Romualdo, founded the photographic studio that still bears their name. Very quickly they began concentrating on portraiture, the reproductions of works of art, and architectural views, copying artworks—paintings and sculptures—housed in museums throughout the country (ill. 64). Their output, based on the diffusion of Ancient and Renaissance models, proved a huge success with art lovers, artists, and museum professionals alike. If the Alinari brothers did much of the photography themselves, as their catalog grew they had to turn to other exponents. Around the same time, the publisher and dealer in engravings, Adolphe Goupil (1806–93), who had worked in Paris since 1829, where he forged an association with Henry Rittner (1802–40), started issuing photographs, with the publication, in particular, of Édouard Delessert's photographs of engravings by Marcantonio Raimondi. In 1858 he created *La Galerie photographique*, the first of his photographic series reproducing artworks. By 1894 *La Galerie photographique* included 1,779 numbers; it was completed by five further series, including *Le Musée Goupil, Les Cartes album,* and *Les Cartes de visite.* In 1869, Goupil's opened a large factory at Asnières, which housed all its activities relating to photography and engraving. There, every photomechanical technique was employed and the firm's printing activities grew to near industrial proportions. Their catalog, catering above all for artists whose paintings they also sold, in Paris and in their branches in New York, London, Berlin, The Hague, and Brussels, fostered the narrative, academic art that proved enduringly attractive to customers at the time. After Paul Delaroche, whose illustrated catalogue raisonné the firm published in 1858, the artist best represented in this series was Jean-Léon Gérôme, who became Goupil's son-in-law in 1863. In each, every one of his works was reproduced, ensuring a significant source of income for the painter and making his art even better known. Beyond the family ties between the two men, the dramatizing aesthetics of Gérôme, his sense of storytelling and suspense, and his precise line—to which coloring remained subordinate—were particularly well served by photography, creating instantly readable images that delighted the public. Presented at the Salon of 1857 and acquired by the Duc d'Aumale, then in exile in England, *Leaving the Masked Ball* thus became one of the most popular works of the time under the more expressive title, *A Duel after the Ball* (ill. 66). In the form of a photographic reproduction, the canvas by Gérôme, like several others by the artist, thus made its way into many

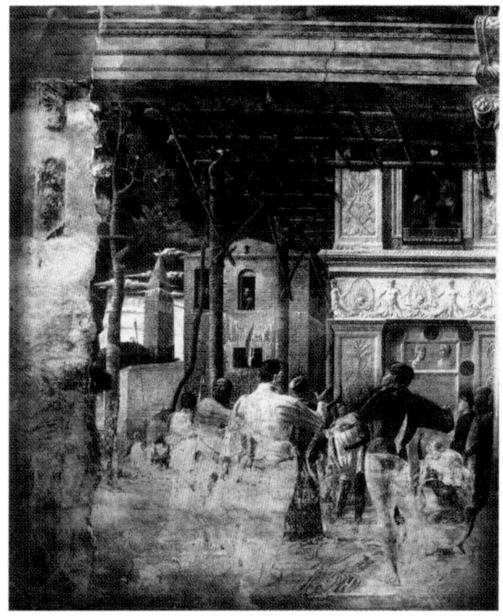

68. Carlo Naya, after Andrea Mantegna, *The Martyrdom of Saint Christopher* (fresco in the Ovetari Chapel, Padua), c. 1870, albumen print, Musée Rodin, Paris.

a middle-class interior, a key element in the development of pictorial taste of the time. Jules Émile Saintin shows a framed photographic reproduction of the painting hanging on the wall of an elegant young woman's apartment (ill. 67).[33]

In 1875, Adolphe Giraudon, a young man of twenty-five, presented to members of the Société Française de Photographie photographs taken in Madrid by Jean Laurent representing a number of historic tapestries. Two years later, Giraudon opened the famous "Photograph Library" in Paris, where, unlike Goupil with his industry-scale use of photomechanical processes, he specialized in selling original photographs. He both commissioned and acquired works by freelancers, who thus often became a chief channel of distribution as they passed their photos on to painters and sculptors, who then built up a catalog of models and other sources of inspiration. The Giraudon company passed into the hands of Alphonse's son, Georges, and continued as a business until 1953.[34] Owing to the efforts of such publishers, the reproduction of artworks, both historic and contemporary, became an important sector of the trade. Just as Delaborde had feared in 1856, photography was to be the most widely used process for copying paintings, propagating traditional classical and Renaissance models and offering a subsidiary source of income for contemporary artists.

In this respect, works by academic painters tended to be preferred over more avant-garde productions: not only for reasons of taste and conformism, but also because, quite apart from the question of color, even the tonal values of impressionist painting were notoriously difficult to reproduce. Hanging over mantelpieces throughout the land, these reproductions implied a new relationship to the artwork intimated by Léon de Laborde already in 1855: "Today photography, or the mechanical art ideally perfected, has initiated the world into the beauties of divine and human creation. Combined, all these processes have brought skillfully reproduced copies of the unique art object even into the peasant's hut."[35]

Government purchases and orders

In 1853, Félix Ravaisson, at that time inspector of the Beaux-Arts, approached the Minister for State Education with a proposal to set up a special commission to study the best way of introducing photography into the teaching of drawing, and replacing engravings of old master drawings with photograph copies. The commission was constituted of several artists, including the sculptor Pierre-Charles Simart and Delacroix; Ingres, though solicited, did not participate. Their findings do not seem to have met with any immediate reaction,[36] though the Archives Nationales do contain traces of several subsequent orders for photographic reproductions of artworks: in 1859, eight copies of the works of Paul Delaroche, photo-

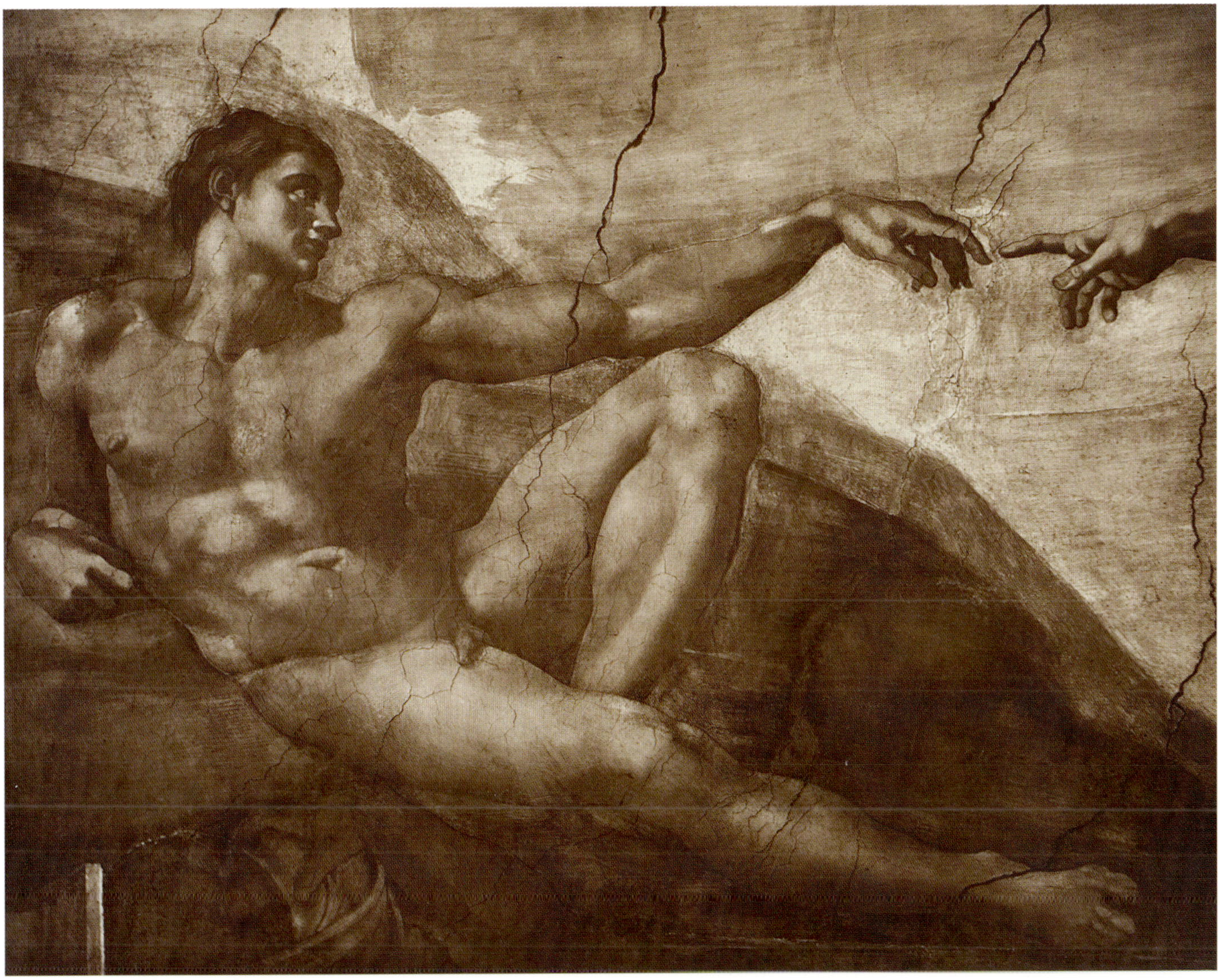

69. Adolphe Braun after Michelangelo, *God Creating Adam* (fresco in the Sistine Chapel, detail), 1869, carbon print, Musée d'Orsay, Paris.

graphed by Bingham, had been acquired (for 4,400 francs; that is, 550 francs each); in 1861, ten copies of the international *Dessins des grands maîtres des galeries de Vienne, Florence, Venise* by Luigi Bardi, each containing 200 photographs, were purchased, one being for the École des Beaux-Arts at Dijon; in 1862, ten copies of Richebourg's album, *Les principaux tableaux de l'exposition de 1861*, the result, as has been mentioned above, of a special order from the artist; in 1864, several copies of the album of *Bas-reliefs antiques du Musée Napoléon*, illustrated by photographs by Charles Marville were distributed to a number of schools of drawing—in Limoges, Roubaix, Nancy, Tourcoing, Strasbourg, Lunéville, Bordeaux, and Caen. In 1873, the state acquired photographs of 120 Ingres drawings by Marville, destined for the Musée Ingres in Montauban. As is clear, if photography seemed a rapid and faithful method for copying works of art, liable to supplant engraving for this purpose at least, the publications illustrated by photographs sold at a high price; even in the late 1860s, for instance, Bardi took 10,560 francs for his album of Italian masterpieces. Such albums of photographic copies of artworks were often extremely costly and their diffusion remained necessarily limited. And yet they played an essential role in the recognition of photography, since it was through this route that the invention entered the art schools and museums.

The painfully slow uptake of photography by French institutions[37]

French museums were singularly slow to embrace photography or to institute a reproduction policy for their collections. Consulting files at the Archives Centrales des Musées, it transpires that, from the beginning of the 1850s to the end of the century, a complex situation arose in which enthusiasm and distrust seem to go hand in hand. Laborde's plans, dating back to 1850, to compile a photographic inventory of the national collection, languished in a bottom drawer; if photographers were permitted entrance to the Louvre without too much difficulty until the early 1860s, it was a long time before an official photographer was assigned there, or a concerted plan tabled to photograph the collections. In Great Britain, Roger Fenton had already been appointed by the British Museum in the early 1850s.[38] Some of the conservators in the Louvre looked on the photography of artworks, of paintings in particular, with suspicion. In reply to a request from Adolphe Braun, Frédéric Villot for instance wrote: "I am not aware that M. Braun has brought improvements to the science of photography such that he is able to obviate the inconvenience that has hereto attended all those who have attempted to reproduce the pictures directly."[39] The quality of the prints Braun had made in Rome, however, show that he had indeed overcome the difficulty of precisely capturing tonal value in painting, and possessed the technical means to convey the awesome masterworks of Michelangelo and Raphael (ill. 69).[40] On July 27, 1866, Nieuwerkerke, the superintendent of Beaux-Arts, issued a decree suspending all photograph permits: "Licenses permitting photography in the galleries of the Louvre have been recognized as harmful to the conservation of the monuments. Photographers have proved extremely negligent in their operations, spreading throughout the rooms they appear to regard as laboratories corrosive substances that damage the parquet flooring and the staircases; as from August 1, all photography permits are withdrawn, without exception, until further notice."[41] This rule, however, was bent for Charles Marville, who had worked in the museum as a photographer from the very early 1850s, and who, with tacit agreement from Nieuwerkerke, gloried in the

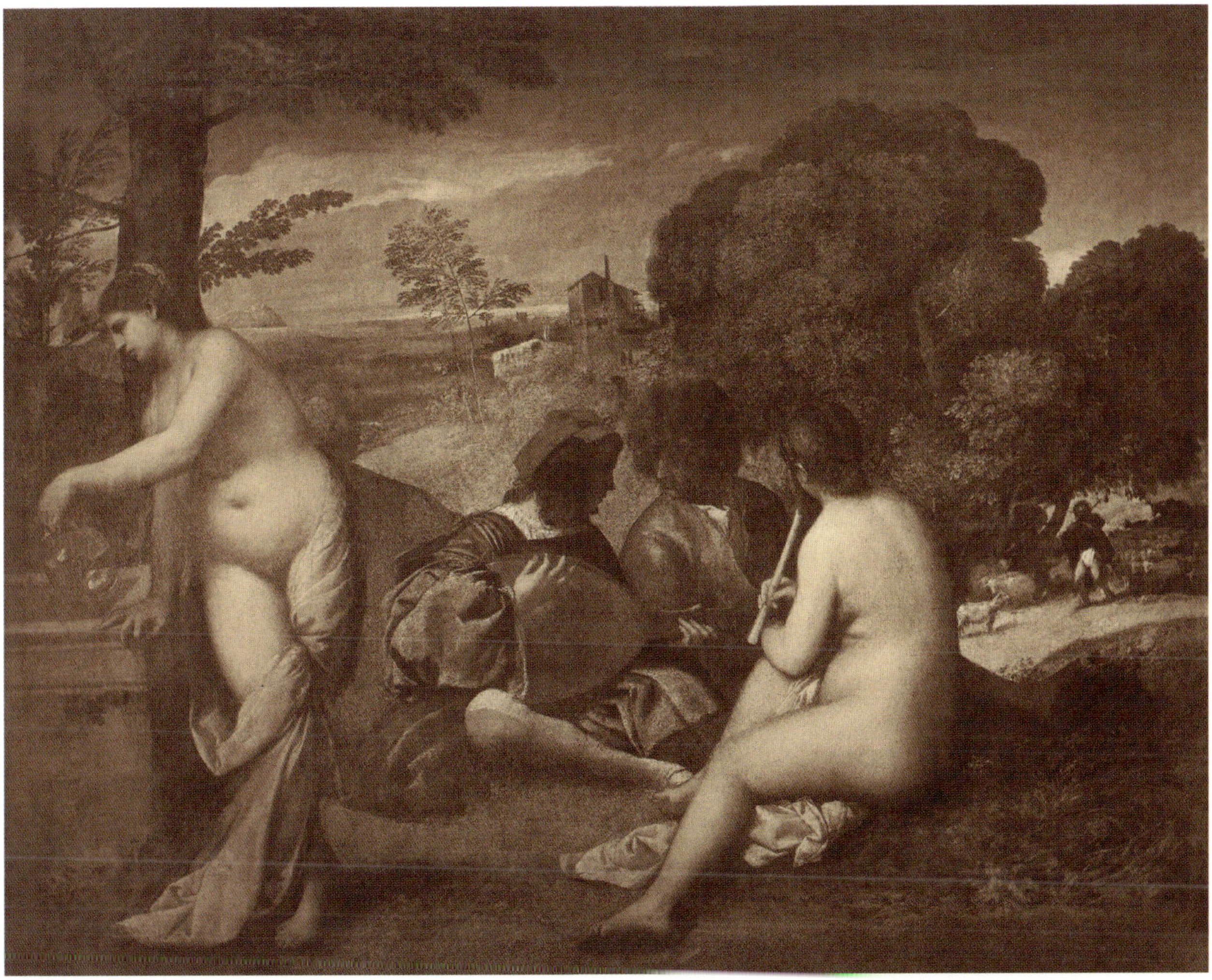

70. Adolphe Braun, after Titian (formerly attributed to Giorgione), *Pastoral Concert*, 1891, carbon print, Musée d'Orsay, Paris.

title "photographer of the imperial museums," and regained access to the Louvre in 1867.

On November 21, 1872, the organization responsible, the Conservatoire des Musées Nationaux, once again authorized photographs to be taken in the museum. Regulations were tightened, though—paintings were not to be moved; the number of photographers was limited to two; and dry collodion alone was permitted (wet collodion demanded more handling on the spot). The museum made demands in return: "Photographers are to deposit in the archives of the Louvre two photographs from each negative taken of the art objects exhibited in the galleries."[42] Only in December 3, 1883 was a contract between the administration of the national museums and Adolphe Braun signed, authorizing the firm to photograph the collections of the Louvre for a period of thirty years (ill. 70).[43]

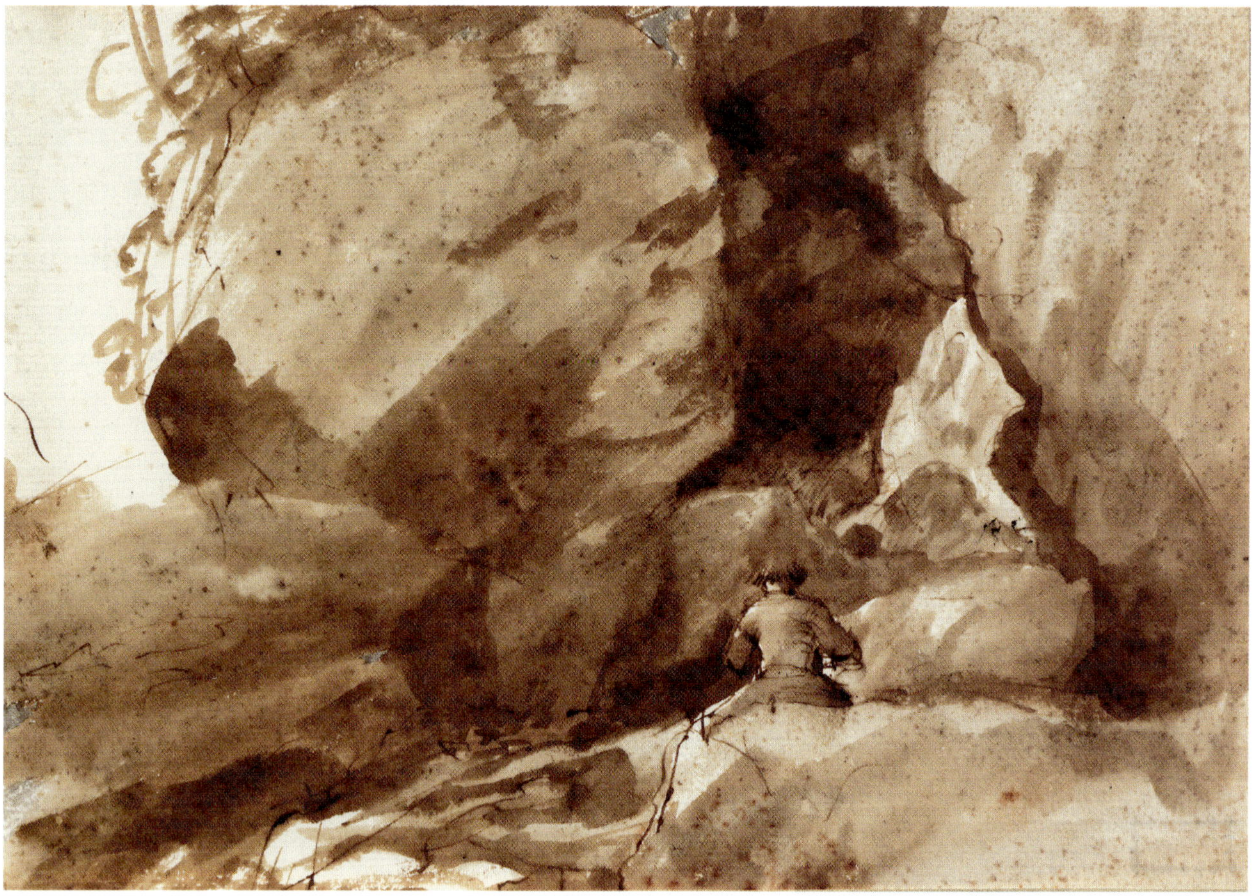

Landscape is a facile genre! Thus is the word out—and the error already enshrined. [1]

REVOLUTIONS IN LANDSCAPE

Starting from a low rung on the ladder of genre, from the turn of the nineteenth century landscape painting began to climb in esteem. Interest in this variety of art did not slacken throughout the century; a favorite with the public, from the 1830s landscape became the genre best represented at the Salon. This was not merely a popular success: undeniably the new predilection for the representation of nature did much to advance the great pictorial revolutions of the century. Once disdained by academe due to its submission to nature and to its dependence—in contradistinction to history painting—on imitation alone, landscape painting raised intriguing questions that went on to irrigate some of the key artistic issues of the era: one was that in this genre the standpoint of the artist determined, de facto, the frame of the depiction. Similarly, a new relationship to nature, initiated in the mid-eighteenth century by Jean-Jacques Rousseau, provided a context in which the emotions in the mind of the walker, painter, or poet might be made manifest in the surrounding landscape.[2] Refuge or shelter, nature seemed, for an artist exploring and describing her, to be an echo of his own feelings. As Chateaubriand wrote in 1795: "Landscape, like the portrait, possesses a moral and intellectual dimension; it too has to be given a voice and it behooves one to convey the reveries or sentiments aroused by different sites through their material execution."[3]

Learning in the midst of nature

The beginning of the century was marked by a desire on behalf of artists to break with earlier, codified representations of landscape and to seek to verify their intuitions in situ. There was, however, nothing novel about either the idea or the practice. In the seventeenth century, Claude Lorrain often showed in his drawings and pictures artists drawing outside in the open air. Recalling his own excursions in the Roman

71. **Facing page:** Claude Gellée, known as Claude Lorrain, *Man Drawing before the Grotto of Neptune at Tivoli*, c. 1640, pen and brown ink, brown and gray wash, Teylers Museum, Haarlem.

countryside, these depictions of painters absorbed in their creation also highlighted the process of abstraction essential to the act of drawing. In the heart of nature, the observation of visual stimuli and the act of recording them were necessarily separate; the talent this required of the landscape painter already elevated him above slavish imitation.[4] Chateaubriand stated the point plainly: "Pupils ought initially to deal with the study of nature herself: it is in the midst of the countryside that they must take their first lessons."[5] The author's advice closely resembles the ideas on landscape painting expounded by Pierre-Henri de Valenciennes in his *Réflexions et Conseils sur la Peinture et particulièrement sur le genre du Paysage* (Reflections and Advice on Painting and in Particular on the Genre of Landscape), published in 1801. The painter invited young artists to study nature before the motif, as he himself had done in Rome; these observations, drawn or painted, were however, to Valenciennes' eyes, just studies intended to supply material for a final picture invariably composed back in the studio.

The creation in 1816 of a *grand prix* for Historical Landscape, founded at Valenciennes' instigation, legitimated the new importance gained by the genre within the Académie des Beaux-Arts. Awarded every four years until 1863, on the first occasion (in 1817) the prize went to Achille-Etna Michallon for his *Democritus among the Abderites* (École Nationale Supérieure des Beaux-Arts, Paris). Such tardy recognition did little to bridge the gap between the accelerating evolution of landscape painting and academic institutions. The presentation at the 1824 Salon of *The Hay Wain* (1821, National Gallery, London) by John Constable, constituted, as Thiers was to stress, a turning point in the perception of landscape among young French painters. The English artist severed all links with the representation of mythological or religious landscape; his subject arose from observation of Suffolk scenery close to where he himself lived. In choosing to place stress on the changing sky and its reflections, he also broke with the postulate of the natural world as eternal and motionless: "Remember light and shadow never stand still."[6]

His manner, his muscular brushwork, as well as the power of his coloring, reinforced the idea of a contingent landscape caught on the wing. Constable did rework his large pictures, the "six-footers," in the workshop, but he executed several preparatory studies out in the open. The final pictures, in a Dutch tradition he explicitly took up, derived much of their value from the attentive examination of nature.[7]

New influences

Théodore Rousseau was one young artist who greatly admired the works of the English painter. A pupil of Guillaume Guillon Lethière, in the Louvre he copied pictures by Claude, as well as Dutch painters then enjoying a critical vogue in France.

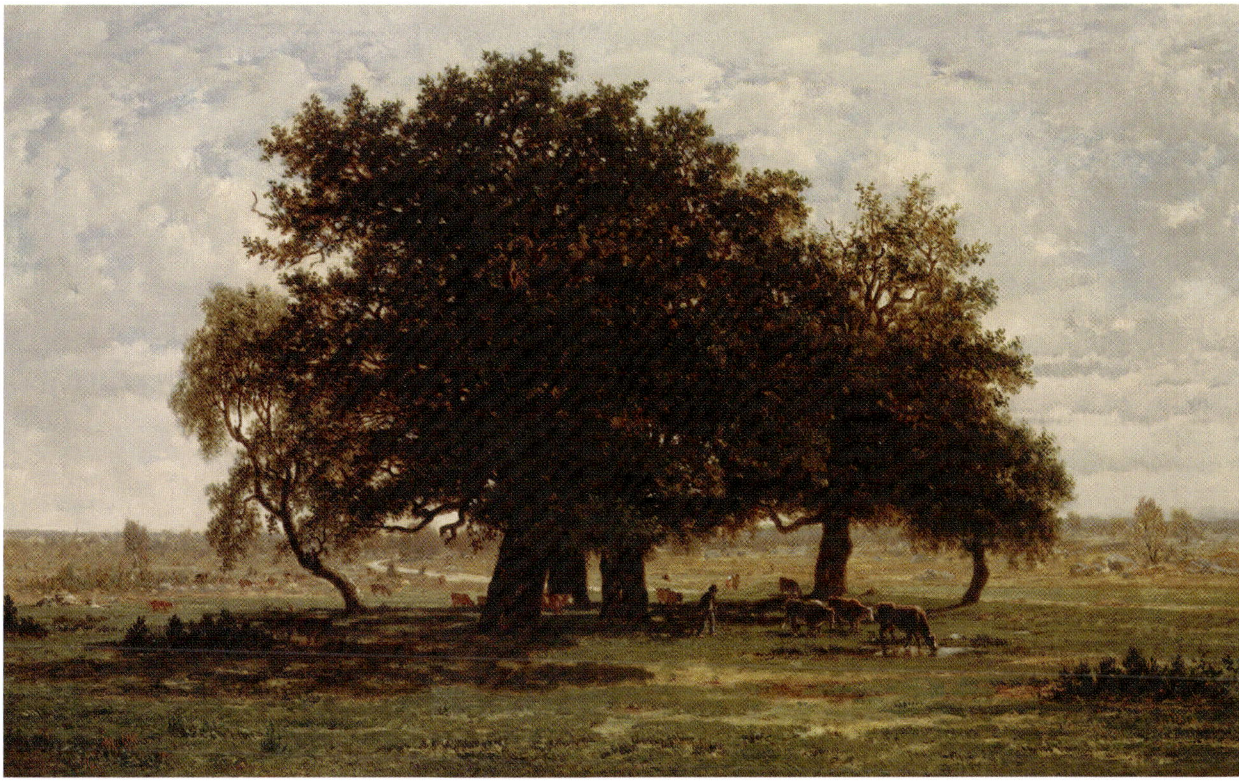

72. Théodore Rousseau, *Great Oaks at Apremont*, 1855, oil on canvas, Musée du Louvre, Paris.

An unsuccessful candidate for the Prix de Rome in Historical Landscape in 1829 (he did not even make it on to the shortlist), Rousseau undertook a journey to the Auvergne, where he executed several *plein air* studies. In 1827—probably thanks to Théodore Caruelle d'Aligny—he had discovered the Forest of Fontainebleau, remaining one of its most faithful denizens and acute observers throughout his life. Asserting the importance of observation of Nature in the open air, he proclaimed his intention to paint "trees which are not a sheath for some hamadryad, but the innocent oaks of Fontainebleau, honest elms of the roadside, humble birches of Ville-d'Avray, and all without the least Greek temple, without the least Ulysses or Nausicaa."[8] The absence of academic subject in his works combined with an inspiration drawn from the Dutch landscapists of the seventeenth century, and the unblinking replication of the subject was bound to set the Salon jury against him. Systematically rejected from 1837 to 1847, he took refuge in a studio in Barbizon, where he worked with Jules Dupré. His Fontainebleau landscapes celebrated a nature unsullied, wild, that industrialization and the hand of man had not yet profaned (ill. 72).

Copying nature

The idea of reproducing a landscape "from nature," in the open air, thus preceded the invention of photography. Before

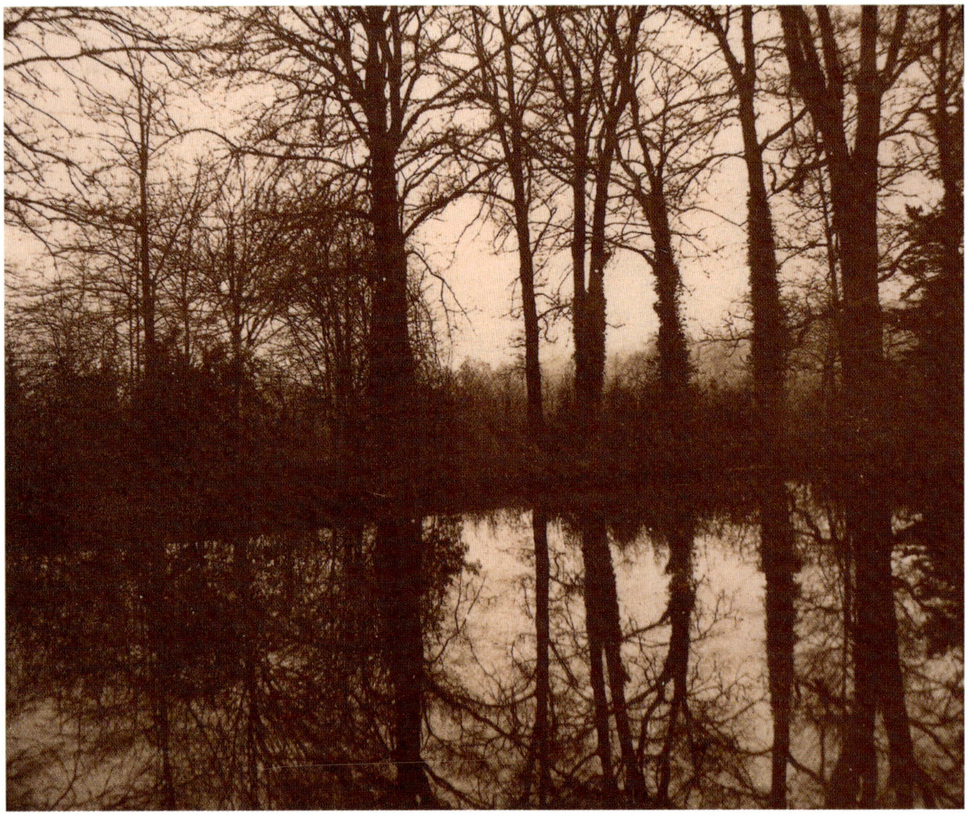

73. William Henry Fox Talbot, "Trees Reflected in the Water, Lacock Abbey," 1843, salt print (calotype), Musée d'Orsay, Paris.

photography, painters had already been confronted by the need to circumscribe the subject of their work in the natural environment. It was the artist's viewpoint that determined the theme of the picture; it was his vision that enclosed it, composed it, framed it. Roland Barthes, in his book *S/Z* on Honoré de Balzac's story *Sarrasine* (written in 1830), underlines the role played by the frame in realist aesthetics, showing how it underpinned the primacy of the pictorial model. Description is a process of placing "the empty frame that the realist author always carries about with him (more important than [an] easel) before a collection or continuum of objects which cannot be put into words without this obsessive operation."[9]

With his customary sarcasm, a caricature by Honoré Daumier poked fun at the difficulties confronted by artists. *Les Paysagistes* shows two painters placed one behind the other with their easels and paint-boxes in the midst of an undulating landscape recognizable as Fontainebleau. The first busies himself, resolutely painting the slice of nature he has chosen; his colleague leans over his shoulder and looks at the easel with an expression of perplexity and disapproval. The caption drives the point home: "Landscapists: the first copies nature, the second copies the first."[10]

The practice of painting in the open air soon became a commonplace. Camille Corot had himself photographed by his

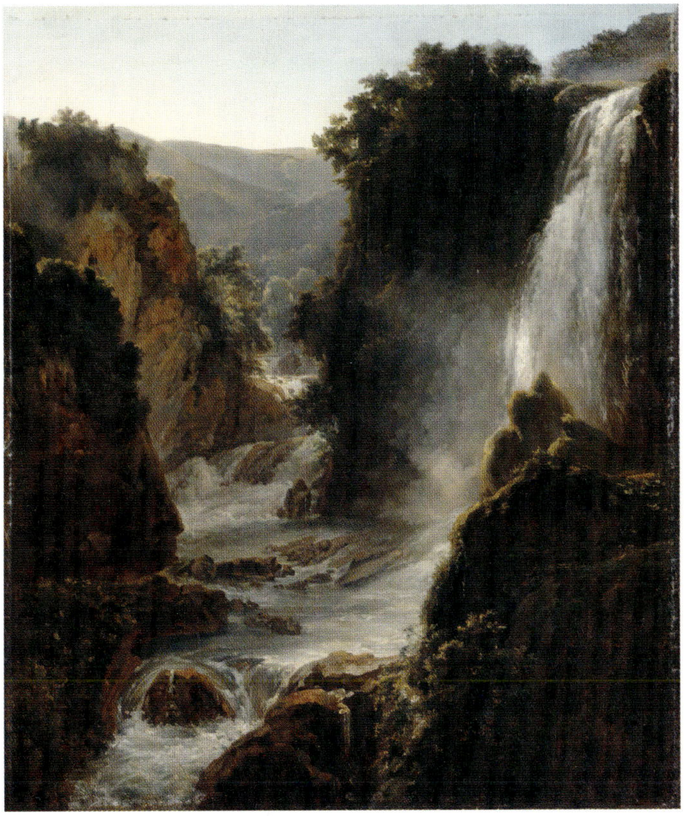

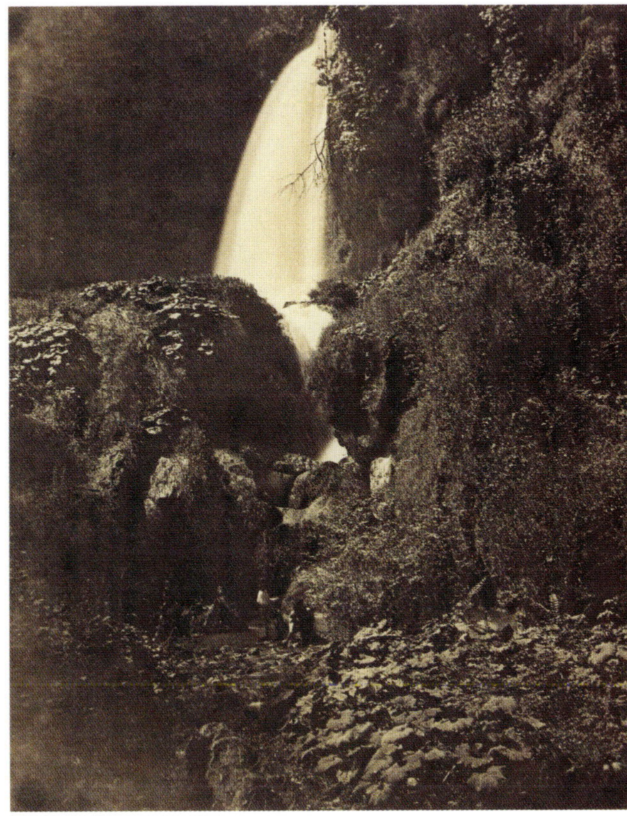

74. **Above, left:** François Souchon, *View of the Great Waterfall at Tivoli*, c. 1830, oil on canvas, Palais des Beaux-Arts, Lille.

75. **Above, right:** Giacomo Caneva, "Tivoli, the Aniene Waterfall," c. 1850, salt print, Musée d'Orsay, Paris.

friend Charles Desavary seated before his easel, brush in hand, in the countryside around Arras; his pictures, however, like the majority of his contemporaries', were finished in the studio. From the very start of the century, the watercolor, made still more popular by the influence of Bonnington in the 1820s, and then by the advent of paint in tubes from the 1850s, encouraged the practice before the motif. If "copy nature!" was the imperative thundered out like an anathema by adepts of academic criticism to painters and, from the end of the 1840s, to photographers, its observance could not dispense with talent. The photographer, still more than the painter, had to construct his subject from natural elements alone, which thus had to be selected with discernment. Since 1843, photographing the park in his property at Lacock Abbey, William Henry Fox Talbot sought to bring out the qualities of precision of his paper process, the "calotype" that allowed him to reproduce not only the foliage of the trees bordering the river but also their reflection in the water (ill. 73). As a critic on *La Lumière* recalled in 1860, "The photographer has to seek out and select this point [of view] even more so than a painter, because, unlike in those of latter, in his pictures there is no chance of adding or subtracting.... Independently of the choice of the site, the photographer still has to choose an hour at which the landscape is best lit, the day when nature will be at her most beautiful."[11] More

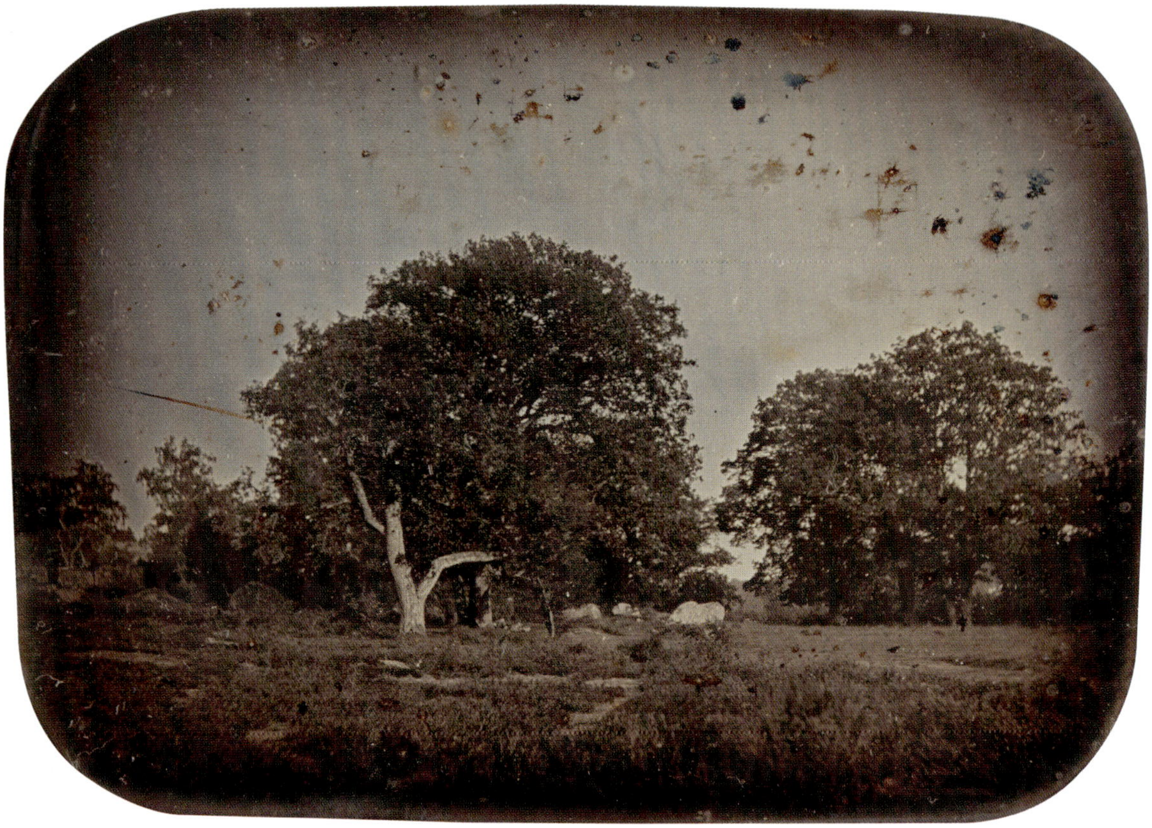

76. Anonymous, "Great Oaks, Fontainebleau," c. 1845–50, daguerreotype, Musée d'Orsay, Paris.

than any other photographic genre, landscape openly contradicted Daguerre's aphorism on the simplicity of use of his process; nature was not merely "reproduced" spontaneously in the camera.

The question of model

In painting, as in photography, the issue of the frame led to that of the model to be followed. Exponents of both learned from the works of earlier artists. The realist perception of landscape was inextricably bound up with the influence exerted by preexistent visions. The classic pictorial model remained vigorous, painters and photographers both borrowing from its compositional rigor and moderate light effects (ills. 74–75). The eye was thus drawn to clearly differentiate the planes and balance the masses. The Barbizon painters and their pictures also influenced the works of their youthful followers in Fontainebleau, among others. They opened their eyes to new subjects, drawn from nature itself, of a realism tinted with a certain lyricism and a marked empathy for the natural realm that also inspired early photographers. The quality of their works, their originality of standpoint, their ability to recreate a landscape affirmed how photography could not be reduced to the model of objectivity François Arago rejoiced in at the

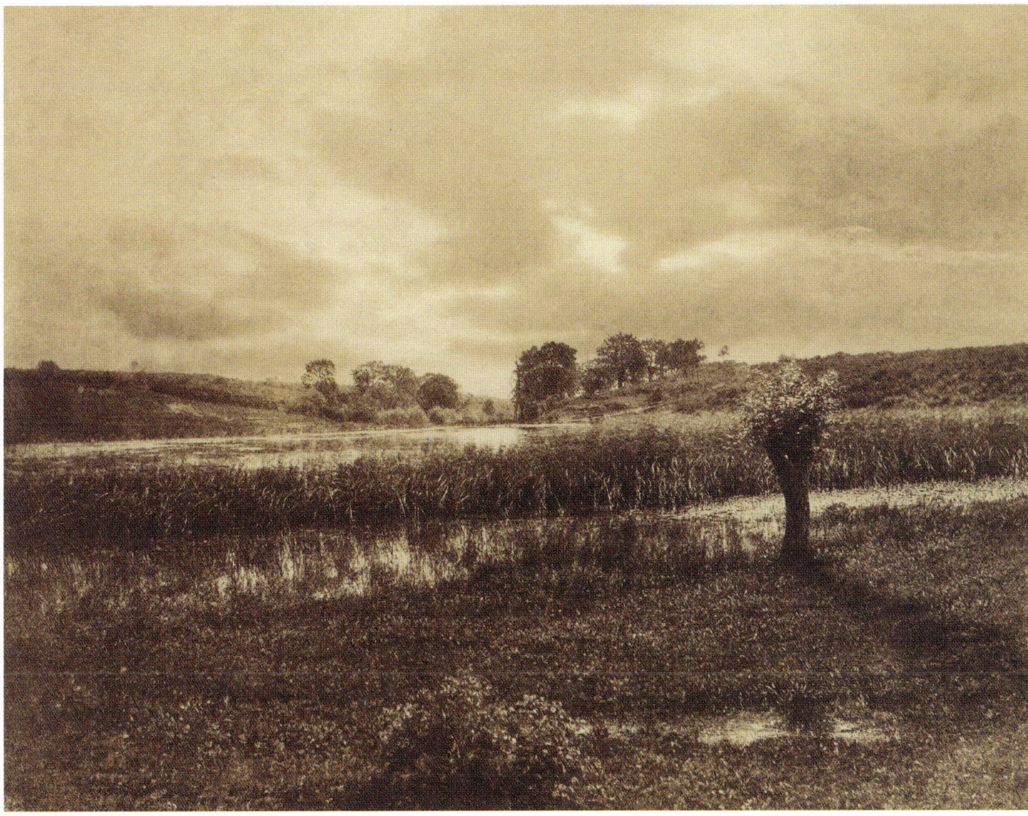

77. André Giroux, "The Ponds at Optevoz," c. 1855, salt print, The J. Paul Getty Museum, Los Angeles.

announcement of Daguerre's invention in 1839. In the other direction, as from the 1850s, photography offered images in which painters in turn identified fresh motifs, a new approach to the moment, and unusual framings.

The Forest of Fontainebleau: an open-air studio

Painters and photographers kept one another's company; it is then probable that they shared visions that by the mid-1850s had precipitated into a "French" conception of landscape that revolved constantly around the same sites.[12] The Forest of Fontainebleau, a kind of open-air studio for landscapists, was just such an exemplary place. Although close to Paris and accessible by train from the late 1840s, it seemed unaffected by the growth of the city, a place where the representation of virgin nature, almost a wilderness, seemed a real possibility. The guides published by Claude-François Denecourt since 1840 had indicated new itineraries, and bestowed names on rocks, trees, and crossroads that could readily be identified. The "Sylvain," as Théophile Gautier affectionately called him, had made "his forest" more familiar and more accessible to all.[13] A daguerreotype dating from the mid-1840s underlines the proximity between painters and photographers (ill. 76).[14] By choosing a gently sloping site, like a proscenium, the photographer magnifies the power of the great stand of oaks, in the way of Narcisse Díaz de Peña or Théodore Rousseau. With no resource other than nature, thanks to this vantage point and a feeling for light, the photographer creates an image of great beauty, whose composition—necessarily decided upon before the picture could be taken—arose from the physical elements of the scenery, yet expressed the artistic ambitions of its creator.

A painter and winner of the Prix de Rome for Historical Landscape in 1826 for *The Hunt of Meleager*, André Giroux took up photography during the 1840s.[15] In subject and rendering, his photographs closely resemble his painted canvases. Critics were lavish in their praise when they were exhibited in 1855 on the occasion of the Exposition Universelle. Ernest Lacan exclaimed, "M. André Giroux is a painter of talent.... Even if one were unaware of the fact, it is easy to deduce it from an examination of his photographic landscapes."[16] He compared Giroux's works to landscapes painted by Rousseau and Dupré. The choice of rural, pastoral subjects from which man is systematically absent echoed the ideal and inviolate nature of the Barbizon School. In its effects—reflections in the water and clouds—as well as in its elevated sky, Giroux's very fine "Ponds at Optevoz," taken in the Dauphiné, is also redolent of canvases by Charles-François Daubigny (ill. 77). In 1854 and 1855 Daubigny painted several landscapes at Optevoz, including *The Lock in the Valley of Optevoz* (Musée des Beaux-Arts, Rouen).[17]

A photographic "theory of sacrifice"

The artistic scope of landscape photography was ardently defended by Gustave Le Gray; as a painter he asserted that the theory of "sacrifice" governing that art also guided the work of the photographer, going on to advocate the advantages of photography on paper and the potential it harbored: "Its [photography's] influence will be immensely far-reaching ... it cleanses public taste by accustoming it to look at nature reproduced as faithfully as possible.... Obviously, I do not in the least mean by this that a good painting must be possessed of the meticulous, microscopic execution of a daguerreotype plate. From my point of view, the beauty of a photograph almost always consists, on the contrary, in the sacrifice of certain details.... Thus in truth only an artist or a man of taste is sure to obtain a perfect work using an instrument capable of capturing the same object in an infinite variety of interpretations, since only he can intuit the effect most appropriate for the subject he reproduces."[18] Le Gray rejected the mechanical vision of the technical instrument and emphasized instead the skill of the photographer, his ability to construct an image not only thanks to a judicious choice of subject matter, but also by "adjusting the focus, the exposure time, [so that] the artist can

78. **Facing page:** Henri Le Secq, "Stream in a Forest," 1852, salt print from a paper negative, Musée d'Orsay, Paris.

79. **Page 118:** Achille-Etna Michallon, *Woman Struck by Lightning*, c. 1819, oil on canvas, Musée du Louvre, Paris.

80. **Page 119:** Gustave Le Gray, "Tree Trunk," 1856, albumen print, Winsberg Collection, New York.

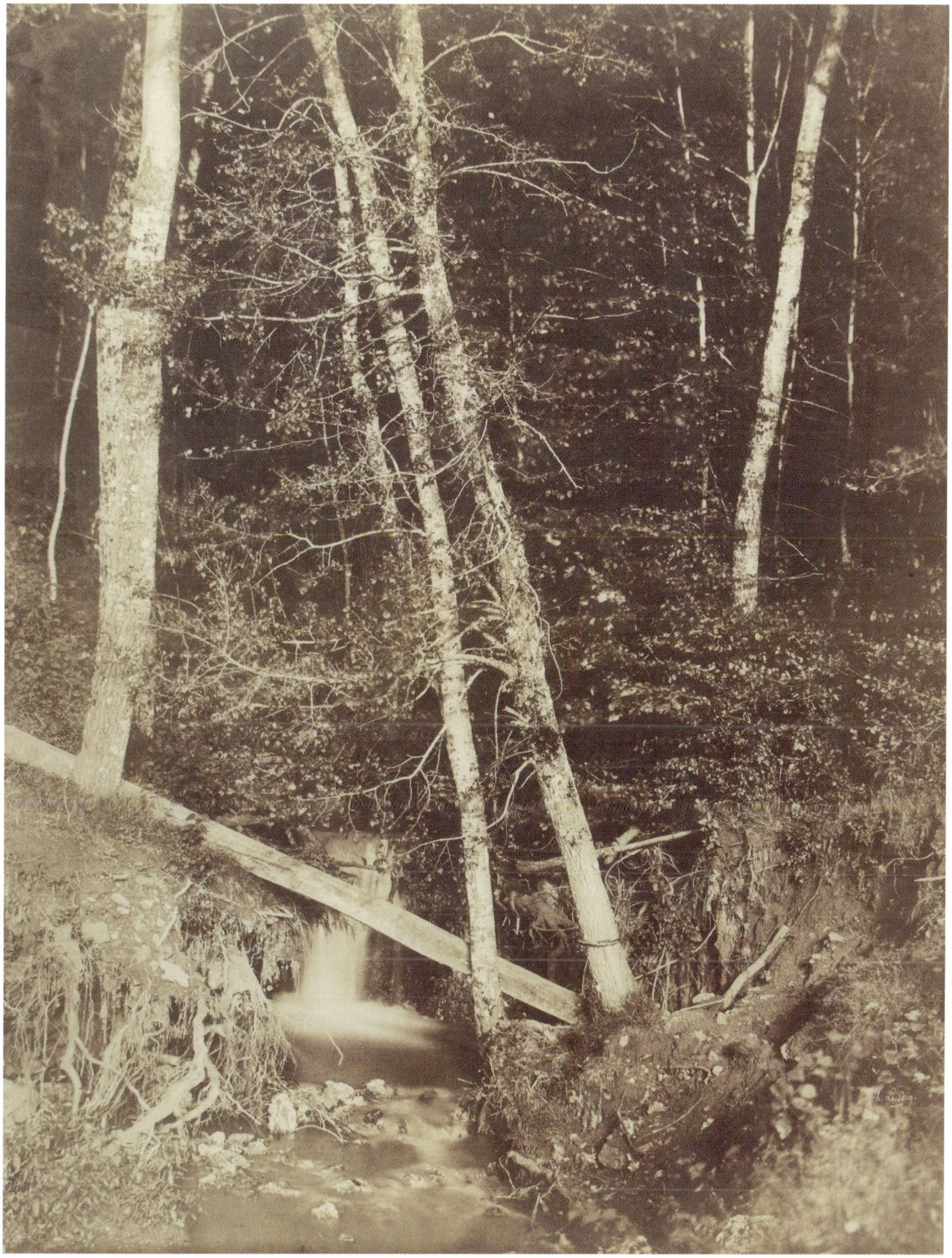

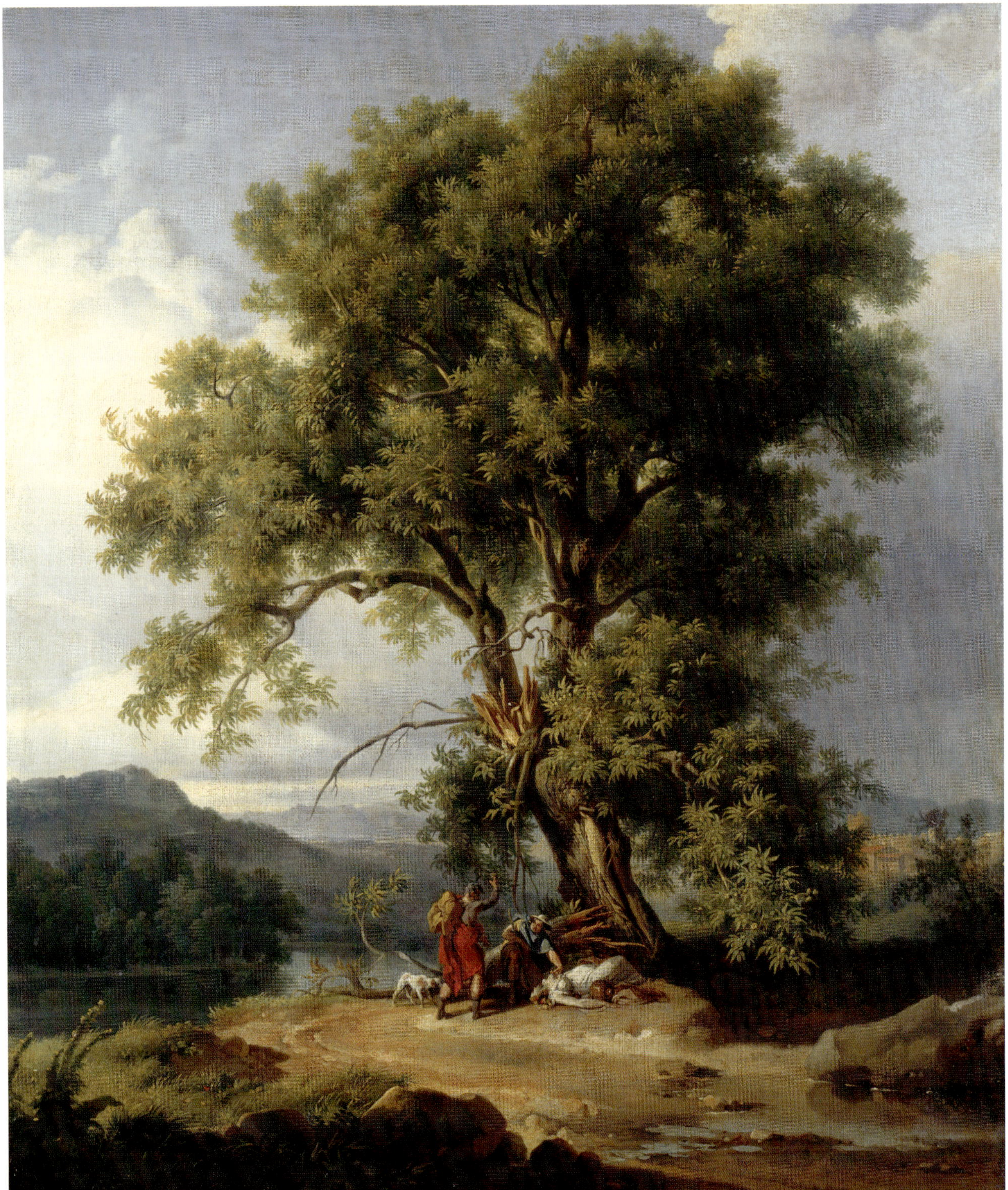

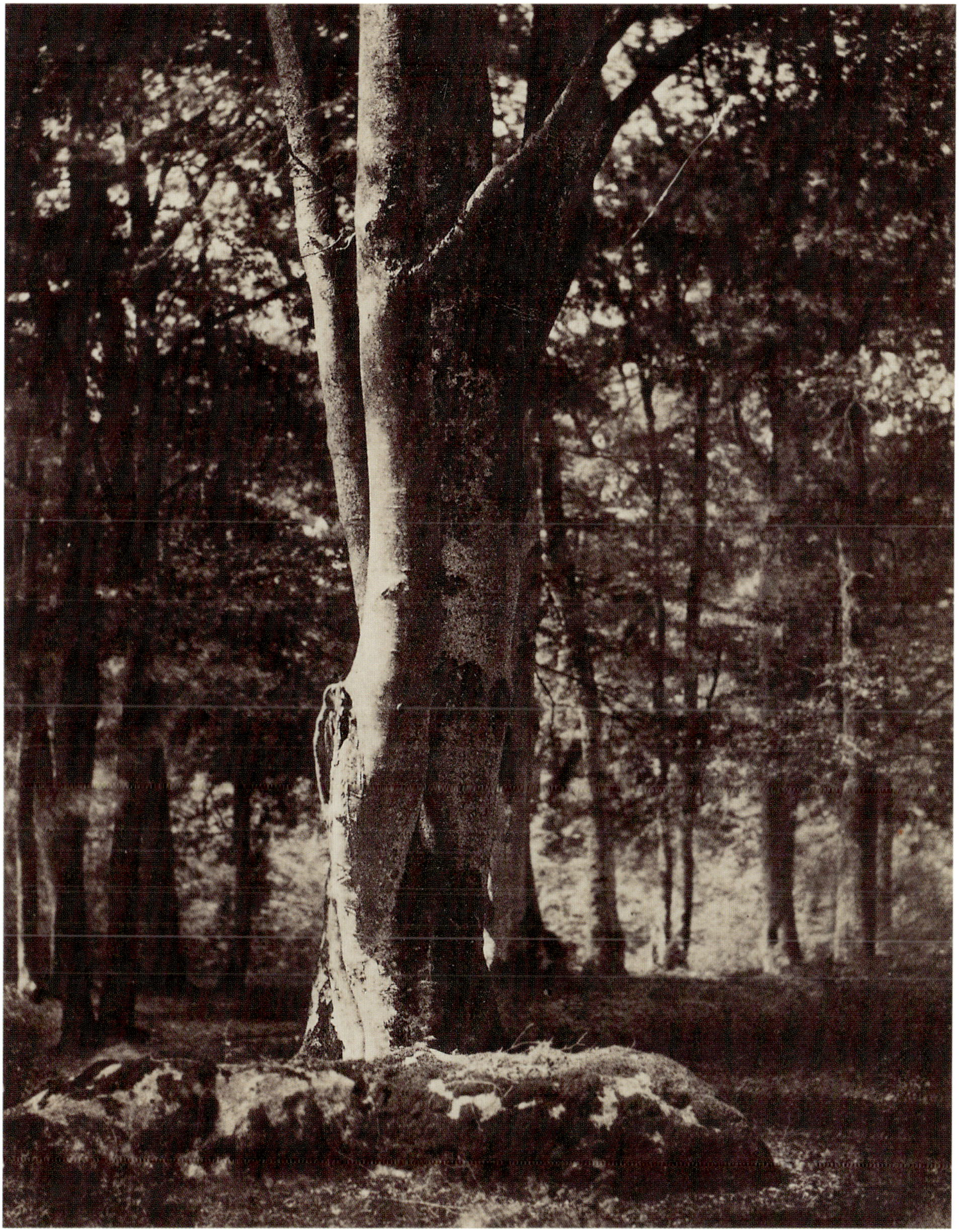

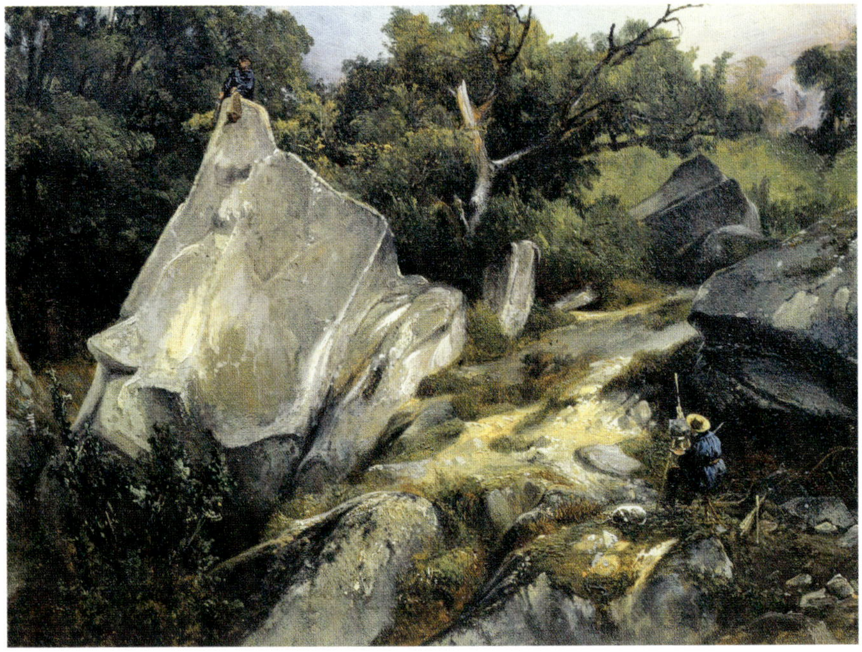

81. Auguste Enfantin, *An Artist Painting in the Forest of Fontainebleau*, 1825, oil on canvas, private collection.

bring out or sacrifice such and such a zone, producing powerful effects of light or shade, or else extreme gentleness and calm." Served by dazzling technical skill, Le Gray's talent as an artist begot images of truly exceptional beauty. Thus, in the course of various sojourns in Fontainebleau, he photographed some of the great trees to which Denecourt had given names (ill. 80) in "portraits" sometimes redolent of earlier models, those of Achille-Etna Michallon in particular (ill. 79). Le Gray's vision is also novel in how he crops the object; a powerful tree, which the frame of the image seems to struggle to contain, is thereby further extolled. Le Gray's subtle use of light, his meticulous attention to the treatment of both negative and printing, draws the eye to the bark, the foliage, the undergrowth. Thanks to qualities such as these, the tree is promoted from motif into subject. Exhibited on several occasions during the late 1850s, Le Gray's photographs engendered models eventually taken up by painters. *The Oak of Flagey* by Gustave Courbet (1864, Murauchi Art Museum, Tokyo) and then Claude Monet's *Oak at Bodmer* (1866, The Metropolitan Museum of Art, New York) learned a great deal from the lesson of Le Gray, as much in the choice of subject as in its treatment.

Intimate visions of landscape

In 1852 and 1853, Henri Le Secq, once a fellow student of Le Gray in Delaroche's studio, realized several views of the forest of Montmirail, near his family estate. His choice of subject is singularly original; rather than an extensive plain opening on to the horizon, he preferred to turn his camera on rock falls or

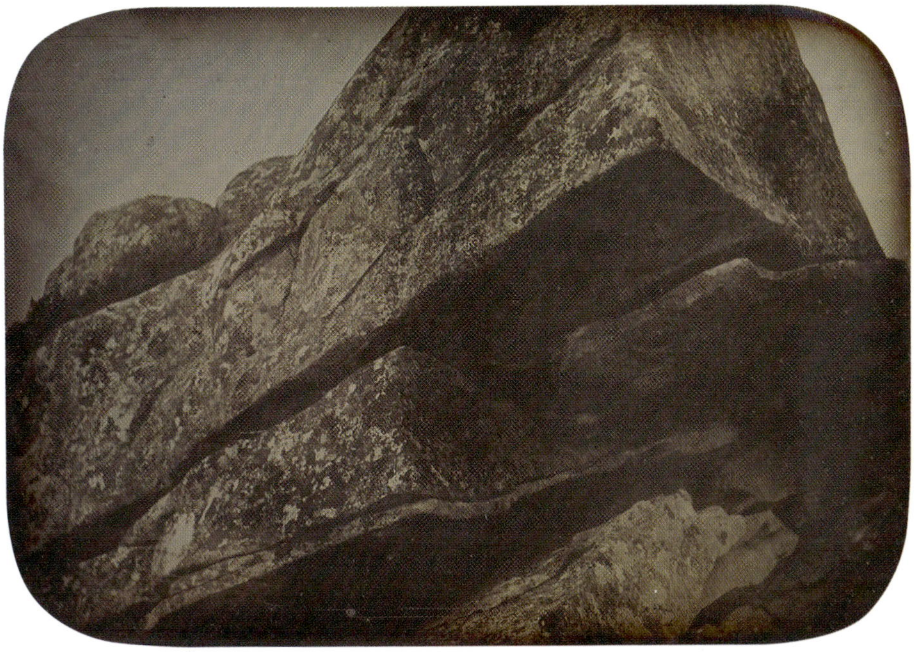

82. Anonymous, "Study of Rocks," c. 1845, daguerreotype, The J. Paul Getty Museum, Los Angeles.

the earthy escarpment of a quarry. For vast avenues, he substituted dense undergrowth, through which spouts a brook, or a coppice traversed by a narrow stony path, a single ray of sunlight poking through a gloomy thicket. His images represent nature in the raw, empty of all human presence save for that of a single observant walker: himself. Such an interpretation of landscape is reminiscent of Courbet, who, at much the same time, was delineating the boulders and crevices of the Franche-Comté. Unbeknownst to each other, but at the same moment, the two men shared the same vision of landscape—unpretentious, emerging at eye level to be selected by an eye intimately familiar with it.[19] These subjects, concentrating on the contrast between light and shade, water and rock, presented an opportunity for Le Secq to demonstrate his masterful handling of light and his talent at gauging exposure times. Added to the sheer quality of the images, the exceptional dimensions of his prints, genuine professional tours de force, exalted the motif. They attracted much praise from critics: "They are studies of trees and plots of land," wrote Ernest Lacan in 1854 on Le Secq's landscape photos. "But the artist was not satisfied with reproducing the trunk or foliage of a tree, or a few meters of grass or stony ground taken randomly out in the countryside. On the contrary, the size of his photographs allow him to obtain complete, interesting motifs, as well as details precious in both breadth and precision. There is air, truth, and life in this photograph, which, on a canvas, would make a charming landscape," (ill. 78).[20] A few years later, an anonymous daguerreotypist turned his lens on such pictorial subjects; keeping the field of his image clear of everything save for the rocks of

Fontainebleau, he spurned more picturesque, pictorial depictions, whose subject tended to be the artist as much as the motif (ills. 81–82). This radicalization of the subject, towards no more than a heap of rocks, endowed the image—as was the case with photographs by Le Secq and paintings by Courbet—with a new temporality divested of all narrative.

Painting and photography: identical frames of reference

The artistic ascendancy of landscape photography ruffled many feathers. Voices were raised proclaiming the unbridgeable divide between pictorial and photographic representations of scenery. Though a founder member of the Société Héliographique in 1851, Champfleury expressed his conviction that photography would never be able to proffer an individual, unique vision: "Ten *daguerreotypeurs* meet up in the countryside and subject the scenery to the action of light. Beside them, ten students of landscape painting set to copying the same site. Once the chemical operation is complete, the ten plates are compared: they depict exactly the same landscape, without variation. On the other hand, after two or three hours at work, the ten pupils ... lay their sketches out next to each other. There is not a single similar one among them."[21] To the author, a painted study conveys a particular facet of personal talent. This talent, as he saw it, owed little to the education received. As he goes on: "Though they might be under the direction of the same master, and whether they absorbed good or bad principles," their diversity derives entirely from the temperament of each artist: "An oak has a different form and color for a sanguine man than for a bilious one.... A thin man does not experience the same feelings before nature as a fat man."[22] Champfleury's point seems rather forced; turned on its head, such chop logic betrays rather the power of the unstated counterargument—that of the competition between painting and photography predicated on a common frame of reference underpinned by identical pictorial models and revolving around similar subjects.[23] That same year, Georges Niel, in a lengthy paean to the landscape painting displayed in the Salon of 1857, also censured what he saw as the aridity of its photographic equivalent: "Photography has all the dryness of a plan, it reeks of death; the hand of man, creativity is lacking. Harmony is destroyed, the light is broken up by the instrument ... there exist a thousand little effects that photography cannot capture. Air will never be photographed."[24] Such a critique rang out all the more sonorously since the arguments Niel deploys in hailing the work of landscape painters—especially Daubigny—resemble those embraced by partisans of photography, by Ernest Lacan in particular: the skill required in choosing a worthwhile site; a flair for capturing light, and so on. The dissimilarity between painted landscape and photography had to be all the more clear-cut since it was essential to defend the former as a genre often envisaged as an "easy" pictorial vein, appreciated for its prettiness but still looked down upon: "The esteem accorded landscapists, even those with talent, does not appear to us to be what it should. Their works charm, everyone agrees on that point; but if there is a prize, a commendation to be awarded, it is routinely attributed to some mediocre piece by a history or genre painter."[25]

New seascapes

The very notion of landscape merges with its representation; in English, the term "landscape" covers both natural scenery and its portrayal in painting. In offering new images, paintings and photographs, artists thus contributed to the emergence of new forms.[26] Human impact on the coastline, industrial as well touristic, profoundly altered the vision of the sea, becoming instrumental in a type of depiction in which the aesthetic agendas of painting and photography commixed. The mid nineteenth-century marine or seascape had roots in two traditions: Dutch painting of the seventeenth century and the romantic vision invented in the mid-eighteenth century, deriving from the notion of the sublime as developed by Edmund Burke and eloquently reiterated by Denis Diderot in his critiques of the Paris Salons. Tremendous storms, fearsome shipwrecks, and distraught sailors readily kindled the "delicious terror" the philosopher extolled. Distanced by painting, the sea kept her rawness and mystery, all the while presenting to the beholder the beauty of her seething waters and the looming magnificence of her tempestuous skies. Flourishing until the end of the 1840s, it was an idea that fed into romantic painting no less than into verse.[27] It was to such painted or composed figurations Charles Baudelaire referred in 1859 when, under cover of offering advice to Eugène Boudin, he wrote of certain marine skies that he recalled: "In the end, all those clouds with fantastic and luminous forms, the chaotic darkness, the green and russet vastness, suspended and superimposed one over the other, these gaping furnaces, these firmaments of black or purple satin ... all these splendors went to my brain like a heady drink or the eloquence of opium."[28]

Fleeting atmospheres

Such romantic exaltation could be tempered by more scientific observations. Baudelaire, for instance, was also intrigued by sky studies that Boudin carried out before the motif in Honfleur or Trouville, and expressed his delight at their meteorological accuracy: "The margins of these studies so rapidly and so accurately rendered ... always bear the date, the time, and the wind; thus, for example: October 8, midday,

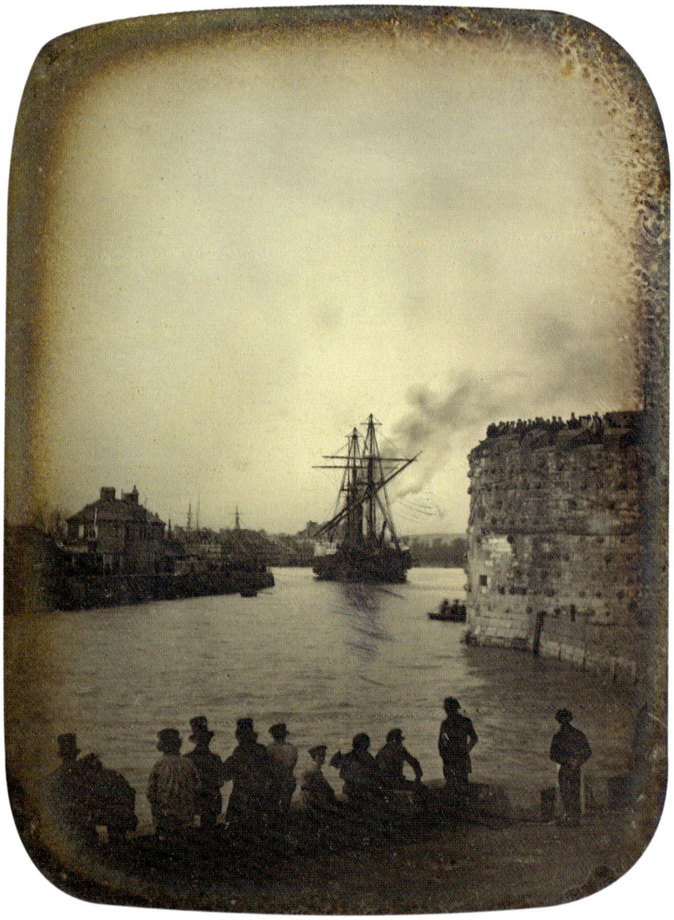

83. Louis-Cyrus Macaire and Jean-Victor Macaire-Warnod, "Vessel Leaving the Port at Le Havre," 1851, daguerreotype, Bibliothèque Nationale de France, Paris.

wind from the N.E. If you ever have the leisure of acquainting yourself with these meteorological beauties, you might check the exactitude of M. Boudin's observations from memory. Hiding the caption beneath your hand, you can guess the season, the time, and the wind. I'm not at all exaggerating. I've seen it done."[29] In 1868, Émile Zola noted the degree to which landscape painting was still irrigated by two apparently contradictory traditions: romantic lyricism, and near scientific precision as to atmosphere. The alliance between romanticism and rationalism thus opened the then highly popular genre to a more involving idiom, capable of showing itself to be at the same time moving and charming, correct but deceptive: "Certain landscapists create scenery in the style of the day, possessed of a sufficient veneer of truth, and which yet is possessed of the piquant blandishments of the lie. The masses adore these tidbits. They do not possess an eye acute enough to discern the falseness of the whole and are hoodwinked by the garish notes ... proclaiming: 'That's really how it is, that's so right!'"[30]

Photographic depictions played a key role—though one little noticed and commented on at the time—in a newfound attention

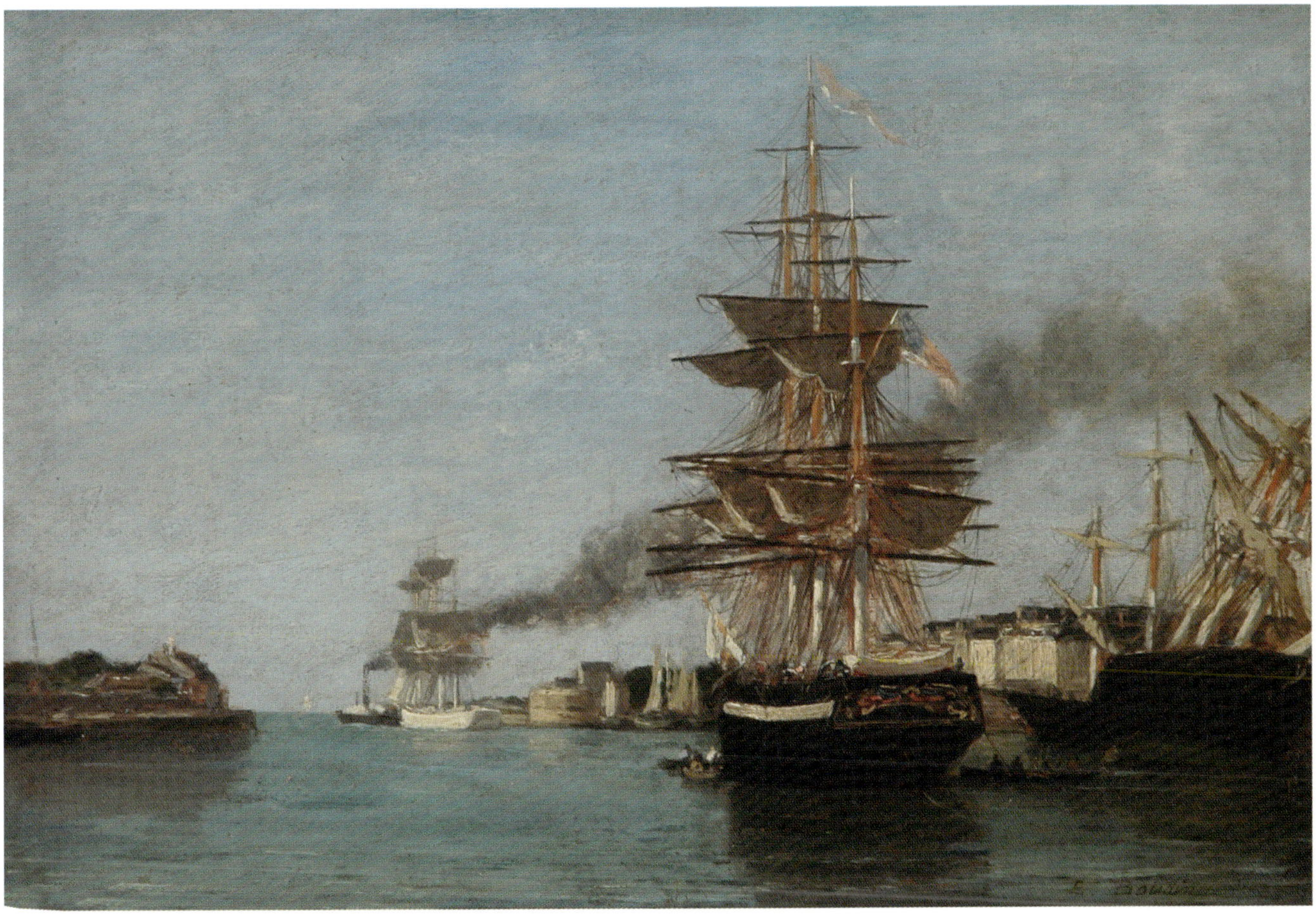

84. Eugène Boudin, *The Port at Le Havre*, 1852–55, oil on canvas, Château-Musée, Boulogne-sur-Mer.

to novel motifs and to the transience of the atmosphere. Obliged to master many technical factors and forced to come to terms with things as they were, photographers tended to draw attention to exactly what they wanted to be overlooked. In photographs of Le Havre in 1851, the Macaire brothers strove to convey a picture of the city's activity as a port; to render the fumes from the great ships casting off from the mole, they developed an accelerator that reduced the exposure time of their daguerreotypes to less than a few tenths of a second. The effect of the steam pouring from the vessel is gloriously captured, down to the last wisp (ill. 83). In all probability, Eugène Boudin saw for himself the Macaires' daguerreotypes in Le Havre and echoes of their photographs seem evident in a picture on the same theme, *The Port at Le Havre*, painted by the artist a few years later (ill. 84). This canvas, like the daguerreotype before it, owes much to the Dutch tradition; built up from the features of the port, Boudin's composition recalls the view chosen by the photographers that emphasized the pier in the foreground of the image and established a gradation of plane and perspective.[31] This artifice steers the viewer's eye towards the infinite and on to the gossamer twist of steam—

ephemeral fumes that amount to a synecdoche of the brothers' technical prowess. An ingenious stratagem, its artistic repercussions are apparent in Boudin's endeavor to capture in paint that same evanescent vapor, surely a consequence of its appearance in photography.[32] By a seeming paradox, it is less the anecdotal and contingent elements offered by photography—in portraits or costumes—that resonate in the works of the Normandy painter, than its more ambitious depictions of the elements, such as sky and sea.

Depicting the sky

For photographers, capturing the sky in an image constituted a horrendous challenge. From 1856 on, Gustave Le Gray managed to convey the ether as an immense but varied phenomenon, quite unlike the leaden and uniformly gray wash to which it was reduced in clumsier hands, due to the saturation induced by overlong exposure times (ill. 85).[33] Le Gray's sea pieces were a favorite with critics and the public alike as soon as they were unveiled in London at the end of 1856 and then in Paris in 1857: "This time, the limits of the possible have been attained; we are by no means surprised to learn that these magic pictures are all the rage and that their fortunate creator has by all accounts already significant orders worth more than 50,000 francs on his books."[34] Le Gray used the subterfuge of combining one negative for the sky and another for the sea, rendering the atmospheric effects to a supreme degree. He succeeded in framing an aesthetic truth that chimed in with public taste, though by dint of a process that had little to do with the supposed "exactitude" of photography. By privileging emphatic truthfulness in the representation of the real, he remained faithful to the tormented vision of romantic art.[35]

In a manner not unconnected with his early training as a painter, Le Gray's mastery of photographic technique gave rise to an entirely original motif. The representation of the ebb and flow of the sea had been high on the list of the aims of photographers almost as soon as the technique was invented. However talented they were, and however short the exposure time, the instantaneous capture of a breaking wave remained out of reach. Even with the briefest exposure, the reproduction of continuity and motion resisted every photographic expedient, generating instead a new image: the surprising sight of waves halted dead in their tracks (ill. 86).[36] The photographic lens surreptitiously freezes the wave for an instant, turning it almost solid. More than ten years later, Courbet too, observing an equinoctial storm at Étretat and recalling the dark fury of the sky and sea, was surely inspired by memories of these photographs, exhibited several times from 1857 to 1860, for his idea of the ocean as telluric outpouring—more like the cliffs of Ornans than any Normandy shoreline (ill. 87). Gustave

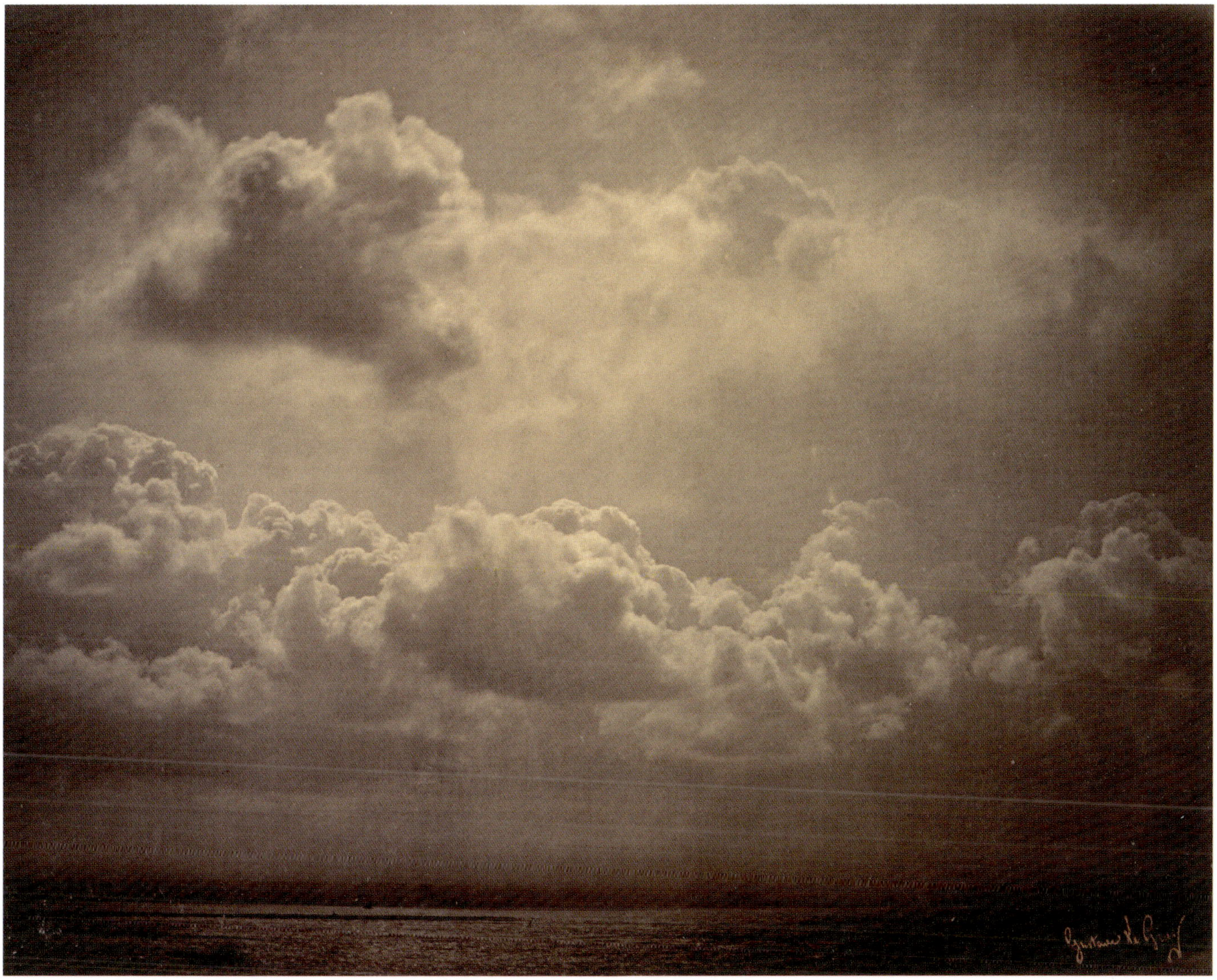

Courbet brought the same tenebrous power to the agitated sky that towers over his frozen waves. Evoked by a paint substance densely applied with the palette knife, the clouds seem gelled in fury, forming against the sea, and separated from it by a firmly laid-in horizon, a solid barrier resembling the outcrops of the painter's native land. These marine canvases had thus become for the painter "*paysages de mer*"—sea landscapes. He thus created some of the most vigorous representations of the Normandy coast, although no precise site is identifiable. The sea as painted by Courbet in his "sea landscapes" is an eternal, not a contingent entity; a sea frozen in its regular movement, but drawing in the eye so it loses itself in amazement. It is a sea whose representation is not realist, but marked by an accent of truth that was thankfully acknowledged by an admiring Paul Cézanne: "[*The Wave*] in Berlin, extraordinary ... with its

85. Gustave Le Gray, "Cloud Study," 1856–57, albumen print from two collodion glass negatives, Musée d'Orsay, Paris.

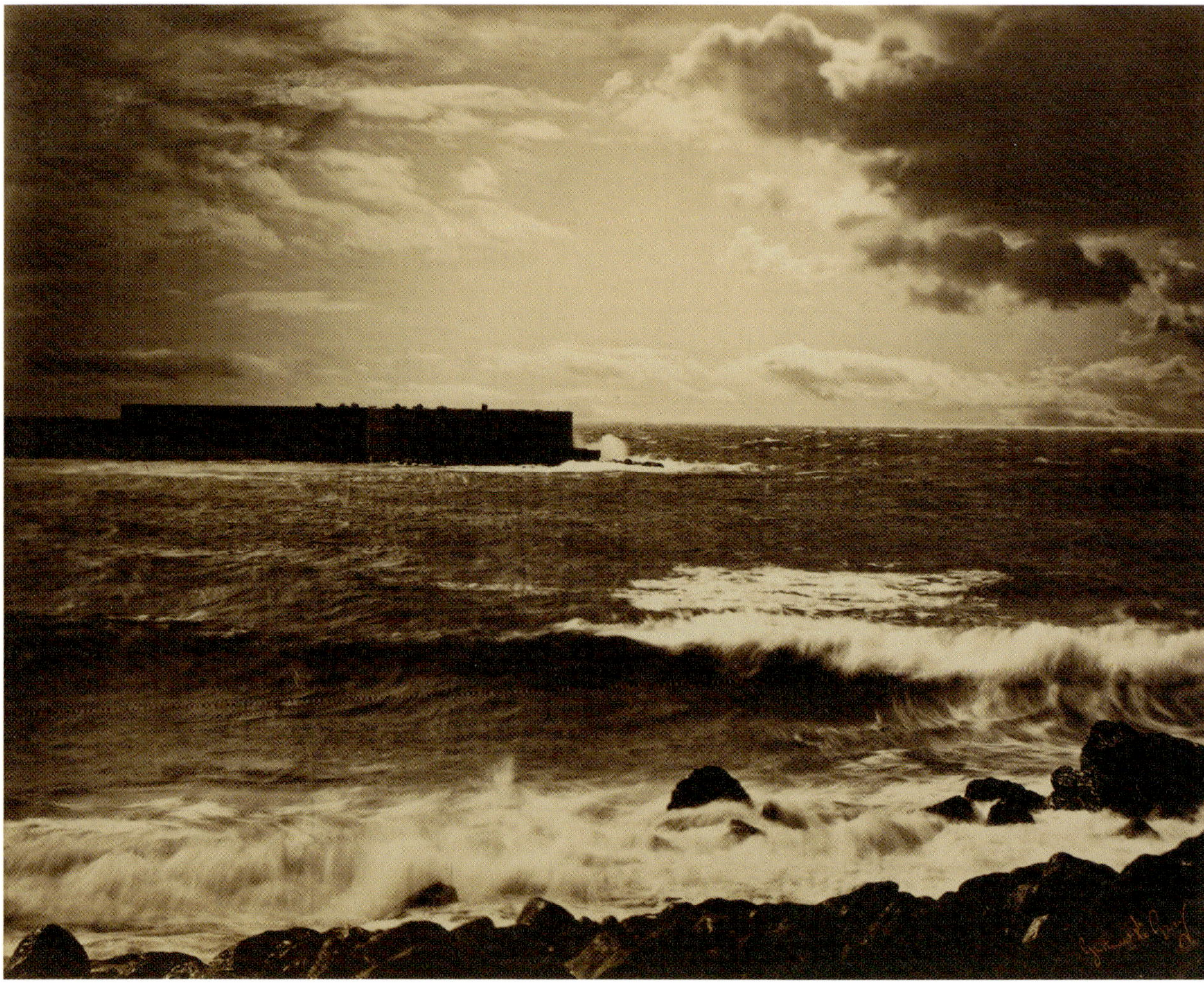

86. Gustave Le Gray, "The Great Wave," 1857, albumen print from two negatives, Musée d'Orsay, Paris.

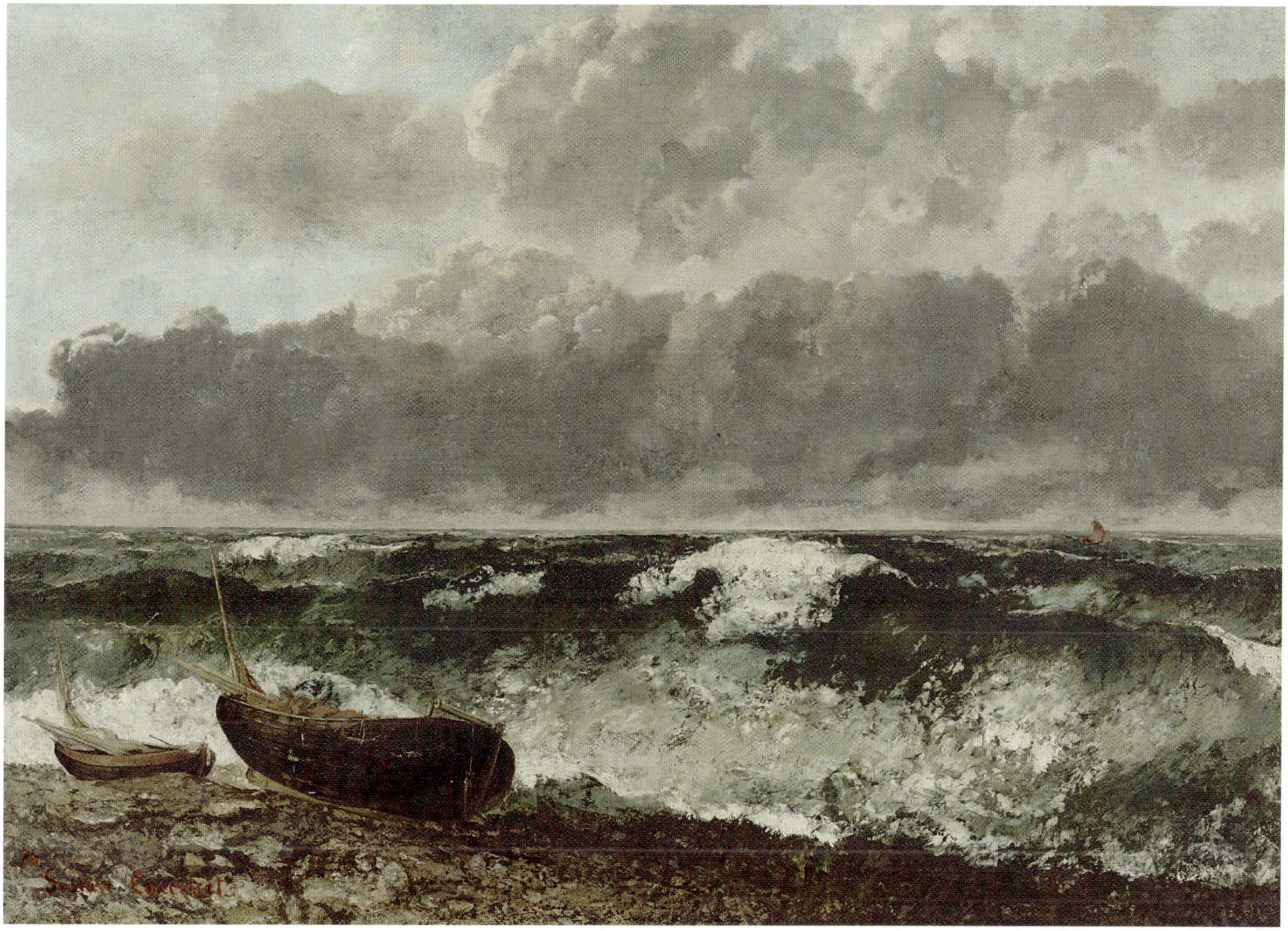

87. Gustave Courbet, *The Wave* or *The Stormy Sea*, 1869–70, oil on canvas, Nationalgalerie, Berlin.

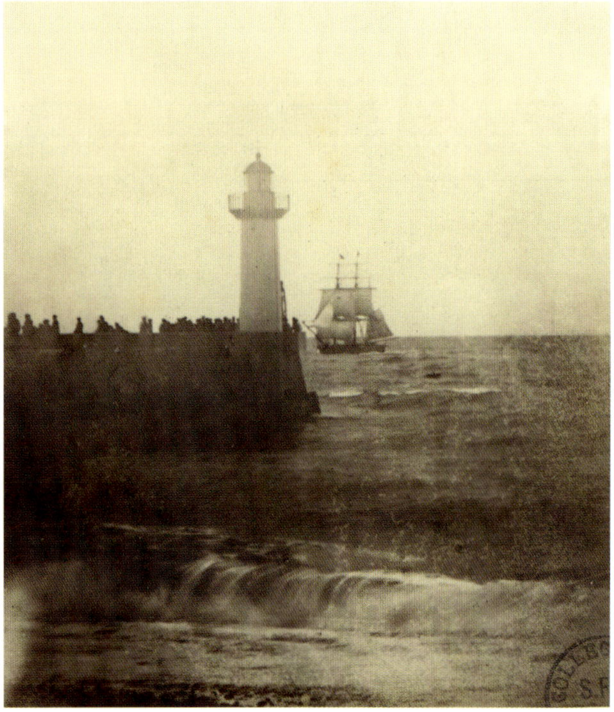

88. Auguste Autin, "The Jetty at Le Havre," 1861, albumen print, Société Française de Photographie, Paris.

foaming tangle, the tide rolling in from the abyss of time, with its sky in tatters and its livid ruggedness. It hits you straight in the chest; you have to take a step back, the whole room reeks of spray."[37]

The series in painting and in photography

In their desire to make show of their technical skill and their ability to capture all but the most fleeting phenomena, photographers vied with each other in conjuring up images of the landscape in transformation. A member of the Société Française de Photographie from Normandy, Auguste Autin sought to render the sky over the sea with the greatest possible veracity. "Sunset Taken in October 1861 at 5 in the Evening," which he sent the association, provides a fine demonstration of his skill. Such precision as to the month and the hour of the day not only highlights the technical tour de force involved; such indications also refer to the fact that the seascape reproduced on this occasion was distinct from its predecessor a minute earlier and its successor a minute later. By inserting duration into representation, photography thus infers a new relationship to time; it is this that in turn opens the door to the idea of series. Remarkably, it is probable that the young Claude Monet—similarly from Le Havre—might have seen Autin's photographs. The frail figures at the mercy of the wind whose outlines he painted in 1866 in a canvas representing the pier of his native city are reminiscent of the slightly blurred shadows

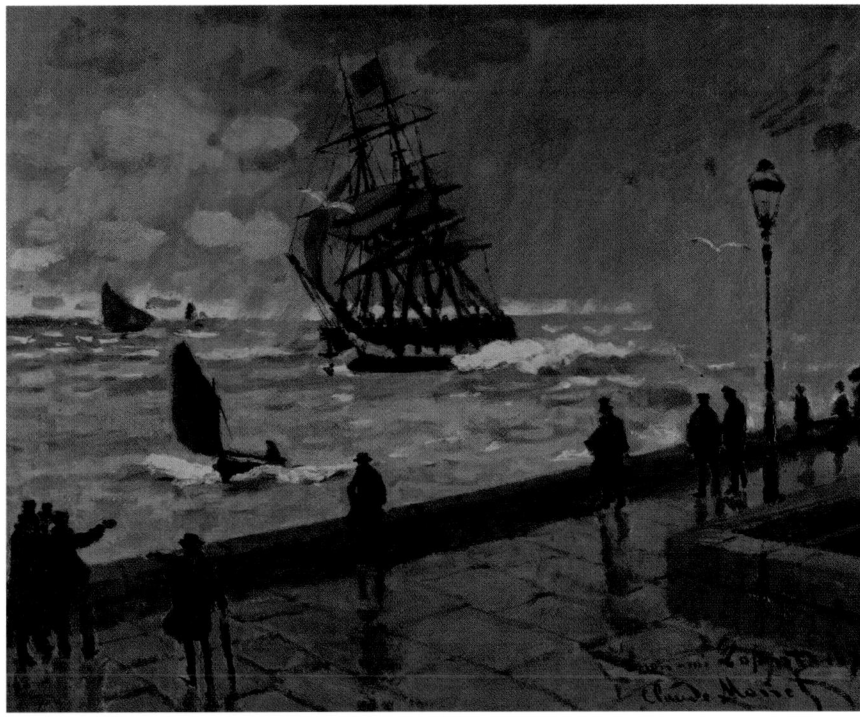

89. Claude Monet, *The Jetty at Le Havre in Bad Weather*, 1866, oil on canvas, private collection.

of the walkers Autin photographed on the pontoon in the same port (ills. 88–89).

This interest in shifting landscapes also motivated Eugène Cuvelier's work in Fontainebleau. A painter like his father, Adalbert, who was a friend of Camille Corot's, he had moved to Barbizon and married the daughter of the innkeeper Ganne, in whose tavern artists visiting the small village on edge of the forest would meet up.[38] Cuvelier carried out many photographs in the great wood, exploring it in harsh as well as in clement months, and acquiring a familiarity with its byways of which Denecourt would not have been ashamed. He excelled in capturing variations in light, the changing hour, the passage of the seasons, and seemed able to seize the very moment that transformed or magnified a particular view. A combination of artistic panache and technical mastery, his talent for capturing the winter light and the white coat of snow covering the rocks and softening their forms is truly exceptional. His interest in variations of a landscape over time and the changing seasons allies his work with that by young painters of his time, such as Claude Monet, Camille Pissarro, and Auguste Renoir.[39] A remarkable group of his photographs recently came to light in New England in the collection of an American painter of the 1860s, who mixed with the founders of the Museum of Fine Arts in Boston. Together with the works of Rousseau, Corot, Dupré, and Courbet, Cuvelier's photographs composed a symbolic image of the Forest of Fontainebleau, out of which was born a new, modern vision of landscape.[40]

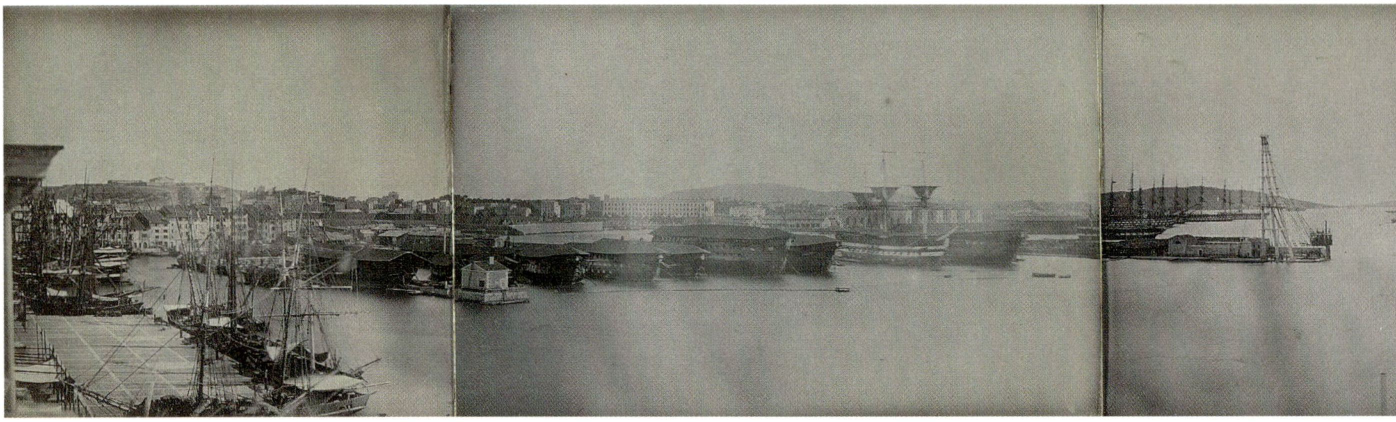

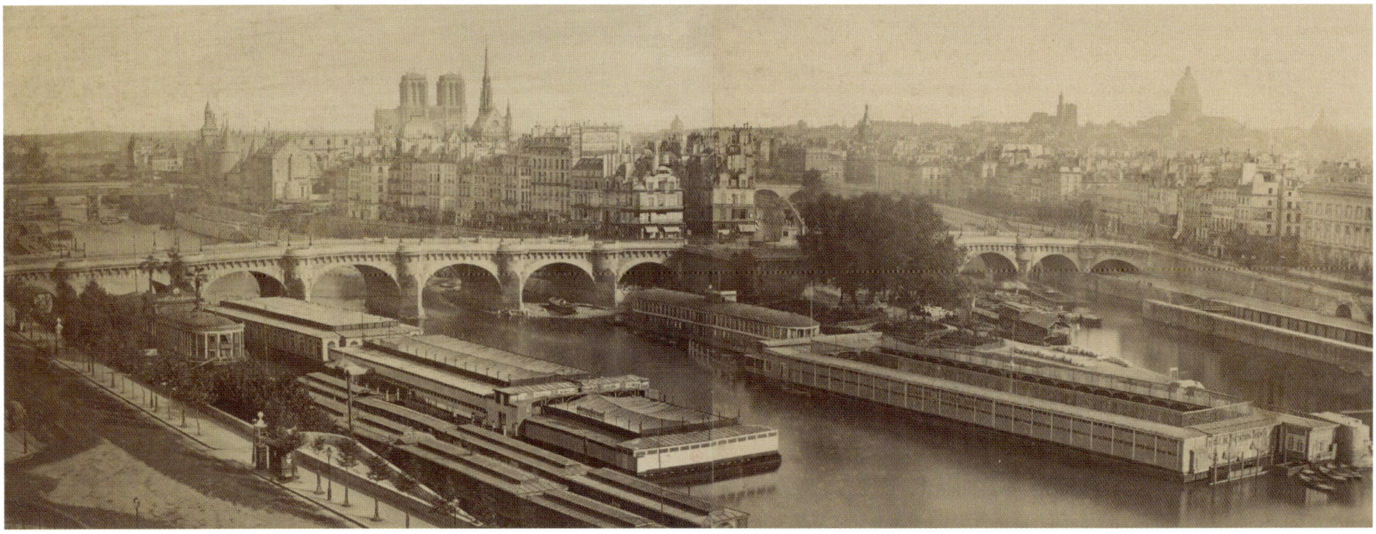

90. **Above, top:** Charles-Isidore Choiselat and Stanislas Ratel, "The Toulon Roadstead," 1845, five daguerreotypes combined to form a single panorama, Musée d'Orsay, Paris.

91. **Above, bottom:** Louis-Auguste and Auguste-Rosalie Bisson, "Great Panorama of Paris," c. 1855, juxtaposition of two albumen prints, Bibliothèque de Fels, Institut Catholique, Paris.

Cityscapes

Invented in the first third of the nineteenth century, photography was contemporary with the growing importance of the city and its radical transformation. Landscape painting, once a purely countryside phenomenon, suddenly, in the middle of the century, became urban. Artists showed monuments in all their glory—a traditional facet of iconography, inevitably linked to the expression of royal or imperial power (Napoleon had dispatched deluxe copies of engraved views of Paris buildings that had recently been erected or renovated to the sovereigns of Europe in attempt to set up comparisons between the French capital and Ancient Athens or Rome, and by extension between his reign and that of Pericles or Cesar). In addition, artists were now trying to represent the city as a whole, laying the emphasis on its sheer size. The influence of the panorama—an optical entertainment that allowed visitors to embrace a vast landscape in one all-inclusive vision—spawned new images in which the city appeared as if through a wide-angle lens.

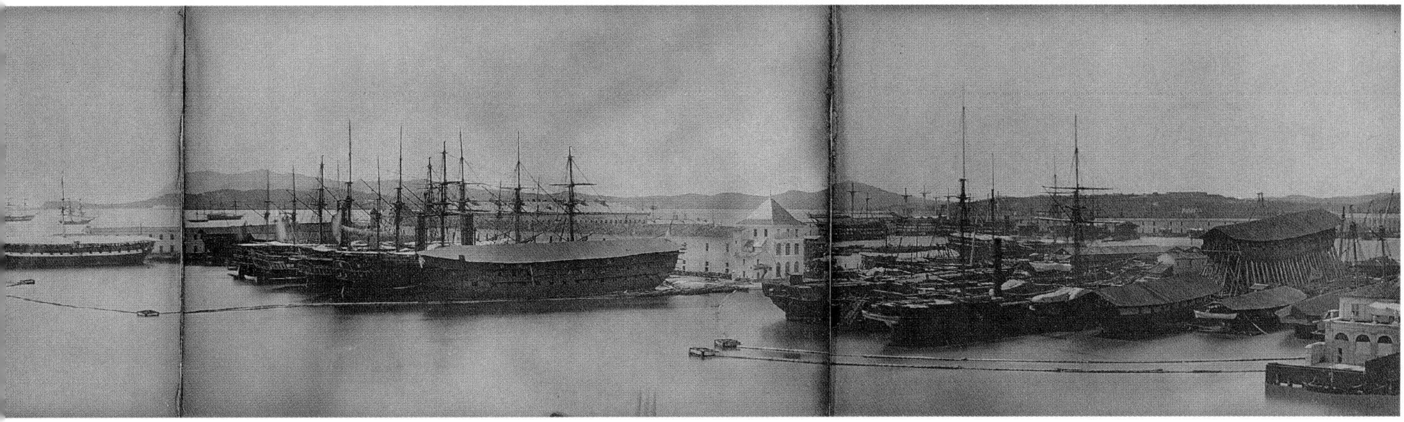

The daguerreotype panorama, invented by Friedrich von Martens (1809–75) in the early 1840s, added new breadth—fully 180 degrees in fact—to the representation of the urban fabric. These images combined amplitude of view with fine-honed details; they attest to the size of the conurbation, showing its meandering course along the banks of the Seine. Thus photography turned to the scientific effects used to create landscape sets for the optical entertainments that were popular at the beginning of the nineteenth century. In 1845, Charles Choiselat and Stanislas Ratel produced an unheralded and exceptional image of the roadstead off Toulon by joining five daguerreotypes end to end to form a single panoramic image. This feat of technical wizardry required painstaking planning to make each plate correspond perfectly with its neighbor (ill. 90). The vast panoramic vista of Paris realized by the brothers Bisson, comprising a pair of photographs taken downstream from the Pont Neuf, showed not only deathless monuments such as Notre-Dame and the Pantheon, but also the bustling activity of the Seine with its barges and washhouses (ill. 91). The work of the longshoremen and sailors, life on the river, and the busy quayside also attracted the interest of the painter Armand Guillaumin, who, from the late 1860s, produced several pictures on allied subjects (e.g., *The Port at Charenton*, 1878, oil on canvas, Musée d'Orsay, Paris).

New motifs, new references

Thus Paris soon became a favored subject for photographers. From the very start of the 1850s, Édouard Baldus, a photographer of German extraction and by training a painter, took a set of views he sold in series. Printed in large formats, these images highlighted architectural monuments, setting them apart from the neighboring houses thanks his work on the negatives. In fact, in a way, Baldus, through his exaltation of isolated monuments, preempts Haussmann's extensive redevelopment plan.[41] From 1854, at the request of the architect Hector Lefuel,

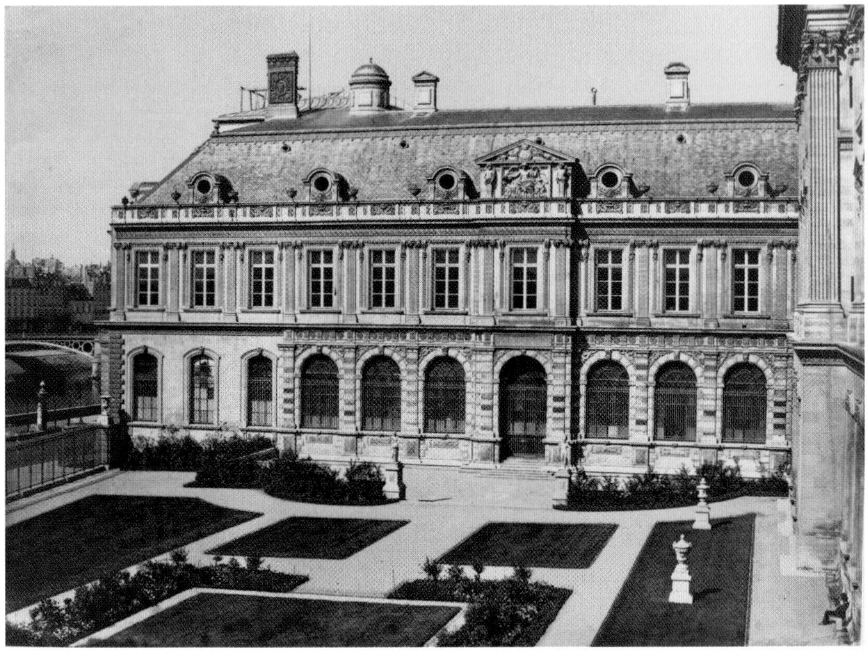

92. Édouard Baldus, "The Louvre, Garden of the Infanta," 1854–57, albumen print, Musée d'Orsay, Paris.

Baldus recorded the renovation of the Louvre. He thus left a visual report on the demolition and rebuilding project, photographing the restored rooms and each new element of the decor. His view of the Garden of the Infant, below the Apollo Gallery, constitutes an unprecedented image. Placing the apparatus at a height carefully judged to emphasize the classically strict disposition of the French-style garden, the clarity and precision of his photograph highlight the lines of the structure (ill. 92). Photographers thus invented a new manner of looking at and representing the urban space; by zeroing in on new motifs, they transformed the frame of reference for landscape.

The impressionists, for the majority born after the invention of photography, started painting in the 1860s, by which time publishers and printers had made photographs widely available and the photographic vision of the 1840s and 1850s no longer presented an innovation. In conjunction with the realist works of the Barbizon School and of Gustave Courbet, as well as with French and Dutch classical art, it had already helped to formulate an array of templates for landscape that carried over into painting. Creations by the first photographers thus contributed substantially to the uptake of new subjects, viewpoints, and framings by the upcoming artistic generation.

Representing the modern city

This new vision of Paris must have been uppermost in Claude Monet's thoughts when, a few years later, he came to paint a picture from a viewpoint redolent of that of a photograph (ill. 93). If photographic images of the modern city presented

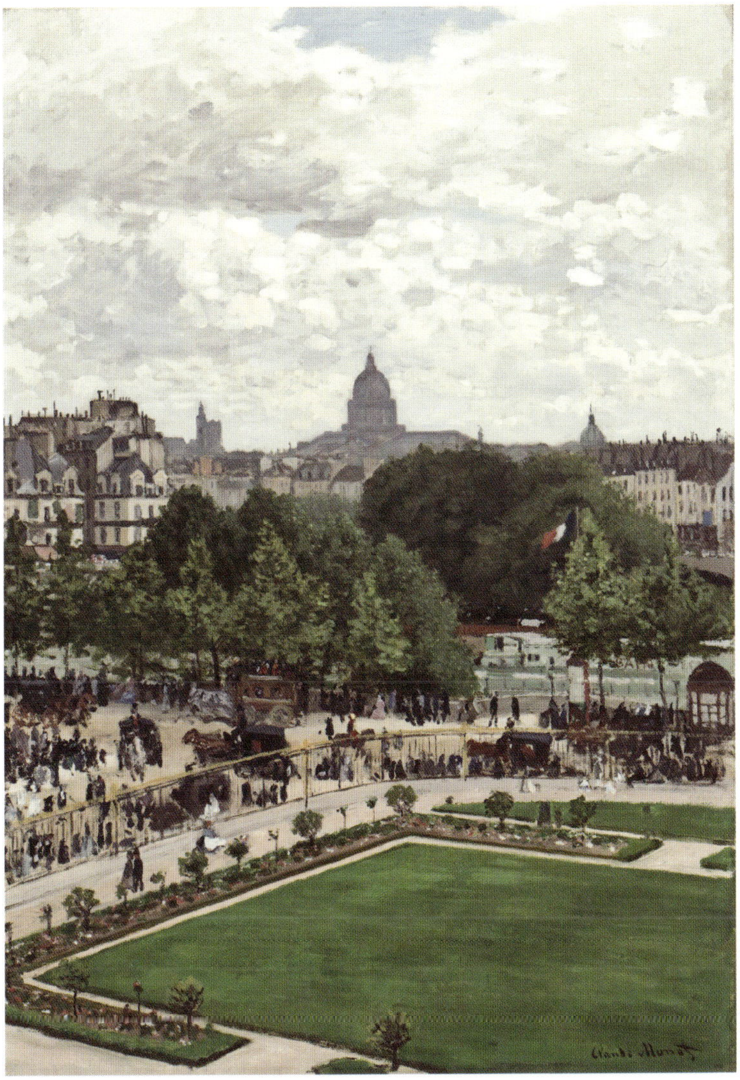

93. Claude Monet, *The Garden of the Infanta* (or *The Garden of the Princess*), 1867, oil on canvas, Allen Memorial Art Museum, Oberlin.

unheralded visual models for the young protagonists of the New Painting, the railroad provided them with unprecedented views of the regions through which it steamed. In 1855, Baldus executed an album commissioned by the Société des Chemins de Fer du Nord (which operated the railroads in Northern France) that was presented to Queen Victoria during Her Majesty's visit to the World's Fair in Paris. It retraced the royal couple's train journey from Boulogne-sur-Mer to Paris in the form of photographs of about fifty sites along the route. These large, remarkably clear plates, well served by the distant viewpoint and rigorous eye of the photographer, reproduced examples of the new industrial architecture, as well as remains of medieval art and examples of pastoral scenery. The photos of stations constituted some of the first images of these new iron monuments, gates to the city, fulcrums around which modern life was increasingly organizing itself (ill. 94). The

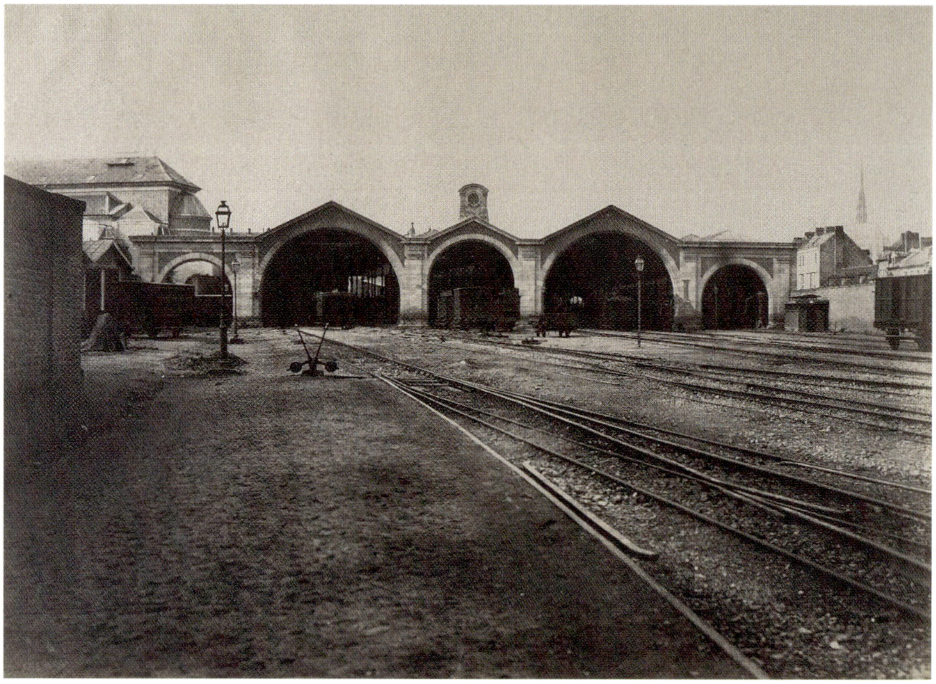

94. Édouard Baldus, "Amiens Station," 1855, albumen print, Musée d'Orsay, Paris.

interest shown for this new motif by impressionist painters is well documented (ill. 95). Younger painters were also sensitive to the redevelopment of the city as it appears in photographs by Charles Marville from 1857. The City of Paris had commissioned him to record the streets and houses earmarked for demolition as well as the new boulevards, streets, and squares opened by Haussmann and Alphand. If Baudelaire and the engraver Charles Meryon reveled in their nostalgia for medieval Paris, unlit and hidden, Monet, Manet, Guillaumin, and Gustave Caillebotte took up their brushes to depict the mushrooming conurbation.[42] Caillebotte saw the long ribbons of asphalt that lay across the city as a visual spectacle that city dwellers enjoyed, leaning over their balconies that stretched out to form long lines strictly parallel to the road.[43]

Conquering the summits

Driven by a desire to outdo one another technically, photographers turned to the awesome terrain of the mountains, where technological complexity was compounded by difficulty of access. Few intrepid souls had ever made their way up to the summit of a mountain in this period; the conquest of the upper realm had begun only at the end of the eighteenth century, before which man had scarcely ventured into places that seemed to open onto a mysterious world beyond our ken. Neither were peaks particularly abundant in painting; the Swiss painter Carl Wolfe and the German Carl Gustav Carus were among the first to explore and represent the High

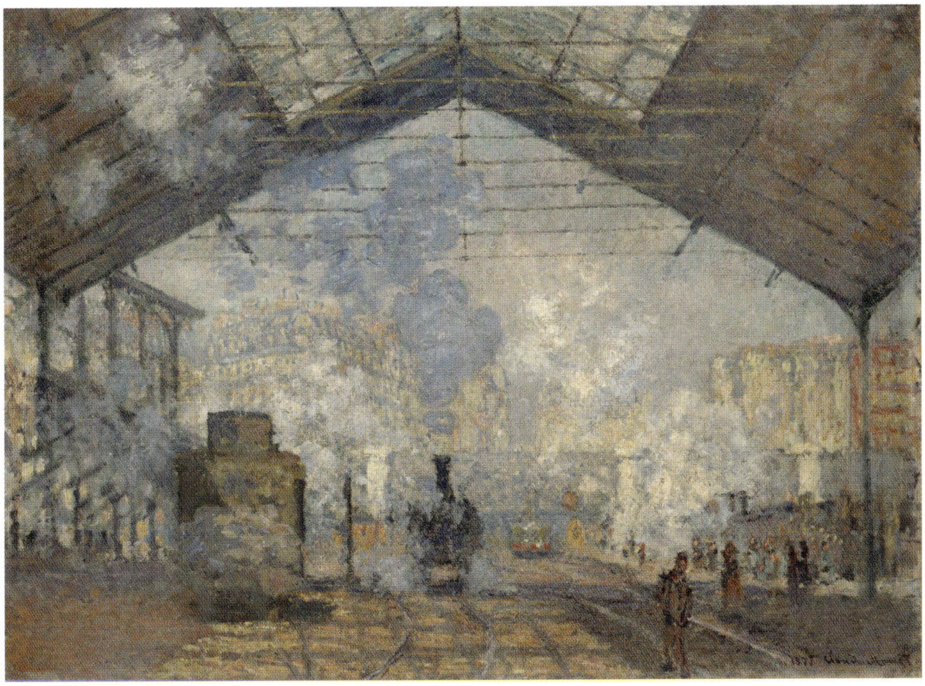

95. Claude Monet, *The Gare Saint-Lazare*, 1877, oil on canvas, Musée d'Orsay, Paris.

Alps. Mountains were, though, an enduring passion of the English writer and art theorist, John Ruskin, a friend of the Pre-Raphaelites, who climbed through the Alps on several occasions from 1833 to 1888. In 1854, in the company of the photographer Frederick Crawley, Ruskin even carried out daguerreotype plates of the landscape around Chamonix. To his mind, only this form of photography seemed to render the reality of a landscape, its "truth to the very letter." On several occasions, he hailed photography as "the most marvelous invention of the century." The view of the "Sea of Ice" speaks volumes as to Ruskin's aesthetic and scientific interests, and to the meticulous attention he paid to the telluric aspects of the landscape (ill. 96). Crawley's viewpoint had been suggested by Ruskin's drawings and inspired an 1859 painting of the same location by Richard St. John Tyrwhitt that appears as a wall decoration in the reading room of the Geology department in the Museum of Natural History of the University of Oxford.[44]

Auguste Bisson took a set of Alpine views at the beginning of the 1860s that were anthologized in albums and presented as a gift to Napoleon III. His large plates embrace the vastness of the panorama, though the presence of mountaineers hints at man's slow victory over the elements. The contrast between the dark silhouettes roped together and the huge, white expanse of the glaciers exemplifies Bisson's technical expertise; the highly reflective surface of the gleaming snow demanded exceptional control of the light. To do this at an altitude of some 10,000 feet (3,000 m) represents no mean feat. In 1911, Léon Gimpel, a photographer working regularly on *L'Illustration*, produced

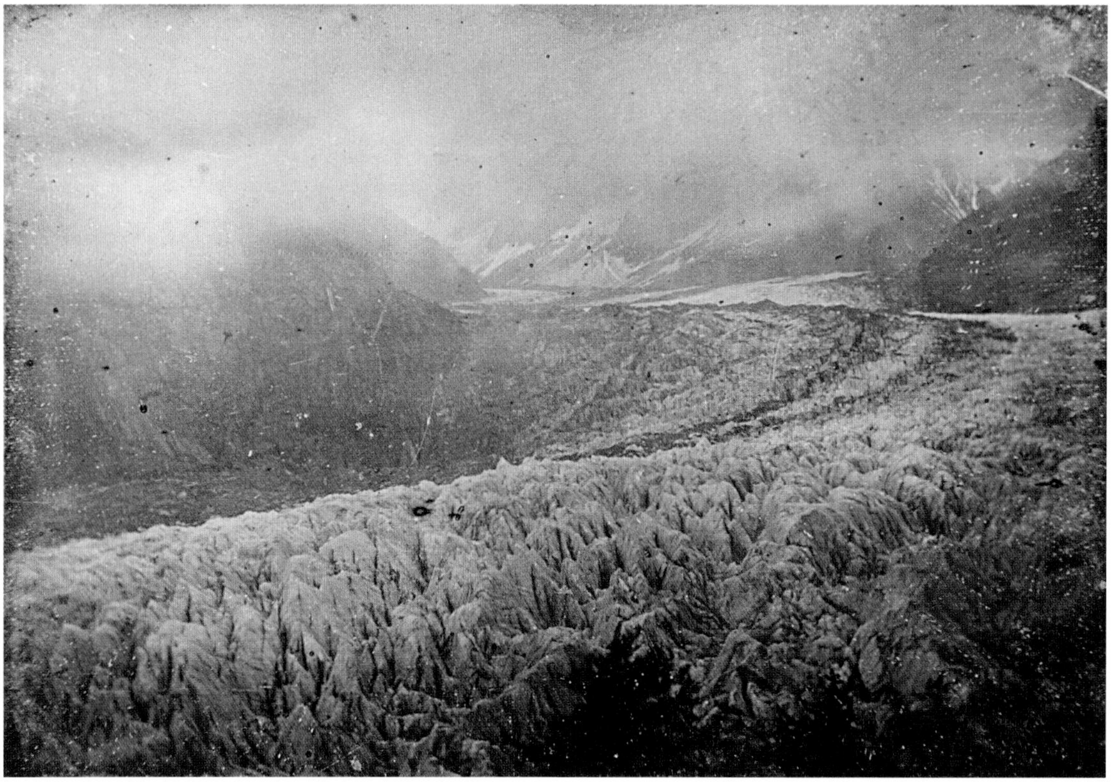

96. John Ruskin and Frederick Crawley, "The Sea of Ice on Mont Blanc," 1854, daguerreotype, Ruskin Library, Lancaster University, Lancaster.

several large autochromes of the glaciers above Chamonix. But this earliest of color processes, patented by the Lumière brothers in 1907, required even longer exposure times. Capturing the luminous variations of the snow remained, as it was half a century earlier for Bisson, an awesome challenge. Artistically composed, some of these photographs were issued. Gimpel was conscious of his images' affiliation with painting, writing: "Never could a painter (be he a pointillist!) have obtained what the autochrome plate afforded me concerning this subject: the seventy million grains of colored starch covering my plate produced (especially when projected as a slide) an extraordinary effect received with great enthusiasm by many viewers."[45] Gimpel thus revealed the mountain in all its facets, from sublime masses and pits to the bluish gleam of the sun and the dazzling flutter of falling snow (ill. 97).

The landscape as history painting

Badly fractured by the fratricidal conflict of the Civil War, the young nation of the United States of America set off to conquer the wide-open spaces of the Wild West in the 1860s. It led to the discovery not only of uncharted territories to clear and break to the plow but also of material with which to enshrine the resurrection and assertion of the state itself, around pioneering values such as courage, individual risk-taking, and a

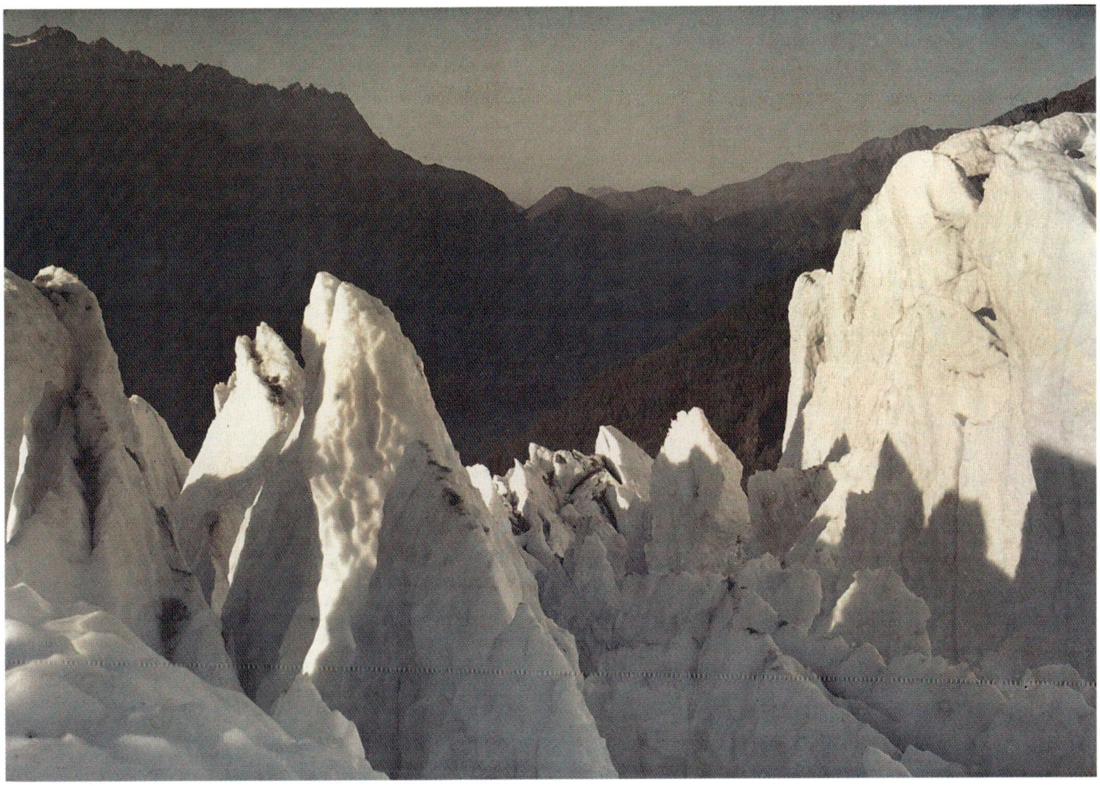

97. Léon Gimpel, "View of the Bossons Glacier," 1911, autochrome, Musée d'Orsay, Paris.

sense of community. In the United States then, the representation of landscape acquired a value similar to that possessed by history painting in Europe.

Photography played an essential role by accompanying and illustrating the exploration campaigns financed by the American government from 1867 to 1879. The large-scale photographs taken on this occasion show virgin tracts of territory devoid of civilization, majestic in beauty and rich in natural resources. Simultaneously they offered a majestic and conciliatory image of the new land, and contributed to the creation of an image of the American West, since reused time and again in literature and at the movies. In the early 1870s, Timothy O'Sullivan realized some extremely original images; turning his camera on vast stretches of sand or clusters of rocks, he underlines the rugged terrain of the lifeless Arizona Desert. Some of these photographs had been ordered by the US Army Corps of Engineers. Proceeding by series, he presented the same landscape from various perspectives, with variations of light, but also—in sometimes bizarre fashion—the impact of man, and even items of photographic material. Transfiguring the luminist visions of the new America, his photography transcends the more banal images of painting. One of his most eye-catching works, *Black Canyon, from Camp 8, Looking Above* (ill. 98), strangely resembles a photographic equivalent of a painting by Martin Johnson Heade, *The Stranded Boat*

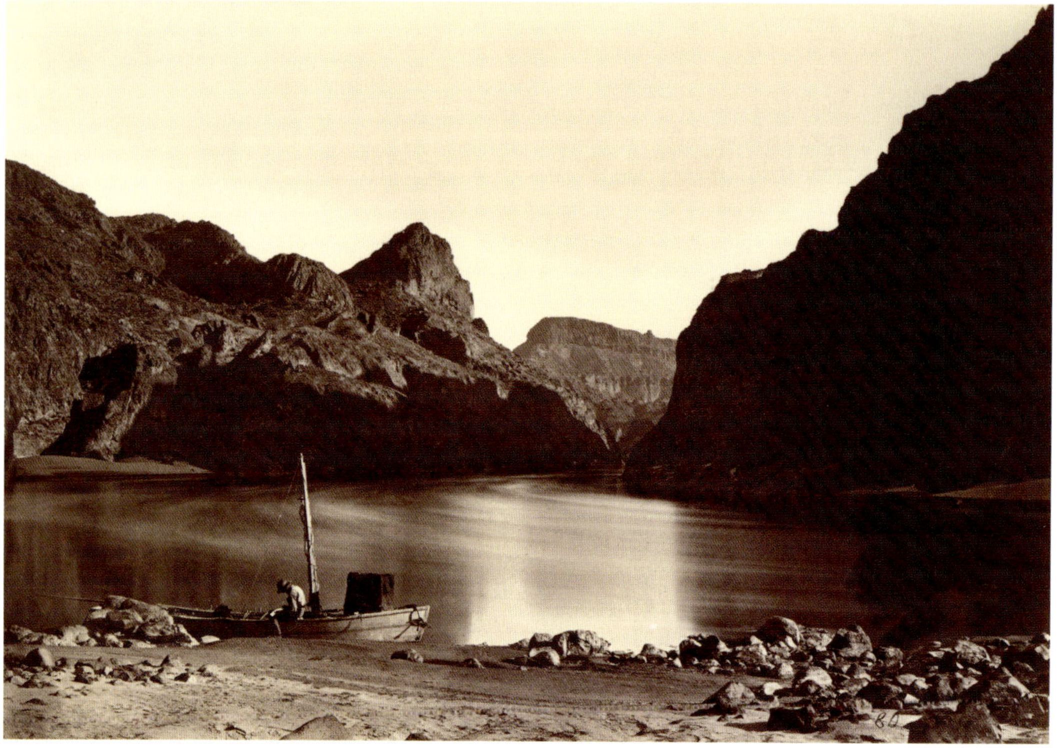

98. Timothy O'Sullivan, "Black Canyon, From Camp 8, Looking Above," 1871, albumen silver print from a glass negative, The Metropolitan Museum of Art, New York.

99. **Facing page:** William Henry Jackson, "The Royal Gorge, Grand Canyon of Arkansas," c. 1880–85, albumen print, Musée d'Orsay, Paris.

(1863, oil on canvas, Museum of Fine Arts, Boston). Characterized by their dramatic opposition between light and shade, images like these gave rise to a new vision of America, whose poetry combined bucolic joy and epic sweep, like an echo of the verse of Walt Whitman. Many years later, Robert Adams described O'Sullivan simply as the "American Cézanne."[46]

Photographers strove to magnify the great spaces opening up before them by placing the stress on their sheer expanse and vertiginous verticals, reminding beholders of the scenery described by Alexander von Humboldt or painted by Albert Bierstadt in the 1860s. The collodion glass negative permitted images of large dimensions that nonetheless conserve remarkable precision in line and volume. Intrepid explorers, photographers had to stagger across the boulders, transporting camera, plates, and developing material with them on the backs of mules. The theatrical viewpoint and composition of one striking image by William Henry Jackson (commissioned by the Denver & Rio Grande Western Railroad Company) exalts the depth and the power of the unfathomable chasm of the Grand Canyon in Colorado (ill. 99). Jackson played a key role in making images of the American West more widely known, contributing works to the Detroit Publishing Company, the first major concern in the United States to market photographic views of the landscape in America.

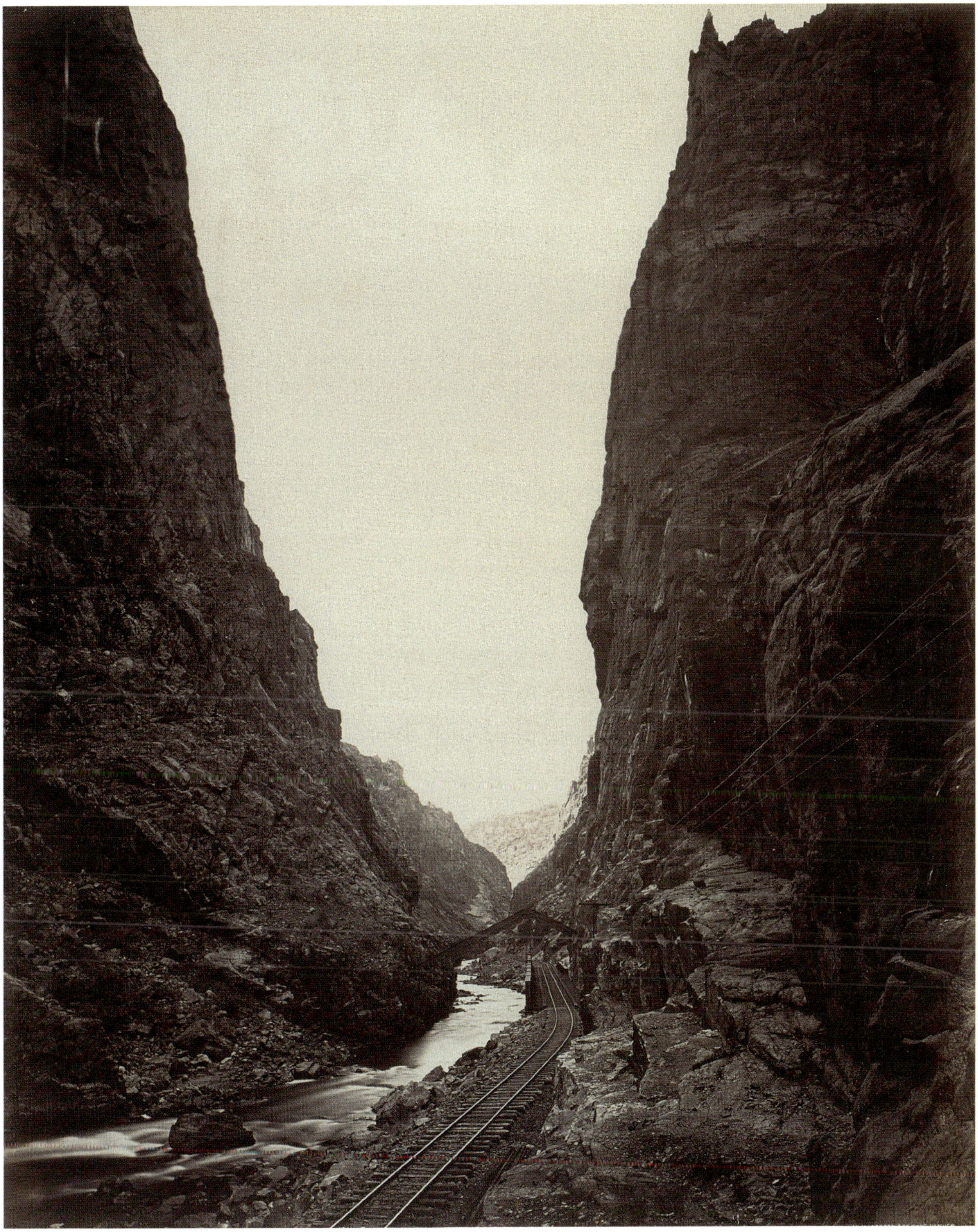

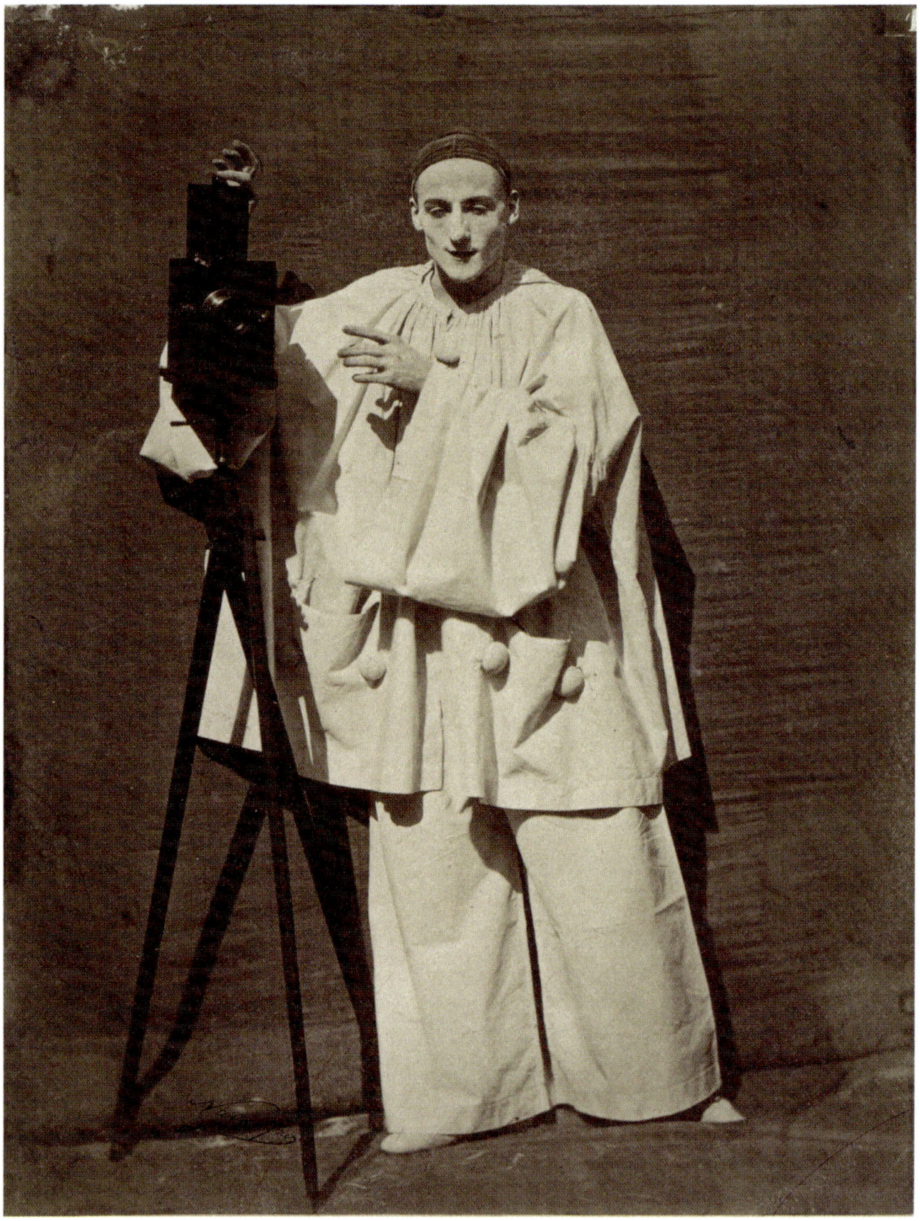

"A seemingly unassuming genre [that] requires great intelligence." [1]

PORTRAITURE

PAINTED PORTRAITS, PORTRAIT PHOTOGRAPHS

Another once minor genre in the hierarchy, in the late eighteenth century the portrait acquired greater importance, a reflection of the elevated status ascribed to the human being in literature and in philosophy. As the individual began to be regarded as an intellect and an active, sensitive personality, the reproduction of the human face took on a crucial role. A successful portrait still needed to capture the outward appearance of the sitter, but now inner truth became no less significant. The dual representation of the features and the soul, however, already benefited from a lengthy tradition—in the sixteenth century, Vasari had distinguished the act of portraying (*rittrare*) from the act of imitating (*imitare*). The ostensibly perfect representation offered by a wax mold, for example, in fact turned out insufficient, as it imparted a solidified appearance to the model's features and failed to capture his expression and true physiognomy.[2] The late eighteenth-century theories of Johann Kaspar Lavater and Joseph Gall, which aimed—from a standpoint then considered scientific—to draw equivalences between facial features and personality, added further impetus to the interest in depictions that transcended mere physical reproduction. The desire for analogical veracity was then compounded by a commitment to introspective truthfulness characteristic of later romanticism. As Hegel underlined: "To reproduce a face by imitation alone, such as it presents itself, at rest, all on the surface, all exteriority, and to reproduce its actual features, those through which the subject's very soul are expressed, are two utterly distinct processes."[3]

The portrait then was increasingly being understood as a tool for investigating the individual soul.

The work of the imagination is arduous and subtle

The artist was expected to be able to read not only the facial features but also the intellect and character of the model, to

100. **Facing page:** Félix Tournachon (also called Nadar) and Adrien Tournachon, "Pierrot As Photographer," 1855, salt print, Musée d'Orsay, Paris.

capture on canvas, beyond a fixed image of the sitter's face, the fleeting passage of their expressions. In 1859 Baudelaire once again poked fun at the bourgeois who claimed that he was the only significant variable in a portrait of quality: "What does one need imagination for to paint my portrait? To paint my soul—so clear, so familiar, so plain to see? I pose, and in reality it is me, the model, who condescends to do the hard work. It is me who supplies the artist with his material."[4] Scornful arrogance, of course, that the critic countered, saying, "The more the material seems positive and solid, the more the work of the imagination is arduous and subtle. A portrait! What could be simpler and yet more complicated, what more self-evident and yet more profound?" In this case, the brush has to be wielded by a psychologically acute mind, and the artist's personal manner and style must come over as palpably as the sitter's features. More than any other pictorial genre, the portrait was the fruit of an encounter between model and painter. A satisfactory portrait ought thus to resemble both. "Every painter," Amaury-Duval stressed in 1846, "possesses a different eclecticism, an eye that belongs to him alone; that is why there are as many varieties of portrait as of painter, and why the same model appears in as many guises as there are artists, all utterly unlike one another, and yet all to the same degree true."[5]

Portraits of a society

More and more people were in a position to order their portrait; long the preserve of the great and the good, the possibility of being portrayed was increasingly extending to the emergent middle class.[6] In 1833, an anonymous critic complained of the abundance of portraits at the Salon: "Painting has this year taken refuge in the *genre picture* and the *portrait* ... Rue Saint-Denis has elbowed its way into the Louvre; the Salon has been stormed by the private sphere. Here are landowners in profile, manufacturers looking you square in the eye, candle-makers in the ceremonial garb of a quartermaster-sergeant with in full view the Cross of Honor they demanded be shown nice and big."[7] The value placed in the family, and in the education of children, now meant pictures showed parents and offspring posing together (ill. 101). The genre had, it is true, been initiated by a splendid royal example: the portrait of *Queen Marie-Antoinette and her Children* by Élisabeth Vigée-Lebrun.

The value of portraiture as a keepsake was now becoming accessible to circles below those of royalty and the aristocracy. The middle classes, like sovereigns of old, could now use a representation to allay absence or stave off death. The paramount issue of resemblance, of mimesis, acquired a second level: at the Salon, the features of an industrialist or tradesman (unlike those of a ruler, the dissemination and endurance of whose image was an important component of personal power) would

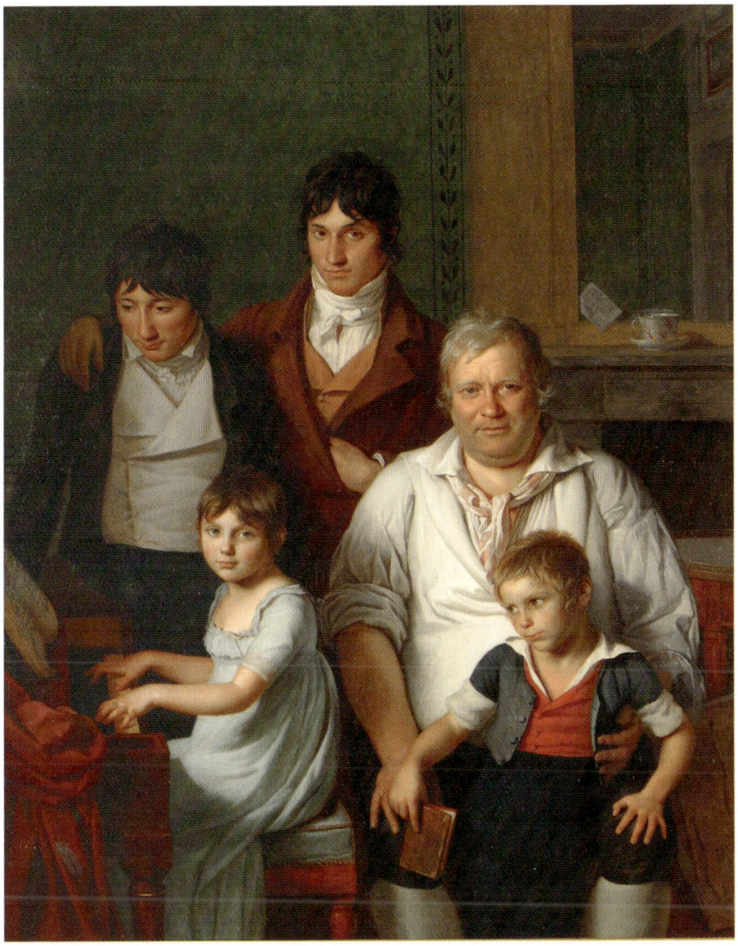

101. Anonymous (French School), *Portrait of a Man with His Children*, c. 1810, oil on canvas, Musée Tessé, Le Mans.

be rarely known to visitors. Thus, in representing a bourgeois, to make him identifiable to those beyond his private sphere, the painter had to rely on the symptomatic characteristics of the class to which he belonged. If the portrait remained a likeness of an individual, it was also increasingly the representation of a society, signaled both by the model's clothes and by the setting in which he or she posed.

The ideal reconstruction of individuals

Winner of the Prix de Rome in 1801, a student of Jacques-Louis David's and thus destined to work in the most exalted sphere of genre (that is, in history painting), Jean-Auguste-Dominique Ingres, for his first contributions to the Salon in 1806, dispatched two pictures, one representing *Madame Rivière*, and the other her daughter, *Mademoiselle Rivière* (now both in the Musée du Louvre, Paris). Ingres affected disdain for his portraits, which, he claimed, he painted solely to earn money and to make his way in society, in the hope that his prestigious sitters might advance his career, in Rome as in Paris.

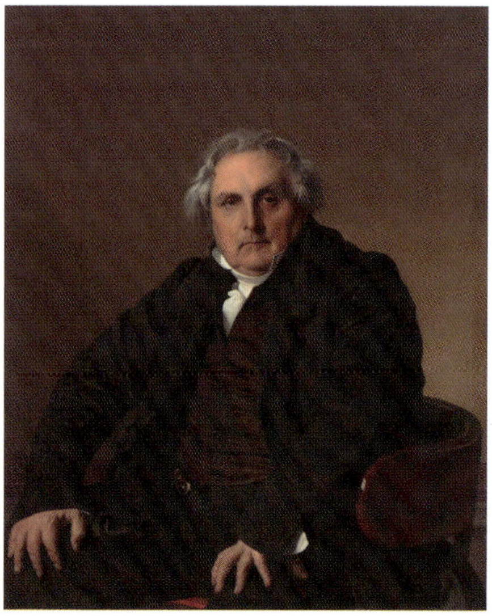

102. Jean-Auguste-Dominique Ingres, *Louis-François Bertin*, 1832, oil on canvas, Musée du Louvre, Paris.

Nonetheless, he went on to present further examples at each annual Salon: illustrious examples include *Louis-François Bertin* (1832, 1833 Salon; Musée du Louvre, Paris) and *Madame Leblanc* (painted in 1823 but unveiled at the 1834 Salon; The Metropolitan Museum of Art, New York). After the critical failure of his *The Martyrdom of Saint Symphorien* (1834, Cathedral of Saint-Lazare, Autun, France), Ingres made up his mind to cease submitting works to the Salon entirely, a decision he never rescinded. He nevertheless displayed portraits at the Bazar Bonne-Nouvelle in 1846 and in an exhibition in the hallowed precincts of the Palais des Beaux-Arts during the World's Fair of 1855, for which he received great critical acclaim. As a very young Baudelaire underlined in 1846, Ingres' talent lay in being able simultaneously to translate inner life and sublimate the model. "The portraits of M. Bertin, M. Molé, and Mme d'Haussonville—are genuine portraits, that is, ideal reconstructions of an individual." [8]

In 1855, Théophile Gautier celebrated the vibrant beauty of the portrait of Mme Devauçay: "The intensity of life here attained by M. Ingres is alarming; these black and tranquil eyes beneath the fine arch of the eyebrows penetrate your soul like two jets of flame. They follow you, they obsess you, they charm you—taking the word in its magical sense." [9] Ingres drew from the lessons of David, a talented portraitist who knew how to bring out naturalism in his models, painting them against a subtly lit, somber background. His pupil invented an individual manner founded on the attentive observation of his sitters and nourished by an admiration for old masters and ancient sculpture alike that fused into a remarkable synthesis of the archaic and the modern. His flair for pose, with the head and shoulders often aslant, for positioning the sitter's hands, as well as his talent for capturing depth in his sitter's gaze, are all emphasized by a choice of costume and decor designed to reflect the model's personality. Faithful to his subjects, Ingres was no less so to his art; showing scant respect for anatomical truth, he enhanced the beauty of his canvases by deforming the hands and the line of the shoulders or by elongating the arms.

The strength of the "Ingres" model

Taking inspiration for the composition from Raphael's *Baldassare Castiglione* (c. 1514–15, Musée du Louvre, Paris), in the light shooting out of the background and the hue of the costume, the portrait of *Louis-François Bertin*, director of *Le Journal des débats*, has become a paragon of the figure of power. The firmness of the pose, the hands pressing down on the knees, reflect the sitter's self-confidence; the buttoned waistcoat, hardly able to contain the press baron's massive body, reinforce the might of the man and of his physique (ill. 102). Exerting a magnetic influence on painters, Ingres'

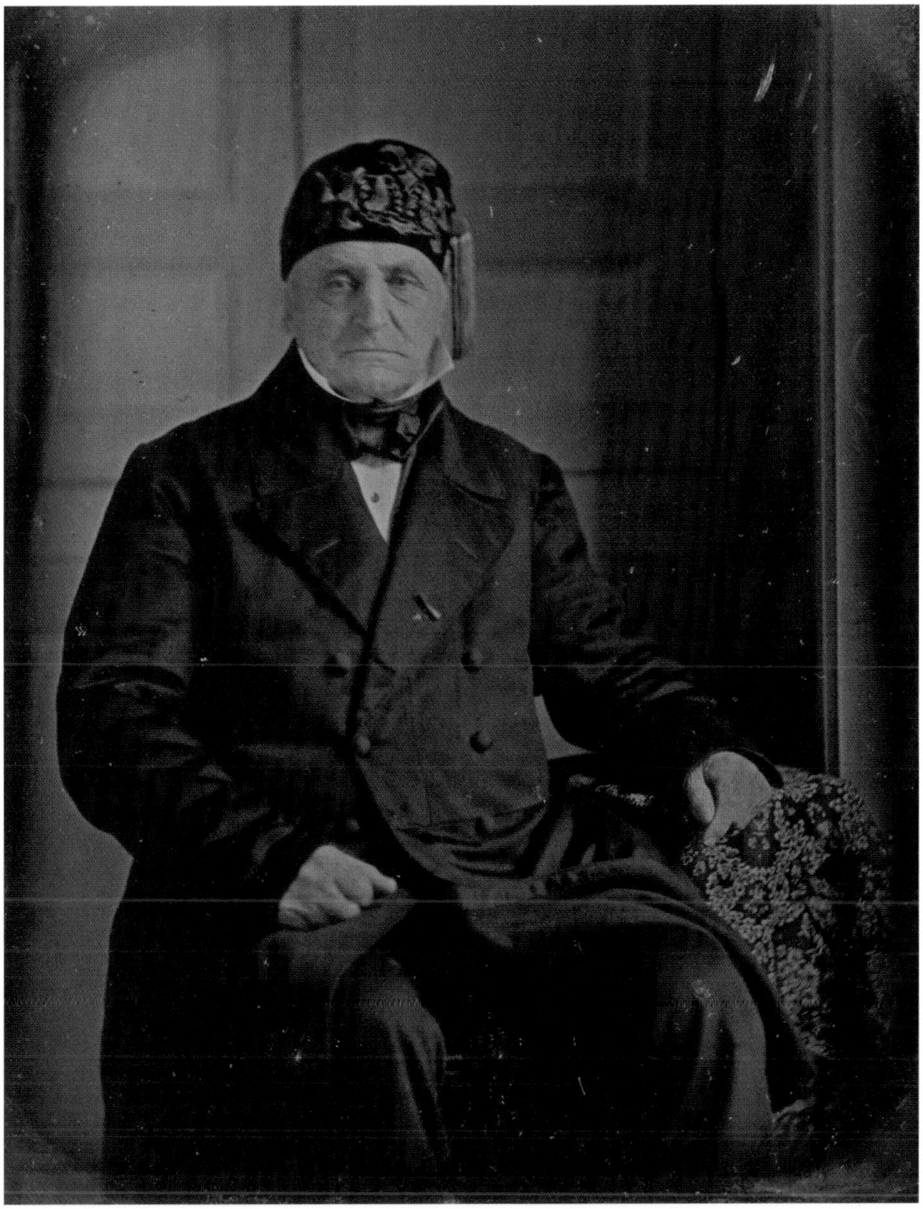

portraits also inspired the work of photographers. Early in the 1850s, Jean-Baptiste Sabatier-Blot, who opened one of the first daguerreotype studios in the Palais-Royal, recalls Bertin's pose in a portrait of M. Naveux de Piennes (ill. 103).

103. Jean-Baptiste Sabatier-Blot, "Monsieur Naveux de Piennes," c. 1850, daguerreotype, Musée d'Orsay, Paris.

In his female portraits, Ingres circumscribed his models' features in firm ovals derived from Renaissance painting, and, combining a feel for individuality with a sense of tradition, he fixed the rules of an enduring type of depiction. The memorable impact of Madame Leblanc's face standing out against the somber ground; the interplay between the textiles—transparent lace, heavily embossed velvet, shimmering calico—consolidates the calm serenity of her three-quarter pose as she sits in

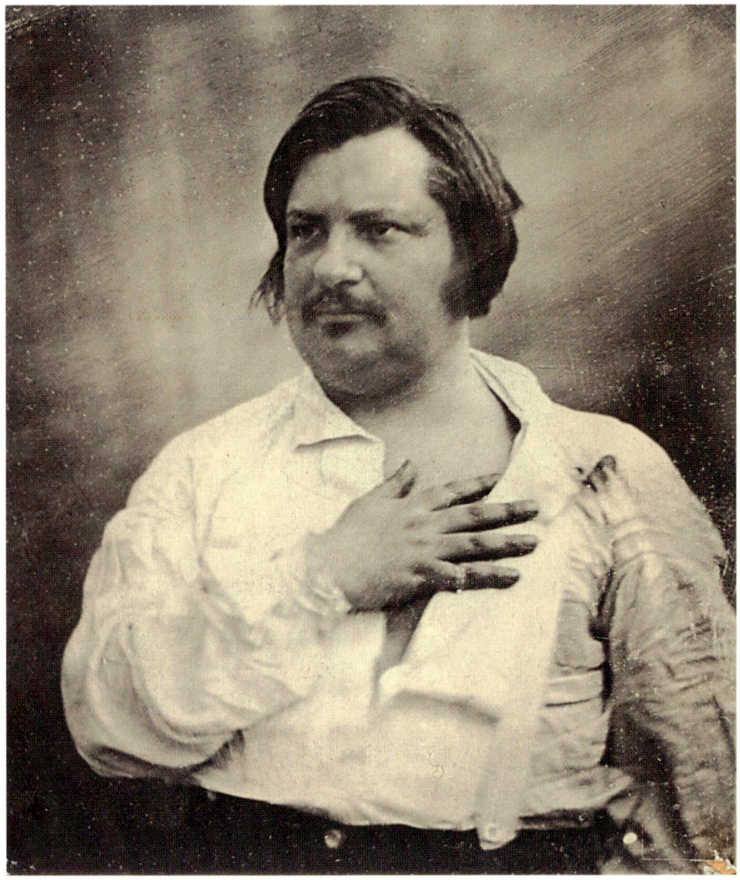

104. Louis-Auguste Bisson, "Honoré de Balzac," 1842, daguerreotype, Maison de Balzac, Paris.

an Empire armchair flanked by a gueridon in the same style. Visitors to the 1834 Salon could be in no doubt as to the young woman's quiet self-assurance in her half-smile and in the way she drapes her arm over the back of the armchair. Thus, even to the majority that could not have known her, the portrait must have felt like a good likeness of the sitter. Ingres demonstrates his talent for translating the singular into the universal, all the while remaining faithful to his belief in harmony, even at the expense of distorted anatomy. The tapering shoulders, the foreshortening of the right arm and lengthening of the left, the size of the hands, the exaggerated protrusion of the eyes are as revelatory of the painter as of the model.

The development of the daguerreotype

As he had suggested to Isidore Niépce, at the very conception of photography, Daguerre thought straightaway of portraiture as a means of ensuring the invention's commercial viability. His in-depth knowledge of the society of the time, as demonstrated by his successes in the theater and diorama, made him confident of the financial opportunities presented by a process that would make portraiture accessible to a large number of the population. The exposure time required by the daguerreotype at the time of its announcement in 1839—several minutes—forestalled the immediate development of this potential and, as was shown above, Daguerre had to seek other ways of publicizing his process.[10] Yet, he was proved right; from the 1840s on, it was indeed portraiture that guaranteed the commercial success, in a preindustrial manner, of the daguerreotype. Eventually, the efforts and researches of the first daguerreotypists, from the autumn of 1839 onward, significantly decreased exposure times. The engraver-medalist Philippe-Fortuné Durand claimed to have been the first to run a photography studio in Lyon in 1840. Hailing from the same city, Camille Dolard, a painter by trade, had set up his daguerreotype portrait studio in 1841. Until about 1842, the daguerreotype remained an activity reserved for adepts; within the following five years, dozens of workshops had been established in Paris and other major French cities. If the word of archivist and curator Léon de Laborde is to be believed, by 1851 there were 100,000 daguerreotype plates being produced every year in France.[11]

Having one's portrait taken thus became accessible to a substantial proportion of the middle and lower-middle classes, a phenomenon that sparked the kind of astonishment ironically pointed up in certain drawings by Honoré Daumier (ill. 35). Photographed in May 1842 by Louis-Auguste Bisson, the novelist Honoré de Balzac, though in general favorable to Daguerre's invention, could not conceal his disquiet at the prospect, afraid that the apparatus might capture his soul as well as his outward appearance. Since Balzac was imbued with the psychological and psychomorphological theories of his time (he was an avid reader of Johann Kaspar Lavater and Franz Joseph Gall, whose theses underpin some of the concepts behind his great saga of novels, *La Comédie Humaine* [*The Human Comedy*]), he might perhaps have been guilty of a little exaggeration. Shared by a number of his contemporaries, this fear was, however, a genuine one at the time, and is more understandable in the light of the extraordinary innovation the new contraption represented (ill. 104).

The frozen pose

The conditions necessary for taking a daguerreotype renewed some of the theoretical reflections on which portraiture was based. Although much reduced, exposure times were still around a minute or so, depending on lighting conditions. To make the best use of the sunlight, photographers worked outside on a terrace or set up their workshop under a vast glass roof. The model had to be immobilized to prevent any movement whatsoever during the pose; the preference for crisp, precise outlines meant that an inopportune shudder could result

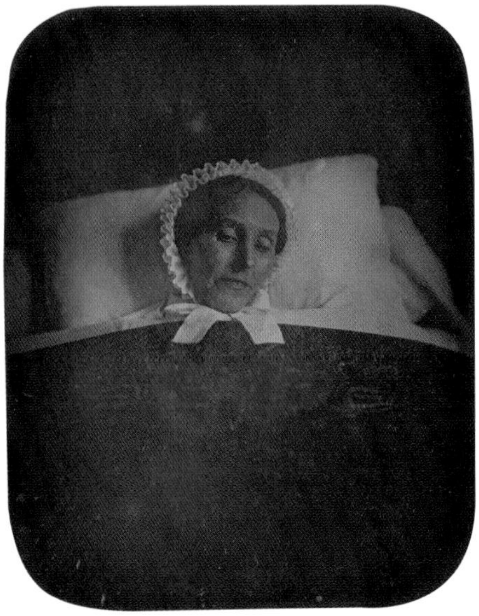

105. Anonymous, "Postmortem Portrait of an Old Woman," c. 1850, daguerreotype (central section of a triptych), Musée d'Orsay, Paris.

in blurring and so ruin the plate. To prevent sitters moving their heads, operators devised chairs with a back fitted with a kind of neck brace; a barbaric device which, if it guaranteed that the sitters' features appeared clearly enough, fixed them in an attitude and expression that marred the overall effect (ill. 34). Inner truth was lacking to the extent that, in celebrating Ingres' talent as a portraitist, his teacher Amaury-Duval uses the daguerreotype as a foil: "The portraits of M. Ingres ... are not a material or petty imitation of nature. Indeed, if the painter set the literal reproduction of what stands before his eyes as his goal, it would make the daguerreotype the most perfect expression of all art. The portrait, on the evidence of its masters, is instead nature interpreted." [12]

Building blocks for a new critique

Like a wax cast, the daguerreotype plate seemed to capture only a single, fixed image of the model's face. In spite of the exactitude proclaimed by Daguerre's disciples and the adepts of photography, such a motionless imprint could never lay claim to the truthfulness of artistic portraiture. In his review of a drawing course published by Élisabeth Cavé, Eugène Delacroix reproached the daguerreotype for showing *too much* and denied it could ever be capable of rendering a truthful account of a human face. "It is still no more than a reflection of the real, a copy misleading due to its very exactitude. The monstrosities it presents rightly shock one, although they are literally those of nature herself; but the imperfections the machine reproduces so faithfully do not strike our eye when we look at the model without such an intermediary; [for] our eye ... already performs the work of an intelligent artist." [13] In her course-book, Madame Cavé emphasized the importance of observing the figure's movements and of varying attitudes in composing a portrait. Delacroix concurred with these remarks: "No work is more delicate. A person moving about, or speaking, does not proclaim her imperfections as does an unspeaking and motionless portrait. One sees a portrait all too often; one sees it more in one day than the original in ten years." And the artist adds, "Examine portraits in daguerreotype. Not one in a hundred is even bearable. Why is that? It's because it is not the regularity of the features that captivates and charms us, but the physiognomy, the expression of the face, because everyone has a physiognomy that strikes us at first glance and which the machine will never convey." A merciless critique of the daguerreotype—and thence of photography generally—was thus being framed which drew on the antimechanist arguments already aired at the invention's announcement. Paradoxically, the photographic portrait, which brought the invention such commercial success and promotion, also held within it the germ of a vein of criticism that refused photog-

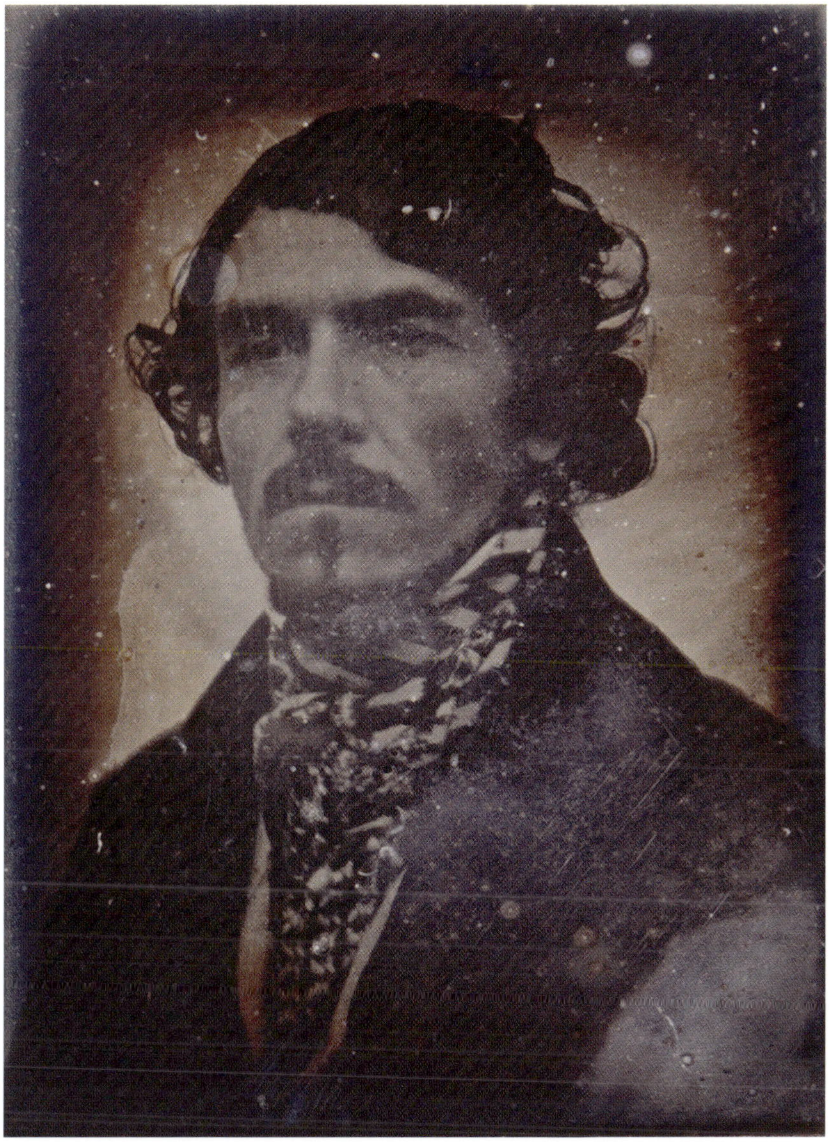

106. Léon Riesener, "Eugène Delacroix," 1842, daguerreotype, Musée d'Orsay, Paris.

raphy all access to the pantheon of the arts.[14] This contempt tended to be all more stinging since the vogue for the daguerreotype had sounded the death knell of the painted miniature and condemned specialists in them to the scrapheap. Photography also did away with a whole class of mediocre painting concerned solely with representing the sitter's features relatively accurately. Only an artist committed to going beyond narrow physical resemblance could now hope to outdo photography.

From an early stage, photographers did everything in their power to counter the glaring disadvantages of the fixed pose and the relatively abbreviated sitting compared to the lengthy process a painted portrait demanded. Thus, like painters, they varied the sitter's attitudes (hence in 1842 the splendid "hand on heart" gesture that Balzac performed for Bisson—

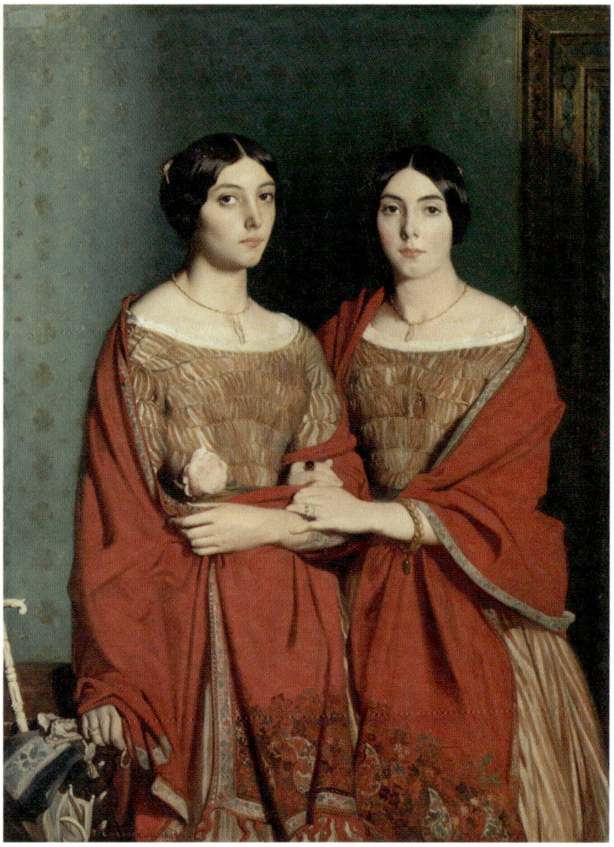

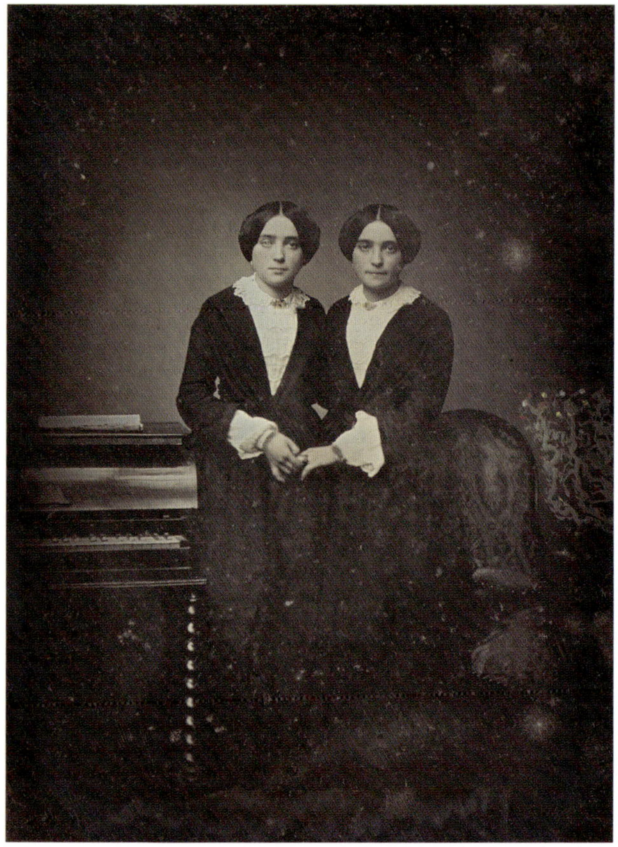

107. **Above, left:** Théodore Chassériau, *The Two Sisters*, c. 1845, oil on canvas, Musée du Louvre, Paris.

108. **Above, right:** Anonymous, "Portrait of Twin Sisters," c. 1848, color daguerreotype, Musée d'Orsay, Paris.

a majestic way of evoking the writer's fear of having his soul stolen by the camera), and evoked the tastes and habits of the model through the language of attire (Delacroix took great care over how his daguerreotype portraits by his cousin Léon Riesener were arranged in this respect [ill. 106]) and/or through elements in the decor.

Last portraits

The fixity characteristic of photography also facilitated the advent of a specific genre, traditionally the preserve of casts and molds: the postmortem portrait. From the mid-1840s, daguerreotypists placed advertisements offering to photograph and immortalize the features of the late lamented in memoriam for the family. For some people in this period, a final image like this would often be their only photographic portrait (ill. 105).[15]

Photographic theories of portraiture

In 1851, Francis Wey attempted to frame a new theory of portraiture in the light of photography, asserting the conceptual and artistic nature of photographic depiction. After a preamble

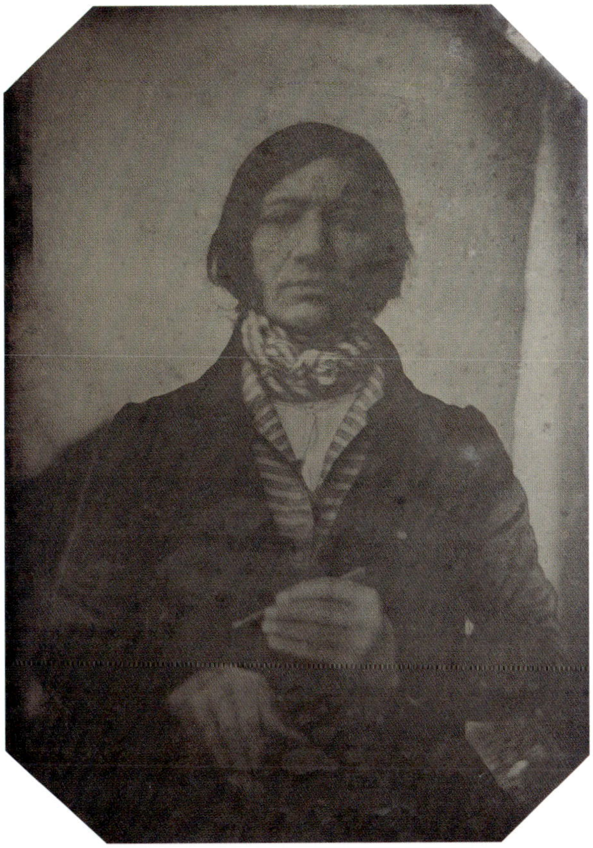

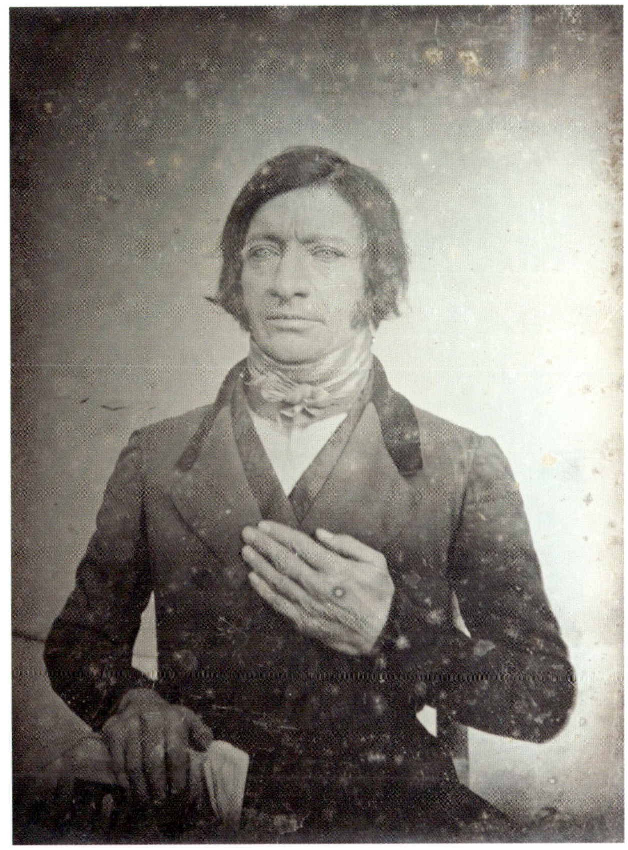

109. **Above, left:** Eugène Le Bœuf, "Self-Portrait with Paintbrush," c. 1840, daguerreotype, J.-G. Bouchaud Collection, Paris.

110. **Above, right:** Eugène Le Bœuf, "Self-Portrait," c. 1840, daguerreotype, J.-G. Bouchaud Collection, Paris.

rehearsing the philosophical and aesthetic complexities behind the concept of resemblance, he went on to write: "The fact that heliography reproduces the features and facets of a face with mathematical accuracy is uncontested.... Nevertheless, we have all seen heliographic portraits perfectly true to life and heliographic portraits that are utterly unlifelike." From this observation Wey deduced that photography, like painting and drawing, required specific qualities, an individual talent testifying to the artistic nature of its creator: "Thus to compete with art, heliography has to call upon the artist's sensitivity, upon his knowledge, conditions that will ennoble and elevate the moral compass of this marvelous discovery."[16] He thus invited photographers to follow painters and acquaint themselves with the works of the masters of the latter art—referring to Titian, Van Dyck, Rubens, and Prud'hon—so as to assimilate their interpretative qualities.[17] "It is necessary for a heliographer to study [his models] from several angles, to expose them in different lights, to choose a pose for them with the utmost care."[18] He went on: "The scope for interpretation is almost as wide as for painting ... it [photography] is spontaneous and, as it excludes corner cutting and correction, it demands a remarkably assured eye. Its exponent ... imbued with all the resources of art ... has to be able to picture the

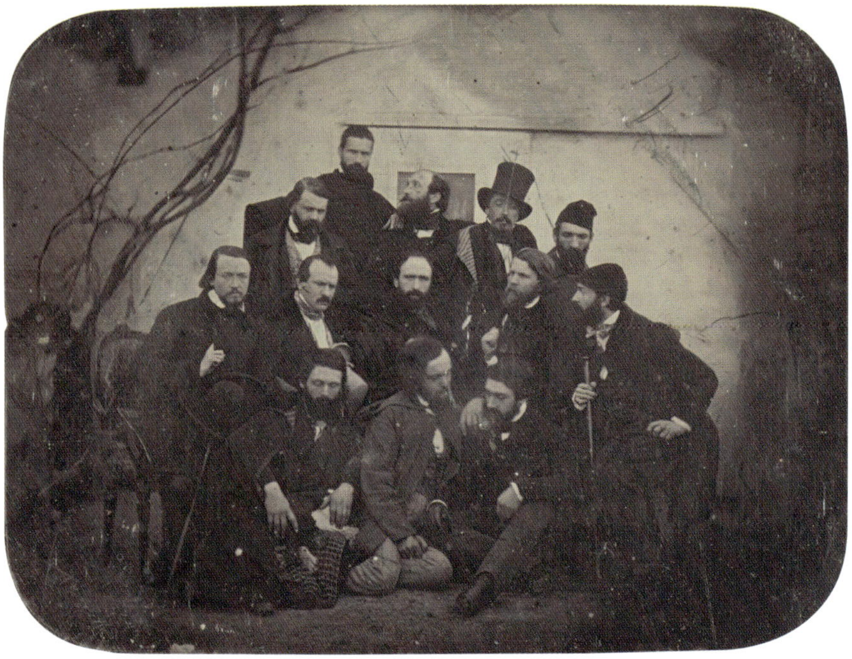

111. Joseph-Philibert Perraud, "Group of Artists in Rome," c. 1846–47, daguerreotype, Musée d'Orsay, Paris.

112. **Facing page:** Hippolyte Bayard, "Portrait of Jules Ziegler in His Garden," 1844, daguerreotype, Société Française de Photographie, Paris.

complete image from whatever nature presents to him." Faithful to the line followed by a review founded in conjunction with the Société Héliographique, Wey's apology for photography on paper centered on dissociating it from the daguerreotype. Without waiting for precepts such as these, however, certain daguerreotypists, to overcome the constraints imposed by length of exposure, had already started resorting to tricks borrowed from painting (ills. 107–8).

Renewing the tradition of the "artist portrait"

As early as 1840, Eugène Leboeuf, a painter and student of Jean-Baptiste Isabey, recalled the lessons of the self-portraits of Nicolas Poussin and David, and portrayed himself elegantly kitted out and with brush in hand (ills. 109–10). In 1843 Hippolyte Bayard, who, despite his persistent rivalry with Daguerre, practiced daguerreotype with skill, carried out a striking portrait of his friend the painter Jules Ziegler, a pupil of Ingres, in his garden (ill. 112). Bayard had him pose seated and wearing a voluminous and improbable headdress, reminiscent of the medieval alchemists that so fascinated the model. Shown in profile, his naturally impressive appearance reinforced in this way, Ziegler, his eyes half closed, looked as though he was meditating. Drawing on the traditional genre of the artist's portrait, the image evoked Ziegler's work (vases standing on the table and the terrace remind viewers of his activity as a ceramist), but it also appropriately underlined the ties between photographer and sitter. Indeed, Ziegler himself practiced the daguerreotype, and later photography on paper; he was in all

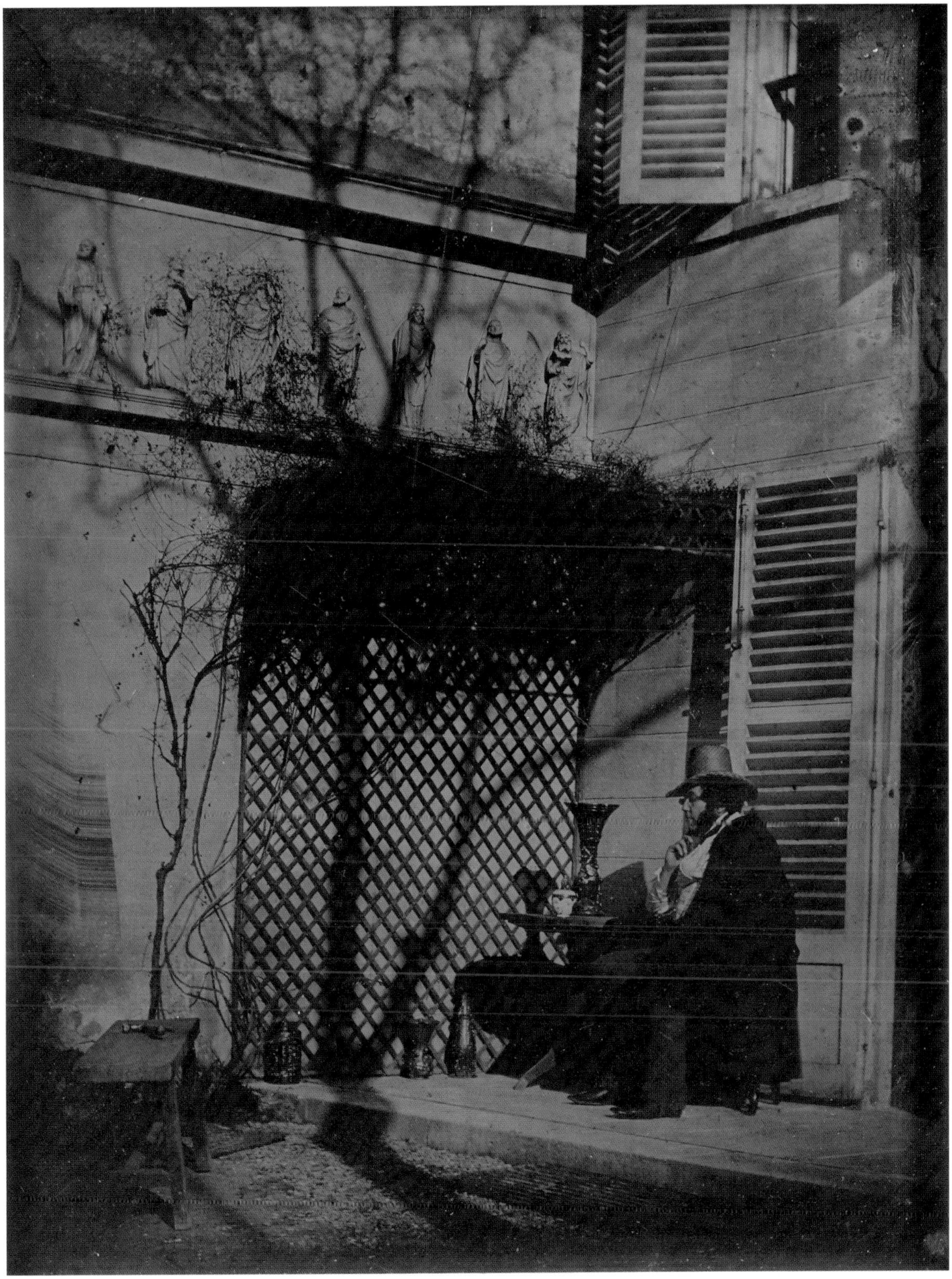

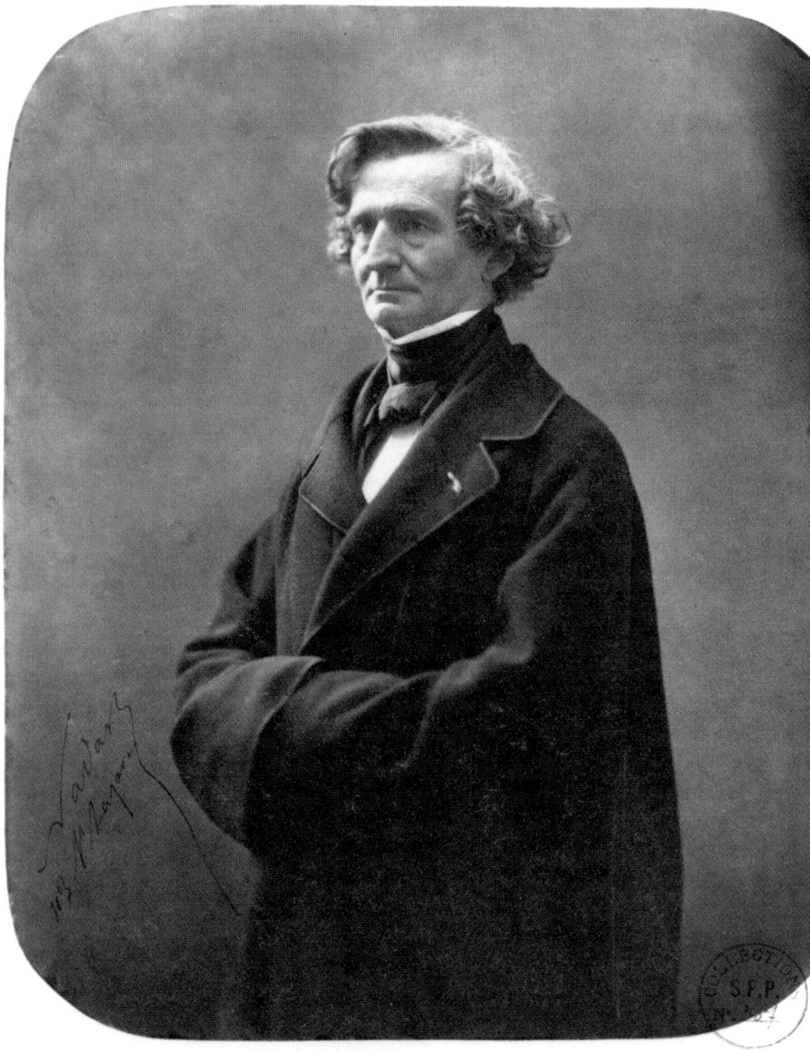

113. Félix Tournachon (also called Nadar), "Hector Berlioz," 1856–57, salt albumen print, Société Française de Photographie, Paris.

probability taught by Bayard himself. The setting insisted on the opposition between light and dark and made much of the theatrical effects cherished by both men in their art. The very place the photo was taken, the painter's garden in Paris, evokes their fondness for a similar daily routine. Bayard's portrait of his friend is both lifelike and sensitive, the intimate, even metaphorical depiction seconding the physical resemblance.

Setting themselves technical conundrums, certain photographers managed to pull off genuine tours de force. In Rome in the mid-1840s, for instance, Joseph-Philibert Perraud realized several group portraits of members of various academies and European schools on their sojourn in the Eternal City (ill. 111).[19]

"A profound intuition of the model's character"

Félix Tournachon, better known by the pseudonym "Nadar," which he adopted for his work in 1838, developed a talent for

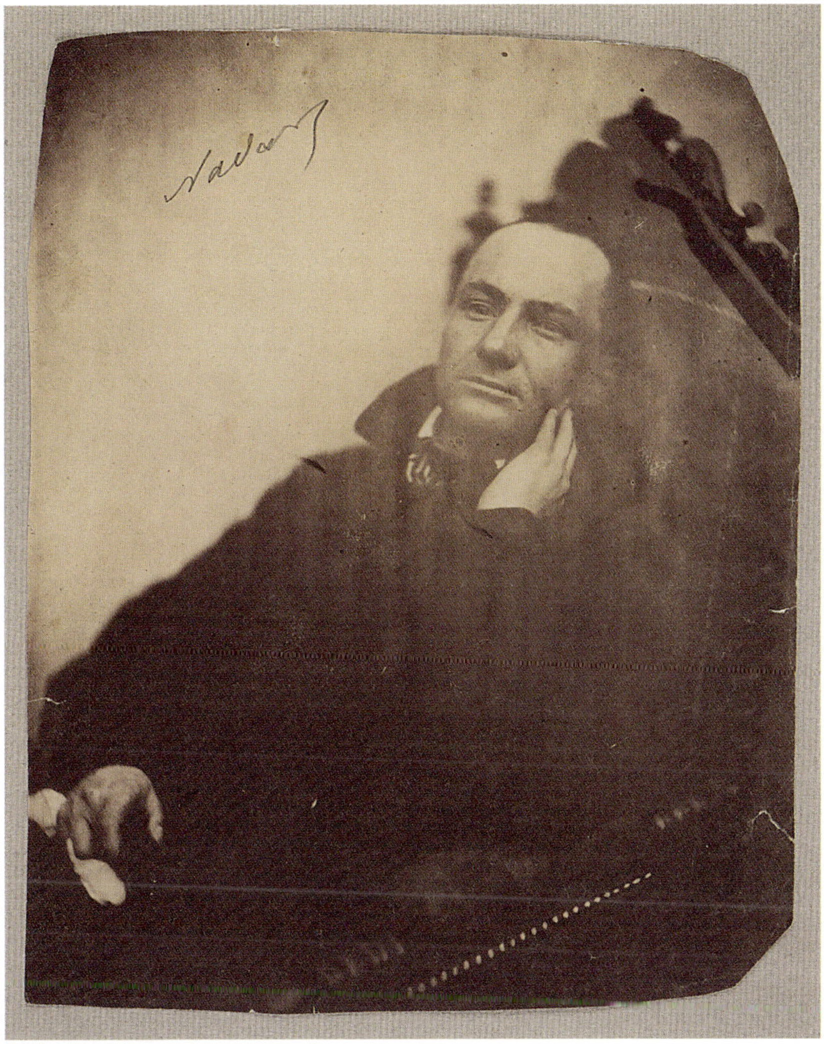

capturing the intimate likeness of his models. Originally from Lyon, and familiar since the late 1830s with the art world of his age, he learnt photography in 1854, by which time he was already a recognized pamphleteer and caricaturist.[20] With his ability to bring out the most striking features of a sitter's physiognomy, and his close links with contemporary personalities from the world of the arts and literature, he took photographic portraits of exceptional quality which display a penetrating and sincere study of his models—the only means, as the photographer himself claimed, to obtain a representative image of their features and character. He thus seemed to have made his own the young Baudelaire's stipulation to painters in his critique of the 1846 Salon that portraitists should strive to acquire a profound intuition of the model's character.[21] Although rejecting Ingres' recourse to decor and accessories, Nadar had nonetheless examined the painter's portraiture attentively; he took over the plain, somber backgrounds in which light seems to emanate

114. Félix Tournachon (also called Nadar), "Charles Baudelaire in an Armchair," 1855, salt print, Musée d'Orsay, Paris.

from the subject, the range of attitudes arranged to translate the sitter's inner life, the skillful manipulation of dress codes. Having discovered that Hector Berlioz did not have the anticipated stature of the composer of *The Trojans*, the photographer draped him in a vast greatcoat that conferred on him the power Nadar felt his talent deserved (ill. 113). Philippe Burty in 1859 could hardly have been more lavish in his praise of these photographs: "It is undeniable that M. Nadar has turned his portraits into works of art in the fullest sense of the term, by the way he lights his models, the freedom of movement and attitude he allows them, by the striving for a characteristic facial expression."[22] A close friend of Baudelaire's, Nadar took several portraits of the dandy poet that convey his extreme sensitivity and his fathomless but debonair melancholia. In "Charles Baudelaire in an Armchair," the skillfully disposed lighting emphasizes the only bright elements in the picture, contrasting with the dark clothes, the face, and the hands that underline the essential role of Baudelaire's wit and gesture in his genius. Protected beneath the mighty arc of their sockets, the black eyes appear not to see the viewer, as if the poet's glance is turned inward to some inner vision, prolonged it seems in the gesture of the left hand gently rising to the cheek (ill. 114). A unique photograph, long kept by Baudelaire, this remarkable image reveals the twin talents of model and photographer, further elevated by their profound understanding of one another. Nadar entertained few doubts about his talent; a few years later, commenting on Ernest Meissonnier's painting of Alexandre Dumas *fils* (1879, Musée du Louvre, Paris), he skewered what he saw as the painter's inability to capture the soul or character of his sitters in portraiture. Wryly, he described Meissonnier as a "minor … suburban photographer," blind to the movements best suited to revealing the inner character of his subjects.[23]

The challenge of expression

The Pierrot series—which was conceived together with his brother Adrien Tournachon in 1854, and which shows the mime artist, Charles Deburau, in the Pierrot costume that his father had invented—highlights Félix's exceptional ability to convey human expression. By adapting the attitudes, gestures, and poses of this new variant on the well-known figure from the commedia dell'arte (ill. 100), the "Nadar" brothers demonstrated how photography, no less than painting, could reveal the abysses of the human heart. Tackling one of the mainstays of academic training, founded on the search for expressions representative of human emotions, the photographs obtained a gold medal at the World's Fair in 1855. Their qualities had already been lauded by Ernest Lacan in *La Lumière*: "Each one of these photographs constitutes an admirably rendered study of expression, doing as much honor to the talent of the

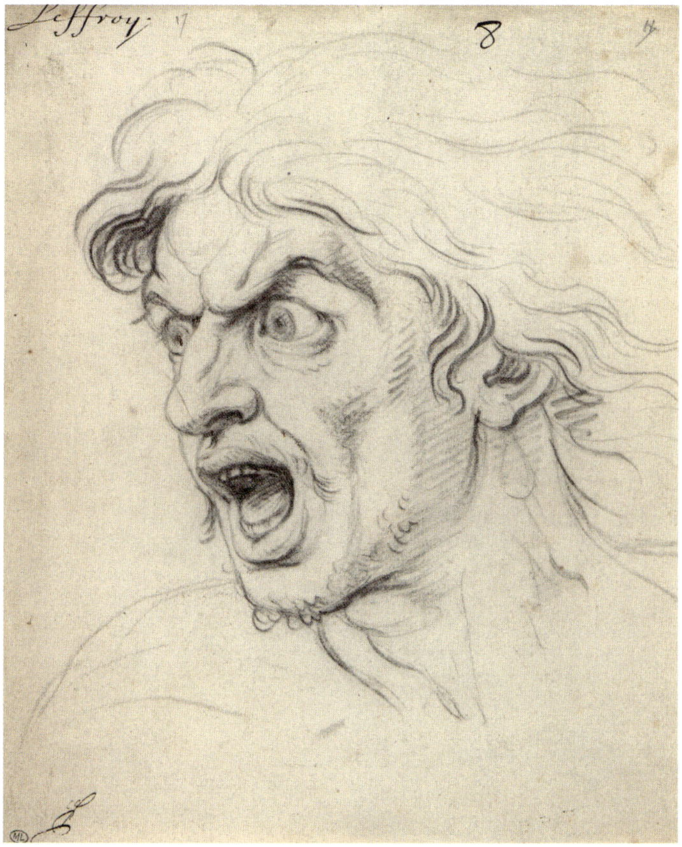

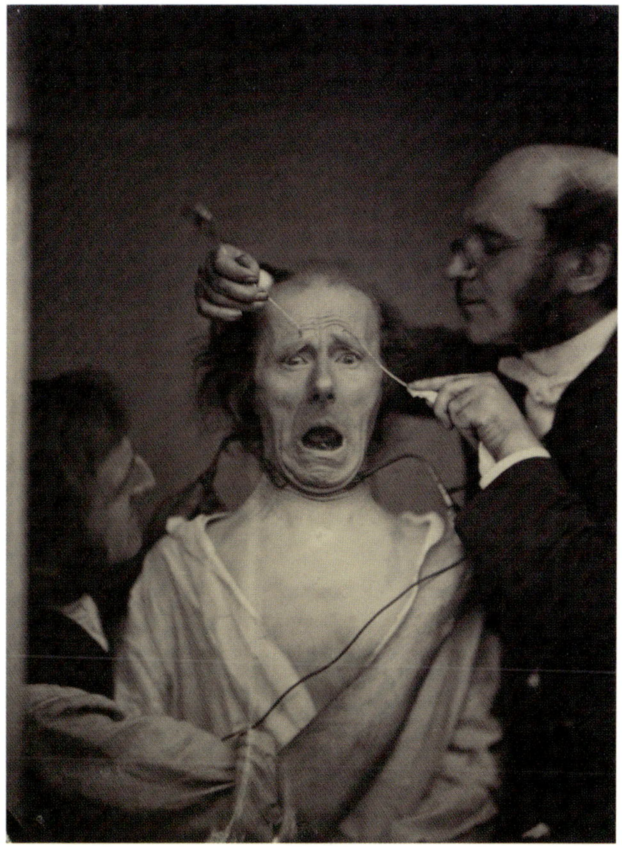

115. **Above, left:** Charles Le Brun, *Fear*, 1727, black chalk, Musée du Louvre, Paris.

116. **Above, right:** Adrien Tournachon and Guillaume Benjamin Duchenne de Boulogne, "Combined contraction of the neck and eyebrow muscles, associated with the voluntary opening of the lower jaw: fear mixed with pain, torture," 1855–56, salt print, École Nationale Supérieure des Beaux-Arts, Paris.

photographers who carried them out as to the inspired artist who acted as their model."[24] Having adopted the pseudonym of Nadar *jeune*, Adrien Tournachon was awarded the gold medal for the photographs; the resulting lawsuit, lodged by Félix, was an early sign of a photographer attempting to establish intellectual rights in his work. In 1857, Félix Tournachon finally won the right to exclusive use of the name Nadar.

The collaboration between Adrien and Dr. Duchenne de Boulogne in 1854 certainly bolstered interest in the expression of feelings and passions through photography. The doctor's research on muscular atrophy led him to embark on the anatomical investigation of living subjects, employing electricity as an instrument of physiological research for the first time. He turned to Tournachon with the aim of recording the results of these experiments in photographs that would thus represent human facial expressions in a wholly unprecedented form. Published in 1862 in *Mécanisme de la physionomie humaine, ou analyse électro-physiologique de l'expression des passions* (*The Mechanism of Human Physiognomy*), these images were later deployed in art schools as a sourcebook of genuine emotional responses.[25] They thus vouchsafed an ostensibly scientific corrective to the series of the passions by Charles Le Brun, which, in the forms of collections of engravings, remained a

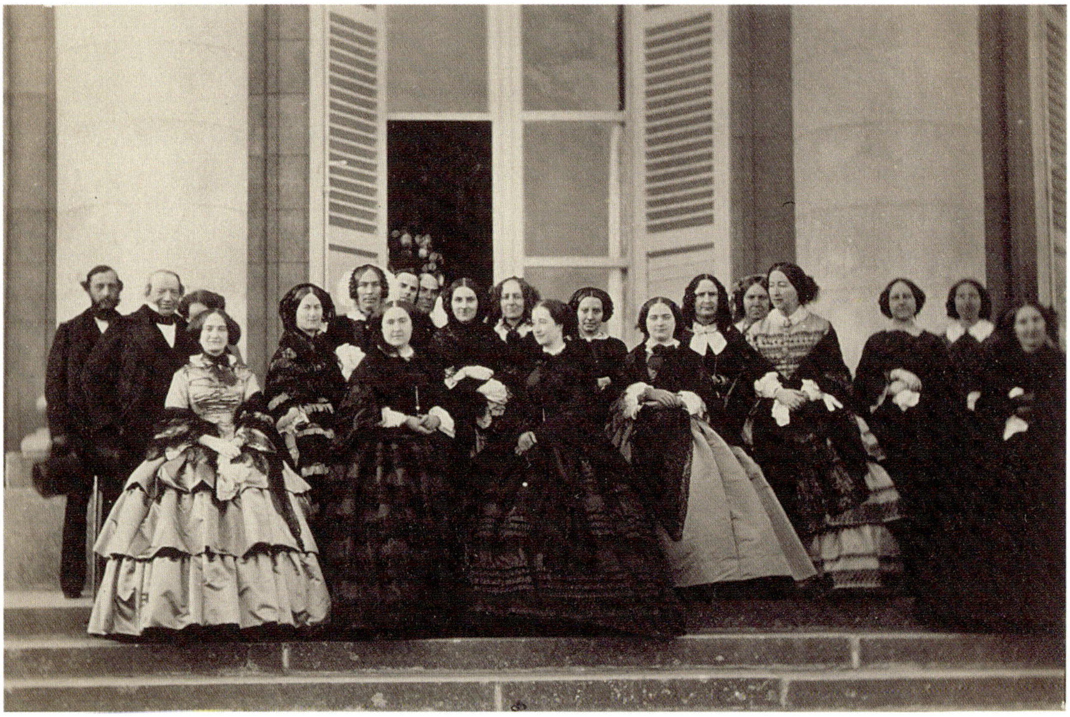

117. Edouard Delessert, "Empress Eugénie and Her Ladies-in-Waiting" (from the Third Series of 1856), October 1856, albumen print, Musée du Château, Compiegne.

stalwart in every art studio. In spite of its positivist character, Duchenne and Tournachon's images, centering on the face of the experimental subject, the light being judiciously deployed to reinforce the contrast between dark ground and the brightly illumined face, betrayed the influence of artistic predecessors on their composition (ills. 115–6).[26]

Royal and imperial portraits: photography earns its letters patent

If the daguerreotype presented an entire echelon of the population with unprecedented access to portraiture, thus modifying the perception of the self and its representation, photography also proposed new images of royalty, in France and Britain alike. Queen Victoria and Prince Albert had voiced interest in the invention as early as 1853, and had even agreed to act as patrons to the newly founded Photographic Society of London. The prince's librarian and founder member of the society, Dr. Ernst Becker, presented to the royal couple Roger Fenton, a trained painter (like so many others of his ilk, he had worked in the studio of Paul Delaroche in Paris) and a photographer since 1850. In 1854, he was chosen by the sovereign and her consort to take an extensive series of portraits of the royal family. Of exceptional quality, and moving in their depiction of the bonds of affection between the couple and their children, Fenton's photographs provide a glimpse into the private world of the British sovereigns (ill. 118).[27]

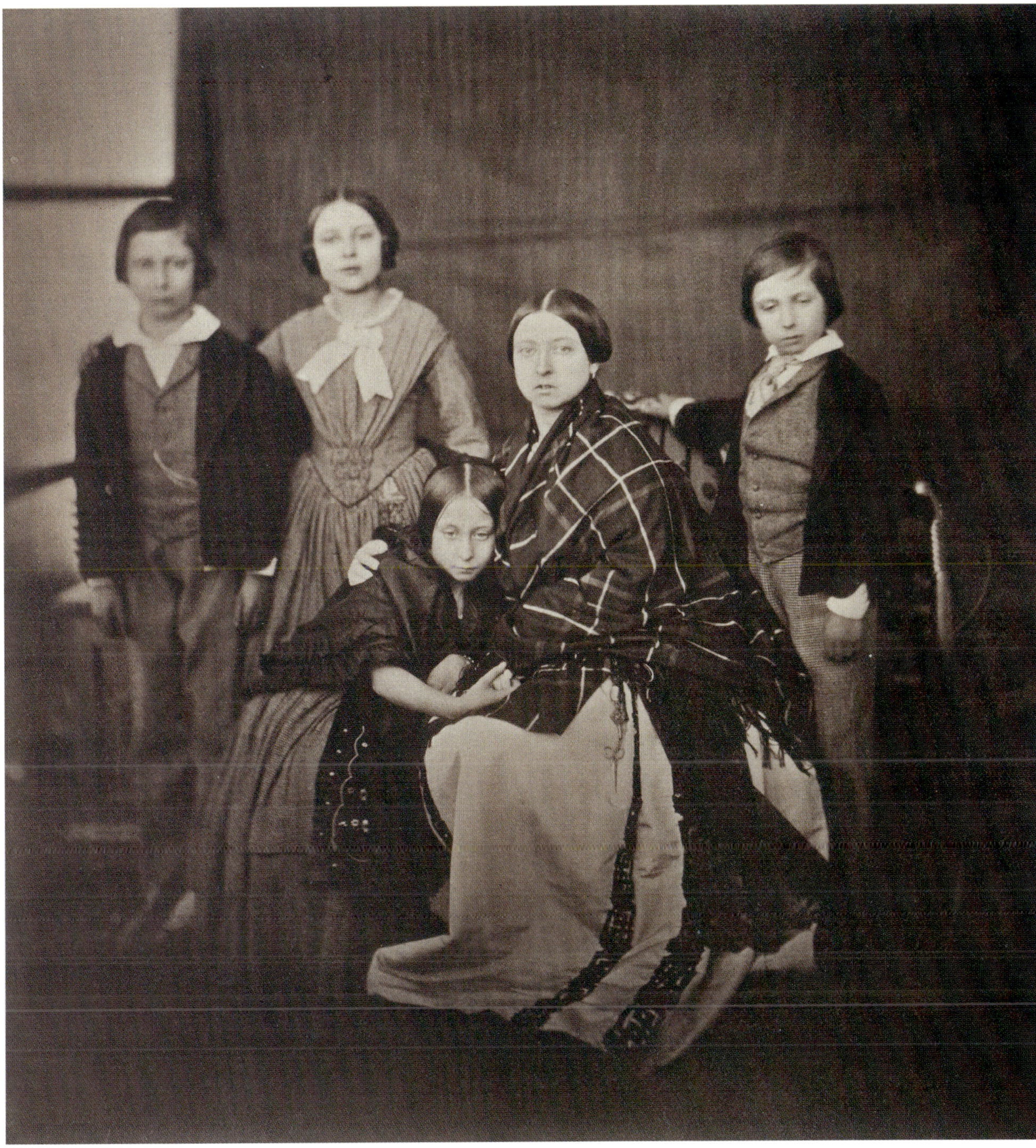

118. Roger Fenton, "The Prince of Wales, the Princess Royal, Princess Alice, Queen Victoria, Prince Alfred, February 8, 1854," 1854, carbon print, The Royal Collection, Windsor.

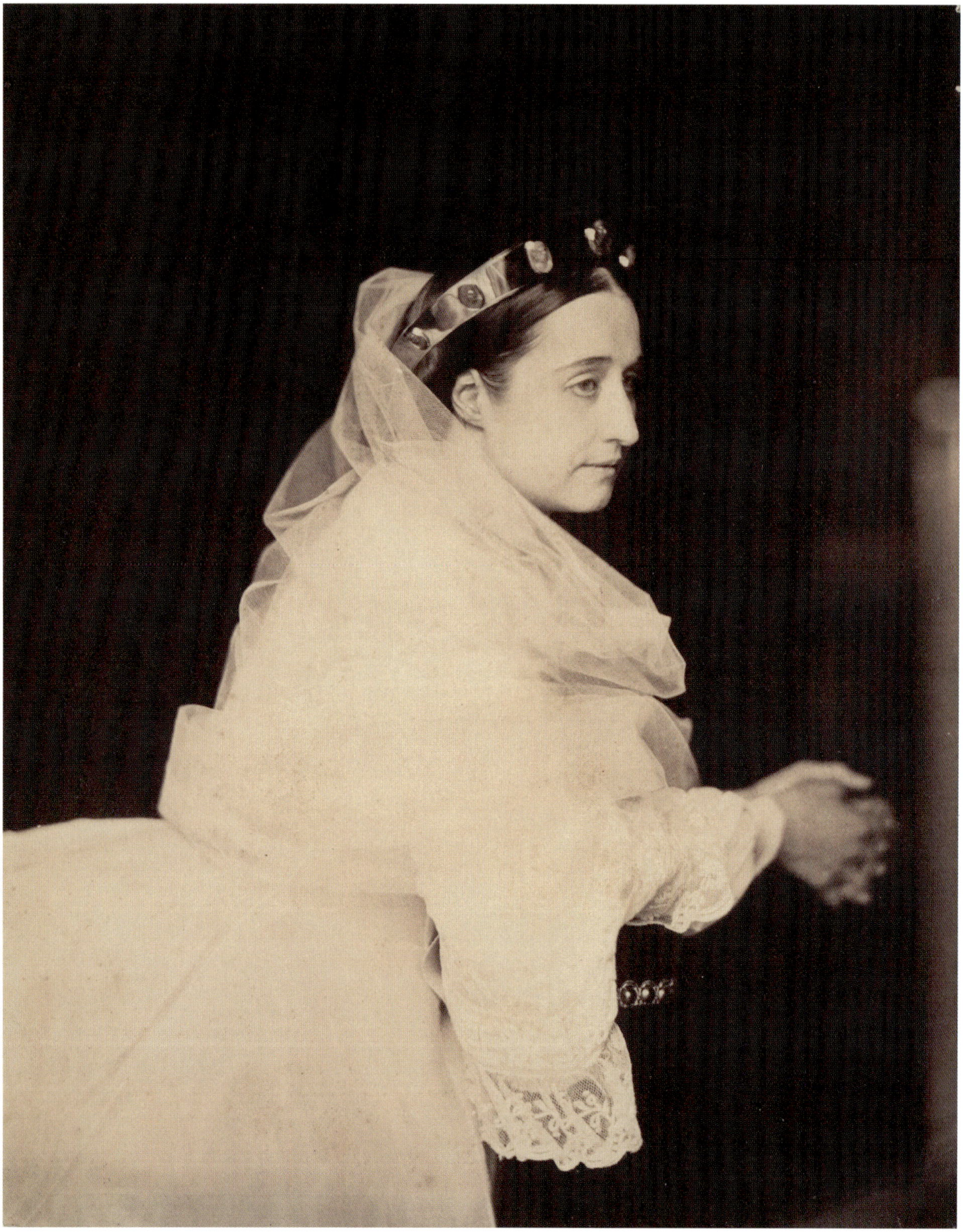

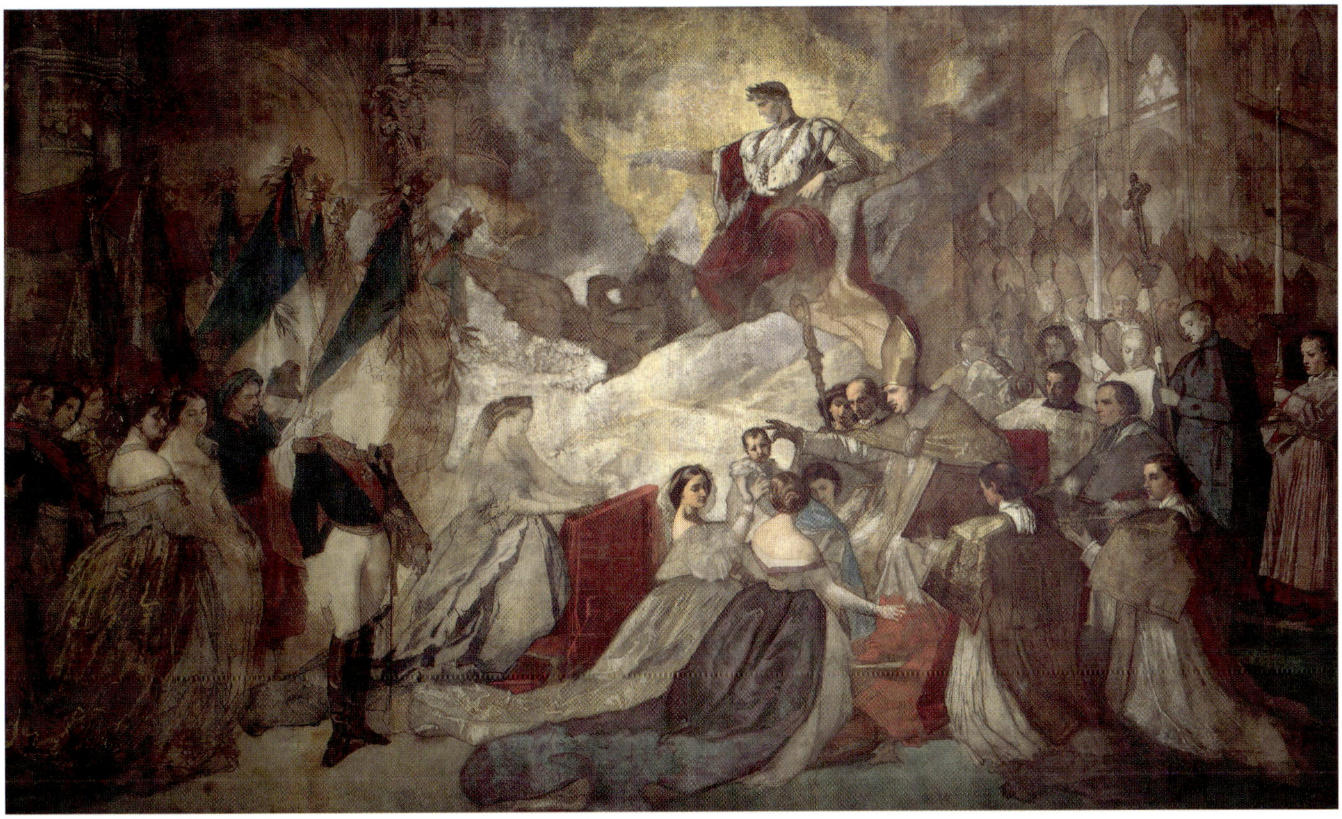

In France, Gustave Le Gray, probably as much by conviction as by opportunism, had shadowed Napoleon III's rise to power. He had been photographing Napoleon I's nephew since 1852, while he was still only prince-president, producing one of his very first official photographic portraits. These useful connections later earned him several commissions from the imperial court. In 1856, the painter Thomas Couture was appointed to carry out a portrait of the Empress Eugénie in commemoration of the birth and baptism of the prince imperial—a rare dynastic event. At Couture's behest, Le Gray (another fellow student in Delaroche's studio) took several photographs of great beauty as preparatory studies for a picture that in the end remained unfinished. The empress's pose and grave demeanor are identical to those bestowed on the august model in the painting (ills. 119–20).[28] Another familiar of the imperial court and a regular guest at the soirees in Compiègne, photographer Édouard Delessert, son of a Paris police commissioner, took several portraits of Eugénie and her ladies-in-waiting posing on the stairs in the Château de Compiègne. These elaborate compositions pay tribute to the glorious attire and adornments of the empress and her confidantes. Delessert's talent also extended to brilliant portrayals of society balls (ill. 117).

119. **Facing page:** Gustave Le Gray, "Empress Eugénie at Prayer at Saint-Cloud," 1856, albumen print, The Metropolitan Museum of Art, New York.

120. **Above:** Thomas Couture, *The Baptism of the Prince Imperial*, 1856, oil on canvas, Musée National de Compiègne.

The commercial success of *cartes de visite*

The photographic works of Nadar and of Gustave Le Gray, in particular, stimulated a critical approach to the artistic conception of portraiture that restated the fraught question of outer and inner resemblance in different terms. From the end of the 1850s, a process invented by André Adolphe Eugene Disdéri, the so-called *carte de visite* (visiting card), profoundly modified attitudes to the genre. Lodged on November 26, 1854, the patent "for the improvement of photography" made it possible to obtain ten photos at once, "so that the time and the expense required ... are divided by ten."[29] Photographic pictures could thus be marketed on a far larger scale than ever before. Disdéri went on to describe precisely its possible application to the portrait, underlining the potential of collodion, including a significant reduction in the time required for a sitting: "These new improvements in photography make it possible to obtain splendid photographs with very moderate outlay.... One of the first uses I made of these improvements was to apply them to the *carte-de-visite* portrait. To this end, I have the subject sit one or more times, since with collodion one or two seconds suffice, so the same person can pose in several positions without tiring. Lastly, I set up my negative with ten identical or different subjects, and then print them out on paper; when they are finished, I cut them out of the paper and stick them on visiting cards."[30] Disdéri established his photography showroom on the Boulevard des Italiens in Paris. Immense, and decked out with an eye to luxury, such venues became the symbol of a fashionable Second Empire, to which thronged not only members of the aristocracy and the upper-middle classes, but also figures from the worlds of literature and theater. Since acquiring the contents of Disdéri's studios in 1995, the Bibliothèque Nationale de France and the Musée d'Orsay have embarked on their systematic classification and study, which is gradually revealing the photographer's working methods. Some pictures appear to have been the subject of veritable mise-en-scènes—as with the portraits of the Countess Hatzfeld and her children, who appear and disappear from picture to picture (ill. 121).

Celebrities pinned in albums like butterflies in a display case

Although it only gave its inventor a brief glimpse of fame and fortune (Disdéri died ruined, losing his money after several ill-judged decisions), his process proved a remarkable and durable success. The vogue for the *carte-de-visite* portrait was not limited to the family circle: people glued into albums not only their nearest and dearest, but also celebrities of the time whose features and expressions soon became more familiar than ever. One critic voiced supposed dismay in 1860: "Today,

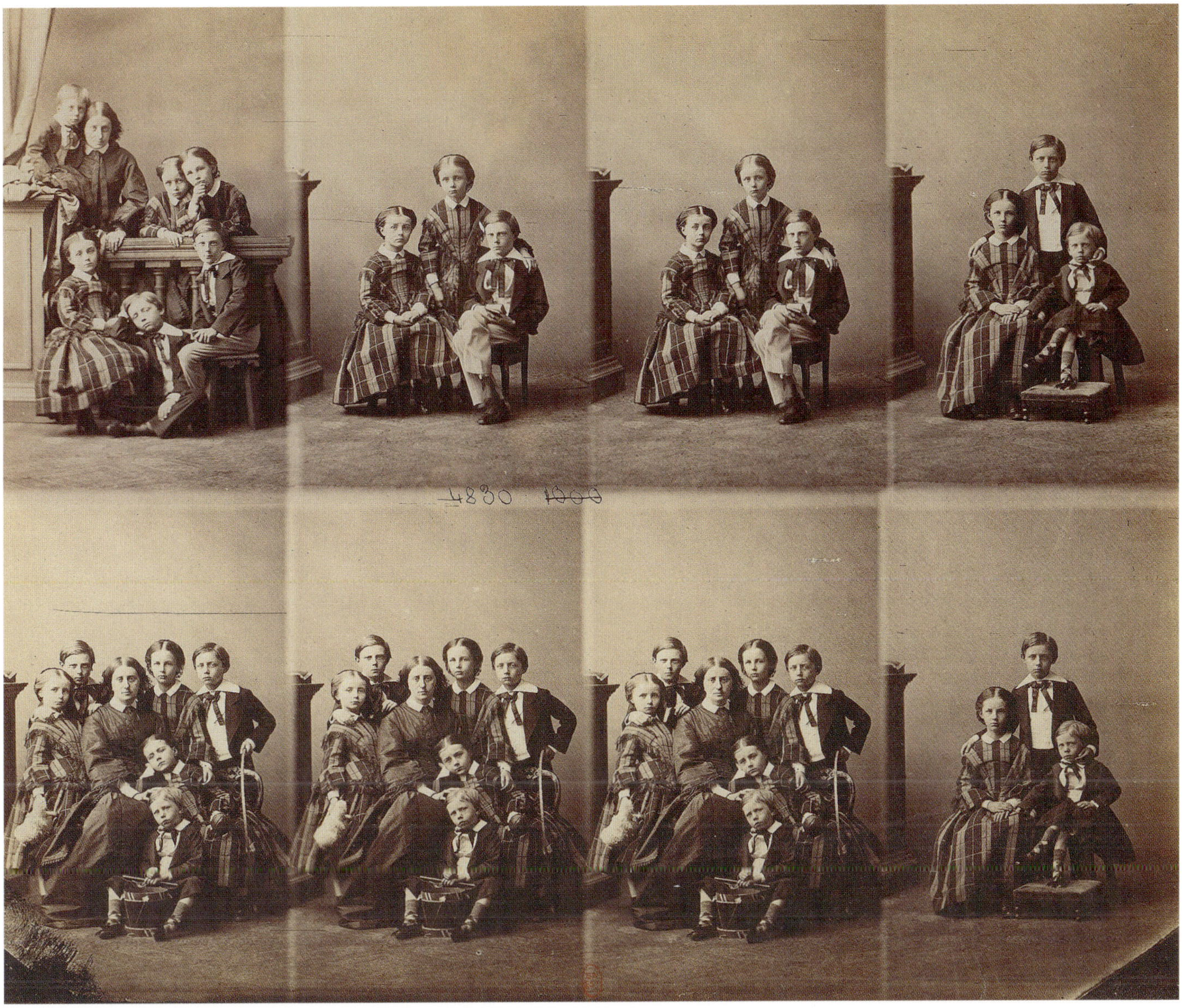

121. André Adolphe Eugène Disdéri, "Countess Hatzfeld and her Children," 1857, albumen print, Bibliothèque Nationale de France, Paris.

it's gone too far. Everyone who is anyone in the arts or in letters, in the aristocracy, the military, at the bar, in finance, theater, government, administration, or demi-monde has their phizz stuck on a little piece of cardboard, sold by the dozen, by the score, or by the gross, and packed off to every town in France and Europe."[31] Or, as Alexandre Dumas senior nicely put it, celebrities could now be found in family albums like so many "butterflies pinned in a display case." The *carte de visite* amounted to a genuine social phenomenon, granting the image a new status and raising questions (still pertinent today) about the disclosure of the self and the rights of a person to their image. It also had far-reaching consequences on the artistic perception of the portrait. The poses adopted by sitters in photographs remained those codified by the painted portrait in the early years of the nineteenth century; the choice of attitudes was nourished especially by models from Ingres. Similarly, if the decors of photographic studios were not invariably as luxurious as those of Disdéri on Boulevard des Italiens, far from it, they still often sought to ape the plush, middle-class interiors of their time, and photograph their customers against a flattering if stereotyped setting. The enduring supremacy of an aesthetics of clarity and precision that banished all but the clearest focus paralleled the precepts of academic painting from which contemporary taste was only slowly freeing itself. After vying with painting for so long—and with considerable success in respect of quantity and commercial reward—photography ended up endorsing the perennial model.

Portraits, types, figures

The interest Pablo Picasso expressed for the *carte de visite* at the turn of the twentieth century (his archives contain a vast and varied collection) is indicative of its ambivalent status. To Picasso, the *carte de visite* appeared as an outdated frame of reference, deriving from a long-vanished pictorial aesthetics (that which many years previously had sought to dissociate itself from photography), thus presenting his painting style with a homothetic model, appealing in its potential for transcendence and transgression.[32] Disdéri's invention had also shifted the border between type, portrait, and figure, by disseminating images of men and women unknown beyond their immediate environment, anonymous figures that could readily serve as typical representatives of their region, trade, or condition. Photographic images of this kind were likely to change status, genre even, once they were extracted, physically and morally, from their original milieu. Removed from the village or district where they were taken, the portrayal became a type, an element of collection or comparison, to be copied or imitated, less for the features of the model than for some characteristic of physique or attire. Its use added a further dimension to the construction of human typology initiated by lithography at the turn of the nineteenth century.

From resemblance to identity

The *carte de visite* also paved the way for a method of legal identification. Thanks to an image bank containing a record of a vast number of subjects, the process offered the possibility to undertake the study of facial features and advance research that was attempting to systemize the supposed links between physical appearance and criminality.[33] It would also offer a tool of identification that could in time become a foolproof method of telling individuals apart: "One of the most

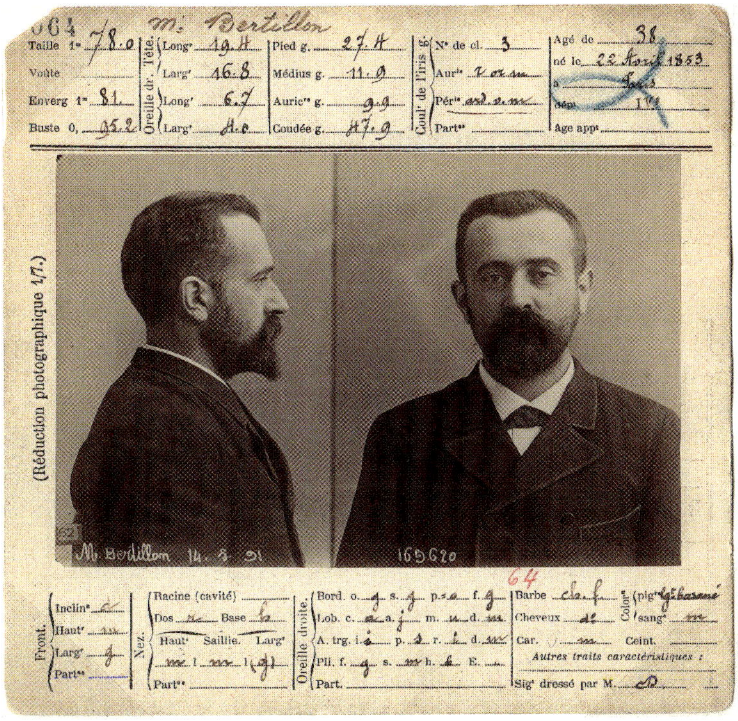

122. Alphonse Bertillon, "Example of an Anthropometric Record, Alphonse Bertillon," 1892, two albumen prints, Archives of the Préfecture de Police, Paris.

irrefutable proofs of identity is the exact representation of the features of the condemned man in a photograph."[34] The arguments rolled out against the resemblance of an individual to his photographic image were identical to those previously marshaled in condemning the daguerreotype portrait in general. Those who advocated the establishment of a photographic database of the entire population were countered by detractors who once again argued for the irreducibility of the human face. Too changeable to be captured in a portrait, they contended that "such a method would besides all too often prove ineffective; that nothing is more fleeting than the human physiognomy, the least modification in facial features transforming the appearance of a man's face; that the age of those condemned to lengthy sentences, who are the most dangerous, would anyhow render photographic images useless."[35]

The development in the late nineteenth century of a system of anthropometry by Alphonse Bertillon was based chiefly on photography. He had proposed that every police inspector be issued with a camera so as to be able to include photographic prints in his report.[36] Overcoming a raft of objections and misgivings, the system eventually carried all before it: the use of the "ID photograph" soon became so widespread that the notion of "proof of identity" has grown into a tautology. In the few decades from 1840 to 1890 the photographic portrait changed paradigm; physical and psychological resemblance was replaced by the utopia of identity; for the authorities, a man was reducible to that intangible component of his selfhood, his depiction on a photograph. Like a cast, a photograph—even though its supporters had, in the name of interpretation, tried to draw a cast-iron distinction between them—increasingly resembled an *impression*, though one preeminently subjected to the representational images of its time (ill. 122).

Painters and the challenge of photography

Over the decades, photography gradually gained predominance in portraiture. Above and beyond commercial success, Daguerre's prediction had come true: any representation betraying too literal a physical resemblance now seemed subordinated to the aesthetics of photography. Confusion between a photograph *from life* and a photographic reproduction of a painting that enshrined the primacy of the drawn line furthered the assimilation of painted portrait and portrait photograph: the artistic renewal of the portrait was again conveyed by transformation, by transgression even. From the 1860s, artists distanced their work from classic photographic models by increasing their canvases to the size of a history painting or royal portrait. Photography had also embraced the traditional artificial markers (pose, attitudes, attire, decor) of psychological penetration. The pictorial translation of the temperament of model and creator—in an idiom increasingly marked by an exacerbated expressionism—was being channeled into visual distortion. The process had its roots, not only in the use of color (a no-go area for photography for a few decades still), but also in a synthetic conception of pose that objectified the model and laid the stress instead on the act of painting; or else the adoption of new formats such as the *kakemono*, inspired by Japanese art, in which the figure, trapped within the frame of its depiction, was elongated into a novel decorative motif. Psychological likenesses thus retreated before a symbolist or expressionist portraiture, the real elements receding before pure pictorial invention (ill. 124).

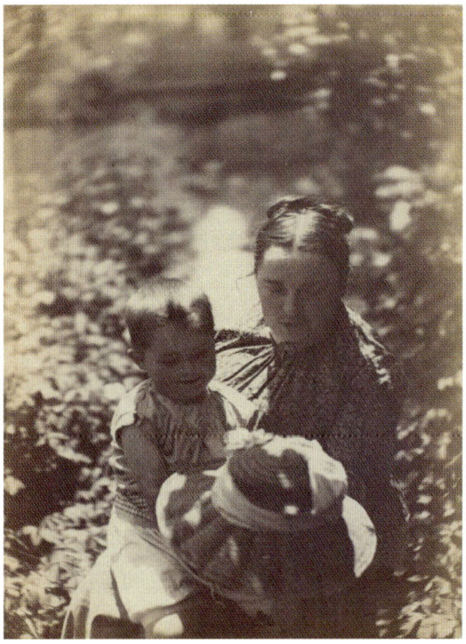

123. Gabriel Loppé, "Maman Grand and Marguerite," c. 1885–90, aristotype, Musée d'Orsay, Paris.

Soft focus and blurring

Portrait photography had long centered on the search for precision and clarity, and hence, by its very nature, a blur amounted to a photographic catastrophe; indeed, the photographer's skill was gauged by his ability to avoid indeterminacy thanks to a control over exposure time and clever lighting. Rejected by commercial photographers, out-of-focus effects were sought after by artists intent on affirming their creativity. As the use of the camera within the family unit continued to increase, such effects surfaced as indicators of intimacy and emotional bonds (ill. 123). The family album containing portraits of friends and relations gathered together by a generally female hand created a new level of familiarity with the personal image; in lockstep

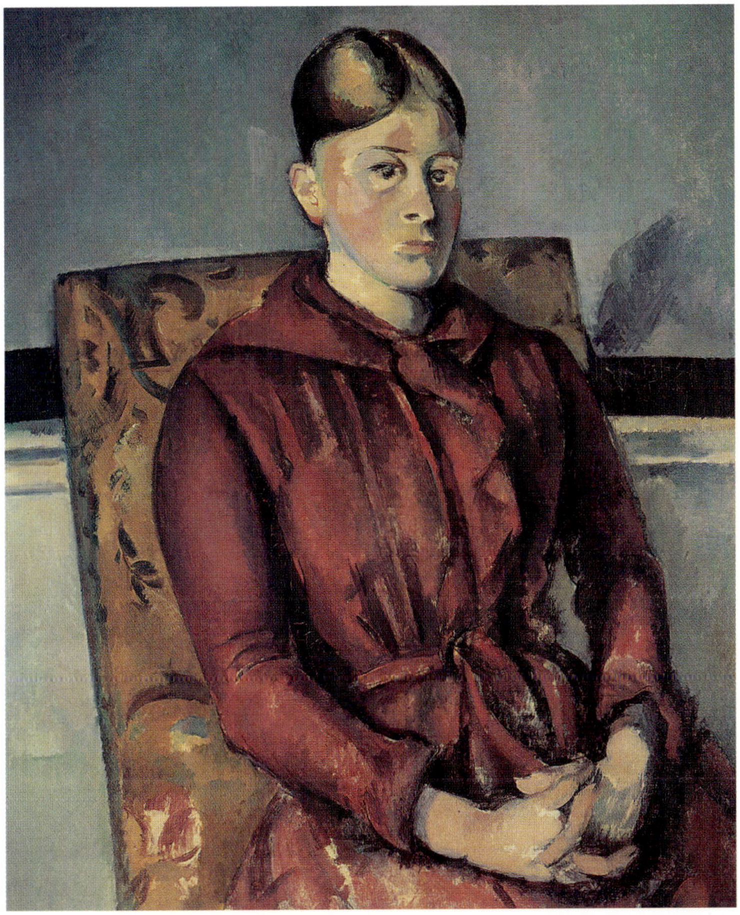

with a narrow codification of social interaction, this variant was essentially comprised of images orchestrated to reflect an idealized conception of family life.[37] The blurring and hence the softening or even partial obliteration of facial features certainly limited their identifying function, but it recalled the romantic conception of portraiture, sensitive rather than exact and closer to recollection than authentication. The romantic author Nodier wrote: "I couldn't quite recall her features as a whole [those of his beloved Amélie], but did I even need to? Who has ever seen the features of the woman he loved as a whole? Who has ever been able to remember them? Though I do not care for portraits, I have, however, to give some idea of Amélie."[38]

The works of the British photographer Julia Margaret Cameron during the 1860s are a rare combination of the intimate and aesthetic dimensions of the soft-focus image. Born into the British gentry and having lived for a long time in India, Cameron started practicing photography rather late in life, when she was around fifty. In all probability the result of an accident in her early trials, her photographs seem to have been taken beneath a piece of "gauze," reinforcing their

124. Paul Cézanne, *Madame Cézanne in a Yellow Armchair*, c. 1895, oil on canvas, The Art Institute, Chicago.

125. **Page 170:** Julia Margaret Cameron, "Alfred Tennyson with a Book," 1865, albumen print, National Media Museum, Bradford.

126. **Page 171:** Edgar Degas, *Princess Pauline von Metternich*, 1865, oil on canvas, The National Gallery, London.

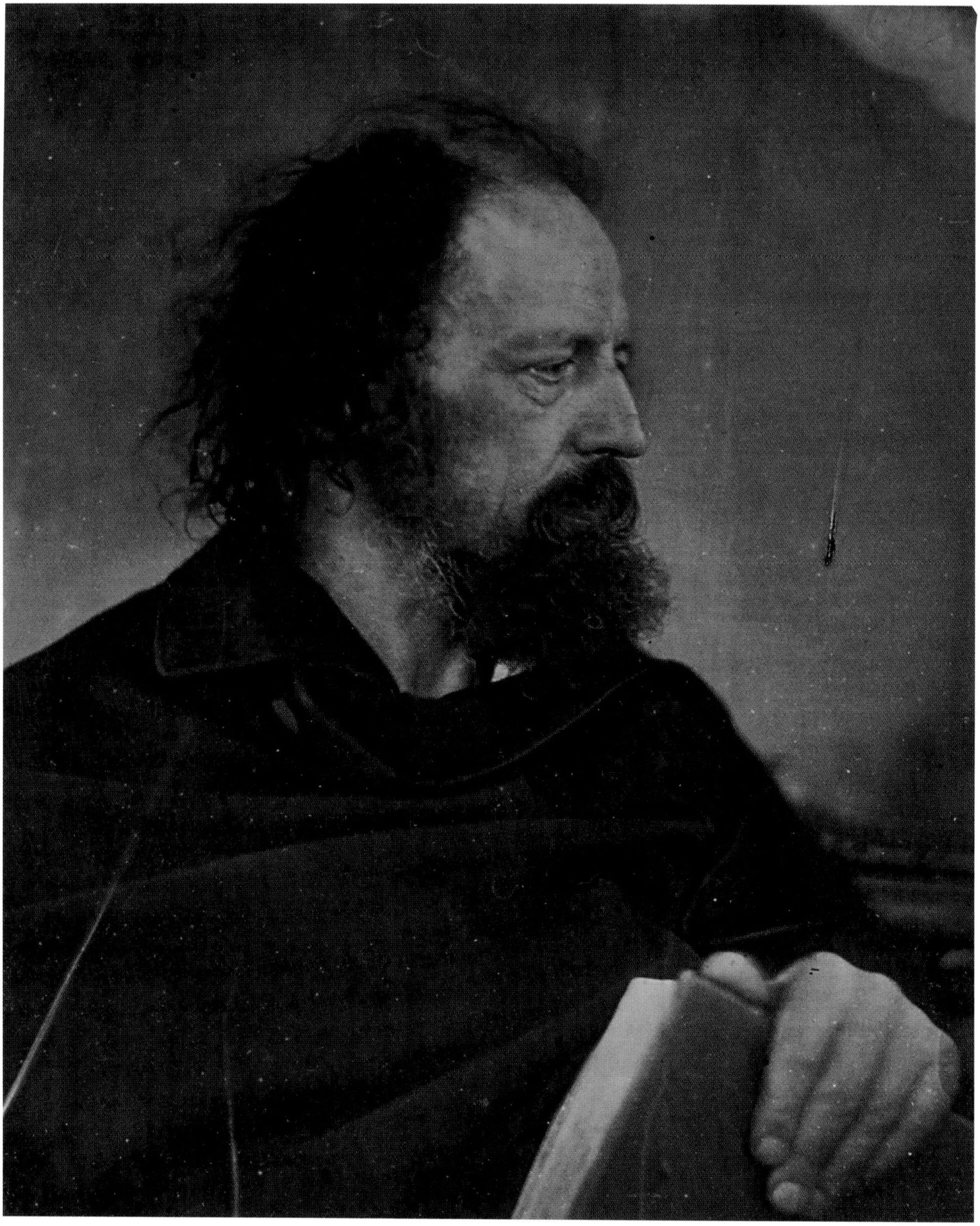

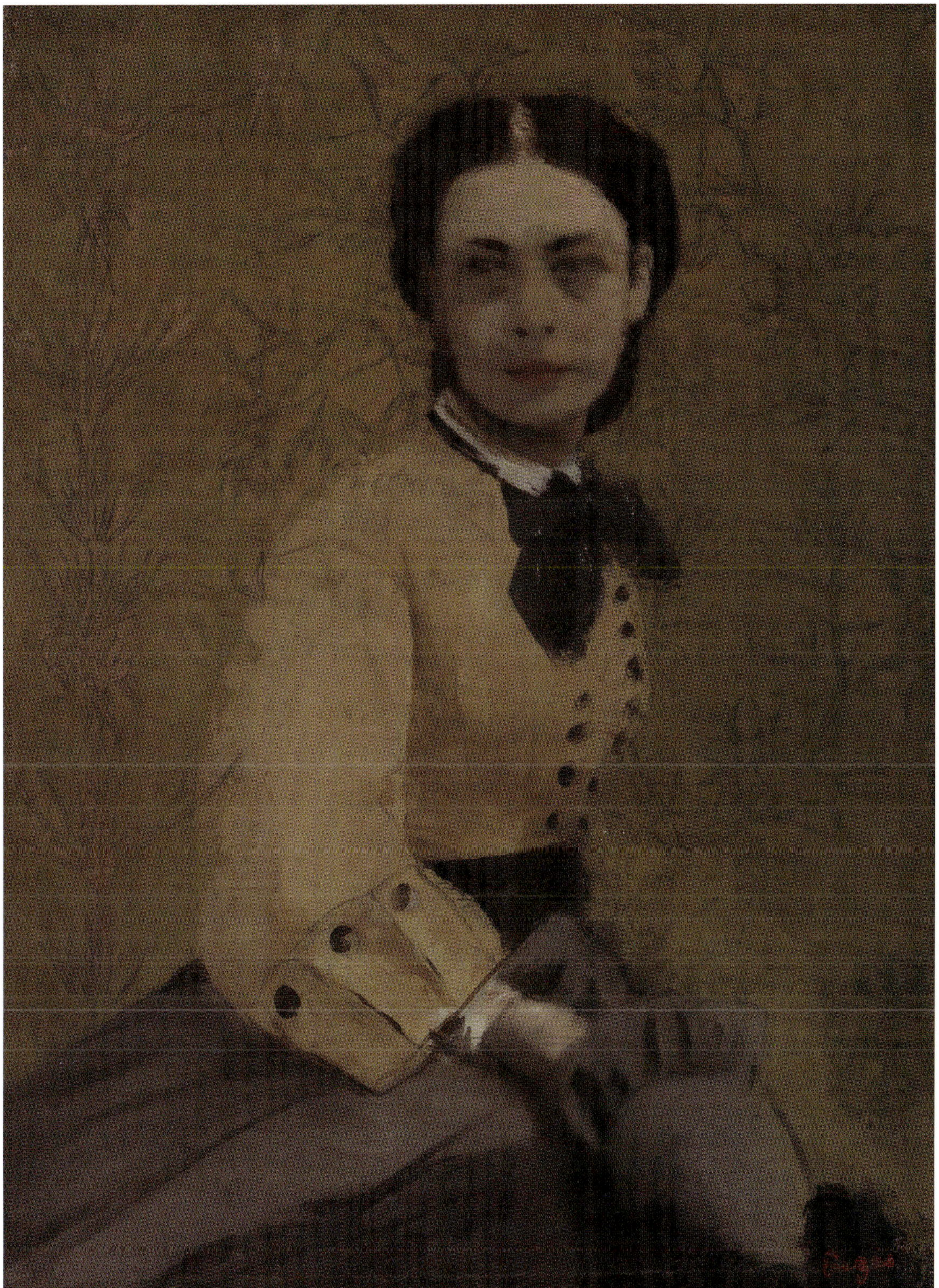
Degas

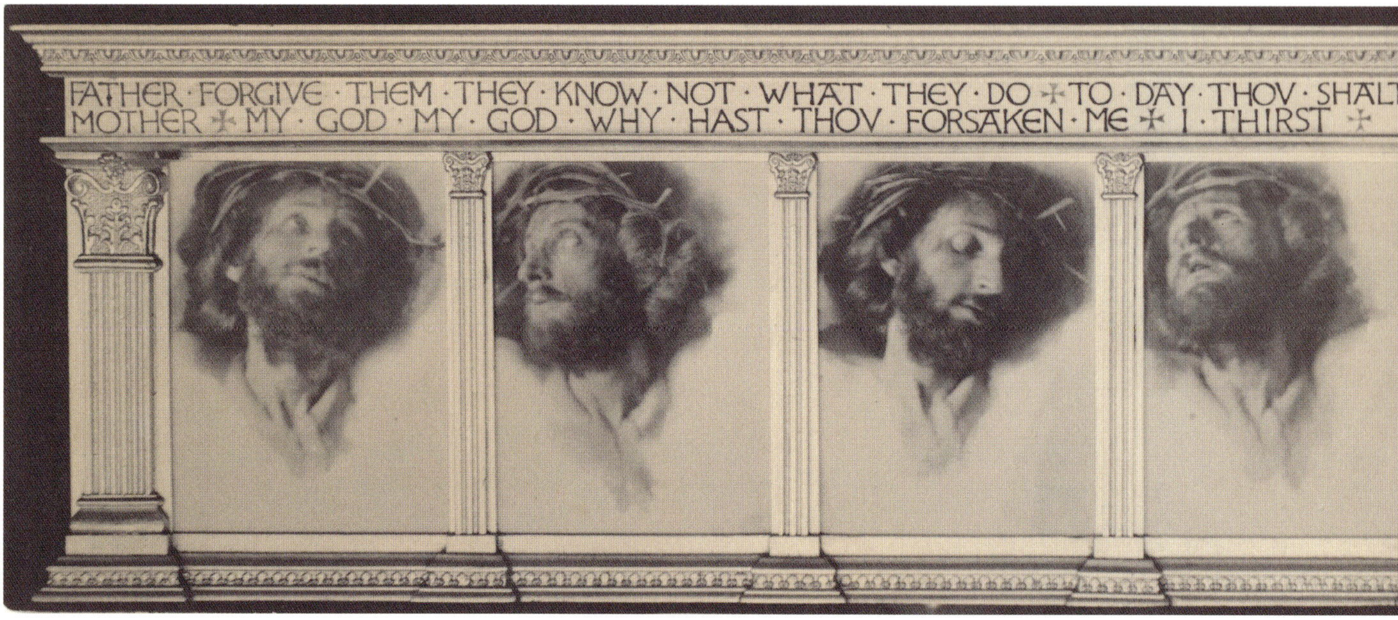

127. Frederick Holland Day, "The Seven Last Words," 1898, platinum print, The Metropolitan Museum of Art, New York.

symbolist atmosphere. A close associate of many poets and painters of the period, members of the Pre-Raphaelite Brotherhood, in particular, she photographed several visitors to her house on the Isle of Wight, producing straight portraits as well as scenes inspired by Shakespeare, Milton, or the poems of her friend, Alfred Tennyson (ill. 125). Exhibited and published, several of her photographs exemplify an aesthetic at odds with representational exactitude. Published by Alfred Stieglitz in his review *Camera Work* from 1901, they exerted a telling influence on the pictorialists.[39]

Banished from trade work, soft focus or blurring is a harbinger of that pictorial aesthetic by which painters make use of fortuitous accidents: integrating photographic errors in his canvas, such artists would distort their models. When Edgar Degas painted the portrait of Princess Pauline von Metternich, wife of the ambassador of the Austro-Hungarian Empire to Paris, he took as his starting point a *carte de visite* taken by Disdéri for which the couple had posed together. Veiling the face of the princess (intelligently unattractive, her contemporaries called her), he blurred her features slightly, just as in a shaky photograph (ill. 126).

The pictorial reaction of photographers

In a reaction against what appeared as the aesthetics of the photographic medium, submission to the exact reproduction of reality, many photographers in Europe and in the United States sought to adopt models from modern painting in their creations. Often gathering together into clubs and societies that began staging exhibitions in the late 1880s and advocating

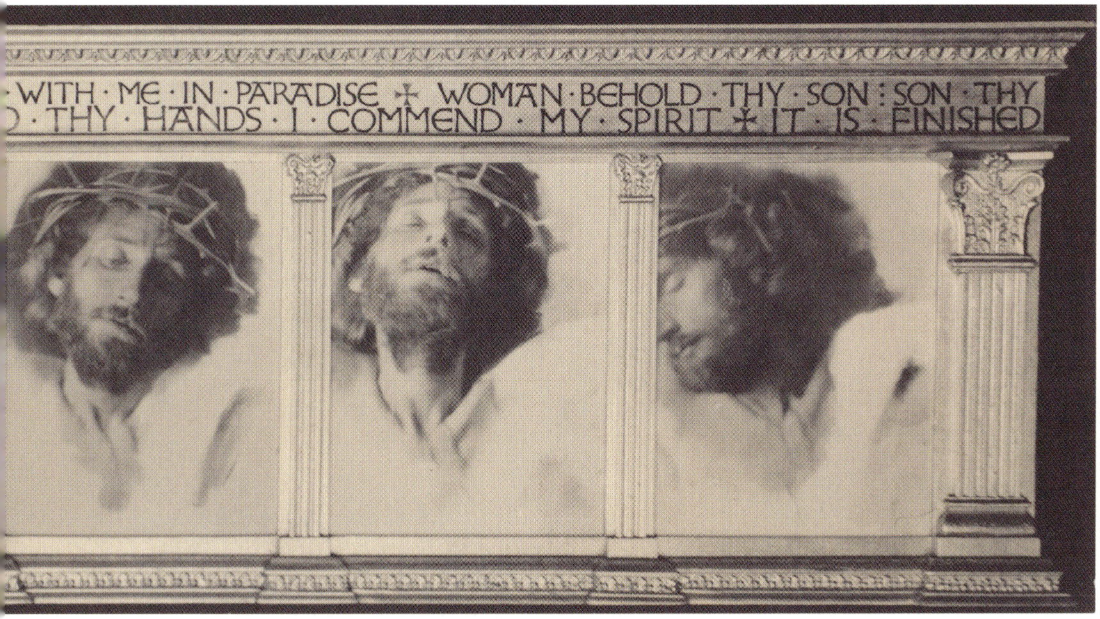

an aesthetic conception of photography, the pictorialists were opposed to its commercial practice. They created images close to symbolist painting that deliberately co-opted photographic processes designed to represent an idea and attain the immaterial. Receptive to the decorative impulse in much art of their period, they also absorbed the influence of *Japanism*. By using subdued lighting, by printing different versions of one and the same negative, by retouching the print after pulling, images were obtained that refer explicitly to contemporary pictorial codes (ills. 128–29). Between 1895 and 1898, Frederick Holland Day embarked on a plan to depict the life of Christ, from Annunciation to Passion, in photography. Acting as his own model, he altered his appearance (growing a beard) and even changed his lifestyle (he fasted rigorously) to achieve the desired effect. Owing as much to the drama and painting of the era as to Scripture, these highly theatrical self-portraits transfigured the art of photography (ill. 127).[40] The pictorialist movement petered out at the end of second decade of the twentieth century, leaving the path clear for a "pure" photographic aesthetics—the "Straight Photography" embraced by Paul Strand. But pictorialist portraiture underlines the complexity of the relationship between photography and painting in the context of a genre by now dominated by the former.

Soft-focus became a properly pictorial quality, wherever reference to a romantic aesthetics founded on recollection seconded the sense of representational rupture. Édouard Manet painted Stéphane Mallarmé, cigarette in hand, the smoke smudging the outline of the writer's face: thus the portrait takes on all the vivacity of a personal memory.

128. **Page 174:** Constant Puyo, "Decorative Profile," c. 1900, bichromate gum, Musée Nicéphore-Niépce, Chalon-sur-Saône.

129. **Page 175:** Paul Haviland, "Florence Petersen in a Floral Kimono," c. 1909, cyanotype, Musée d'Orsay, Paris.

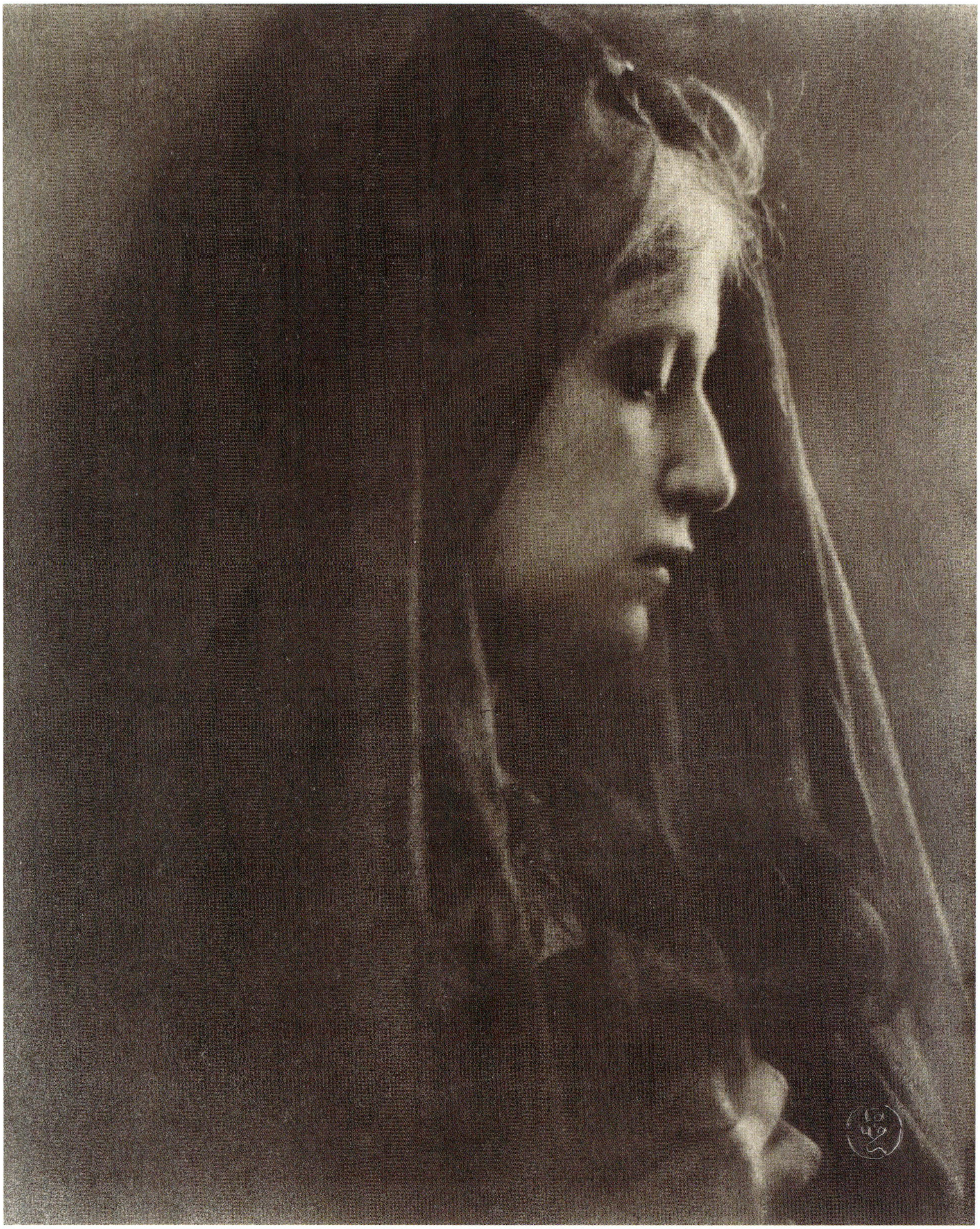

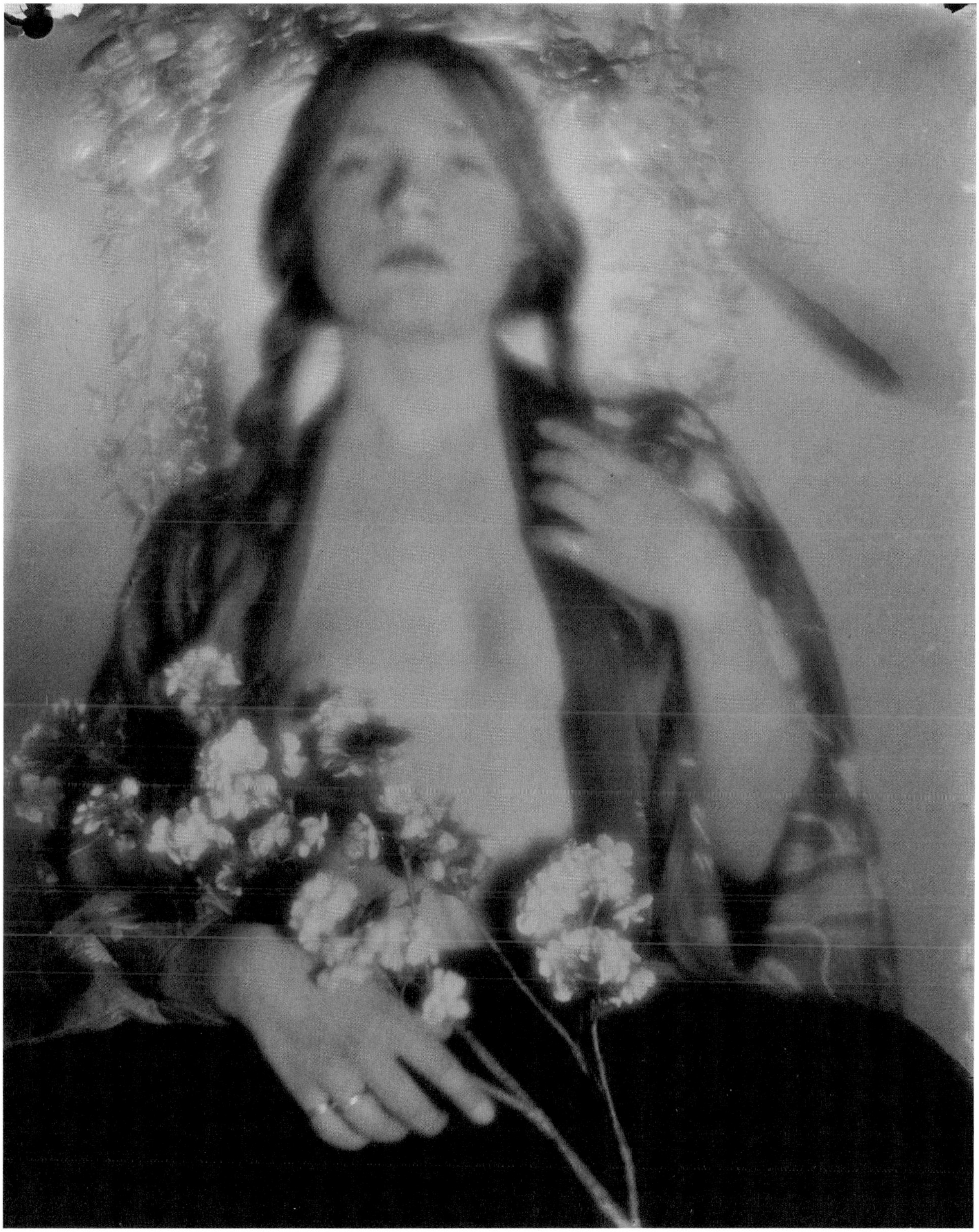

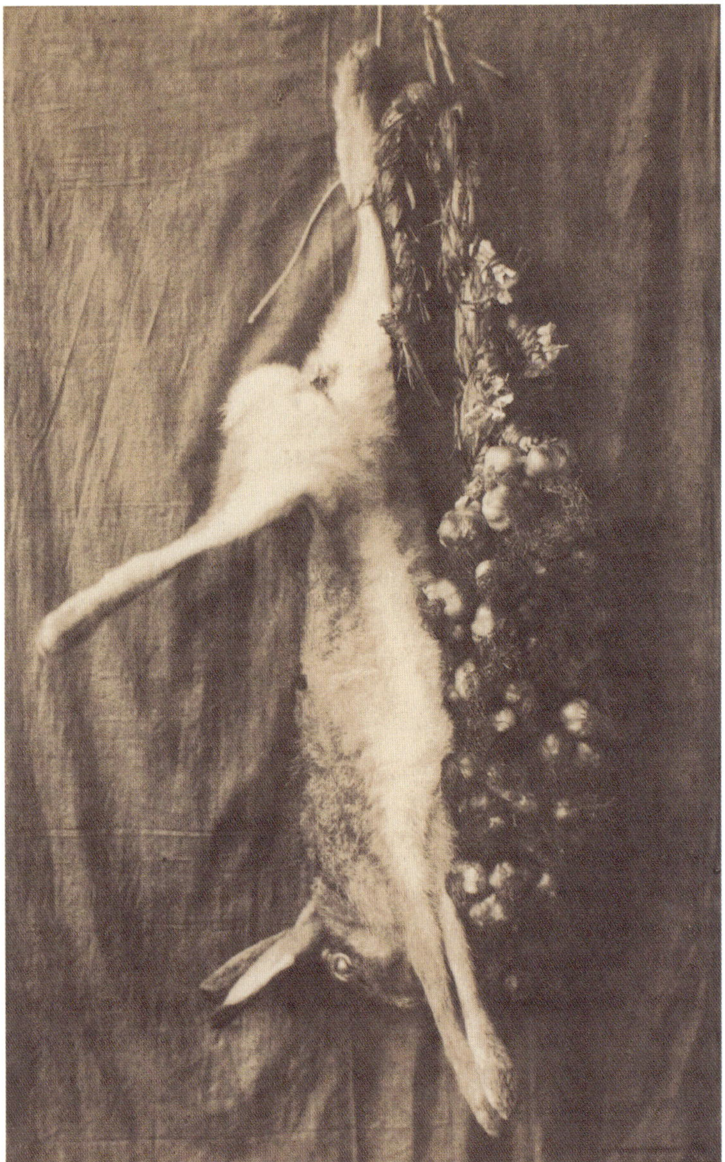

"These kinds of compositions, in addition to the general techniques of the art, possess their own peculiar brand of poetry. For one can also provide a good likeness of the elegant profile of a vase, of the grace of a garland; the art of drawing a cloth is no more arbitrary than that of drawing a figure. I just find that the rules are less obvious, more secret."[1]

STILL LIFE

In his *Salon de 1767*, Denis Diderot thus underlines the singular charm of painted still lifes, the poetry of their compositions. It is an approach that foreshadows a move away from the unfavorable view of the Académie des Beaux-Arts, which, since Félibien, had relegated the genre to the lowest level of the hierarchy, since it required only the reproduction of *inanimate* nature. A connoisseur of the works of Jean-Siméon Chardin, whom he described as a magician, the critic hailed the extraordinary talent and meticulousness of the artist when it came to depicting inanimate objects. In Diderot's view, such an artist went beyond mere resemblance and had sought—rather than the mere mimetic representation of things—to bring out their grace and subtlety, the delicate melancholy of their forms and arrangements.

Seemingly so uncomplicated, in respect of aesthetic judgment the genre presented a number of puzzles. The first is encapsulated in the name itself. Vasari called works by Giovanni da Udine "*cose naturali*": thus the object was seen as identical with its transcription. In the seventeenth century, the term *stilleven*—"calm" or "still life"—appeared in the Netherlands to refer to "pieces with flowers, fruit, and fish." It was taken up in English and in German (*still Leben* or *Stillleben*). Such expressions treat nature as a living thing. Endowing it with specific qualities, of tranquility and peace, they call upon an idea of duration; selecting a specific state among the elements implies that the calm they exalt in the painting followed some earlier disorder in the arrangement and preceded their subsequent decay. The name thus reflects the symbolic, religious, and meditative components of pictures of objects. Such assemblies, combining natural and manufactured objects, the produce of the land and of the sea, conjure up the diversity of the world and the transience of life, symbolized by the fragile state of the things the painter portrays in one brief instant of their blooming. In France, the term *nature morte*, taken up in

130. **Facing page:** Eugène Cuvelier, "Still Life with Hare and Garlic Cloves," c. 1862, salt print, Musée d'Orsay, Paris.

Italian (*natura morta*), gained currency in the eighteenth century, although Diderot still preferred to write of *nature inanimée*. In the course of the seventeenth century the genre was taken up widely in the form of the Vanity (or Vanitas), where sacred or religious connotations outweigh the uncomplicated representation of objects.[2] In Spain, they are defined by the rugged, simple nobility of the term *bodegón*, which implies something like "pantry piece."

Illusionism

The second complexity underlying still life is due to the criteria used for its appreciation and evaluation. The genre had become indissociable from virtuosity with the brush. If one can believe the anecdote concerning the well-meaning rivalry between the painters Parrhasius and Zeuxis, recounted by Pliny, this was already the case in antiquity: "[Parrhasius,] it is said, entered into a pictorial contest with Zeuxis, who represented some grapes, painted so naturally that the birds flew towards the spot where the picture was exhibited. Parrhasius, on the other hand, exhibited a curtain, drawn with such singular truthfulness, that Zeuxis, elated with the judgment which had been passed upon his work by the birds, haughtily demanded that the curtain should be drawn aside to let the picture be seen. Upon finding his mistake ... he admitted that he had been surpassed, for that whereas he himself had only deceived the birds, Parrhasius had deceived him, an artist."[3] The quality of the representation results from the painter's skill in weaving an illusion; still life thus merges with trompe l'oeil. Pliny's anecdote became a commonplace; in 1781, commenting on a piece by Gerard Van Spaendonck, *Picture Representing a Vase Carved in Low Relief, Filled with Flowers and Fruit* (private collection, Paris), Diderot reports the remarks made by the young Duke of Enguien, then nine years old: "[He] stood enchanted before the fine vase of flowers. He was introduced to the artist: *Ah, Monsieur*, said the young prince with gracious and ingenuous wit, *would you be so kind as to let me have one of them?*"[4]

Thus, the pictorial representation of objects was inextricably linked to the idea of a technical tour de force, of control and mastery. Virtuosity, however, should not be the unique aim; too great a resemblance in a canvas endangers its qualities of insight, the melancholy depth of its subject. The challenge, in which Chardin excelled, was "not to smell too much of the palette," but to achieve an agreeable balance (ill. 131). By the beginning of the nineteenth century, still life had lost the cachet accorded it by critics in the previous century; the genre seemed consigned to the lady's boudoir or limited to flower painters. Commentators on the Salons seldom even distinguished it as a category in their accounts.

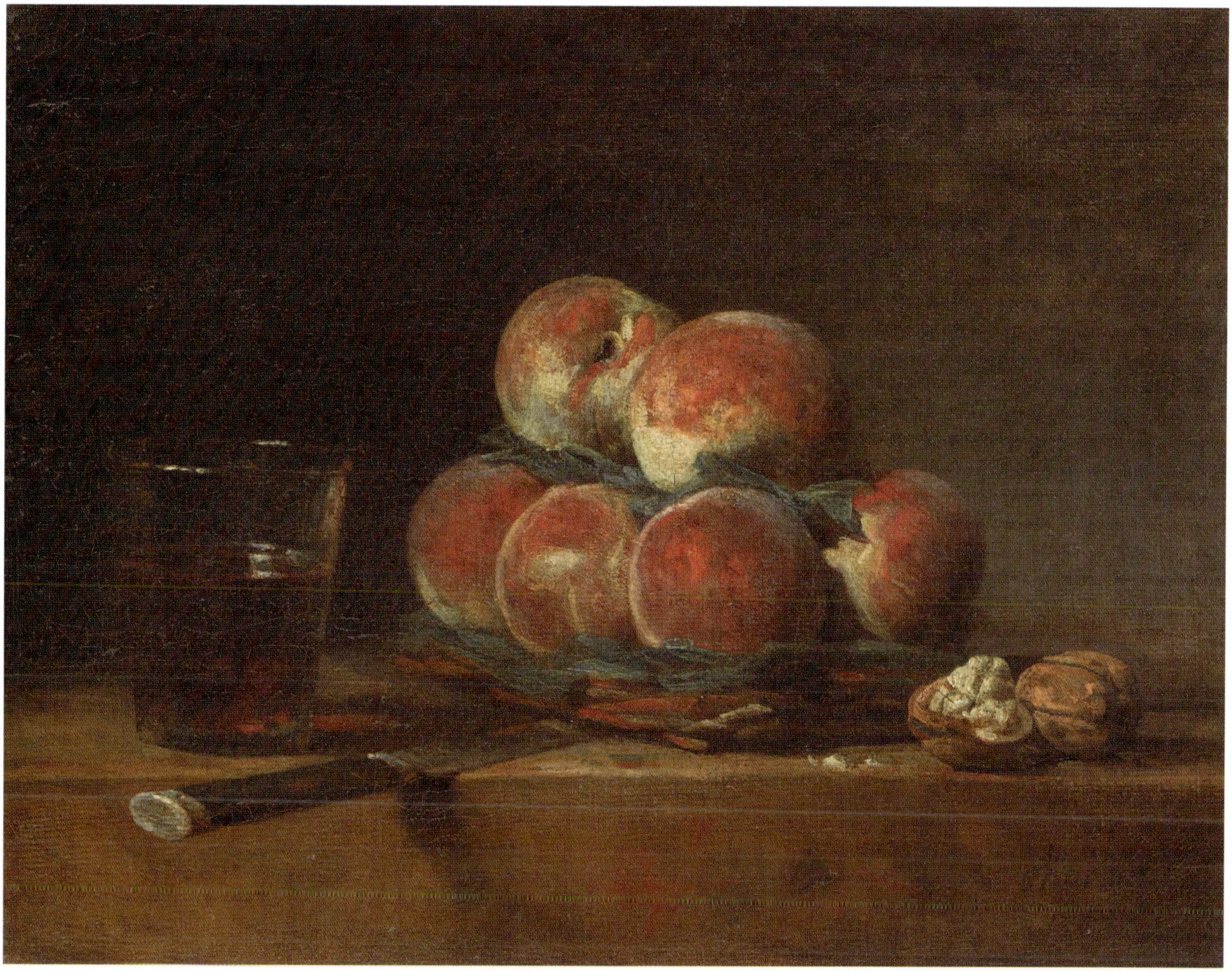

131. Jean-Siméon Chardin, *Basket of Peaches*, 1768, oil on canvas, Musée du Louvre, Paris.

One of the earliest photographic subjects

The reproduction of objects was naturally among the first photographic subjects.[5] Every major contributor to the invention tried his hand at it. This was due, of course, to the constraints imposed by lengthy exposure times that demanded subjects that did not move. One of Nicéphore Niépce's heliographs—probably contemporary with the "View from the Window at Le Gras"—shows a laid table that is known by a heliograph taken by his nephew Niépce de Saint-Victor.[6] It has often been held that such a choice is purely the product of external circumstance: this is, it would seem, far from the truth. In fact, none of the very earliest variants—daguerreotype, "photogenic drawing," heliography—relates to the reproduction of a random sample of everyday objects. On the contrary, each inventor chose a specific natural element, doubtless in

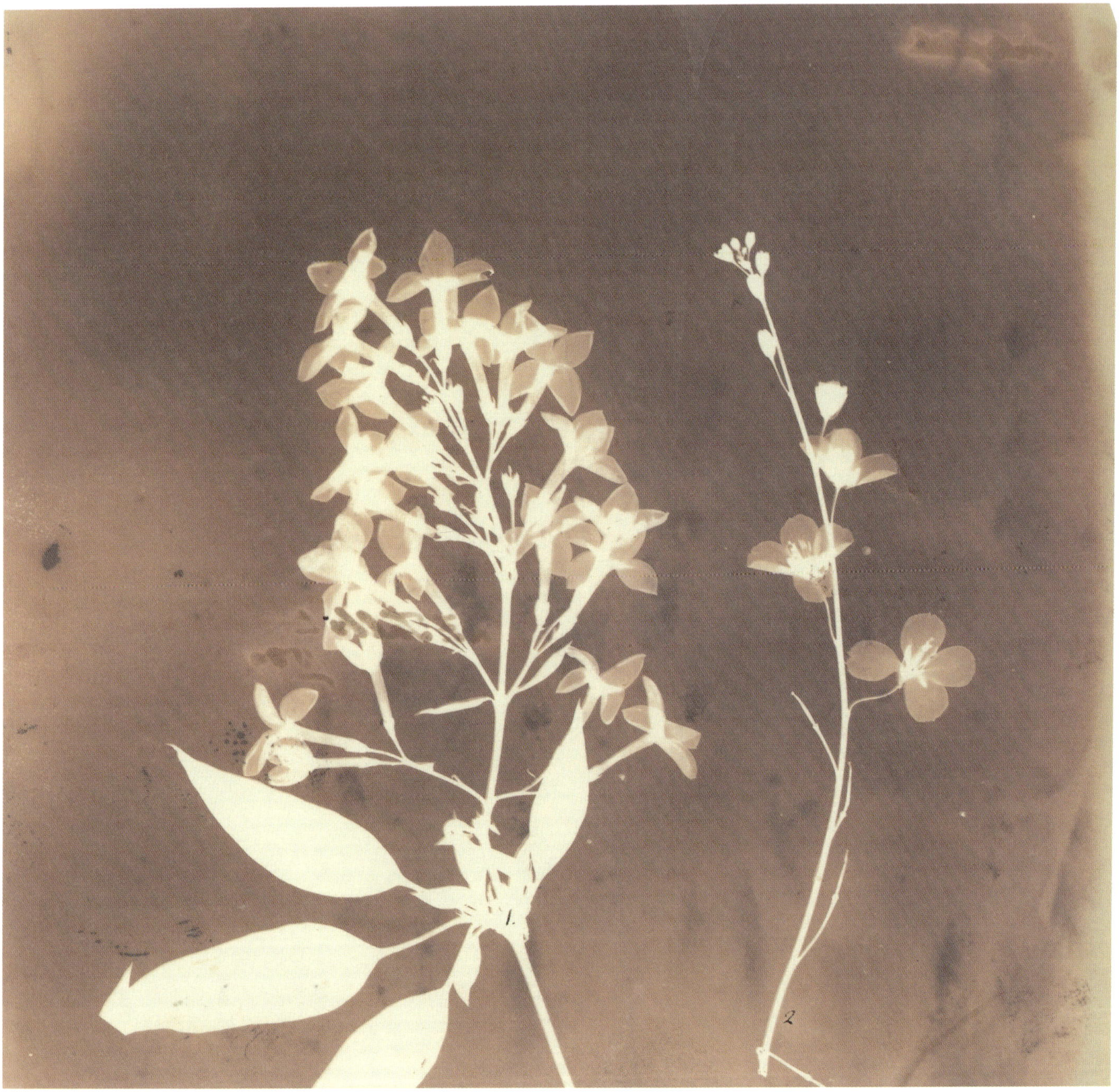

132. William Henry Fox Talbot, "Heliophila," 1839, photogenic drawing, The Metropolitan Museum of Art, New York.

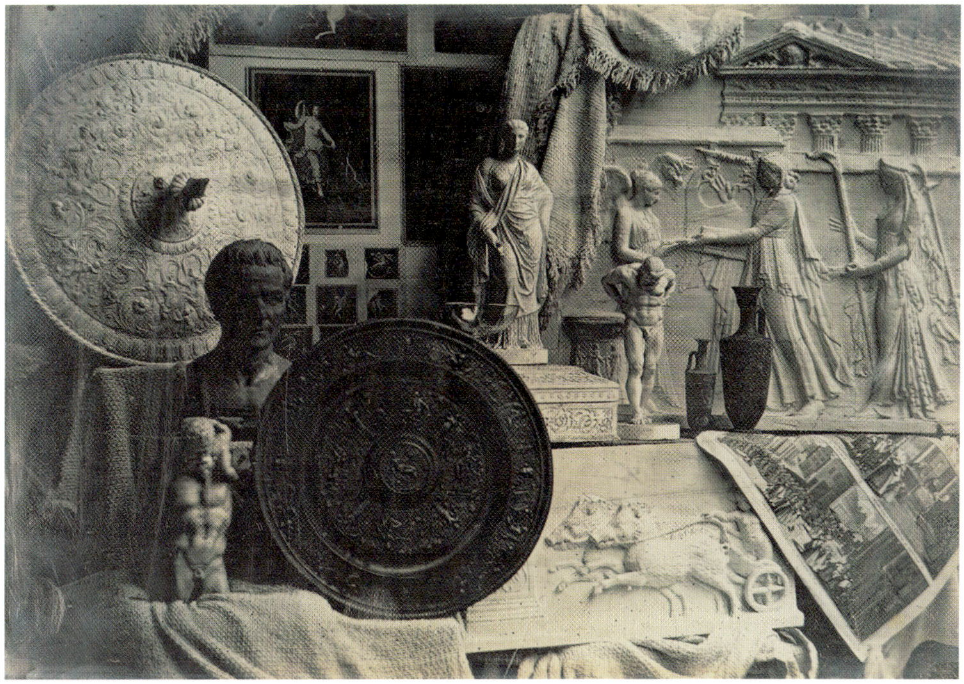

133. François-Alphonse Fortier, "Still Life," 1839–40, daguerreotype, Société Française de Photographie, Paris.

keeping with his tastes and interests, which offered him a way of showing off the process and his skill. Niépce's "*Table dressée*" (Set Table) is thus reminiscent of still lifes painted by Chardin in the mid-eighteenth century, much appreciated by the enlightened middle class to which the Burgundian gentleman belonged. William Fox Talbot's representations of leaves and flowers, meanwhile, reflect the Englishman's keen interest in botany. The depiction of foliage, delicately placed as if on a sheet from a herbarium, presents a fine demonstration of photographic flair, and fostered Talbot's ambition to have his new invention regarded as an advanced and irreplaceable scientific tool (ill. 132).

Daguerre's plates, on the other hand, seem to evoke at once a cabinet of curiosities, the bric-a-brac in a painter's studio, and the arcana of the alchemist's laboratory. The light falling on these arrangements of plaster casts, engravings, and other articles wonderfully conjures up the forms and reliefs, as if to affirm the skill of the operator in overcoming every constraint. The artistic intention too is tangible; the images composed by the French inventor and his early followers exude a subdued, melancholic nostalgia. But these daguerreotypes do not refer to concrete pictorial models. In fact, Daguerre zeroes in on elements painters tended to relegate to the background (ill. 133). Perhaps he was inspired by Tony Johannot's lithograph, printed on an early page of the first number of the romantic journal *L'Artiste* (ill. 9), where objects—vase, engravings, books, pictures—are piled up in carefully calculated disorder on a console. In 1841, Eugène Isabey introduced

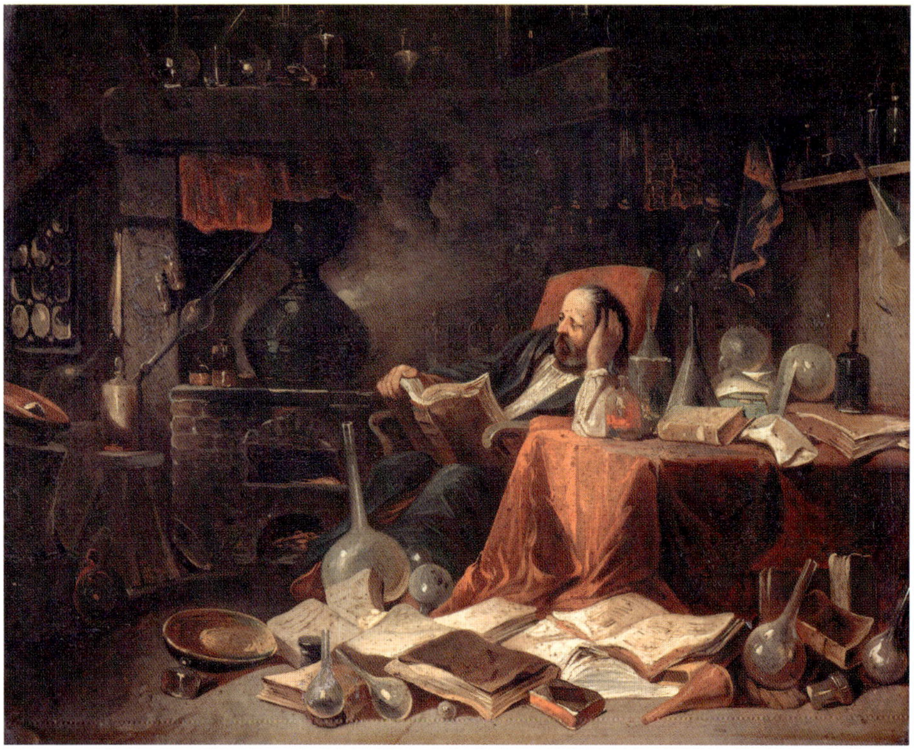

134. Anonymous, after Eugène Isabey, *The Alchemist*, after 1841, oil on canvas, Musée Magnin, Dijon.

"The Alchemist" at the Salon, the picture proving a great success with critics and the public at large (ill. 134). The objects gathered on the table on which the scholar leans absorbed in his reading form a composition rather close to Daguerre's images.

Though it clearly addressed reality, fledgling photography also wanted to keep faith with the definition Diderot advances of pictorial inspiration: "The art of raising a corner of the veil and showing men part of a neglected or rather of a forgotten world.... The inspired man himself is sometimes uncertain whether the thing he has uncovered is a reality or a figment of the imagination."[7] Daguerre's metonymic process thus offered the possibility of disclosing—"developing"—a long-lost world.

Hippolyte Bayard also took as his subject the representation of objects; his early prints on paper from 1839 are composed of molds and casts, the familiar paraphernalia of the painter's workshop. No doubt these artistic evocations of their daily life spurred the interest of academicians from the Beaux-Arts in photographs taken using his process, in which plaster casts appear behind a haze that blurs their outlines as if in a charcoal drawing (ill. 135). From the outset, the very first photographic representations of objects—an admixture of virtuosity, the desire to promote the validity of the invention, and aesthetic inspiration—were placed squarely in the territory of art. They thus derive from the genre of still life such as Charles Sterling defines it: "an authentic Still-life

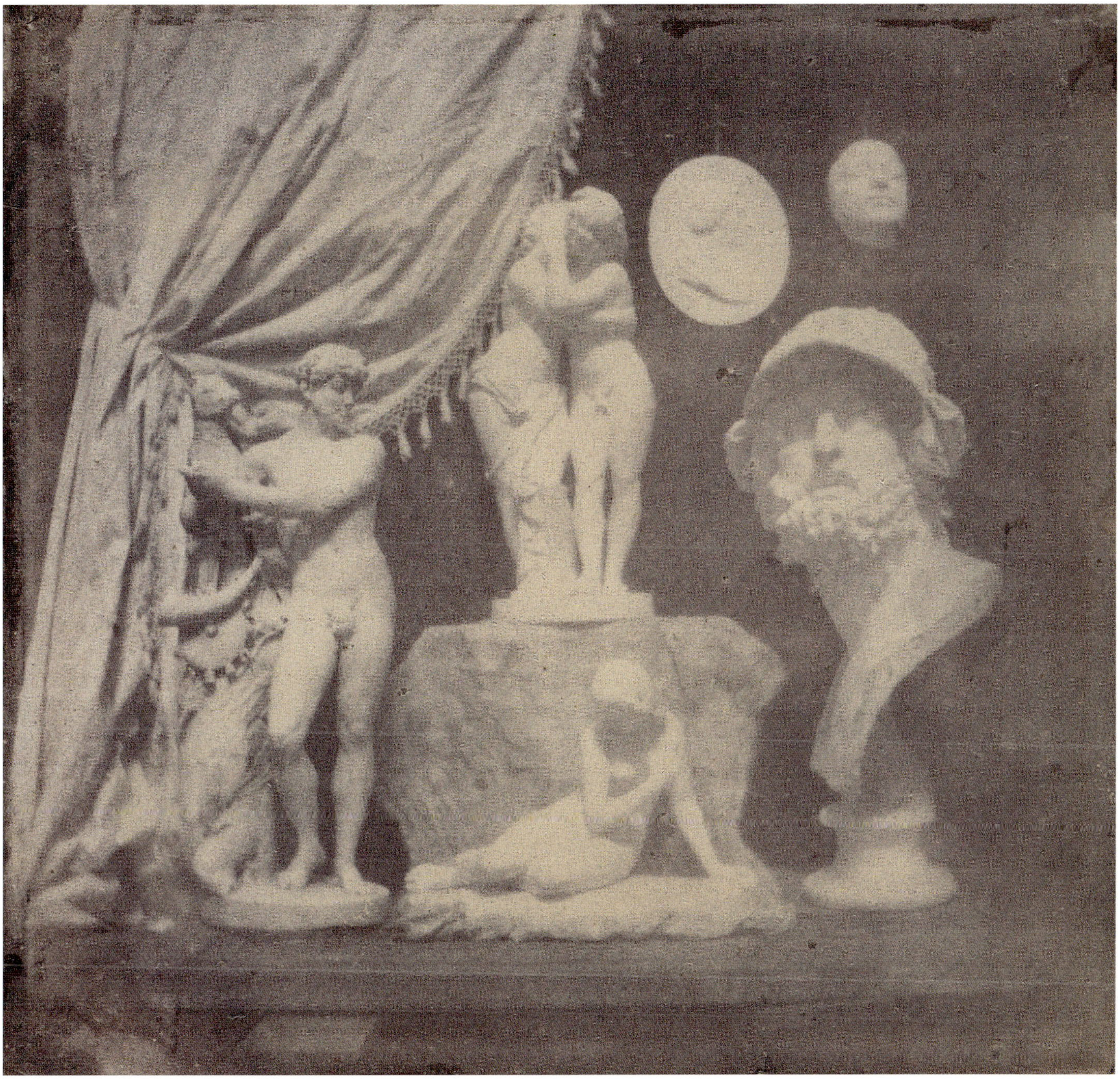

was born the day a painter made the fundamental decision to organize into a plastically self-sufficient work a group of inanimate objects.... The fact that, depending on the era and the medium in which he worked, they are freighted with all kinds of intellectual allusions, changes nothing with respect to the profound intention of the artist: that is, to arouse in us a poetic emotion through the beauty glimpsed in inanimate objects and their arrangements."[8]

135. Hippolyte Bayard, "Still Life with Casts," 1839, Bayard paper process, Musée d'Orsay, Paris.

The manifestation of a particular virtuosity

As the manifestation of a specific type of photographic skill, however, these compositions remained distinct from painted still lifes. The latter provided an opportunity for artists to deploy a dazzling spectrum of colors that conveyed and/or embellished the variety of forms and materials depicted. But color, of course, was long in coming to photography; not before the early years of the twentieth century, in 1907, was a patent lodged for the first color photographic process, the autochrome plate developed by the brothers Lumière. While the black-and-white snapshot gained ground, photographers in color, forced back into the straitjacket of extremely long exposure times, returned to precisely calibrated compositions, inspired by the subjects and idioms of painting (ill. 136). Photographers were thus long obliged to substitute tone for value, and play with direct light or chiaroscuro and subdued or clear-cut shadows. They had to be able to tell exactly how an object would react to photographic reproduction. When taking pictures of his family collection, Talbot already noted that he had to be careful when choosing objects to place in the same image, because of the way different substances and colors reflect the light. The sheen of white or blue porcelain demanded reduced exposure times and subdued light, and thus had to be kept away from glass objects that required prolonged exposure and strong illumination.[9]

Photographic still life associated a taste for erudition with a liking for inventories; special emphasis was thus placed on groups and collections of objects. Even today Daguerre's celebrated image "*Coquillages*" (Shells and Fossils) keeps its fair share of secrets: for example, it is not known to whom these shells and fossils belonged. Elaborately arranged on parallel shelves, they remind one of a scholar's study in the late eighteenth century; did the inventor, in an attempt to highlight the new medium's ability to render form and relief accurately, choose such subjects to impress a scientific audience? The brio with which Daguerre dosed the exposure allowed him to carefully regulate the quantity of light falling on the objects that thus seem to emerge directly from the image.[10]

As Talbot stated in the plates for *The Pencil of Nature*, photography might be of great help to collectors and connoisseurs in the compiling of inventories or catalogs of their collections, providing irrefutable proof of their possession: "The whole cabinet of a collector might be depicted on paper in little more time than it would take him to make a written inventory ... and would a thief afterwards purloin these treasures ... it would certainly be evidence of a novel kind."[11] To bolster this contention, he took several pictures of artifacts at his Lacock Abbey estate ("Articles of Glass," "Articles of China"). The most astonishing—showing some fine pieces of silverware

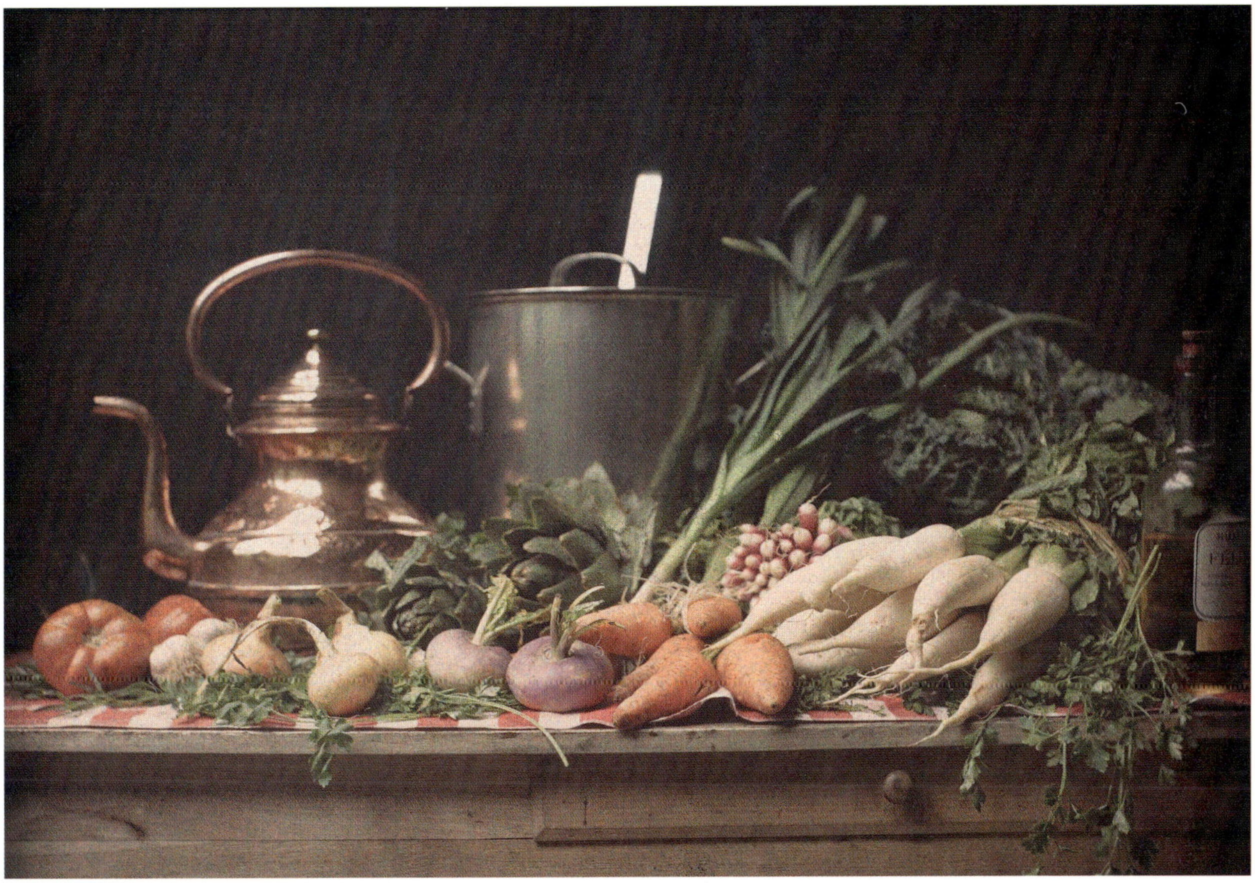

136. Auguste and Louis Lumière, "Still Life with Vegetables," 1907, autochrome, Musée d'Orsay, Paris.

lined up on shelves—was not actually published in *The Pencil of Nature*. To reproduce such objects presented an immense photographic challenge, since the reflective surface of the cutlery must have played havoc with the light. Talbot doubtless had to undertake many trials before achieving a satisfactory outcome in which every object appears distinctly. The photographer must have been beguiled by the idea of taking a picture of silver while employing a process based on the use of a solution of that very metal; through its subject, the image thus appears as a metaphor for the invention itself.

If the still lifes by Adolphe Bilordeaux, reflecting the taste of their time and incorporating casts, fossils, paintings, and ceramics, are vaguely redolent of an assortment of articles from an artist's workshop, the photograph presented by Robert Jefferson Bingham in London in 1856 under the title "Still Life of Antiquities" shows objects actually now part of the Armand Signol Collection in Tours. Far from smacking of the inventory, however, the objects are arranged before a large, dark-colored silk curtain, whose sobriety greatly enhances the forms.

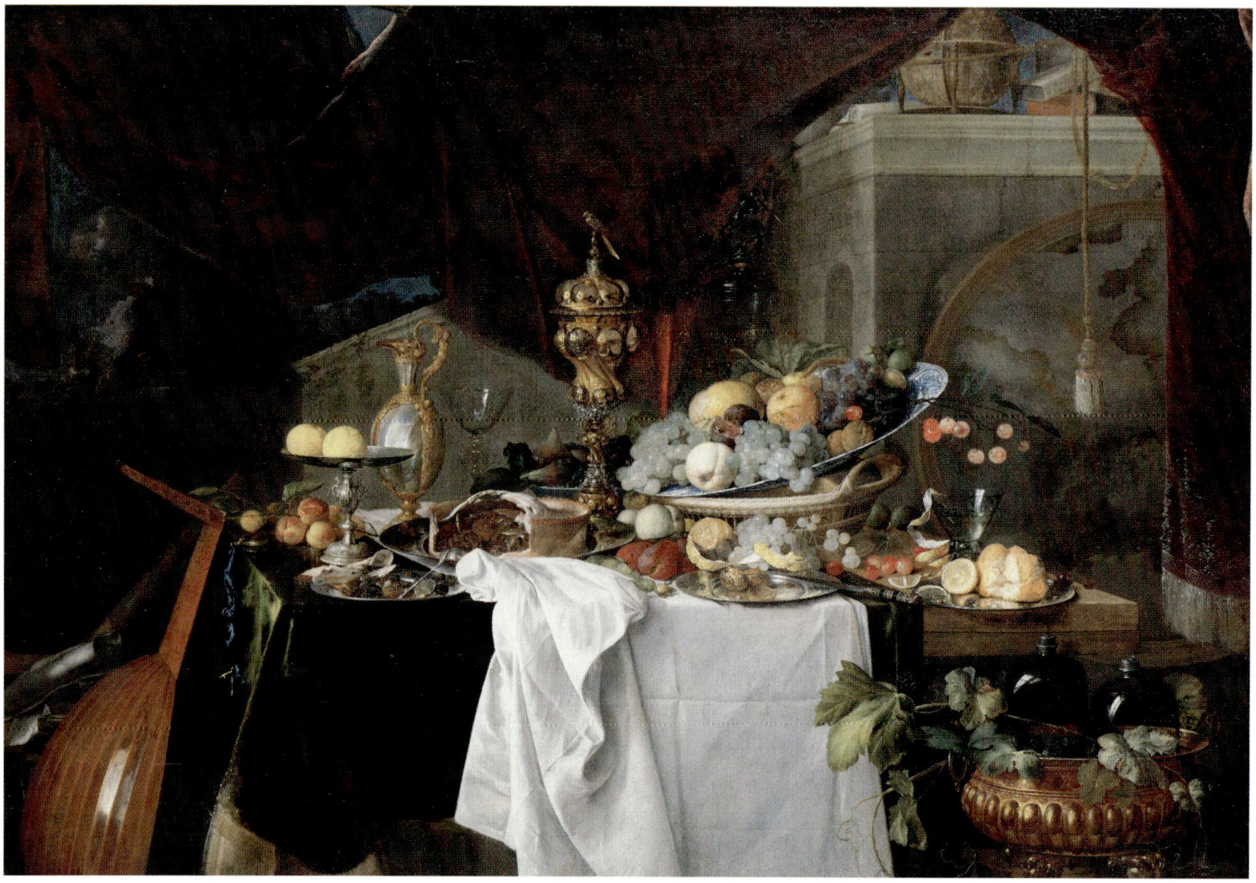

137. Jan Davidsz. de Heem, *A Table of Desserts*, 1640, oil on canvas, Musée du Louvre, Paris.

A new taste in the middle of the century

The renewed interest in Dutch painting in France from the 1840s—advocated in particular by the critic Théophile Thoré—as well as the growing taste for eighteenth-century French art, did much to improve the status of still life, by reminding the general public, artists, and connoisseurs alike of the beauty of models from previous centuries. The exhibition in 1860 of the collection belonging to Dr. La Caze in Martinet's Paris gallery on Boulevard des Italiens, followed by the physician's bequest to the Louvre in 1869, paved the way for the rediscovery of *natures mortes* by Chardin. From the end of the 1850s, Louis La Caze, via his friend the painter François Bonvin, had opened his house to many young artists, who were thus able to gain access to earlier artistic models; one case in point was Henri Fantin-Latour.[12] In 1852, Louis-Desiré Blanquart-Évrard had included in his *Études photographiques* (a portfolio of photographs for artists and amateurs) a "Still Life with Rabbit," which bears the imprint of pictorial precedent.[13] In the 1850s, Henri Le Secq carried out forty "*Natures mortes*," whose affiliations with painting transpire in the choice of composition, the thematic of flowers, fruit, and precious objects,

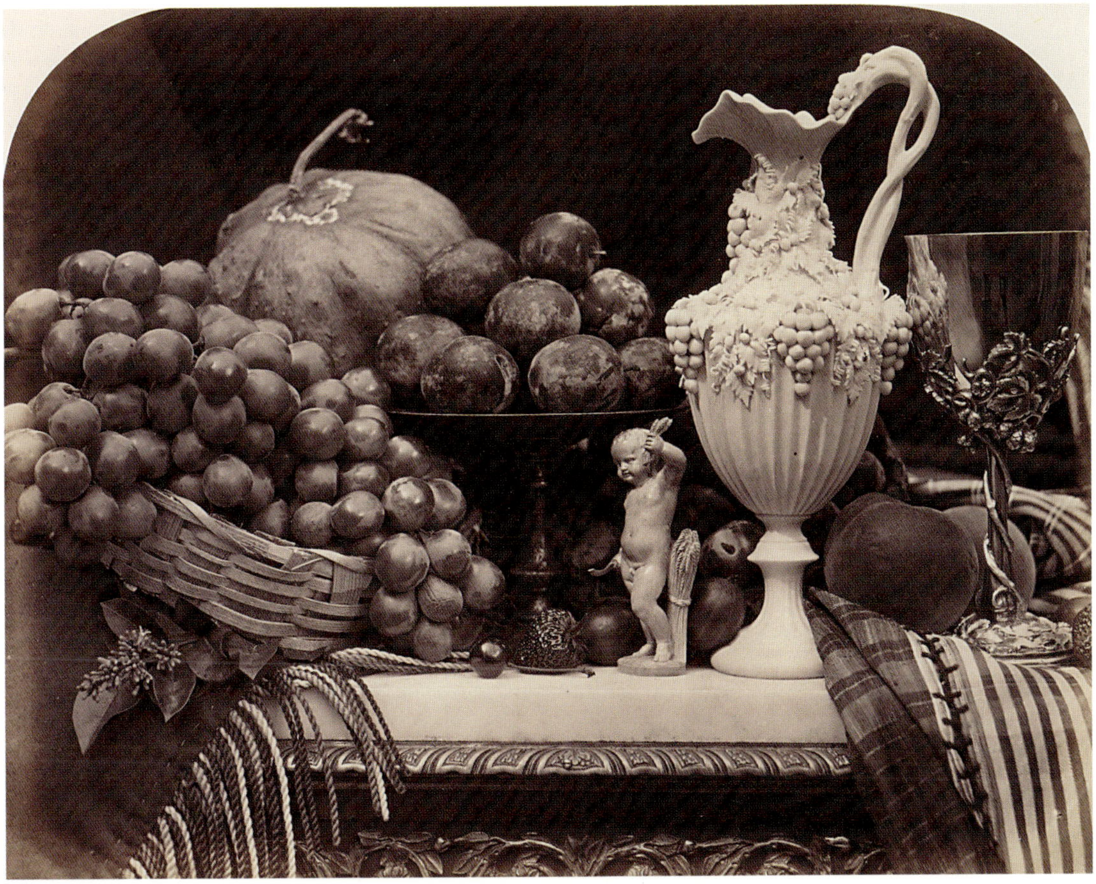

138. Roger Fenton, "Still Life, Tankard with Fruit," 1860, albumen print, National Media Museum, Bradford.

and in a subtle feeling for light where the values seem ready to vie with the panache of seventeenth- and eighteenth-century canvases in their depiction of surface and material.[14]

In 1859 and 1860, Roger Fenton composed the most splendid photographic still lifes of the era. Inspired by models from painting (Fenton had absorbed the lessons not only of the Dutch masters, but also of British painters of the time; in particular George Lance, whose pictures he had reproduced), each one of these photographs was composed with scrupulous attention as to the choice of the fruits and objects, their disposition, number and appearance. By placing the lens close to the subject, Fenton endowed it with remarkable power, drawing in the eye and encouraging it to explore the satisfying rhythms of form and texture; such masterful control of light and reflectivity is unparalleled at the time and conveys the investment, at once aesthetic and commercial, the artist placed on such images. Fenton unveiled his still lifes for the first time in 1860 at the seventh exhibition of the Photographic Society in London, pricing them at the higher end of the scale, on a par indeed with the celebrated photographs he had taken of the Crimean War in 1855 (ills. 137–38).[15]

Hunting pieces

In the mid-nineteenth century, hunting pieces or *tableaux de chasse* enjoyed a new lease of life. Photographers and painters alike started rehashing decorative variations that were dear, for example, to Claude-François Desportes. Charles Nègre, in about 1858, composed several still lifes with game, where dead birds languish on a cloth with a foliage pattern that blends with the real plants and the feathers. The material effects, combining fabric, plant, and plumage, underline the dexterity of the photographer in the same way they did the sensitivity of the painter. The "trophies" that Eugène Cuvelier took at the beginning of the 1860s are revelatory of their creator's desire to affirm the artistic dimension of his work; the meticulous way he deploys the paper negative confers exceptional depth and density to his splendid "Still Life with Hare and Cloves of Garlic" (ill. 130). Photographers were also asserting the artistic import of their works by explicitly designing them to be hung on a wall, like paintings. Thus, in around 1870, Adolphe Braun produced several large hunting trophies (30 × 22 ½ in./76 × 57 cm), designed to decorate the walls of a dining room; such carbon prints provided a relatively long-lasting mural decor (ill. 139).[16] Photographing his painter friend Richard Ansdell in his studio with, next to him, a large dead bird he is about to start sketching, William Henry Lake's composition deliberately conflates portrait, genre scene, and still life, thereby highlighting the singular creative potential of photography.

Patterns for models

Motifs of flowers and fruit were much appreciated by textile manufacturers, silk weavers, and wallpaper manufacturers for their designs. At the beginning of the nineteenth century, the great factories of Lyon often turned to painters to commission new patterns. Some, like Antoine Berjon, who exhibited several still lifes at the 1810 Salon, grew into admirable talents. Such qualities of accuracy in observation and rendering of subject remained rare, though, and manufacturers often complained of receiving hackneyed motifs lifted from existing repertories in drawings, engravings, or lithographs. In addition, they would deplore the fact that studies tended to be divorced from their natural setting and the motif cropped and devitalized. Adolphe Braun, who designed patterns for textiles in Paris, founded his own company in 1834, before moving to Mulhouse in 1843, where he worked for the Dolfuss factory. By the end of the 1840s, he had learned photography and produced several pictures for the company's designers. In 1854, he published three hundred *Fleurs photographiées* (Photographed Flowers), gathered into six albums. Like many of his colleagues, he grew the flowers that appear in these compositions in his own greenhouse.

139. **Facing page:** Adolphe Braun, "Hunting Piece with Hind," c. 1867, carbon print, Musée d'Orsay, Paris.

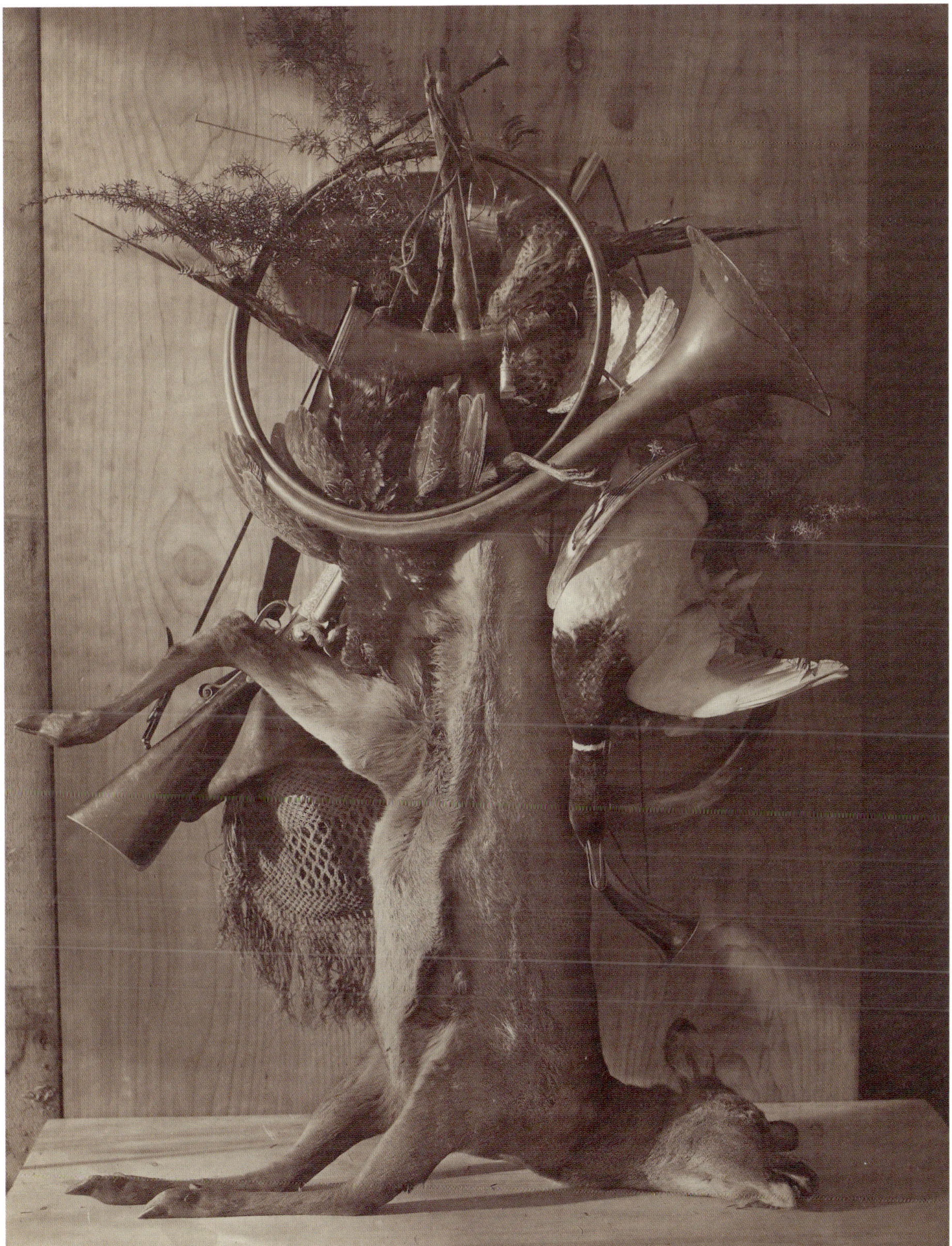

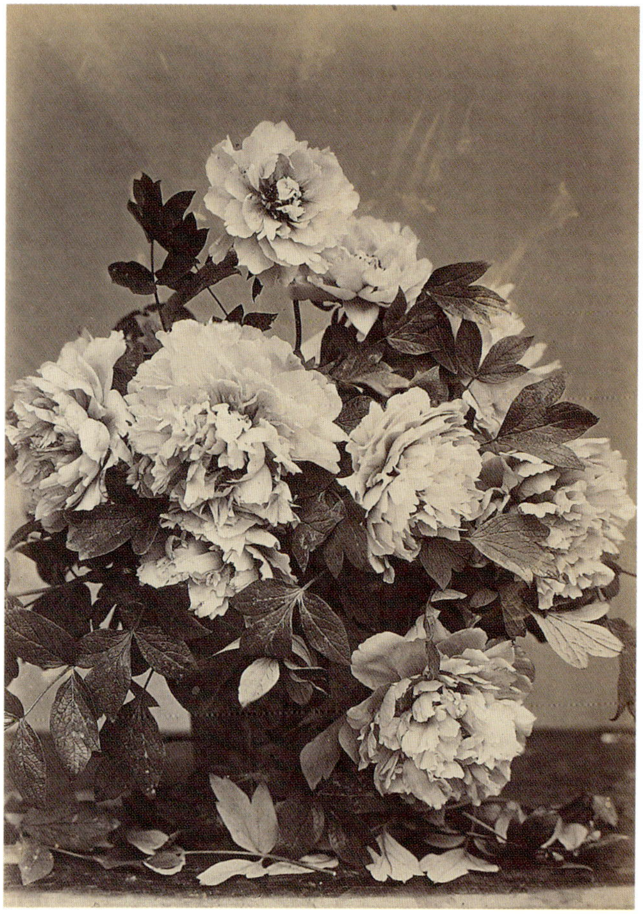

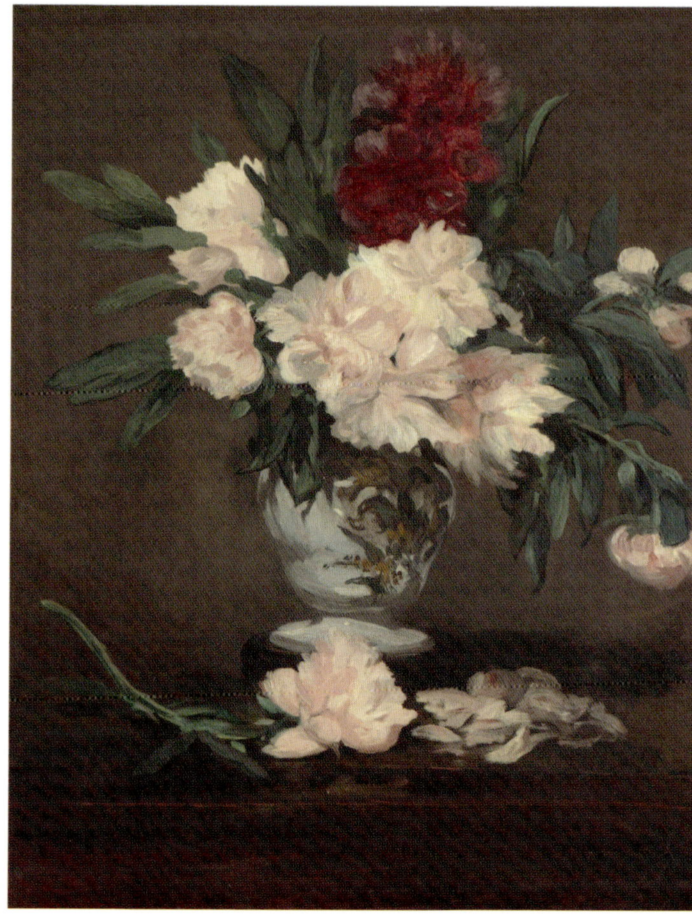

140. **Above, left:** Charles Aubry, "Nine Peonies," c. 1864, albumen print, Musée d'Orsay, Paris.

141. **Above, right:** Édouard Manet, *Peonies in a Vase*, c. 1865, oil on canvas, Musée d'Orsay, Paris.

To him, photography appeared as an excellent instrument for obtaining studies at once truer to nature and more conducive to the creative impulse. Scrupulously composed, these works, in which various flowers are arranged against a uniform gray background, were acclaimed on their presentation at the 1855 Exposition Universelle by critics, gaining an award from the jury: "M. Braun is one of those artists," wrote Ernest Lacan in his review, "who, under the modest title of *dessinateur* [draftsman], has contributed markedly in France to the development and success of the textile industry by providing major manufacturers with compositions that are masterpieces of taste and artistic intelligence."[17] Henri-Victor Regnault, then director of the Sèvres Manufacture and president of the Société Française de Photographie, presented one of Braun's albums at the Academy of Sciences. The exorbitant cost of such albums—more than thousand francs a copy—made them inaccessible to amateurs, but Braun signed a contract with the publishers Alexis Gaudin et Frères to produce some photographs in smaller formats.

Such success was sure to come to the notice of Charles Aubry, a designer specializing in drawings for cloth and lace, and a close friend of the painter and sculptor Albert Carrier-Belleuse

(1824–87). During a stay in Great Britain at the beginning of the 1850s, the sculptor had observed the changes afoot in the teaching of drawing in the kingdom's art schools. Piloted by Henry Cole, the scope of these reforms was increased by a plan born from the triumph of the 1851 Exhibition: to open a museum dedicated to the industrial arts: the future South Kensington Museum (now the Victoria and Albert Museum). The Circulation Gallery that Cole set up also provided schools with molds, casts, and photographs that thus offered new models to artists, decorators, and manufacturers. It is probable that Carrier-Belleuse, some of whose works had already been reproduced in photographs, reported on these interesting innovations to Aubry. So it was that, in 1864, the latter established a company devoted to the production of plaster casts and photographs of plants and fruit. That same year, in an effort to draw attention to his activities, Aubry presented some of his finest works in an album to the prince imperial (Department of Prints and Photographs, Bibliothèque Nationale de France, Paris). Although a certain number of these photographs were indeed purchased by art schools and commercial concerns (the Dolfuss Manufacture in Alsace acquired a number, as did the Gobelins Manufacture, whose holdings are today housed in the Musée d'Orsay), Aubry's business did not meet with the acclaim he had hoped. The quality of the pictures was never in question; with a reduced depth of field and brightly lit, his floral arrangements were graceful and sensitive. But he could not resist varying the motif, producing pictures too diverse in composition, in material and formal effects, to serve as worthwhile models. He replaced the invariable neutral ground preferred by Braun by a panoply of backdrops; sometimes the shadow of an easel or of some other object not in shot can be glimpsed. Too complex to be iterated by screen printing or stamping, Braun's photographs betray a receptiveness to the painted still lifes of his time, such as those of Fantin-Latour and Édouard Manet (ills. 140–141). Expropriated in 1867, and evicted from his Paris workshop, in 1869 he penned a rather pathetic letter to Nadar—with whom he was not even acquainted— pleading with the great portraitist to help him sell off his wares, which Aubry was willing to let him do.[18]

The several hundred pictures of flowers and vegetables taken between 1895 and 1910 by the British gardener Charles Jones were most probably motivated by the idea they would serve as models. The intention behind their collection is not exactly known, but the advertisement Jones took out in *Popular Gardening*, offering to reproduce gardens belonging to the members of the public, implies he was no dilettante. Yet it appears that Jones never exhibited. If he composed a number of still lifes closer to pictorial traditions, the majority of his spectacular photographs amount to veritable portraits of flowers and vegetables, taken in close-up, against a uniform ground from which each plant stands out in its glory.[19]

The work of Karl Blossfeldt, a professor in the decorative arts studio of the Berlin Kunstakademie, embraced similar ideas. Carried out in connection with his work as a teacher of sculpture, his photographs spawned entirely new models. Against a white or black ground, the plants are shot in extreme close-up under a bright light, exacerbating the contrast in value and underlining the contours (ill. 142). A great favorite in Germany from the 1920s, Blossfeldt's images are often associated with the tenets of the Neue Sachlichkeit (New Objectivity). He had started working, however, at the end of the 1890s, and harks back to the pictures of Braun and Aubry in France. His oeuvre is not unconnected with the aesthetic approach of Ernst Haeckel, who demonstrated the existence of aesthetic forms in the natural world in a book published in 1899, *Kunstformen von der Natur* (*Art Forms in Nature*), which went on to have a notable impact on art, architecture, decoration, and furniture design in the early twentieth century. It was in a similar context in Vienna in 1902 that Austrian photographer Martin Gerlach issued a portfolio of photographs for artists and decorators entitled *Formenwelt aus dem Naturreiche* (*A World of Forms from Nature*). These photographs present a break with both still life and the natural portrait, and forge entirely novel motifs by associating diverse plants and animals, including insects, on the same plate in images reminiscent of the neutral yet penetrating vision of the microscope. Some of Gerlach's photographic plates directly inspired decorative drawings, feeding into the work of the Wiener Werkstätte and the Vienna Secession.[20]

A new relationship to the object

The pursuit of a specifically photographic type of virtuosity brought with it new motifs that gradually moved away from the models of pictorial still life. John Beasly Greene, an archaeologist of American extraction, trained in photography with Gustave Le Gray; better known for archaeological views of Egypt now preserved at the Musée d'Orsay and in the library of the French Institute in Paris, in 1854 he took interesting pictures of composed assemblages. On a plank placed on a Paris balcony (the city and its roofs offer an original backdrop to this type of depiction) stand a glass, a ceramic flask, and a bottle. Far from being fortuitous, this peculiar miscellany of objects recalls the difficulties Talbot had mentioned of reproducing in the same image glassware and light-colored blue or white porcelain. Independent of any pictorial model, Greene's work constituted a photographic challenge but was also not without an aesthetic dimension, reinforced by the way in which the objects are boldly delineated against the indistinct background of the Paris skyline. The constraints of exposure time made the manner in which the objects are apprehended distinct from painting compositions since antiquity. By deploying processes other

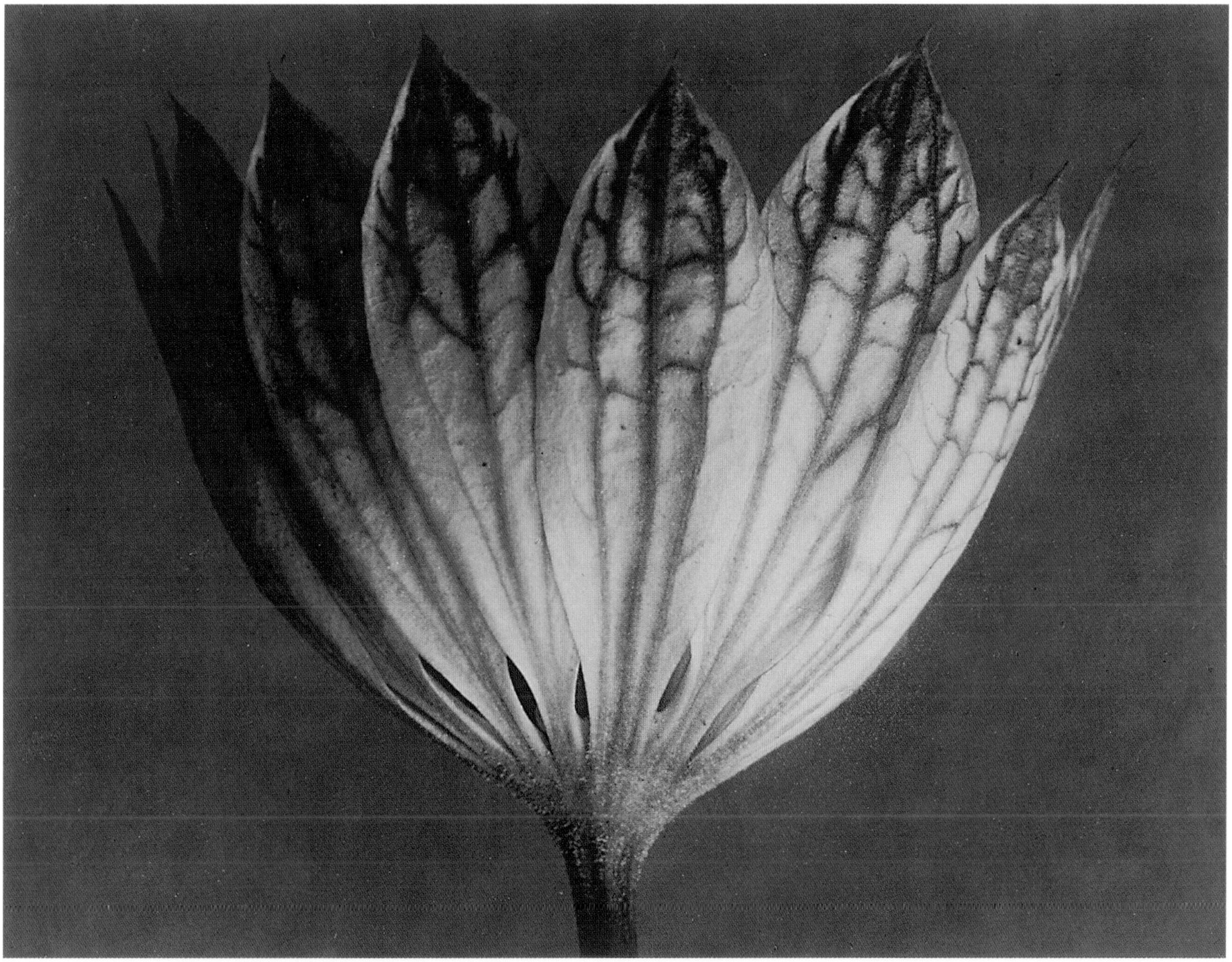

142. Karl Blossfeldt, "Astrantia major," c. 1915 (for the print), silver print from a glass negative, Musée d'Orsay, Paris.

than pictorial to produce the representation, the new mode of perception rejuvenates the relationship to the reproduction of inanimate things. Such photographs, by privileging clarity of view, lay the emphasis on outline and form (color is still of course absent), and thus on the subtle juxtapositions and values. The patience—stamina, even—of the photographer is put to the test, setting up a singular relationship to the passing of time.

To propose parallels between Greene's doggedness and the single-mindedness demonstrated by Paul Cézanne in his still lifes would be an exaggeration; an analogy with the photographic model, as such, does not greatly enhance our understanding of the unprecedented genius from Aix. It is possible to venture, though, that Cézanne might have been sensitive to the new rapport with the object—in terms of perception as much as method of representation—that was precipitated by the photographic model.

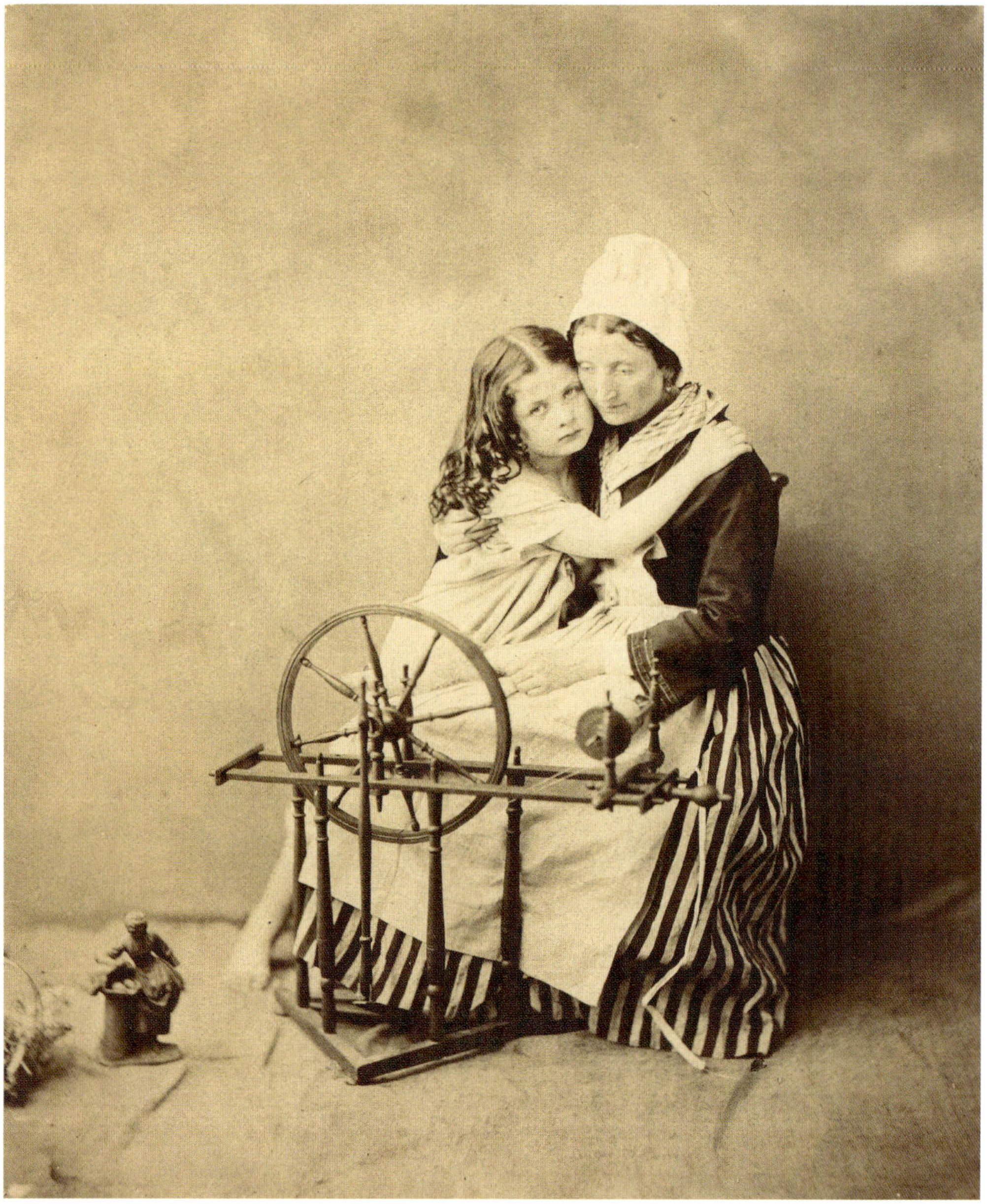

"It is no paradox to state that all genres without exception have now been reduced to just one: genre.*"* [1]

GENRE PHOTOGRAPHY

PHOTOGRAPHIC ARRANGEMENTS AND TABLEAUX VIVANTS

Whether in regret or in satisfaction (like Paul d'Ivoi, who, in 1857, proclaimed genre to be the "true monarch of art" [2]), Second Empire critics agreed on the fact that "genre" had invaded every artistic category. By 1861, Maxime du Camp could write, "The divisions we have devised are entirely arbitrary, because each species of painting has become so mixed up; history painting has descended down to genre painting and genre painting has penetrated landscape to such an extent it is extremely hard to establish any kind of standard or hard and fast classification." [3] A basic definition appeared all the more out of the question since "genre" (qua a genre) now seemed omnipresent. Recent university research covering the vast number of works claiming to fall into this category, in booklets issued on the occasion of the Salons, has discovered that they dealt with very different themes and came from the hand of extremely diverse artists, thus underlining just how difficult it had become to circumscribe its limits.[4] The depiction of human beings seems to have been the only common criterion, one whose extension—much remarked upon by contemporary observers—hardly made it a cast-iron tool of discrimination. The success of genre painting was due essentially to its capacity to translate and transmit simple emotions, thus occasioning the empathy of the beholder without any undue effort of comprehension on his part: "It is [the genre painter's] task to use analysis to plumb the human soul more deeply; he can succor, assist, and instruct in simple, moving scenes from neglected lives." [5]

The issue of narrative

The example of Jean Baptiste Greuze survived intact; by endowing his models with the attitudes and expressions that history painting usually attributed to the representation of glorious deeds, by weaving scenes from daily life into a narrative fabric, the painter profoundly modified the appreciation of genre

143. **Facing page:** Félix-Jacques Moulin, "The Spinner or The Woman at her Spinning Wheel," 1853, albumen print, Musée d'Orsay, Paris.

painting generally; hailed by Denis Diderot, Greuze thus pushed the frontiers of genre which now centered on its ability to move the viewer, not without a certain theatricality. Indeed, the stage itself was not immune; in 1761, in the middle of Act II of a performance of *Les Noces d'Arlequin*, the actors froze in the positions and attitudes Greuze bestowed on his figures in *L'Accordée du village* (*The Village Engagement;* 1761, Musée du Louvre, Paris), which had been a hit at the recent Salon. This interest in storyline and the exaltation of finer feelings was taken up by many history painters from the very start of the nineteenth century. Saluting the virtuous spirit of Saint Louis, Fleury Richard, a pupil of Jacques-Louis David's and leader of the Troubadour school that sourced much of its material from the growth of interest in the Middle Ages, painted a scene in which the king's courage is outweighed by filial devotion (*The Deference of Saint Louis*, 1808, oil on canvas, Musée Napoléon, Arenenberg). The artist's fondness for faithfully rendering the decor and costumes of the thirteenth century prettified the picture to the point of undermining the grandeur of the *exemplum virtutis* and turning it into something more like a family tearjerker. The historical canvases of Paul Delaroche celebrated this taste for narrative and the search for an immediate emotion where historical fact plays second fiddle to anecdote. His first success at the Salon of 1824, *A Sick Joan of Arc Interrogated by the Cardinal of Winchester* (ill. 6), shows not the armor-clad virgin of Orleans, but a fragile girl terrorized by the terrible English minister as he questions her. The theatrical feel of the canvas is manifest; Winchester and Joan of Arc seem perched on a proscenium elevated above the viewing line; alighting solely on the main characters, the light plunges the unseen wings into the shadow. The same year Léon Cogniet presented a *Massacre of the Innocents* (ill. 13) at the Salon. Divided into two sections, the canvas presents a pair of distinct tableaux: on the left, Herod's soldiers—obeying their order to slaughter all newly born males—hunt down the mothers and their young children; on the right, the same size as the historical scene, a terrified young woman cowers behind a stretch of wall, grasping on to her child and trying to stifle his cries with her wrap. The biblical event is thus presented from the personal point of view of one unfortunate woman. Visitors to the Salon could immediately identify with her distress and fear of the terrible fate awaiting her and her son, all the more so since the wall concealing them from the eyes of their pursuers seemed to offer scant protection.

The primacy of subject matter

In the course of the July Monarchy history painting therefore became diluted by a preference for anecdotal storylines peppered with dramatic incidents that guaranteed the immediate comprehension of a public with a penchant for emotional frisson rather than moral edification. It was the increasingly uncertain distinction between the grand manner and genre that made for the success (at least among the general public) of the latter at the annual Salon. The bourgeois, as Théophile Gautier pointed out in 1858 in his account of Paul Delaroche's posthumous retrospective, was concerned primarily with subject matter: "Paul Delaroche was always too preoccupied with the subject. In this one could say that he was bourgeois.... If a visitor to a gallery, stopping in front of a picture, instead of looking at it and delighting in it, first of all flicks through his booklet to find out what historical scene or anecdote it represents, you can say, without fear of error, 'This man surely does not like painting.'"[6] The artist thus sought to transcribe the most readily intelligible facts, those whose comprehension—as in a tableau at the theater—depends solely on the scene illustrated. The recourse to easily identifiable expressions made manifest a range of definable emotions; the quotation of precise details made it possible to locate the representation in time as well as in space, thus bestowing critical importance on the costumes and accessories. In fact, often it was only these that distinguished a historical from a contemporary episode or an Oriental scene from one set in Brittany or Provence. More than just an indication, a detail had to produce meaning. In his generally positive appraisal of *The Assassination of the Duc de Guise* (1834, oil on canvas, Musée Condé, Chantilly), Gautier took stock of the tendency, comparing the painstaking exactitude of the painter to photography: "Like everyone else, indeed more than everyone else, we admired this marvelous little masterwork, *The Assassination of the Duc de Guise*, a history picture of astonishing truthfulness, a *photography* of an entire era, taken across the centuries, a retrospective drawing one would think made by an eyewitness."[7]

Portrait and genre: translating expressions

From the first stirrings of the invention, photography quickly appropriated every idiom of "genre." The search for a lifelike expression lay at the heart of portraiture, all the more since the rigid pose necessitated by long exposure times made this difficult. So, very early on, group portraiture embraced the artifices of the genre scene to counteract the risks inherent in the technique. In 1840, Eugène Leboeuf composed several open-air scenes showing various members of his family gathered around a rather elegantly set table (daguerreotypes, 1841, private collection, Paris). A daguerreotype recently acquired by the Musée d'Orsay shows three men around a chessboard. The pretext of the game allowed the photographer to present a range of attitudes from intense reflection to amused mockery (Anonymous, "A Game of Chess," daguerreotype, Musée d'Orsay, Paris).

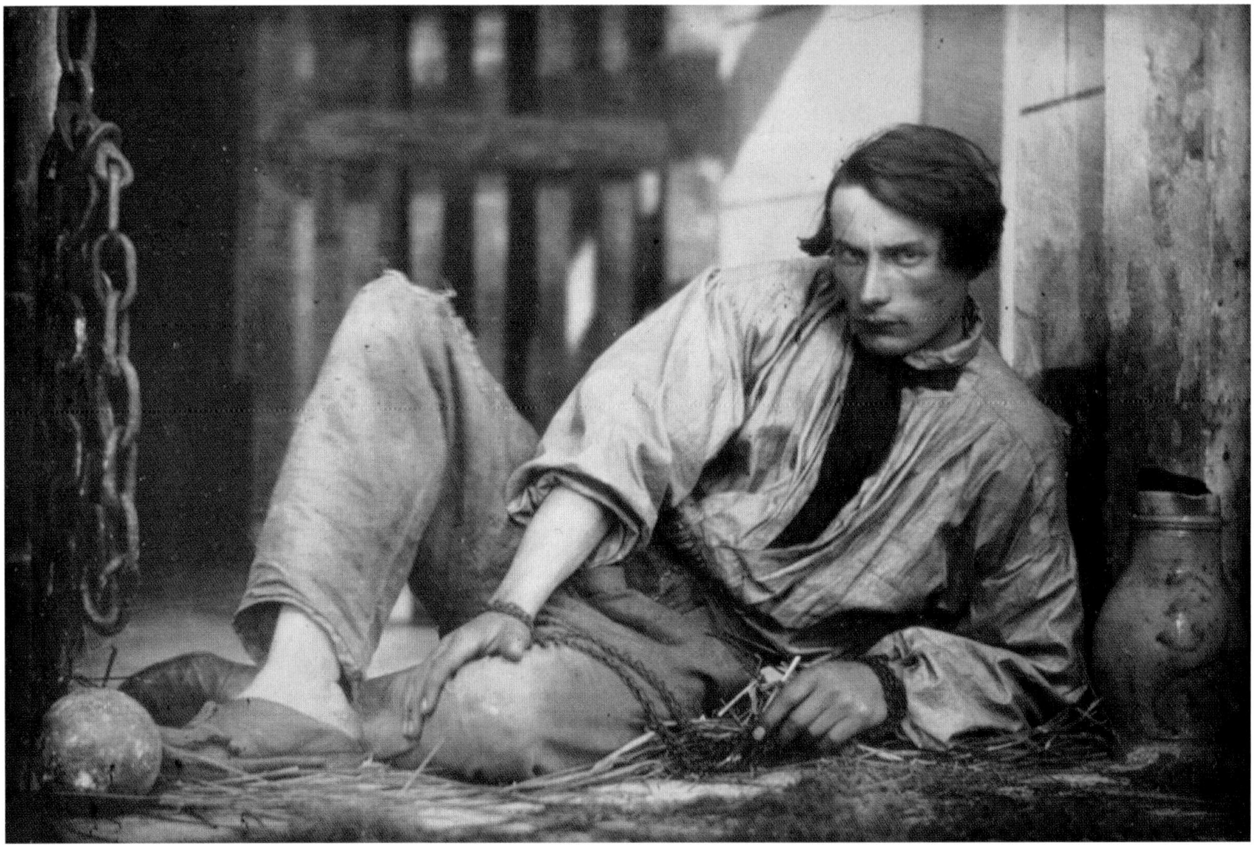

144. Adolphe Humbert de Molard, "Louis Dodier As a Prisoner," 1847, daguerreotype, Musée Gatien-Bonnet, Lagny.

Several years later, British photographer Henry Peach Robinson summed up the difficulties facing the group portrait: "The arrangement of a portrait group of figures is one of the most difficult things to succeed in accomplishing perfectly in photography; more difficult, certainly, than the composition of a picture that would take a much higher rank in art, but of which the materials were more under the command of the artist as regards selection and disposition. The portrait group is often nothing better than a pile of humanity fitted together like a dissected puzzle; a heterogeneous conglomeration of human atoms, and sometimes dogs, not one of which has any artistic relation to another; agreeing in nothing except that each individual of it shall keep rigid and stare at the lens."[8] In this context, to produce a successful image, photographers were obliged to resort to a level of artifice. The portraits Louis-Adolphe Humbert de Molard realized of his steward Louis Dodier in around 1847 underline how the pictorial trappings of genre made it possible not only to mitigate the technical constraints arising from lengthy exposure times, but also to promote the aesthetic role of the model, his appearance and features. Two daguerreotypes show Dodier in working clothes seated on a chair: in the first he seems wrapped in thought, a little forced, perhaps toying with the

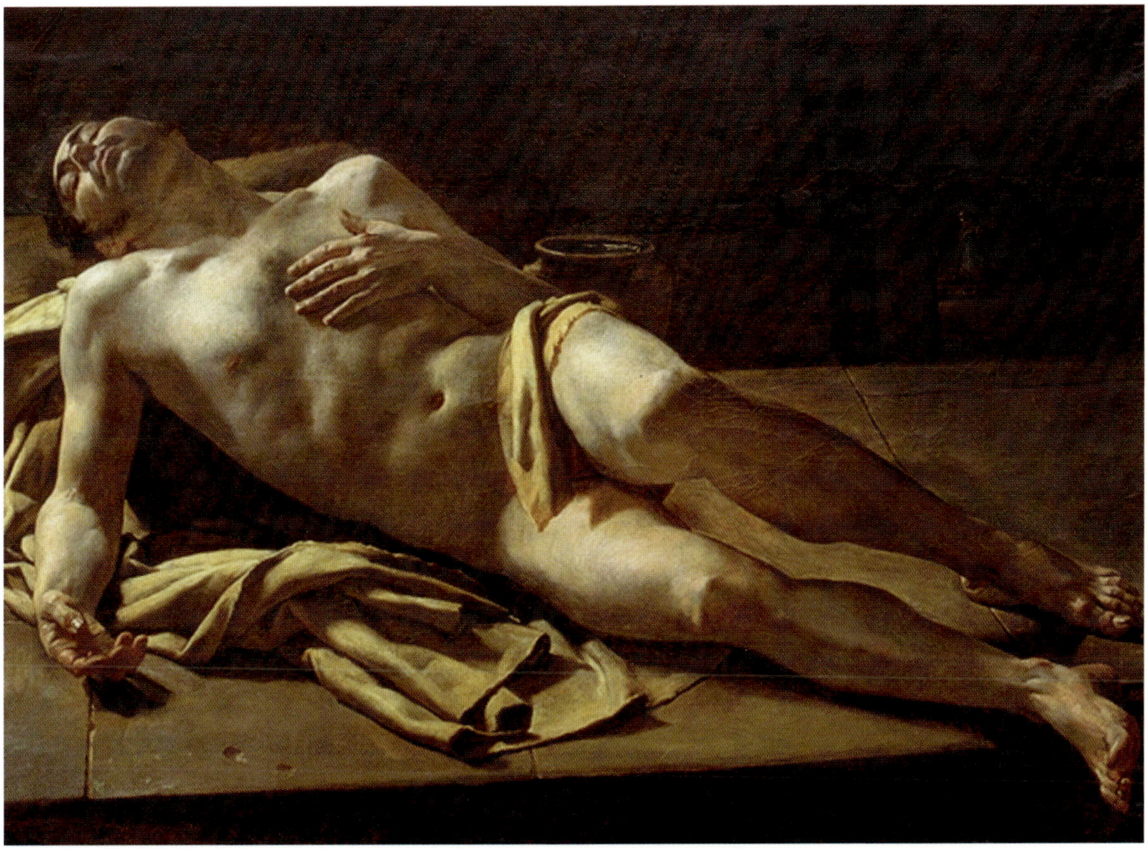

145. François-Joseph Heim, *The Prisoner*, 1827, oil on canvas, Musée Municipal, Semur-en-Auxois.

photographer; in the second, he sits bolt upright, eyes raised, tools in hand, undoubtedly closer to how he was in everyday life (Louis-Adolphe Humbert de Molard, "Portrait of Louis Dodier, with a Hand Held to His Cheek," and "Portrait of Louis Dodier, Face to the Front, with Tools," c. 1845–46, daguerreotypes, Musée d'Orsay, Paris). If the young man's face seems pleasing and honest enough, it has nothing of the dark beauty emanating from his most successful portrait, in which he mimes a prisoner in fetters (ill. 144).[9] The influence of painting is manifest in Dodier's pose as well as in the lighting and a feeling of enclosure that enhances the drama and which resembles a picture by another pupil of David's, François-Joseph Heim (ill. 145). The scene was carefully composed and beyond its pictorial and literary models—Scott's romantic drama is never far away; the photograph exalts the intensity of the steward's physical presence. The result is disconcerting. Technical modernity here serves a romantic aesthetic drawing on the worlds of poetry and of painting.

Inventing reality

Genre also permitted photographers to display their talent for conjuring up new realities that a discovery subjected to the

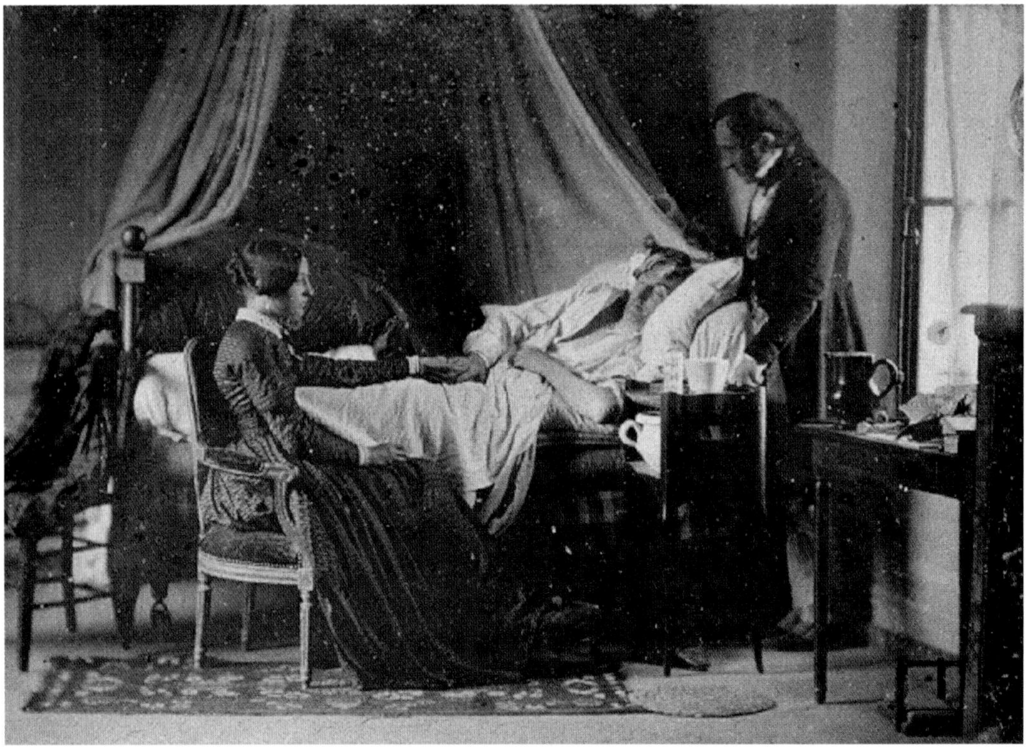

146. Adolphe Humbert de Molard, "The Patient at Lagny," 1849, daguerreotype, Musée Gatien-Bonnet, Lagny.

laws of exactitude seemed virtually to impose on them. Thus they could demonstrate their inventiveness and creativity.

Humbert de Molard composed a daguerreotype scene of a visit to a man confined to bed in which he appeared himself (ill. 146). The tableau is inspired by Dutch painting in particular and illustrates a household drama guaranteed to stimulate an emotional response. It also draws attention to the virtuosity of the photographer in mastering the difficult lighting conditions inherent in indoor photography.[10] This picturesque-cum-technical exploit was much appreciated by contemporary photographers. Molard here displays exceptional qualities as much in the composition of the scene—the curtains around the bed, the position of the visitors, their dignified and attentive attitude all reinforcing the theatricality of the episode—as in the use of the summer sunlight entering by the window and creating a soft glow in the room, illumining—without dazzling—each face, the patient's especially. In one photograph reminiscent of numerous engravings inciting the beholder to religious virtue, Camille Dolard shows himself as a hypochondriac receiving succor from a sister of charity.

Genre photographs

In an account of photographs shown by Félix-Jacques Moulin in 1853, Ernest Lacan makes use of the pictorial category and describes them as "genre photographs" (ill. 143). In his article, he refers to the pictures of Charles Nègre, the photographer who, in his eyes, had invented "photographic genre": "A painter of talent, who is at the same time a photographer of the first rank, with the intelligence of an artist, M. C. Nègre has understood how certain scenes lend themselves magnificently to being reproduced with the lens. His 'Ragman' and 'Chimneysweeps' created the photographic *genre*. M. Moulin has followed his lead, and, by almost exclusively plowing this new furrow, has proved himself worthy of a place among his fellows. He is the photographer of *genre*." (For Charles Nègre's "Ragman," see ill. 37.) Lacan's remarks show how photographic and pictorial genre alike aimed to create empathy in viewers, seeking to arouse emotions based on feelings shared by the greatest number, such as family relationships: "['The Spinner'] is a work full of charm and... her laboring hand has stayed, her distaff escapes her grasp, and all because her daughter, a delectable child... has come up to her, probably suffering some childish fear, and is hugging her with chubby white arms."[11] He concludes by recalling how the work was inspired by Dutch painting, whose recent vogue had popularized scenes of daily life: "This scene is not just a delicious composition; it is also an admirably well realized photograph. Ineffably simple, the group is very skillfully posed. The two heads possess a touching and lifelike expression; that of the woman is wholly in the sentiment of Gerard Dow [*sic*]."[12]

In 1854, Nègre published a lengthy article in *La Lumière* concerning the sale of the collection of the Baron of Mecklenburg to the Hôtel Drouot auction house. Containing some thirty canvases, the collection was entirely devoted to Flemish and Dutch art: "What exquisite taste, what experience, what willpower is required to gather and preserve a relatively small number of works of the first order so that together they resolve into a harmonious whole?"[13] The painter and photographer revels in the simple but to his eyes perfect manner in which Rembrandt and his contemporaries convey everyday existence and authenticity in their models: "[Rembrandt's] first models were peasants, men who lived outside in nature, possessing neither the culture nor the conventions of city life, who, coming to the cellar that served as his workshop, would present before the young painter heads bursting with frankness and health. Rembrandt painted this exuberant nature without constraint, without check, in complete independence of mind, and his work is captivating in its truth, warmth, and life; it is these fundamental qualities that form the bedrock of his talent." On the face of it, these lines echo Nègre's own photographic creations. In recommending the same fidelity to the model as Rembrandt, Nègre stresses the importance of selecting faces that can convey the artist's intention—a choice even more crucial for photographers than for painters, since the former are unable to tinker with the sitter's real appearance.

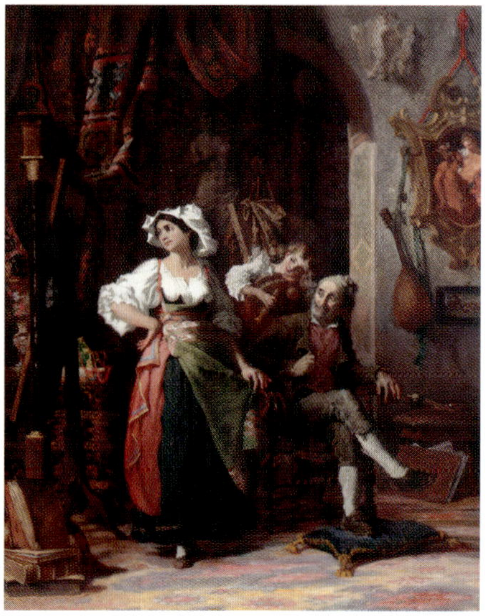

147. Auguste Dutuit, *Models in a Studio in the Painter's Absence*, 1869, oil on canvas, Musée des Beaux-Arts de la Ville de Paris, Petit Palais, Paris.

Composing scenes that were inspired, like Nègre's photographs, by humble folk in the street, the British photographer of Swedish extraction, Oskar Gustav Rejlander, shows himself particularly attentive to the expressions of his models, choosing poses and attitudes that emphasize their inner pathos. Rejlander too was inspired by the genre painting of his age, but also by vaudeville in works whose anecdotal content is designed to arouse shared emotions ("Hard Times," 1860, albumen print, George Eastman Collection, Rochester, NY; "Armer Joe" ["Poor Joe"], c. 1860, albumen print, National Media Museum, Bradford). Some of his photographs inspired works by end-of-century naturalist painters who saw them as ideal models for a combination of realism and a respectable level of pathos (Jules Bastien-Lepage, *Pas mèche* [Nothing Doing], oil on canvas, 1882, National Gallery of Scotland, Edinburgh).

Costumes and dressing-up

Not only did the models' features call for careful selection: there was also the choice of an appropriate costume. Indeed, attire was often the only way of distinguishing a scene set in Brittany from one taking place in Italy or the Orient; the garments in which the subjects were dressed thus diversified what was a limited range of attitudes. The attention paid to clothing became all the more intensive after the 1840s, with the increasing interest in ethnology and folklore.[14] In the light of this fledgling research, it became important that the detail on a cap or on a piece of embroidery appeared absolutely exact. Painters and photographers thus often accumulated a vast mass of costumes and accessories. The posthumous inventory of Julien Vallou de Villeneuve records a bequest to the committee of the Société des Artistes peintres, sculpteurs, architectes, graveurs et dessinateurs (Society of Painters, Sculptors, Architects, Engravers, and Draftsmen) of "divers costume models for a lump sum of 60 francs, including: costume for an Italian girl, a skirt or bolt of cloth colored scarlet with a broad ribbon along the edge, part of the costume for an Italian woman from the uplands; costume for an Oriental woman: a long calico blouse, a short veil with little white flowers, a Moresque bodice in green silk; fragments of costumes for Spanish women; garments for Swiss women from Bern; a coat for a Greek woman; several corsets from the time of Louis XV; a skirt for a Normandy countrywoman."[15] Similarly the stock of photographs belonging to Jean-Léon Gérôme and his son-in-law, Aimé Morot, include several showing a dummy sporting historical costumes used by the painters.[16] Sometimes with a tinge of humor, genre painters made much of this taste for fancy dress and exploited the function of costume in producing meaning. Canvases, like the one exhibited by Auguste Dutuit at

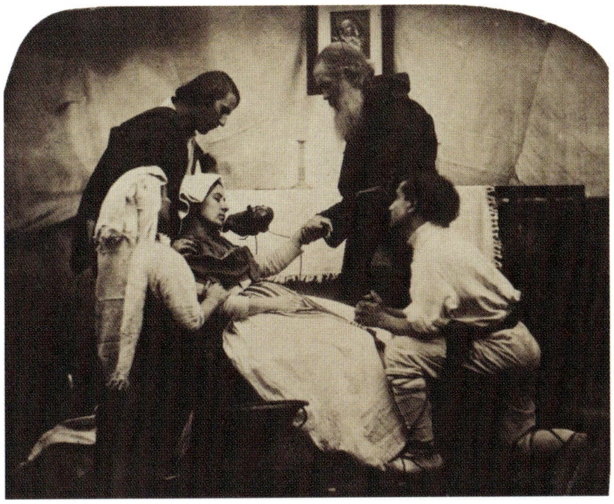

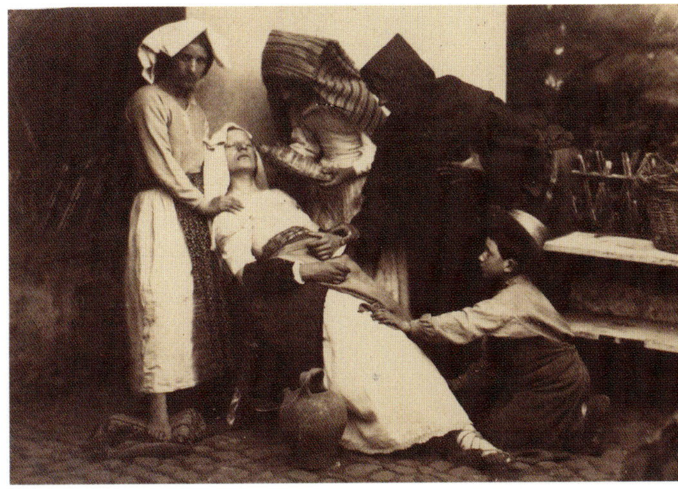

148. **Above, left:** Giacomo Caneva, "The Last Rites," c. 1850, salt print, Dietmar Siegert Collection, Munich/Kalamata.

149. **Above, right:** Anonymous or Edmond Lebel, "Models Dressed in the Italian Style Composing a Pictorial Scene," 1850–59, albumen print, Musée d'Orsay, Paris.

the Salon of 1869, show in one and the same studio a countrywoman from the Abruzzi, an eighteenth-century *petit marquis*, and a youthful Breton shepherd, whose regional and historical differences depend entirely on clues from their attire (ill. 147).

The charms of Italy off the beaten track

The interest in the ordinary people of Italy as a subject developed greatly during the 1820s. Its first interpreters were a number of David's pupils, including Léopold Robert, François-Joseph Navez, and Jean-Victor Schnetz, but soon throughout Europe pictures were overflowing with country girls from the mountains, women fortune-tellers, and *pifferari* (pipe players). These artists turned out charming or melancholy genre scenes, sometimes with a religious pretext, in compositions that remained rooted in the academic tradition, where the costumes did not infringe the rules of the old masters by being only moderately exotic: examples include *The Vow to the Madonna* by Jean-Victor Schnetz, painted in 1831 for the church of Saint-Étienne-du-Mont in Paris (oil on canvas, Musée du Louvre, Paris), and *The Pilgrims in Rome* by Paul Delaroche, (1842, oil on canvas, Poznán). The obligatory tour through the Peninsula undertaken by young artists to study the vestiges of ancient and Renaissance Italy now became an occasion to record the charms of a picturesque populace. In 1843, the young Jean-Léon Gérôme accompanied his master Delaroche; the delight afforded him on this voyage of discovery, which took him to Rome, Venice, and then Naples, is recorded in his *Notes*: "Aged eighteen, I was then in Italy. I had no illusions as to my studio studies which were indeed very weak.... I made studies of architecture, landscapes, figures, animals.... This year is one of happiest and most profitable of my life, and at that time

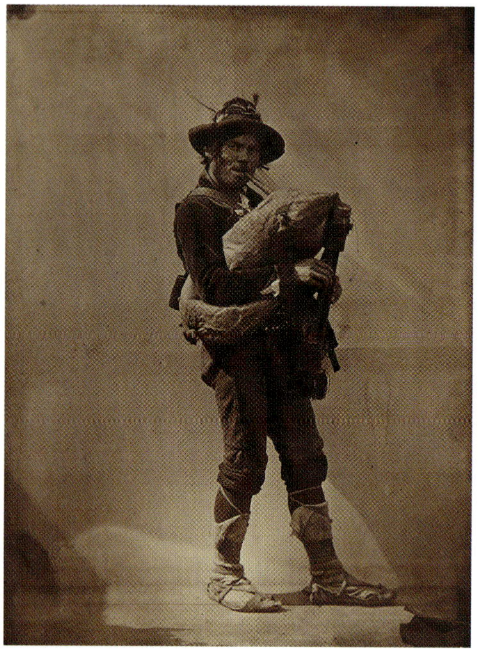

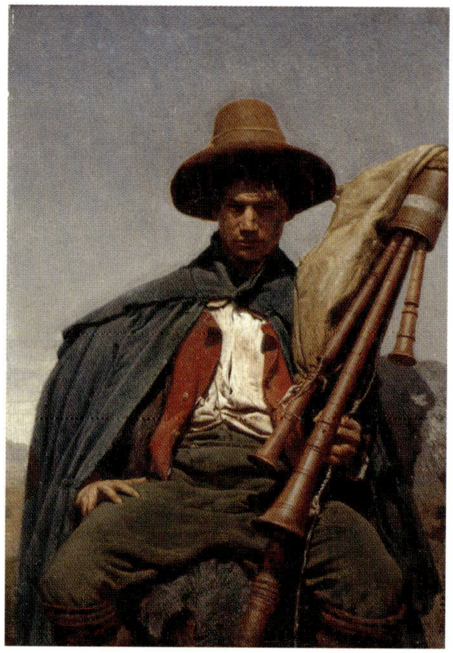

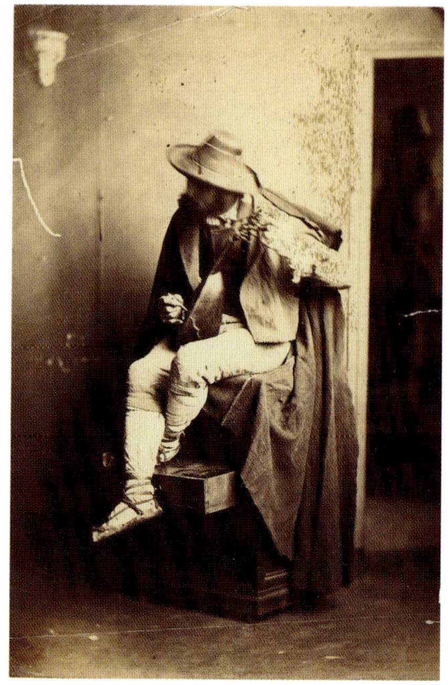

150. **Above, left:** Adrien Tournachon, "Pifferaro," 1855, salt print, Société Française de Photographie, Paris.

151. **Above, center:** Jean-Léon Gérôme, *Pifferaro*, 1856, oil on canvas, Musée des Beaux-Arts, Nantes.

152. **Above, right:** Edmond Lebel, "Jules Picavet Dressed in the Italian Style Posing in the Studio," c. 1863–68, albumen print, Musée d'Orsay, Paris.

I undoubtedly made serious progress."[17] He produced many pencil sketches, as testified by a touching little notebook that remains in the hands of his heirs.

Photographers too delighted in these amiable motifs of daily life in Italy. Giacomo Caneva took many posed scenes with models dressed in traditional costume. Intended for artists as well as collectors, these photographs took their cue from painting (ills. 148–49). A peasant from the Abruzzi, the *pifferaro*, named after the flute with which he would scrape a living playing in villages, became one of the stock figures of this well-tempered picturesque. His tanned, somewhat somber, even disturbing presence, and wild-looking attire saved such genre scenes from insipidity. Easily identifiable with his instrument, sporting broadcloth breeches and leather gaiters, the *pifferaro* was a familiar figure in Paris studios belonging to painters and photographers alike. An artist's model, he was also the subject of many photographic studies. Charles Nègre produced several showing young musicians—or models rigged out like them. Adrien Tournachon presented two full-length photographs of a *Pifferaro* at an exhibition of the Société Française de Photographie in 1857 (ill. 150). Gérôme painted *pifferari* on several occasions and the theme became a recurrent one in his oeuvre in the 1850s. The artist was sufficiently fond of such figures to unveil canvases featuring them at successive annual Salons (ill. 151). Gérôme based these *pifferari* as much on photographic models as on his personal memories of Italy; the extreme degree of accuracy in the costumes might well have derived in part from photography. He also perhaps found in

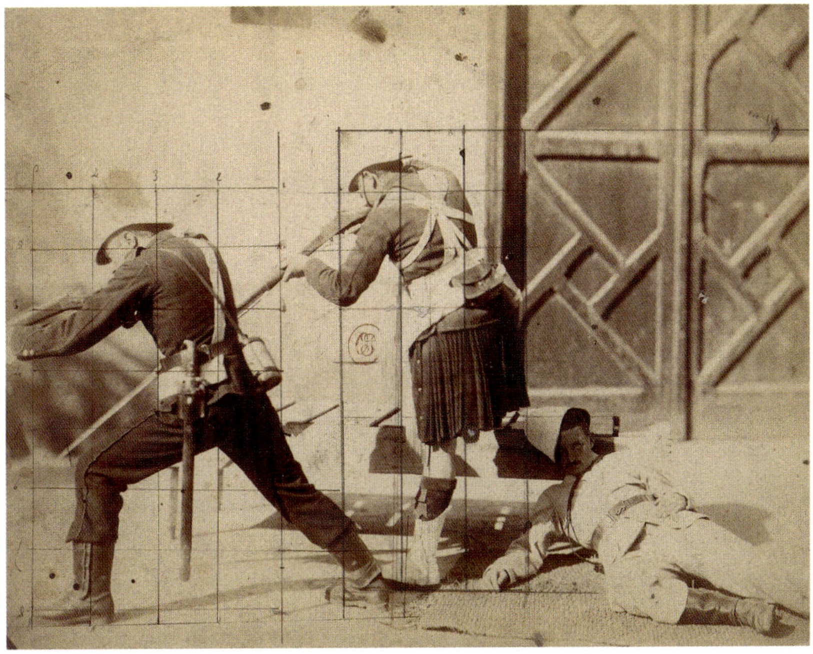

153. Olivier Pichat, "Two Soldiers," c. 1870, albumen print (squared up), Musée d'Orsay, Paris.

Tournachon's work the rather brutal lighting of the figures, which exacerbates outlines and reduces relief. Commenting on the *Pifferari* painted in 1857 (Stanford Museum), Théophile Gautier notes: "Photography, if only it could provide color at the same time as form, could not be more exactly truthful."[18] A picture of the painting was taken by Robert Bingham in 1859 for the "Photographic Gallery" of Goupil & Co., being sold by the publisher in this form until at least 1904, a photographic incarnation that further increased the *pifferaro*'s popularity.

A miniature photographic theater

In addition to aping scenes from genre painting, all the more successful since the dimensions of such canvases were often scarcely much greater than those of a photograph, some photographers accentuated the stage effects still further. Above and beyond the theatrical artifices of costume and set, photography lifted another veil, revealing a hidden, more private auditorium: the painter's studio. The genre scene was thus duplicated. On one and the same photograph, a composition inspired by painting, and evidencing the aesthetic qualities of the new invention—as well as its capacity to provide models or study material for artists and connoisseurs—overlaps with the portrayal of a place whose description had become a commonplace in both literature and painting. Several photographs in collections that belonged to painters even record the decor and the subterfuges that lay behind their realization. Thus, posing for his cousin the painter Edmond Lebel, Jules Picavet dressed as a Sicilian bandit: standing proud, his somber figure

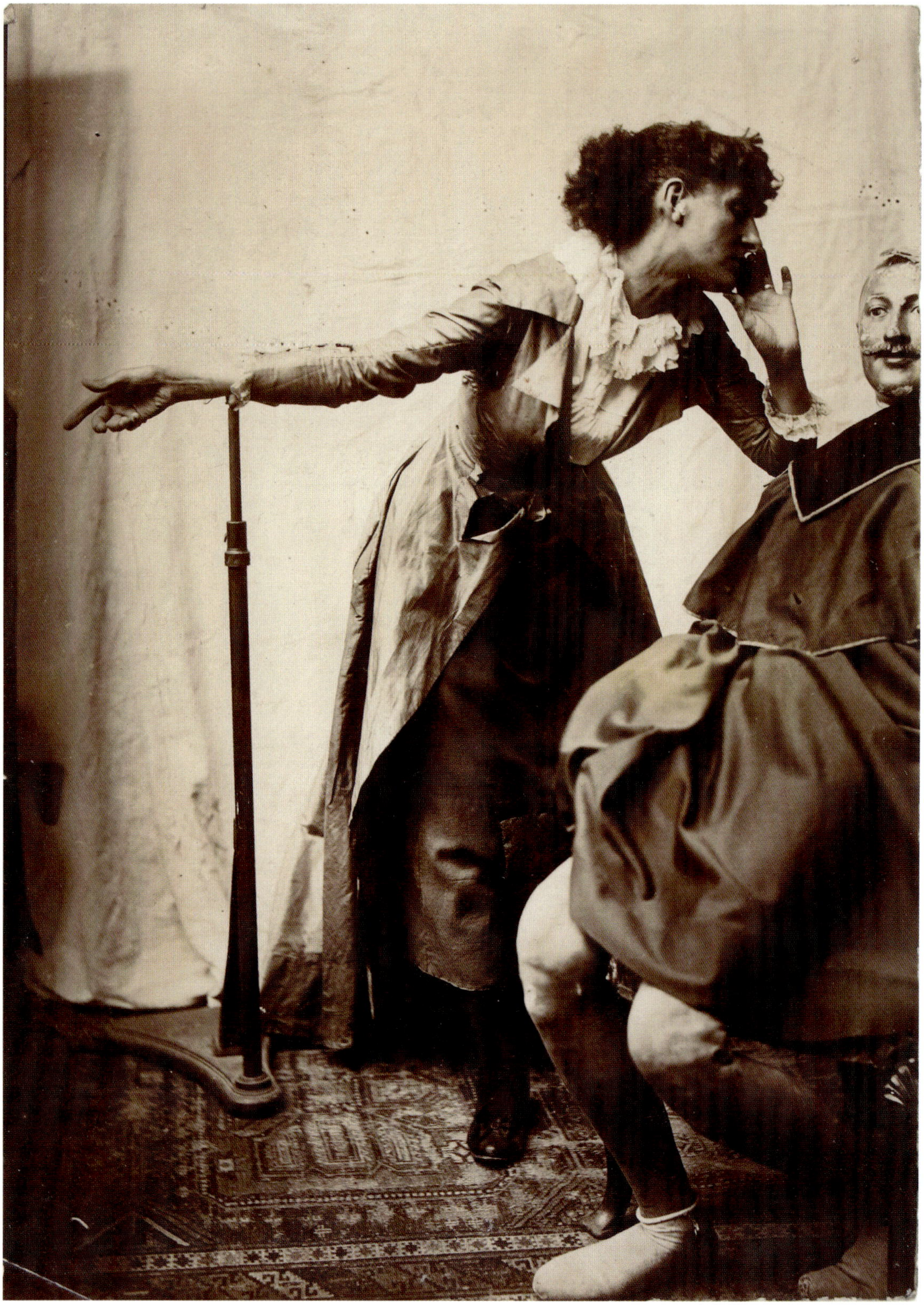

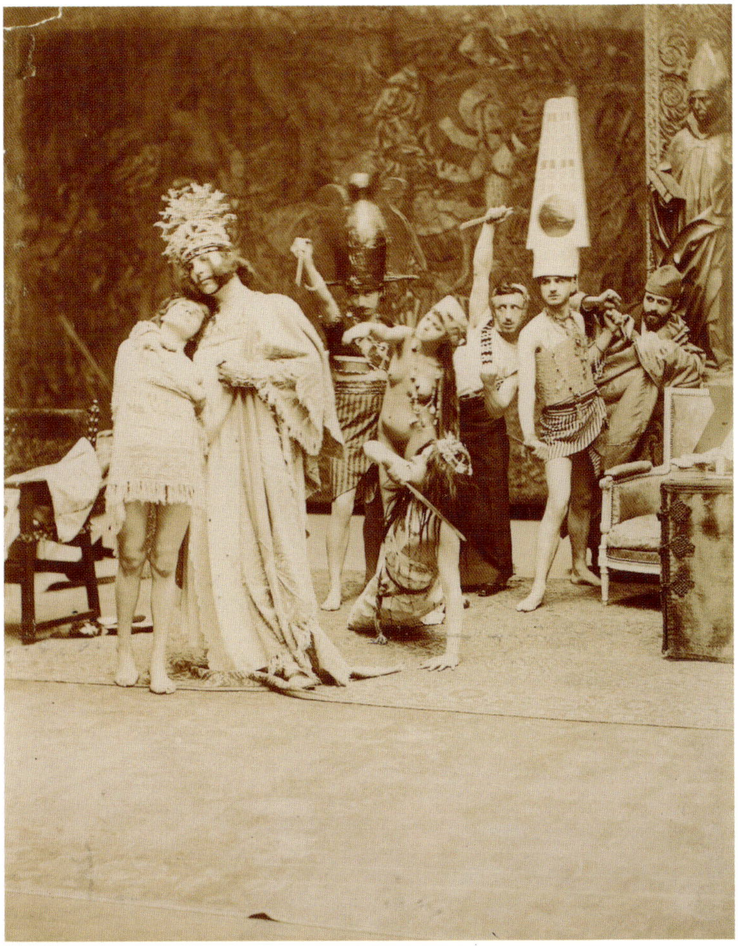

is ennobled by the melancholic pose given to him by the artist. If the photograph depicts this figure plausibly enough, no effort was made to conceal the studio bric-a-brac on which the model perches: piles of boxes, frames, and blankets (ill. 152). On a photograph intended to be used as a model for one of his canvases, the military painter Olivier Pichat carefully arranged the poses, costumes, and attitudes of two British soldiers. He must have been relatively satisfied with the final result since he squared it up for reproduction; but bizarrely the photograph leaves, in full view, the carpet on which one of the "victims" of the skirmish has collapsed (ill. 153).

Less well known is the charming rendezvous set up in a photograph belonging to the painter François Brunery, a pupil of Gérôme's much appreciated for canvases representing court ecclesiastics, often in the seventeenth century—a clever theme that combines religious seriousness and gimcrack, cardinal crimson, and gossamer lace. In a workshop stands a woman, one arm maintaining her pose, leaning over a dummy decked out in an ample chasuble to whisper in its ear. This meeting between a living model in fancy dress, and a carefully attired

154. **Facing page:** François Brunery, "Woman in a Dress and Lace Chemise, Leaning over a Dummy Wearing Priestly Vestments," c. 1900, silver print, Musée d'Orsay, Paris.

155. **Left:** Anonymous, "Murder Scene with Seven Figures: Study for a Painting set in Ancient Egypt," c. 1880, citrate print, Musée d'Orsay, Paris.

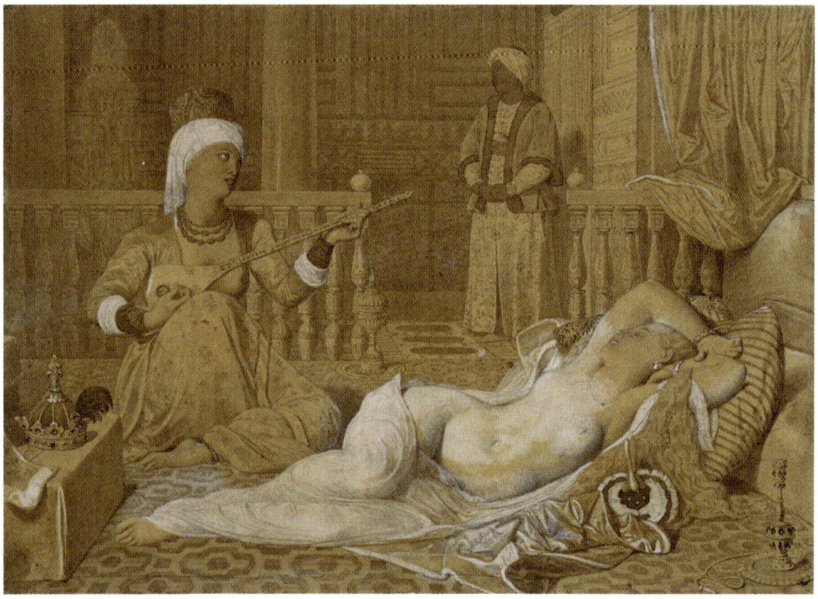

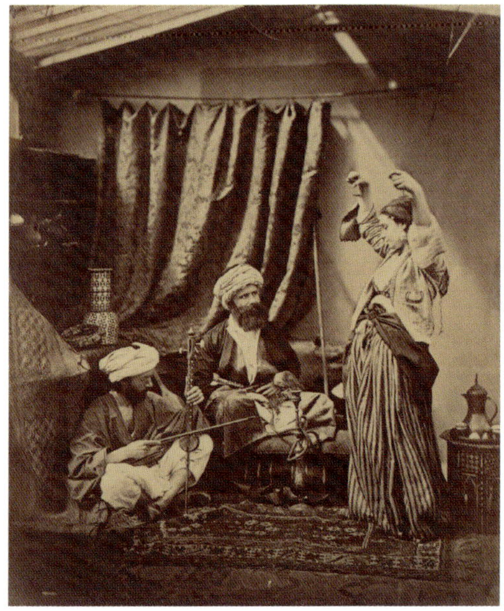

156. **Above, left:** Jean-Auguste-Dominique Ingres, *Odalisque with Slave*, 1858, lead pencil, pen and brown ink, and brown wash with white highlights on pasted and mounted tracing paper, Musée du Louvre, Paris.

157. **Above, right:** Roger Fenton, "Pasha and Bayadere," 1858, albumen print, The J. Paul Getty Museum, Los Angeles.

mannequin in wood and rags, dressed to appear as lifelike as possible, conjures up a simultaneously strange and intimate atmosphere that Brunery's actual paintings lack (ill. 154).[19]

Tricks of the trade

Ostensibly models for a history painter, five anonymous photographs now in the Musée d'Orsay raise a smile by the incongruity of the scenes represented and the amateurism of costumes that smack of papier-mâché, cardboard, and hastily run-up cloth. They evoke almost as much the preparation for one of the fancy-dress balls young artists were so fond of at the time as material for an academic painting. In a vast studio hung with tapestries, various figures wearing costumes aping those of ancient Egypt strike a pose: pharaohs, queens, or high priests. It is not known precisely what the photographer was trying to represent: just some young artists dressing up and larking about? Or did the artist pose them in view of some vast Egyptian scene? The declamatory aspect of their attitudes reminds one most of pantomime (ill. 155).

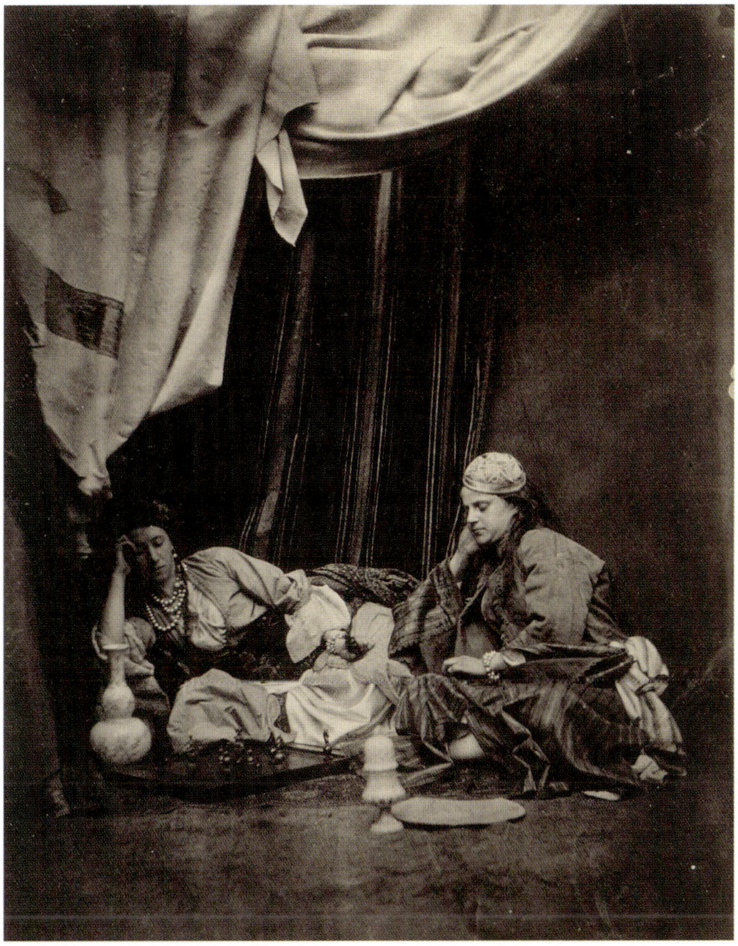

158. Attributed to Achille Bonnuit, "Orientalist Tableau Vivant: Two Women Drowsing," c. 1865, albumen print, Musée d'Orsay, Paris.

Photography thus produced new images that mimicked those of painting but which also—deliberately or no—revealed the tricks and dodges used in studios. The emergence of a *suppressed* reality in compositions, in which the referent remains academic painting, with its poses and attitudes, led to the invention of novel subjects, opened up new fields, which were soon exploited by painters in the late nineteenth century and into the early twentieth century.

Tableaux vivants

The mimetism of painting, together with the role-playing implied in creating this type of photographic image, has led one modern critic to employ the term "tableaux vivants" in their connection—a reference to the then fashionable variant of charades, in which actors would act out the poses and attitudes of a painting, as members of the Théâtre Arlequin had done in 1761 for the picture by Greuze.[20] The expression appeared in French at the beginning of the nineteenth century and was taken up in particular by Théophile Gautier in 1839 in his

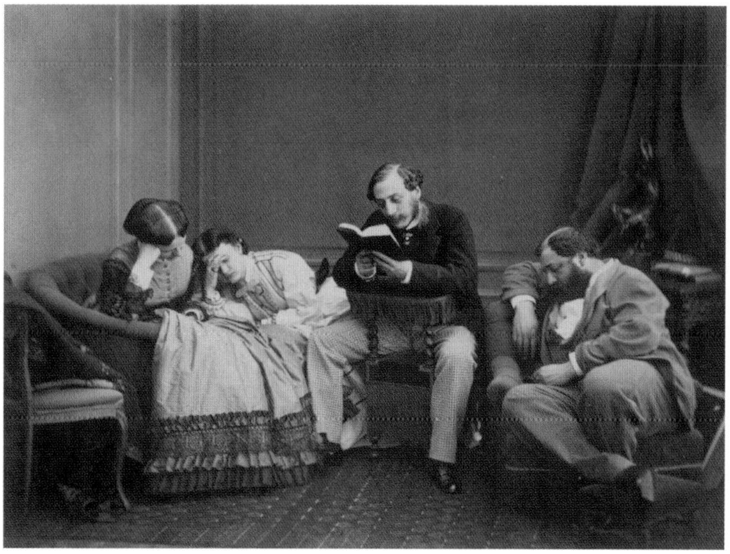

159. Count Olympe Aguado, "The Reading," 1862–64, albumen print, Musée d'Orsay, Paris.

short story *The Golden Fleece*. Apparently not used by contemporary commentators on photography, the term nonetheless designates a proven practice.

Avid readers of *The Thousand and One Nights*, painters found the imaginary Orient a plentiful and seductive source of inspiration. In 1858, Roger Fenton took several Orientalist scenes in his London workshop on Albert Terrace. Posing in some himself, he was assisted by his friend the painter Frank Dillon, who went on to acquire a complete set of the results. Scrupulous attention to truthfulness is here conjoined with a degree of imagination, in particular as regards the choice of artifacts and costumes. If some of these originated in the Middle East (which Fenton, though an inveterate traveler, had never actually seen), others seem to have been concocted in the workshop. The inspiration was decidedly pictorial. Fenton, who had studied in France as well as in Great Britain, here reinvents scenes derived from Ingres, Delacroix, and Chassériau. When they were displayed in London in January 1859, however, the critic of the *Photographic Journal* dealt with them as if they were faithful, first-hand testimonies of the Orient: "They are favourable examples, being admirable illustrations of Eastern scenes of actual life. Their execution, also, is worthy of Mr. Fenton's well-known fame."[21] Such confusions rendered the distinction between accurate images taken in the East and the imaginings of some fantastical vision still more problematic (ills. 156–57).[22] Achille Bonnuit, a painter at the Sèvres Manufactory, and belonging to the group around Henri-Victor Regnault and Louis Robert, took several hundred photographs that his immediate circle later collected into albums. The subjects are a cross between family snapshot and tableau vivant. Several examples of this type of work are tinged by Orientalist accents close to those of painting (ill. 158).

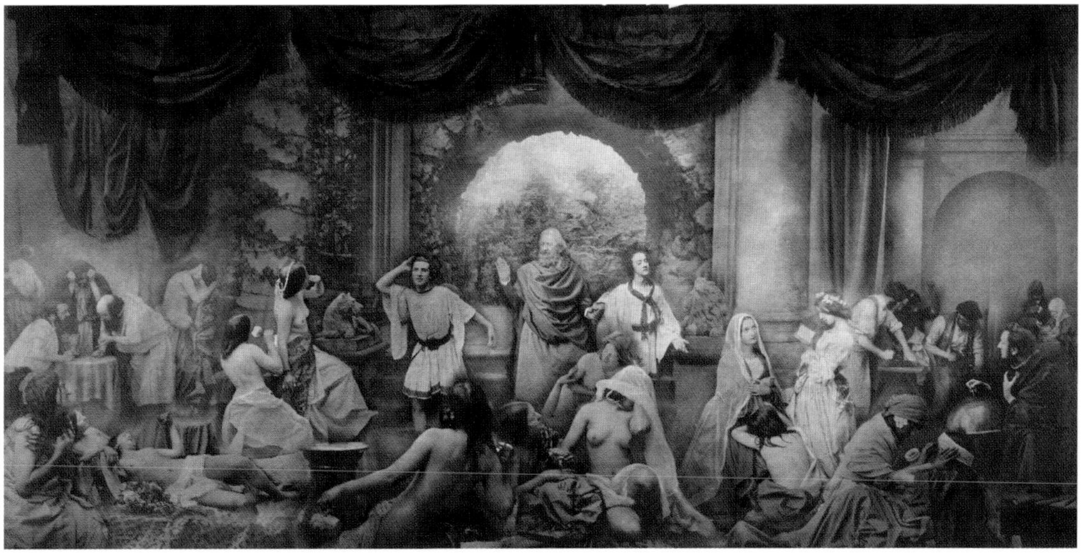

160. Oscar Gustav Rejlander, "The Two Ways of Life," 1857, carbon print from thirty negatives, National Media Museum, Bradford.

The pictures taken by Olympe Aguado, an intimate of the imperial family who trained in photography with Gustave Le Gray, show how flimsy the border between parlor game (charade and tableau vivant), family portraiture, and photographic genre scene was becoming, making their artistic appreciation and classification a thorny issue. Using himself as well as his relations—his brother, wife, and sister-in-law particularly—as models, Aguado composed several pictures in which the models' attitudes were scrupulously arranged. The result is both attractive and intriguing; in spite of the sitters and the location being duly noted, in spite of attire that is clearly in the contemporary fashion, as Michel Poivert has observed, these photographs, in which representation appears to lack a solid and readily identifiable referent, never seem quite real (ill. 159).[23]

Victorian fantasies

British photographers harbored unquestionable pictorial ambitions. It is these that underpinned their efforts to construe images that go beyond the pure reproduction of reality. The reputation and influence of Oscar Gustav Rejlander played a notable role in England. It was, for example, with Rejlander that Reverend Charles Lutwidge Dodgson—better known as Lewis Carroll—learnt the rudiments of the technique. Starting out as a painter, Rejlander took up photography in the late 1840s. In 1857, he stated his claim for photography as a creative medium in a large-scale piece assembled from no less than thirty-two glass negatives, *The Two Ways of Life*, whose subject, inspired by Renaissance painting, contrasts the virtues of a sober existence with the ills of dissipation. Rejlander combined references to the grand pictorial tradition with the technical skill required to seamlessly integrate an unusually large number of negatives

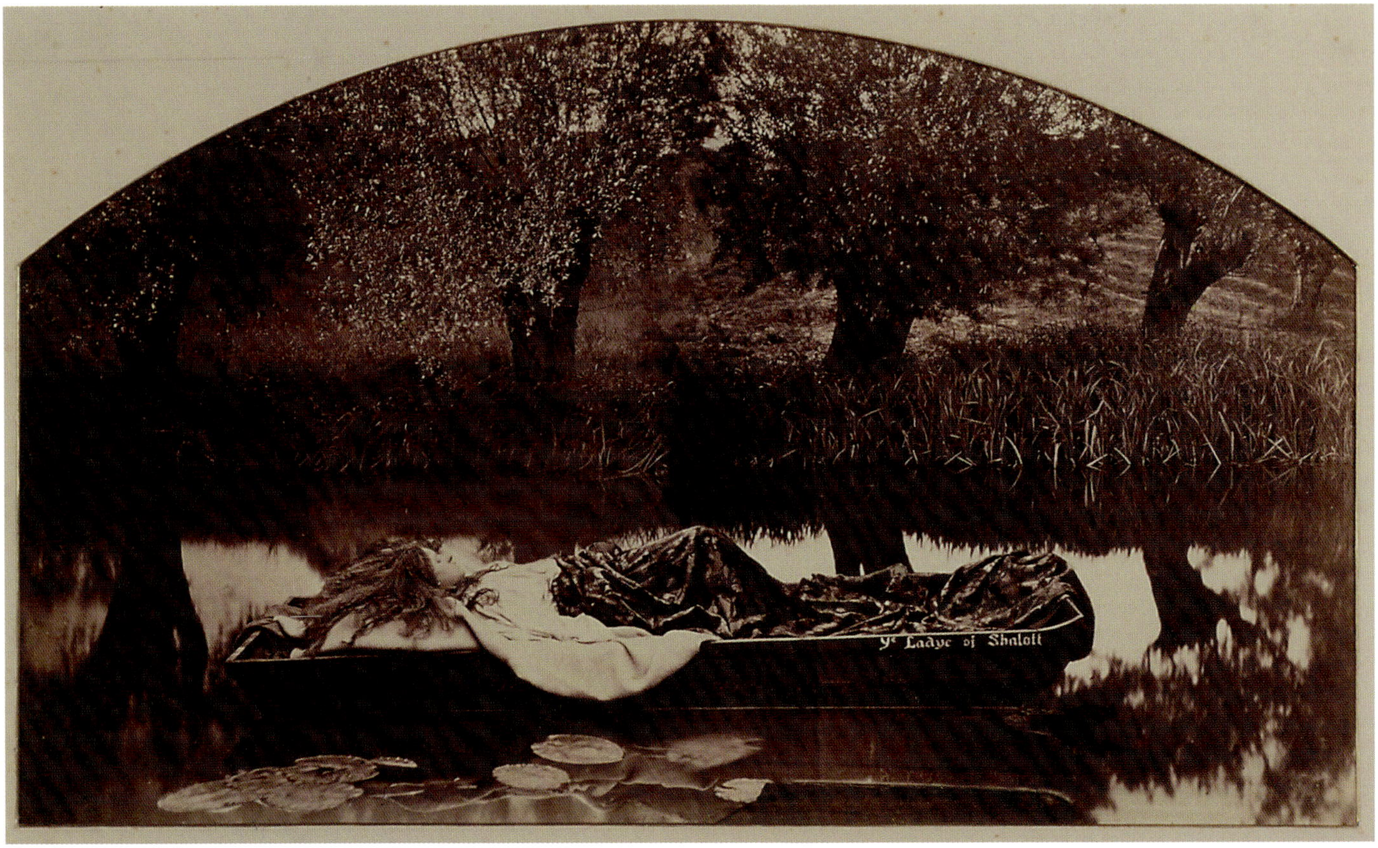

161. Henry Peach Robinson, "The Lady of Shalott," 1860–61, albumen print, National Media Museum, Bradford.

into a single image. The complete work was exhibited in 1857 at *The Art Treasures*, a major international exhibition in Manchester that displayed many masterpieces of British art. The numerous models were diversely arranged about a vast stage, as in a theater. In spite of its narrative ambitions, diversity of pose, and episodic composition, the reality effects produced by the costumes, and the emphasis laid on the physical appearance of the models, are more redolent of genre painting than of the grand manner (ill. 160). The ostensible source is the seminal allegory of the invention portrait recorded by Pliny: "[the daughter of the potter Butades of Sicyon,] deeply in love with a young man about to depart on a long journey, traced the profile of his face, as thrown upon the wall by the light of the lamp. Upon seeing this, her father filled in the outline, by compressing clay upon the surface, and so made a face in relief, which he then hardened by fire along with other articles of pottery."[24] Light and shadow; imprint, trace, reflection: Pliny's text reads like a prescient allegory of photography. In the scene as Rejlander presents it, two models act out Pliny's anecdote. In its effort to elevate the status of photography, this theatrical piece amounts to a veritable allegorical tableau vivant.

Determined to demonstrate that their practice possessed something beneath its veneer of technique, many English

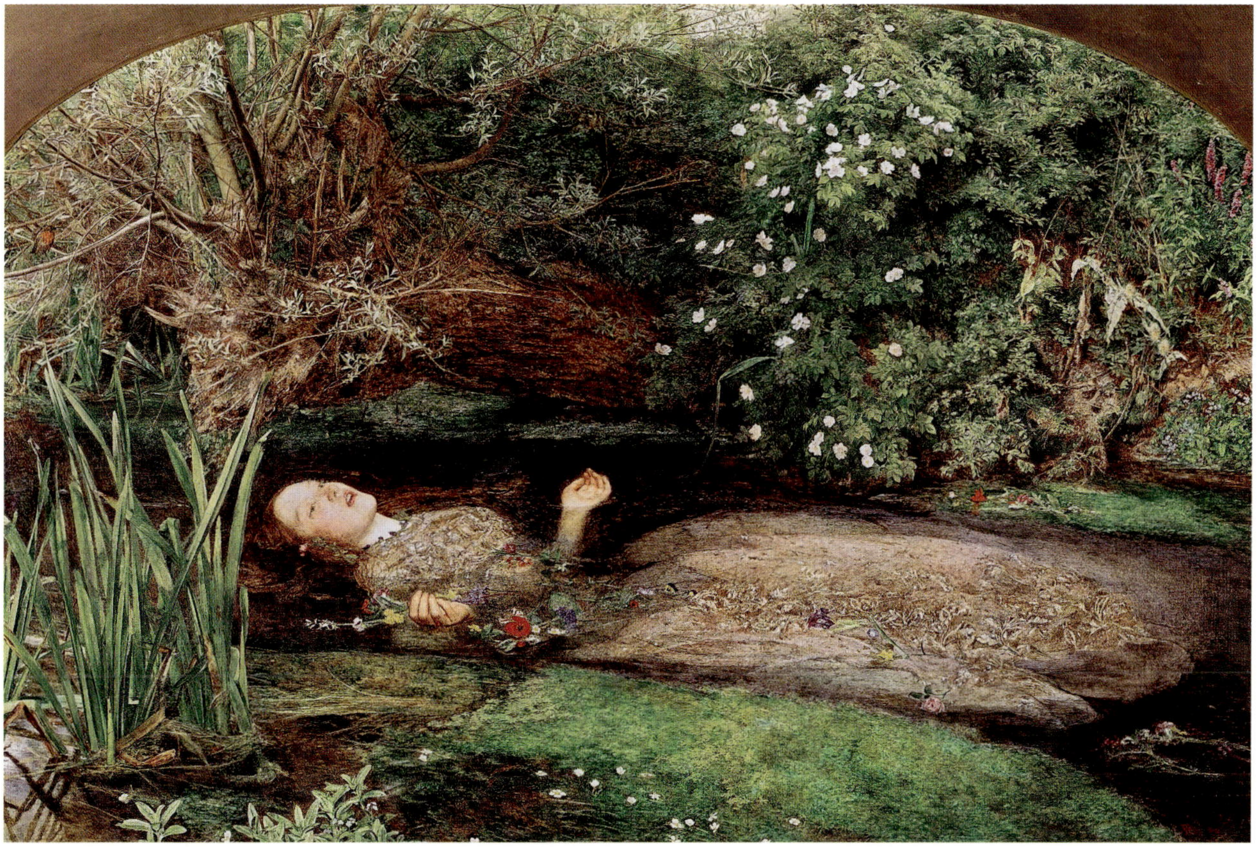

162. John Everett Millais, *Ophelia*, 1851–52, oil on canvas, Tate Britain, London.

photographers adhered to the ideas of Talbot, who, like his successors, had promoted artistic amateur photography over its professional, commercial equivalent, cultivating scenes that parallel those of painting, the theater, or literature as a ready means of ennobling their personal productions and of moving away from reality.[25] Contemporaries of the Pre-Raphaelites (some photographers formed part of their circle; Julia Cameron, for instance, was a close friend of the painter William Holman Hunt), they turned to the same written sources—Shakespeare, Milton, and Tennyson in particular—and, like them, married scrupulous attention to detail with a quest for imaginative, not to say outlandish compositions. In his conception of The *Lady of Shalott*, the heroine of a poem by Lord Alfred Tennyson, Henry Peach Robinson was much inspired by John Everett Millais's *Ophelia* (ills. 161–62). Like Rejlander, Robinson often abutted several glass negatives in the same photograph, drawing the scenes beforehand to ensure the composition was harmonious and correctly framed. One of his most famous pictures, "Fading Away" (ill. 163), shows a tearful family assembled around an expiring girl—probably a young victim of tuberculosis, then a devastating disease. Robinson had already photographed the figure of the girl in 1857 under the title "She Never Told Her Love" (albumen print, Musée

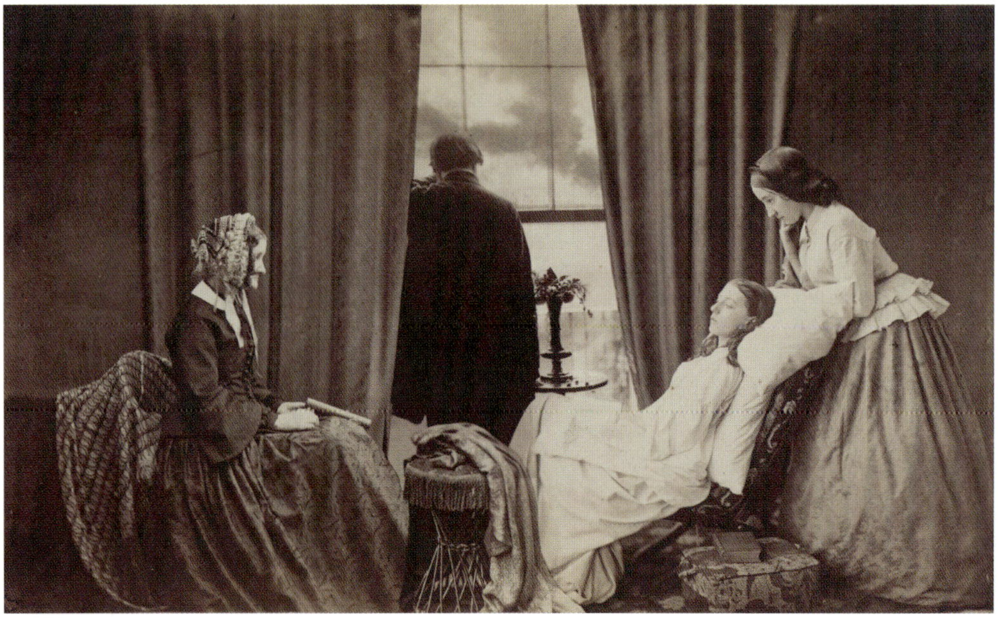

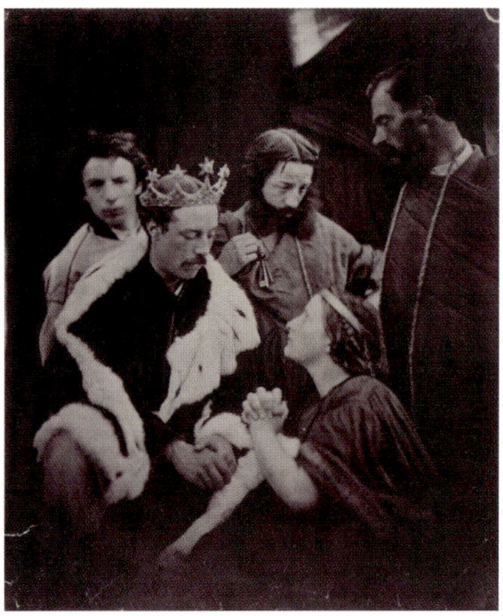

163. **Above, top:** Henry Peach Robinson, "Fading Away," 1858, albumen print from five negatives, National Media Museum, Bradford.

164. **Above, bottom:** Julia Margaret Cameron, "Queen Philippa Interceding for the Burghers of Calais," 1872–74, albumen print, National Media Museum, Bradford.

165. **Facing page:** Julia Margaret Cameron, "The Return after Three Days," 1865, albumen print, National Media Museum, Bradford.

d'Orsay, Paris), a motif close to the depictions of ill-fated and clandestine love affairs of which Dante Gabriel Rossetti and his entourage were so fond. Julia Margaret Cameron's photographic oeuvre also has its roots in literature, often taking inspiration from biblical texts or Shakespeare; she illustrated *King Lear*, for example. Unlike Rejlander and Robinson, her photographs were developed from a single negative, with her friends and relations donning costumes and posing for the scene (ill. 165).[26] Sharing this taste for fancy dress with the painters Holman Hunt and David Wilkie Winfield, she was extremely attentive to accuracy in costume and to making the model's expression fit the character (ill. 164). A close friend of Alfred Tennyson, she had the idea of composing a photographic version of his poem *The Idylls of the King*, inspired by Arthurian legend. Scrupulous as to her selection of models, Cameron was adept at eliciting and capturing the expression best adapted to the narrative episode. Conceived uniquely for the photograph, here the Victorian drawing-room entertainment of the tableau vivant takes on a profoundly poetical and symbolic significance. Rather than the performed imitation of a picture, it becomes the channel for a highly individual body of work in which the paragon of painting is transformed by the physical charisma of her models and by a new relation to time. All these tableaux vivants are tinged with a searing, almost fateful melancholy, further exacerbated by their timeless atmosphere. In her predominately frontal compositions, Cameron places her lens very close to the subject. Here, for the first time, in the service of a new and subtle vein of aesthetic grace, the hitherto photographic accident of "soft focus" is used to significant artistic purpose.

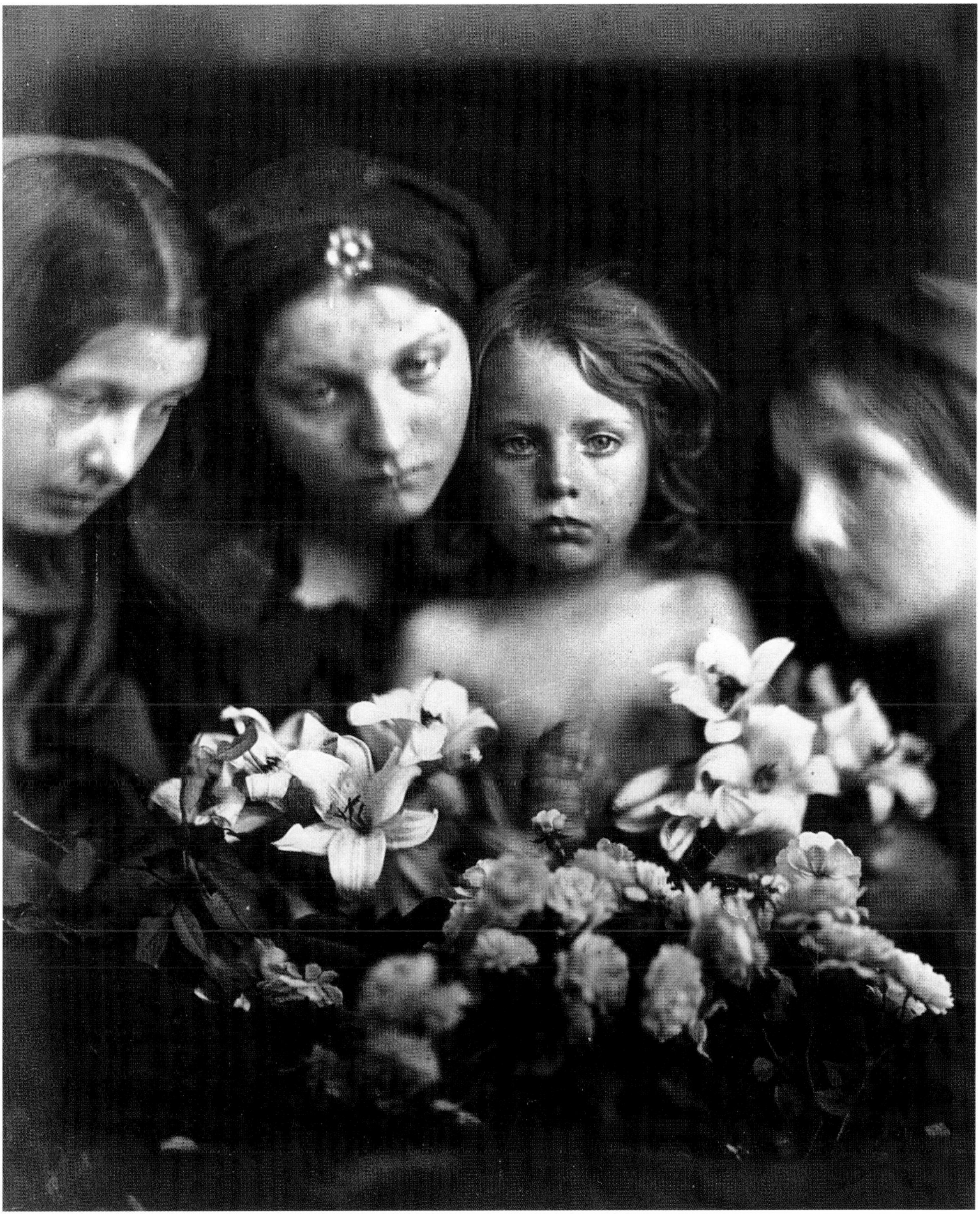

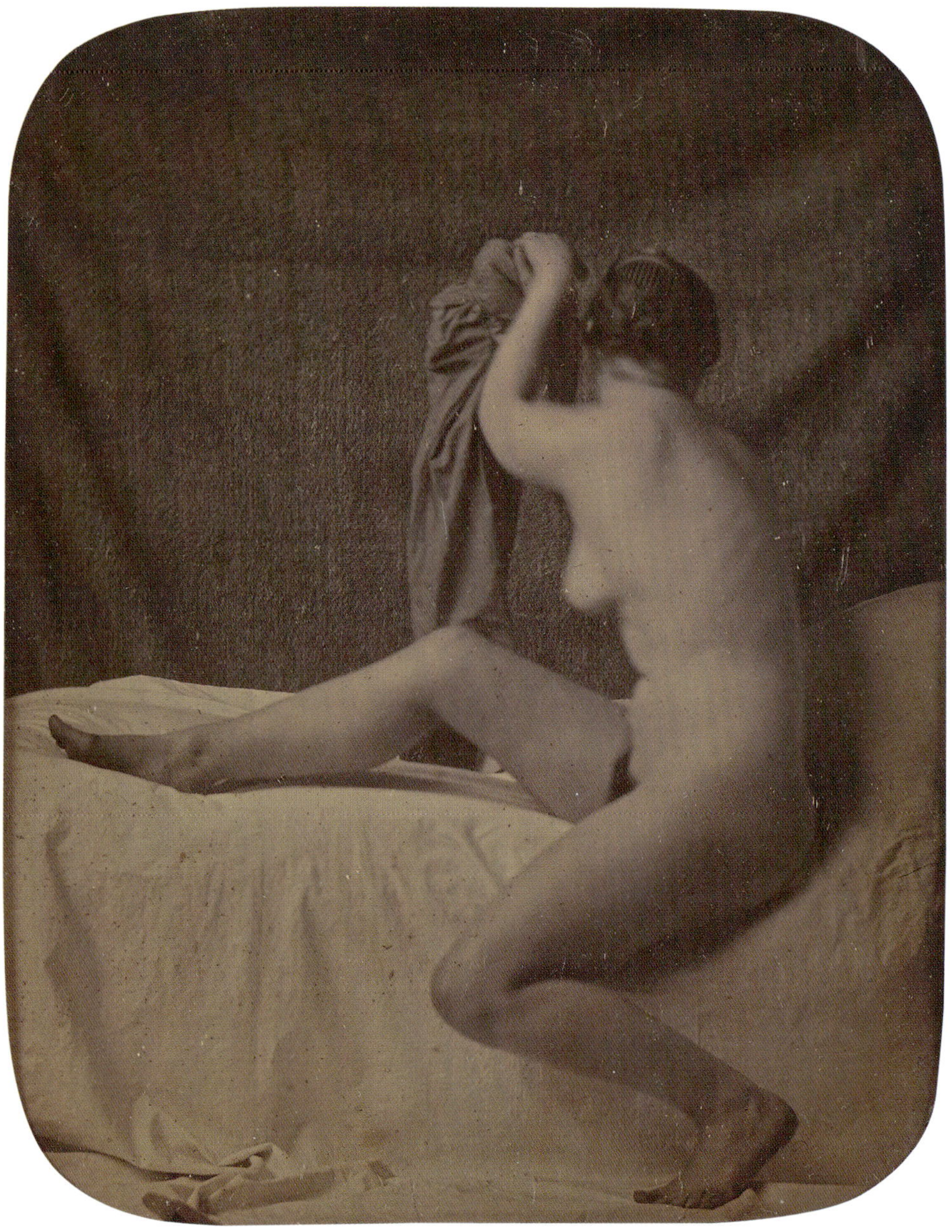

"Photography . . . obliges Artists to divest themselves of the old routines and to dispense with the old formulae. It has opened our eyes and forced us to look at what we never saw before. . . . Because of it, Truth has emerged from the well; she will never return to it again."[1]

PHOTOGRAPHING THE NUDE

THE AMBIGUITIES OF A GENRE

In the early nineteenth century, the representation of the naked human form was already part of a deep-seated tradition in painting and sculpture in which, above and beyond naturalistic reproduction, a number of concerns were intertwined: philosophical (the confusion between beauty and truth), religious (the choice of an ideal figuration of the divinity), and moral (the transmission of acceptable models for young artists). Since the late seventeenth century in France, art education in the academy had arrived at a conception of the drawn, carved, or painted nude that prescribed a lengthy program of training for young artists, during which their eyes and hands, but also their minds, were gradually engaged by ceaseless copying of antique and Renaissance precedents in the form of drawn, engraved, or cast copies. Access to the live "model" class was permitted only to those young artists who had demonstrated not only their skill and know-how, but also their comprehension and acceptance of the canons of antiquity. Moreover, living models would then ape poses in antique or Renaissance works; thus life imitated its representation. Accuracy in depicting physical proportion, in rendering its symmetry, and in showing how muscles and tendons attach to the skeleton was learned in the shadow of earlier depictions that served as benchmarks. As Sébastien Bourdon had decreed in the mid-seventeenth century: "It is advisable that, after drawing a figure after nature and having put into it everything he has learned to do, the student should lay in a further version of the same figure [Polykleites' *Doryphoros*] on a spare sheet of paper.... He should then check, with compass in hand, whether what he has drawn after nature conforms to the measures given by the classical style."[2] By extension and in accordance with the teaching rules promulgated by the institution, in the eighteenth century an "academy" became a term indicating "the imitation of a live model, drawn, painted, or modeled."[3]

166. **Facing page:** Anonymous, "Nude Woman Viewed from the Rear," c. 1850, daguerreotype, Metropolitan Museum of Art, New York.

Physical beauty, moral beauty

Copied from preexistent models, this idealized nature was transparent: bodily beauty showed that of the soul. Since the Renaissance the allegorical figure of "Truth" had possessed the attributes codified by Cesare Ripa: "Truth: a totally naked beauty gazing on the sun [which she] holds in her right hand.... She is painted nude to show that she is naturally innocent and that she requires no explanation to make herself clear.... Being that immortal Sapience that nothing can resist, she is in consequence stronger than anything else in the world."[4] The purpose of drawing—purified painting, according to Giorgio Vasari—was to reveal this hidden beauty. The process of art thus boiled down to an epiphany. Beauty was of a divine and sacred essence; as Pliny pointed out, it rises above individual nature. To paint Helen in the temple of Juno Lucina, in Crotona, the painter Zeuxis "examined every girl in the city naked and chose five, painting what was the most beautiful in each."[5] Ideal nudity, although an image of truth, thus appears less a matter of analysis than assembly. Early on in the nineteenth century, it was the idea of composing an artificial beauty by recombination that invested the anecdote about Phryne, famous since antiquity, with fresh significance, due to its connections with the issue of depicting nudity.[6]

Phryne, a courtesan in fourth-century BCE Athens, was famous for a beauty so dazzling that the sculptor Praxiteles selected her as a unique model for a Venus that the inhabitants of Kos had commissioned from him; horrified by the nudity of the goddess, however, they refused it. The piece was acquired by the town of Cnidos, where it became, according to Pliny, one of the most admired sculptures in the world.[7] Led before an assembly of the Athens Areopagus to answer the charge of impiety, Phryne exposed her naked beauty to the judges and was promptly acquitted: the perfection of her physique was thought to correspond to that of her soul and devoutness. Bodily and moral beauty were thus considered as one and the same.

The invention of a genre

A foundation stone of art teaching, the nude played a vital essential role in the noblest pictorial genre: the grand manner of history painting. Since the Renaissance, the purpose of the representation of female nudity had been to embody mythological divinities, Venus and Danae in particular, or else scenes from the Old Testament, such as Susanna at her bath observed by the elders, or Bathsheba at her toilet. Eighteenth-century French painters had tended, however, to make the loves of the gods look a light and frivolous affair, not devoid of eroticism. Some complained that moral elevation had been replaced by libertine seduction, a reflection of taste at Louis XV's court. The vigorous revival of history painting in the second half of the eighteenth century sought to

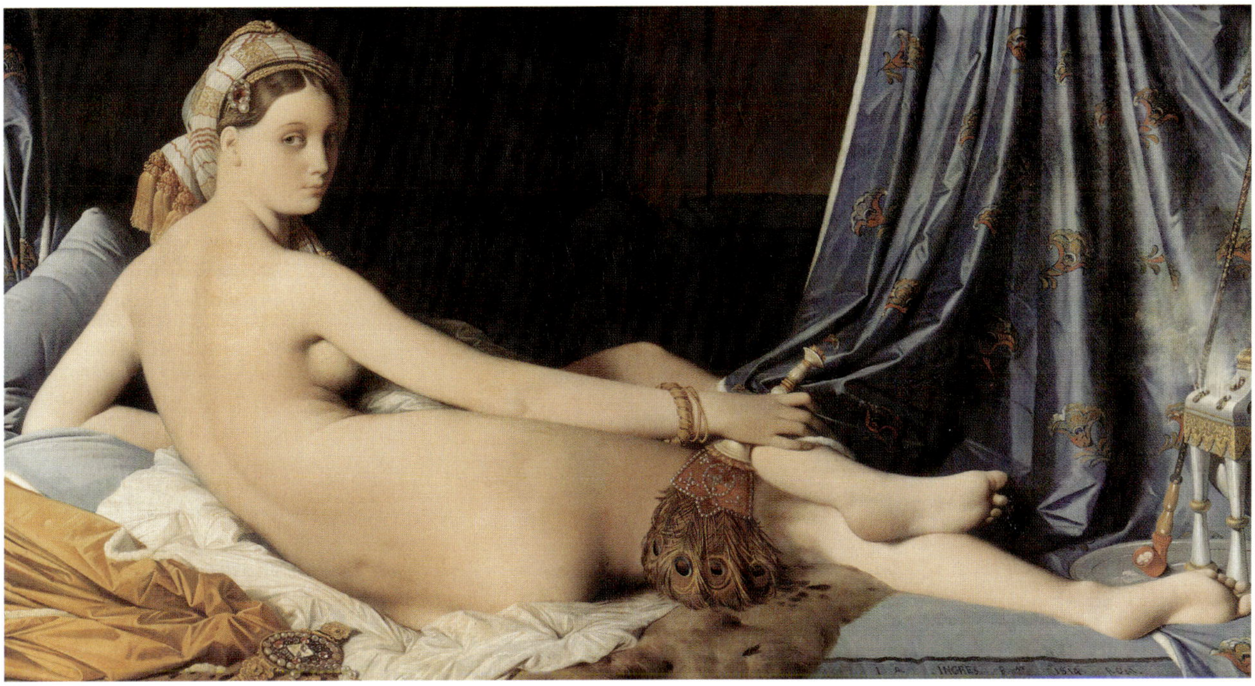

167. Jean-Auguste-Dominique Ingres, *The Grande Odalisque,* 1814, oil on canvas, Musée du Louvre, Paris.

moralize its content by exalting examples of virtue.[8] Divine dalliance was ousted by grave scenes from the history of the Roman Republic. In the wake of Johann Joachim Winckelmann, author of the first thorough history of the art of antiquity published in 1763, references to the ancient world were tinged with a delicate, polished grace that fed into many depictions of couples, such as Cupid and Psyche, Apollo and Hyacinth, or the languid Endymion lying in readiness for Selene. The presentation of Jean-Auguste-Dominique Ingres' *Grande Odalisque* at the Salon of 1819 marked a watershed. Painted in 1814 for Caroline Murat, Napoleon Bonaparte's sister and then Queen of Naples, the picture was never delivered to its patron due to the political events that led to her husband's overthrow. If the pose is redolent of the reclining nudes of the Renaissance and the seventeenth century, the flexibility of the lines of her body is similar to that of the naked sculptures of Antonio Canova; no precise subject, however, guides its composition: gracefully prone, this female figure refers to no particular divinity. The shimmering fabric on which she lies, the turban wrapped round her head, the feathery fan in her hand all bespeak of an imaginary Orient that exalts her sensuality. Although free of mythological reference, Ingres's nude was admitted to the Salon where it was lauded by academic critics, in spite of occasional misgivings about the anatomical deformation of the back (ill. 167). The Ingres model proved an enduring inspiration to many artists throughout the nineteenth century. The representation of the female nude thus became a pictorial genre in its own right. It was, however, less its suitability to the subject (often confined to a vague title) that counted than a "manner" dominated

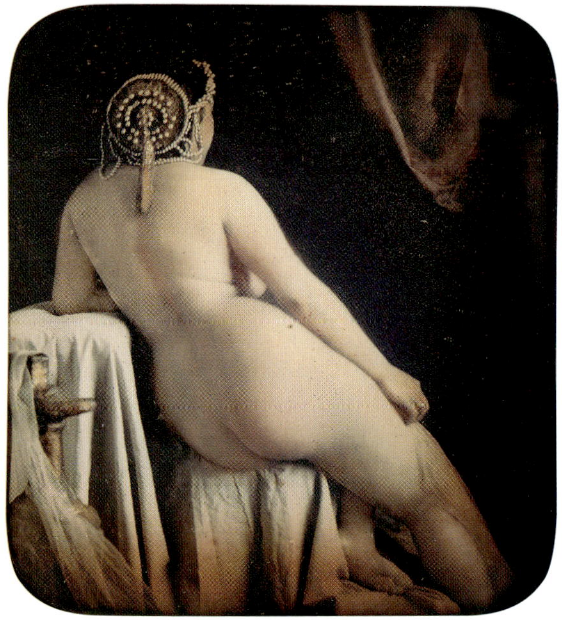

168. Bruno Braquehais, "Female Nude with Pearl Headdress" (detail), c. 1858, colored stereoscopic daguerreotype, Thérond Collection, Paris.

by line and a marmoreal finish that banished all flaws, asperities, hairs, and shadows. Reference to ancient models thus passed from meaning to intention; outward appearance, alone, remained the paragon. Flesh was expunged; the real woman was scarcely to be seen behind the model.

The "shamefulness" of nude photography

The invention of photography in 1839 and its rise during the 1840s played an essential role in the perception of the painted nude, on both the aesthetic and moral levels. In necessarily being concerned with a living model standing before the lens, the new process placed real women within the scope of representation. This incursion was felt all the more strongly, since early photographers liked to draw on the repertoire of poses of antique and academic painting in their works.

The history of nude photography is a relatively recent phenomenon. For a long time, art historians neglected such images, finding them too prettified, or too licentious, to be deserving of their attention. In this they concurred with Academy inspector Émile Bernard, who, at the end of the nineteenth century, was of the opinion that: "The nude, the necessary foundation of the arts of drawing, sculpture, and painting, would be shameful in photography."[9] Over the last twenty years, however, several studies have attempted to make up lost ground and assign to the photographic nude a rightful place between the two poles of artistic creation and erotic titillation.[10] The question remains disconcerting, however: the photographic reproduction of the female nude body is not an image that can be looked at, contemplated, or studied just like any other. The frontier between an "academy"—a study intended

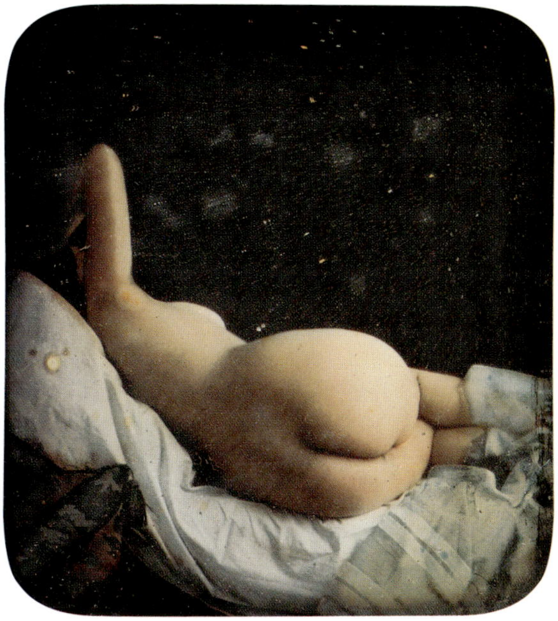

169. Bruno Braquehais, "Reclining Female Nude from the Rear" (detail), c. 1856, colored stereoscopic daguerreotype, Thérond Collection, Paris.

to be worked up into a painting, by analogy with the studies after nature and before the model realized by art students—and an erotically charged object is imprecise and problematic. In 1882, in his *Introduction à l'Exposition des Beaux-Arts de 1882* (Introduction to the Fine Arts Exhibition of 1882), Champfleury was still distinguishing between what he called "elegant nudities *à la parisienne*"—that is, erotic, or at least suggestive images—and true "academies."

The nude in daguerreotype: the thorny question of genre

For the daguerreotype, the question of genre was, as Sylvie Aubenas has shown,[11] particularly delicate, dangerous even. Indeed, for having neglected the fact, in 1851 photographer Félix-Jacques Moulin was condemned to a month in jail and a fine of 100 francs for having taken licentious images, in all probability stereoscopic daguerreotypes. It should be noted that the seller—the optician, Malacrida—was more severely punished than the photographer. Even more than the creation it was the circulation and publicizing of these photographs that was pursued by the law and in the courts.[12] The advertisement Moulin placed in *La Lumière on* May 11, 1851 maintains the ambiguity between the object of artistic study and erotic image, conflating the two entities in an ambivalent couple of lines: "Daguerreotype. Portraits of pretty women and novelty subjects for watches. Studies after nature for artists. Moulin, 31 bis rue du Faubourg Montmartre. Delivery to the provinces and abroad."

The nature of the daguerreotype—a unique, nonreproducible, relatively costly image—was not particularly well adapted for use by artists in search of a model or wishing to record a sitter's pose in the studio. The daguerreotype as object, however—something

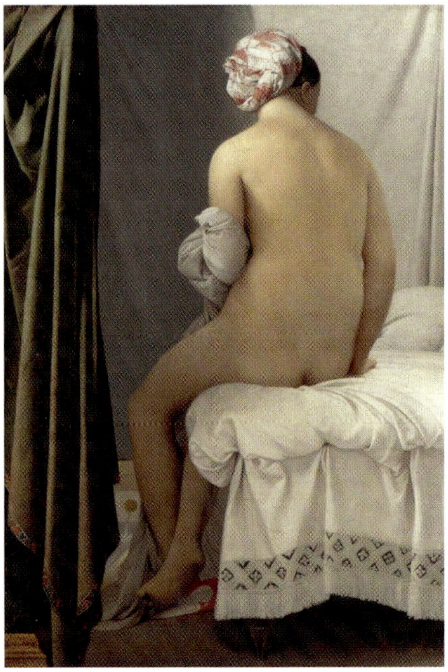

170. Jean-Auguste-Dominique Ingres, *The Bather* (also called *La Baigneuse Valpinçon*), 1808, oil on canvas, Musée du Louvre, Paris.

precious to be hidden away under lock and key in a lined box—spoke of secret cabinets, of places of pleasure where viewer becomes synonymous with voyeur. The Peeping Tom effect was accentuated in 1850 with the appearance of the stereoscopic daguerreotype, developed by David Brewster and further improved and marketed in France by the photographer Jules Duboscq, his father-in-law the optician Soleil, and Abbé Moignot. Vision through a stereopticon's lenses is a more private, more solitary experience. Creating the illusion of relief, the apparatus, simple to use, shows the body from every angle, every line and curve, every swelling and hollow. Colorized, these images reinforce the appetite for reality and exacerbate the exclusive nature of the photograph (ills. 168–69). Thanks to the colorist (generally a woman, thought better suited to meticulously applying the pigments to the plate), jewels and diadems were bedecked with gold and gems, complexions turned pink and fleshy. The opulence of the interiors, the abundance of fabrics and veils, the countless accessories, and the complexity of the mise-en-scène can leave little doubt as to the true aim of the majority of such nude daguerreotypes. They were clearly intended to give pleasure to the eye and show the beauties of the flesh, rather than for wholesome artistic study. The references deployed, however, tended to be pictorial, evoking phantasmagorias of an Ingresque Orient, or arousing sensual recollections of a canvas by François Boucher (ills. 170–71). The overlap between medium and subject, between mode of vision and object, was perfect, guaranteeing enduring success for the erotic stereoscopic daguerreotype that continued unabated throughout the 1850s, in spite of the advent of photography on paper that had by then supplanted Daguerre's process elsewhere.

A whiff of sulfur

Quite apart from titillating or suggestive images, there existed a rather sizable body of more frankly erotic, even pornographic daguerreotypes, that no longer lifted the veil but crudely ripped it off, and in which sensual allusion was ousted by the representation of the sex act. These pornographic daguerreotypes were the heirs of the licentious engravings of the eighteenth and early nineteenth centuries.[13] Nonetheless, a photographic representation goes a step farther than an engraving; burin and acid reduce the pornographic impact even of an explicit image. The lens, and the sensitized plate of the photographer capture such scenes in all their rawness. This is no painter's or engraver's fantasy: what the photograph shows once occurred.[14] This innovation transformed the codes governing the representation of nudity. Such images brought a whiff of sulfur to any reproduction of the naked body.

An aesthetic oxymoron

The artistic, academic nude was one of the earliest subjects to be tackled by daguerreotypists in France. In 1843, the optician and

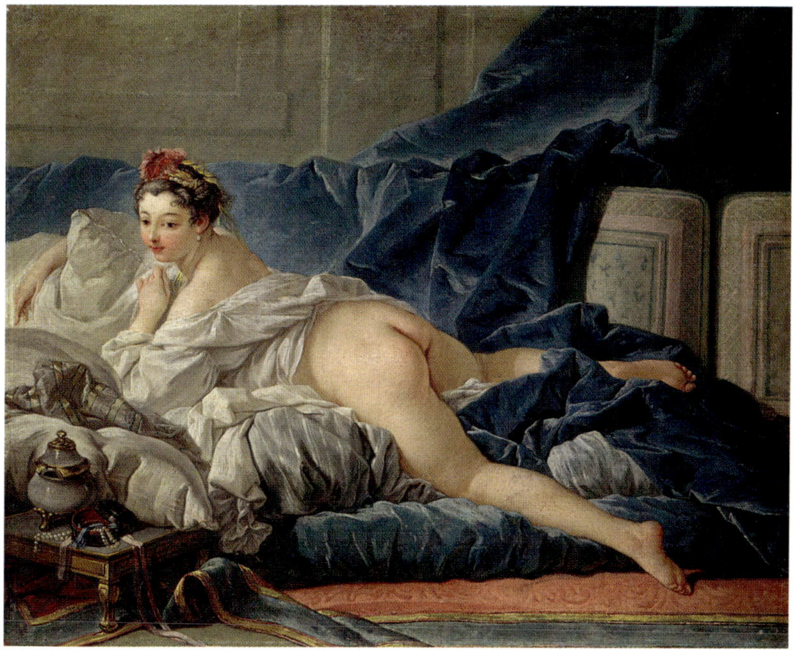

171. François Boucher, *The Odalisque*, c. 1745, oil on canvas, Musée du Louvre, Paris.

photographer Nicolas-Paymal Lerebours indicated in his manual, the *Traité de photographie,* that he had already carried out several nude photographs intended for use by artists in 1841: "The first academies made two years ago met with some success, and the majority are now in the possession of artists of the first rank."[15] The idea of substituting photographic models for drawings and engravings was then practically contemporary with the invention of the technique. In 1850, Eugène Delacroix noted in his *Journal*, "Laurens informs me that Ziegler has taken a large quantity of daguerreotypes, among which some of naked men. I shall go and ask him to lend me some."[16] Alas, neither of these examples has apparently survived, or at least has not come to light so far. If the majority of nude daguerreotypes were of the erotic variety, however, several pictures were intended to be employed by artists as study material after nature (ill. 166). Such works are parsimonious in both accessories and backdrop; no drapery, no jewels, no vases or perfumes conjure up the delights of the harem. The photographer's efforts are entirely centered on composing the image, on exploring the lines of the subject, and on adjusting the light and shadow so as to enhance the pose. The discomfort surrounding these early nude photographs—whatever genre they belonged to—arises from the presence of an actual model before the lens, from the fact that she was necessarily a real woman, one who lived and breathed. By freezing a single, indubitable yet since vanished instant, photography fused eroticism and mortality in a reciprocal process described by Georges Bataille: "Such is the essence of both death and of eroticism. Both of them escape us: and they escape the very moment they reveal themselves."[17] Anxiety was also aroused by the hiatus between the nature of the images as

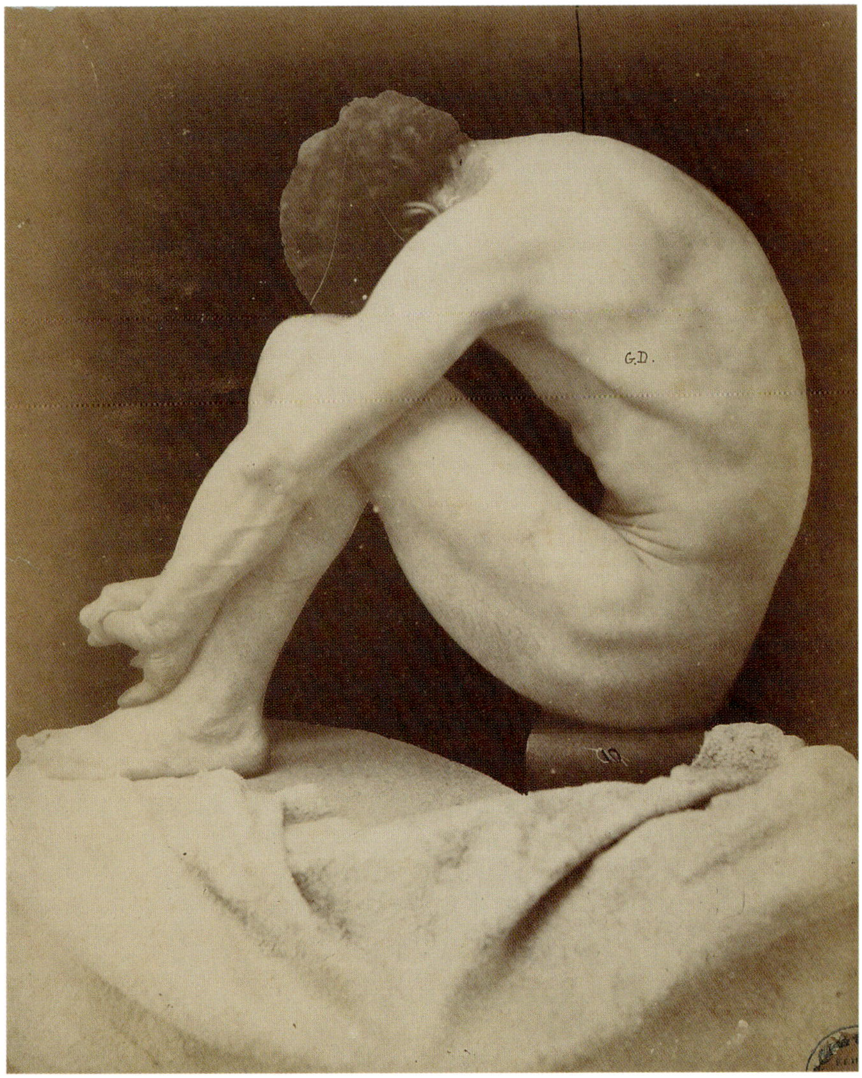

172. Gaudenzio Marconi, "Seated Male Nude," 1869, albumen print, École Nationale Supérieure des Beaux-Arts, Paris.

objects of pleasure and an iconography that conforms to the canons of the academic painting of the period. By ignoring the gap between representation and flesh, this divided loyalty—to the real and to the ideal—inescapably disturbs the beholder. Nude daguerreotypes thus coined an aesthetic oxymoron: between, on the one hand, a real, authentic body, an image of a (once) living body; and, on the other, the reflection of a figment of the imagination, a depiction of an actual body subjected to the canons of academe.

Models stripped bare for the camera

While, due to the ease with which prints could be reproduced, it was photography on paper that earned the photographic nude its artistic status, the development came freighted with moral and legal implications. That familiar art world figure,

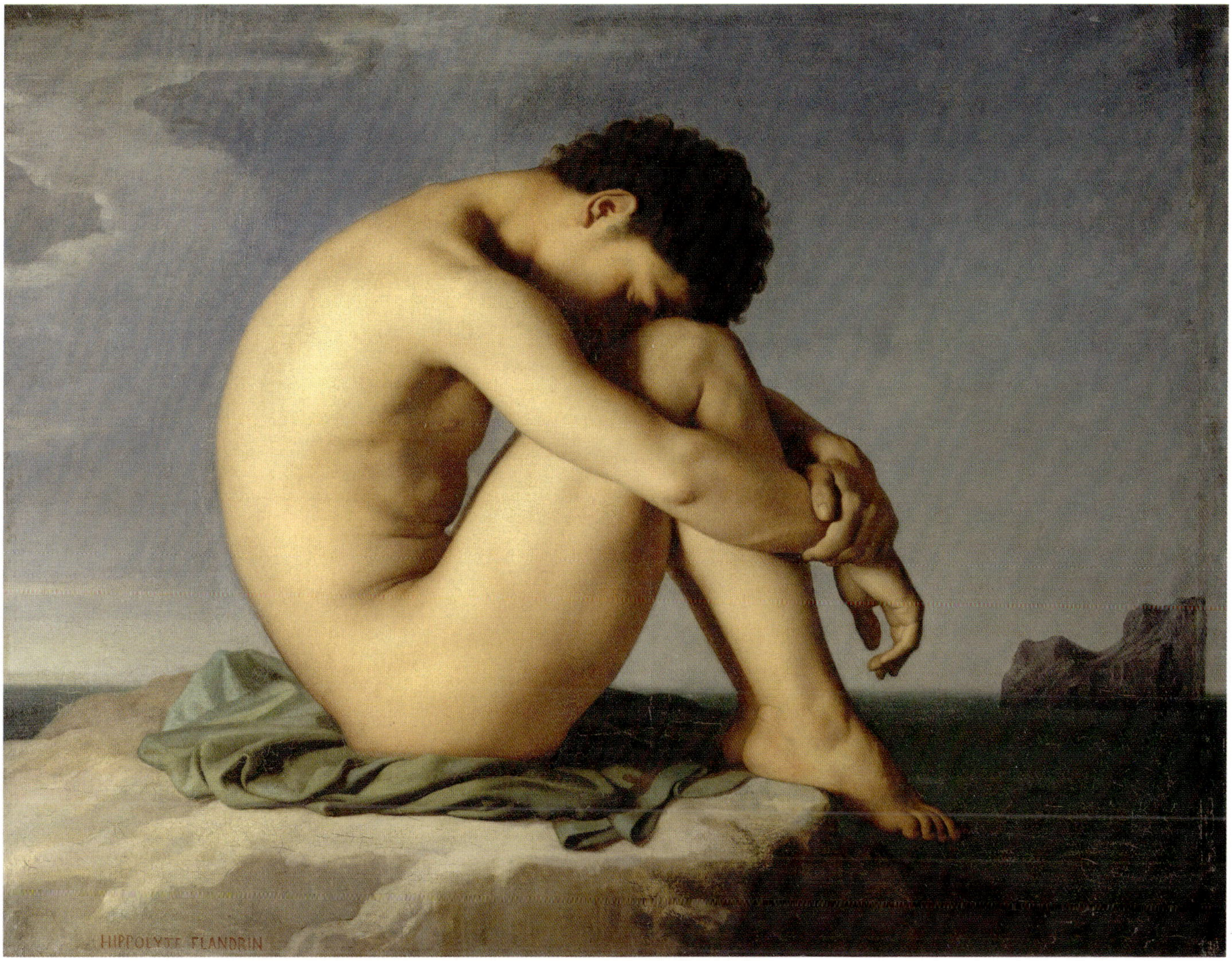

173. Hippolyte Flandrin, *Young Man Sitting by the Sea. Study Figure,* 1836, oil on canvas, Musée du Louvre, Paris.

the model, now climbed down from the studio walls. The ambivalence between "academic" and erotic images seemed all the more inextricable because, since its invention, the new process had proclaimed itself as the exact reflection of reality. A woman represented in a photograph—whatever her pose (inspired by the classical style or by Renaissance painting), the nature of the lighting, or the intention of the photographer—had to have removed her clothes before taking up her position before the lens. Photography thus revealed the living woman standing behind the "model," which the artifice of painting tended to dissimulate. In 1889, Paul Dolfuss, in a work dedicated to *Modèles d'artistes*, noted: "The beautiful girls who pose 'in the all together' . . . often mar the beauty of their body by the deplorable ugliness of their head. They are not very attractive, despite the purity of their lines."[18] A decree on the press dated February 17, 1852, which reiterated edicts that since 1819 regulated the sale of paintings, engravings, and drawings "contrary to morality," was rolled out by the authorities to crack down on the creation, open display, and sale of licentious photographic images. A register today housed in the Paris Préfecture de Police, and including various reports drawn up by the constabulary until 1869, highlights how difficult it proved for officers of the law to clearly demarcate the border between obscene and permissible images.[19]

The ambiguity was due as much to the photographer's avowed intention, conveyed by the choice of pose, of model, the arrangement of the decor and the lighting, as to the perception of his work by his contemporaries. In 1852, an event took place that demonstrates exactly how the photographer's intentions and references to poses close to those of painting could not always protect him from unwanted consequences. In an attempt to forestall legal proceedings, Félix-Jacques Moulin (in this anticipating the obligation of copyright registration, which was formally instituted with respect to photographs only in the 1930s) deposited at the Bibliothèque Nationale two photographs, one representing a naked young woman standing with her clothes scattered about her.[20] They were inventoried as "Studies after Nature"—an observation likewise inscribed in the captions to the images—and which gave a formal basis to their "artistic" purpose.[21]

"Academies" and "studies from nature"

The production and dissemination of images for artists proved a linchpin in the growing recognition of photography as a source of models. The commission convened by Félix Ravaisson in 1853 had underlined the role photography might play in the teaching of drawing in high schools, not only through the reproduction of masterpieces but also through studies taken from nature: "Photography can in addition help the pencil and the graver, be it by replicating drawings by good artists, or by providing instant reproductions of masterpieces of painting or representations of nature."[22] Ravaisson's recommendations remained dead letter, at least in official circles. Photography only entered the institution of the École des Beaux-Arts in the 1880s (for the morphology course). But, from the 1850s, several photographers, such as Moulin, produced images for artists described as "academies" or "studies after nature." Some, notably Gaudenzio Marconi, even claimed to be "photographer at the École des Beaux-Arts."[23] Marconi, in order to accredit his status at the institution more securely, gave his models poses copied from famous academic pictures; thus the material he provided fostered their imitation (ills. 172–73).

New models for painting

In December 1853, Louis-Camille d'Olivier, who studied painting with Léon Cogniet, set up a photographic society, whose object was "to spread the taste for photography among the public, to popularize its productions, and to apply it in a practical manner to the arts, sciences, and industry."[24] Founder members included Cogniet, Adrien Dauzats, and the medievalist architect Jean-Baptiste Lassus. It seems that this society did not meet with the success he had envisaged. In 1854 and 1855, he deposited under the reference "Société photographique, 18 rue de la Pépinière" several photographs of female nudes whose sensitive poses and intelligent lighting, together with the skillful manner in which they enhance the dark brunette beauty of his model, endow them with a rare power and aesthetic quality. The girl's swarthy complexion and her abundant and thick pubic hair represent a complete break with the academic canon, from which all pilosity is rigorously excluded, and where flesh possesses the smooth and artificial whiteness of marble. Variations on the traditional figure of the reclining nude, Olivier's works—thanks to the carnal presence of their sitter—present a new treatment of a pictorial commonplace.[25] From this fusion of academic pose and physical authenticity a new archetype emerged, at once representational and transgressive. In the 1860s, such works probably fed into the approach to the naked figure by Courbet (in the *Nude* painted in Saintes in 1862 and today in a private collection) and then of Manet (*Olympia* dates from 1863), whose reclining females renew a hackneyed pictorial theme. Instead of smoothing out the physical idiosyncrasies of their models, they strove to emphasize them, along with the materiality of the paint on canvas. Critics denounced the "dirty flesh" of Olympia; infringement of the dominant aesthetics was seen to amount to a moral failing. To place a prostitute in a pose recalling a Venus—the painter deliberately indicating her profession by her name, her insolent look, the black woman next to her, and the presence of the wrapped bouquet—proved all the more shocking because the body, like in a nude photograph, remains as it was, unretouched, uncorrected.

Truth and artifice in painting and photography: the example of Courbet and Vallou de Villeneuve

A few years previously, a comparison between Courbet's *Bathers* (ill. 174) and Julien Vallou de Villeneuve's photographs of Henriette Bonnion—the model who posed for the woman viewed from the rear—brings out the complex nature of the issue of representing the nude in photography and in painting, in the light of its dual relationship with "ideal beauty" and reality. Henriette Bonnion could be found in the studios of both artists—at the photographer's probably from 1852 (although the photographs deposited by Vallou date from 1854), and in the painter's at the end of 1852 or the beginning of 1853, when Courbet decided, as he wrote to his parents, "to do only nudes," with a view to the Salon exhibition of 1853.[26] Following the tremendous scandal surrounding *A Burial at Ornans*, thanks to which, in spite of the barrage of criticism, his name had become one to be reckoned with in the art world, his intention was to tackle pictorial tradition head-on by attempting to renew the canons of the nude. It is not known whether at this time Courbet used a photograph by Vallou de Villeneuve, as he was to do in 1854 for the nude female figure in *The Painter's Studio* (Musée d'Orsay, Paris), or if the pose of the woman, inspired by those in the Sources or the Nymphs, was arrived at independently by the two artists. The photographs even include the strip of white linen that Courbet said he added on his canvas so as "to frighten [the public] just a little." Still, if model and pose evidently appear close, their treatment differs. Where Courbet undeniably delighted in conveying, magnifying even, his model's powerful, fleshy physique, unflinchingly portraying the folds of skin on her back and the massive rump and thighs, Vallou, on the other hand, erases the woman's heavy contours by retouching them with a brush. Paradoxically, it is photography that cheats reality and painting that reveals it. The paradox is only apparent, though. A comparison between Courbet's canvas and Vallou's photographs indicates that photographic and pictorial truth alike were both based on a unique interpretation on their creator's part (ills. 174–75). Courbet's use the following year of one of Vallou's photographs from the same series for the female model in the center of *L'Atelier* throws further light on the relationship between painting and photography. The relationship is not one of original and copy; it is rather that this shared approach to tradition and reality furthered Courbet's determination to forge a new artistic language. When Courbet asked Alfred Bruyas, his patron in Montpellier and owner of *The Bathers*, to send him: "That photograph of a nude woman I told you about. She will stand behind my chair, in the middle of the picture,"[27] the painter was choosing to revert to a type of model that would enable him both to satisfy the imperative of faithfully representing reality (a real woman had posed for the photograph) and address the exigencies of the pictorial tradition through standard poses and conventional symbolism. The treatment of Courbet's nudes in the 1850s appears all the more radical as, instead of simply turning his back on the pictorial tradition, he transgresses it. And it was photography, through its reliance on long-established canons whose relation to reality it distorted, that opened the door for him.[28]

Transgression and transcendence

Marked by a sense of transgression, Courbet's use of photography was also orientated towards transcendence. *The Origin of the World*, painted in 1866 for Khalil Bey, the Ottoman Empire's representative in France and an enlightened collector (he had amassed a collection of contemporary art of great quality, including works not only by Courbet, but also Ingres and Delacroix), was inspired by pornographic photographs, like those taken by Auguste Belloc and

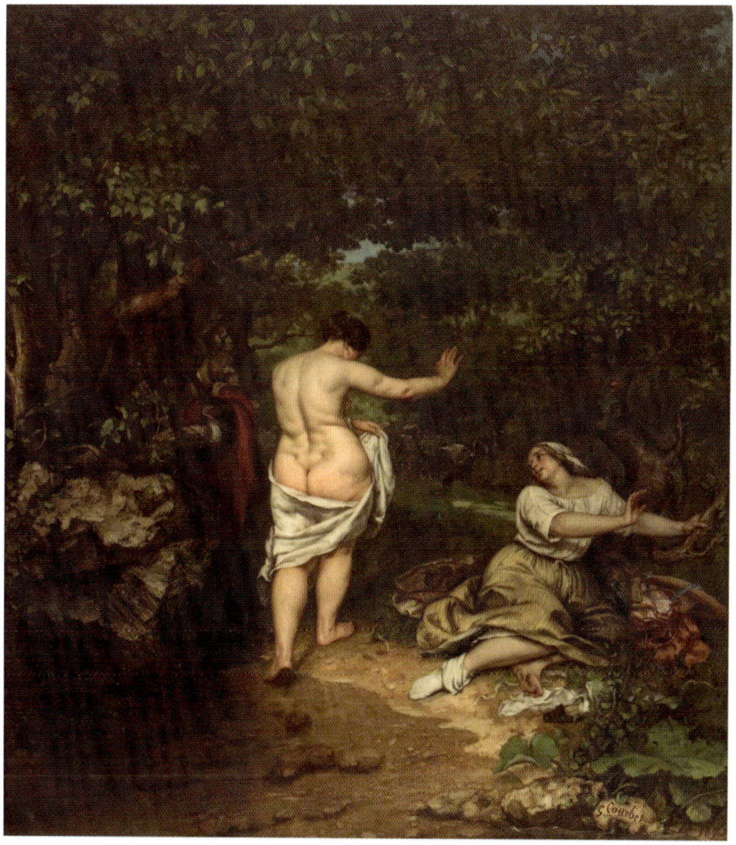

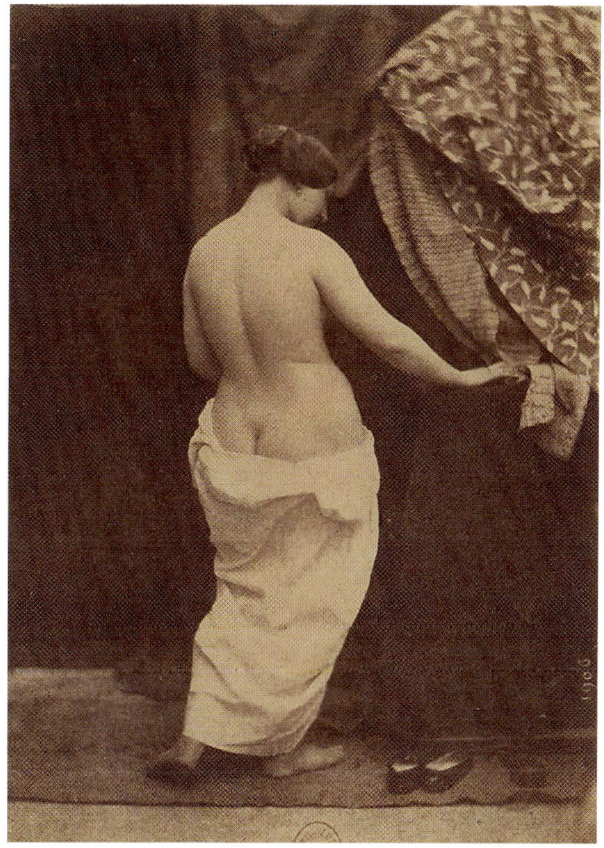

seized by the Paris police in October 1860,[29] and presented poses wholly foreign to painting.

Intended for private viewing, the innovation of stereoscopy endowed these images with the artifice of relief. Pulled up, the petticoat forms a frilly screen round the genitals, a hem of social femininity that frames the uncovered nudity. Though exposed, these "nudes" were not naked; the full, lace-rimmed underskirts, the white stockings pulled tight, the floral pattern on the seat cover, betrayed, underscored even, the fact that the models observed the fashions and ostensible proprieties of the Second Empire, turning them on their head. The printing, like the hand coloring, was painstaking; Belloc's prints clearly prove his brio as a photographer. Yet, instead of mollifying the censor, such technical qualities aggravated the situation, since the masterly perfection of the image served something unspeakable (ill. 176).

Though the composition is framed and posed as it is in the photograph, the greater economy of detail in Courbet's canvas is striking. The artist avoids all allusion to contemporary fashion, eludes all contingency. The truncated body does not belong to any particular woman; it is a representation of the eternal feminine. By elevating the photographic metonymy in painting, Courbet transforms, transcends the pornographic representation of genre. The erotic immediacy, the voyeurism attaching itself to the

174. **Above, left:** Gustave Courbet, *The Bathers*, 1853, oil on canvas, Musée Fabre, Montpellier.

175. **Above, right:** Julien Vallou de Villeneuve, "Study after Nature, Nude no. 1906," 1852–53, salt print, Bibliothèque Nationale de France, Paris.

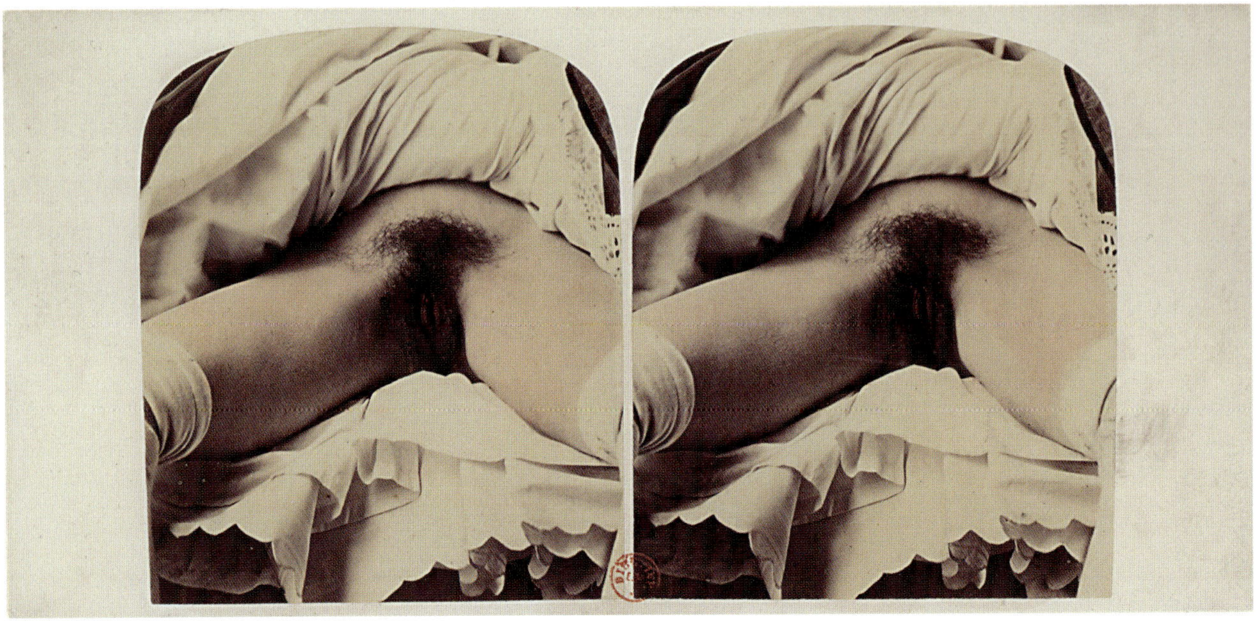

176. Auguste Belloc, "Erotic Nude," c. 1860, color stereoscopic albumen print, Bibliothèque Nationale de France, Paris.

stereoscopic eyepiece, is supplanted here by a more subtle delight based on the sensuality of the paint itself (ill. 177). If it is now known both from the painter's correspondence and the recently discovered inventory of the workshop at Ornans that Courbet had gathered a collection of several hundred photographs of nude women, the pictures themselves have never been found, probably victims of the prudishness of his sister, Juliette. It is likely, however, that the artist had acquired them as sources for paintings, rather than for scabrous purposes. In any case, as Castagnary wrote, for Courbet woman was always secondary to painting.[30]

The nudes of Eugène Durieu and Eugène Delacroix

Eugène Delacroix was already an established and recognized painter in 1839 by the time the process of photography was announced; his relationship to it was complex and multilayered.[31] In 1842, his cousin Léon Riesener produced several daguerreotype portraits in which Delacroix certainly lent a hand (ill. 106).[32] The new invention is mentioned relatively frequently in his *Journal*, though unfortunately the period contemporary with the invention is lacking, since the years 1832–47 have to date not been unearthed. His remarks are far from uncritical; the painter expresses the fear that the precision in detail of the daguerreotype might saturate the eye and harm the realization of an artist's most important quality: the imagination. He did feature, however, among the members of the Société Héliographique set up in 1851, thus fostering his interest in the development of photography and in its artistic potential, and in September 1850, as has been noted previously, he had expressed interest in borrowing some of Ziegler's daguerreotypes of naked men.[33] It was around the same time that, through

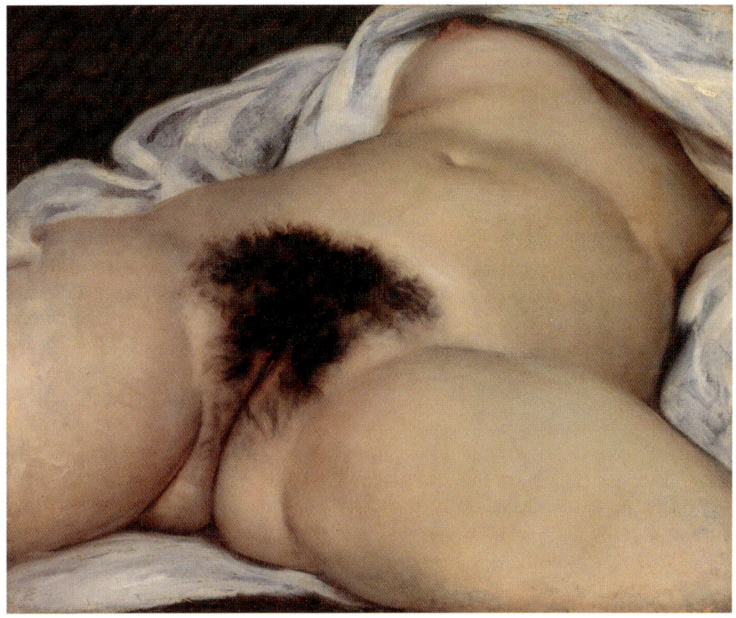

177. Gustave Courbet, *The Origin of the World*, 1866, oil on canvas, Musée d'Orsay, Paris.

the Committee for the Arts and Religious Buildings, Delacroix met Eugène Durieu, an assiduous civil servant and unusual amateur artist, a member of the Société Héliographique in 1851, then a founder of the Société Française de Photographie in 1854.[34] It was on the occasion of two sittings on the Sundays June 18 and 25 of that year that Durieu took a set of photographs in the presence of Delacroix and under his instructions. These prints were collected into a portfolio known as the "Durieu Album," today housed in the Bibliothèque Nationale de France.[35] Sylvie Aubenas divides the thirty-two photographs comprising the album into four sections: a photograph of a man taken by Durieu alone, perhaps in 1853; a first series of twenty-six photographs in which a man and a woman pose together; two photographs of a young woman alone, posing as a odalisque; and finally three albumen prints, probably carried out by a photographer other than Durieu. The man in the most extensive series, whom Delacroix called the "*Bohémien*," was—as his musculature and the facility with which he strikes his poses show—doubtless a professional model. The young woman was the brown-skinned model whom Olivier was to employ the following year. In the photographs taken by Durieu, however, she does not possess the carnal, disconcerting presence bestowed upon her by Cogniet's pupil. Perhaps this was on the initiative of Delacroix, who was wary of the impact of the model on the painter and his work, writing for instance in his *Journal*: "It is this effect [of unpretentious naivety and solidity] that can be obtained from the use of models and from nature generally; it is also the rarest thing in the majority of pictures where the model plays a major role. He or she attracts everything and nothing remains left for the painter."[36] The young odalisque has been identified as being Mlle. Hamely, a young model who also posed for Félix-Jacques

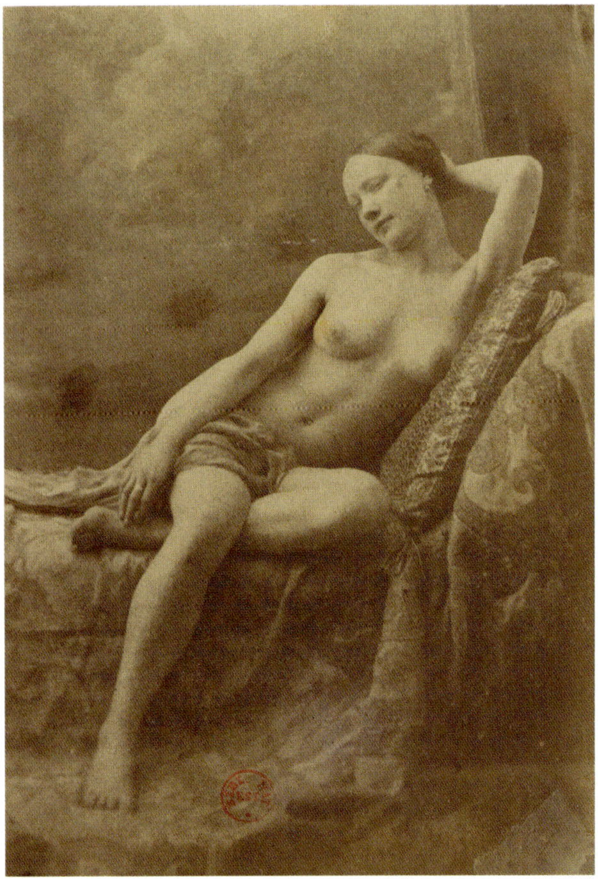

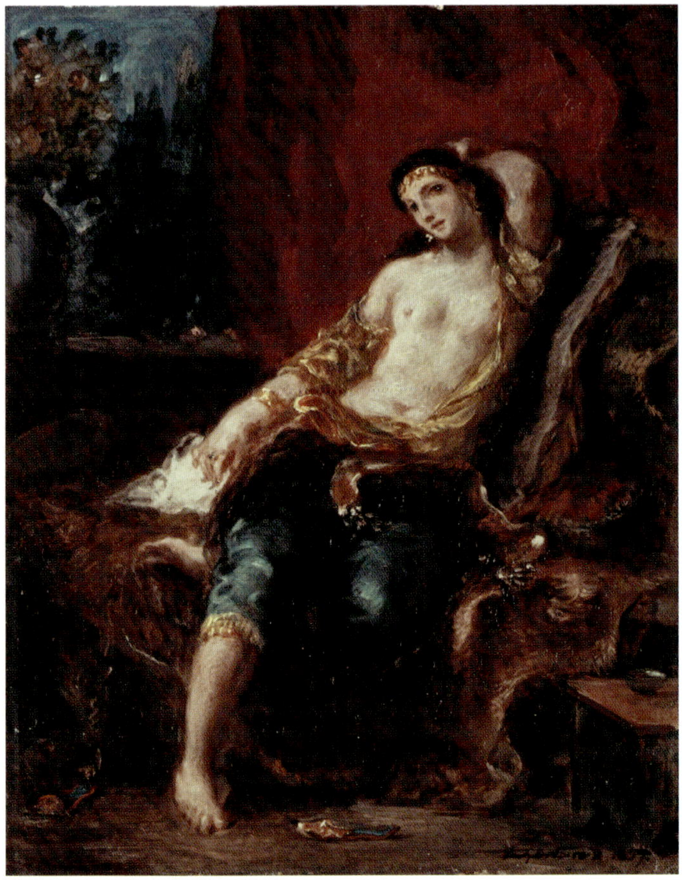

178. **Above, left:** Eugène Durieu, "Female Nude Sitting on a Divan, with Head Leaning on One Arm," 1853, salt print, Bibliothèque Nationale de France, Paris.

179. **Above, right:** Eugène Delacroix, *Odalisque*, 1857, oil on wood, private collection.

Moulin in 1852 and 1853, as well as for Adrien Tournachon, Nadar's brother, during the winter of 1854–55 (ills. 178–79).

Imagination beyond imitation

Delacroix seems to have directed proceedings at these sittings; indeed, the negatives in the album differ from the photographs realized by Durieu. The pared-down details, the command of lighting, and the firmness of the pose endow them with a unique quality. It was also surely Delacroix who encouraged the use of paper negatives, though glass was at this time the more widespread process; the velvety, cloudy texture of paper blunts the lines and reduces the contrast in the image. This group of studies was used by the painter for drawing, like manual or mental exercises. Several passages in the *Journal* mention the artist traveling with them or looking at them (ills. 180–81). Such photographic studies were not intended to be copied slavishly, a notion that the painter reviled in any case. As he wrote in 1853: "On the imitation of nature, that great foundation stone of every school ... the entire question reduces to this: is imitation undertaken to delight the imagination, or to simply to satisfy an odd kind of conscience, which for the artist consists in feeling self-satisfied

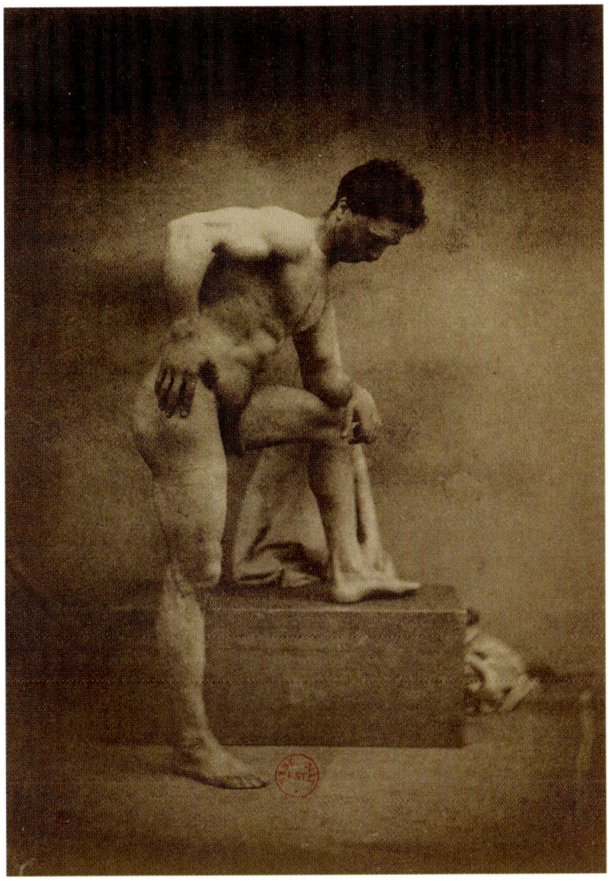

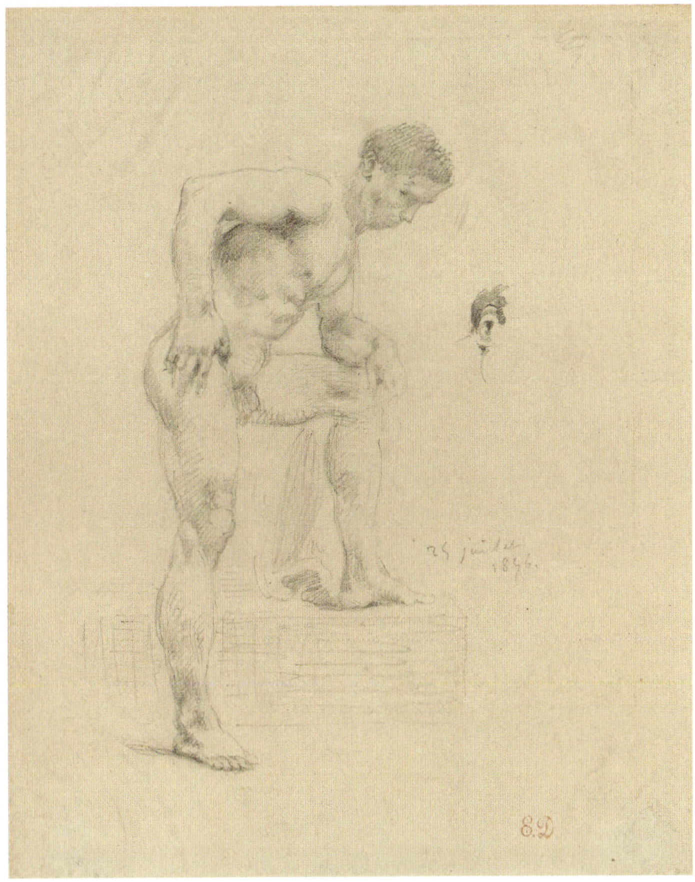

180. **Above, left:** Eugène Durieu, "Male Nude Standing, in Profile, with One Foot Placed on a Chest," 1853, salt print, Bibliothèque Nationale de France, Paris.

181. **Above, right:** Eugène Delacroix, *Nude Man Standing Turning to the Right, his Left Foot on a Plinth,* 1856, lead pencil, Musée du Louvre, Paris.

once he has managed to copy the model before his eyes as exactly as possible?" [37]

"A shameful little thing"

Jean-Léon Gérôme's relations with the photographic nude were very different; at the same time more immediately dependent, but also more involved, as they were rooted in the very basis of the academic tradition he defended so fiercely throughout his career as a painter and teacher. As a student in the studio of Paul Delaroche in the early 1840s, he had rubbed shoulders with several young men who were later to number among the foremost photographers of their time: Gustave Le Gray, with whom he struck up a close friendship, Charles Nègre, Henri Le Secq, Édouard Baldus, and Roger Fenton. He was thus perfectly familiar with the new invention; thanks to his friendship with Le Gray, by the late 1840s he had experience not only of the effects and results, but also of the principles of the process.[38]

The fact that he relied on a photograph for the nude in *Phryne before the Areopagus* (ill. 183) was surely no coincidence. This painting—one of the most widely commented-on works at the Salon—relied on the story of the appearance of the all too

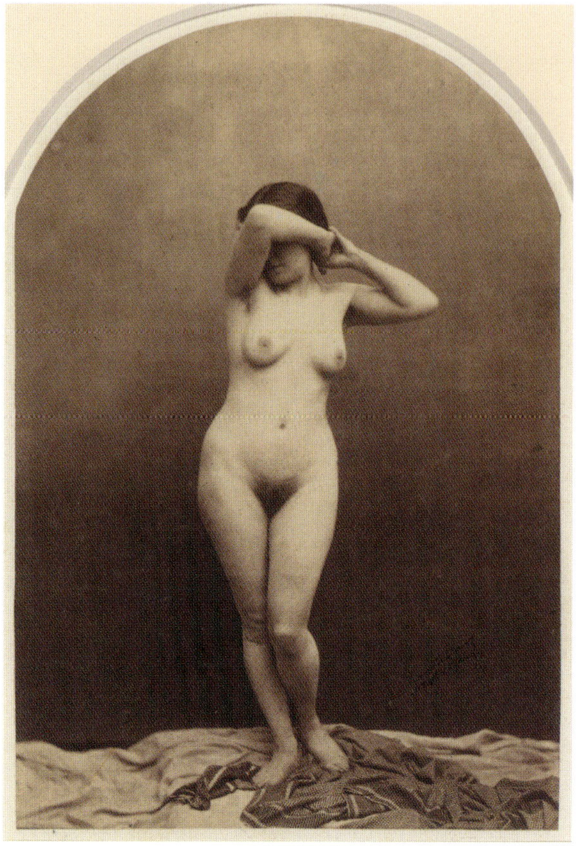

182. Félix Tournachon (also called Nadar), "Nude Study for Jean-Léon Gérôme's *Phryne*," 1861, albumen print, The Metropolitan Museum of Art, New York.

beautiful hetaera before the court of Athens. As we saw above, this ancient story constituted an allegory of the representation of nudity as an amalgam of aesthetics and morality, of human figuration and divine apparition. Gérôme's interpretation was simultaneously completely faithful and singularly personal. If he sought to reproduce the world of Ancient Greece as closely as possible, if he bestowed on Phryne the smooth, white curves of a statue, he was not above taking certain subtle liberties with archaeological verisimilitude.[39] But Gérôme played fast and loose with history too, to the point of distorting the very meaning of the heroine appearing naked. Far from proudly assuming her superb goddess-like beauty, Gérôme's Phryne, embarrassed at finding herself thus divested of her clothes before so many male eyes, puts her face in her hands. Émile Zola, like Edgar Degas, was outraged at this aesthetic misinterpretation. If the first described her as a "modern little miss unexpectedly caught changing her chemise,"[40] the latter summed up disapprobation with the work in these words: "What can one say of a painter who makes Phryne appearing before the Areopagus into a shameful little thing who has to hide herself away? Phryne hid nothing, she could not have hidden, since her nakedness was precisely the cause of her glory."[41] The use of a photograph ordered from Nadar implies that Gérôme may have had in mind, not only the well-worn reference to the ancient

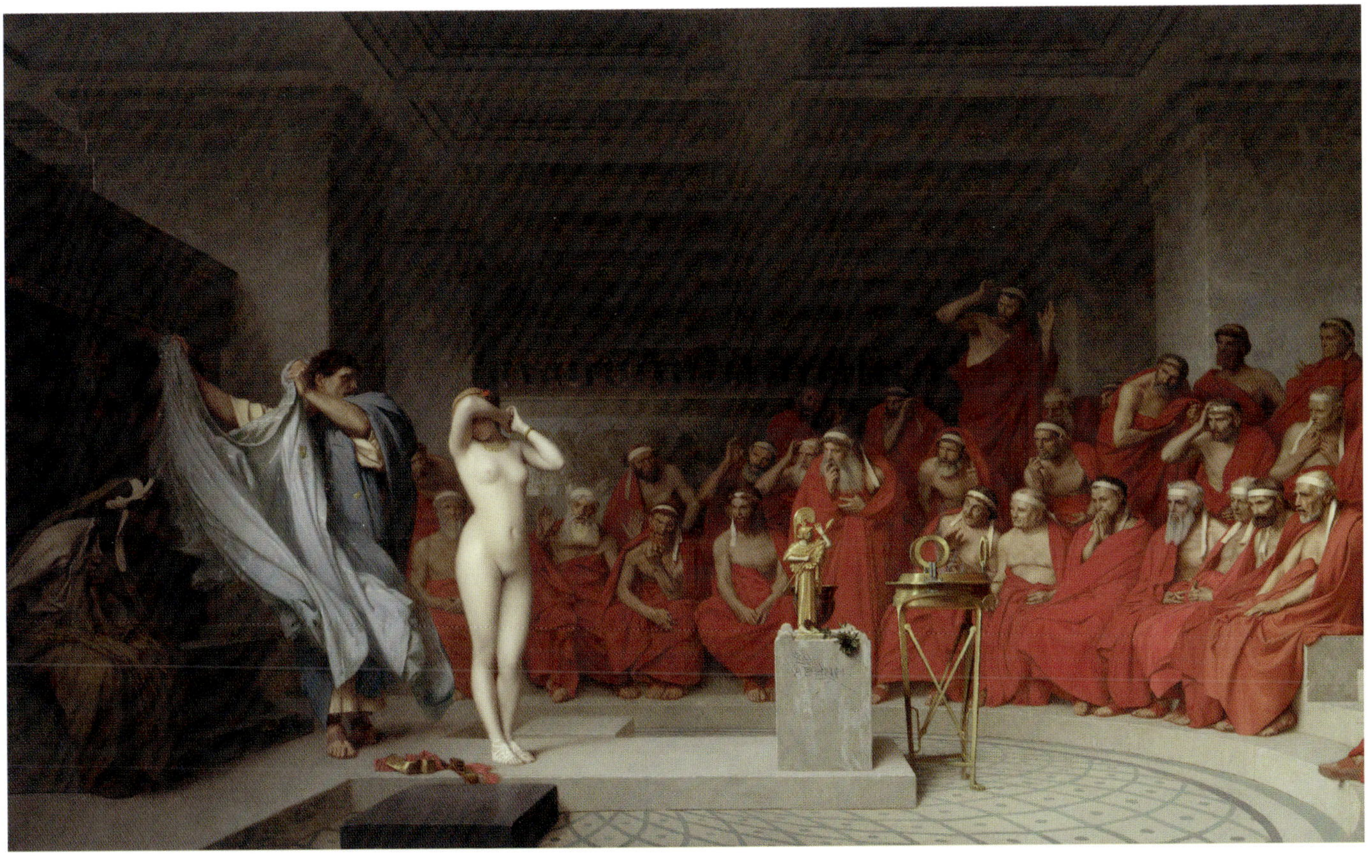

183. Jean-Léon Gérôme, *Phryne Before the Areopagus*, 1861, oil on canvas, Kunsthalle, Hamburg.

example of Phryne herself, but also an allusion to a more recent debate centering on photography and its role in painting. At the painter's own request, Nadar had his model—a woman called Marie-Christine Roux or Leroux—adopt the agreed pose. If her modest dissimulation amounts to misinterpretation in painting, in photography it seems instead to point up the latent ambiguity surrounding the academic and the erotic nude. Thus, if the ancient Phryne could expose her nakedness with pride, the modern, photographic Phryne has to cover up her face, since otherwise she might have to answer in court for infringing the law regulating the display of licentious photographs (ills. 182–83).[42]

The Triumph of Truth

Phryne was not only an epiphany; she was also an allegory of Truth. The theatrical gesture of her lawyer Hyperides, although de facto unlikely, had the impact of veracity.[43] By divesting the young woman of her clothes, he revealed the Truth. The representation of Truth was one of the stock subjects of Gérôme's later period, to which he devoted a series of three canvases in 1895–96. These representations of Truth were those of an ageing painter, whose manner and style had been radically called into question by a new generation of painters—by the impressionists in particular, a group he fiercely opposed. The title of a since lost canvas, *Truth Killed by Liars and Histrions*, refers to this artistic rivalry. And Gérôme began the sequence in 1895, the year after the State's acceptance of the Caillebotte Bequest, in the teeth of the academic painter's frantic efforts to have it rejected (see *Truth at the Bottom of a Well*, 1895, oil on canvas, Musée des Beaux-Arts, Lyon). In Gérôme's eyes, the entry into a public collection of canvases at odds with the traditional pictorial approach offended his intellectual attachment, to "making true" his obsession with exactitude and accuracy. In 1906, in the first biography dedicated to the painter, Charles Moreau-Vauthier grandiloquently underlines the importance the painter afforded these canvases.[44] "Truth, this is the noble goddess the master ever revered, the one he always followed. She was depicted in a picture above his bed, and his face was turned towards this image when he was found lifeless, one arm raised, frozen in death, in a supreme gesture of respect and farewell."[45] (*Truth Climbing out of the Well Armed with her Martinet to Punish Humanity*, 1896, oil on canvas, Musée Anne-de-Beaujeu, Moulins). The subject also rekindles the old realist battles of the artist's youth. Gérôme probably had in mind Louis Auvray's devastating remark about the large woman in a picture by his much-despised antagonist Courbet, *The Bathers* (ill. 174): "Since Truth comes out of a well, the very least she might be is washed."[46] The foreword he wrote in September 1902 for Émile Bayard's *Nu esthétique* (Aesthetic Nude) shows that Gérôme remained sensitive about this debate and confirms the major role of photography in the conception of his work: "Photography, which has made great strides in recent times, obliges artists to divest themselves of the old routines and to dispense with the old formulae. It has opened our eyes and forced us to look at things we never looked at before, thereby rendering an immense and appreciable service to Art. *Because of it, Truth emerged from her well; she will never return to it again*."[47]

Books of models

Even before the publication of Bayard's *Nu esthétique*, photographers had already been offering collections of nude models, men, women, and children, for the use of artists. In Vienna, Herman Heid founded his first studio in 1864 before taking over Györgi Klosz's company in 1868. He was to present his photographs at many exhibitions and from 1878 they were distributed by the firm of Giraudon. To facilitate the choice of pose and attitude, these plates could incorporate up to twenty-five images on a single sheet. The negative was preceded by a letter indicating the series: "E" for women and children and "F" for men. Round about the same period, the publisher Calavas started marketing plates featuring photographs by

184. **Facing page:** Herman Heid, "Plate with Twenty-Five Vignettes of Nude Male Models," c. 1880, albumen print, École Nationale Supérieure des Beaux-Arts, Paris.

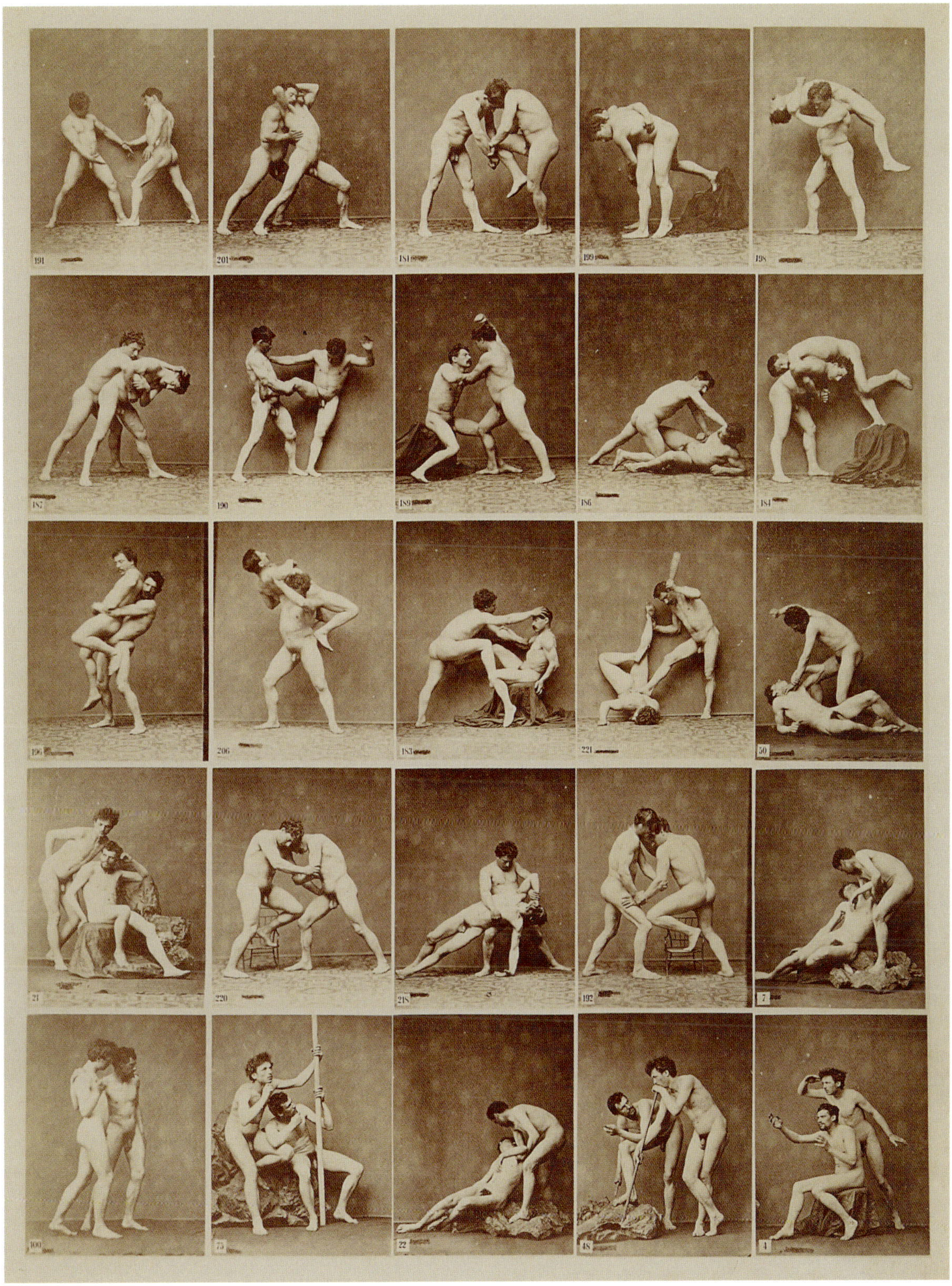

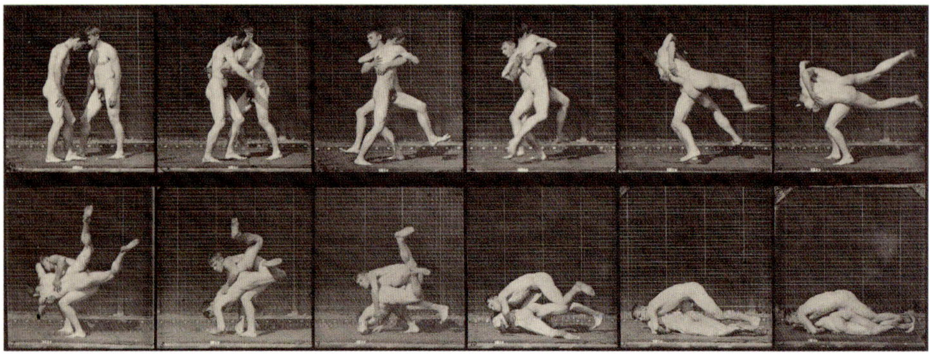

185. Eadward Muybridge, "Two Men Wrestling," from the album on the deconstruction of movement *Animal Locomotion*, 1887, photomechanical print, Musée d'Orsay, Paris.

186. **Facing page:** Jean-Marc Nattier, *Two Wrestlers*, c. 1730, black chalk, École Nationale Supérieure des Beaux-Arts, Paris.

Heid and others by Jean-Baptiste Igout, each bearing a handwritten number. Although intended for the same usage, photographs by Heid and Igout differed in style and context: the first had his models take very conventional poses against a neutral ground, without trappings, whereas the second had them strike their poses in a decor awash with accessories. The École des Beaux-Arts in Paris possesses a series of Heid's negatives inscribed for the "anatomy class."[48] The poses chosen were thus thought sufficiently close to those used in drawing lessons for them to serve as a teaching aid (ill. 184).

An artistic movement?

If the stereoscopic daguerreotype added the magic of relief to the precision of the image, "chronophotography" made it possible, by combining a sequence of photographs taken very rapidly, to record and decompose movement. Developed in the late 1870s, chronophotography allowed Étienne-Jules Marey, professor at the Collège de France, to advance his medical and physical theories. In his laboratory the renowned physiologist set up his camera painstakingly so that each movement might be captured and examined in detail. He also lavished immense care on how his models were dressed; black garments with an arrangement of white stripes broke the motion up into identifiable sections and prevented the eye becoming distracted by the individual characteristics of the model or by details in the decor that Marey completely screened off.[49]

If Marey's forays into chronophotography formed part and parcel of his scientific researches, the case of Eadweard Muybridge is less straightforward. Starting to use the photographic gun in 1878 to take a succession of pictures, the virtuoso Muybridge composed his images as scenes, complete with backdrops, themes, and a profusion of accessories that renders analysis for the purposes of anatomical observation all but impossible. What is one to make, for example, of plates showing a naked woman sweeping with a broom or carrying water? In spite of Professor Marks mentioning "scientific exactitude" in his foreword, these plates in *Animal Locomotion*—

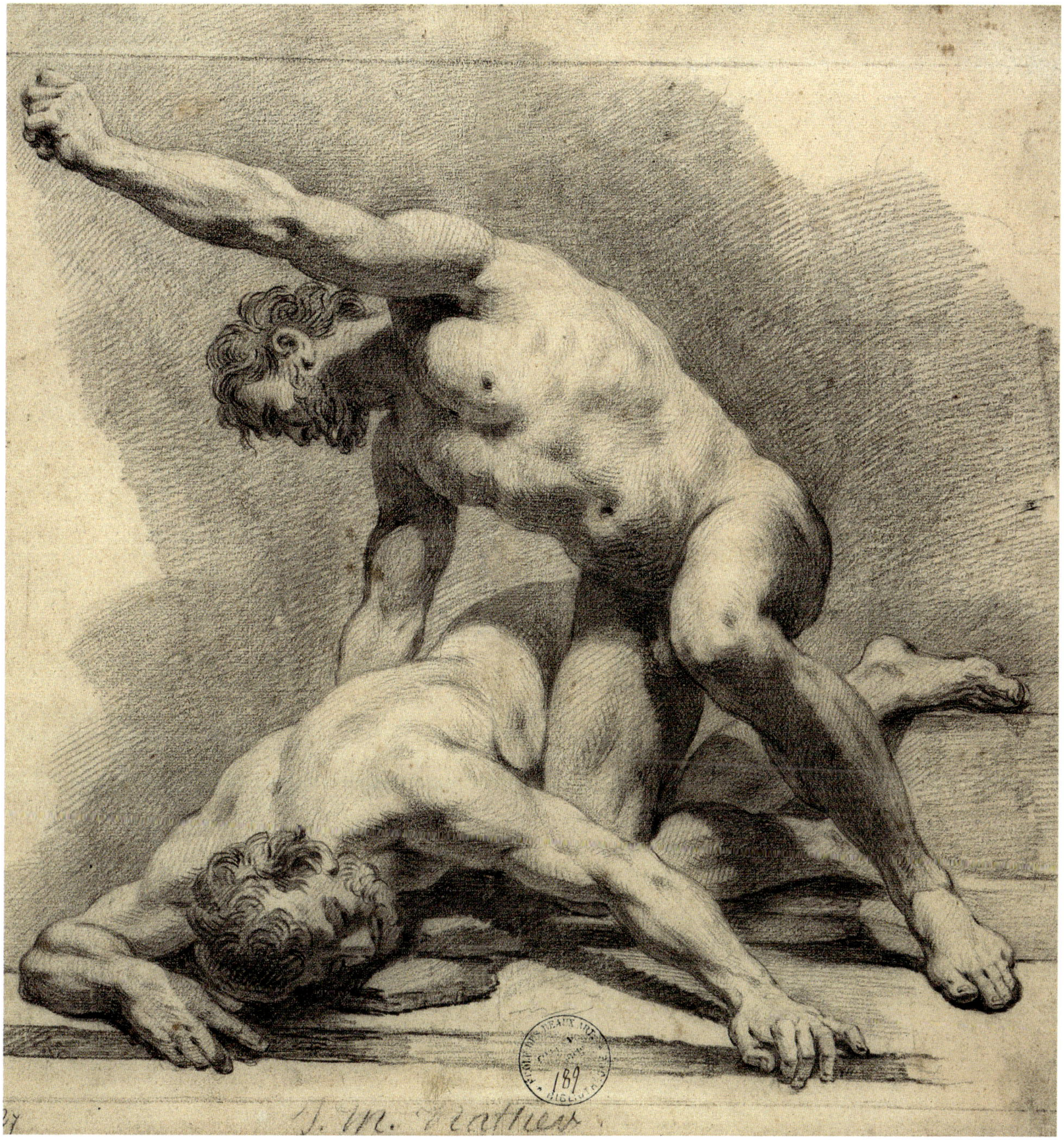

published in 1888, and with subjects and poses inspired by the genre scene and by the academic tradition—seem to originate less in science than in imagination (ills. 185–86).[50]

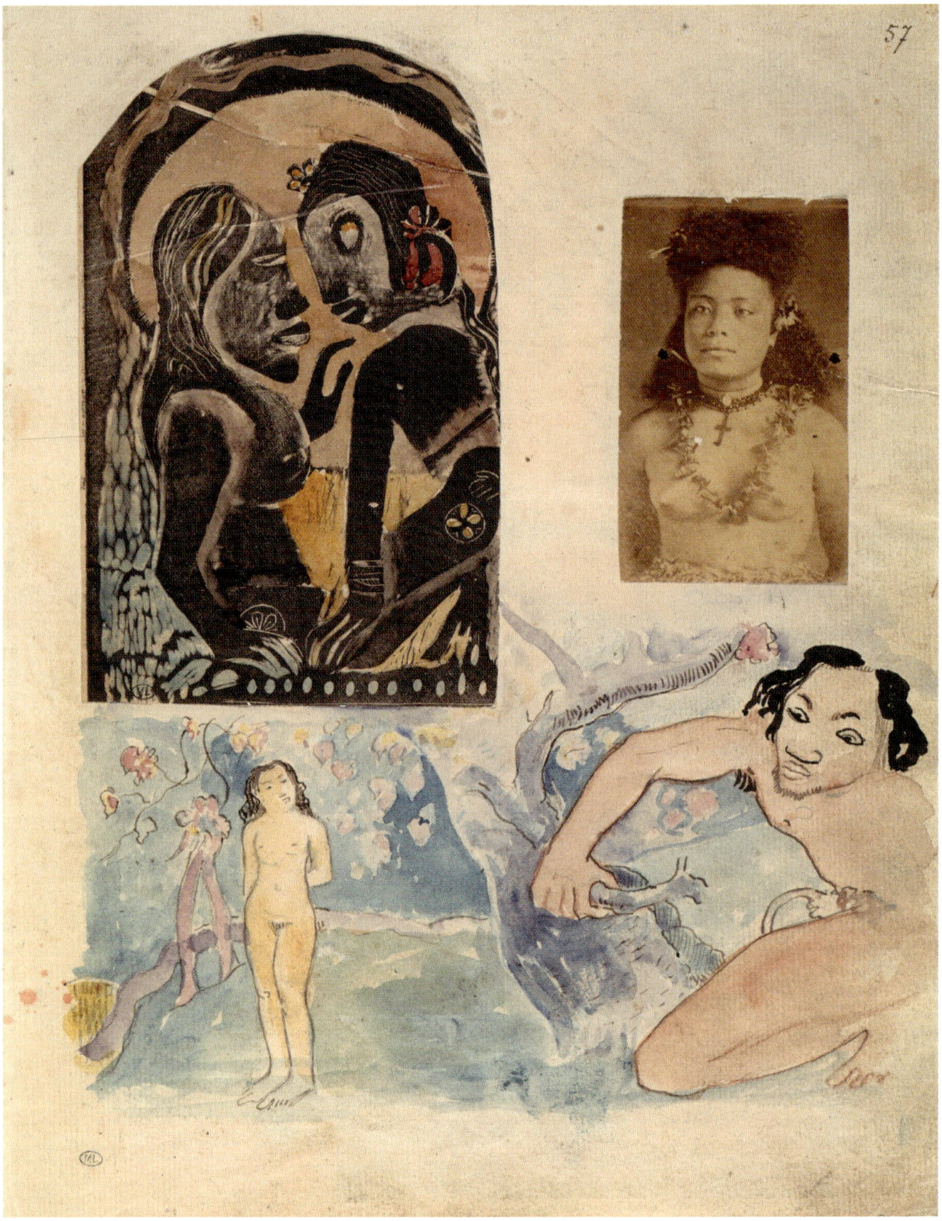
57

"Photography, in some hands, can become an instrument of art as good as any brush, pencil, chisel, or graver." [1]

STUDIES AFTER NATURE

PHOTOGRAPHY IN THE PAINTER'S STUDIO

Nature: an inept mistress whom one has to keep in mind

To become an artist in the nineteenth century, the student entered a kind of apprenticeship that inculcated the accepted forms into his eye, mind, and hand. Old master drawings reproduced as engravings, masterpieces of ancient, Renaissance, and classical sculpture in the form of casts set the yardsticks to which the pupil had to adhere. The expression "study after nature" alludes to the necessity hammered into the aspiring artist of regularly comparing his productions with reality. Molière uses the term in *La Critique de l'École des femmes* (Critique of the School for Wives) in 1663: "When you paint men, you have to paint them after nature; people want portraits to be good likenesses; and you have done nothing if the people of your world cannot recognize themselves in them." [2] At the end of the eighteenth century, Pierre-Henri de Valenciennes exhorted the young landscape painter to remain true to nature: "To hone his talent [the artist] ought to make several studies of the landscape after Nature. The great painters of history did not neglect this important aspect. This kind of study teaches one how to let air into one's pictures, to paint the local color suited to the light and shade of every moment of the day. The reminiscences one conserves of Nature prevent one from slavishly copying the effects of chiaroscuro presented by the model … unlit by the sun and without the air of the atmosphere." [3] These studies were to be treated solely as exercises and were never intended to replace the artist's inventiveness, curbed as always by academic custom and respect for pictorial tradition.

Although imperfect, nature represented—as Charles-Alphonse Dufresnoy underlined in a text often quoted and reprinted at the Académie des Beaux-Arts—the absolute benchmark: "Do not be so strongly attached to Nature that you leave nothing for your studies nor for your Genius; but likewise, do not believe that your Genius and the memory of things you

187. **Facing page:** Anonymous and Paul Gauguin, *Tahitian Woman and Couples in the Countryside, Noa-Noa*, 1893–97, watercolor, carved wood, albumen photograph, Musée d'Orsay Collection, held at the Musée du Louvre, Paris.

have seen can alone provide you with enough to make a beautiful picture without the assistance of this inept mistress, Nature, whom you should always have before you as a witness to the truth."[4] Constant crosschecking against nature was thus, as various authors emphasized, an imperative—as much for portraiture as for landscape. In 1831, in his *Dictionnaire des artistes de l'école française du XIXe siècle* (Dictionary of Nineteenth-Century Artists of the French School), then on its opening volume, Charles Gabet frequently employed "*études d'après nature*" to refer to the representation of landscape; the increasingly frequent practice of painting in the open air encouraged artists to exhibit works designated by this expression alone. Gabet also employed it for life-class studies.[5]

Throughout the eighteenth century, engraving remained an important vehicle for the diffusion of drawings made *after nature* and intended for study or practice. In 1828 an ordinance issued by Charles X stipulated the tasks and obligations of any student in engraving awarded a boarding scholarship at the French School in Rome: "To assiduously attend life classes and to devote themselves to the study of the classical style, [he] will be expected to send in at the end of his first year two figures drawn after nature and two drawings of figures after the classical style."[6] (This obligation was renewed for the second year of the four-year scholarship.) Such practices meant that students exercised their talent for thinking up works of their own, all the while building up a repertory of models.

The earliest daguerreotype studies

Praised as soon as it was invented for its exactitude, a quality many commentators considered ontologically intrinsic to the new process, photography very quickly appeared as an ideal medium for providing artists with studies that would represent nature perfectly. As early as the 1840s, the daguerreotype was regarded as a ready source of reproductions of living models for painters. For his friend, the young painter Rosa Bonheur, Louis-Auguste Bisson realized a series of horses and dogs, as well as some cattle, including one gloriously spectacular bull.[7] Veritable animal portraits that showcase their subjects—often selected from among the prizewinners at agricultural shows (as shown by handwritten notes on the back of some of them)—these pictures are genuine tours de force in which the photographer manages to capture not only the essential form of the animal, but also its vigor and power (ill. 188).

Bartholdi's studies for Gérôme

Photography on paper offered a new impetus to these studies and it was thanks to this more convenient medium that photography entered artists' studios. Certain painters worked

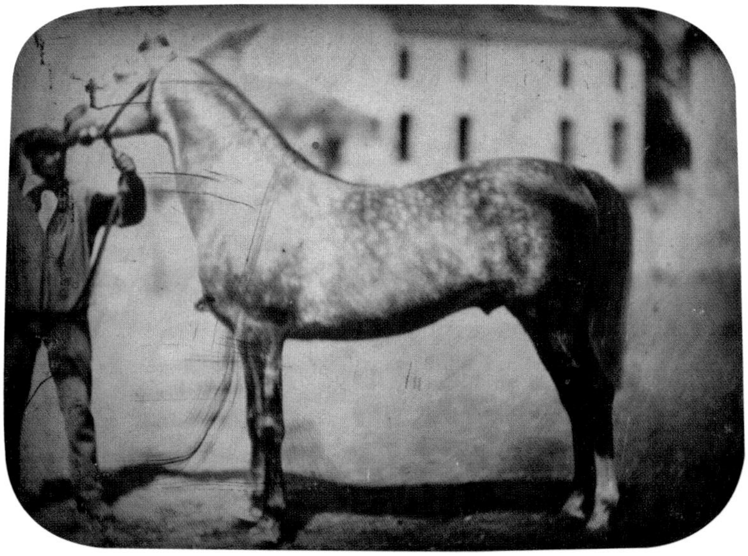

188. Louis-Auguste Bisson, "Studies of Horses: Horse Held by a Man," c. 1844–48, daguerreotype, Musée d'Orsay, Paris.

closely with photographers, whose efforts were carried out under the artist's direction; Eugène Delacroix working with Eugène Durieu for a number of photographs of naked models is a case in point.

In 1855, Jean-Léon Gérôme set off for Egypt with the barely twenty year-old Auguste Bartholdi. For his young friend and himself, the painter had obtained a government mission to gather materials "for the study of antiquities from various lands [Egypt, Nubia, Palestine] and the photographic reproduction of the principal monuments and the most remarkable types of their divers races."[8] The positive reception that had been accorded Blanquart-Évrard's publication in 1852 of photographs taken by Maxime du Camp—during his journey to Egypt, Palestine, and Syria in the company of the novelist Gustave Flaubert in 1849—certainly played a key role in the brief with which Gérôme and Bartholdi were entrusted. Thanks to du Camp, the utopian dream François Arago expressed in July 1839 at the time of the presentation of the daguerreotype to the Chambre des Députés was becoming a reality, if on paper rather than metal. The remit Gérôme and Bartholdi were given seems to have been rather hazy; at the time, it does not seem that the two artists even submitted a report; judging by the photographs taken by Bartholdi, they neglected to "reproduce the principal monuments" of Egypt (apart from the colossi of Memnon), and they failed to bring back any portraits of indigenous peoples. It was, for both of them, their first voyage to the Orient and the whole tour was marked by the delight and astonishment of discovery. Bartholdi nonetheless returned with a hundred or so pictures taken in Egypt and across the Yemen; the first batch he took with Gérôme, the second alone. He kept all the images, together with their paper negatives,[9] having given a copy of the prints to his traveling companion.

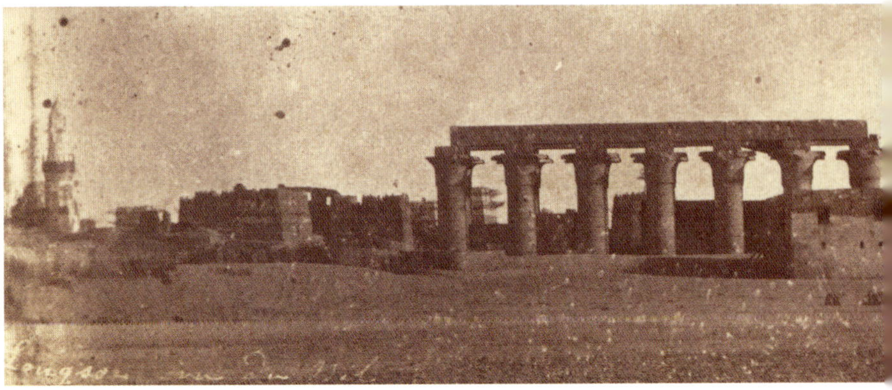

The influence these photographs were to exert on the painter proved seminal. Unlike the majority of his fellow painters, often reticent concerning the use of photography in their pictorial work, Gérôme made no mystery of it. Théophile Gautier and Paul de Saint-Victor both mentioned such materials in their reviews. It seems Gérôme resorted to it to boost his reputation as an "ethnographic painter," one who painstakingly reproduced what he had seen in the East and that photography—that paragon of exactitude—had recorded. He thus embraced the supposed virtues of the new invention for his own benefit. Such economy with the truth meant his ostensibly faithful visions of a fantasy Orient were accepted by his contemporaries as real. It would seem that Théophile Gautier, for one, was taken in: "The young artist, accompanied by a few friends, has traveled up the Nile in one of the river's *canges*, vessels fitted out so picturesquely and commodiously that journeying through Egypt is a veritable pleasure cruise. Having advanced, as you are aware, to the perfection it achieves today, photography dispenses artists with the necessity of copying monuments thanks to photographs that are absolutely faithful and to which a judicious choice of point of view and moment can impart a most superb effect."[10]

A model for new images

Far from copying what the photographs depict (Bartholdi's prints, in addition, showed only a few of the great monuments mentioned by Gautier), Gérôme used the composition of the shot and certain details to construct new painted images. For example, in *Horse Dealer in Cairo* (1867, oil on panel, Pioneer Museum and Haggin Collection, Stockton), he juxtaposed two buildings Bartholdi had taken in Yemen, where as we saw the artist himself never went, to produce a vision of the streets of Cairo, with a *mashrabiya* latticework window and a dilapidated course of stonework, which appeared "truer" to him than the reality of the mushrooming city he witnessed. The recourse to photography in the conception of *The*

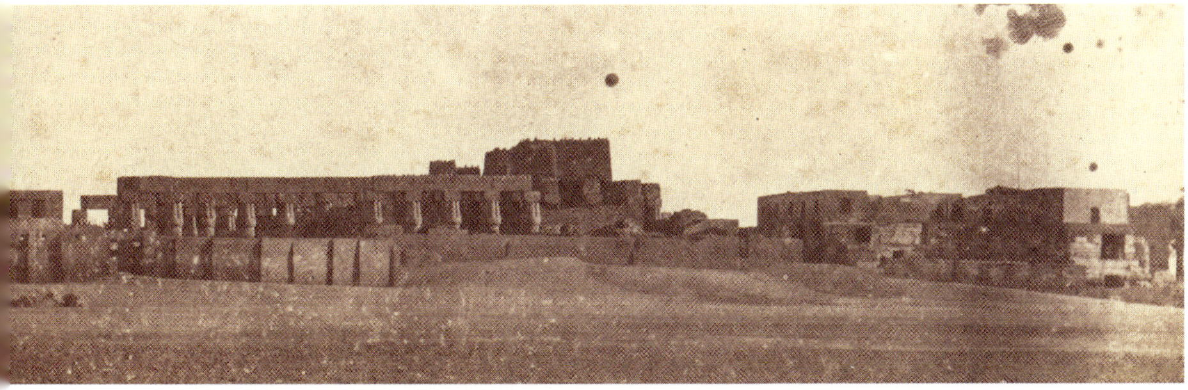

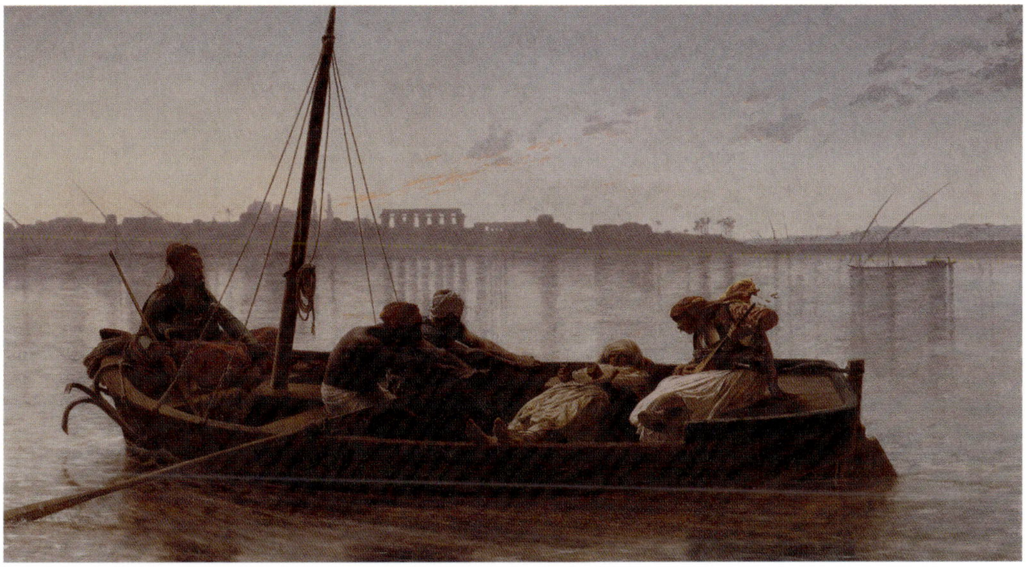

Prisoner (ill. 190) was of a more subtle kind. The scene represents the wild and sensual Orient of *The Thousand and One Nights* hugely popular among Gérôme's contemporaries. A bound prisoner lies at the bottom of a *cange* as the boat slips down the Nile; his warder, a fierce Arnaut (or Arvanite), sings, accompanying himself on an instrument. Famous for their brutality as much as for the panache of their costume, a wide white skirt flaring up beneath an embroidered jacket, these Arnauts were mercenaries in the Ottoman army. A great success at the Salon of 1863, the picture won accolades from critics for the accuracy of a scene that felt like a snapshot from Gérôme's stay in Egypt. This was in fact far from the case; such an image could never have been seen in Egypt. Iconographically, the work refers to a painting by Paul Delaroche set in France, *The State Barge of Cardinal de Richelieu* (1829, oil on canvas), inspired by Alfred de Vigny's 1826 novel, *Cinq-Mars* (*Cinq-Mars; or a Conspiracy under Louis XIII*). From photography Gérôme lifted the panoramic viewpoint that opens up the space to show the rippling waters and the wake behind

189. **Above, top:** Auguste Bartholdi, "Luxor," 1856, salt print, Musée Bartholdi, Colmar.

190. **Above, bottom:** Jean-Léon Gérôme, *The Prisoner*, 1861, oil on canvas, Musée des Beaux-Arts, Nantes.

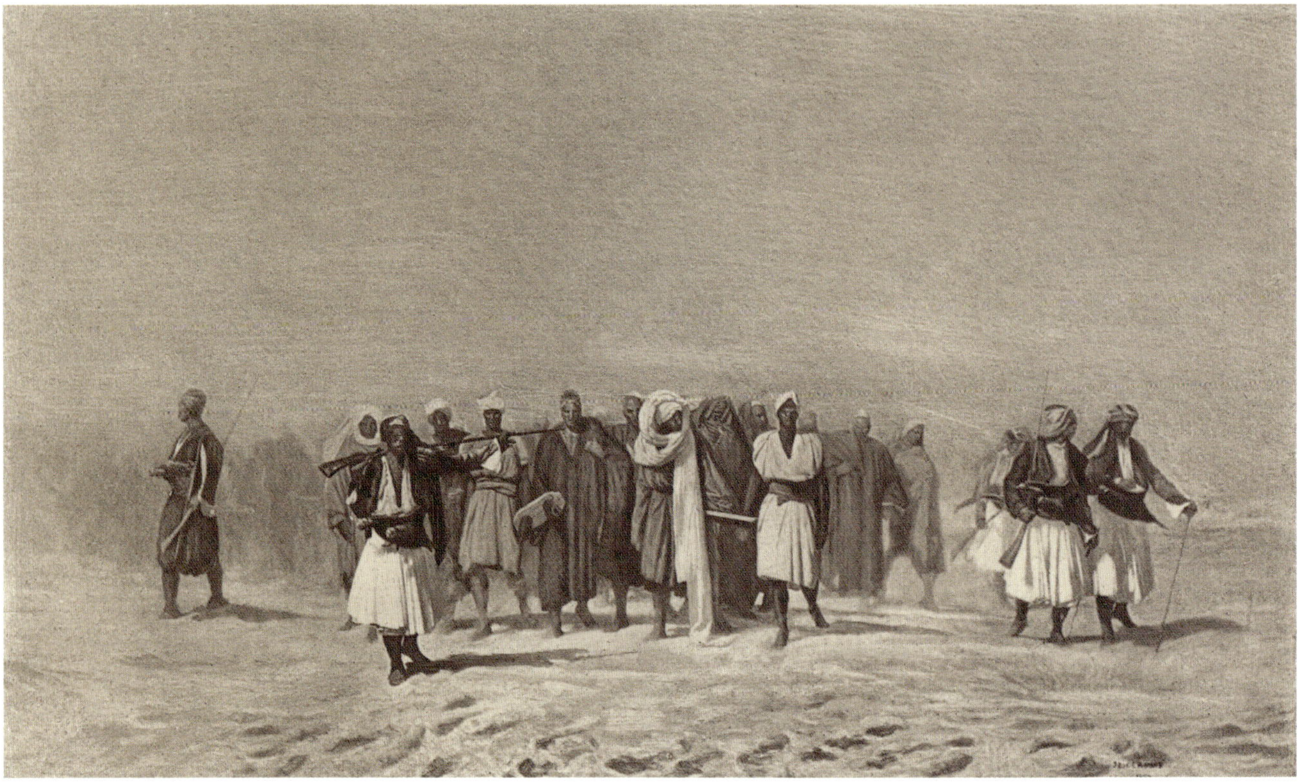

191. Adolphe Goupil (publisher), after Jean-Léon Gérôme, *Egyptian Recruits Crossing the Desert*, 1857, engraving, Musée Goupil, Bordeaux.

the boat. As on photographs by Bartholdi, the background to the picture is closed off by the ruins of an archeological site (ills. 189–90). As Gérôme had not met Arnauts in the Egypt of 1855 (in fact he had two models dressed in the costumes of this Ottoman corps photographed in his studio back in Paris), their attire is very close to that presented in many romanticized illustrations. From the end of the 1850s, the Arnaut was to become a familiar figure in the painter's oeuvre; Gérôme depicted him striking various attitudes, some in keeping with his martial origins, others less fearsome (ills. 191–92).

Gustave Moreau's carefully staged images

Scrupulously attentive to their conception, Gustave Moreau often reworked his pictures and, reluctant to part with them, many remained in his studio throughout his lifetime. "I wish," he wrote in 1885, "to accumulate evocative Ideas in my works… year by year, I add 'incremental details as the Idea comes to me.'" During the 1880s, Moreau had several photographs taken of male and female models by his friend and secretary, Henri Rupp. Painstakingly selected by Moreau, and close to figures planned in preliminary drawings, the subjects' attitudes could then be transferred into the artist's elaborate compositions inspired by ancient history or mythology. The poses obeyed precise constraints; the ropes tying some of the

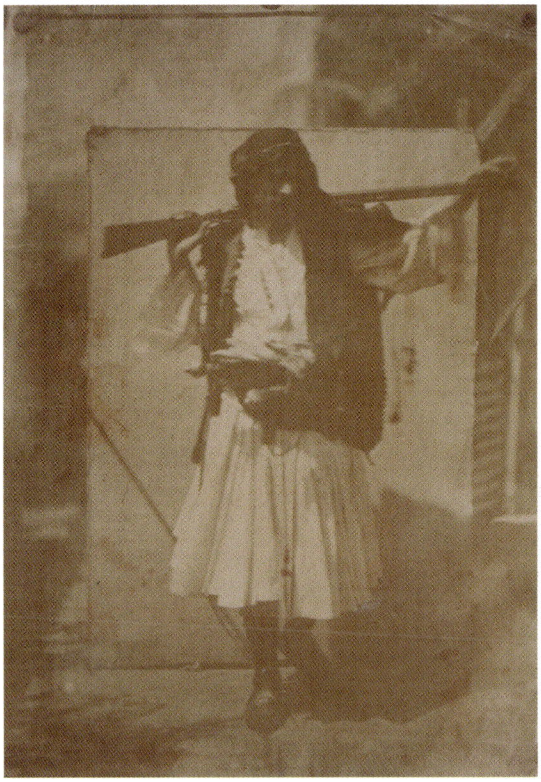

models to studio stools testify to their enforced immobility. If he was attentive to the positions of his subjects, Moreau proved more flexible as to their sex and age: he had a very young man pose for his Jason and a young woman for one of his companions. These photographs show how an artist who called himself an "assembler of dreams" would take inspiration from the real, but adapted it in his visions of marmoreal and androgynous demigods, transforming, for instance, a retiring young man into an all-conquering hero (ills. 193–94).

192. **Left:** Anonymous, "Male Model Dressed in Eastern Clothes, with a Rifle on his Shoulders, on the Roof of a Workshop", c. 1856, salt print, Musée d'Orsay, Paris.

193. **Page 248:** Attributed to Henri Rupp, "Male Model Posing for *The Argonauts*, Figure for Jason," c. 1890, albumen print, Musée Gustave-Moreau, Paris.

194. **Page 249:** Gustave Moreau, *The Argonauts*, before 1895, oil on canvas, Musée Gustave-Moreau, Paris.

Blanquart-Évrard's albums

Certain painters assisted in the conception of photographic studies they later employed to plan a picture. This use often went further than simple copying. From the early 1850s, the possibility of realizing several prints from a single negative encouraged photographers and publishers to issue studies for artists in the form of printed plates often gathered into portfolios.

In 1850, Louis-Désiré Blanquart-Évrard founded the first photographic printers in the environs of Lille. From 1851 to 1856, he published, under the title "albums," several collections of photographs intended for artists. Already referred to above, the *Album photographique de l'artiste et de l'amateur*, published from 1851 to 1853 in twelve installments, included views of

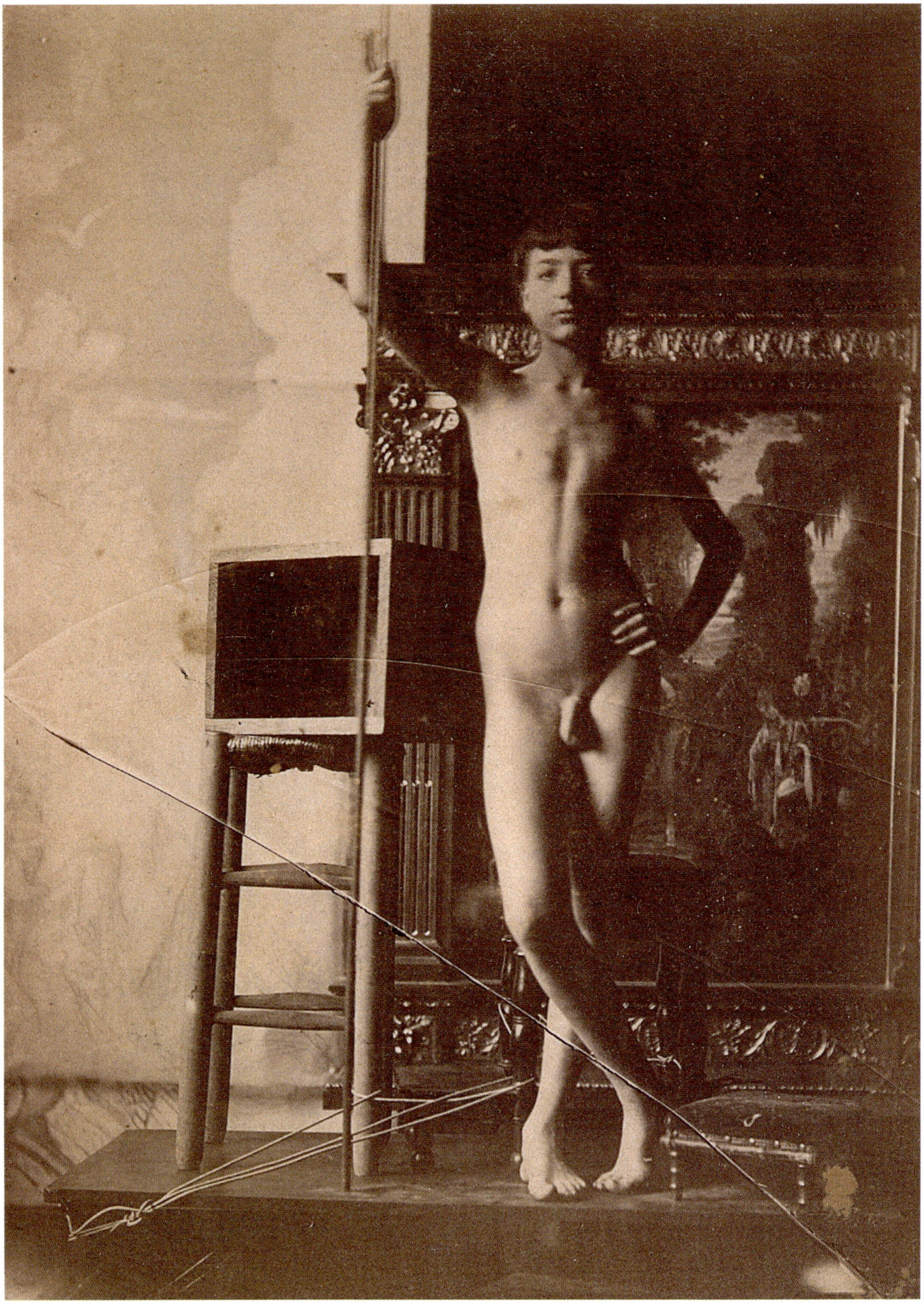

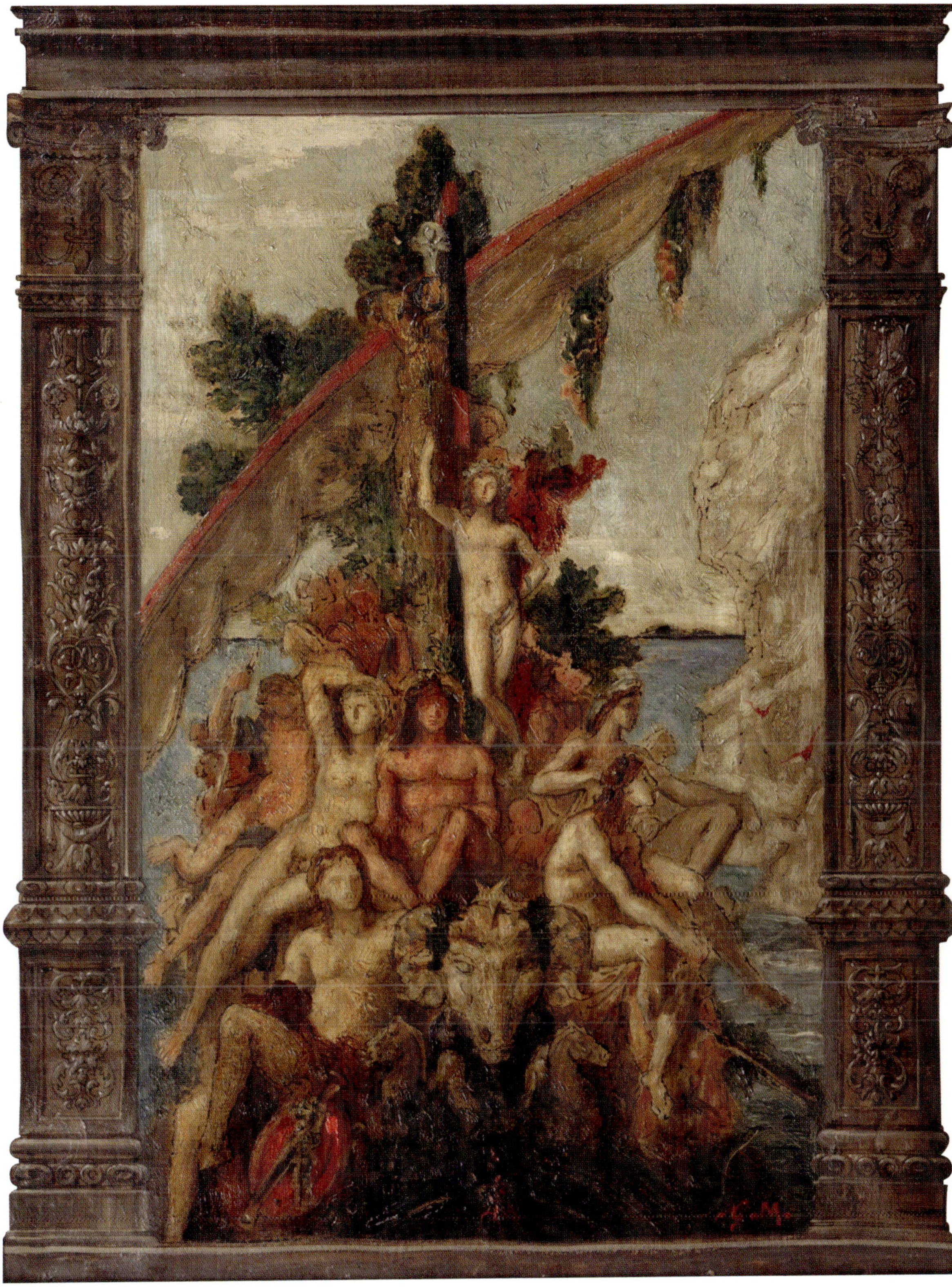

architecture and reproductions of artworks—paintings, drawings, and sculptures.[11] Blanquart-Évrard also brought out the views taken by Maxime du Camp in Egypt in 1850. The titles of several of his publications imply that they were meant to be studies for artists: in 1853 came *Études photographiques* (Photographic Studies), including one very beautiful "Clearing"; in 1853 and 1854, under the title *Études et paysages* (Studies and Landscapes), there appeared photographs of the scenery around Fontainebleau and the environs of Paris. Among the photographers whose work was published by Blanquart-Évrard were Charles Marville and Henri-Victor Regnault. Pioneering though it was, his business did not in the end prove profitable, production costs being all the higher due to the fragility of the support and their tendency to fade over time.

Photographic studies after nature

His project, however, paved the way for more profitable outlets for photographs with artistic ambitions. In 1866, the Maison Giroux—a firm specializing in the supply and trade of materials and studies for artists—brought out the first installment of *Études photographiques* by the photographer Ildefonse Rousset. The foreword, by Louis Jourdan, underlines the aesthetic purpose of these photographs: "Others... ascribed artistic value [to photography] in the belief that its productions, because they are able to attain a notable degree of truth, are worthy of being classified as works of art—art being, after all, none other than the most elevated and most ideal expression of truth."[12] Rousset's portfolio featured landscapes and genre scenes inspired by rustic life and agricultural labor. It thus disseminated images close to pictures painted in Barbizon or in the Forest of Fontainebleau that drew on a repertoire that deliberately set out to show man and the landscape living in peaceable, even idyllic union. As Jourdan pointed out, his studies were as painstakingly composed as a finished picture; the presence of a pair of these photographs, "Two Fishermen on the River Bank" and "Landscape, River," in a collection that once belonged to the painter and engraver Théophile Chauvel (today in the Musée d'Orsay) testifies to their use by artists at the time.[13]

A printer and publisher of engravings since forming an association in 1829 with Henry Rittner, from 1842 Adolphe Goupil became interested in photography, co-publishing *Les Excursions daguerriennes* (Daguerreian Travels) with the optician Noël Paymal Lerebours. From 1853, the Maison Goupil published several important sets of photographs, whose themes reflect those in their print catalog; the subjects included ancient monuments (*L'Égypte et la Nubie* by Félix Teynard); architecture (*Monuments, vues générales et tableaux* by Édouard Baldus, *La Cathédrale de Reims* by Henri Le Secq, *Vues de*

Paris by the brothers Bisson); landscapes (*Études diverses* by Gustave Le Secq, *Vues des Pyrénées* by Joseph Vigier, *Vues d'Auvergne* by André Giroux), and the reproduction of works of art (*Notice sur la vie de Marc-Antoine Raimondi* by Benjamin Delessert, *Catalogue raisonné de l'œuvre de Paul Delaroche* by Robert Jefferson Bingham). Creating *La Galerie photographique* (The Photographic Gallery) in 1858 (the first of five series of reproductions of artworks), Goupil gradually specialized in this field to the point of becoming one of the most significant publishers, not only in Paris, but also in London, New York, and The Hague, where he also opened branches.[14]

Adolphe Giraudon and his "Photographic Library"

In 1877, a young man of twenty-seven, Adolphe Giraudon, opened a "Bibliothèque Photographique," whose vocation was to furnish artists and scientists with the widest selection possible of photographic reproductions. Conveniently located just opposite the École des Beaux-Arts at 15 rue Bonaparte, Giraudon's company was soon competing head-on with the commercial and publishing supremacy of the firms of Braun and Goupil. In order to carve out a position against better-armed competition, Giraudon sought to supply his customers with images they could not find elsewhere. The site of his store encouraged several photographers, such as Neurdein and Co., to sell their products through him. Thanks to his way with people, Giraudon had soon set up a network of correspondents, adding to his catalog many reproductions of art and studies after nature. His first advertisement in 1880 mentions: "COLLECTIONS AFTER NATURE—SCENES FROM THE FIELDS: instantaneous reproductions of peasants and country-women, harvesters, haymakers, shepherdesses, washerwomen, etc.... Created by an artist in his leisure hours, the collection is remarkably fine and offers an invaluable resource to the landscape artist. ANIMALS AND LANDSCAPES ... COSTUMES ... ACADEMIC STUDIES."[15] The "academic studies" had been taken by the Austrian photographer Hermann Heid, whom Giraudon represented in France.[16] Over the years, his catalog swelled to become one of the richest and most exhaustive, providing artists, scientists, and amateurs with a profusion of the most varied photographs, covering every field: reproductions of artworks, but also landscapes, monuments, academic, and genre studies. Giraudon was also the Paris agent for the Italian firm of Alinari; for French photographers who had set up in the Lebanon, Félix Bonfils and sons; for the Venetian photographer Carlo Naya; for Juan Laurent, a Frenchman working out of Madrid; for the German Georgio Sommer, living in Naples; for Pascal Sebah, living in Istanbul, etc. As he proudly asserts in his catalog for 1889, twelve years after his store was established, he was thus equipped to "fulfill all the needs of the

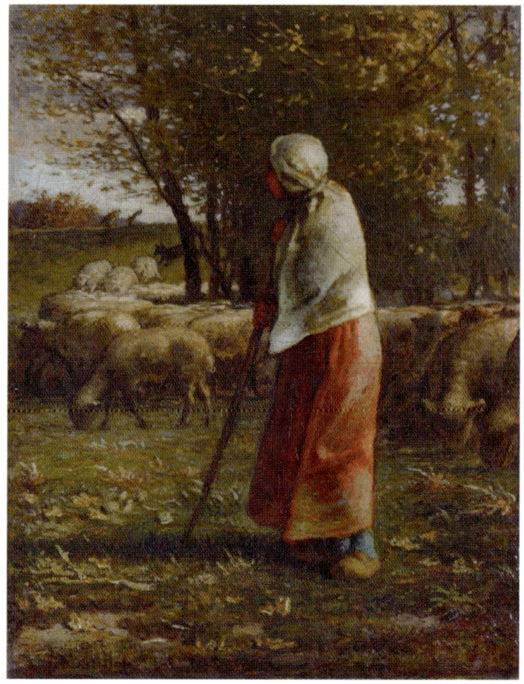

artist, as much as in the supply of useful documents as from the point of view of art history teaching."[17] At this time, Giraudon stocked more than seven thousand studies after nature as artistic aids. One of the most original sections in his catalog consisted in "scenes from the fields," carried out by an anonymous artist, as the advert says, "in his leisure hours." Taking their cue from the works of Jean-François Millet and the Barbizon painters, these subtly composed photographs show models posing in the open air. The evocation of a tranquil, paradisiacal nature, where agricultural labor was an effortless joy, flattered the tastes of contemporary artists and hobbyists. In their turn, these pictures nourished images in paintings at the end of the century, by which time realism had lost ground to a more sanitized view of country life (ills. 195–96).[18]

Painters' collections of photographs

Today interest in artists' art collections is growing. The desire to understand better the nature of the sources on which creative artists draw and to analyze their conceptual processes has motivated many studies. Long neglected, the photographic collections of painters provide a novel subject of research that often casts much-needed light on the relations between painting and photography. The task of reconstituting their contents, however, even virtually, is often arduous. It is extremely rare for a given collection to have come down to our day intact; auction sale catalogs and probate inventories mention them succinctly, at best, a single line often designating an entire batch

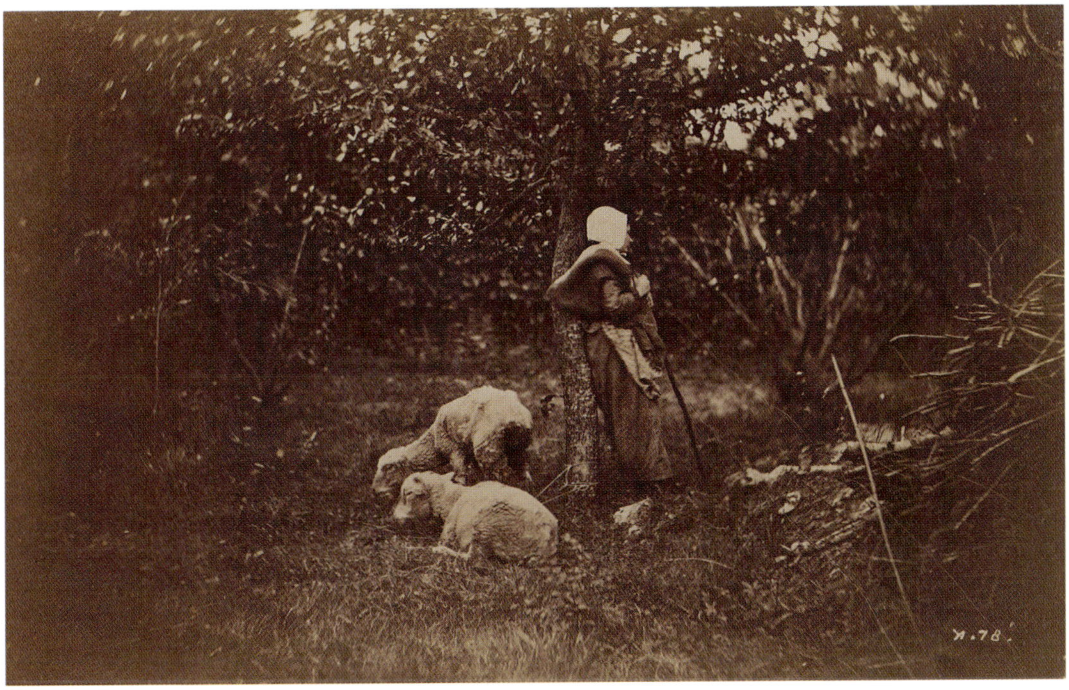

195. **Facing page:** Jean-François Millet, *The Little Shepherdess*, c. 1870, oil on canvas, Musée d'Orsay, Paris.

196. **Above:** Anonymous, Adolphe Giraudon (publisher), "Shepherdess and Two Sheep," 1877–78, albumen print, Musée d'Orsay, Paris.

or lot of photographs. The correlation between an actual image and a reference to it in correspondence, a diary, or some other testimony often remains hazardous. The weakness of the provenance histories of the photographs sold today, which seldom venture back beyond the immediately preceding owner, complicates the historian's task still more. The study of collections once belonging to artists and now preserved in museums has opened up some interesting if inevitably incomplete lines of research.[19] Analysis undertaken by Georges Vigne and latterly Florence Viguier at the Musée Ingres in Montauban, and by Geneviève Lacambre and then Marie-Cécile Forest at the Musée Gustave-Moreau in Paris; the enthralling exhibition organized in 2008 by Christophe Leribault at the Musée Delacroix in Paris; research by Richard Kendall, Malcolm Daniel, and Sylvie Aubenas on Degas; the online launch of the holdings of the Musée d'Orsay that visually combines photographs from same workshop—by Édouard Lebel, Théophile Chauvel, and Gérôme, for example; and Anne Baldassari's research centering on the Picasso Archive: all have exposed the sheer quantity of photography existing in nineteenth-century studios.[20]

Painters' imaginary museums

Reproductions of works of art were present in most collections; they were used for reference, as an aid to drawing exercises, and were often appended to print collections. Delacroix, for instance, probably acquired reproductions of Rubens's

Raising of the Cross, photographed by Eugène Desplanques and published in the portfolio *Les Tableaux célèbres* by Blanquart-Évrard (ill. 65). The painter noted in his *Journal* that he had seen a reproduction of a Rubens on one of his walks through Paris: "Thursday, November 24. Went for a walk this evening in the Galerie Vivienne [an arcade], where I stopped at a bookshop to look at some photographs. I was attracted by a photograph of the *Raising of the Cross* by Rubens, which interested me greatly; the inaccuracies are more apparent when they are they are no longer saved by execution [i.e., by the the engraver's interpretation] and colour. The sight of this masterpiece, or rather the recollection of my feeling when I actually saw it [in Antwerp], kept me happily employed for the rest of the evening."[21] Photographic reproduction here comes to the aid of the artist's memory and, by reminding him of a much-admired canvas, sparks an emotion. Delacroix's reaction underlines the role of photography in his sensitivity and in the constitution of his memory: "If the invention ... of the daguerreotype [had occurred thirty years ago] perhaps my career would have been fuller. The ability to paint at any moment without the trouble of a palette, and the lessons the daguerreotype can provide anyone painting from memory offer priceless advantages."[22] The singular manner in which photography reproduces paintings—without the intermediary of grooves or ridges—revealed the work in a wholly novel manner. In fact, Delacroix was less taken with the exactitude of the process than by how it left unaltered inaccuracies that an engraver would have smoothed over in his interpretation. If, as he had written in *La Revue des Deux Mondes*, addressing the subject of the teaching of drawing on September 15, 1850, he mistrusted the exaggerated precision of the daguerreotype, here he delighted in its faithful rendering of Rubens's manner.[23]

Several decades later, Paul Gauguin assembled a collection of reproductions of artworks, including paintings and sculpture, and of monuments. Taking them with him to Tahiti in 1891, these photographs constituted a kind of private museum on which he relied in many works. Unfortunately, no precise inventory or description has come down to us; historians have to base their investigation on crosschecking testimonies of witnesses against photographs actually unearthed in Tahiti. Although eager to get to grips with this new world, the wellspring that would renew his art, for a number of compositions Gauguin would still take inspiration from monuments, sculptures, and paintings in these photographic reproductions. Thus the rhythm in several paintings and drawings is derived from that of the Parthenon frieze (*The Vanilla Grove, Man and Horse*, oil on canvas, 1891, Solomon R. Guggenheim Museum, New York). In 1889, while still in Paris, he had been struck by the architectural reconstructions in the Colonial Exhibition at the World's Fair. He visited them on several occasions and made drawings inspired by features in

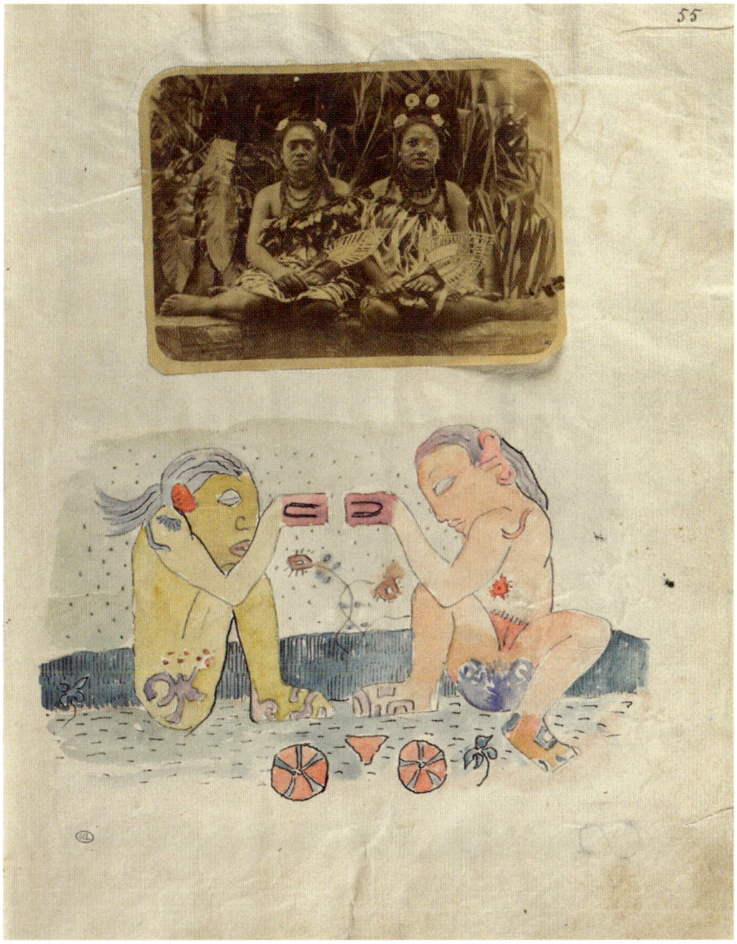

197. Anonymous and Paul Gauguin, *Polynesian Women and Goddesses, Noa Noa*, 1893–97, albumen print and watercolor on buff paper, Musée d'Orsay collection, held at the Musée du Louvre, Paris.

the temple at Angkor Wat.[24] He also acquired a group of photographs of the temple of Borobudur in Java; in Tahiti, female figures from a reproduced frieze inspired the sinuous poses and graceful attitudes for several works.

Photographic images in Gauguin's Noa Noa

In Polynesia, Gauguin was on a quest for *sauvagerie*, that rawness that in the West had been forgotten. Disembarking in Papeete he was then grievously disappointed to encounter an island where Western civilization, through religion and education, had already begun to erode local customs and traditions. He was interested in photographs taken by settlers and travelers in Tahiti, though. At the end of the 1860s, a naval officer aboard the *Astrée*, Paul-Émile Miot, had taken a number of photographs of Polynesian populations for the purposes of ethnographic study. Of extraordinary quality, his pictures display singular sensitivity to his models, whose personalities—above and beyond any scientific intention—Miot adeptly manages to capture and convey to the viewer.[25] Their languid and melancholic beauty is somewhat redolent of the sensations that imbue Gauguin's Polynesian period canvases. Disenchanted with Tahiti, which he considered to be perverted by civilization, Gauguin went off in quest of Maori culture, now buried beneath the ashes of modernity, becoming interested in their ancient religion with its multifaceted and complex pantheon, including mysterious spirits called *tupapau* that greatly intrigued him. He attempted to give the latter material form in several pieces, such as the glorious *Manao Tupapau* (aka *The Spirits of the Dead Watching*, 1892, oil on canvas, Albright Knox Collection, Buffalo). Back in Paris, Gauguin embarked on an original enterprise: a kind of instruction book that would introduce a culture so different from that in the West. This was *Noa Noa*, a "world book," whose very form exemplifies the extraordinary richness of its inspiration and sources. With its mix of drawings, watercolors, engravings, and photographs, it translates in a variety of images not only the diversity but also the richness of a universe that captivated him and kept him spellbound even after his return (ills. 187–97).[26]

Like Gauguin, Gustave Moreau also accumulated a huge number of photographic reproductions of paintings, sculpture, and architecture. Their variety demonstrates the breadth of sources that fed into large-scale works in which a vast assortment of details confers a decorative, dreamlike appearance. Photographs from his collection served not only as models but also as actual media, as he often drew directly onto prints, embellishing for instance a reproduction of Leonardo's *Saint Anne, the Virgin and Child* with marginal drawings.

Models for painting, models for photography

Both containing a significant number of prints, the collections once belonging to the painters Edmond Lebel and Théophile Chauvel and conserved in the Musée d'Orsay constitute a rewarding object of study. A pupil of Léon Cogniet's, and a painter who exhibited at every Salon in the 1860s and 1870s, a favorite of the emperor's cousin Princess Mathilde for his pieces inspired by the common people of Italy, Edmond Lebel assembled a voluminous collection of photographs that was fortunately kept by his heirs and has since entered the French State collection. Many of them were acquired in Italy by the painter during one or other of his various sojourns. Genre scenes recreating the attitudes and poses of an idealized, indigenous Italy are numerous and of varying quality. Lebel also possessed prints by the photographer Giacomo Caneva (1813–65), who was by training a painter, and who had settled in Rome in the mid 1840s; in 1845, he appears on the roster of the Caffè Greco—that mecca of artistic life in Rome at the time—as a "painter and photographer." Taken for the artists to whom he sold them, his photographs feature picturesque scenes posed for by models sporting traditional costumes. Caneva also took some magnificent landscapes, close in terms of subject matter (the waterfalls at Tivoli, trees bordering the Appian Way), as well as in manner (a feeling for light and composition), to earlier, pictorial works. The presence of photographs by Caneva in the collection gathered together by Lebel underlines the way that in the mid-nineteenth century models would pass back and forth between painting and photography. Themselves irrigated by the lessons of both classical and romantic painting, Caneva's photographs in turn served as templates for paintings. Lebel painted canvases of the same type, also taking photographs, first in his Paris studio and then in the early 1870s in Italy.[27] Thus, Caneva's studies after nature played a dual role as models for Lebel: as a memory aid for paintings of the Italian lower classes, which he, in common with many contemporary artists, nostalgically associated with his time in Italy, and as a spur to the novel artistic practice of photography, in which Lebel retains Caneva's dense, grave manner.

The French painter's collection included in addition photographs of models by Pietro Thyge Boyesen, a Danish artist who had moved to Rome, and a group of *cartes de visite* by Frattodi, as well as landscapes and architectural views by Gioacchino Altobelli, Gustavo Eugenio Chauffourier, and Bonis. The number of photographs—about two hundred in the Musée d'Orsay—shows how interested Lebel must have been in images that formed a repository he could mine whenever he required material to recreate in Paris the ancient and modern Italy he had visited.[28] This treasure trove was all the more precious since it was allied to pictorial models and thus fostered, not just models to be copied, but fully composed scenes whose artistic nature is already palpable.

The "studies after nature" collected by Théophile Chauvel as a reflection of his artistic world

The collection of Théophile Chauvel, a painter and engraver close to the school of Barbizon, is representative of the kinds of studies after nature available in Paris during the 1860s and 1870s, and demonstrates how images taken by photographs and sold by booksellers, in stores selling artists' materials, printers and publishers found their audience and their purchasers. Chauvel was a customer in Giraudon's shop, buying photographs of models inspired by Millet and also a group of nudes taken by Heid. Numbering more than two hundred items, his collection contains many photographs related to the new representation of landscape and the countryside—trees, rocks, and animals, as well as models in costume—that illustrate the wide dispersal of contemporary artistic trends. Chauvel had acquired prints of the Forest of Fontainebleau by Charles Marville, Constant Famin, and Achille Quinet, with subjects and compositions recalling the naturalistic approach of Théodore Rousseau, Narcisse Diaz de la Peña, or Jules Dupré. Such acquisitions show that Chauvel, himself so familiar with the region (he had met Camille Corot there), remained faithful to his pictorial sources. These photographs show the extent to which this artistic universe had been taken up by others; closely related to his own creations, such images could be treated as ersatz sketches or study drawings.[29] They also constitute a new paradigm since, in their search for continuity with painting, they invent authentically photographic representations, benefiting from the invention's potential as well as being limited by its constraints. For example, pictures by Foncelle representing a rough sea and clouds scudding through the sky refer directly to photographic works by Gustave Le Secq in the 1850s; they also sought to reveal the ability of photography to seize the movement of the waves and sky, and so triumph over the obstacle presented by lengthy exposure times.

This taste for the Barbizon School went beyond the borders of France. From the mid-nineteenth century, the realist revolution in the apprehension of landscape experienced a real vogue, fostered especially by the painter William Morris Hunt, who stayed in Paris in the 1850s and exhibited at the annual Salons. He played a key role in the constitution of North American collections as the buyer on behalf of the Allston Club (an association in Boston of painters, art lovers, and collectors) of Jean-François Millet's *Sower* and Gustave Courbet's *La Curée* (or *The Quarry*; both pictures are today in the Museum of Fine Arts, Boston). The recent sale of the photograph collection belonging to the financier and amateur painter John Chandler Bancroft, consisting of very fine prints by Adalbert and Eugène Cuvelier, shows how the new aesthetics extended into photography.[30] A friend of the American painter Whistler, Bancroft had garnered a vast collection of paintings.[31]

The problematic recognition of painting's "very humble maidservant"

These "studies after nature" confirm the ambiguity of the role and position of nascent photography with respect to its elder sister. The issue of the recognition of photography depended largely on its uptake by painting studios; the implication being that it was, as Baudelaire had ironically framed it in 1859, "the very humble maidservant of painting," and that photographers had to accept the aesthetic models and genres of the existing art. Photography thus followed dutifully in the footsteps of its predecessor. So the interest of photographic studies after nature derived less from the supposed exactitude of their reproduction of nature than from their capacity to embody preexisting pictorial references. Not so much a mimetic reflection of the real, such photographs—by their choice of subject and composition, by the carefully staged poses—instead tended to offer an artful rearrangement of reality. Productions by photographers intended for artists took their cue first and foremost from classical and academic models, though without totally ignoring developments in landscape and genre by the new so-called realist school.

In fact photography's subsidiarity with respect to painting was less to its disadvantage than Baudelaire's anathema might imply; photography, by reiterating the forms and iconography of painting, spawned a new vein of creativity founded on a novel relationship to reality and on the overcoming of technical problems. This in turn might engender images utterly distinct from pictorial precedents. Their attraction today for amateurs and collectors stems from the way they open a window onto the artistic practice of the time. Lifting the veil on how paintings were made in a nineteenth-century studio, they throw a light on the secrets of the painter's craft.[32] The growing amount of interest in collections of artists indicates that, far from being insulated from contemporary painting, photography was closely associated with it, in various registers, some going far beyond mere imitation or copying. Painters thus made use of photography to build up private museums in which reproductions of artworks rubbed shoulders with nude and landscape studies. And so, from the middle of the nineteenth century on, a new mode of representation was gradually accepted in painting circles—whatever the individual artist's opinion on photography happened to be.

New models from science

With its links to contemporary scientific concepts, photography had a part to play in the creation and diffusion of new archetypes.

Jean-Martin Charcot's weekly public demonstrations at the hospital of La Salpêtrière attracted not only doctors and psychiatrists, but also artists, painters, and writers. Interest in psychoses and their effect on an individual's attitudes and expressions had been growing since the beginning of the nineteenth century. In the late 1870s, Charcot took on as an assistant a young house physician with a gift for drawing, Paul Richer. In his *Études cliniques sur la grande hystérie* (Clinical Studies on "Grand" Hysteria) published in 1885, Richer reproduces sketches made during these public consultations, as well as drawings after photographs by Albert Londe. The photographer expounded on his interest in the experiments undertaken by the physician and the challenges they represented for photography: "In his private clinic for diseases of the nervous system, Professor Charcot sees a host of patients afflicted with paralysis, hysteria, epilepsy, chorea, etc. Taking studies that divide up and analyze their tremors and attacks presents photography with a

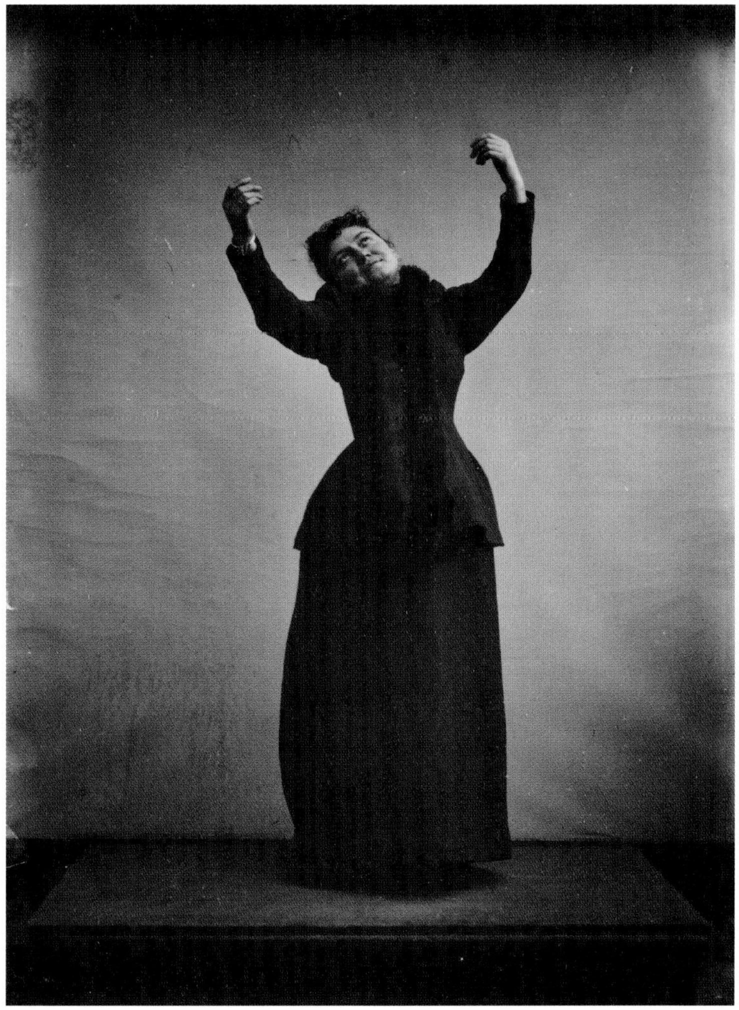

198. Albert Londe, "Woman in a Selected Pose," c. 1882, modern print from gelatin-bromide silver glass negatives belonging to a series, École Nationale Supérieure des Beaux-Arts, Paris.

considerable challenge. Hence the need for a special apparatus able to take a sequence of photographs at irregular intervals, as close or as far apart in time as required."[33] Inspired by Muybridge and Marey's chronophotographic inventions, the process developed by Londe produced a series of images taken against a dark background that highlight a single model exemplifying the attitudes and episodes of a hysterical attack (ill. 198). The status of these images remains disconcerting; if some appear to have been carried out at the behest of Charcot, others were in probability performed by an actress, perhaps even Londe's own wife, who thus imitated each phase of the illness.[34] Through photography, La Salpêtrière's dramatic performances became "images" and thus available for use as artists' models. Charcot's research and the photographic iconography it spawned exerted a notable influence on late nineteenth-century artists. Symbolist painters redeployed the exalted expressions and excessive gestures of the hysteric, transposing them pictorially in depictions of religious ecstasy or the tremors of love (ill. 199).[35]

From the end of 1870, Eadweard Muybridge was using motion-capture in his experiments; the researches of Étienne-Jules Marey on movement also proved of immense import to artists. To add credence to his physiological theories, by 1882 French scientist had developed a "photographic rifle" to take a rapid sequence of consecutive images. That same year, he started publishing the results the journal *Nature* and publicizing his activities at the Station Physiologique in Auteuil in a series of lectures, in particular at the prestigious Collège de France. Edgar Degas kept a watchful eye on this research as it chimed in with his artistic interest in movement, which culminated in a series of sculptures. Though Degas tended to keep his counsel on the subject, in 1897 he nonetheless mentioned to the journalist François Thiébaut-Sisson, in reference to some early studies of horses: "Marey had not yet invented the device which visually separates the imperceptible movements of a bird flying or a horse galloping or trotting."[36]

Several pictures published by Muybridge in *Animal Locomotion*, as well as others reproduced in 1892 by Marey in *Le Mouvement*, which anthologizes two decades of earlier research, show girls dancing in a rhythm and with gestures reminiscent of images by Degas. The artist took a keen interest in photography, taking it up in the mid-1890s, though he seems to have been unconcerned with representing motion. He was also an avid collector who accumulated an impressive mass of paintings, drawings, and prints of high quality, which were dispersed in November 1918, after his death. It is also probable that he collected photographs and knew the published work of Muybridge and Marey.[37]

Appointed professor of anatomy at the École des Beaux-Arts, Paul Richer—with the assistance of Albert Londe—pursued Marey's studies. Such motion-analysis enriched the representation of anatomy by emphasizing the muscular deformations arising from movement. Thus, more than sixty years after its announcement by Arago, the photographic process finally made its entrance into the École des Beaux-Arts.[38]

Turning the most ephemeral experiences into permanent images, the unprecedented scientific models derived from photography were taken up by many painters of the period. Such studies after nature loosened the conventional classifications rooted in the traditional approach; as a potential template, photography already went beyond pictorial archetypes, generating—though still predicated on codes inspired by painting—a new aesthetics. Over the course of the twentieth century the introduction by artists of photographic images not intended for the purposes of art (as they co-opted advertisements, press photographs, and other published materials and integrated them into their pieces) was in fact a distant echo of the presence of photography—more prevalent than had hitherto been imagined—in the studios of the preceding century.

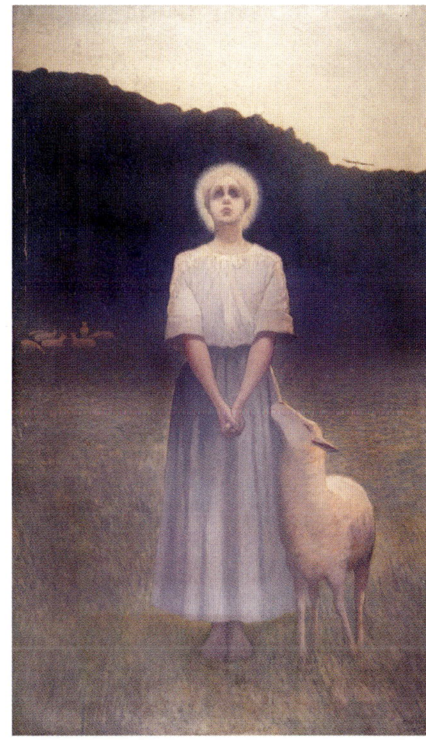

199. Alphonse Osbert, *Vision of Saint Genevieve*, 1892, oil on canvas, Musée d'Orsay, Paris.

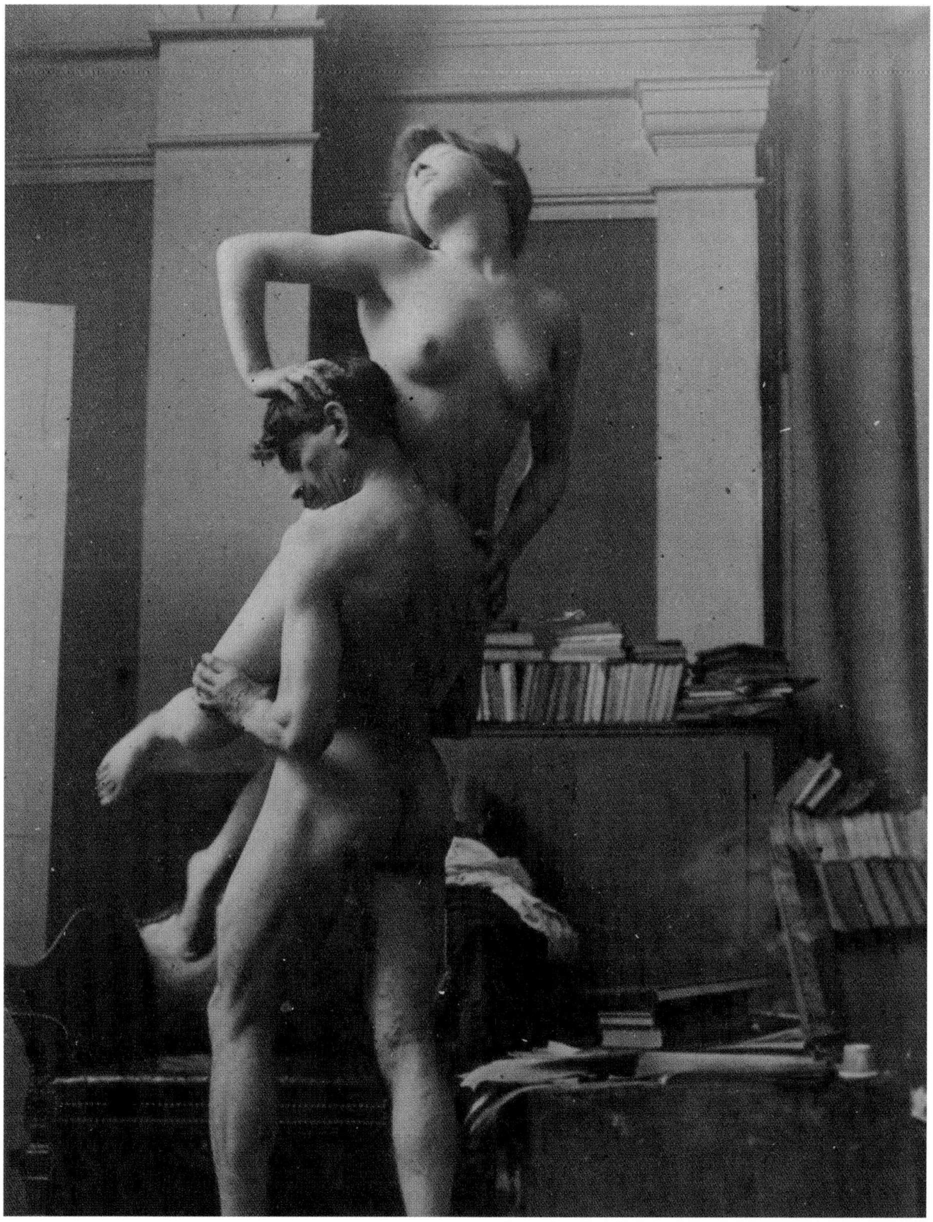

"The artist photographer is someone who, having devoted his life to the study of an art such as painting, architecture, engraving, etc., sees in photography a new instrument for representing his impressions, for imitating nature in all her poetry, richness, and beauty, or for reproducing the masterpieces that human genius has set upon the earth. He is usually a painter: he is always a man of intelligence and talent."[1]

PAINTER PHOTOGRAPHERS

When, in 1853, critic Ernest Lacan sought to characterize the various types of exponents of photography, he divided them into four categories: the photographer proper, the artist photographer, the amateur photographer, and the scientific photographer. His analysis emerged in the context of the invention's recognition (in particular the artistic ambitions of processes on paper), though Lacan was also concerned with setting up an association dedicated to the promotion of photography which would find room for "operators" of every stripe.[2] In Lacan's opinion, the indubitable paragon of artistic photography was Gustave Le Gray. By this time the talented Le Gray—a painter by training and a former pupil of Paul Delaroche—was playing an essential pedagogical role. In his Paris workshops near the barrier of Clichy, and then on Boulevard des Capucines, he received pupils from the best circles and trained some distinguished examples of what Lacan dubbed the "amateur photographer," such as Olympe Aguado: "When you visit such an artist photographer, you find him surrounded by a rather numerous troupe who executes his orders and assists him in his manipulations, all the while emulating his every move and gesture. These are his pupils. They will one day form part of that category we have dubbed 'amateur' photographers... [and] are undergoing training." By underlining the vitality of Le Gray's workshop (it clearly resembled his master's studio, since Delaroche's had been one of the busiest of the July Monarchy), Lacan was pleading for the artistic status of photography, based on the fact that, like painting, it could only be learned at the end of a lengthy period of selfless toil.

"Like a mistress whom one cherishes but hides"

In his sketch of the "artist photographer," Lacan distinguishes two attitudes adopted by the disciples of Niépce and Daguerre. The first seeks to conceal his passion for photography, "like a

200. **Facing page:** José Maria Sert, "Nude Study, Couple," c. 1905–10, silver print, Musée d'Orsay, Paris.

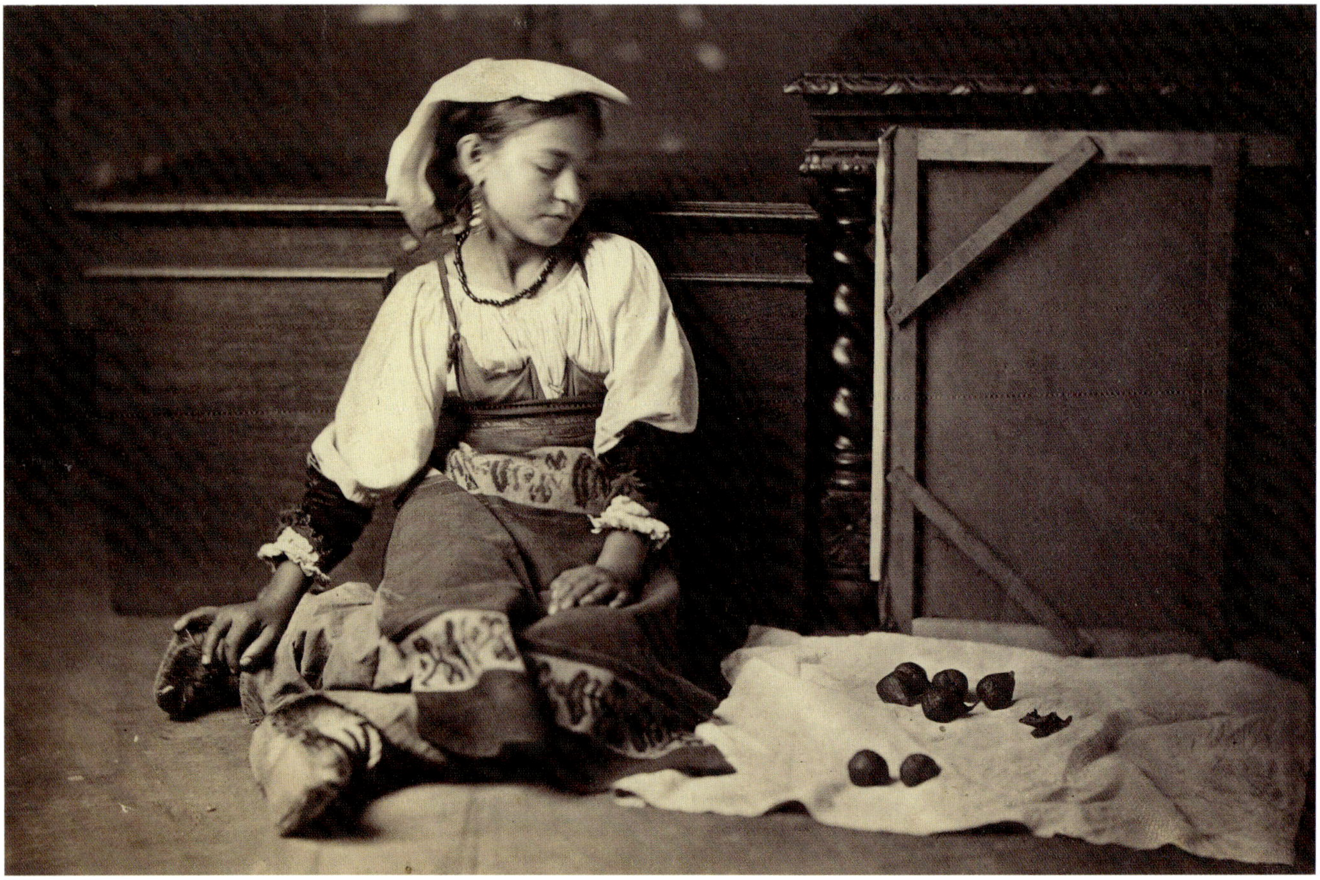

201. Edmond Lebel, "Model for *Young Girl Selling Figs and Nuts*," c. 1863–68, albumen print, Musée d'Orsay, Paris.

mistress whom one cherishes but hides," whereas the second strives to make his photographic work as visible as possible, to the point of abandoning "painting and dedicating himself totally to the charms of photography," as Le Gray did. A certain freedom in tone and attitude was part and parcel of this type of talent, as Lacan noted: "As each individual preserves his independence and yields only to his inspiration, his taste and his imagination; he thus preserves his originality."

Over the course of the decades, photography remained a clandestine but much-cherished second love for several painters. Although interest in the photographic output of painters has accelerated in recent years, the knowledge of their practice remains piecemeal and often depends on the chance discovery of their photographic production. No analysis of the subject can hope to be exhaustive at present; in the wake of future studies, many additions will, we hope, be made to the various examples dealt with here. In general, the painters whose photographic works are referred to here never even mentioned their photographic activity; or at the very least, they did not seek to exhibit it publicly as they did their painting. Their interest in photography, however, went well beyond its sporadic practice, even as enlightened amateurs. The photographs they left are often of first-rate quality, and they exemplify the singularity of their talent and betray the effort they expended in creating them. If there are too few examples to attempt a meaningful typology,[3] it seems reasonable to distinguish first those for whom photography appears as an instrument used to constitute a repertory of models or sketches for their pictorial work: that is, studies after nature employed in turn as material for their paintings. The subordination of photography to pictorial art in this case does not at all mean that these artists were without any particular aptitude for photography. Still, the interest of their output derives not from the fact that they show such-and-such a scene, but that they reveal the strategies underlying the creative process, with photography serving as a window onto their painting. Frozen in the apparatus, these studies become images in their turn, while the poses adopted form scenes, like in a private theater of the creative mind. Photography thus preserves a part of the artistic process that would otherwise remain invisible; their harmony and quality show that the attitudes, the expressions, and often the costumes had been carefully selected: there could have been nothing fortuitous about the scenes composed by Edmond Lebel, Alfons Mucha, and José Maria Sert.

Edmond Lebel's photographs: reproducing and reinventing Italy

Originally from Amiens and a student at the École des Beaux-Arts in Paris, where he attended Léon Cogniet's studio, the painter Edmond Lebel exhibited at the annual Salons on several occasions after 1863. His canvases were often based on recollections of his stay in Rome at the beginning of the 1860s, where he had accompanied a childhood friend and fellow student, Jules Lefebvre, winner of the Prix de Rome in 1861; they were in tune with the taste of the period for the picturesque charms of vernacular Italy. Lebel was protected by Emperor Napoleon III's cousin, Princess Mathilde.

His involvement in photography, however, was unknown until the discovery in 2006 of a collection of more than five hundred photographs, including reproductions of works of art, a group of studies after nature, as well as several dozen photographs taken by Lebel himself.[4] He was most probably introduced to the process by his father, Désiré, an engraver and the founder of an art school in Edmond's birthplace, who entered into an association with Eugène Disdéri in 1857. Edmond, once back from his travels through Italy, settled in Paris, near Batignolles. His studio served as a theater for various "scenes" in which his friends dressed up and acted. Photography also provided him with an opportunity to select poses and attitudes for figures in paintings that often literally replicate the positions his models adopted for the camera. Lifting the veil on how these scenes were staged among studio jumble (books used to support a model's foot, cases of painting materials, etc.), the photographs possess a more relaxed feel than Lebel's finished pictures. They seem to reflect Ernest Lacan's remarks in 1853, when he mentions the charming disorder characteristic of the artistic workplace: "If you enter [the 'artist photographer's'] studio, you will immediately notice an agreeable disorder, the inevitable consequence of the restless spirit of him who occupies it." In one, the painter's young son, Albert, poses, chin in hand, half reclining on a rough wooden sideboard and dutifully absorbed in the attitude requested of him by his father; caught by the camera, the subject then reappears in a canvas of 1875, *The Ponte Rapido in Cassino*. A dusky little girl, whom one can spot in several of Lebel's pictures, was photographed dressed as a young Italian countrywoman in a composition that recurs a few years later as a painting, *Young Girl Selling Figs and Nuts* (ill. 201).

The quest for the right scene

The care taken in setting up the scene and the pretty costumes often look at odds with the frames standing against the wall and general mayhem of the studio visible in the background. Lebel must have used the medium in a search for exactly the right scene—one truthful enough to be worthy of painting. He thus exemplifies how important photography could become to an artist, even one from an academic circle, in his working practice. Back in Italy a few years later, in April 1871, Lebel made several views of the village of San Germano, near Naples. Arranging the compositions with precision, and painstakingly regulating the photographic conditions, he reimagined for the lens some uncompromising and severe-looking market scenes (Musée d'Orsay, Paris).

The photographs of Alfons Mucha: in the service of painting

By a lucky coincidence blending filial fidelity and a happenstance of the history of taste, Alfons Mucha was among the very first artists of the nineteenth century to be recognized for photographic work undertaken in the margins of his pictorial oeuvre. Thanks to the generosity of his son, Jiri, four photographs on paper entered the collections of the Musée d'Orsay a matter of months after the decision to establish the museum had been ratified.[5] Nearly thirty years later, access to the collections of the Mucha Foundation (established by the painter's heirs)—and thus to the hundreds of glass plates preserved there—offers an opportunity to investigate Alfons Mucha's photographic practice further and reconsider the nature of his production. The painter took up photography in the mid-1880s,[6] continuing to take pictures until the beginning of the 1930s.[7] He took hundreds of images, storing the plates in wooden boxes. Some of the prints are squared-up, showing that they were intended as an aid for his painted compositions. Though a skilled photographer, the painter cannot be said to have constituted a photographic oeuvre as such.

Photography is never mentioned in Mucha's theoretical writings which nevertheless contain a detailed—if sometimes rather turgid and narrowly academic—plea for the importance of observation and exactitude in composition. Thus, his photographic activity remained inextricable from his art as a painter, rather than possessing an autonomous existence. Mucha didn't apparently entertain relations with the photographers of his time, be they late nineteenth-century pictorialists or postwar futurists or realists. He never exhibited his photographs, keeping them to himself as he would a study drawing; nor did he, it seems, exchange information on technique or on the results obtained within one of the many photographic clubs and societies which then existed. Likewise, there is nothing to show he might have gathered a collection of photographs, studies after nature realized for the use of artists. His only models seemed to have been those he himself composed and printed.[8]

Mucha's little photographic theater

Neither a body of work, nor an original hobby, and wholly subordinated to his painting, Mucha's photographic activity unfolded on the fringes of the professional circles of the day. It nonetheless remains highly individual—unique, even. First of all in terms of quality, since the painter placed in the service of photography his acute sense of composition and mastery of light; and then by its sheer extent and regularity, since, over nearly forty years, he took several hundred negatives, each the basis of a major work. His steadfast if undemonstrative confidence in the technique of photography bestows on his practice a value equivalent to that of drawing, a practice he advocates in several passages of his writings. His assiduity is remarkable in itself; indeed few artists bound the photographic model so closely to their pictorial art.

Mucha was astonishingly meticulous about setting up his scenes: before embarking on his vast compositions, he would have every detail acted out like a tableau vivant before the lens; as far as one can judge from the photographs, he would have made a first-rate theater director. He implemented this working method in 1899, when painting the interior for the Bosnia-Herzegovina Pavilion for the Paris Exposition Universelle of 1900.[9] His skill as a photographer was put to most effective use in his masterwork, the twenty canvases that made up his patriotic and artistic profession of faith, entitled *The Slav Epic*, begun in 1911. Preoccupying the painter until the end of his life, this cycle became celebrated for its hugely ambitious scope. Mucha wanted this combination of historical and legendary scenes to illustrate the history of a people whom he saw as victims of history, split into several nations, treated as a pawn by the European powers before 1914, and ill-served after World War I by the arbitrary political decisions enshrined in the Treaty of Versailles. The style of these immense pictures can hardly be termed realistic: the power of the compositions, the tangle of figures, their chromatic impact are a far cry from the kind of descriptive history painting based on edifying anecdote that had become the norm in Europe in the second half of the nineteenth century: even when he turned his hand to the grand manner, Mucha remained first and foremost a genius of decoration.

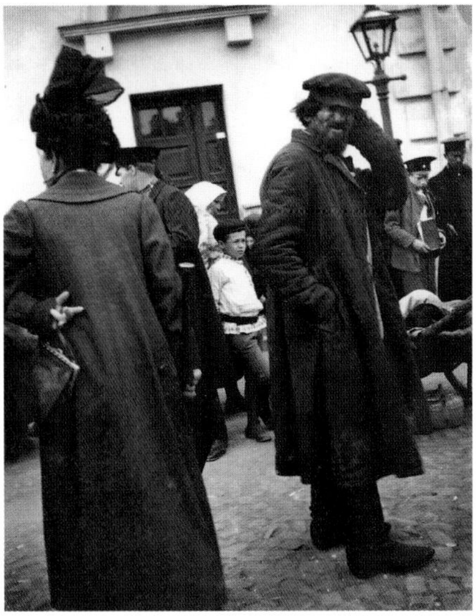

202. Alfons Mucha, "Street and Figures in Moscow," 1913, silver print, Mucha Trust Collection.

The scrupulous observation of reality

The discovery of a substantial number of preparatory photographs for *The Slav Epic* cast fresh light on the development of the oeuvre. The principles underlying it seemed to have been of various orders. Like many others, of course, Mucha used photography to constitute an accurate record of details in costume and decor. A visionary, Mucha was nevertheless committed to the scrupulous observation of reality; but this was a reality that could just as readily be carefully recomposed in the studio as taken from life. On a journey to Moscow in 1913, he took many views of the city's streets and inhabitants (ill. 202). These photographs constitute the bedrock of the preparatory material for paintings—thumbnail sketches taken from life that allowed Mucha to compose and adjust his scenes later, like in a photographic "theater," staging them outside as well in the studio. In fact, the Moscow photos did not directly lead to the realization of a canvas: Mucha did not copy them. In a singularly original manner, the real world the painter observed underpinned a second reality, reinvented by and through photography. The gestures and attitudes recorded were reworked and reenacted in the studio before the lens.

Mucha was extremely fussy about the positions and expressions adopted by his models. Photographing every stage, he noted the variations between the scenes, keeping only the desired attitudes for the finished picture. His theoretical appreciation of art was nourished by the academic tradition of the depiction of the passions. He described in his *Lectures on Art* how joy and sadness had to be conveyed, even at the cost of a measure of exaggeration and in a manner the viewer can readily understand, particularly when the figures form part of a large-scale composition: "If, for example, one wants to show merriment, one has to keep in mind that joy causes all the muscles to relax, the eyes to open wide, the nostrils to dilate, the mouth to gape, the chest to puff out, the arms to be

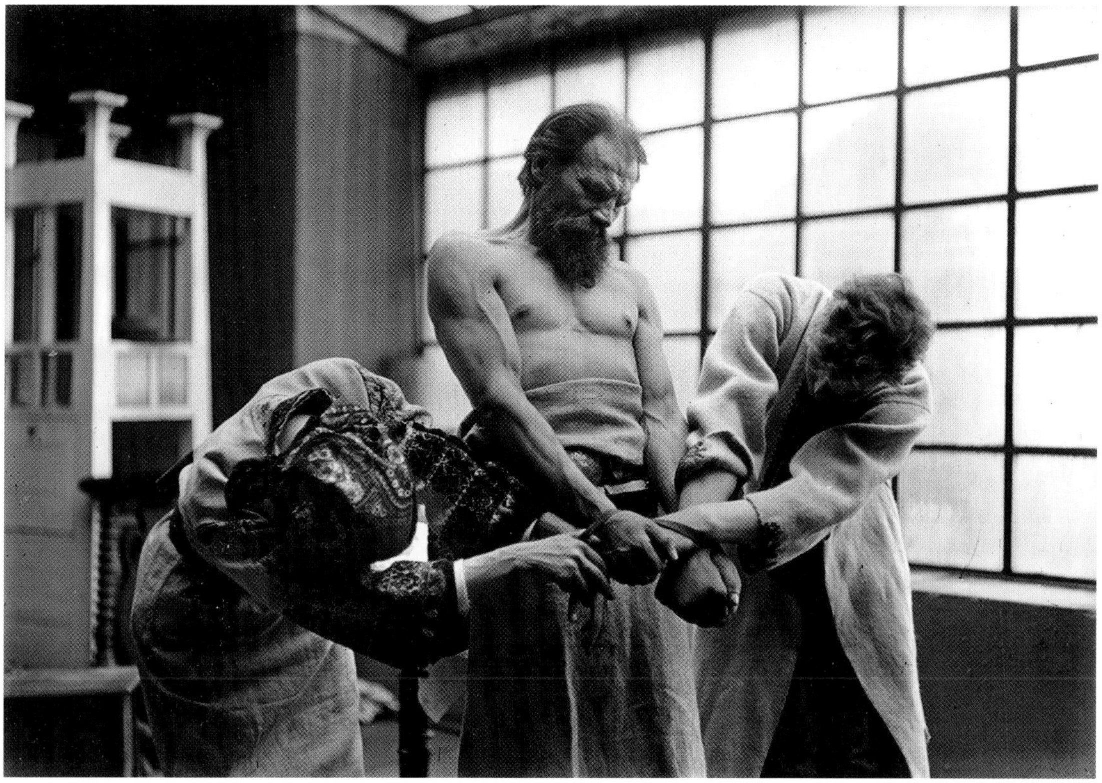

203. Alfons Mucha, "Three Models in Mucha's Studio, including a Man with his Hands Bound," 1911, albumen print, Mucha Trust Collection.

thrown out.... If, on the other hand, one wants to express sadness, one must imagine the person prey to sorrow leaning or seated, because the muscles of his legs, paralyzed, are unable to bear him."[10] The gestures made by the model stand for the emotions he sought in his pictures: for example, for one of the first canvases in the cycle dating to 1912, *Sun Worship in Rugen* (also known as *Svantovit Celebration on the Island of Rugen*), he photographed a male model stripped to the waist with his hands bound. Mucha used the photograph less to reproduce the exact features of his model than to capture the savage determination of men whom no chain can fetter (ill. 203).

The challenges and pitfalls of theatricality

Mucha's painstaking attention to the poses of his models bestows a peculiar character on his photographs that the finished paintings do not possess. Examined for themselves, which was never the case while the painter was alive, these photographs—in spite of their subordination to the painted oeuvre—acquire a new dimension that relates to the painter's desire to compose the most exact scene possible before taking up his brush. If photography betrays the creative methods of the painter, the use to which these pictures were put—plans for future paintings—spawned an independent aesthetics. Models for paintings, the subjects photographed seem to be actors in

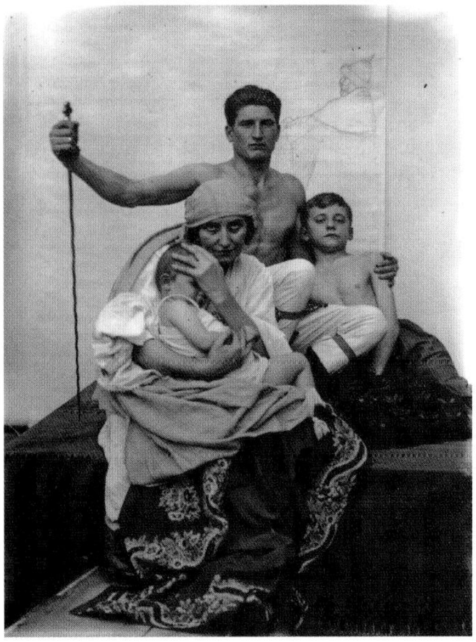

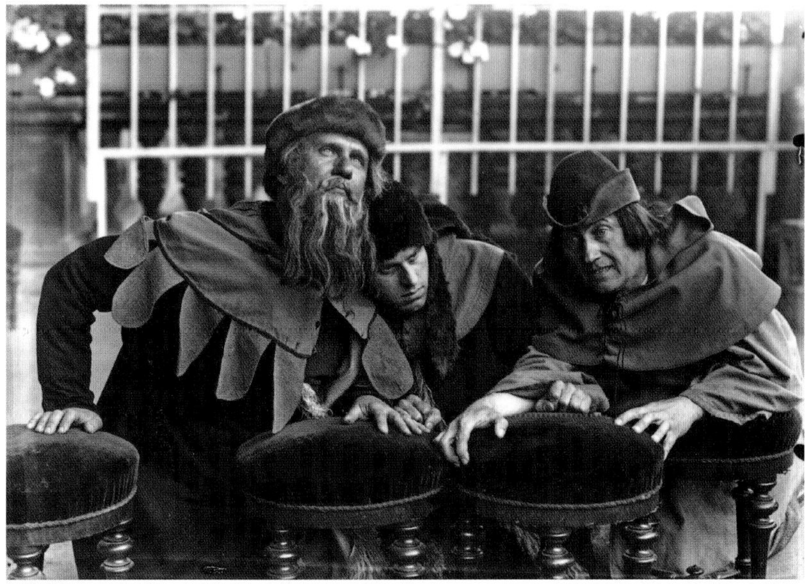

204. **Above, left:** Alfons Mucha, "Family Posing for *The Slav Epic*," c. 1913, modern print from a glass negative, Mucha Trust Collection.

205. **Above, right:** Alfons Mucha, "Three Men in Costumes Leaning on Stools," c. 1915, modern print from a glass negative, Mucha Trust Collection.

a recomposed scene: studied as such, the photographic theater invented by Mucha is thus not free from a degree of dramatization. Sometimes the effect is carried over into the complete piece; as in the photograph of two young male models taken for the canvas dedicated to *Mount Athos*, which preserves the suppleness and distinction of the two young servants in the canvas, thanks to an economy of detail and subtle lighting that emphasizes their smooth torsos and rippling muscles (Alfons Mucha, "Young Men Standing in the Studio," c. 1920, modern print from a glass negative, Mucha Trust Collection). The proud beauty of the young man who on several occasions poses as a knight protecting his loved ones gives the images an appeal that the painter eliminated in the final canvases. Mucha excelled here in capturing the sheer physical presence of his model, his natural assurance in assuming the pose and in varying his attitudes and expressions. Drifting away—unconsciously perhaps—from his initial intention, Mucha here highlights the subject's features and graceful form, his photographer's eye getting the better of his demands as a painter (ill. 204).

Contrariwise, other scenes in the photographs appear rather comic, and thus totally at odds with the artist's primary intention: the effect arises from the way the photographic medium reproduces the individual features of the sitter. It may also derive—in particular in a series of photographs probably connected to *Master Jan Hus Preaching at the Bethlehem Chapel*—from the disconnect between the elaborate costumes inspired by the Middle Ages and the modern articles scattered about the spare workshop. Three acolytes at the ceremony were photographed, duly attired in keeping with their role, outside Mucha's studio in Prague, leaning on wooden stools (ill. 205).

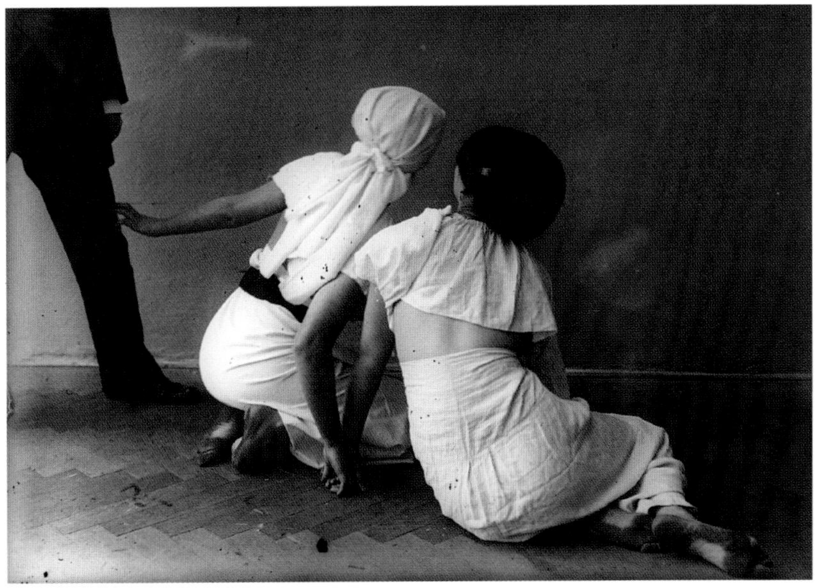

206. Alfons Mucha, "Seated Girls in White from the Back," c. 1911, modern print from glass negatives, Mucha Trust Collection.

The incongruous modern furniture, with its lathed turned feet and velvet-covered seats, reinforced by the flower stand in the background, underscores the chronological hiatus between the scene being reenacted and its photographic reproduction. All illusion is shattered; no longer in character, the grimacing faces of the three models appear contemporary with the painter.

Toward a specifically photographic aesthetic

A substantial proportion of the appeal of Mucha's works derives from their admirable sense of rhythm. The artist often drew comparisons between painting and the musical phrase, often expounding on how it was crucial to envisage the composition as an organic whole: "It is important to grasp that a finished composition, like a sentence or a musical score, must have a beginning and an end—that it must be, in other words, inscribed between two predetermined lines."[11] In photography, rhythm represents a serious challenge: essentially, it freezes, solidifies the world; it is thus that it attains exactitude and precision. It was indeed often for this reason that its users chose it. But on several occasions in his photographic reproductions, Mucha succeeds in capturing the physical and gestural rhythms of his models. In an empty studio bathed in light, he dressed up two girls in white and had them dance for the camera. In order to capture their rhythmical movements for his *Sun Worship at Rugen*, he took many photos, employing several episodes of their graceful pas de deux in paintings that conserve much of their dynamism (ill. 206). In a large unfurnished room, with no decor, furniture, or accessories, and attired in white linen of no recognizable period, the nimble gestures made by the slender girls draw supple forms captured by Mucha's lens. Derived from his use of lighting, Mucha's sense of movement here transcends not only the intrinsic limits of photography, but also the secondary nature of the technique with respect to painting. And so, fostered by his talent as a painter, he proposes—if not perhaps deliberately—the fundamentals for a specifically photographic aesthetics.

The true photographer's vision

In his Bohemian studio in 1926, Mucha photographed a circle of young boys on their kneees, with their arms raised and clasped in a fervent gesture (Alfons Mucha, "Circle of Young Boys Kneeling," modern print from a glass negative, Mucha Trust Collection). This precisely codified scene was intended as a study for the last canvas in *The Slav Epic* and constitutes both the artificial recreation of the event and its original occurrence: before the lens, Mucha does not so much recreate an image for a painting, as invent the moment. Ostensibly the restatement of a preexisting model, the youngsters' ardent adoration appears to be *real*. By focusing solely on the ring of slim but vigorous blond children, sparsely lit in strongly contrasting chiaroscuro, the painter—here turning photographer—manages to conjure up not only the materialized appearance of the scene, but also its abiding spirit. The desire for resemblance, which led Mucha to use photography in elaborating his complex canvases, here becomes a vision in itself, just as in his paintings.

José Maria Sert: behind the scenes

Of Catalan origin, the painter José Maria Sert frequently employed photography as an aid to artistic creation. Although he too remained close-lipped on the practice, he seems to have resorted to it throughout his life. More than six hundred photographs, taken from 1900 to 1945, were rediscovered thanks to the Paris gallery owner Michèle Chomette (the Musée d'Orsay holds around a dozen). Taken in studio, these photographs present poses for monumental frescos—in the cathedral at Vich, for example—or for private house interiors. The vigor of his male models as they contort their bodies, the power of their movements endows these photographic memoranda with a particular force that is exalted by the harsh lighting (ill. 200). Beside professional models, Sert also took pictures of assistants and friends, sometimes combining living bodies with lay figures or even crèche figurines in photographs that go behind the scenes in his painting practice. The prints sometimes bear the traces of their use in the studio: annotations; lines from when they were squared up; drawing-pin holes; outlines run over with pencil; redrawing in colored pastel; highlights in white gouache. They are the fruit of painstaking preplanning, each gesture being accentuated for the benefit of the camera, sometimes rather melodramatically. As Michèle Chomette has commented, "the formal structure of the image proceeds from the beauty of a scaffolding removed at the painting stage, thus becoming the prerogative of photographs that resemble a kind of experiment in art." [12]

Revealing the substructure

Often of modest dimensions (between 3 ½ × 4 ¾ in. and 9 ½ × 11 ¾ in. [9 × 12 cm and 24 × 30 cm]), the size of these photographs is a far cry from the temptation of gigantism that haunted the mural works by Sert that they helped to create. They facilitate the analysis of his often busy paintings by dividing up their complex construction into separate scenes. These photographs—whose singularity and power are reinforced by the use of lighting—thus afford a breakdown of the pictorial act. The subtly handled blacks and grays give the photographs a graphic acuity lacking in paintings where Sert often yields to a penchant for gold and bright colors. The deconstruction provided by his photographs shines a new light on his conception of art, showing it as unexpectedly modern. The "underside" of the picture as revealed in the photographs demonstrates how, for the demands of his painting, Sert—much like a theater designer, or, during this same period, a cinematographer—transformed his studio. The images embrace "an all-round view of the 'set,' complete with fixed props, machinery, pulleys, bars from which mannequins hang, and the struts to which the figurines are fixed." [13] (José Maria Sert, "Study for *On to Victory*, interior of the chapel in the Alcázar, Toledo," 1939, squared-up silver print reworked with black pastel, Galerie Michèle Chomette, Paris). Freezing the scene he wishes to paint, dissecting it, his photographs amount to a series of stills recording its genesis.

Francesco Paolo Michetti's "photographic sketches"

The role of photography in the artistic life of the Italian painter Francesco Paolo Michetti was more discreet, more restrained, less bombastic. Hailing from the Abruzzi, he had been a pupil of Domenico Morelli's in Naples. Marked, like so many European painters of his generation, by the approach of the French impressionists, his handling in landscape painting is brushy and high-keyed. The Alinari Museum in Florence houses several hundred photographs, often stereoscopic, coming from the painter's archives. It seems that Michetti took up photography in the late 1880s, with several pictures of female models posing dressed or in the nude in his studio (ill. 207). Between 1895 and 1910, the majority of the surviving photographs were taken outside. Links between contemporary canvases by the

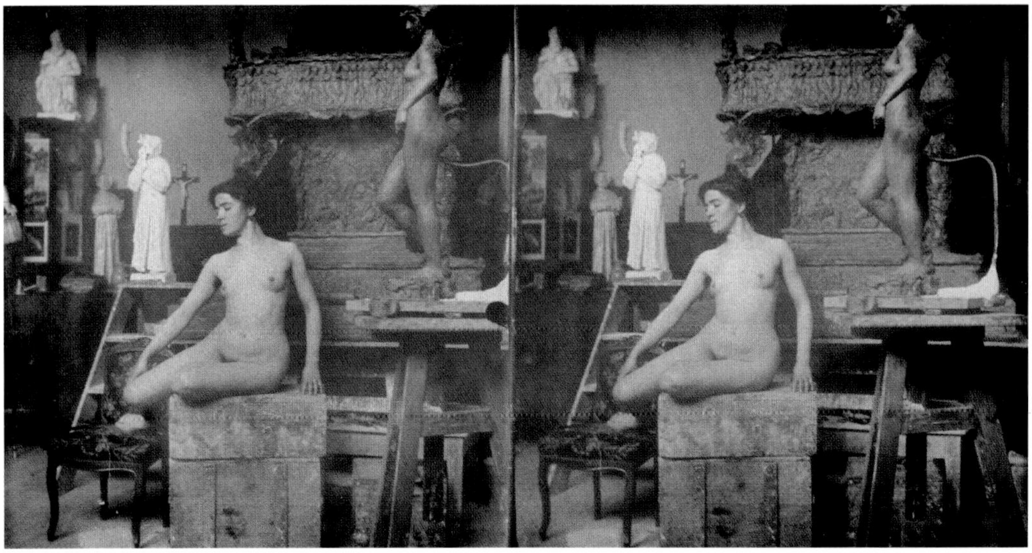

207. Francesco Paolo Michetti, "Model Posing in the Studio," c. 1890, stereoscopic albumen print, Museo Alinari, Florence.

painter, or their sketches, can often be pinpointed; while there is no doubt that Michetti's photographic activity regularly accompanied his work in painting, the lack of precise dates on the photographs means it is not known whether they provided the artist with initial ideas for a piece or material for a project he already had in mind.[14] Some of the pictures clearly resemble notes taken in the midst of nature (rocks, foliage, grass); they are all potential material for a painting, just like a thumbnail sketch penciled into a notebook. Others seem to relate more closely to painted studies; this is the case in particular for a group of photographs showing several young women bathing, alone or in the company of children. The sensuality of these images—in which the girls' freedom of movement and the pleasure they take in abandoning themselves to the water is palpable—is further accentuated by the warm sunlight of the south. Half naked, holding swathes of white cloth to their waists, Michetti's models appear as genuine modern Venuses (ill. 208). The precision intrinsic to the technique of photography, contrasting the dark gleam of the sea with the dazzling whiteness of the sky, simultaneously underlines the presence of the young women, while keeping them in the distance. On the other hand, the painted sketches of similar subjects have the look of fleeting memories of a scene; rapidly laid in with a few brushstrokes, they feel more unreal, but also more fragile, as if they belonged to the artist's private world.

André Derain: imparting new depths

Photography was a constant in the working practices of the painter André Derain. It seems that he first owned a camera in 1910, carrying out many landscapes and views in studio (ill. 209). His niece Geneviève Taillade has it that he sought

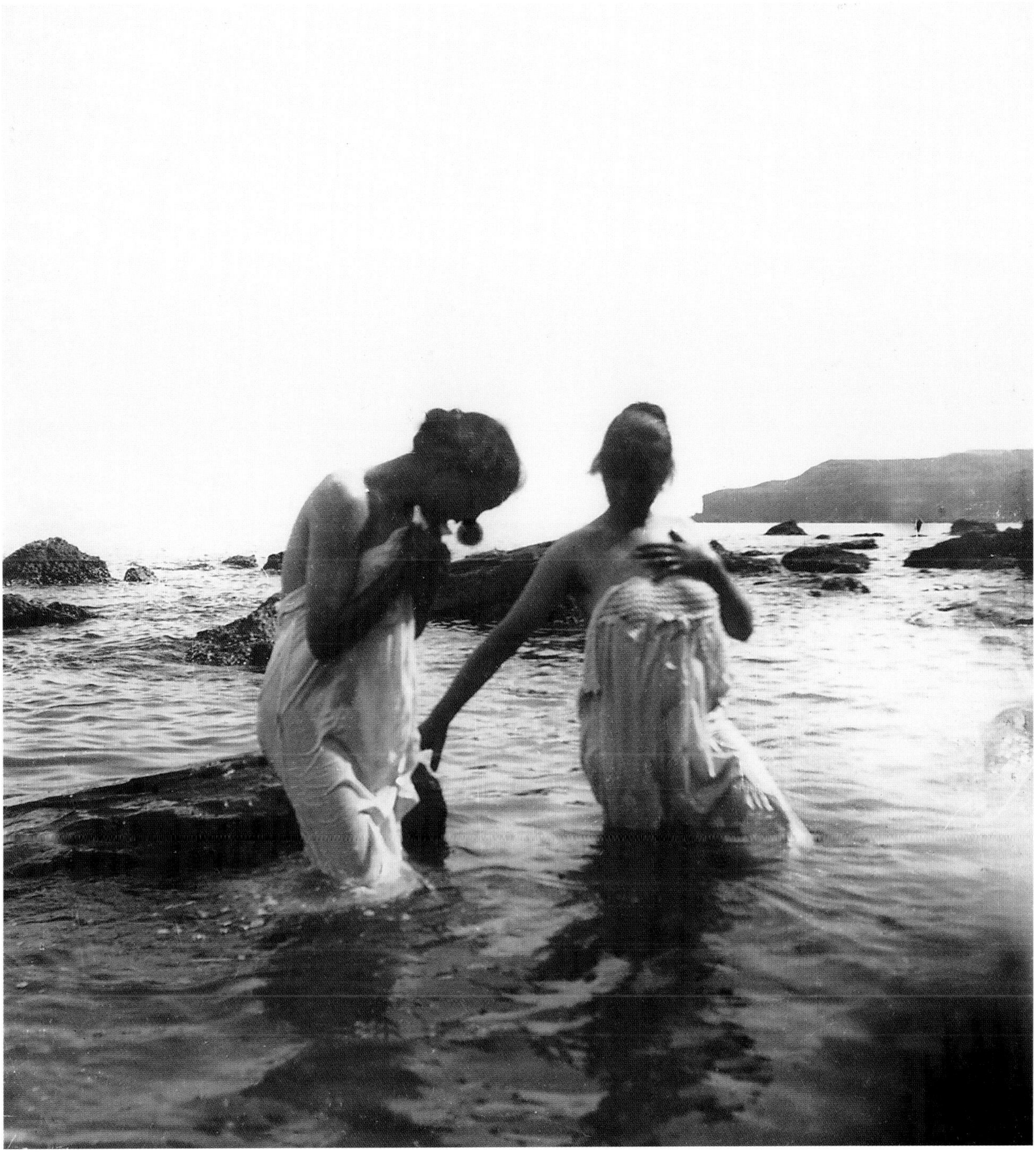

208. Francesco Paolo Michetti, "Bathers Coming Out of the Water" (detail), c. 1895–1900, stereoscopic albumen print, Museo Alinari, Florence.

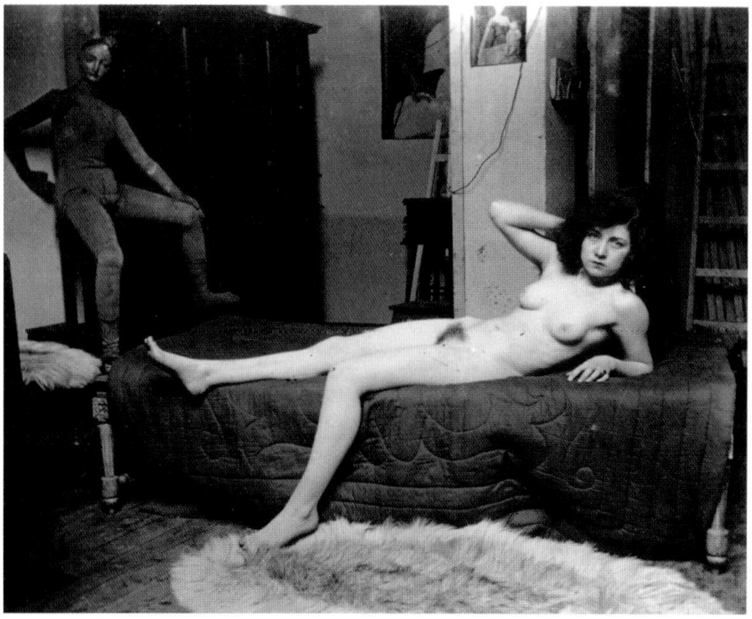

209. André Derain, "Female Nude in the Studio Seated next to a Dummy," c. 1920, silver print, private collection, Paris.

in photography not so much an aide-mémoire as a different way of looking at things. His photographic observations were meant to supply new qualities that might reinvigorate his painting, and indeed, the memory of a photograph was often to impart new depth to his pictorial output (André Derain, "Bridge at Cagnes," 1910, silver print, private collection). "In photographs taken by Derain, it is as if different ways of seeing cohabit rather than succeeding, or transforming one into the other; as if the man was like a pendulum, forever swinging from one way of seeing to the next, without acquiring any certainty [and] hostile ... to all theory."[15] In 1903, one of Derain's first significant canvases in terms of accomplishment and recognition, *The Ball at Suresnes*, had its roots in a photograph, several copies of which were unearthed in the family archives, with one print being squared up. Probably taken by a photographer close to the artist, its theme is echoed in a letter Derain wrote to Maurice de Vlaminck: "I write to you at the back of a little smoke-filled restaurant chock-a-block with soldiers where guys from up north are playing the accordion and dancing. It would interest you and might amuse you too.... You're at the end of your tether? Me too. I can only see needs—not even desires: even in a sound or a color or an idea. I can see nothing any longer except for an inert revolt, with, in some way or another, death at the end."[16] Faithful to the composition of the photographic image, the high-keyed color of the uniforms in the canvas reinforces the feeling of inanity and despair that gripped Derain during his years of military service. Prior to the painting, this scene of grating jollity had been already reduced to two dimensions, to the flatness of an image, by photography (ills. 210–12). In the pictorial work of artists

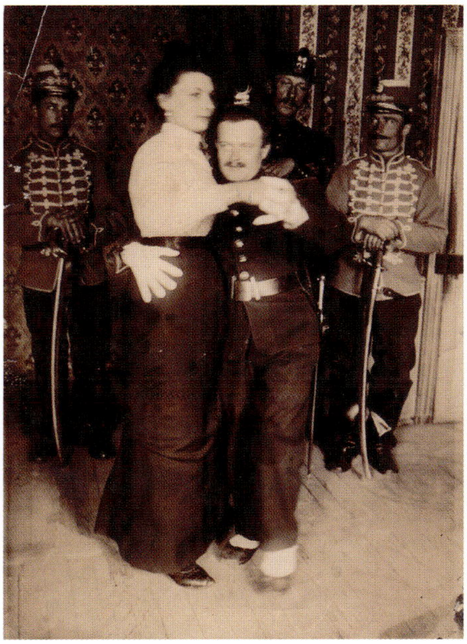

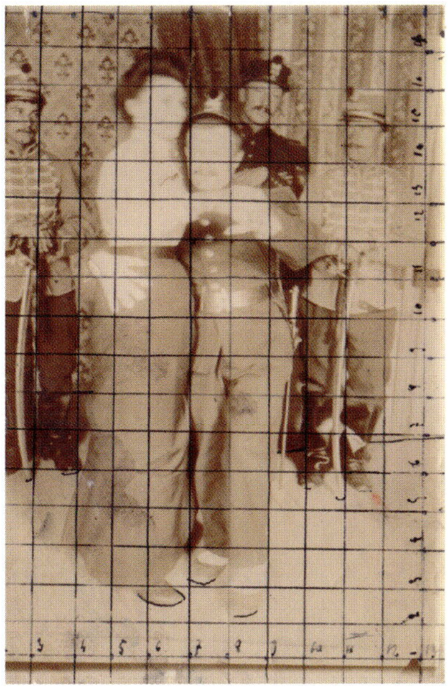

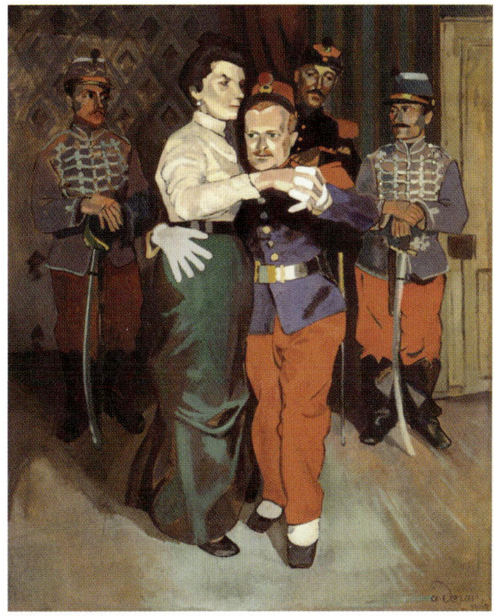

such as these, photography resonated profoundly; although its practice remained bound up with their painting, they regarded the process as a means of conceiving and developing a new perspective on the world and its representation. If photography did not always burgeon into new creations, it provided a means for enriching the process of artistic invention. The ongoing examination and study of their photographs confirms that they tended to distinguish the use of photography as a device and as an image, placing one or other of these aspects in the service of their painted oeuvre. Their practice of photography was not limited to the reproduction of reality; instead, the process afforded a temporal or spatial dimension that provided the conditions for its realization. Beyond the immediacy of copying, it was photography's "depth of field" that many painters-cum-photographers preserved in their work.

210. **Above, left:** André Derain, "Study for *The Ball at Suresnes*," 1903, silver print, private collection, Paris.

211. **Above, center:** André Derain, "Study for *The Ball at Suresnes*," 1903, silver print squared-up, private collection, Paris.

212. **Above, right:** André Derain, *The Ball at Suresnes*, 1903, oil on canvas, Saint Louis Art Museum, Saint Louis, MO.

Edgar Degas' photographic oeuvre

Although his photographic practice was extremely limited in time (apparently to around the years 1895 and 1896, by which time the artist was more than sixty and with a firmly established reputation), Edgar Degas left to posterity a large number of photographs which have gradually come to light. Though further surprises undoubtedly await us, they already form an original group with interesting links to his conception of art. The painter appears to have begun taking photographs in the summer of 1895, while staying at Mont-Dore.[17] Like the majority of contemporary artists he was well acquainted with the photographic process. In the 1860s he had posed for a *carte de visite* portrait and, a few years later, used a photograph of

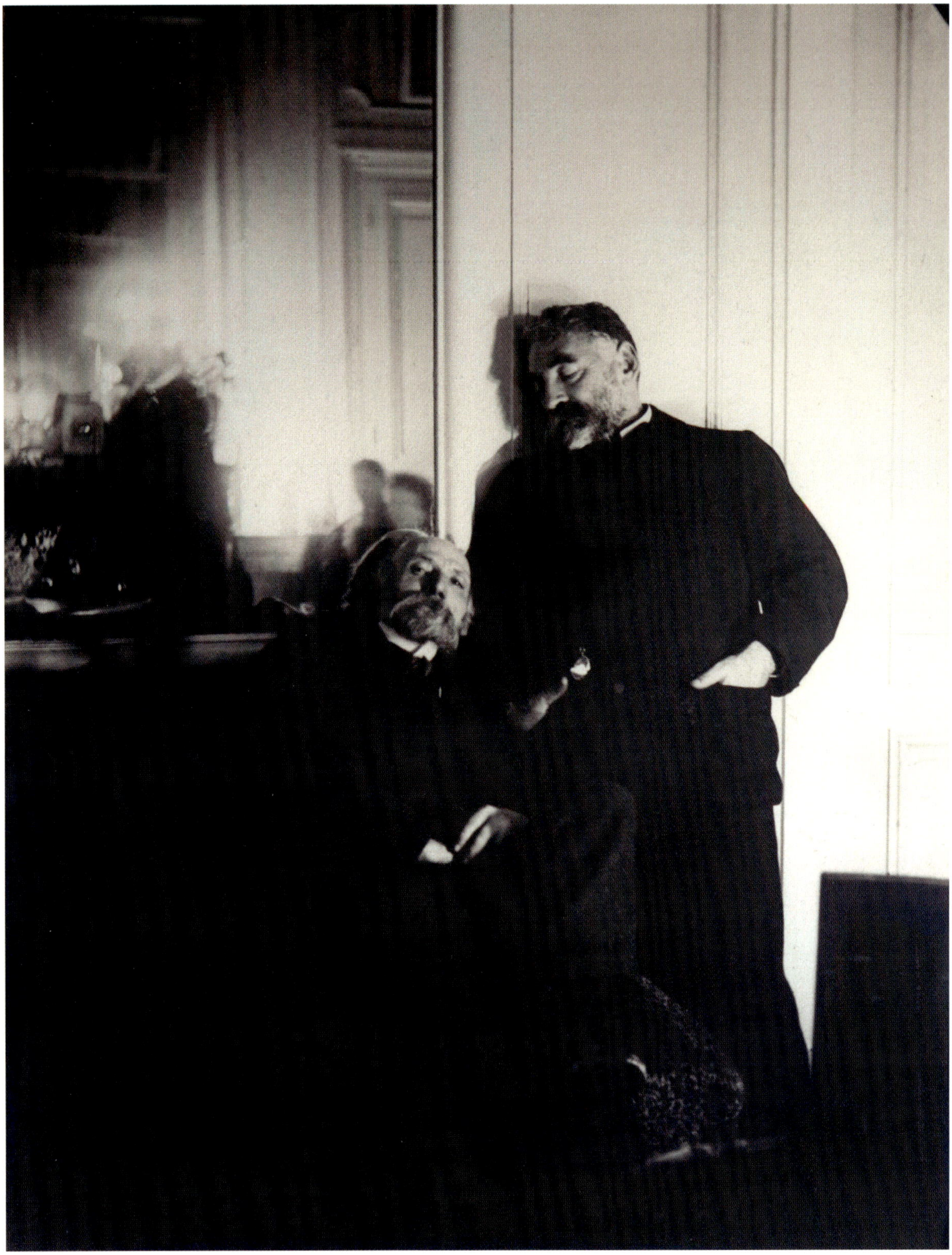

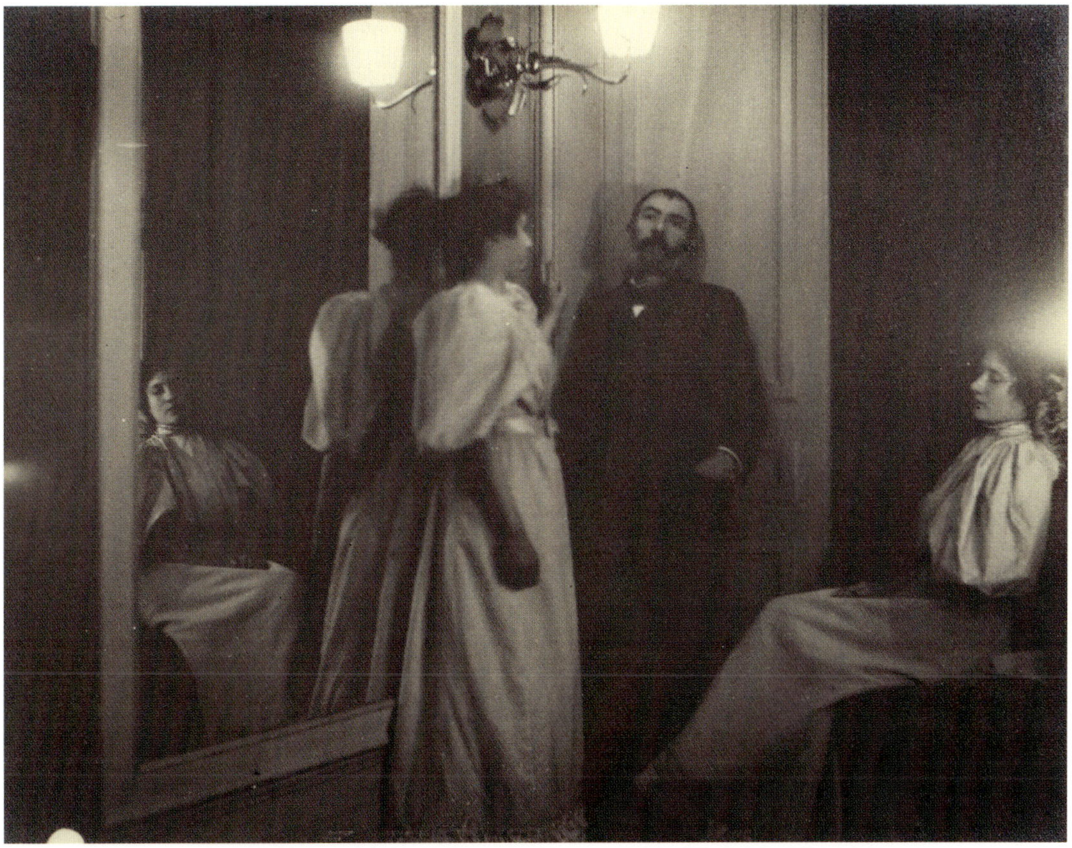

Princess von Metternich for a painting. In 1885, together with Élie and Daniel Halévy, he composed, with the Lemoinne girls, a tableau vivant aping Ingres' *Apotheosis of Homer*, and employed the services of a local photographer, Walter Barnes, to capture it. The reasons why the artist purchased a camera and practiced photography so intensively for a few months (Daniel Halévy reports in his *Journal* for November 1895 that Degas spent most evenings with them taking pictures) are not precisely known. Was it, as Malcolm Daniel suggests, to keep up contacts with his close relations and to be able—as he did at the Mont-Dore when he created a portrait of one of the tutors of his cousins, the Fèvres—to send portraits of his kith and kin to absent friends? It seems likely. Over the years, Degas became more and more attached to those he had known for a long time—to his family, but also to friends such as the Halévys (he had met Ludovic Halévy while they were at school together at the Lycée Louis-le-Grand), as well as to his allies and companions in the painting world, Julie Manet and her cousins, the Gobillards (the daughter and nieces of Berthe Morisot), the poet Stéphane Mallarmé, Auguste Renoir, the painter Henri Lerolle and his family. Was it, as has also been advanced, to try to compensate for eye trouble, of which he despaired and which unfortunately was only worsening? He

213. **Facing page:** Edgar Degas, "Auguste Renoir and Stéphane Mallarmé," 1895, silver print, Institut National d'Histoire de l'Art, Paris.

214. **Above:** Edgar Degas, "Portrait in a Mirror of the Painter Henry Lerolle and His Two Daughters, Yvonne and Christine," 1895, silver print, Musée d'Orsay, Paris.

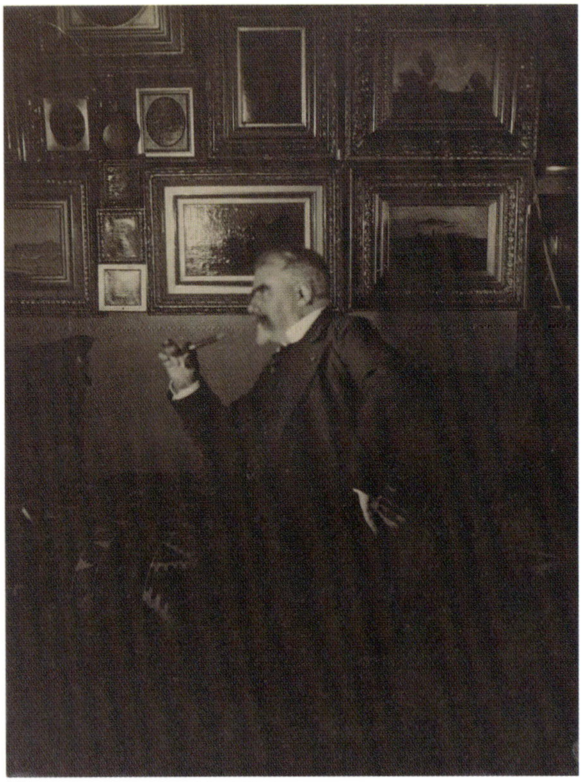

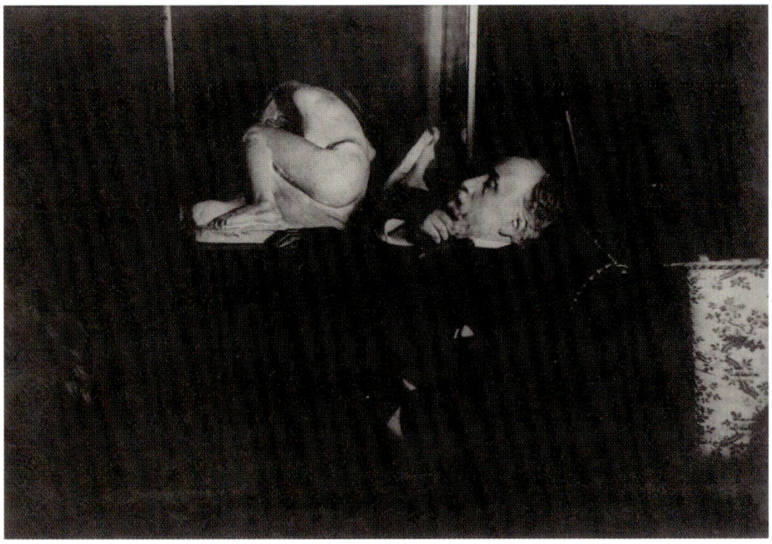

215. **Above, left:** Edgar Degas, "Henri Rouart in Front of His Pictures," 1895, silver print, Musée d'Orsay, Paris.

216. **Above, right:** Edgar Degas, "Self-Portrait with a Statue by Bartholomé," 1895, silver print, Musée d'Orsay, Paris.

may have been reassured, however briefly, to think of photography as a kind of ersatz eye, a crutch to his failing sight. It might also have seemed to him to be a diverting occupation for autumn and winter evenings, when fading light prevented him from painting and drawing.

Degas' lengthy sittings

Various witnesses—Daniel Halévy, in particular—and the photographs themselves, show the immense care Degas lavished on their planning, sittings, and realization.[18] He handed the task of printing and enlargement over to Guillaume Tasset and his daughter Delphine, who had run an art supplies shop on rue Fontaine, in Paris, since 1885. Degas' decision to keep and to show only such large, dense, and rich printings (measuring up to 11 ¾ × 15 ¾ in. [30 × 40 cm]) demonstrates the store he placed in photographs too large to be locked away in any "family album." [19] Their models were struck by the length of the sittings. They would wait interminably while the painter arranged their pose and attitude, and regulated the lighting. After some early fiascos, Degas had learned that—unlike with painting, where mistakes can be erased or retouched—a photograph had to work first off, and therefore it called for meticulous preparation. His very fine photograph taken on December 16, 1895, of Mallarmé standing beside Renoir, seated in Julie Manet's drawing room, shows the attention the painter-photographer lavished on lighting the shot. As Paul Valéry wrote eloquently on the back of a print in his possession, the models had to be patient: "This photograph was given to me by Degas, whose camera and specter can be glimpsed in the mirror. Mallarmé stands next to Renoir seated on the divan. Degas inflicted on them a pose of some fifteen minutes beneath the glare of nine oil lamps" (ill. 213). Degas was also greatly drawn to the reflections made possible by photography, on several occasions placing a mirror behind or in front of his models to reflect the light; the resulting halo effect blurs the features, creating the ghostly atmosphere that Valéry noted; as if, to pass the time, his subjects were engaged in some kind of spiritualist séance, a leisure pursuit that was much in vogue among the artist's contemporaries. The mirror duplicates the specular processes of photography, forcing viewers to examine the image and explore its problematic (ill. 214).

A theatrical aesthetic

Degas' portrait photographs did not serve as matrices for later paintings or pastels. They evinced—among other things in respect of their treatment of light—a singular aesthetic quite distinct from that of his paintings. His practice of photography, however, did accompany his pictorial creation, and on occasion underpins it.

Just as Degas had been attracted to the study of motion by sculpture, so an interest in the theater may have drawn him to photography.[20] The meticulous preparations necessitated by portraiture led him to compose scenes in which the expressions and attitudes of his subjects look as if frozen (ill. 215). His photographs certainly served as a way of isolating fragments of the world surrounding him, as if cut out from some larger episode that he observed from a distance, examining those close to him just as he had scrutinized dancers or musicians in the theater. His photographs are often framed in a manner reminiscent of his paintings, cutting a picture in the background into two, off-centering the image to the left or right, leaving visible a rug or the floor to act as a kind of proscenium. Degas the photographer preserves all the perspicacity of Degas the painter; his portraits never flatter his models, instead collecting, rather than "catching" (if one thinks of the prolonged sittings demanded by an artist who scorned the snapshot), their subject's true character. Neither did Degas go easy on himself; his self-portrait with a sculpture by Bartholomé, *The Weeping Girl*, a plaster for a monument at the Père-Lachaise cemetery, shows him half reclining, pondering, his features haggard and aged. The light landing on the piece by his sculptor friend alludes to the key role played by sculpture as an artistic practice in Degas' ideas. The whiteness of the plaster accentuates

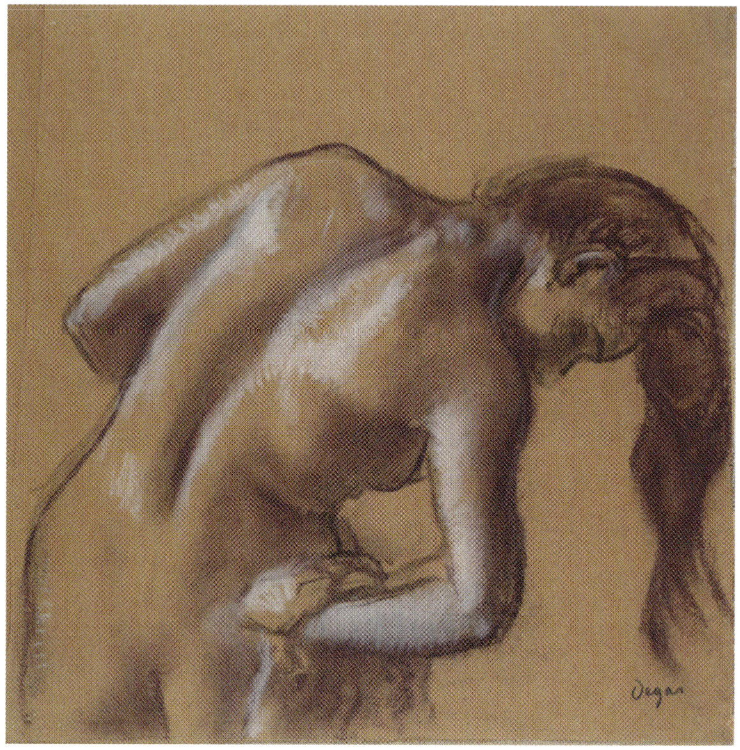

217. Edgar Degas, *Woman Drying Herself*, c. 1892, charcoal and pastel with white highlights, The Metropolitan Museum of Art, New York.

218. **Facing page:** Edgar Degas, "After the Bath, Woman Drying Her Back," 1895, silver print, The J. Paul Getty Museum, Los Angeles.

Degas' pallid face; a large mass standing before the artist's broad forehead, the statue appears, thanks to the photograph, like the excrescence of some melancholy thought (ill. 216).[21]

Apart from large-size portraits, it seems that Degas also took several photographs of nudes, more directly related to his painting. One beautiful photograph, preserved at the J. Paul Getty Museum, may be compared to several pastels of similar subjects (ills. 217–18). The young woman's pose is quite different from those adopted in photographs of academic nudes designed for painting studies. The twisted bust, the bent knees, and straining muscles underline Degas' interest in the transformations undergone by the human body during motion, changes that modify its form and perception. There also exists a photograph of a truncated woman. Only the torso is visible; plunged into shadow, the head is missing. The acephalous model is thus reduced to a motif for painting.

Fernand Khnopff's guilty secret

Throughout his life, Fernand Khnopff did all he could to hush up his practice of photography; in 1916 he even gave a lecture at the Academy of Fine Arts in Brussels in which he denounced the claims of the invention to artistic status.[22] Linked to the symbolist movement, concerned with the representation of ideas and symbols, and desirous of elevating his art above mere naturalistic reproduction, *officially* Khnopff considered

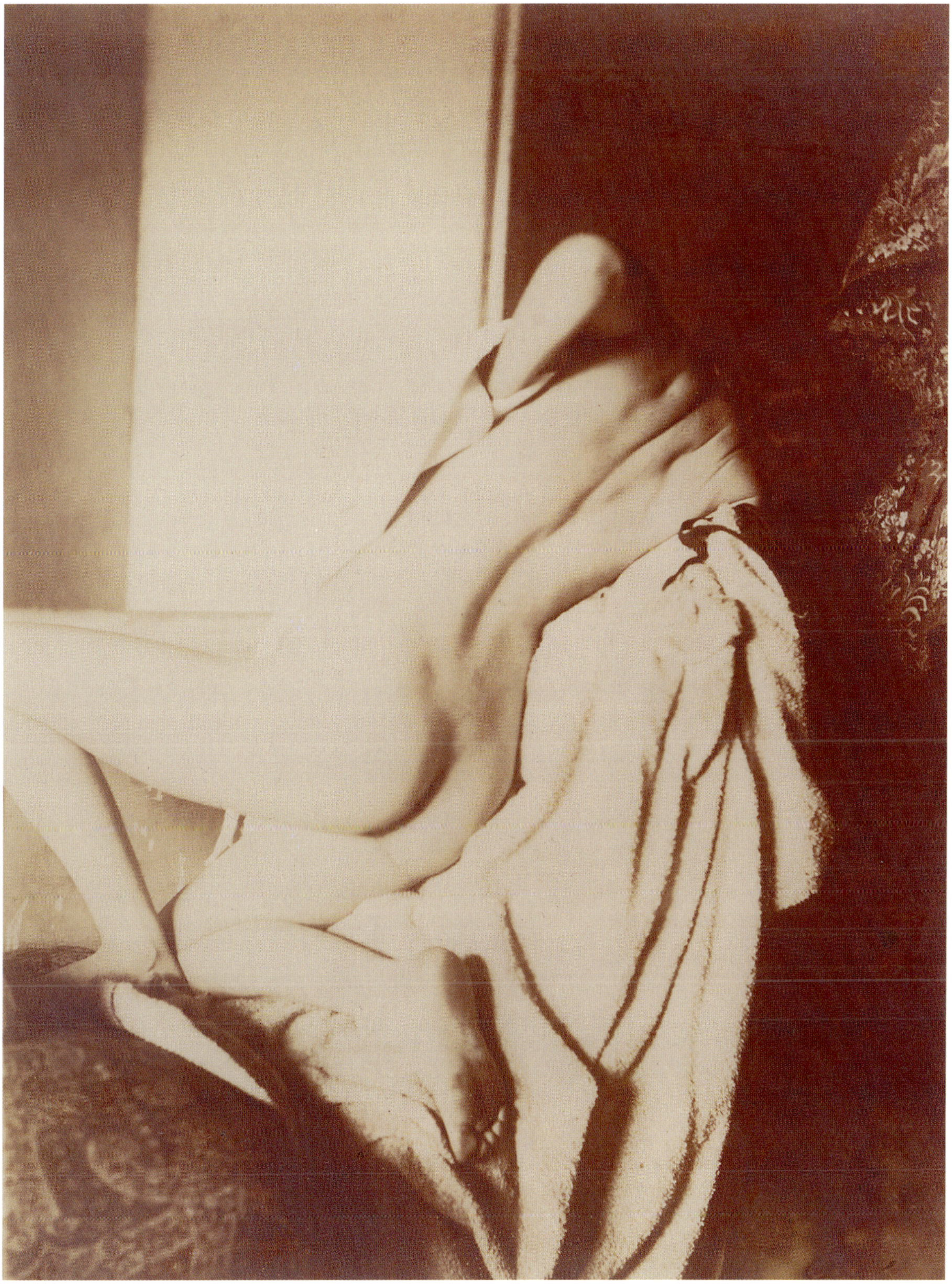

photography as a medium slavishly rooted in the commonplace, all imitation of which would be disastrous. On his death, however, a group of more than forty photographs of his sister Marguerite, of whom he was more than especially fond, were discovered in his studio; beside pictures he had himself taken, many photographic reproductions of his paintings were also found. The clandestine practice of an activity that the artist rejected so violently is intriguing, and his photography would deserve more extensive analysis. As studies for paintings, Khnopff's photographs are characterized by their theatrical quality; some are clearly photographed performances in which the brother "directed" the sister (ill. 219). Their sense of mystery—reinforced by the opposition of swathes of light and shadow, and by their deployment of complex imagery in which everyday reality plays no part—are reminiscent of the tableaux vivants devised by Juliet Margaret Cameron and Lewis Carroll during the 1860s and 1870s. If Khnopff saw these photographs simply as models for pastels and paintings that combine their compositions and gestures, they also preserve the memory of the little plays the artist dreamed up and in which the young woman acted (ills. 220–21). Artfully staged, in Khnopff's eyes these images must have acquired a dual value: quite apart from their role in his artistic work, they also conserved the memory of joyous times spent with a sister who remained so dear to him that, in spite of his own marriage, he never truly recovered from the shock he felt when she departed the family home. However much he affected to loathe photography, the painter sensed the complex relations his art maintained with reminiscence and buried memories. He produced a frontispiece for an edition of *Bruges-la-Morte* by his friend Georges Rodenbach, who had chosen to illustrate his novel—in which a widower pines for his late wife in the city of canals which gradually merges with the image of the dead woman—with photographs by the Neurdein brothers.[23] Khnopff's large painting, *Memories* (1889, oil on canvas, Musées Royaux des Beaux-Arts, Brussels), in which Marguerite is represented in various poses and costumes, and for which Khnopff took several photographs that he kept by his side, undoubtedly exploits the twofold ambiguity of images that are at once studies for paintings and family keepsakes; by occulting the photographs, Khnopff concealed both the secret of his pictorial method and his troubling affection for his sister.

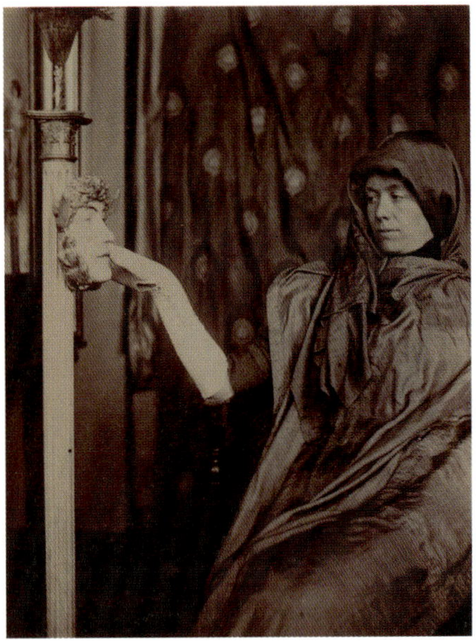

219. Fernand Khnopff, "Marguerite Posing for *The Secret*," before 1902, aristotype, Musée d'Orsay, Paris.

New uses for photography

In 1888, the Kodak 1, a user-friendly camera containing a one-hundred-frame film roll, was developed and marketed by George Eastman. His firm, founded in Rochester, undertook development and printing; the Kodak 1 totally transformed the practice of photography, making it at once more available

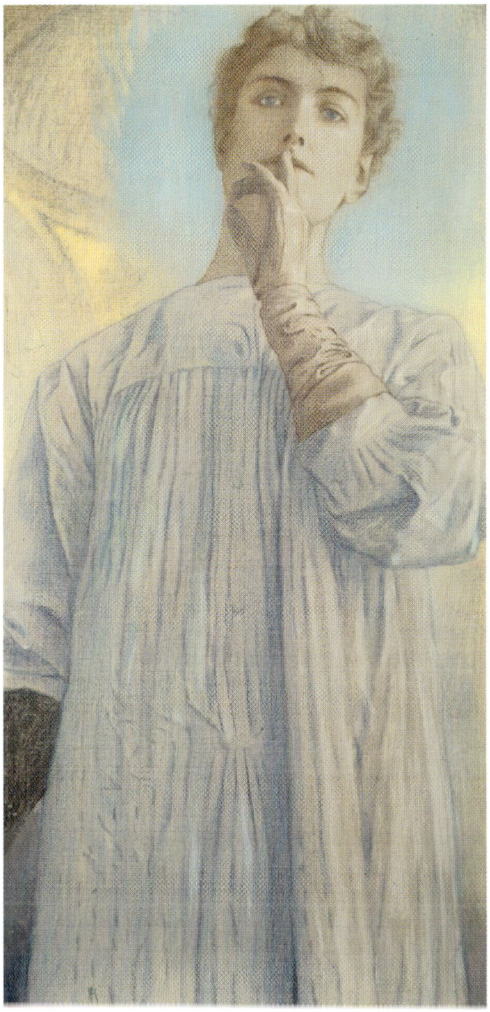

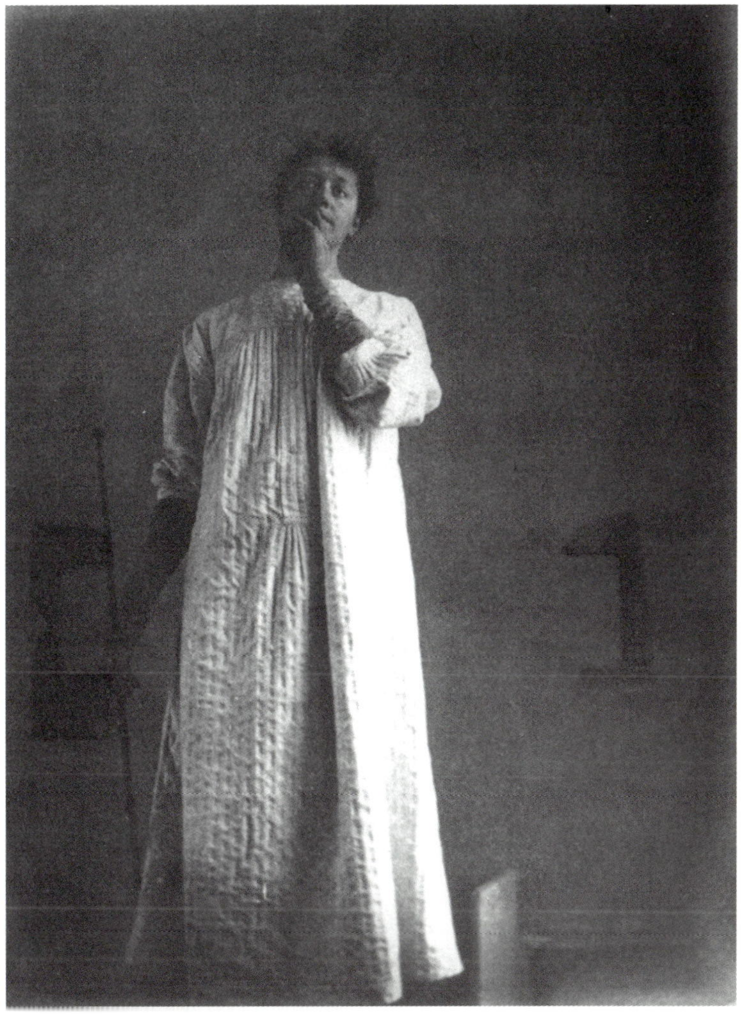

220. **Above, left:** Fernand Khnopff, *Silence*, 1890, oil on canvas, Musées Royaux des Beaux-Arts, Brussels.

221. **Above, right:** Fernand Khnopff, "Marguerite posing for *Silence*," 1890, aristotype, Musées Royaux des Beaux-Arts, Brussels.

and less complicated. The hobby of photography spread like wildfire through the United States and Europe, promoted by sales campaigns that trumpeted the simplicity of Kodak's apparatus. Thanks to the rapid uptake of this invention, photography—hitherto a leisure pursuit for well-heeled and skilled people—became accessible to millions of enthusiasts from middle-income Western families. Thanks to its short exposure times, the gelatin-bromide process could record rapid events (running races, cycling, and jumping, as well as disorder of all kinds), freezing and solidifying even the most fleeting moments. Now, as well as photographs taken by professionals, people could look at photos by family members, introducing a note of intimacy into the notion of the photographic image. The snapshot was taken up by many painters, whose work in photography is now being rediscovered and investigated. Naturally, the place of photography within a given artist's activity varies widely; if its use for creating models persisted, sporadically at least, the frequent, perhaps daily use of the camera gave the practice a wholly new dimension. The fact that the medium now became a family pursuit proved particularly interesting for artists who liked to draw inspiration from everyday life. A wholly distinct conception of photography by painters thus appeared: if sometimes lacking pre-established artistic intention, the enduring transformation of an instant into an image, thanks to its capture by the photographic apparatus, presented painters with a novel repertory.[24]

Édouard Vuillard, "an explorer of the everyday"

This was markedly the case for Édouard Vuillard, who once called himself "an explorer of the everyday." The painter began taking photographs in the mid 1890s, continuing until late in life, in the 1930s. The Vuillard family archives contain hundreds of imperfectly classified prints that the artist had conserved.[25] It is not known how the artist first came to photography; perhaps, like many of his contemporaries, it was simply to preserve souvenirs of happy events among his tight-knit family. The birth of his niece Annette Roussel, daughter of his sister Marie and brother-in-law the painter Ker-Xavier Roussel, may well have encouraged him; indeed, few photographs survive from before the little girl's arrival on November 30, 1898. For decades, Vuillard photographed family get-togethers, meals with friends, and holidays by the seaside, often in the company of his friends the Hessels, Lucie and Jos. Although he mentions his photographs rarely in his *Journal*,[26] the few occurrences show that he thought them important enough to want to do the developing and printing himself. It also seems that he would often take them out subsequently, in particular in moments of distress. The sorrow he felt at the death of his mother in 1930 was not alleviated by looking at the dozens of photos he had taken of her over the years.

In the eyes of his entourage, his camera seems to have been the inoffensive tool of a retiring, warm-hearted uncle, a faithful and quiet friend. A gentle sort, the "doux Vuillard" thus felt protected, the apparatus serving as both a rampart against and a window onto the world in which he lived. His photographic production was, however, far from anodyne, and not without artistic significance. In 1963, Annette Vaillant wrote how photographs by Vuillard were instantly distinguishable from those taken by any other member of his family or his circle of friends: "M. Vuillard and my father each had the same Kodak. A camera in pitted black leather, the corners rounded smooth, whose garnet-colored interior spouted out like an accordion.... Though of the same format, it is impossible to mix up prints by our two photographers. For some inexplicable reason, some resemble Vuillard so much that they could only be by him and by nobody else."[27] And it is true; such photographs do resemble him: not only in their subjects

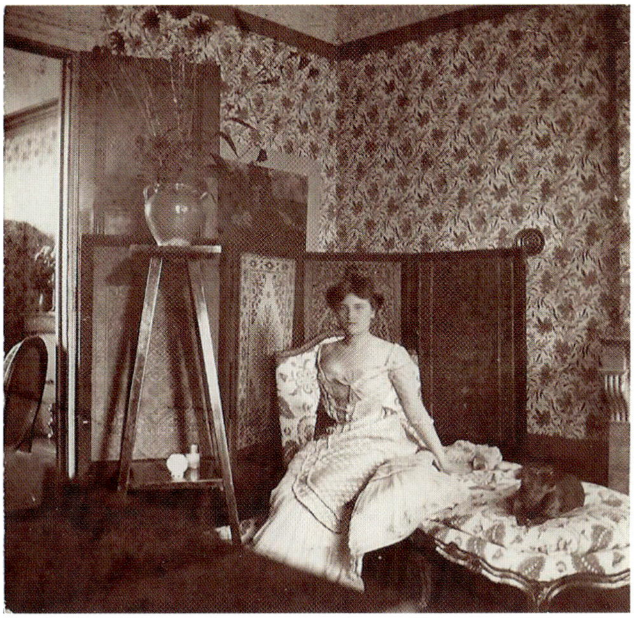

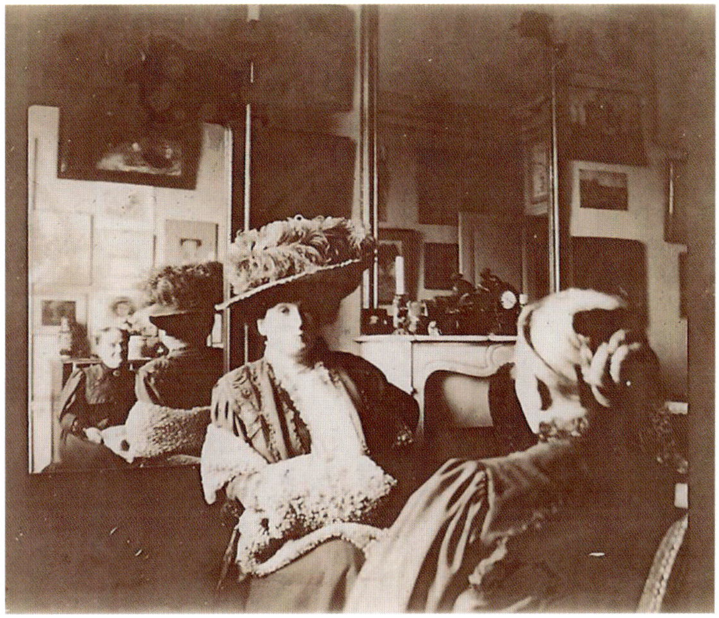

222. **Above, left:** Édouard Vuillard, "Misia Natanson Seated on a Duchesse Divan, in Rue Saint-Florentin," 1899, silver print, private collection.

223. **Above, right:** Édouard Vuillard, "Lucy Hessel visiting Madame Vuillard, Rue de La Tour," c. 1904–8, silver print, private collection.

(drawn from daily life), and by the recurrence of female models (his adored mother, the piquant Misia Natanson, his dear niece, Annette, or Lucie Hessel), but also by their perspicacity (ill. 222). Carefully staged and painstakingly arranged (in spite of the fast film, there is nothing fortuitous about Vuillard's images, the sense being that he must have waited patiently for just the right moment to open the shutter), the photographs prolong the detached and somewhat ironical tone of the Nabis period (ill. 223). Their theatrical effects, like the delicate reflection of the (all too) elegant hat of Madame Hessel in the mirror on the wardrobe in Madame Vuillard's modest interior, are rather reminiscent of the stage sets and decors Vuillard worked on with Aurélien Lugné-Poe in the 1890s.[28]

An impressionist of memories

For Vuillard, his photographs were at once a way of revealing and of preserving the routine of daily life, the everyday events that fertilized his imagination.

As he wrote in August 1893 in his *Journal*, he found more charm in his immediate environment than in any newly discovered place: "Why do the mind and the emotions find what is genuinely new in the most familiar places?" (ills. 224–25).[29] Vuillard's photographs thus form a substrate of the work of memory and reminiscence that underlies his creative practice. André Chastel rightly describes the painter as "an impressionist of memories, his pictures already bear the imperceptible impression of remembrance."[30] And, as Guy Cogeval has proposed, Vuillard, like Marcel Proust, was also engaged in the task of exhuming the past; his painting, like Proust's language,

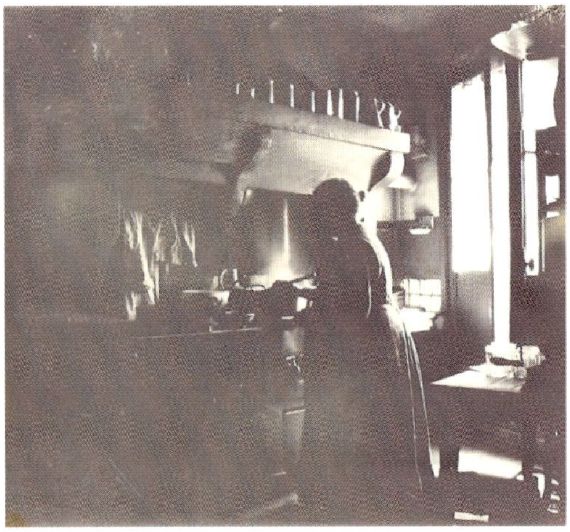

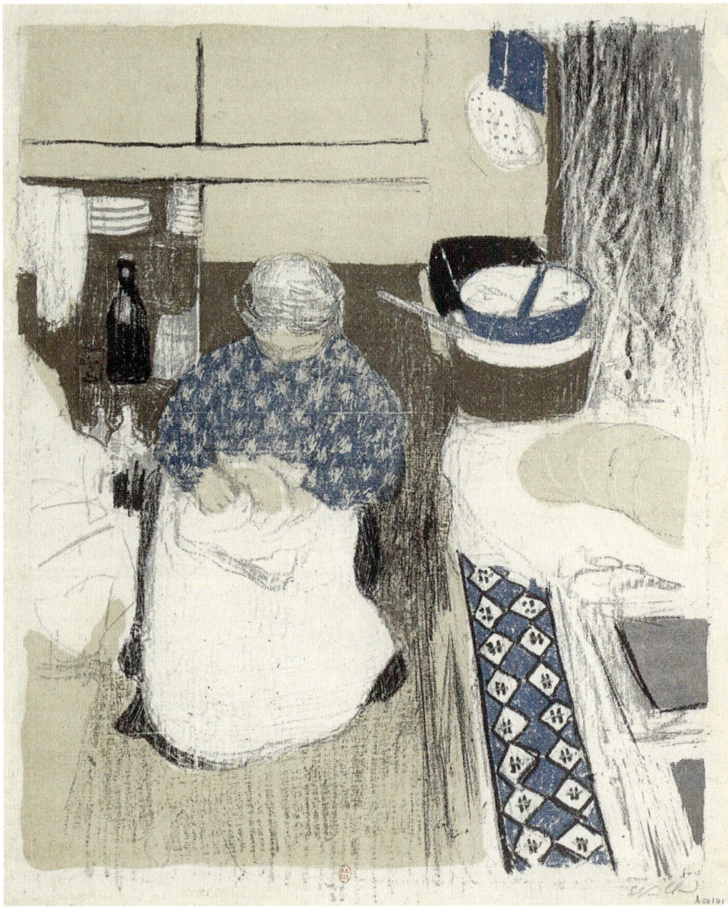

224. **Above, left:** Édouard Vuillard, "Madame Vuillard Cooking, Rue des Batignolles," 1897, silver print, Archives Vuillard, Paris.

225. **Above, right:** Édouard Vuillard, "The Cook," 1896, color lithograph, Bibliothèque Nationale de France, Paris.

forms a mnemonic rhapsody in which traces of different past events become entangled. "Real life, life at last laid bare and illuminated ... is literature, and life thus defined is in a sense all the time immanent in ordinary men no less than in the artist. But most men do not see it because they do not seek to shed light upon it. And therefore their past is like a photographic darkroom encumbered with innumerable negatives which remain useless because the intellect has not developed them. But our life, if it means awareness of our own life, also means awareness of the lives of other people—[since] style for the writer, no less than color for the painter, is a question not of technique, but of vision."[31] These reflections of the narrator in *À la recherche du temps perdu* (Remembrance of Things Past) seem to echo a note Vuillard made in his *Journal* for September 24, 1922, after spending some time looking at his photographs: "It is those indefinable circumstances, those arcane encounters, those facts visible to oneself alone [and] others that are so familiar or so evident that one is unaware of them, which constitute the essence of the work. It is easy to discover by oneself that it is these ceaseless and intangible events that constitute the bedrock of our true character."

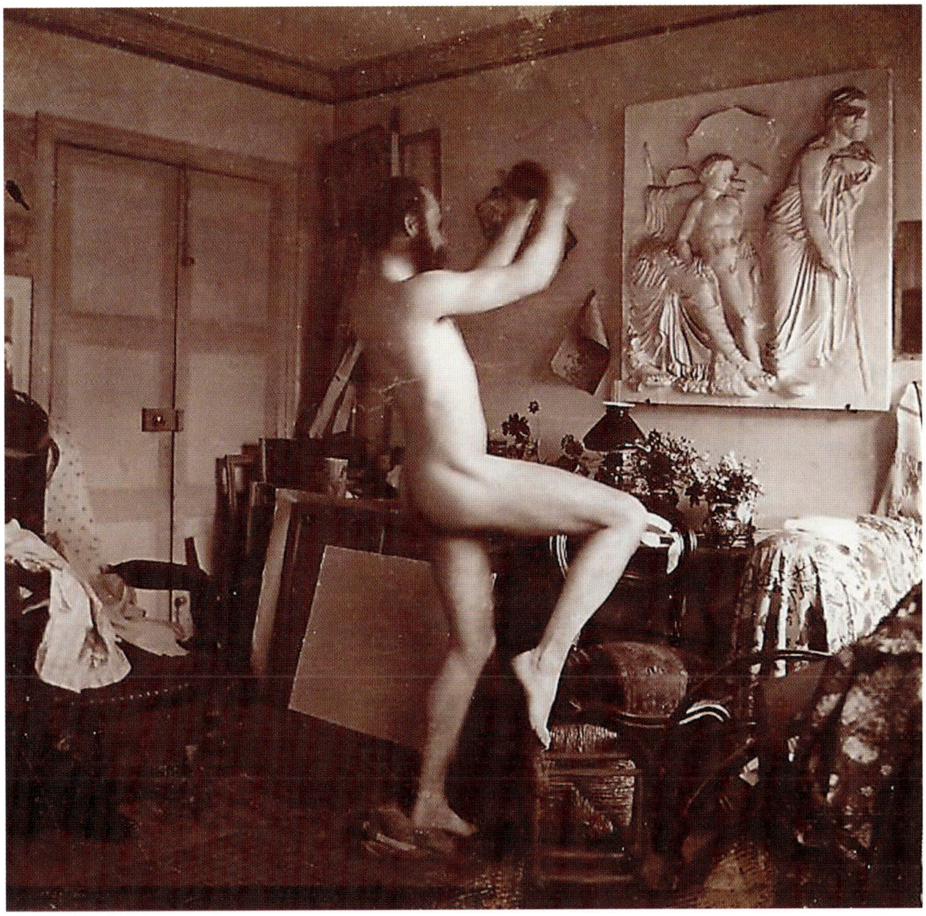

226. Édouard Vuillard, "Ker-Xavier Roussel Naked, Rue Truffaut," c. 1900, silver print, private collection, Paris.

"Spontaneity is the fruit of conquest"

When Vuillard took photographs he sought less to seize a moment than to manufacture a memory. He enjoyed capturing the repetition of habitual scenes: eating lunch, shelling peas, preparing meals, lighting the stove, a woman doing her hair. Vuillard did not make use of the Kodak's advantage of speed; he preferred regularity to fortuitousness. "Spontaneity," as Paul Valéry elegantly phrased it, "is the fruit of conquest." As Annette Vaillant once again observes, Vuillard's photographs served as a "memorandum for a discreet individual for capturing (if only exceptionally and to document his memory) some unprocessed element that he then shifts and incorporates—timeless—into some slowly transfigured scene that perpetuates a long-vanished youth, that reappropriates the past—by way of the secret alchemy of color—giving it a life, an unfathomable pulse that neither old age nor death can extinguish" (ill. 226).

Nonetheless, in a phrase in his *Journal* for September 1917, Vuillard appears to reduce his photographs to little more than notes for paintings. "Using photography like Delacroix used nature," he writes, alluding to a remark the Romantic painter made to Baudelaire: "Nature is just a dictionary in which one looks up the meanings of a word" (Édouard Vuillard, "Lucy Hessel and Marcelle Aron in front of a Haystack at Amfreville," 1907, silver print, Vuillard Archives, Paris; Édouard Vuillard, *Panel for Prince Emmanuel Bibesco, the Haystack,* 1907–8, tempera on canvas, Musée des Beaux-Arts, Dijon). Be that as it may, the practice of photography may well have reassured him at a time when he feared that painting was getting beyond his powers; he felt the renewed successes of Pierre Bonnard after World War I, and the profound faith of Maurice Denis, as a rejection of his own talent.

Vuillard felt protected by his practice of photography since it placed reality at a sufficient distance for him to be able to treat life as an object of analysis and study, all the while allowing him to remain safe and undisturbed among his family and friends. Vuillard's photographs *do* constitute a family album, but one made by a painter who devoted his oeuvre to the expression of intimacy and companionship. His photographs thus reveal the close correspondence between a man who was a painter, "director," and photographer, and his personal affinities. Transforming everyday life into images, Vuillard's photographic work offered him a way of recording "the extraordinary in the ordinary," as Jacques Aumont has prettily phrased it.[32]

Pierre Bonnard's "snapshots"

The photographic oeuvre of Pierre Bonnard, unknown until then, only came to light following a donation by the painter's grand-nephew, Antoine Terrasse, to the Musée d'Orsay. In 1987, Philippe Néagu and Francoise Heilbrun brought out a basic catalog to coincide with an exhibition at which part of the collection was unveiled at the new museum.[33]

Bonnard probably started taking photographs in 1890. It is likely that the oldest known example is a portrait of his cousin, Berthe Schaedlin, on a bicycle. The entrance into the French public collection of all the negatives and the prints kept by the artist's family confers on Bonnard's photographic practice a truly exceptional institutional and artistic status—cases like these remain rare for artists of such significance.

This unique position has led to two contrary, if equally erroneous, analyses of Bonnard's photographic output. The first, in investing them with an overblown status, distorts the importance of the artist's practice by presenting modern prints after surviving negatives in dimensions significantly greater than those of the extant printings. Bonnard, unlike Edgar Degas and Édouard Vuillard, seems to have been relatively unconcerned with the quality of his prints. To exhibit in outsized formats photographs whose original dimensions did not exceed 1 ½ × 2 ¼ in. (4 × 6 cm) bestows on them a solemnity and aesthetic ambition that their creator never intended. So

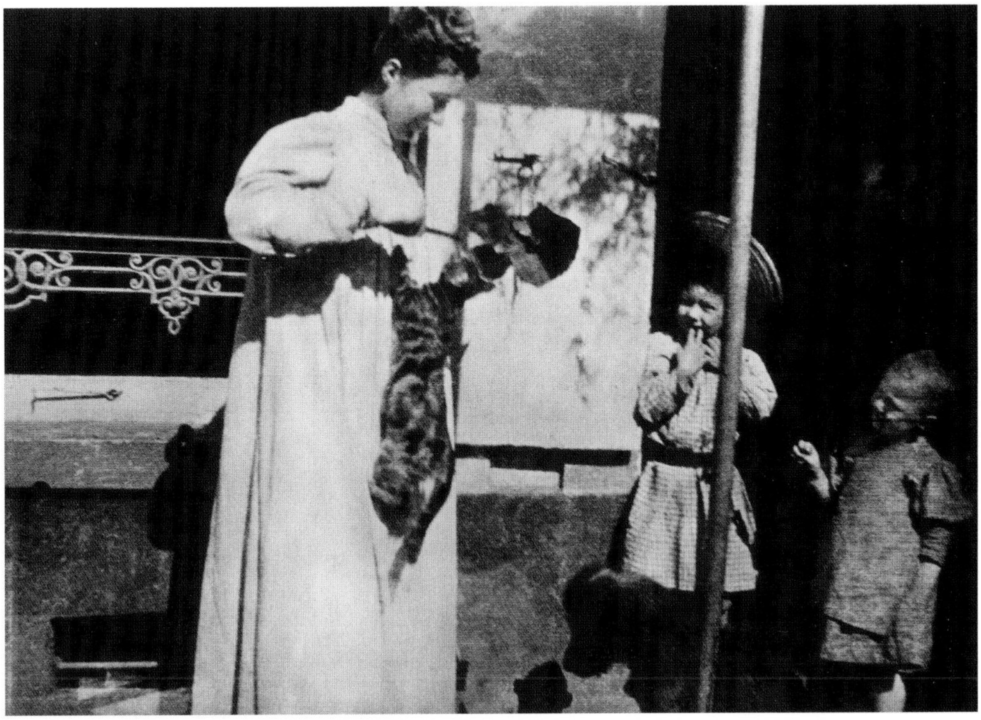

227. Pierre Bonnard, "A Cat Jumps up on Andrée Terrasse's Dress, Renée and Robert Observe the Scene," 1897, modern print from gelatin-bromide silver glass negatives, Musée d'Orsay, Paris.

much emphasis on one selected photograph obscures the collection as a whole.

A polar opposite approach has led other commentators to treat the painter's photographs in a cavalier fashion and reduce them to the level of banal family snapshots, more documentary than artistic. Such a hasty dismissal may have been fostered by the fact that few of Bonnard's photographs can be directly related to his painting or printmaking, and that he did not practice the technique for very long; the majority of his photographs were carried out before 1905.

Thus, in spite of being studied at a relatively early stage, an in-depth analysis of Bonnard's photographic output remains pending. Recent interest in the family photographs replaces the pictures of the Terrasse nephews playing in the garden at Noisy-le-Grand or Grand-Lemps in a more receptive creative context, by examining them, not only from the artistic, but also from the social perspective (ill. 227). Such a study may make it possible to understand them as a whole, in their succession, and not in the artificiality of isolated blowups.

Through the prism of intimacy

The photographs of his partner and model Maria Boursin, known as Marthe, whom Bonnard met in 1893 and married in 1925, after living with her for many years, may be analyzed separately from the search for immediate links they might have with pictures or lithographs. Taken between 1899 and

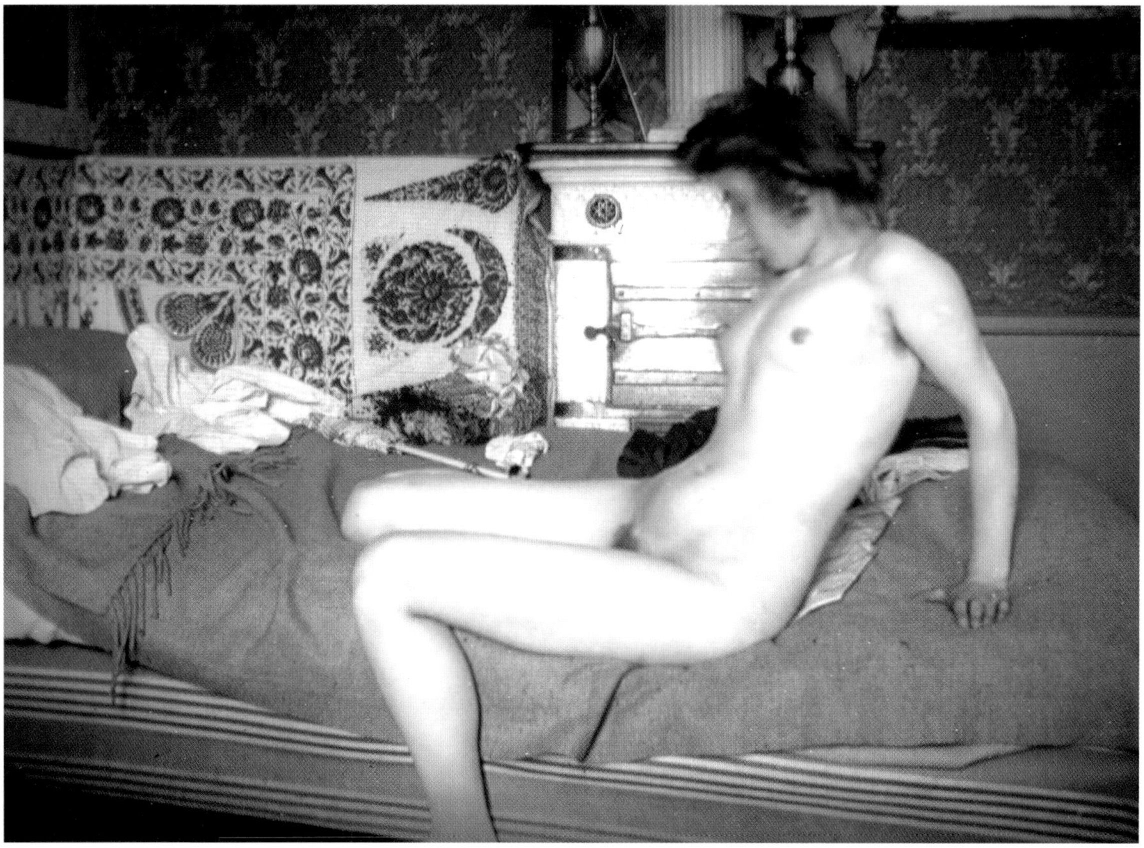

228. Pierre Bonnard, "Marthe in Profile, Seated, Her Left Leg Hanging over the Bed," c. 1899, modern print from a gelatin-bromide negative, Musée d'Orsay, Paris.

1901, they apparently form two distinct series, one of interior photographs taken in the painter's Paris apartment on rue de Douai, the other containing views taken in the garden of a house in Montval, to the west of Paris, which Bonnard rented in summer 1900. Not posed, and sometimes hurriedly composed, the lighting and decor being in all probability quickly prepared beforehand, the viewer is first struck, then intrigued by the benign simplicity of these photographs of Marthe in the bedroom on rue de Douai; their tangible sense of intimacy confers on his beloved a uniquely sensual authenticity, emphasized still more by the unabashed ease with which she takes each pose (ill. 228). Several illustrations for Paul Verlaine's collection of poems *Parallèlement*, published in 1900 by Ambroise Vollard, might be compared to these images of Marthe, though it is not known whether it is the photograph that spawned the lithograph or whether, perhaps more probably, the photograph and the print draw on one and the same source—the artist's deep love and desire for his model. As was the case with Vuillard, Bonnard did not treat photography as a model, but rather as a tool for looking at and apprehending the world around him in a new way. As for his Nabis companions, this was a world that can only be discovered and then divulged through the prism of intimacy, as revealed—

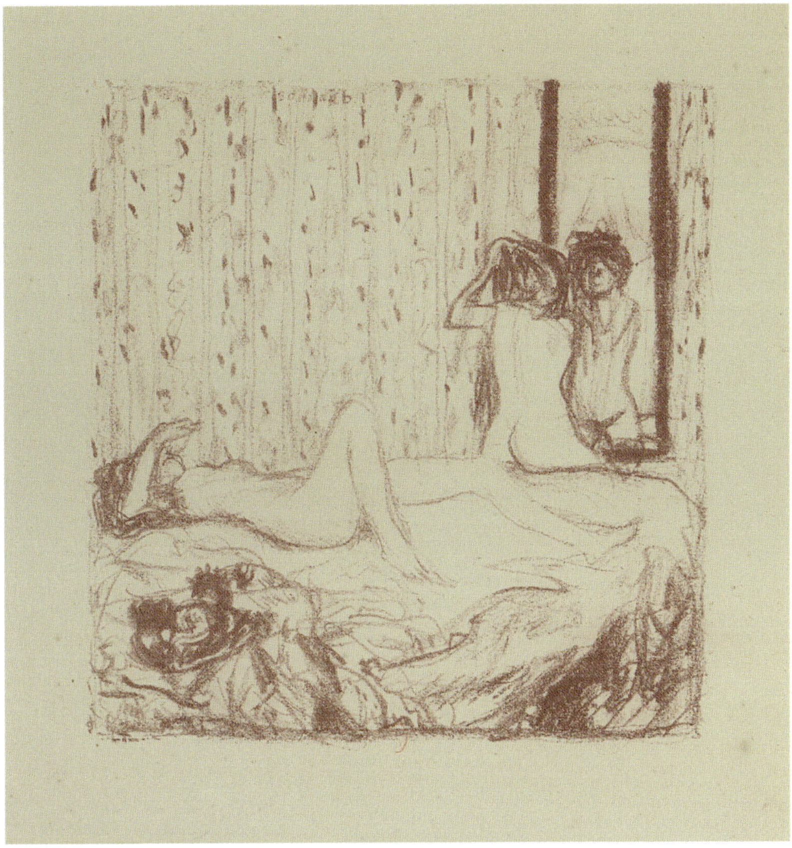

229. Pierre Bonnard, "Woman Lying Down and Woman Seated Before a Mirror," taken from *Parallèlement* by Paul Verlaine, c. 1900, lithograph in red, Bibliothèque Nationale de France, Paris.

unadulterated and unvarnished—through the intermediary of photography.

Beyond any immediate correspondence, the photographs of Marthe are contemporary with a body of pictorial work in which the representation of love, in its everyday, but nonetheless subtle and poignant manifestations, was a recurrent theme. The *Blue Nude* (c. 1900, oil on panel, Musée d'Orsay, Paris) and "Woman Lying Down and Woman Seated Before a Mirror" (ill. 229) show their model, as ever Marthe, in a pose just as abandoned as in the photographs. As it is once again in the emotionally charged *Man and Woman* (c. 1900, oil on canvas, Musée d'Orsay, Paris), where the backdrop is provided by the painter's Paris apartment. It is on record that over the course of his career Bonnard grew increasingly sensitive to the representation of commonplace things in his immediate surroundings. The most out-of-the-way parts of a bourgeois apartment—the bathroom, the lavatory—become places to paint life, bodies, or faces, his own or those of his companion. Sometimes they are elevated to the sublime, as in the splendid series showing Marthe washing; others are searing, like the excruciating *Self-Portrait*, an admirable, derisory image of a self caught in the trap of creeping old age (Pierre Bonnard, *The Boxer,* 1931, oil on canvas, Musée d'Orsay, Paris).

The photographs taken in the garden at Montval are among Bonnard's most attractive images. Their quality arises once again from the freedom of movement and pose of the naked bodies of the artist and Marthe, further enhanced by the natural light from a summer sun that dapples the greenery and blazes down on the glowing figures of a man and a woman (ill. 230).[34] Perhaps it was a reminiscence of the iridescent light emanating from their bodies in these photographs that gave the artist the idea several years later of painting Marthe floating in the bathtub, her body so luminous that it seems to have dissolved.

His interest in the most secret places, in unpretentious interiors, his talent for observing them as from a distance, a distance not devoid of elegance, bestows on Bonnard's photographic output a unique status. It should be analyzed neither as a function of mimetism, nor of reproduction, but through the notion of intimacy in its most nondescript form. The painter's photographs are perhaps just family snapshots taken at a time when the purchase of a camera coincided with both a widening of the family circle—the birth of his sister Andrée's children—and the invariably overwhelming discovery of love. But, if they seem commonplace, it does not mean they are insignificant. On the contrary: to look at them today such as they were taken (small in size, poorly printed, sometimes crudely pasted down) is to appreciate them in all their simplicity—rejecting the temptation to transform them—by magically printing them up in a format close to that of the canvases, into perfect images. Their true value will only be grasped when they are studied as a whole. For Bonnard the practice of photography surely never acquired an importance equal to painting; but its study provides a new view of the work of a painter who is a manifestly more complex figure than his immediately seductive pictures let on. This does not mean seeking an "*ut pictura, ut photographia*" (as is painting so is photography); it means reconsidering how painting and photography overlapped in the artist's creative world.[35]

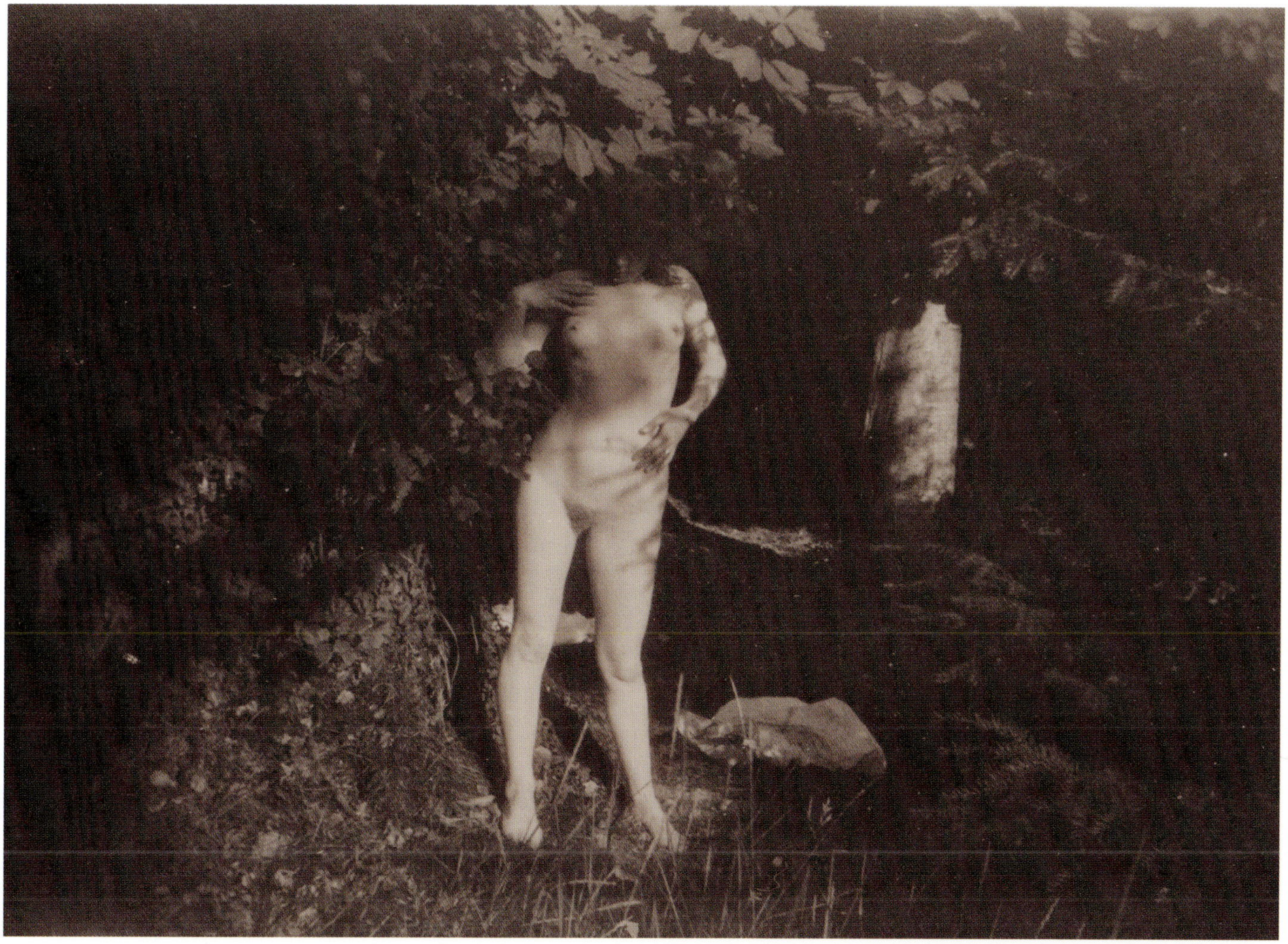

230. Pierre Bonnard, "Marthe Standing in the Garden at Montval", c. 1900, gelatin-bromide silver print, Musée d'Orsay, Paris.

NOTES

INTRODUCTION

1. Théophile Gautier, "Exposition photographique," *L'Artiste,* March 8, 1857, 193. On Théophile Gautier and photography, see Stéphane Guégan, "'Ces bonheurs-là n'arrivent qu'aux habiles,' Théophile Gautier et la photographie artistique," *48/14, Revue du Musée d'Orsay* 28 (Spring 2009): 6–23.
2. The selected bibliography on page 320 together with the endnotes will provide references to the most important works.
3. "Rétrospective de la photographie, 1839–1900," *Exposition internationale de la photographie contemporaine,* Musée des Arts Décoratifs/Louvre, Pavillon de Marsan, January 16–March 1, 1936. See on this subject the article by Quentin Bajac, "Nouvelle vision, ancienne photographie," *48/14, Revue du Musée d'Orsay* 16 (Spring 2003): 74–83.
4. See on this André Jammes's interview with Serge Lemoine and Quentin Bajac published in *48/14, Revue du Musée d'Orsay* 16 (Spring 2003): 84–101, and Dominique de Font-Réaulx, "Les Audaces d'une position française, Un Siècle de vision nouvelle à la Bibliothèque nationale, 1955," *Etudes photographiques* 25 (May 2010): 70–105.
5. Aubenas, *L'Art du nu au XIXe siècle.*
6. Galassi, *Before Photography.*
7. Pinson, *Speculating Daguerre.*
8. At a seminar directed by Julie Ramos around the subject of tableaux vivants, INHA, Paris, October 2011–May 2012. Contributions to the seminar are forthcoming.
9. Barthes, *Camera Lucida.*
10. Billeter, *Malerei und Photographie im Dialog von 1840 bis heute*; Pohlmann, *Eine andere Kunst? Eine andere Natur!*
11. The collection of photographs belonging to Edmond Lebel was acquired in 2006 by the Musée d'Orsay thanks to the generosity of the painter's heirs. The daguerreotypes associated with Auguste Mestral were sold in Paris by public auction on June 6, 2012, through the good offices of Pierre Bergé Associés.

BEFORE PHOTOGRAPHY

1. Alfred de Musset, *Rolla*, first published in 1833.
2. Thiers, "Salon de 1824," in *Adolphe Thiers, critique d'art*, 149. Looking back some ten years, Thiers had in mind the last Salon to be held under the First Empire, that of 1814, at which Géricault unveiled his *Wounded Cuirassier Leaving the Field* (Musée du Louvre, Paris), which, in its subject, style, and manner already marked a clean break with the art of David and his pupils.
3. Several recent studies of high quality have been devoted to artistic life during the French Restoration: Chaudonneret, *L'État et les artistes*; Yon, Mollier, and Reid, *Repenser la Restauration*; Sébastien Allard, *Le Louvre à l'époque romantique*; Kopp and Couty, eds., *Romantisme et révolution(s)*; Bouillo, *Le Salon de 1827, classique ou romantique?*; Allard and Chaudonneret, *Le Suicide de Gros.*
4. *The Hay Wain* (National Gallery, London); *A Canal in England, Landscape* (Huntington Library, Gallery, San Marino, CA); *View near London: Hampstead Heath* (Tate Britain, London).
5. The combination of an optical device, the camera obscura (devised in the late fifteenth century in Italy and thereafter employed by painters for architecture and landscape to correct lines and elevations), with a chemical process that might fix the images formed on it.
6. Galassi, *Before Photography*; Brunet, *La Naissance de l'idée de photographie.*
7. Stendhal, "Critique amère du Salon de 1824 par M. Van Eube de Molkirk," *Salons* 59. Delécluze, a pupil of David's turned critic, published his reviews in *Le Journal des débats*, Adolphe Thiers in *Le Constitutionnel*. Stendhal's text on the Salon came out in *Le Journal de Paris*, over seventeen numbers from August 29 to December 24, 1824.
8. Louis Ulbach, "Paul Delaroche," *Revue de Paris* 26 (April 1, 1857): 349–72, cited in *Paul Delaroche, un peintre dans l'histoire* (Paris: RMN, 1999), 266.
9. Hugo, "Préface," *Cromwell*, 89. The italics are Hugo's own.
10. Ibid., 73.
11. Immanuel Kant, *Observations sur le beau et le sublime*, translated by Hercule Peyer-Imhoff (Paris: JJ Lucet, 1796); Charles de Villers, *Aperçu rapide des bases et de la direction de la philosophie de Kant* (Paris, 1801), and *Philosophie de Kant ou principes fondamentaux de la philosophie transcendantale* (Paris, 1802); Humboldt gave his lectures in German at the Institute in 1798. On Kant's reception in France, see F. Azouzi and D. Bourel, *De Könisberg à Paris : la réception de Kant à Paris (1798–1804)* (Paris: Vrin, 1991).
12. Ibid., 48.
13. Antoine Chrysostome Quatremère de Quincy, *Essai sur l'imitation* (Paris, 1825), translated by J. C. Kent as *An Essay on the Nature, the Means and the Ends of Imitation in the Fine Arts* (London, 1837).
14. Note on the exhibition of 1819, Archives Nationales, Paris, O3 1402.
15. Ibid., 147.
16. Étienne Delécluze, "Beaux-Arts, Exposition du Louvre 1824 no. 1," *Le Journal des débats* (September 1, 1824): 3.
17. The remarkable and now historic exhibition, *De David à Delacroix*, RMN, Paris, 1974, already underscored the richness of Restoration Salons and showed how the diversity of styles and genres of the works presented therein profoundly altered the preconditions of painting.
18. Jean-Dominique-Auguste Ingres, *Écrits sur l'art* (Paris: La Bibliothèque des Arts, 1994), 35. Ingres's remarks are undated.
19. "L'Artiste, le savant et l'industriel," *Oeuvres complètes de Saint-Simon et d'Enfantin* 10 (1867): 210. The text initially appeared in the collection *Opinions littéraires, philosophiques et industrielles.* For an analysis of these texts, see McWilliam, *Dreams of Happiness.*
20. Georges Matoré, "Les notions d'art et d'artiste à l'époque romantique," *Revue des Sciences humaines* 16, 62–63 (April–September 1851): 120–37.
21. Concerning the essential role played by the journal *L'Artiste*, see the thesis by Adrien Goetz, 1997, unfortunately as yet unpublished. The article distilled from it provides a preliminary and exceptionally interesting approach to the subject: Adrien Goetz, "L'Artiste, revue de combat des années 1830," *De l'utopie au désenchantement, Romantisme et révolution(s)*, vol. 2, Les entretiens de la Fondation des Treilles (Paris: Gallimard, 2009), 165–94.
22. Cited by Laurent Jullier and Guillaume Soulez, *Stendhal, le désir de cinéma*, followed by *Privilèges du 10 avril 1840 de Stendhal* (Paris: Séguier/Archambaud, 2006), 21.
23. Hugo, "Préface," *Cromwell*, 90.
24. Roland Barthes, *S/Z*, trans. R. Miller (New York: Hill & Wang, 1974), 55 and 54.
25. See on the subject Crary, *Techniques of the Observer*, and Laurent Mannoni, *Le Grand Art de la lumière et de l'ombre, le cinéma.*
26. Chateaubriand, *Lettre sur le paysage en peinture.*
27. See on this Grunchec, *Les Concours des prix de Rome, 1797–1863.*
28. The history of the many and complex links between painting and the theater in the Romantic era remains as yet unwritten. The exhibition at the Musée Cantini, Marseille, in 2009, "De la Scène au Tableau," organized by Guy Cogeval and Marie-Paule Vial, provides interesting insight. For an analysis of the Romantic theater, see Naugrette, *Le Théâtre romantique.*
29. Thiers, "*Salon de 1824*," 112–13. The italics are Thiers's own.
30. Stendhal, "*Salon de 1824*," 67–68.
31. The intriguing article by Linda Whiteley rehearses a precise analysis of the role played by these Paris dealers, "Art et commerce d'art en France avant l'époque impressionniste," *Romantisme* 40 (1983): 65–76.
32. Balzac, "Pierre Grassou," 272.
33. The study of the connections between Daguerre's diorama and the painting of the era has not been thoroughly addressed. The forthcoming PhD thesis by Stephen Pinson on Daguerre, presented at Harvard University and supervised by Henri Zerner, will surely provide some initial pointers. Less ambitiously, two articles attempt to draw out the links between the diorama, the invention of photography and Romantic theater and painting: Dominique de Font-Réaulx, "Le vrai sous le fantastique," *Études photographiques* 16 (May 2005) 152–65, and "L'invention de la photographie, avatar du romantisme," *De l'utopie au désenchantement, Romantisme et révolution(s)*, vol. 2, 325–46.

34. Stendhal, "Salon de 1824," 64.
35. Originally published in 1914 and thus marked by the ideas of the age in which it was written, Léon Rosenthal's work nonetheless remains an informed and vivid account of the art world during the July Monarchy. See Rosenthal, *Du romantisme au réalisme* (reprinted 1987).

THE BIRTH OF PHOTOGRAPHY
CONCEPTION, ANNOUNCEMENT, AND RECEPTION

1. Paul Delaroche, quoted by Arago in *Rapport de M. Arago sur le daguerréotype lu à la Chambre des députés le 3 juillet 1839 et à l'Académie des Sciences, séance du 19 août* (Paris: Bachelier imprimeur, 1839), 34.
2. Frizot, *A New History of Photography*; Bajac, *La Photographie, du daguerréotype au numérique*.
3. Louis Figuier, *Exposition et histoire des principales découvertes scientifiques modernes* (Paris: Victor Masson, 1851) and *Les Merveilles de la Science* (Paris: Victor Masson, 1868); Gaston Tissandier, *Les Merveilles de la photographie* (Paris, Hachette, 1874); Adrien Mentienne, *La Découverte de la photographie en 1839, description du procédé faite aux Chambres législatives* (Paris: Pierre Dupont, 1892); Georges Potonniée, *Histoire de la découverte de la photographie* (Paris: P. Montel, 1925).
4. François Brunet, *La naissance de l'idée de photographie*, and André Gunthert, "L'inventeur inconnu. Louis Figuier et la constitution de l'histoire de la photographie française," *Études photographiques* 16 (May 2005): 6–18.
5. Letter of May 5, 1816, cited by Rouillé, *La photographie en France, textes et controverses: une anthologie, 1816–1871*, 24.
6. Helmut Gernsheim, "La première photographie au monde," *Etudes photographiques* 3 (1997): 6–25. The first publication dates from 1977, in *History of Photography*, under the title "The 150th Anniversary of Photography."
7. On François Arago and his stage management of the announcement of Daguerre's process, see Brunet, *La naissance de l'idée*, surely the most penetrating and rounded study of the question. An article by Ann McCauley, "L'invention de la photographie et le politique," *Études photographiques* 2 (May 1997): 6–43, and an introduction by Roubert, *L'Image sans qualités* are also well worth perusal. The recent article by André Gunthert, "Spectres de la photographie—Arago et la divulgation du daguerréotype" (put online June 2, 2010), stressing Arago's scientific interest in Daguerre's invention, provides food for thought as well. See also: Bajac and Font-Réaulx, *Le Daguerréotype français, un objet photographique*.
8. [Arsène Houssaye], "Diorama, la Vallée de la Goldau," *Journal des artistes* vol. 2, 13 (1835): 202–3; Emmanuel Viollet-le-Duc to Eugène-Emmanuel Viollet-le-Duc, Paris, September 28, 1836, in Eugène-Emmanuel Viollet-le-Duc, *Lettres d'Italie adressées à sa famille, 1836–1837* (Paris: Léonce Laget, 1971), 167.
9. Taylor, "Photography and an Age of Paradox," *Impressed by Light*.
10. Plantureux, *Joseph Hamel chez Talbot, Niépce et Daguerre*.
11. Arago, François, *Rapport de M. Arago sur le daguerréotype lu à la Chambre des députés le 3 juillet 1839 et à l'Académie des Sciences, séance du 19 août* (Paris: Bachelier imprimeur, 1839).
12. See in the anthology, p. 308, Daguerre's text published in 1838 as he attempted to set up a subscription to fund his invention.
13. Arago, *Rapport de M. Arago*, 52.
14. Ibid., 35.
15. Isidore Niépce, *Histoire de la découverte improprement appelée daguerréotype, précédé d'une notice sur son véritable inventeur, Nicéphore Niépce* (Paris: Astier, 1841). It is amusing to see how the tension between partisans of Niépce and Daguerre lives on: a series of popular articles devoted to the major events in the invention of photography published in summer 2011 in the French weekly *Télérama* kicked off with a piece devoted to Nicéphore Niépce, "the true inventor," followed the next week by a page devoted to the "unjustly forgotten" Hippolyte Bayard; the timeline says little about Daguerre, envisaged by the author of these articles as a "usurper."
16. Tissandier, *Les Merveilles de la photographie*, 24–25.
17. Paul-Louis Roubert, "Hubert ou l'honneur de Daguerre," *Études photographiques* 16 (May 2005): 41–49. For long in the shadows, this individual was identified by Stephen Pinson as Alphonse Eugène Hubert, architect, the author of a manual entitled *Le Daguerréotype considéré sous un point de vue artistique, mécanique et pittoresque* (Paris: Alph. Giroux, 1840).
18. In 1844, in the foreword to *Pencil of Nature*.
19. See the text publicizing Daguerre's subscription, reproduced p. 308 herein.
20. Arago, *Rapport de M. Arago*, 31.
21. The correspondence between Alexander von Humboldt and François Arago betrays their lack of confidence in the paper-based processes of both Talbot and Herschel, who was nonetheless a colleague of theirs. See Hamy, *Correspondance d'Alexandre de Humboldt avec François Arago 1809-1853*. Part of the correspondence between the two scientists is housed in the library of the Institut de France, Paris. Ms. 2115: 1–126.
22. Arago, *Rapport de M. Arago*, 36.
23. Letter of October 5, 1835 from Daguerre to Isidore Niépce, quoted by Brunet, *La naissance de l'idée*, 49.
24. The first to quote from the correspondence between Niépce and Daguerre was Tissandier. The letters have since been published by Kravets, *Documentii po istorii izobretenia fotografii*. Helmut and Alison Gernsheim based their researches—which always refer to Kravets' publication—on these (Helmut and Alison Gernsheim, *The History of Photography*). Niépce's entire correspondence has recently been the object of an exhaustive edition: Bonnet and Marignier, *Niépce, correspondance et papiers*.
25. Quoted by Tissandier, *Les Merveilles de la photographie*, 149.
26. Charles Chevalier, *Souvenirs*, quoted by Taillandier, ibid., 53.
27. A line drawing by Charles Bouton, *Le Laboratoire de Daguerre*, dated 1824, offers a glimpse into Daguerre's alchemical cave. It is now conserved at the International Museum of Photography and Film in George Eastman House, Rochester, NY.
28. Adhémar, "Introduction," *Daguerre et les premiers daguerréotypistes français*, 1. The publication in April 2012 of Pinson's eagerly-awaited work *Speculating Daguerre* allows us to appreciate the connections between Daguerre's various inventions.
29. Delécluze, *David, son école et son temps*, 401.
30. See note 31 in the chapter Before Photography (Whiteley, 1983), 65–76.
31. In his recent book Stephen Pinson (2012) expresses the opinion that the diorama was also partially related to new developments in lighting being undertaken at that time by painters and in museums. One also recalls the way *The Rape of the Sabine Women* was exhibited by Jacques-Louis David at the beginning of the nineteenth century and of the artist's determination to present the painting using original light effects. In addition, Pinson advances that, in the mind of Daguerre and of Charles Bouton, the invention of the diorama might also have seemed to herald a new type of museum.
32. Daguerre, *Historique et description des procédés du daguerréotype*.
33. Jules Janin, "*Le Daguerotype*," [*sic*] *L'Artiste* 2nd series, vol. 2, March 1839: 145. See the text in translation in the anthology at the end of the present volume, pp. 308–9.
34. More satisfactorily than anyone else, it was Roland Barthes who, with his customary brilliance and sensibility, analyzed the ontological relationship between photography and time, the "*it was so*," which he describes in his posthumously published text on photography (Barthes, 1980).
35. On Raoul-Rochette, see Perrot, "Notice sur la vie et les travaux de Désiré Raoul-Rochette," *Comptes-rendus de l'Académie des Inscriptions et belles lettres* 50th year, 9 (1906): 638–701.
36. Quoted by Arago, *Rapport de M. Arago*, 33. The letter from Delaroche to Arago was printed in *La Lumière* on January 15, 1866: 1.
37. As cited by Recht, *La Lettre de Humboldt*, 10.
38. Ibid.
39. "Rapport sur les dessins produits par le procédé de M. Bayard, séance du 2 novembre 1839," *Le Moniteur*, November 15,

1839, 2. The report is signed, as well as by Raoul-Rochette, by Picot, Schnetz, Petitot, Debret, Guénepin, Desnoyers, Richomme, Nanteuil, and Huyot, the commission being composed of painters, sculptors, and architects.
40. In *Procès-verbaux de l'Académie des beaux-arts* (1839): 18 (Paris: Bibliothèque de l'Institut).
41. Janin, "*Le Daguerotype*," 145.
42. Ibid.
43. The reference is to the English painter John Martin, whose vast compositions with dramatic effects of crowds, shadow, and light, rather similar to those of the diorama, proved a huge success when they were shown in Paris.
44. Janin, "Le Daguerotype," 147.
45. Frédéric Goupil-Fesquet, *Voyage d'Horace Vernet en Orient* (Brussels: C. Muquardt, 1844). Unfortunately, to date, the images taken by Goupil-Fesquet in Egypt on the advice of Horace Vernet have not come to light. They were the first photographs to be taken in the Orient, from autumn 1839, together with those carried out at the same time by the Canadian Joly de Lotbinière. See also Aubenas and Lacarrière, *Voyage en Orient*.
46. See Bajac and Font-Réaulx, *Le Daguerréotype français*.
47. Charles Letaillé, *Le Daguerréotype de la jeunesse* (Paris, 1839).
48. Auguste Le Gallois, ed. *Paris daguerréotypé par Méphistophélès* (Paris, 1840).
49. A. M. Reybert, *Daguerréotype des reines, histoire universelle de tous les peuples civilisés* (Paris: Mme. Lepage, 1840), VIII. The italics are Reybert's own.
50. See on this subject the very precise chronology established by Marie-Sophie Corcy listing the patents and announcements made by daguerreotypists, in Bajac and Font-Réaulx, *Le Daguerréotype français*, 399–405.
51. "Des nouveaux procédés de la photographie," *L'Artiste* (1841): 244–45.
52. Töpffer, *Réflexions et menus propos d'un peintre genevois ou essai sur le beau dans les arts*, 379–406.
53. Ibid., 383.
54. Ibid., 384.
55. Ibid., 382.
56. Étienne Delécluze, "Exposition de 1842," *Journal des débats*, March 25, 1842. François Bouchot had died in February of the same year. Delécluze trained as a painter in the studio of Jacques-Louis David, whose history he published. Abandoning painting, he became one of the most influential critics of the age and a personality in artistic circles; his salon on Rue Chabanais was attended by many luminaries from the literary and artistic worlds. Delécluze was, in addition, Eugène-Emmanuel Viollet-le-Duc's uncle on his mother's side.
57. Théophile Thoré, *Salons de 1844, 1845, 1846, 1847, 1848* (Paris: A. Lacroix, 1868), 105.
58. Henri Delaborde, *La Revue des deux mondes* (April 1, 1856): 617–38, quoted by Paul Périer in 1857, "De la photographie comme art," published in *La Revue photographique*, and reprinted in *Bulletin de la Société française de photographie*, 1857, vol. 3; Charles Baudelaire, "Le public moderne et la photographie, Salon de 1859," *Critique d'art*, 277. Several recent analyses of Baudelaire's text have cast light on its complexities. See especially Jérôme Thélot, "Le rêve d'un curieux, la photographie comme fleur du mal," *Études photographiques* 6 (May 1999), and Paul-Louis Roubert, "Edition commentée du Public moderne et la photographie de Charles Baudelaire," *Études photographiques* 6 (May 1999): 22–32.
59. Charles Chevalier, *Mélanges photographiques, complément des nouvelles instructions sur l'usage du daguerréotype* (Paris: Charles Chevalier, 1841), 1. On the commercial exploitation of the daguerreotype, see Bajac, in Bajac and Font-Réaulx, *Le Daguerréotype français*, 41–54.
60. A. Desplaces, "Lettres sur le Salon," *L'Union* 29 (January 29, 1851). On this subject, see the brilliant analysis by Roubert, *L'Image sans qualités*.
61. Étienne Delécluze, "Feuilleton de l'Exposition de 1850," *Journal des débats* (January 7, 1851): 28–31.
62. Louis Esnault, "Salon de 1850," *La Chronique de Paris* (February 16, 1851). Concerning the reception of *Un enterrement à Ornans (A Burial at Ornans)*, see the description of the painting in the catalog to the exhibition, *Gustave Courbet (1819–1877)*, 2007 (cat. 47).
63. Jules-Antoine Castagnary, *Gustave Courbet* (Rezé-les-Nantes: Bertrand Tillier, 1882 [repr. 2000]), 40.
64. On the creation and rapid demise of the Société Héliographique, see André Gunthert, "L'institution du photographique, le roman de la Société héliographique," *Études photographiques* 12 (November 2012): 37–63.
65. Francis Wey, "Album de la société héliographique," *La Lumière* 15 (May 18, 1851): 58. On this, see Paul-Louis Roubert, "Le daguerréotype en procès," in Bajac and Font-Réaulx, *Le Daguerréotype français*, 119–131.
66. Le Gray, *Photographie, traité nouveau*, 2.
67. The word "*calotypist[e]*" is a neologism coined from "calotype," the term used by Talbot to designate his paper process. Forged from the conjunction of two Greek words, "calotype" might be translated by "beautiful image." On the calotype in France, see Aubenas and Roubert, *Primitifs de la photographie*.
68. On more than one occasion in his speech to the Chamber, Arago stresses the "almost mathematical precision" of the daguerreotype, "the perfect imprint of the optic image."
69. The words used in 1839 by Louis-Joseph Gay-Lussac, chemist, physicist, and friend of Arago.

EXHIBITING PHOTOGRAPHY

1. Henri de Lacretelle, "Revue photographique II," *La Lumière* (March 20, 1852): 1.
2. This exhibition, mentioned by Vernon Heath in 1892, the only eyewitness to the event to leave an account, is also supposed to have featured a lecture by the physicist Faraday.
3. "Exposition au profit du tremblement de terre de la Martinique," *Le Constitutionnel* (August 3, 1839): 2. This benefit exhibition was to have opened in June of the same year, i.e. before the promulgation of the law covering photography by the Chambre des Députés at the beginning of July. The date of June 24, 1839, however, circulated for a long time among first exponents, then historians, of photography; it seems that Bayard himself nurtured a confusion that afforded him a chronological advantage over Daguerre.
4. See note 39 of the chapter The Birth of Photography.
5. It is not known exactly how Bayard came into contact with the organizers of this event. Perhaps the photographer was introduced by Amaury-Duval, a painter and pupil of Ingres, or he might have made an approach on his own initiative.
6. On these "Expositions des produits de l'Industrie," and on their importance in the development and distribution of the decorative arts, see in particular *Un âge d'or des arts décoratifs* (Paris: Réunion des musées nationaux, 1991).
7. *Rapport du Jury de l'Exposition des Produits de l'Industrie de 1844*, 7: 383. On this occasion the daguerreotypists Jean-Baptiste Sabatier-Blot, Philippe Derussy, and Louis-Auguste Bisson received awards for their work.
8. Laborde thus distinguished "heliographs on metal plates" [daguerreotypes] from "heliographs on paper," and colored heliographs. His report was published in *La Lumière*, the journal founded by the Société Héliographique on March 2, 1851.
9. *Rapport du Jury de l'Exposition des Produits de l'Industrie de 1849*, ninth commission "Beaux-Arts," 7: 529–35. Sabatier-Blot, Bisson, and Derussy once more received awards for their daguerreotypes. Hippolyte Bayard, Gustave Le Gray, and Guillot-Saguez were commended for their photographs on paper.
10. *Travaux de la Commission française sur l'industrie des nations, Exposition universelle de Londres*, vol. 8 (Paris, 1856).
11. Ibid., 481.
12. The "Exhibition of Arts and Manufactures" took place in the Assembly Rooms from December 1839 to January 1840. Twenty of Talbot's "photogenic drawings" were also shown. See on this subject the excellent and informative site hosted by Roger Taylor with backing from the De Montfort University, Leicester, "Photographic Exhibitions in Great Britain, 1839–1865," which lists all the exhibitions to show photographic prints during this period.

13. "Exhibition of Recent Specimens of Photography" December 22, 1852–January 29, 1853. Notable exhibitors included Henri Le Secq, Gustave Le Gray, and Henri-Victor Regnault.
14. *Art-Journal Advertiser,* April 1, 1852, quoted by Taylor, *Impressed by Light*, 47.
15. "The point is not simply to set up an agreeable and practical photographic club but a real association that would possess as many advantages for art as the Geographic Society has for advancing knowledge in its field" (see note 4 in the present chapter).
16. This exhibition featured nearly a thousand numbers. Several French photographers presented their work; Le Gray showed in particular *La Grande Vague*; Pierre Ambroise Richebourg exhibited numerous photographic reproductions of contemporary paintings, including *The Duel after the Ball* by Jean-Léon Gérôme (1857, Musée Condé, Chantilly).
17. *La Lumière* (February 9, 1851): 2.
18. On the creation of the Société Héliographique and its rapid dissolution, see André Gunthert, "L'institution du photographique, le roman de la Société héliographique," *Études photographiques* 12 (November 2012): 37–63.
19. Henri de Lacretelle, "Exposition, association des artistes boulevard de Bonne-Nouvelle," *La Lumière* (March 27, 1852): 1.
20. The Salon of 1850 opened at the end of December; due to the exceptional political situation, it was still on by the time Wey published his article.
21. Francis Wey, "De l'influence de l'héliographie sur les beaux-arts," *La Lumière* (February 9 and 16, 1851): 2. A translation of the article is printed in the anthology at the end of the present volume, pp. 309–10.
22. Henri de Lacretelle, "Revue photographique I," *La Lumière* (February 28, 1852): 1.
23. Lacretelle, "Revue photographique II."
24. "Exposition universelle, 1er Article," *Bulletin de la Société française de Photographie* (1855): 146.
25. Ibid., 147.
26. "Exposition universelle, 3ème Article," *Bulletin de la Société française de Photographie* (1855): 200.
27. Ibid., 171.
28. Ibid., 200.
29. Théophile Gautier, "Exposition photographique," *L'Artiste* (March 8, 1857): 193–95.
30. The claim to exclusive rights over the name Nadar, "Mémoire pour la revendication de la propriété exclusive du pseudonyme Nadar," *Mémoires du tribunal de Paris* (December 12, 1857), is quoted in Rouillé, *La Photographie en France*, 239–40.
31. On arts' policy in Le Havre during the nineteenth century, see the remarkable overview by Isolde Pludermacher, *Les conditions du développement de la vie artistique au Havre au XIXe siècle,* monograph of the École du Louvre edited by Jean-Pierre Mohen and Anne Roquebert, 1997–98. The exhibitions of 1837 and 1839 each hosted fifty or so exhibitors, for the most part from the city itself.
32. The booklet for the exhibition reads: "Macaire, Jetée du N.O. Havre, épreuves daguerriennes." I would like to express my gratitude to Annette Haudiquet, head curator and director of the Musée Malraux in Le Havre, for having communicated this information.
33. Municipal exhibition of the town of Le Havre, catalog of paintings, sculpture, and drawings.
34. Philippe Burty, "Exposition de la Société française de photographie," *La Gazette des beaux-arts* 2 (May 15, 1859): 209.
35. Figuier, *La Photographie au Salon de 1859*, 2.
36. On the connections between Figuier and Wey, see André Gunthert, "L'inventeur inconnu. Louis Figuier et la constitution de l'histoire de la photographie française," *Études photographiques* 16 (May 2005): 6–18.
37. Figuier, *La Photographie au Salon de 1859*, 6–7.
38. Including in particular printing, music, and geography, but also the arts of medicine.
39. Alphonse Davanne, "Exposition universelle de 1867, classe 17 [*sic*] Epreuves et appareils photographiques," *Bulletin de la Société française de Photographie* 14 (August 1868): 189.
40. Léon Vidal, "Classe 12, la photographie," *Classe III, procédés des lettres, des sciences et des arts*, 1900 Exposition universelle (exh. cat.), 143–44.
41. See on this subject, Quentin Bajac, "Nouvelle vision, ancienne photographie," *48/14, Revue du Musée d'Orsay*, 2003, no. 16, 2003, 74–83. On page 76: "The World Fairs of 1867 and 1878 appeared keener to hail the most recent scientific applications of the technique than to offer a historical perspective on the invention."
42. On this, see the exhibition catalog, Lisa Mintz Messinger, ed., *Stieglitz and His Artists: Matisse to O'Keefe* (New York: Metropolitan Museum of Art and Yale University Press, 2011).

REPRODUCING PAINTINGS

1. Paul Delaroche, quoted by Arago in *Rapport de M. Arago*, 33.
2. Fortunately, since the early 1990s studies have begun to fill the gap in our knowledge; those by Ann McCauley, Stephen Bann, Anthony Hamber, Pierre-Lin Renié, and Laure Boyer, in particular.
3. In 2005, Roland Recht, professor at the Collège de France, held a seminar on the subject of the photographic reproduction of works of art that has opened up new and fruitful fields of research.
4. Jules Janin, "*Le Daguerotype*," [*sic*] *L'Artiste,* 2nd series, vol. 2, March 1839, 147. See the text in translation in the anthology at the end of the present volume, pp. 308–9.
5. Léon de Laborde, "Rapport du Jury central de l'Exposition des Produits de l'Industrie de 1849–II," *La Lumière* (March 2, 1851): 14.
6. Francis Wey, "De l'influence de l'héliographie sur les beaux-arts," *La Lumière* (February 9 and 16, 1851): 3. A translation of the article is printed in the anthology at the end of the present volume, pp. 309–10.
7. Francis Wey, "Un voyage héliographique à faire," *La Lumière*, (March 23, 1851): 2.
8. Ibid., p. 1.
9. On the intricate links between printmaking and photography and the complicated situation concerning painting and its dissemination during the July monarchy and the Second Empire, see Bann, *Parallel Lines*, and "Photographie et reproduction gravée, l'économie visuelle au XIXe siècle," *Études photographiques* 9 (May 2001): 22–43.
10. Wey, "De l'influence de l'héliographie," 3.
11. Henri Delaborde, *La Revue des deux mondes* (April 1, 1856): 617–38, quoted by Paul Périer in 1857, "De la photographie comme art," published in *La Revue photographique*, and reprinted in *Bulletin de la Société française de photographie*, 1857, vol. 3, 172.
12. The italics are Paul Périer's.
13. Périer, "De la photographie comme art," 169.
14. See Laure Boyer, "Robert J. Bingham, photographe du monde de l'Art sous le Second Empire," *Études photographiques* 12 (November 2002).
15. Louis Figuier, *La Photographie au Salon de 1859* (Paris: Imprimerie C. Lahure, 1859), 43.
16. Philippe Burty, "Exposition de la Société française de photographie," *Gazette des beaux-arts* (1859): 211.
17. *L'Artiste* (March 7, 1858)
18. Ernest Lacan, "Exposition universelle, Photographie, 7ème article," *La Lumière* (October 27, 1855): 1.
19. The presentation in 1865 at the École des Beaux-Arts in Paris, at a posthumous exhibition of the work of Hippolyte Flandrin of the photographic reproductions and decorations carried out by the painter for the nave of the church of Saint-Germain-des-Prés, underlines the extent to which the reproductive qualities of photography were already being appreciated.
20. Wey, "Un voyage héliographique," 2.
21. Central Archives of the Musées Nationaux, Palais du Louvre, series Z 18.
22. The Salon of 1850–51 and that of 1852 took place in the Palais-Royal. The 1853 Salon was held at the Hôtel des Menus Plaisirs. Owing to the preparations for the Exposition Universelle, there was no Salon in 1854; the following year it was absorbed into the exhibition that included contemporary and historic works at the Palais des Beaux-Arts. Subsequently, until the 1880s, the Salon was staged in the enormous Palais de l'Industrie on the Champs-Élysées, which had stood

vacant since the end of the Exposition Universelle.
23. Correspondence, June 27, 1862. The Arcade database at the Archives Nationales holds the images of artworks commissioned by the state. This valuable tool retraces the history of these orders for photographs.
24. Bingham had received a British government order to take photographs of the objects on display.
25. See on this subject, Taylor, "Photography and an Age of Paradox," *Impressed by Light*.
26. *Revue universelle des arts* (1855): 316.
27. *La Lumière* announced the publication of the portfolio devoted to Camille Corot in its August 27, 1853 number, page 139. The article underlines the novelty of the project and the importance of reproducing original canvases in photographic form: "It was claimed that photography ... was limited to the mere reproduction of portraits, of sites and scenery, of prints, engravings, line drawings, sculptures, and monuments; but it was prohibited from even thinking of tackling works of painting."
28. Jules Barbey d'Aurevilly, *Oeuvre critique* 2 (Paris: Les Belles Lettres, 2006), 705.
29. It appears that Silvestre also ordered photographs (portraits or reproductions of artworks) with a view to further biographical summaries. An album of photographs now in the Rare Book Reserve in the Bibliothèque Nationale de France contains several prints with links to Silvestre's project.
30. Undated letter [early May 1855] from Gustave Courbet to his parents, in Ten-Doesschate Chu, *Correspondance de Courbet*, 130–31.
31. In 1862, two letters from Courbet addressed to Léon Isabey—the architect of the Pavillon du Réalisme—and to art dealer Jules Luquet refer to Richebourg's unsettled bills, probably concerning unpaid photographs (Ten-Doesschate Chu, *Correspondance de Courbet*, 193 and 196).
32. Aubenas, *Le Concours du duc de Luynes*.
33. Concerning photographic reproductions of artworks published and marketed by Goupil, consult Pierre-Lin Renié, "Goupil et Cie à l'ère industrielle: la photographie appliquée aux oeuvres d'art," *État des lieux* 1: 115–42.
34. Le Pelley-Fonteny, *Adolphe et Georges Giraudon, une bibliothèque photographique*.
35. Léon de Laborde, *Travaux de la Commission française sur l'industrie des nations, Exposition universelle de Londres*, vol. 8 (Paris : Imprimerie impériale, 1856), 450–503, cited by Rouillé, *La Photographie en France*, 223. Laborde's text exerted a profound influence on Walter Benjamin for his *Work of Art in the Age of Mechanical Reproduction,* written in 1935 and published posthumously in German in 1955.
36. Félix Ravaisson, *De l'enseignement du dessin dans les lycées, rapport du 28 décembre 1853* (Paris: Imprimerie P. Dupont, 1855).
37. Font-Réaulx, *L'oeuvre d'art et sa reproduction photographique*.
38. On issues surrounding the reproduction of artworks in Great Britain, see Anthony Hamber, *A Higher Branch of the Art*. The equivalent for France remains to be written.
39. Archives des Musées Nationaux, Palais du Louvre, Paris, series C 19, January 25, 1865.
40. Philippe Jarjat, "Photographier les fresques de Raphaël au Vatican en 1869: Histoire et usages des images d'Adolphe Braun," *Studiolo* 3 (2005) (Rome: Académie de France à Rome/Somogy), 219–45.
41. Archives des Musées Nationaux, Palais du Louvre, Paris, series T 18.
42. Ibid., series T 18.
43. Ibid., series Z 34. The work of cataloguing and classifying the photographic holdings of the relevant department in the Louvre will surely offer material for the understanding and analysis of the bonds between musical and photographic institutions in the nineteenth century.

REVOLUTIONS IN LANDSCAPE

1. Niel, *Le paysage au Salon*, 6. See the text in translation in the anthology at the end of the present volume, p. 316.
2. On the links between literature, painting, and music at the turn of the nineteenth century, see *L'Invention du sentiment* (Paris: Réunion des Musées nationaux, 2002).
3. Chateaubriand, *Lettre sur le paysage en peinture*, 12. Written in 1795, this letter was only published in 1830 in the first volume of the French edition of the writer's complete works.
4. See Van Tuyll, *Claude Gellée dit Le Lorrain: le dessinateur face à la nature*, 12–23.
5. Chateaubriand, *Lettre sur le paysage en peinture*, 11.
6. Quoted by Clark, *Landscape into Art*, 32. For an original approach to the issue of the representation of landscape and of its appreciation, see also Coetzee, *Paysage sud-africain*.
7. See Anne Lyles, ed., *Constable: The Great Landscapes* (London: Tate Publishing, 2006).
8. Alfred Sensier cited in the article "Théodore Rousseau," *La Grande Encyclopédie*, vol. 30, 1885–1902.
9. Roland Barthes, *S/Z*, trans. R. Miller (New York: Hill & Wang, 1974), 55.
10. Lithograph issued in *Le Charivari* of May 12, 1865.
11. "L'art et la photographie," *La Lumière* (May 19, 1860): 77.
12. From 1855 onward numerous photographers began to haunt the forest. A favorite site for their studies, they took countless views of the woodland to serve as models for painters. The collection of a painter-engraver close to the Barbizon School, Théophile Chauvel, demonstrates the uptake of these photographs by the art world of the time (see pp. 257–58 of the present volume).
13. On this subject, see Challe and Marbot, *Les Photographes de Barbizon*; Schama, *Landscape and Memory*, 585–653; Georgel, *La Forêt de Fontainebleau, un atelier grandeur nature*.
14. The daguerreotype is attributed by some today to Gustave Le Gray. This attribution is, however, still to be confirmed.
15. His father, the painter Adolphe Giroux, a pupil of David's, ran a "stationer's, colorman's and picture gallery" in Paris, at 7 rue du Coq-Saint-Honoré. He supplied artists with canvases and paints, sometimes in addition selling their works; in 1839, the Giroux firm joined up with Jacques Louis Mandé Daguerre, with whom the Girouxs probably had family ties, to sell the inventor's design for a camera. On Giroux, see Pomarède, Grishin, and Canguilhem, *André Giroux (1801–1879)*.
16. Ernest Lacan, "Exposition universelle, photographie, 4ème Article," *La Lumière* (October 6, 1855): 157.
17. André Giroux received a commendation for photographs exhibited during the 1855 Paris Exposition Universelle, the award being accompanied by the following comment: "M. Giroux, of Paris, for his highly picturesque landscapes that reveal a taste of a distinguished artist," in "Extrait des rapports du jury mixte international de l'Exposition universelle," *La Lumière* (May 2, 1857): 71.
18. Gustave Le Gray, "Photographie, traité nouveau, théorique et pratique," (Paris, 1852), 1–3, cited by Rouillé, *La Photographie en France*, 98–99.
19. See Cars and Font-Réaulx, *Gustave Courbet (1819–1877)*, particularly the opening pages of the chapter on landscape.
20. Ernest Lacan, "Revue photographique, MM. Le Secq, Soulié, Tiffereau," *La Lumière* (July 29, 1854): 119.
21. Champfleury, *Le Réalisme,* quoted by Philippe Ortel, "Réalisme photographique, réalisme littéraire, un nouveau cadre de référence," in *Jardins d'hiver. Littérature et photographie*, ed. M.-D. Garnier, 72–74. Writing in 1857, once again the author refers to daguerreotype, though by this time it had been entirely supplanted by photography on paper. Perhaps he had in mind the uniqueness of the daguerreotype plate, as against the "heliographic" print or collodion photograph; or else, as for many of his contemporaries, "daguerreotype" served as generic term to cover all forms of the process. It is this latter hypothesis that seems the more likely.
22. See on this subject the enthralling article by Ortel "Réalisme photographique," 55–78.
23. Ortel "Réalisme photographique," 73.
24. Niel, *Le Paysage au Salon*, 17.
25. Niel, *Le Paysage au Salon*, 1.
26. Corbin, *Le Territoire du vide, le désir de ravage*.

27. On this question, see the excellent article by Gloria Gloom, "The Sea as Metaphor in Nineteenth-Century France," *Manet and the Sea*, exh. cat. (New Haven, CT: Yale University Press, 2003), 35–53, and McNamara, ed., *The Lens of Impressionism*.
28. Charles Baudelaire, "Salon de 1859," *Critique d'Art*, 325–26.
29. Ibid., 325.
30. Zola, "Mon Salon 1868," *Écrits sur l'art*, 213.
31. Eugène Boudin's copies of the Ruysdaels in the Louvre (Eugène Boudin, after Jacob Van Ruisdael, *Tempest Near the Dykes in Holland*, 1853, Musée André-Malraux, Le Havre) are worthy examples of his talent. The positive reception given to the canvases by contemporary Dutch painter Johann Barthold Jongkind in Paris in the 1860s was also one stream in an advancing tide in favor of the pure depiction of nature.
32. If Boudin himself practiced photography, as is implied by the letter sent by Berthoud in 1854, he did not deploy it in the manner adduced by his friend: "You've been taking photographs, you say. It must be really useful to you, above all for figure groups." Quoted by Anne-Marie Bergeret-Gourbin, "Eugène Boudin, 1845–1865, entre Honfleur et Le Havre," *Eugène Boudin en Normandie* (Honfleur: Musée Eugène-Boudin, 1998), 41. Gustave Hamelin had opened a daguerreotype studio in Honfleur by 1843.
33. A few seconds or so, thereby excluding the depiction of scudding clouds.
34. *La Revue photographique* (February 5, 1857), 213.
35. Aubenas, *Gustave Le Gray (1820–1884)*. References to Dutch seventeenth-century landscape were frequent. Photographic prints by Le Gray showing the sky may remind viewers of the spectacular luminous effects in works by Jacob Isaacksz. van Ruisdael, such as *The Ray of Sunlight*, painted in about 1660 and which the photographer could have admired in the Louvre.
36. On the aesthetics stemming from "instant" photography and on the obsessive pursuit of the depiction of movement, see the catalog to the exhibition at the Bibliothèque Nationale de France, *La Révolution de la photographie instantanée, 1880–1900* by Aubenas and Gunthert. A view of the motion of the sea was taken for the first time by Étienne Jules Marey in 1891 in the Bay of Naples, *La Vague* (The Wave).
37. André Fermigier, *Courbet* (Geneva: Skira, 1971), 113.
38. Camille Corot learned how to use *cliché-verre*, a process that combines the techniques of gravure with those of photography with Adalbert Cuvelier and Constant Dutilleux. See Deschamps, ed., *Gravure ou photographie?*
39. See Challe, Gauss, and Weidemann, *Eugène Cuvelier.*
40. These prints were sold at auction at Sotheby's, New York, on April 13, 2007.
41. See Daniel, *Édouard Baldus.*
42. Works by the young Auguste Renoir and Claude Monet in the 1860s show how sensitive they were to such new subjects; see, for example, the dramatic shadow effects in the former's *Le Pont des Arts*, painted in 1867 (Norton Simon Museum, Pasadena).
43. In Marseille, the photographer Adolphe Terris received a commission comparable to Marville's in which he detailed the redevelopment of the city during the Second Empire.
44. See Staley and Newall, *Pre-Rapahelite Vision.*
45. Léon Gimpel, *Quarante ans de souvenirs photographiques,* held at the Société Française de Photographie. On Gimpel, see Gervais and Font-Réaulx, *Léon Gimpel, les audaces d'un photographe.*
46. Robin Kelsey, "Les espaces historiographiques de Timothy O'Sullivan," *Études photographiques* 27 (2011): 4–33.

PORTRAITURE
PAINTED PORTRAITS, PORTRAIT PHOTOGRAPHS

1. Baudelaire, "Portrait-Salon de 1859," *Critique d'art*, 315.
2. See Pommier, *Théories du portrait, de la Renaissance aux Lumières.*
3. G. W. F. Hegel, *Aesthetics*, vol. 2, section 3, ii, c ("Painting"); quoted in Aubenas and Biroleau in the introduction to the catalog *Portraits/Visages*, 6.
4. Baudelaire, "Portrait-Salon de 1859," 314.
5. Amaury-Duval, "De Monsieur Ingres, à propos de l'exposition Bonne-Nouvelle," *La Revue Nouvelle* 7 (February 1, 1846): 90.
6. On this subject, see exh. cat. *Portraits publics, portraits privés* (Paris: Réunion des musées nationaux, 2006)
7. Anonymous, "Salon de 1833," *La Mode* (March 16, 1833), 245–46.
8. Baudelaire, "Le musée du Bazar de Bonne-Nouvelle," *Critique d'art*, 72. The year 1846 was when a young Baudelaire cut his teeth as a critic. The portrait of Count Molé is now in the Louvre, while that of Mme d'Haussonville is in the Frick Collection, New York.
9. Théophile Gautier, "L'Exposition universelle de 1855," *Le Moniteur universel* (July 12, 1855). The portrait of Mme Devauçay dates from 1807 and is conserved in Musée Condé, in Chantilly.
10. In 2003 a polemic flared up concerning a portrait dating perhaps from before 1839 and ascribed to Daguerre. The attribution is far from certain (see André Gunthert et Jacques Rocqencourt, "Note sur le portrait de M. Huet," *Études photographiques* 6 [May 1999]: 143). It remains the case, however, that the inventor did try his hand at portraiture before abandoning it as a way of publicizing his invention, as demonstrated in a letter to Isidore Niépce dated January 1838. The mediocre quality of the plates probably dissuaded him from continuing.
11. Quentin Bajac, "Une branche d'industrie assez importante," and Sylvain Morand, "Le daguerréotype en province," in Bajac and Font-Réaulx, *Le Daguerréotype français, un objet photographique*, 41–54 and 103–18.
12. Amaury-Duval, "De Monsieur Ingres," 89.
13. Eugène Delacroix, "Revue des arts," *Revue des Deux Mondes* (September 1850): 1140. Delacroix wrote in his *Journal:* "It would be terrible if the eye saw like the daguerreotype."
14. See on this subject the chapter The Birth of Photography, on the reception of the invention of photography.
15. See Héran, *Le Dernier Portrait.*
16. Francis Wey, "Théorie du portrait, I," *La Lumière* 12 (April 27, 1851): 1–2.
17. This he invited artists to do through the expedient of comparing photographic reproductions of old masters in what was a virtual restatement of the arguments developed in his debut article for *La Lumière,* "De l'influence de l'héliographie sur les beaux-arts," published on February 9 and 16, 1851, on the photographic reproduction of works of art.
18. Wey, "Théorie du portrait, II," *La Lumière* 13 (May 4, 1851): 2.
19. To date, the exact number of group portraits of artists taken in Rome by Perraud is unknown. In addition to the one reproduced here, another representing some Swedish artists is in the Fine Arts Academy in Stockholm, and another in that of Copenhagen; a fourth plate recently resurfaced on the art market (Millon Sale, Hôtel Drouot, Paris, November 10, 2011, lot 49). The appearance in June 2012 of a group of daguerreotypes carried out in about 1848 by the circle around the photographers Auguste Mestral and Gustave Le Gray will cast new light on how artists made use of the invention of photography to produce images of a subtly staged intimacy. (Sale on June 6 2012, at the auction house of the Hôtel Drouot, Pierre Bergé Associés.) The parallel between a drawing by Hippolyte Flandrin showing him with his brother, the landscapist Paul Flandrin, in a pose very close to that on Chabrol's daguerreotype also underlines the way in which photography made its way into the painter's studio. The drawing is preserved at the Department of Graphic Arts in the Louvre, while the daguerreotype is in the J. Paul Getty Museum, Los Angeles.
20. Published in March 1854, the portrait caricatures of the *Panthéon Nadar* was intended to enshrine the lasting glory of three hundred contemporary writers in the manner of the great Romantics.
21. See on this subject, Philippe Néagu, "Nadar et la vie artistique de son temps," *Nadar, les années créatrices, 1854-1860* (Paris: Réunion des musées nationaux/Musée d'Orsay, 1994), 104–29.
22. Philippe Burty, "Exposition de la Société française de photographie," *Gazette des beaux-arts* 2 (1859): 210.
23. Nadar, *Salon de 1877,* quoted by Néagu, "Nadar et la vie artistique," 127–28.

24. Ernest Lacan, "Exposition universelle, photographie, 11ème Article," *La Lumière* (January 19, 1856), 1.
25. See on this subject Catherine Mathon, *Duchenne de Boulogne*. Duchenne de Boulogne's experiments took place in the Paris hospital of La Salpétrière under the aegis of the celebrated Professor Charcot. Darwin adapted the pictures as illustrations to his work *The Expression of the Emotions in Man and Animals*.
26. See the exhibition catalog *Figures de la passion* (Paris: Musée de la Musique/Réunion des musées nationaux, 2002).
27. Roger Taylor, "Mr Fenton Explained Everything: Queen Victoria and Roger Fenton," in Baldwin, Daniel, and Greenough, *All the Mighty World*, 74–89.
28. See Aubenas, *Gustave Le Gray*.
29. André Adolphe Eugène Disdéri, "Brevet d'invention." The patent is cited by Rouillé, *La Photographie en France*, 354–56.
30. See on Disdéri, McCauley, *A.A.E. Disdéri and the Carte de Visite Portrait Photograph* and *Industrial Madness: Commercial Photography in Paris, 1848–1871* (New Haven: Yale University Press, 1994); Sylvie Aubenas, "Le petit monde de Disdéri, un fonds d'atelier du Second Empire," *Études photographiques* 3 (November 1997).
31. Audigier, 1860, p. 2. An advertisement for the photographer Pierre Petit in 1862 mentions a fee of 40 francs for 50 portrait *cartes de visite*. If this appears high compared to the day-rate for a workman (between one and two francs), it was not beyond the means of members of the lower-middle and middle classes.
32. Baldassari, *Le Miroir noir*.
33. The most famous of these attempts is the notorious *Homme criminel* by Cesare Lombroso, published in 1876. Lamentably, the researches of the Italian physician and physiologist were of profound and enduring influence, not only on public perceptions, but also in military dictatorships and police states generally to the detriment of their (supposedly) scientific aims.
34. Le Ministre de la Marine et des Colonies, "Instructions relatives à la photographie des condamnés," August 11, 1871, quoted by Rouillé, *La Photographie en France*, 481–82.
35. Ministère de l'Intérieur, direction de l'Administration pénitentaire, le conseil de l'Inspection générale des prisons, "Proposition du directeur de Clairvaux d'acheter un appareil photographique pour chacune des maisons centrales," November 20, 1863, Archives Nationales, Paris F7 12708.
36. Teresa Castro, "Une cartographie du crime : les images d'Alphonse Bertillon," *Revue hypermedia, histoire de la justice, des crimes et des peines*, posted online May 6, 2011; see also Hamilton and Hargreaves, *The Beautiful and the Damned*, and Berlière and Fournier, *Tous fichés*.
37. An exhibition centering on the family album in the nineteenth century, entitled "Figures de l'intime," but sadly without a catalog, was held at the Musée d'Orsay in 2003.
38. Nodier, *Souvenirs de jeunesse,* quoted by Anne-Marie Roux, "Le désir de peindre de Nodier," in Joseph-Marc Biasi, ed., *Le Portrait* (Rouen: Université de Rouen, 1987), 106–7.
39. Ford, *Julia Margaret Cameron*.
40. Michel Poivert, ed., *La Photographie pictorialiste en Europe, 1888–1918* (Rennes/Cherbourg: Musée des Beaux-Arts/Le Point du Jour, 2006).

STILL LIFE

1. Denis Diderot, "No. 82, Bellangé, *Un Tableau de fleurs et de fruits*," *Salon de 1767* (Paris: Éditions Hermann, 1995), 297.
2. The catalog of Charles Sterling's exhibition *La Nature morte de l'Antiquité à nos jours* [1952] remains seminal (reissued as *Still Life Painting from Antiquity to the Twentieth-Century* [New York: Harper & Row, 1981]).
3. Pliny the Elder, *The Natural History*, 6252 (xxxvi, 10).
4. Denis Diderot, *Salon de 1767*: 337.
5. Philippe Kaenel, "La Nature morte photographique," in Frédéric Elsig, Laurent Darbellay, and Imola Kiss, eds., *Les Genres picturaux, genèse, métamorphoses et transpositions* (Geneva: Métis Presse, 2010), 197–213; Aubenas and Versavel, *Objets dans l'objectif*. Philippe Kaenel is preparing a book dedicated to the photographic still life from 1839 to the present day.
6. Helmut Gernsheim, "La première photographie au monde," *Études photographiques* 3 (1997): 8.
7. Diderot, *Salon de 1767:* 311.
8. Sterling, *Still Life Painting*, "Introduction," 24.
9. "It may be remarked that white china and glass do not succeed well when represented together, the picture of the china, from its superior brightness, is completed before that of the glass is well begun," William Henry Fox Talbot, *Athenaeum* 904 (February 22, 1845): 202.
10. The subject can be compared with the taste for shells that started in the eighteenth century from Antoine Watteau to Dezallier d'Argenville. The subject of Daguerre's image might be related to gouaches by Alexandre Isidore de Barde—in particular, to the *Choice of Shells*, now in the Louvre.
11. The text accompanies plate 3 of *Pencil of Nature,* June 1844; see Larry Schaaf, "William Henry Fox Talbot," *Sun Pictures* 17 (New York: Hans P. Kraus, Jr. Fine Photographs, 2007).
12. Faroult, *La Collection La Caze*.
13. Several photographers took still lifes to provide models for artists and connoisseurs. Two cases in point are Jules Boitouzet in 1854 and Eugène Chauvigné in the 1870s. The aesthetic, academic, and social issues behind such "studies after nature" are addressed in the chapter Studies After Nature.
14. On this subject, see Sylvie Aubenas, "Henri Le Secq et la nature morte," *48/14, La Revue du Musée d'Orsay* 16 (Spring 2003): 52–63.
15. Pam Roberts, "Roger Fenton and the Still Life Tradition," *All the Mighty World: Photographs of Roger Fenton* (New Haven/London: Yale University Press, 2005), 91–98.
16. See *La Beauté et la Mort, natures mortes animalières de la Renaissance à l'époque moderne/Von Schönheit und Tod. Tierstillleben von der Renaissance bis zur Moderne* (Karlsruhe: Staatliche Kunsthalle, 2011), especially the article by Rapahël Abrille on photographic still life.
17. Ernest Lacan, *Esquisses photographiques à propos de l'Exposition universelle et de la guerre d'Orient* (1856): 217. Braun received a gold medal at the Universal Exhibition of 1855.
18. On Charles Aubry, see McCauley, *Charles Aubry, photographe*. Aubry's letter to Nadar is reprinted by Rouillé, *La Photographie en France*, 407–9.
19. See Sexton, Johnson, and Waters, *The Plant Kingdom of Charles Jones*; Charles Jones's photographs today feature in a number of private collections.
20. Mahler-Lechner, *Martin Gerlachs "Formenwelt aus dem Naturreiche."*

GENRE PHOTOGRAPHY
PHOTOGRAPHIC ARRANGEMENTS AND TABLEAUX VIVANTS

1. Ernest de Toytot, "L'art en 1867," *Le Contemporain* 13 (August 1867): 253.
2. Paul d'Ivoi, "Salon de 1857," *L'Estafette* 238 (August 26, 1857).
3. Maxime du Camp, "Peinture de genre – Paysanneries – Paysage," *Salon de 1861* (Paris: 1861), 81.
4. Michaël Vottero, "La peinture de genre en France sous le Second Empire et les premières années de la Troisième République, 1852–1878," under the general editorship of Barthélémy Jobert (thesis, Paris-IV – Sorbonne, presented November 14, 2009).
5. Eugène Loudun, *Le Salon de 1857* (Paris: J. Tardieu, 1857), 27.
6. Gautier, "Paul Delaroche," *Histoire du romantisme*, 258.
7. Ibid., 256. The italics are mine. Probably knowingly, Gautier is playing here on a twofold—historical and contemporary—anachronism. In fact, Delaroche painted the canvas in 1834—that is, fully five years before Daguerre's process was made public. By the time of writing in 1857, Gautier's observations are sufficiently remote from the events to be able to refer not only to the role played by Delaroche in the announcement of photography, but also, as he points up here, to the manner in which the new invention furthered the desire for exactitude that was characteristic of the period.
8. Robinson, *The Studio*, 73.
9. Humbert de Molard probably produced several versions of the scene; a plate very similar to Lagny's is today held in the Musée d'Orsay, Paris.

10. A study by Rembrandt, *Saskia in Bed*, now in the Fondation Custodia in Paris, represents a subject close to Humbert de Molard's daguerreotype. Though Molard could never have seen it, this coincidence nevertheless emphasizes the interest of photographers in scenes from daily life.
11. Ernest Lacan, "La photographie de genre, épreuves de M. Moulin," *La Lumière* (August 20, 1853): 135.
12. That is, the Leiden painter Gerard Dou (1613–75).
13. Charles Nègre, "Écoles flamandes et hollandaises, Rembrandt, Ruisdael, Hobbema, etc...," *La Lumière* (December 16, 1854): 200–201. The sale took place on December 11, 1854. It included in particular the portrait of the Burgomaster Six by Rembrandt, now in Amsterdam. A recent piece of first-rate academic research has been devoted to pictorial criticism in the pages of *La Lumière*. Awarded the Roland-Barthes Prize in 2010, we sincerely hope it will soon benefit from publication: Ève Le Paon, "La Critique picturale dans *La Lumière*," under the general editorship of Barthélémy Jobert (research paper, Paris–IV – Sorbonne, September 2008).
14. "Ethnology" as a term and as an object of study appeared in French at the end of the eighteenth century; the adjective "ethnological," like the Anglicism "folklore," became current by the late 1840s.
15. Posthumous inventory undertaken on June 8, 1866 (Minutier des Notaires, Paris). My gratitude goes to Marc Durand, researcher and archivist at the French National Archives, for his invaluable assistance.
16. On this subject, see work by Françoise Tétart-Vittu, particularly her contribution to the symposium "Regarder Gérôme," held at the Musée d'Orsay, December 9 and 10, 2010, "De l'atelier à la collection d'armes et de costumes, le peintre antiquaire."
17. Quoted by Sophie Harent, *Dessins de Jean-Léon Gérôme* (Paris: Somogy, 2009), 38.
18. Théophile Gautier, *L'Artiste* (July 5, 1857): 248.
19. A very curious group of plates—formerly gathered into an album and including sometimes colored photographs cut out and tipped in—shows staged scenes of torture and martyrdom inspired by paintings. Known since the beginning of the 1990s by the title *Obsession*, a great deal concerning this collection remains shrouded in mystery. At the crossroads between family album and genre scene, the uniqueness of these images makes them all the more intriguing. Their origin and date have proved difficult to pin down. See Dominique de Font-Réaulx, "Une obsession photographique, digression autour d'une acquisition de la collection de photographies du musée d'Orsay," *48/14, La Revue du Musée d'Orsay* 28 (Spring 2009).
20. See Vouilloux, *Le Tableau vivant*. See also the paper on mime and the theory of physiognomy by Martial Guédron, "De la figure humaine comme 'tableau vivant,' mimiques, genres et postures dans les théories physiognomoniques (XVIIIe–XIXe siècle)" (paper presented at the seminar "Le Tableau vivant ou l'image performée," organized by Julie Ramos and Léonard Pouy, INHA, Paris, January 10, 2012).
21. *Photographic Journal* (February 1, 1859): 35.
22. On the ambiguity between an observed East and an imagined Orient, see especially Dominique de Font-Réaulx, "Le désir de faire vrai, Gérôme et la photographie," and Sophie Makariou and Charlotte Maury, "Le paradoxe du réalisme, Gérôme en Orient," *Jean-Léon Gérôme* (Paris: Skira-Flammarion, 2010), 212–21 and 257–65.
23. Michel Poivert, "L'hypothèse du tableau volé, une utopie photographique," *Olympe Aguado photographe (1827–1894)* (Strasbourg: Musées de Strasbourg, 1997), 170–72.
24. Pliny, XXXV, 43.12.
25. See Quentin Bajac, *Tableaux vivants. Fantaisies photographiques victoriennes*; Diane Waggoner, ed., *The Pre-Raphaelite Lens: British Photography and Painting, 1848–1875* (Washington: The National Gallery, 2010).
26. Ford, *Julia Margaret Cameron*.

PHOTOGRAPHING THE NUDE
THE AMBIGUITIES OF A GENRE

1. My italics. See Cars, Font-Réaulx, and Papet, Introduction, *Jean-Léon Gérôme, l'histoire en spectacle*, 18. See also "*La Vérité sortant du puits armée de son martinet pour châtier l'humanité,* de Jean-Léon Gérôme, Allégorie réaliste des quarante dernières années de la vie artistique du peintre," in *La Vérité nue*, exh. cat., Musée Anne-de-Beaujeu, Moulins (Moulins: 2012), 38–47.
2. Mérot, *Les Conférences de l'Académie royale de peinture et de sculpture au XVIIe siècle*, 267.
3. Claude-Henri Watelet and Pierre-Charles Levesque, *Dictionnaire des arts de peinture, sculpture et gravure* (Paris: 1788–91, reissued Geneva: Slatkine, 1972), vol. 1: 1–2. On the issues surrounding art teaching using models, see Emmanuel Schwartz, "L'École des Beaux-Arts au XIXe siècle et l'enseignement 'd'après le modèle,'" in Aubenas et al., *L'Art du nu au XIXe siècle, le photographe et son modèle*, 12–23, and Comar, *Figures du corps*.
4. Cesare Ripa, *Iconologie des principales choses qui peuvent tomber dans la pensée*, trans. Jean de Baudouin (Paris: c. 1600), 195–96.
5. Pliny the Elder, *Histoire naturelle*, 352.
6. See Vouilloux, *Le tableau vivant*; Édouard Papet, "Phryné au XIXe siècle: la plus jolie femme de Paris?" in *Praxitèle*, exh. cat. (Paris: Musée du Louvre, 2007), 362–79.
7. Pliny the Elder, "On Precious Stones," *Histoire naturelle*, 369. Praxiteles' original is lost, but numerous Roman copies of the *Aphrodite of Cnidos* survive, including a superb example in the Louvre.
8. See Michel, *Le Beau idéal*.
9. Cited by Aubenas et al. in *L'Art du nu au XIXe siècle*, back cover.
10. The pioneering study is the article by Sylviane de Decker-Heftler, "Le nu photographique, art impur, art réaliste," *Photographies* 6 (December 1984). One should add the exhibition catalog mentioned in note 9 (*L'Art du nu*), as well as Nazarieff, *Early Erotic Photography*, and the book devoted exclusively to the daguerreotype by Adam, *Die erotische Daguerreotypie*.
11. Sylvie Aubenas, "Le nu académique existe-t-il en daguerreotype?" in Aubenas et al., *L'Art du nu au XIXe siècle*, 24–29.
12. Xavier Demange, "Nu et nudité: le nu devant la loi," in Aubenas et al., *L'Art du nu au XIXe siècle*, 38–41.
13. Jean M. Goulemot, "Des mots et des images: l'illustration du livre pornographique. Le cas de Thérèse philosophe," in "Erotisme et pornographie," *Revue de la Bibliothèque nationale de France* 7 (January 2001): 28–33.
14. Barthes, *La Chambre claire*.
15. *Traité de photographie. Derniers perfectionnements apportés au daguerréotype* (Paris and London: 1843), 86.
16. Dated September 17, 1850: Delacroix, *Journal* (Paris: Plon, 1996), 268. This is the painter and ceramist Jules Ziegler, a pupil of Ingres, an amateur photographer and friend of the photographer Hippolyte Bayard, who took pictures of him in his garden.
17. Bataille, *Les Larmes d'Eros*, 43.
18. Paul Dolfuss, *Modèles d'artistes* (Paris: Marpon and Flammarion, 1889), 173. Dolfuss here rehashes the well-worn cliché about the relationships between painter and model that—with their customary tartness—the Goncourt brothers had already addressed in *Manette Solomon*, surely the novel that presents the most realistic vision of life in a mid-nineteenth-century art studio.
19. Archives of the Préfecture de Police, Paris (Register BB3).
20. These photographs were lodged by Moulin on September 29, 1852, with the numbers 3465 and 3466; the first showed "two naked women from the back" and has never been recovered.
21. One abiding reference to unclothed women in the artist's studio again derives from Dutch painting, since Rembrandt drew or engraved posed naked models on several occasions.
22. Félix Ravaisson, *De l'enseignement du dessin dans les lycées, rapport du 28 décembre 1853* (Paris: Imprimerie P. Dupont, 1855). The committee assembled by Ravaisson included the sculptor Pierre-Charles Simart, the painters François Édouard Picot, Hippolyte Flandrin, and Eugène Delacroix, as well as the director of the porcelain factory at Sèvres, Alexandre Brongniart. Though Ingres' presence had been solicited, he declined the invitation, citing exhaustion owing to overwork.

23. Of Italian origin, the photographer settled in Paris in 1868, on rue des Beaux-Arts. He took over the workshop of Auguste Belloc, retailing some of his photos under his own name. Marconi took numerous nudes, photographing men, women, and children in poses often inspired by the classical style, in keeping with the teaching he falsely claimed to have received in his advertising.
24. Alexis Gaudin, "Société photographique," *La Lumière* (December 10, 1853): 1.
25. Théodore Chassériau's *Sleeping Nymph*, painted in 1840, already displays the subject's body hair (Musée Calvet, Avignon).
26. At the 1853 Salon, Courbet presented three canvases: *The Sleeping Spinner* (Musée Fabre, Montpellier) and, as was his avowed intent, two remarkable large pictures of nudes—one female, *The Bathers,* and the other male, *The Wrestlers* (Szépmüvészeti Múzeum, Budapest). Sylvie Aubenas (Aubenas et al., *L'Art du nu au XIXe siècle*) shows how easy it was for models to move from one workshop to another; the way models might be passed from a studio belonging to a painter to one belonging to a photographer furthered the exchange of ideas and forged connections.
27. Letter dated November–December 1854, in Ten-Doesschate Chu, *Correspondance de Courbet*, letter 54-7: 119–20.
28. See Dominique de Font-Réaulx, "Courbet et la photographie : l'exemple d'un peintre réaliste, entre vérité et réalité" in Aubenas et al., *L'art du nu au XIX*e *siècle*, 84–91, and "La tradition transgressée, les nus de Gustave Courbet," in Cars and Font-Réaulx, *Gustave Courbet (1819–1877)* (Paris: RMN, 2007), 337–39.
29. Archives of the Préfecture de Police, Paris (Register BB3). "1,200 obscene cardboard-mounted photographs; a number of boxes in the shape of books bearing the title *Oeuvres complètes de Buffon*; 3,000 obscene photographs on paper; 307 negatives used for the production of the aforementioned obscene photographs; four albums containing a certain number of photographs representing naked women; 102 photographs on paper (large format) representing naked women in licentious positions." In the 1860s, twenty-six of these photographs were deposited in the "Enfer" (the "Special Collections") of the Cabinet of Prints in the Imperial Library. If hundreds of other photographs have disappeared, been destroyed or else purloined by police officers, the Buffon bindings have survived as proof of provenance.
30. A singularly transgressive group entered the collections of the Musée d'Orsay in the early 1990s in the shape of an extremely curious album by Charles Jeandel. Following some banal family snapshots, the album goes on to present images taken in a painter's studio in which naked women are shown tied up and forced to adopt complicated and uncomfortable poses. Enhanced by being printed as cyanotypes, these photographs remain enigmatic. See Hélène Pinet, "Les Photographies de Charles Jeandel, un si funeste désir," *48/14, La Revue du Musée d'Orsay* 16 (Spring 2003): 84–93.
31. The catalog of the exhibition organized by Christophe Leribault in 2008 at the Musée Delacroix in Paris, Christophe Leribault, ed., *Delacroix et la photographie* provides remarkable information concerning the diverse aspects of the painter's relationship to photography.
32. See p. 151 of the present volume.
33. Eugène Delacroix, *Journal*, vol. 1: 548.
34. See Sylvie Aubenas, "Les albums de nus d'Eugène Delacroix," in Leribault, ed., *Delacroix et la photographie*, 22–51.
35. Another album, containing forty or so photographs, some by Durieu, has been discovered in a private collection. It demonstrates the scope of Delacroix's photograph collection. Research undertaken by Fiona Le Boucher has identified a number of these pictures, which in all probability belonged to the painter—in particular photos by Julien Vallou de Villeneuve and Louis-Camille d'Olivier.
36. Delacroix, *Journal*, October 12, 1853: 686.
37. Ibid., 689.
38. See the chapter Reproducing Paintings in the present volume and ills. 52–53.
39. See Papet, "Phryné au XIXe siècle, n. 5, and "Phryné devant l'Aréopage," in Cars, Font-Réaulx, and Papet, eds., *Jean-Léon Gérôme*, 104–5, cat. 45.
40. Zola, "Nos peintres au Champ de Mars," *Écrits sur l'art*, 184.
41. Georges Janniot, "Souvenirs sur Degas," *La Revue universelle* 14 (October 15–November 1, 1933): 172.
42. See Dominique de Font-Réaulx, "Étude de nu pour la Phryné de Jean-Léon Gérôme," in Cars, Font-Réaulx, and Papet, eds., *Jean-Léon Gérôme*, 108, cat. 46.
43. An ensemble of three different garments, Greek attire could not in fact have been removed in a single gesture in the manner implied. Here dramatic impact takes precedence over exactitude.
44. The fact that the painter chose to send two successive versions to the Salons 1895 and 1896 speaks volumes as to their importance in his eyes.
45. Charles Moreau-Vauthier, *Gérôme, peintre et sculpteur, l'homme et l'artiste d'après sa correspondance* (Paris: Hachette, 1906), 6.
46. Auvray, *Exposition des beaux-arts, Salon de 1869*, 56. Auvray, who was close to Gérôme, was in 1869 still classifying Courbet among the "strays," together with Manet, James Tissot, and Gustave Moreau.
47. The italics are mine. See note 1 of this chapter.
48. Catherine Mathon, cat. 152, 153, and 154, in Comar, *Figures du corps.*
49. On Marey and his devices, see the groundbreaking analysis by Mannoni, *Étienne-Jules Marey, la mémoire de l'oeil.*
50. Marta Braun, "Muybridge le magnifique," *Études photographiques* 10 (November 2011): 24–49.

STUDIES AFTER NATURE
PHOTOGRAPHY IN THE PAINTER'S STUDIO

1. Louis Jourdan, "Préface," in Rousset, *Études photographiques,* 4. Part of this text is printed in the anthology at the end of the present volume, p. 318.
2. Molière, *La Critique de l'École des femmes* (Paris: Gallimard, "Bibliothèque de la Pléiade," vol. 1, 1956), 541.
3. Pierre-Henri de Valenciennes, "Etudes d'après nature," *Élémen[t]s de perspective pratique à l'usage des artistes (*Paris, 1799), 293.
4. Charles-Alphonse Dufresnoy, "XIX. Qu'il ne faut pas trop s'attacher à la Nature mais l'accommoder à son Génie," *L'Art de peindre,* ed. Roger de Piles and Charles-Antoine Jombert (Paris, 1751), 30–31.
5. Charles Gabet, *Dictionnaire des artistes de l'école française du XIX*e *siècle* (Paris: Librairie Vergne, 1831).
6. "Ordonnance du Roi qui règle les travaux et les obligations des élèves Graveurs qui sont envoyés à l'École de France de Rome après avoir remporté les premiers grands prix," *Bulletin des Lois* 253 (August 30, 1828): 257–58.
7. Gérard Lévy Collection, Paris.
8. Archives Nationales, Paris, F17 2935 B.
9. The whole group was bequeathed to the Musée Bartholdi in Colmar, where both the prints and negatives are still held.
10. Théophile Gautier, "Gérôme, tableaux et études, et croquis de voyage," *L'Artiste* 3 (1856): 34. Paul de Saint-Victor, "Salon de 1857," *La Presse* (July 11, 1857): 3
11. See the chapter Reproducing Painting. Blanquart-Évrard's activities have been thoroughly examined by Isabelle Jammes in *Blanquart-Évrard et les origines de l'édition photographique.*
12. Jourdan, "Préface," *Études photographiques*, 1.
13. Both photographs are albumen prints now in the Musée d'Orsay, with the inventory numbers PHO 1982 62 30 and PHO 1982 62 31.
14. The subject is addressed in our chapter Reproducing Painting. For Goupil and photography, reference may be made to Pierre-Lin Renié's enlightening books and articles.
15. Monique Le Pelley Fonteny has devoted a remarkable volume to an inventory of all the photographs published by Giraudon: *Adolphe et Georges Giraudon*. The department Cher has acquired Giraudon's original stock for its archives. In the aforementioned work, see the introduction by Catherine Mathon and Hélène Pinet on photograph publishers, "Les éditeurs-photographes," 12–17.
16. See the chapter devoted to the nude in photography in the present volume.
17. Le Pelley Fonteny, *Adolphe et Georges Giraudon*, 27.
18. See also the excellently documented and illustrated sale catalog by Ken and Jenny Jacobson, *Étude d'après nature.*
19. Over the years some collections belonging to painters have unfortunately been dispersed; thus, several years ago,

a very fine album having once belonged to the brothers Hippolyte and Paul Flandrin was sold on the Paris market and regrettably dismembered. It contained in particular several splendid prints of trees by Émile Pécarrère.

20. Georges Vigne, "À propos de daguerréotypes de Millet récemment retrouvés: quatre tableaux d'Ingres revisités," *Bulletin du Musée Ingres* 63664 (1991): 56–63; Anne de Mondenard, "Du bon usage de la photographie," *Ingres* (Paris: Musée du Louvre/Gallimard), 2006; Leribault, *Delacroix et la photographie*; Daniel and Aubenas, eds., *Edgar Degas, photographer*; Kendall and DeVonyar, *Degas and the Ballet*; Baldassari, *Le Miroir noir*; Elizabeth C. Childs, "Paradise Redux: Gauguin, Photography, and Fin-de-Siècle Tahiti," *The Artist and the Camera, Degas to Picasso*, ed. Dorothy Kosinski, 119–141; and Childs, *In Search of Paradise Painting and Photography in Fin de siècle Tahiti*. A proportion of Gustave Moreau's collection of photographs is accessible on the Joconde website hosted by the French Ministry of Culture; the collection of photographs at the Musée d'Orsay is accessible on the museum website, under the heading "Collections."

21. Eugène Delacroix, *The Journal of Eugène Delacroix*, 224, and Christophe Leribault and Fiona Le Boucher, "De Raphaël à Delacroix, l'artiste face aux reproductions photographiques," *Delacroix et la photographie*, ed. Christophe Leribault, 108–19.

22. Delacroix, *Journal*, 1: 689.

23. In 1850, Delacroix thus observed (ibid.): "The monstrosities it [the daguerreotype] presents rightly shock one, although they are literally those of nature herself; but the imperfections the machine reproduces so faithfully do not strike our eye when we look at the model without such an intermediary; for, unbeknownst to us, our eye corrects the unwelcome inaccuracies of strict perspective [and] already performs the work of an intelligent artist."

24. Douglas W. Druick and Peter Zegers, "Le Kampong et la Pagode Gauguin à l'Exposition universelle de 1889," *Actes de colloques Gauguin* (Paris: École du Louvre/Musée d'Orsay, 1991), 101–42.

25. A substantial proportion of the photographs taken by Paul-Émile Miot during various campaigns for the French Navy are now held in the Musée du Quai Branly, Paris.

26. Philippe Peltier, "Gauguin et Tahiti," *Art tribal 3* (Summer–Autumn 2003): 56–73.

27. See the chapter Painter Photographers in the present volume.

28. Cartier-Bresson, *Éloge du négatif*.

29. Thomas Galifot, conservator at the Musée d'Orsay, dedicated an exhibition, unfortunately with no catalog, to Théophile Chauvel's collection (Musée d'Orsay, Paris, May 7–November 8, 2010).

30. Sale Sotheby's New York, April 13, 2007.

31. William B. Siegert, "Whistler and John Chandler Bancroft," *The Burlington Magazine* 136 (October 1994): 675–82. See also *In the Forest of Fontainebleau: Painters and Photographers from Corot to Monet*, exh. cat. (Washington: National Gallery of Washington, 2008).

32. In this sense, studies of collections of photographs owned by painters might be examined in the context of the many nineteenth-century literary works concerned with artists' studios that show how interested their contemporaries were in their working methods. See on this subject Hamon, *Imageries*, in particular chapter 3 on image-making in the artist's workshop: "La fabrique de l'image: l'atelier."

33. Albert Londe, "Appareil photo-électrique," *Bulletin de la Société française de photographie* (May 4, 1883).

34. Comar, "Désordres comportementaux," *Figures du corps*, 380–93. Georges Didi-Huberman, *Invention de l'hystérie*.

35. Rodolphe Rapetti, *Le Symbolisme* (Paris: Skira-Flammarion, 2006).

36. François Thiébault-Sisson, "Degas sculpteur par lui-même," *Le Temps* (May 23, 1921), 3. See Kendall and DeVonyar, *Degas and the Ballet*.

37. Degas' photographic output is addressed in the chapter Painter Photographers. For Degas' own collections, see *The Private Collection of Edgar Degas*, exh. cat., (New York: The Metropolitan Museum of Art, 1997).

38. In Germany, the painter Ottomar Anschütz also developed a photographic process designed to record animal motion. An art photographer by training, his photographs were sold in France by Giraudon. Théophile Chauvel acquired several that are now held by the Musée d'Orsay. The photographic collections of the Kunst Akademie, Berlin, also contain several prints by Anschütz.

PAINTER PHOTOGRAPHERS

1. Ernest Lacan, "Le Photographe, esquisse physiologique. III. Du Photographe artiste," *La Lumière* (January 8, 1853): 11.

2. Paul-Louis Roubert, "Les fonds de la distinction. Le financement des sociétés photographiques du XIXe siècle," *Études photographiques* 24 (November 2009): 18–41.

3. A number have already been the subject of specialized studies; see for instance: Barilli, *L'ultimo Michetti, Pittura e Fotografia*; Roseboom, *George Hendrik Breitner*; Gaillemin, *Alfons Mucha*; Michèle Chomette, *José Maria Sert (1874–1945), L'Envers du décor—un peintre à l'épreuve de la photographie* (Paris: Galerie Michèle Chomette, 2012); Marquet, *Derain et la photographie*. See also Heilbrun, *A History of Photography. Photography at the Musée d'Orsay*.

4. The lion's share of this collection was acquired by the Musée d'Orsay in 2006, thanks in particular to the generosity of Edmond's great-grandson, Vincent Lebel. It would reward more exhaustive study; an exhibition or monograph, for instance. It would be particularly interesting to relate this body of work to Léon Cogniet—his teacher, godfather, and stalwart of the Société Photographique created by Louis Camille d'Olivier. Ongoing research undertaken by Marisa Defonte at the École du Louvre under the direction of Dominique Jarassé and the present author will doubtless cast some much-needed light on this aspect.

5. These were the following: "Three male models posing for the Pavilion of Bosnia-Herzegovina" (PHO 1979 77), "Girl at prayer, model for the Pavilion of Bosnia-Herzegovina" (PHO 1979 78), "Model kneeling in Mucha's studio" (PHO 1979 79), and "Model posing for the program for the Exposition Universelle of 1900" (PHO 1979 80). They numbered among the first photographs to be inventoried in a museum collection which, for the first time in France, treats photography as one of the fine arts, on a par with painting, sculpture, and architecture. Moreover, they had hardly entered the collection before they were presented at an exhibition of Mucha's work that raised the curtain on the future museum devoted to the second half of the nineteenth century. Its curators thereby celebrated an artist whose work in painting and line—his posters especially—was then extremely popular, late 1970s art lovers being particularly receptive to the sinuous female figures in his vast, colorful compositions, the fruit of close observation of reality, combined with a fertile imagination. Beyond this, to dedicate such an event to an artist who could be at once a painter, illustrator, decorator, and photographer offered the museum's conservators a heaven-sent opportunity to stress the notion of interdisciplinarity, one of the keystones of the Musée d'Orsay's philosophy. Thus it was that at an early stage, more than six years before the museum even opened in the station erected by Victor Laloux (a contemporary building of Mucha's vast decors for the 1900 World's Fair), Mucha revealed himself to a novice audience—ignorant perhaps of photography in the nineteenth century generally—as a photographer. See Laclotte, ed., *Mucha, 1860–1939*.

6. The earliest surviving photographs date from his time in Munich, in 1886.

7. He possessed several cameras, keeping a 12 × 9 and an 18 × 13 from the mid-1890s; he printed from the glass plates himself, without enlarging.

8. Quite apart from taking pictures to serve as an aid to composing his paintings, Alfons Mucha was also an amateur photographer, on several occasions taking shots of painter friends with whom he lodged on Rue de la Grande Chaumière in 1895. The prints testify to his close relations with some of them, with Gauguin in particular, whom he photographed on several occasions, in his underpants at the piano, or in fancy dress in the company of Mucha himself, with his friend, the

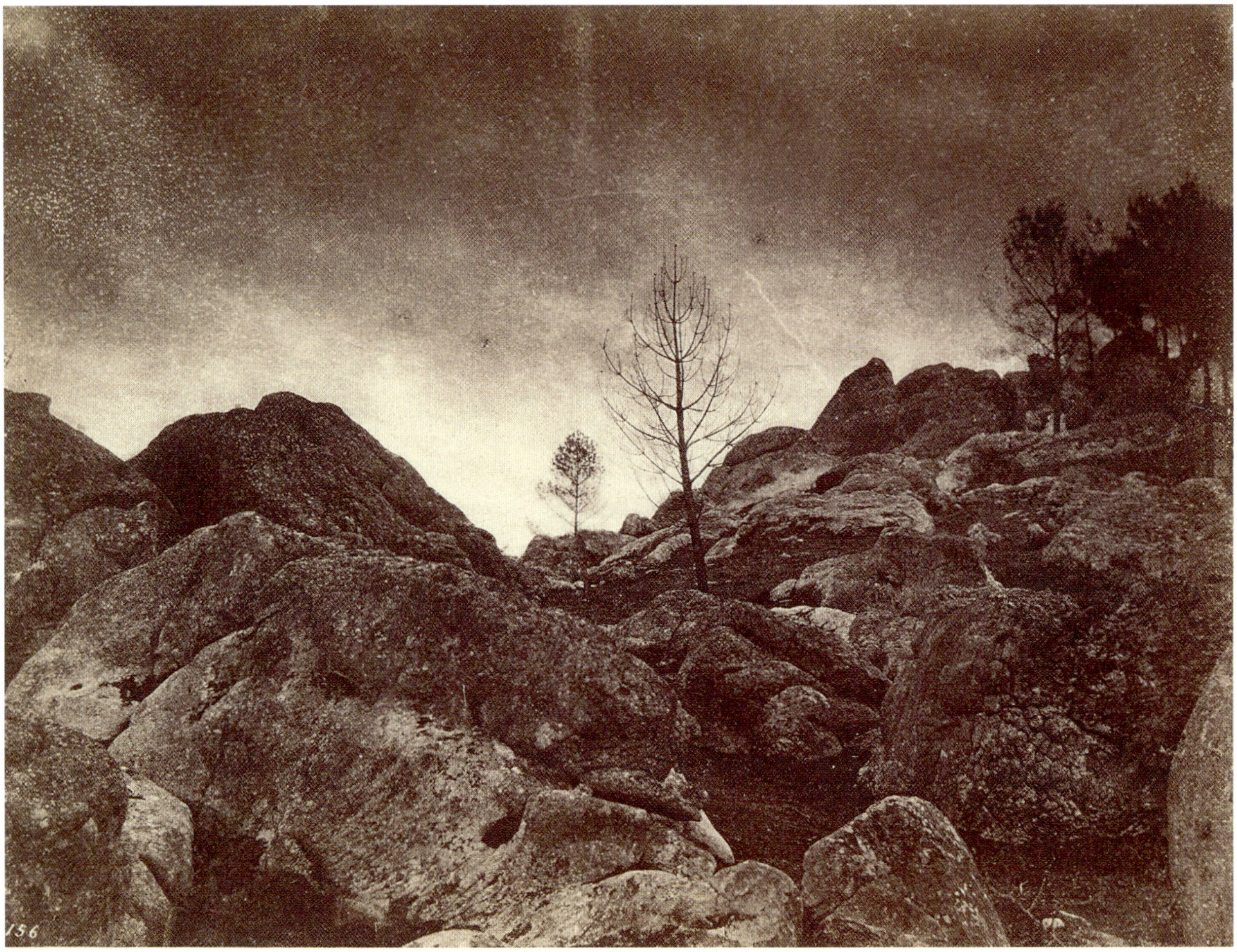

231. Eugène Cuvelier, "The Forest of Fontainebleau, Storm," 1860, salt print, Musée d'Orsay, Paris.

painter Ludek Marold, or with Gauguin's then partner, "Annah la Javanaise." The freedom of the models' attitudes and their extempore costumes capture the joyous atmosphere that must have reigned in the studio and show how perfectly at home Mucha had become in the Paris art scene. Amusing and touchingly homely, they seem to have been taken with no specific intention in mind.
9. Alfons Mucha, *Girl Kneeling*, 1900, modern print from a glass negative, Mucha Archives; a print from this plate is conserved in the Musée d'Orsay.
10. Alfons Mucha, *Lectures on Art* (London: Academy Editions; New York: St. Martin's Press, 1975), 47.
11. Ibid., 49.
12. Chomette, *L'Art de la fresque de José-Maria Sert, 1874–1945: photographies inédites*, and Lacave et al., *José-Maria Sert, Un Titan à l'œuvre (1874–1945)*, exh. cat. (Paris: Éditions Paris Musées, 2012).
13. Chomette, "Communiqué de presse," *Sert, L'envers du décor.*
14. Barilli et al., *L'ultimo Michetti, Pittura et Fotografia*.
15. Marquet, *Derain et la photographie*, 29.
16. Quoted in Marquet, *Derain et la photographie*, 18.
17. The Italian painter Federico Zandomeneghi wrote to his compatriot Diego Morelli that Degas had taken four portraits of him the previous winter. These portraits have never been found. Concerning Degas and photography, see Daniel and Aubenas, eds., *Edgar Degas, Photographer* (New York: The Metropolitan Museum of Art, 1998).
18. Daniel Halévy, *Degas parle*, ed. Jean-Pierre Halévy (Paris: La Palatine éd., 1960; new ed. Paris: Editions de Fallois, 1996). Loyrette, *Degas*.
19. According to the surviving evidence, when Degas exhibited his photographs at Tasset's it was apparently less a public exhibition than an opportunity for the painter's close family and his friends to see them. See on this subject Théodore Reff, "Degas chez Tasset," in Daniel and Aubenas, *Edgar Degas, photographer*, 74–79.
20. Eugenia Parry Janis, "Edgar Degas' Photographic Theater," in Daniel, ed., *Edgar Degas, Photographer*, 52–73.
21. Bruno Gaudichon and Anne Pingeot, *Degas sculpteur* (Paris: Gallimard, 2011).
22. Hoogue, *Autour du symbolisme*, Françoise Heilbrun, "*Le Secret* de Fernand Khnopff, acquisition de deux photographies," *48/14, La revue du musée d'Orsay* 20 (Spring 2005).
23. George Rodenbach, *Bruges-la-Morte* (Paris: Flammarion, 1892). See Edwards, *Soleil noir*.
24. The book published under the general editorship of Elizabeth Easton deals with the links between pictorial creation and photographic practice among some of these artists (Easton, *Snapshot*).
25. Guy Cogeval, ed., *Édouard Vuillard*; Easton, *Snapshot*. We ourselves have classified and inventoried the photographs by Édouard Vuillard conserved in the family archives, under the direction of Guy Cogeval, during preparations for the catalogue raisonné of his work by Guy Cogeval and assisted by Mathias Chivot, published in 2003 by the Wildenstein Institute.
26. Édouard Vuillard's *Journal*, conserved at the library in the Institut de France, is presently being edited by Guy Cogeval and Thomas Schlesser.
27. Annette Vaillant, "Les photographies d'Édouard Vuillard," *L'Oeil* (April 1963). Annette Vaillant was the daughter of Alfred Natanson, one of the founders—with his brothers Thadée and Alexandre—of *La Revue blanche*. Thadée, Misia Godebska's first husband, Alfred, and Alexandre were all close friends of Vuillard's.
28. Guy Cogeval, "Le célibataire mis à nu par son théâtre, même," in *Vuillard*, 105–35. As Guy Cogeval writes, "Vuillard would provoke what he wanted to paint." This must also have been the case when he took photographs.
29. Fossier, *La Nébuleuse nabie*.
30. André Chastel, "Au-devant de Vuillard," *Vuillard*, exh. cat. (Lyon: Musée des Beaux-Arts; Paris: Flammarion, 1991), 15–51.
31. Marcel Proust, *Le Temps retrouvé* (Paris: Gallimard, 1972), 895. Translation from, Marcel Proust, *Remembrance of Things Past*, trans. C. K. Scott Moncrieff and T. Kilmartin, vol. 3, *The Captive, The Fugitive*, and *Time Regained* (New York: Vintage, 1982), 931.
32. Aumont, *L'Attrait de la lumière*, 39.
33. Heilbrun and Néagu, *Pierre Bonnard photographe* (Paris: Réunion des Musées Nationaux/Philippe Sers éditeur/Vilo, 1987). The accession of more than 400 negatives and photographs into French public collections accompanied the renewed interest for the Nabis painters and their circle in general, sparked by the opening of a French museum dedicated to the art of the latter half of the nineteenth century.
34. The photographs must have provided material for the lithographs drawn by Bonnard for the edition of *Daphnis and Chloe*, a paragon since antiquity of eternal love, published in 1902 by Ambroise Vollard.
35. Investigations undertaken recently by Clément Chéroux on photographs by Edvard Munch has paved the way to such an approach; see Chéroux and Lampe, *Edvard Munch, l'oeil moderne*. It should encourage further studies on the photographic output of painters and, in particular, to resume and expand research started on the photographs of Maurice Denis (a painter who also belonged, like Vuillard and Bonnard, to the Nabis brotherhood), which are now conserved, thanks to the generosity of the painter's heirs, in the Musée d'Orsay. Similarly, an exhibition dedicated to the photographs of the Dutch painter George Hendrik Breitner, conserved at Rijksmuseum, Amsterdam, "George Hendrik Breitner (1857–1923), pioneer of street photography," which took place at the Institut Néerlandais in Paris in autumn 2011, has created a line of inquiry that would reward further investigation. Then there is the travel album of the painter Henri Evenepoel containing photographs taken in the late 1890s in Algeria and now held in the Musée d'Orsay, which would benefit from more thorough examination.
These are just a few of the dozens of paths that are bound to open up in the future, thanks to the ongoing interest in photography by established painters. Such studies will surely cast a new light on many of the observations made in the present volume.
The selection made here is in the nature of a preliminary exercise; it is subjective and does not aspire to cover the full range of the studies undertaken over the last few years on photography by painters of the second half of the nineteenth century.
One might cite the study of the photographs by the American painter Thomas Eakins (1844–1916), a more recent approach dealing with his compatriot Frederic Edwin Church (1826–1900), and the analysis being undertaken in Berlin around photographs by the painter Heinrich Zille (1858–1929), as well as the photographic prints now in a private collection in Paris by the Austrian painter Carl Rudolph Huber (1839–96).
It is to be hoped that each of these corpus will benefit from a specific study; an overview covering the totality would struggle to classify and individualize them.

ANTHOLOGY

Jacques Louis Mandé Daguerre
ADVERTISEMENT FOR THE DAGUERREOTYPE
1838

The discovery I announce to the public is one of the few which, by their principles, their results, and the positive influence they are bound to exert on the arts, surely number among the most useful and extraordinary inventions.

It consists in the spontaneous reproduction of images of nature received in the camera obscura, not with their colors, but with wonderful finesse in gradation of tone.

It was M. Nicéphore NIÉPCE, of Châlon-sur-Saône, already well-known for his love of art, for his many and useful inventions, and for his sudden and unexpected death that stole him away from his family and from science on July 5, 1833, who unearthed, after long years of research and relentless toil, the principles behind this significant discovery: he had managed, after countless and infinitely diverse experiments, to obtain an image of nature using an ordinary camera obscura; but his apparatus, failing to achieve the clarity necessary, and the substances with which he operated not being sensitive enough to the light, his efforts, though surprising in their results, remained nevertheless in abeyance.

For my part, I had already been dealing in similar researches. It was in these circumstances, in 1828, that relations were established between M. NIÉPCE and myself, in consequence of which we formed a company with the aim of cooperating on the improvement of the discovery.

I brought to the firm a camera obscura I had modified for the purpose, and which, extending greater clarity to a larger zone of the image field, did much to advance our subsequent success. Certain significant modifications I afforded the process, joined to the unflagging researches of M. NIÉPCE, held the promise of a happy outcome, when death separated me from a man whose vast and profound knowledge was combined with every quality of heart; may I be permitted here to pay to his memory, which will ever remain dear to me, due tribute of esteem and regret.

Appreciably affected by this loss, I temporarily forsook our endeavors; but soon, further prosecuting it with ardor, I attained the goal we had set ourselves.

This seemingly gratifying result still did not, however, render the effects of nature with sufficient exactitude, because the operation had to remain subjected to the action of light for several hours.

Even in this state, the discovery was still extraordinary, but it harbored little promise of any great utility.

I knew that the only means of succeeding completely was to attain a rapidity such that it could produce the same effects in space of a few minutes, so that the natural shadows would not have enough time to change, and to render the process less arduous.

It is the resolution of this principle that I announce today; this other process, whose basis is entirely different and to which I gave my name, calling it the *DAGUERREOTYPE*, is, in terms of speed, clarity of image, nuance of tone, and, especially, perfection of detail, far superior to the one invented by M. NIÉPCE, despite all the improvements I had brought to it, since, as a comparison, the difference in sensitivity to light is 1 to 70, and compared to the substance known by the name "cerargyrite," it is 1 to 120.

In its present state, to acquire a perfect image of nature necessitates but a short space of time amounting to some three to thirty minutes at most, according to the season in which one operates and the greater or lesser intensity of the light.

The imprint of nature would be reproduced far more promptly in lands where the light is stronger than in Paris, such as Spain, Italy, Africa, etc., etc.

Employing this process—with no acquaintance with drawing and no inkling of chemistry or physics—anyone is able, in a matter of minutes, to take the most detailed vistas, the most picturesque sites, since its means of execution are simple and call for no special knowledge in their application; one needs only care and a little familiarity to succeed perfectly.

Using the DAGUERREOTYPE, everyone will be able to take views of their chateau or country house: one will be able to assemble collections of all kinds, all the more precious as art cannot vie with them in terms of exactitude and in perfection of detail, and they now have been made light-fast; one will even be able to take portraits: in this admittedly the mobility of the model presents a stumbling-block to complete success.

Suited to every application, this groundbreaking advance will not only be of immense interest to science, it will also provide fresh impetus to the arts, and far from harming those who practice them, it will prove of great utility.

Society people will find it a most diverting occupation; and though the result is obtained using chemical means, it is a little pastime that is sure to appeal greatly to the ladies.

Finally, the DAGUERREOTYPE is not an instrument used to draw nature, but a chemical and physical process that offers her a means of reproducing herself.

DAGUERRE,
Painter, inventor, and director of the Diorama.

Nota. On January 15, 1839, an Exhibition comprising some forty photographs [*épreuves*] recording the results of the DAGUERREOTYPE is to opened at the same time as a subscription, the conditions regarding which will be announced on this occasion.
Pollet, Soupe, and Guillois, Printers, rue Saint-Denis, 380.

Jules Janin
LE DAGUÉROTYPE [*SIC*]
(THE DAGUEROTYPE)
1839
L'Artiste—Journal de la littérature et des beaux-arts

And finally, we could see with our own eyes, touch with our own hands the incredible and admirable invention of Daguerre. It is not necessary to deal as we do with the details of the fine arts to have become acquainted with Daguerre. His name is popular throughout Europe; he started out as a skillful painter; but that art was not enough for him and he wanted to find something beyond painting. That something was the Diorama. Through the sheer power of an art that he ameliorated still further, Daguerre draws us deep into pictures that, prior to his efforts, were just surface. With him by your side, you entered ancient ruined churches; you climbed mountains, descended into dells; you traversed rivers and seas; this magician walked you though the most curious capital cities without your tiring; a man of talent if ever there was one, he played with all multifarious effects of light and color, controlling them as he liked, as if he were their sovereign lord. Presented with such novel spectacles, the public stood dumbfounded in amazement and admiration. And the painters said to each other: what a pity that Daguerre, that great artist, now busies himself making pictures more beautiful than any painting! Daguerre answered approval and reproach alike with a smile, for only he knew what he was aiming for. . . . You will now see to what mysterious goal such unremitting efforts led Daguerre. By dint of much study, this celebrated painter has managed to become a great chemist: he had doubtless observed that such and such a nuance, vigorous in the light of day, faded as the light faded, only to disappear completely. He knew, moreover, as we all do, about the action of the sun and light on color [pigment]. He thus proposed, with that keen perseverance called genius, a solution to the following conundrum: To find a color [pigment] so constituted that the sun, no, more, that the light alone would partially remove, while the other zone would resist and remain unchanged in its place; to force daylight to act on this shadow, as would the divine graver of some immaterial Morghen, and thus to cast, on a plain, dark plate, form and life; to force the sun—the eye of the world—to be no more than an ingenious workman engaged at the orders of a taskmaster! This is indisputably the strangest, most intractable, most incredible problem a man has set himself in recent times. For the difficulty—we do not say for the utility of the result—the inventor of the steam engine comes only second.

At the end of what incredible series of tests, trials, researches, and adventures of all sorts did the inventor of the Daguerotype achieve the result we are about to describe to you remains his secret. Later on, he will explain himself to all Europe, when France, the most liberal and disinterested nation in the world, presents this most noble gift to the continent.

Be that as it may, it could only have been through perseverance and genius, and after an infinite number of trials, that M. Daguerre arrived at the following result: he composed a certain black varnish; this varnish is spread on a certain type of plate; the plate is exposed to daylight, and at once—and whatever the shadow projected on this plate, land or sky, or running water, a cathedral lost in the clouds, or stonework or paving, the imperceptible grain of sand floating on the surface—all these things, large or small, all equal before the sun, are, that very instant, engraved in this kind of camera obscura that preserves their every imprint. Never did the draftsmanship of the greatest masters produce drawings like it. If the mass is admirable, the details are infinite. Just think: it is the sun itself—enlisted on this occasion as the all-powerful agency of a wholly new art—that produces this unbelievable prodigy. In this case, it is no longer the unreliable eye of man that searches out some distant shadow or light; is no longer his trembling hand that reproduces on shifting paper the changing scene of the world that is lost in the great void.

Now one no longer has to spend three days beneath the same point of the sky or land to come away with little more than a distorted shadow. The marvel occurs in an instant, as swift as thought, as fast as the sunbeam that strikes the far-off waterless mountaintop or the scarcely budding flower. There is that beautiful passage in the Bible. God says: *Let there be Light and there was Light.* At this hour, you might say to the towers of Notre Dame: come to rest there, and the towers will obey; and thus they obeyed Daguerre, who, one fine day, took them home, all of them, from the enormous stone on which they are founded to the slender and light spire they bear up into the air and that nobody had ever seen—save for Daguerre and the sun. . . .

Art can have no quarrel with this new rival. Note this well: there is no question here of some coarse mechanical invention that at most reproduces the masses without the shadows or details, the result being simply to save oneself a few hours of manual labor. No, what we have here is the most delicate, glorious, and complete reproduction to which the workings of God and the works of man could aspire. Observe once more that this reproduction is far from being even and uniform, as might be believed. On the contrary, not a single one carried out employing the same process resembles its predecessor; the hour of the day, the color of the sky, the limpidity of the air, the soft warmth of spring, the rugged austerity of winter, the fiery shades of autumn, the reflection of crystal waters, all the accidents of atmosphere are gloriously reproduced in these marvelous pictures which one would think conjured by the breath of an aerial genius. . . .

Now do I need to tell you of the endless applications of this immense discovery, which will perhaps prove to have been the glory of the century? The Daguerotype is destined to reproduce the most beautiful features of nature and of art, just as printing reproduces the masterpieces of the human mind. It is engraving in the reach of each and everyone; it is a pencil as pliant as thought; it is a mirror that records all that falls on it; it is a faithful memory of every monument, of every landscape in the universe; it is the ceaseless, spontaneous, tireless representation of the hundred thousand masterpieces that time has laid low or set up upon the surface of the globe.

The Daguerotype will be an essential companion for travelers who cannot draw and for artists who do not have the time to draw. It is destined to make available, in our homes and at low cost, the most beautiful works of art of which we can have at present only exorbitant and inaccurate copies; before long, and if one has no wish to act as one's own engraver, one will pack off one's offspring to the museum, telling him: "You've got three hours to fetch me a picture by Murillo or Raphael." People will write to Rome: Send me by the next mail the dome of Saint Peter's and the dome of Saint Peter's will be dispatched to you through the post. If you pass through Antwerp and admire Rubens's house, you could send your architect that unrivaled example of Flemish fancy: This, you will announce, is the house I want built; and, in this faithful drawing, the architect will discover one by one all the ornaments of a stone that became lace beneath the sculptor's chisel. Henceforth, the Daguerotype will suffice for all the needs of the arts, for all the whims of life. You will be able to take home—and without her even knowing—the white house in which your mistress hides. You will yourself take a copy of M. Ingres's splendid portrait in which M. Ingres reproduces the fine head of this noble writer who enjoys all the honors of the European press, and you will say: What does it matter to me that this portrait was not produced by engraving? I have something much better than an engraving, what I have is as good as a drawing by M. Ingres.

Francis Wey

DE L'INFLUENCE DE L'HÉLIOGRAPHIE SUR LES BEAUX-ARTS (ON THE INFLUENCE OF HELIOGRAPHY [PHOTOGRAPHY] ON THE FINE ARTS)

February 9, 1851

La Lumière

Some two months ago, one of the most skillful exponents of the new process of photography, M. Le Gray, sent the jury of the 1850 exposition nine photographs on paper, representing landscapes and portraits after the life and taken from pictures. Once the astonishing perfection of the results had been duly admired came the awkward task of classifying pieces worthy of being set side by side with the most accomplished works of art, but which were attained by a purely theoretical process, not related in any direct way to the practice of drawing. Arranged among the lithographs, the works of the skillful heliographer were referred to under this heading in the booklet to the current exhibition. . . .

The first judges had regarded them as works of art; the second classified them among the products of science. But a subcommission then intervened, which, considering the question from a different point of view, had M. Le Gray's drawings withdrawn.

Evidently, heliography derives from chemistry and physics; but, no less evidently, this discovery, improved as it is on a daily basis, is bound to have an immediate and significant impact on the realm of art.

At one time called upon to examine the most recent results obtained by studious, zealous, and most experienced gentlemen, we were struck dumb with astonishment. Photography is, up to a point, the link between the daguerreotype and art properly called. It seems that by moving over to paper, the mechanism has attained a level at which it can intelligently combine effects; it is simpler in execution, interprets nature, and adds to the reproduction of the planes and lines the expression of feeling and the facial features.

Indeed photography can now tackle a vast range of tones; from the fugitive and vaporous, yet still precise, indications of a breath of air, such as M. Vidal managed to capture it, to the violent and contrasting relief of Rembrant [*sic*], and to an intensity of tone that would defy every resources of engraving. Such is the flexibility of this instrument that it can address equally well the most antagonistic genres, the most diverse qualities, and even the most individual manners. In a series of landscapes and other subjects, we saw in turn works by Joyant and Piranesi, Decamps, Metzu, Corot, Ruysdael, and Marilhat hatch out fortuitously from the sole imagination of nature. It is as if—suddenly tractable—she actually enjoys paying homage to the many painters who have feted her so diversely. . . .

A consoling, bizarre fact! That consecrates more or less everything public opinion has over time seen fit to praise. Thus pure aesthetics can lose nothing by this challenge; it can in fact only gain in boldness, in experience, while the inferior layers of art, those whose doubtful triumphs depend on routine and manual procedures, and which limit themselves to sterile tradition, will be dissolved and destroyed. . . .

At root, what seems in fact to be being steadily eliminated is the tangible mark of manipulation, the artifice of the process, the complexity of the act.

Unless it vies with drawing or appears impressed by a powerful emanation of color, to our eyes engraving has become cold; the classic vigor of intaglio [*les tailles*] is being appreciated less and less; lithography, more immediately comparable to drawing in the normal sense, has progressed by leaps and bounds.

It is in these circumstances that heliography presents itself: what will it produce? Indisputably, some old genres will disappear; a revolution will take place, gradual, profound, and salutary like all revolutions worthy of the name. But is it already possible to gather some inkling of what the future holds? Undoubtedly it is.

Let us then in four brief words elucidate the final outcome: truly original artists, far from feeling threatened, will find in the new invention unforeseen resources and will prosper greatly. The *tradesmen, the mechanicals*, as people used to call them, will be crushed.

Photography *translates* brilliantly: to improve on its results, one has to be able to both translate *and* interpret. It [photography] is thus ideally suited to bringing out the personal qualities of draftsmen such as M. Desmaisons, who copies Vidal with such flair; M. Sonlanges-Tessier, who has, this very year, recalled Decamps with such suppleness of line; M. Mouilleron, the eagle of lithography, whose especial qualities allow him to assimilate the compositions he takes as his inspiration; M. Anbry-Lecomte, who delights by his charming dexterity, by the finesse and precision of his pencil, and M. Français, that most subtle commentator of our landscapists. This last can furnish us with a telling example. To choose just one, it is certain that photography would reproduce M. Corot's *Morning* with incomparable fidelity; but it could not complete the image, or interpret its spirit; it could not enlighten its poetic intention and add to it the impression of a personal and heartfelt reflection, as M. Français does in his lithograph.

Nevertheless, photography is eminently adaptable, especially as regards the reproduction of nature; sometimes it proceeds by masses, scorning detail as does a skillful master, [thereby] justifying the theory of sacrifice; and in some places it emphasizes form and in others tonal opposition. Such intelligence of the imagination is much less abundant in daguerreotypes on metal plates. And there is more: however material [daguerreotype] may seem, a photographer's personal tastes transpire in his work; photographs obtained by artists are superior to those made by the merely diligent. The first select their subjects better, pick out those effects for which they have an innate feeling, and indeed the influence of the individual is perceptible enough for connoisseurs looking at a plate usually to be able to ascertain the identity of the adept who obtained it.

Armed with these explanations, let us now concisely broach a curious subject: that of the various branches of the arts endangered by photography; then let us identify which branches of art are likely to benefit from this invention. We will not bother ourselves with [distinguishing] what will remain unaffected or outside its influence, since it will leave nothing intact and it will be felt in every area.

The most salient, most destructive repercussions relate to drawings, engravings, and lithographs representing cities, monuments, churches, ruins, bas-reliefs, and architectural subjects generally. On this terrain, the combat will be one-sided: a mediocre heliograph of the gateway to Chartres or Bourges [cathedrals] will always preferable, in terms of detail, realism, relief, and precision to even the most accomplished engraving. For this sort of subject, visual reproduction is everything, and photography heralds its ideal and perfection.

Such is the almost fantastical power of this process that it allows someone examining an architectural drawing to explore it as if before the object itself, and even to discovery elements that went unnoticed on site. A recent happenstance at once clarifies and exemplifies this assertion.

Fifteen months ago, M. Baron Gros, then ambassador plenipotentiary to Greece, fixed, by means of daguerreotype, a point of view taken from the Acropolis in Athens. Scattered around stood ruins, carved stones, fragments of every kind. Once back in Paris, following a delicate and honorably discharged mission, M. Baron Gros looked once again over his travel souvenirs and through a magnifying glass inspected some debris piled up in the foreground of his view of the Acropolis. Suddenly ... he lighted upon an ancient and extremely curious figure on a stone that hitherto had escaped his notice.

It was the hollowed-out contour of a lion devouring a snake of such remote age that this unique monument has since been ascribed to an art close to the era of the Egyptians. The microscope [*sic*] made it possible to discern this invaluable piece of evidence revealed by the daguerreotype and recorded large enough to be scrutinized some seven hundred leagues from Athens.

Thus this extraordinary mechanism seizes not only what one sees, but also what the eye cannot make out; so that, just as in nature, the viewer, when the object in its entirety no longer assuages his curiosity, advances closer and closer and, with the aid of a graduated lens, perceives infinitesimal details.

It is then understandable that heliography, applied to a plane surface such as a painted canvas, reproduces the image and its aspect with mathematical precision. It thus presents a precious resource for obtaining excellent reduced copies for the use of engravers, though the very superiority of the result condemns any other copy with inherent shortcomings and limited to mere imitation—that is, without the cooperation of thought through which a particular cast of mind elevates the translation of the model—to extinction. Morghen, Nicolas Chaprou, the engraver of Raphael of Urbino's *loggie*, undoubtedly provides a more exalted and more complete idea of the master's work that any daguerreotype could do. A portrait copied by Nanteuil or Drevet, after Mignard or Rigault, lives again, breathes with a second life—and hence the engraved portrait of Bossuet is superior to the original. Heliography cannot go beyond its model: it is a faithful helpmeet, not an intellect. But we sense that this material process, invincible in the limits of its field, practically eliminates all imitation confined to imitation and nothing more. Any draftsman, any lithographer, or any engraver deprived of artistic inspiration is thus likely to see himself supplanted and, between two machines, the most accurate, the fastest, the least expensive, will be necessarily preferred.

Is it not strange and providential that revolutions occasioned by the progress of human intelligence take place so opportunely and present themselves at the precise juncture a problem stands before it? Under the liberal and not particularly enlightened regime that has governed the arts for twenty years, the number of artists has greatly increased, while talent has been scattered about like so much loose change. Whoever knows someone of influence is able to put their auspicious mediocrity to good use and to set oneself up as an artist it is enough to possess some small practical skill and acquire renown by joining a coterie. Hence the ever-swelling mob of painters siphoning off funds from the state. . . .

This discovery—I hasten to say to intimidate those of vulgar ambition—will bring the inferior orders of art to inevitable destruction.

The comparison between feeble works and the pure and veracious reproduction of nature will regenerate public taste and train it to be more selective. A photograph of a print will always be preferred to a vile painting, because it will offer greater satisfaction.

The well-heeled—who used to have the means only for a shoddy portrait of doubtful likeness—will inevitably embrace photography, so clear, so precise, so lifelike in its products. And when one can for a moderate price acquire an exquisite image of a landscape one loves, of a place where one once dreamed, of the slope over which rises one's native roof, of a picture one once savored, tawdry pictures, cack-handed drawings, and lackluster engravings will be forsaken.

How many decent people will see themselves constrained to abandon as without profit and glory, and to seek their fortune elsewhere, thereby freeing—as might have been said in former times—the path that leads to the temple of the arts; and in the end they do right by quitting painting, which is for them a mere perfidious seduction and which should never anyway provide a livelihood for mediocrities!

(Continued in the following issue)

Francis Wey
UN VOYAGE HÉLIOGRAPHIQUE À FAIRE (A HELIOGRAPHICAL VOYAGE WORTH TAKING)
March 23, 1851
La Lumière

At a recent meeting of the Société Héliographique, one of our most competent colleagues, M. Fortier, was pleased to share with us a photograph on paper of Leonardo da Vinci's *Last Supper* obtained by means of a glass negative of admirable finish, clarity, and precision. This minor masterpiece, obtained from a far larger engraving, startled the artists present because it blended the firmness of the graver with the softness of mezzotint [*manière noire*], translating, if with greatly accentuated relief, details that even the most experienced hand would have been helpless to bring out. Heads the size of a chickpea were expressive and eloquent; the general effect preserved much of the tranquillity of the original and its merit is entirely concentrated in the miniature.

Any lover of gravure would be happy to have a diamond of this caliber in his collection: what would have happened had the picture not been engraved [and] if the original had been relegated, invisible if celebrated, to some out-of-the-way gallery!

Science has advanced to the point that it appears able to render eminent services to the arts. It behooves us to awaken both the zeal of heliographers and the solicitude of the government. The perfection of the work of M. Fortier has proved to us that the time has come to address these questions.

There exist unpublished pictures, badly reproduced paintings, rare masters known only to travelers or mentioned by biographers. To engrave each to perfection would be too costly; to acquire the canvases, impossible; while copying is a task no less onerous, of which few artists are capable. There even exist some—and these are by no means the least perplexing to study—that can neither be copied, nor engraved successfully; the majority of the Gothic masters are of this type. Two cities possess treasures in this genre: in the north, Bruges, and in the south, Pisa.

Although the museum of the Louvre boasts one of the most opulent collections in the world (the gallery in Madrid [the Prado] is second, if not first), the museum of France is poorly endowed with respect to those painters of the late Middle Ages; mystical artists—astonishing products of Christian inspiration—who opened and closed a tradition to which we can never return.

The processes of engraving are powerless to bring out the strange, naïve, and indefinite feeling alloyed to a certain polished dryness, a meticulous and ingenuous execution that in their works is nonetheless subordinated to thought. If the painter-copyist or engraver is knowledgeable and skillful, he will change the character of the model; and, if not, he will be unable to copy it. The only solution to these difficulties is heliography and it is on this terrain that it is destined to perform miracles. . . .

Photography thus offers us an inexpensive, sure, and mathematical means of acquiring, to the great benefit of scholarship and critical history, valuable information concerning those masters by whom France does not possess a single picture.

Would it not be feasible to devote one of the halls in the Louvre set aside for the drawings collection to this kind of acquisition? An official compendium of masterpieces gracing various European museums and the consecration by the State of the heliography of the nation, this room would exert a dual attraction: by completing a collection of monuments of the arts made by every known process, and by assuaging the desire of the public for faithful reproductions. In this fashion, masters whose absence is regretted would take their place next to their followers and irrevocable gaps [in the collection] would be partly filled.

This then is our wish: its realization requires some rather extensive excursions. Passing on to its application, we propose an example that will be followed: let us set out on a journey; no sooner have we left than we arrive.

To reach Bruges hardly takes much longer; the expedition would be inexpensive, and life in this Gothic necropolis formerly honored with the title "Venice of the North," very reasonable. Everything there seems to have been created for the artist—apart from Venice, Rome, and Florence, Bruges is the most intriguing city in the West.

There exists in the Bibliothèque Nationale a manuscript of Froissard's *Chronicle* rich in illuminated miniatures of the fifteenth century: they feature battles, palaces, courts in session, and fleets of ships; churches beneath whose walls unroll the lively and variegated ribbons of splendid processions rich in nuance; and, finally, entire cities, with their tracery pinnacles, their stepped gables, their cinnabar-colored roofs festooned with bouquets of stone; their galleried convents with pointed-arched cloisters, their tall thin arrow slits, their sturdy crenels, and their posterns flanked by turrets. Of these cities of yesteryear, preserved by the image-makers of the Middle Ages, nothing has survived. One of the most ornate, the most Oriental, the most fairy-like in the Froissard manuscript is, undoubtedly, Bruges. It is represented therein two or three times. But, O, wonder! Time, that vigilant scythe, time has forgotten her. This city, so fantastic that one walks through it in disbelief, seems to have awoken from an enchanted slumber that held her in thrall, forgotten by life, for three centuries. A man from Bruges, leaning over Froissard's manuscript, would be able to recognize his district, his house, his very door; he would hardly suspect that this faithful view were not painted yesterday, and on seeing the costumes, he would just think it was the season of the great *kermesse*, when the populace dresses up in clothes from the time of Mary of Burgundy. . . .

Enter a home: there you will find tall, dark, beeswaxed wooden wardrobes, big, old-fashioned sideboards, four-poster beds in which Van Eyck had the Virgin sleep, and the Venetian glass Metzu, Mieris, and Rembrandt turned crimson to brighten the faces and color the cheeks of their tipplers.

I can only compare Bruges—though it possesses a wholly different character—to Oxford, the city with twenty-two Gothic colleges about which we will speak another time.

A heliographic journey to Bruges would thus be rewarding in more than one respect: in this bizarre place, where stand superb churches, convents, a town hall, squares, and palaces, each a silversmith's caprice, every street is lined with monuments. Viewed in its entirety, from its roofs, Bruges is reminiscent of a medieval frontispiece.

But, having copied the most notable monuments, the most picturesque vistas in this incomplete necropolis that has forgotten both to live and to die, this city entirely built in pink brick, faded here and there, all embellished with arabesques, frames, and stone figurines in even, calm tones, with no discordant notes or errant restoration, heliography would now have to perform a still more important task, the principal aim of our voyage.

In about the year 1450, nine years after the death of Jean Van Eyck, at the time of the Duke Philip of Burgundy, a painter from Bruges made a name for himself with a portrait of Isabella of Aragon.

In the guidebook to the Louvre, this artist, little known in France (where he is represented by a mean and entirely apocryphal daub), is designated by the name of Hemmelinck. He signed his works Memling or Hemling. The first letter has given rise to argument.

Jean Hemling [*sic*] is—permit me the expression—the angel of Christian painting in the Northern Gothic School. He is the Fiesole [Fra Angelico] of Flanders. Well informed for his time, he plied Spain, Italy, Germany. His taste was remarkable and he foreshadowed the style in his manner. His life was an adventurous one. By turn painter and soldier, he fought in the wars of Charles the Bold; he was present at the debacle of Nancy, and, physically and financially ruined, ended up seeking refuge in his fatherland, at the hospice of Saint John, founded long before for poor yeomen returning maimed from Palestine, and which, remaining much as it was in the time of Count Baldwin, now houses victims of the crusade against poverty.

To pay for his upkeep, Hemling devoted his brush to his hosts; he left wonders that decorate one of the rooms in the hospice and the gallery in the Academy of Saint Luke. We know Van Eyck, but we remain in ignorance of Hemling, who is his superior, if not in color, then at least in drawing, the grace of his accoutrements, the splendor of his compositions, but most especially in the surprising depth of the expressions and the exquisite charm of his physiognomies.

At the view of faces so gentle, so alive in their mysticism, so strongly impregnated with thought, that the mild fire of the soil warms and colors, making them so attractive that one cannot tear away one's eyes, I whispered to myself: Here is a peerless master, one whom no contemporary art could hope to interpret. Indeed, so strange a combination of reality and ideal would be hard to imagine.

I have though seen a few lithographs, a few engravings after Hemling, and even some copies in oils, but these imitations only confirm my opinion: they give no idea whatsoever of the master and capture nothing of his art.

To deal with this fantastic painter, one needs to resort to alchemy. How [Memling] proceeded is scarcely comprehensible; all will be revealed by the sorcery of science.

Almost six foot tall, Hemling's chief work is *The Marriage of Saint Catherine*. It is a monument in itself: opened, one of the two panels represents the beheading of Saint Jean the Baptist and the other the vision of Saint John [the Evangelist] on Patmos. Once shut and locked like a cupboard, the outer panel presents portraits of two hospice's administrators, together with four nuns at prayer. I am not sure whether the envelope is not preferable to the picture within, though that is the finest piece of Gothic I have ever seen in my life.

Other works by Hemling include: *The Hunt of Saint Ursula*, a series of subjects representing the German legend of the eleven thousand virgins taken from Sigebert: this charming composition, invaluable for the history of costume, is also to be recommended for its very exact views of Basel, Rome, and Cologne. It is a masterpiece of miniature, an iconographical drama of the keenest interest, a monument unique in the world.

The Adoration of the Magi, a *Saint Martin*, ex-votos, a bust of the *Sibyl Sambethe*, a *Deposition*, complete Hemling's authentic oeuvre to be found at the hospice of Saint John. The other pictures ascribed to him appear to me to be later work by another hand.

The Academy of Saint Luke possesses pieces of supreme beauty: a *Saint Christopher*, with two shutters in grisaille representing the donor, his spouse, their children, and servants. Hemling excelled in endowing his portraits with character and plausibility, those guarantors of honorable resemblance. He is Holbein, but simpler, more elevated.

Finally, the Baptism of Christ, marvelous in execution and teeming with ornate details.

There exists another picture by Hemling, in the Church [Basilica] of the Holy Blood of Christ; it is a figure of *Charity*, a portrait, half-size, of a lady making the offering of a purse. Never has elegance in attire been pushed so far: the lady's pious, moved, dignified, and diffident air places this portrait in the first rank. I know of no more striking expression.

Jean Hemling, or Memling, is a most rare master; he marks the apogee of a long-vanished tradition. France has nothing by him. To engrave him, I repeat, is almost impossible, and the labor required extremely costly.

The entire output of this artist is hidden away in Bruges, because the two small panels known by his name, one in the gallery in The Hague and the other just acquired by England, are of much disputed authenticity. To make Hemling known in our country would be a useful act and of little expense when one considers what a journey [to Bruges] costs and the benefit art would derive from it.

For the price of a shoddy engraving after some trivial subject, like those ordered year after year by the directorship of the fine arts; for the price of just one such daub (and those who paint them are not paid to have them subsequently disappear), one might by means of photography obtain Hemling's engraved work rendered to complete perfection.

We will keep the administration of fine arts informed of other excursions no less advantageous and no less as economic: it owes, it seems to us, some encouragement to heliographers, ever keen to advance a discovery so glorious to our motherland; for them too, it ought—by enrolling heliography among its peaceable conquests—to assert our priority, our superiority in this regard. It should also be added that honor would accrue to any administration that launched such a salutary initiative, one so just and so meritorious.

If ever our voice is not heeded, then our heliographers—for whom no sacrifice is too great to enhance so marvelous a discovery—will one day strike out on campaign on their own and gain admittance among the arts in that fashion.

Heliography, in addition to presenting artists with new obstacles to overcome (in respect of natural truth), will oblige them to make fresh efforts, its compensation coming in the form of other priceless gifts, and ensuring their gratitude by restoring long-forgotten geniuses to their deserved glory.

Francis Wey
THÉORIE DU PORTRAIT
(THEORY OF THE PORTRAIT)
April 27, 1851
La Lumière

Who has not heard the story of the hoax perpetrated by a portrait painter that provided a sharp lesson for those who dared disparage his talent? One day, weary of unjust criticism on the part of the model's family and friends, he invited them to see his work, pretending to have made adjustments. Arriving in the dimly lit studio, they all took their seats in front of the opulently framed canvas placed before a splendid backcloth of dark-colored damask. One of the company complains that the portrait too somber, the other too pallid; one is dissatisfied with the eyes, the other with the hairstyle; the model seems older, say some; he has put on weight, say others. In short, they all agree on only one point: the resemblance is imperfect. But suddenly the portrait bursts out in laughter and the head of the original pokes out of the frame painted in trompe-l'oeil.

Whether contrived or not, this anecdote has comforted many an artist and served more than once to take a pernickety judge down a peg or two. For my part, I think the tale true: but, though I might be taxed with being paradoxical, I am on the side of the hoodwinked. To my lights, they were right: the portrait was not a good likeness.

Logic requires that to resemble an object means to exist in a different condition from that same object, and that Jacques and Paul *resemble* neither Paul nor Jacques—any comparison requiring at least two different terms. But let us leave the philosophical argument aside and boldly affirm that, materially, the copy of a figure is likely to strike the beholder by its interpretative power more forcefully than would, under certain conditions, reality itself.

Allow me to briefly justify this assertion: The fact that heliography reproduces the features and facets of a face with mathematical accuracy is uncontested. It is the face itself that is conjured up and lives again such as it is. Nevertheless, we have all seen heliographic portraits perfectly true to life and heliographic portraits that are utterly un-lifelike.

From this seemingly unconscionable fact, it arises that, in spite of its precision, the scientific instrument of the daguerreotype requires, on the part of those who operate it, a flair for interpretation, a feeling for effect, light, physiognomy—that is, all the qualities inherent in art.

Thus to compete with art, heliography has to call upon the artist's sensitivity, upon his knowledge, upon faculties that will ennoble and elevate the moral compass of this marvelous discovery. Even equipped with a perfect instrument, a heliographer without taste, unaware of the workings of the great masters, will take uncouth portraits, inadequate likenesses of unsympathetic aspect and vulgar effect, at once niggardly and rudely commonplace. M. Mestral understood this very well when he said to me once: The exercise of the daguerreotype led me to seek in the great painters of Flanders, Spain, and Italy, qualities, artifices of accoutrement, aims I had never even previously dreamed of.

Is it not an acknowledged fact that heliography agreeably reproduces certain faces but makes others appear ugly? People say it's like a lottery. We are far from this opinion: nature leaves nothing to chance. It is simply that some heads need to be exposed to a certain light, to be shown in a certain attitude, or more or less strongly lit, etc. And the pose and the effect appropriate for one face or complexion do no favors to a head of another color or of different shape. A portrait somewhat ungainly taken full face might have been delightful presented in three-quarters. Cheeks like these need a penumbra, but for this very different complexion one should provide the glare of daylight. The surface of this man's features demand to be strongly set down; another will improve if mitigated by shadow. That the heliographer is capable of making someone beautiful or ugly is undeniable; but this potential lies in the hands of the artist.

The aesthetic theory of the daguerreotype, however, remains to be written. In establishing its foundations, it is essential to start with painting and to understand exactly what is constituted by resemblance; and to seek out—from our ideas, our instincts on this matter—the essential differences between resemblance and reality; and then, in the footsteps of uncontested masters from various centuries and diverse lands, to retrace the traditions of the beautiful.

Processes exist, such as the *physionotype*, or the invention of M. Collas, by means of which one can obtain an exact cast of a head. Suppose that these processes were brought to perfection and put to use to create the bust of a certain person: the result will be of mathematical precision. It will lack color: a skillful painter will make off with the bust and, mixing on his palette just the right tones for each part of the figure and comparing what he does with the model to ensure himself of their conformity, will then place them on the marble and blend them in with all conceivable artistry. The eyes, the cheeks, the clothing, the hair will be painstakingly applied; the bust will be illuminated so as to appear as real as possible in respect of its color, its form. In a word, in this manner, perfection on this particular road to reality will have been attained.

Would the product of this operation be an ideal resemblance? No.

Such an object would be repulsive, even if the model's appearance were not. The eyes would see something barbaric, a grimacing parody of life, without expression, without animation; outraged, the imagination would never recognize in such a thing the individual as it would like him to be pictured.

A likeness, then, is something else. Resemblance is not mechanical reproduction but an interpretation that translates for the eye the image of an object such as the mind pictures it with the aid of memory.

Hence resemblance is not equivalent to a material fact. It is an abstract idea: the result of an interpretation; it is not necessarily subordinate to absolute precision; far from it—it is likely to lend greater resemblance by some well-chosen liberties. You will as often as not be unable to recognize a portrait of a man you have only vaguely glimpsed; but you will more probably identify him from a caricature since its simplicity would stay in your memory with more force.

Just as the intellectual effort required to appreciate a resemblance is instinctual and independent of our will, so the artist who produces a likeness is subjected to involuntary impulses. All the while he is endeavoring to copy, he is unconsciously interpreting. What he sees is recreated in a certain manner in his thought, and it is this thought that he renders palpable. This essential point needs emphasizing. All of us have noticed that a portrait does not bear an equal likeness for everyone. The opinions to which it gives rise depend on the degree of intimacy and on the nature of the feelings that govern the relationship between each beholder and the original. From which the following proposition can be deduced: the most skillful artist is the one who is capable of providing the interpretation closest to the general impression. . . .

It has often been observed that the majority of faces from a particular era display similarities and people may be overheard saying: Look at that passerby, doesn't his face look as though it's stepped out of the age of the Medici? Or, that girl has the profile of a fifteenth-century medal, etc. . . .

But from the fifteenth to the eighteenth centuries, the races have surely not actually changed: and yet the reign of Louis XIV and that of his successor did not produce a single head that resembles those in paintings of the Middle Ages. From age to age, it is taste and the doctrines of the beautiful that alter; the fundamentals of the ideal, inextricably entwined with the arts of copying, are modified; style transforms; people see things differently.

Successive fashions leave tangible traces—and this even in recent times. From 1788 to 1794 were published engraved portraits, almost all in profile, of the majority of the outstanding figures of the Constituent and Legislative Assemblies and the Convention. The foreheads in all these portraits, save for two or three—and the collection is a vast one—recede: that was the fashion. How did this happen? The artist, seeking a pose, chose one whose appearance seemed to him the most striking and, in that age, this was one where the forehead appeared to slant. Then, under the weight of that idea, he unconsciously exaggerated it still further.

For the last twenty-five years, Gall's system has propelled artists to the opposite extreme: the plane of the forehead aspires to the vertical; and now deformed by an artifice no longer perceived because it has become common practice, in portraits this part of the face functions like a page of advertisements taken out on behalf of the genius of the model. And so the age of broad foreheads has been ousted by a mode for scatterbrains—just as Byronian youth has succeeded the dandified troupe of madcap *Muscadines* and *Incroyables*.

At the time of the Renaissance and during the Empire, the face of any woman was adorned by a Greek nose; from Mignard to Rigault, the Greek nose disappeared and faces waxed round. In the Gothic period, ovals, and likewise every form, were elongated, and the features grew smaller. Contemporaries of David, Gros, and Gérard tended to enlarge their proportions.

Under Louis XIV, bulging noses lie very close to mouths that are small with round lips: the nose is a pink beak sitting on a cherry it is getting ready to peck. It is obvious that in all these various eras, people naively thought they were just depicting and, unconcerned, sought a likeness, but taste and fashion gave rise to bias.

The interpretation of effects and the color provides still more disparate observations.

Some schools, like the Germans, see everything in light; others, like the Spaniards, sought darker effects; the Bolognese modeled in half-tones dissolving into a gentle glow; Ribera, Velázquez, and Rembrandt proceeded primarily through energy of contrast, tearing a blaze of light from the abyss of shadow.

Some construct their planes by tailing off the lines; others concentrate on outlining the features and—depending upon which of these two considerations each acts—they are dubbed colorists or draftsman [*dessinateurs*], without the use of these terms implying any particular perfection. Titian is a colorist; [but] he undoubtedly drew better than Holbein and than many modern painters classified among the draftsmen. Nature, one avers, shows scant concern with such distinctions.

These considerations permit one to advance:

1. That absolute reality, were it even possible, is far from constituting an essential for what is known as *truth in art*;

2. That resemblance is merely an interpretation subordinate to taste, to fashion, to the prejudices of the age, and to the preconceptions of judges of the artist's work;

3. That a materially unimpeachable copy, were it to contradict such ideas, would be likely to appear much less truthful than a less accurate interpretation conceived to afford satisfaction to the mind.

If these postulates are allowed, it will be conceded that art and heliography are destined to mutually exchange many invaluable lessons.

The potential for realism of the daguerreotype [*daguerrien*] process will mitigate the missteps of convention; it will prevent fashions, fads, or the manias of some artist from imposing, as used to be the case in former times, a banal stereotype of the human face; it will accustom the eye to variety in outline, to originality in character; it will extend the resources of art by accustoming it to seek out dissimilarities instead of congruities in a range of faces.

In addition, heliographers, forced to penetrate the secrets of interpretation in art and to add ideal resemblance to mathematical accuracy, will be obliged to show intelligence in placing the models before the camera and to ensure that the conditions of lighting, effect, taste, style, and attitude are those best adapted to result in an at once appealing and striking image.

In point of fact, the heliographer, lest he produce graceless marvels, cannot dispense with the theory of painting, without which his coldly mechanical work will lack appeal, want life and interest, and—as often as not—appear to educate eyes less faithful than a painting more remote from pure reality.

Photographers will be prevailed upon to interpret these theories—the elements for which are scattered throughout the old master tradition—and ponder them afresh; they will have to assimilate them and find for them new applications.

It is upon this range of ideas that an aesthetics of heliography will be founded; it is to this that we will endeavor to call to the attention of practitioners [of photography] by applying the experience of the [painting] schools to the portrait genre.

(Continued in the following issue)

Francis Wey

THÉORIE DU PORTRAIT II (THEORY OF THE PORTRAIT II)

May 4, 1851

La Lumière

A figure can be sketched out in our mind's eye in ten different guises; our neighbor can be depicted in such a fashion that his abstract image, were it made tangible, would scarcely be recognizable for anyone.

Prior to the experience of heliography, such ideas might not have been advanced with any certainty; they will soon be accepted into the domain of accepted truth. One of our collaborators, M. Renard, has provided me with a precious piece of information in this connection. One day, in the space of some one and a half hours, he obtained three portraits on metal plates of a lady that were, in differing degrees, considered as good likenesses by the model's friends; and yet it proved impossible to persuade people who had never seen the original that these three photographs even represented one and the same face.

The beholders were convinced that they could distinguish three utterly distinct individuals, judging one of these three ladies to be ugly, another of plain aspect, and the third of exceptional beauty. Patently, satisfying as it did the conditions of art, it was this last that constituted the sole good portrait, since, though no less accurate than the other two, it captured all the charm of the [sitter's] physiognomy.

It thus follows that a heliographer must study his models from several angles, expose them in different lights and choose their pose with utmost care.

Up to now, it seems to have been enough to draw one's hands behind one and pull in one's knees and elbows in an effort to palliate exaggerated perspective. These material precautions are no longer sufficient. In regard of such preliminary arrangements, the mind has a more significant role to play.

The scope for interpretation here is almost as wide as in painting. Moreover, as regards heliography, it has to be spontaneous and, since it excludes corner cutting and correction, it demands a remarkably assured eye. Its practitioners, infinitely imbued with all the resources of art, have to arrange their models meticulously and to be able to picture the complete image from whatever nature presents to them.

Most faces, according to whether they are adequately or dimly lit, gain or lose in roundness of character: the majority of faces have a good side from which they are best viewed. How many times in the withdrawing room have we not run into a person so brightly illuminated that at first we were unable to recognize them; or glimpsed a woman who at first appears to us very ordinary, and who later, by inclining her head or changing her position, suddenly reveals a rare beauty. . . .

Thus, for the heliographer as much for the painter, a twofold problem arises: to conjoin both resemblance and charm to reality. Choosing among all the various aspects of reality is, for a photographer, to interpret.

Such selection is subordinated to certain general laws of suitability.

One can divide the models presented by nature into three categories: Those who impress by their purity, by the hallmarks of nobility; others by their physiognomy, complexion, or a certain liveliness. The first are subjects for style and awaken thoughts of the beautiful; the second recommend themselves by their grace—they are pretty figures. And lastly, there exist, and in very large numbers, faces which are neither beautiful nor ugly and which offer nothing particularly striking.

To reproduce models of the first class one must eschew raking light, overcomplicated shadow effects, and seek instead an aspect which, in simple, broad planes, allows the viewer to grasp the peaceful and noble harmony of their lines, without obscuring or fragmenting them.

A head in which fancy dominates, a sprightly little phiz, calls for an exactly contrary method. Here, the shades, a warming sheen, skillfully disposed pale tones are marshaled to mask the irregularity of their features and coalesce so to offer up an image of movement, expression, and life.

Do not think that nondescript and vulgar heads are to be despised. The models from this third species provided the Flemings of yesterday with some of their most dazzling successes. For it is rare to find a mortal creature who has not inspired, if just once, tender feelings. Now, anything that has been loved possesses some more or less perceptible, more or less fugitive grace, and it is the burden of art, which is passion par excellence, to submit to and convey the attractions of this kind of illusion. To reproduce a face such as we each picture it offers undeniable proof of talent; but to see it, to reveal it from a novel, agreeable, original point of view and to strike viewers by the truth of this interpretation, to lead them to perceive it as one saw it oneself—this is the lot of genius.

It is this tour de force that characterizes the art of Rembrandt, Velázquez, and a handful of others. Through unprecedented effects, powerful contrasts, bright lights, and deep shadows they manage to make a head so striking, that, on seeing it, one has no thought of analyzing each feature. To achieve this feat, it is clear that great artists paid attention to the figure's attire and took care about on which portion of the face they wanted the light to stream. A want of rotundity is dissolved in tones almost equivalent to those in the ground or on the accessories; the relief is strongly brought out, the modeling energetically rendered, while the eye, struck by such unity, neglects to scrutinize and investigate more deeply. On being presented with a portrait of a likeness of a rather unprepossessing man, the beholder, subdued by the genius of the painter, will exclaim: How magnificent!

It is to colorists that it falls to make the laurel bloom on this ungrateful land. And, in this connection, it should be noted that, in its finest productions, photography has to date indeed uttered a panegyric to those schools dedicated to the worship of color. MM. Le Gray, Mestral, and some imitators have each tackled head-on—in accordance with the particular character of each head—the portrait à la Van Dyck, à la Rembrandt, etc.

For the rest, the part played by personal taste is so tangible that some of our leading colleagues can with a brief glance at a photograph distinguish which of them took it. The day such discernment became feasible, heliography was able to claim for itself the honor of having created genuine artists.

One condition for art that requires pondering is that of *style*.

Nothing can be more contrary to this than unthinking prolixity in detail. The shops along the banks of the Seine, the Palais National and the boulevards deal in these bourgeois *chinoiseries*, in which a head, sacrificed to a puerile profusion of tawdry accessories, is reduced to playing second fiddle. A foliated hanging, a flowery waistcoat, watch-chains, charm bracelets, a checkered tie, a table groaning beneath papers, inkstands, statuettes, Japanese vases. etc.—all these constitute distractions which, most of the time, the public might judiciously be spared. When a painter is faced with such impedimenta, he is permitted to temper with local color the crudity, garishness, or gaudiness such objects might possess. In this respect, moreover, the more proficient lean towards sobriety.

But the daguerreotype does not lend itself to such salutary sleight of hand. The more twinkling and fiddly such unconscionable details appear, the more it brings them out, the more objectionably it reproduces them. To the point that the head, the chief subject, is occluded, tarnished, losing its interest and unity; everything shimmers, without the mind being able to concentrate on any one thing.

The theory of *sacrifices*, so largely practiced by Van Dyck, Rubens, and Titian, must be even more rigorously applied by the heliograph artist. These great painters ordinarily make their heads gleam amid an atmosphere of dark-hued haze; then their backgrounds, darkening as they descend, merge along the shoulders with folds of clothes loosely indicated in solid, somber impasto. They avoid dryly outlining the human body from head to foot and their portraits never remind one—as do certain daguerreotypes—of fried whiting chucked on a silver dish.

What is the purpose of all these sacrifices relating to the distribution of light and the suppression of certain details? It is to focus attention on the faces; to render them clearer, and to instill into them the gleam of life. What people want in a portrait is the sitter himself: artists want us to be able to reach him unhindered and for him to stop us in our tracks. Their interpretation, truer than absolute reality, by dispensing us from undergoing something we would never ask of nature, conforms to an inclination of our mind.

This preeminent law of the theory of the portrait—which painters ignore in due proportion to their want of talent—has been transgressed by the majority of heliographers, and this is why their portraits repulse by a vague sense of vulgarity, by a lack of *presence*, and have excited our curiosity without affording us the satisfaction we expect of a work of art. . . .

Photographers readily impute the difficulty of introducing liveliness and physiognomy into their portraits to the slowness of a process that imposes such lengthy immobility on its model. . . .

A background of an even shade allows one to press home the shadows with vigor and enhances the light; in the lion's share of cases, any course of action chosen should be unequivocal. A drape of purplish tone provides, if I am not much mistaken, a good-quality backdrop, since red, the base of the range, is brought to the fore by the daguerreotype apparatus; at the same time, blue, combined with the red and veering to purple, tempers the hue, making it a little cloudy. One needs air behind a portrait. . . .

It would be just as salutary to learn how to present heliographic prints better, and this may be achieved, either by perusing portfolios of engravings, or by examining collections of original drawings laid on Bristol board or with paper surrounds and tastefully framed. . . .

Unflinching reality is so seldom flattering that it is necessary to disguise it; it has to be excused by every conceivable contrivance. Art delights in sustaining our illusions, offering itself to our imagination like a golden dream.

And let it not be forgotten: feeling, charm can make their presence felt everywhere, can betoken themselves all things, and public favor is sometimes won through a host of little artifices that it does not even notice. The goal is to convince one's judges; but it is prudent to start by earning their acceptance.

In short, heliographers, if they truly wish to nail their colors to the mast of portraiture, must needs search for style, grace, and a knowledge of the effects. . . .

In our opinion, present-day portraitists have as much to gain as heliographers from the study of the old masters, and the latter have less far to travel to elevate themselves to the ideal than the former have to approximate to reality—something that is receding in the face of three glaring defects, characteristic of the entire contemporary generation. These three vices—now established as articles of faith—are: pretentious banality (in studio parlance, *cliché*); Gothic dryness; and brutality: it is these that have replaced the grace, the purity of line, and the vigorous effects of the colorists of earlier ages.

Gustave Le Gray
PHOTOGRAPHIE, TRAITÉ NOUVEAU, THÉORIQUE ET PRATIQUE (PHOTOGRAPHY: A NEW THEORETICAL AND PRACTICAL TREATISE)
1852

(Pages 1–3)
Among the inventions of our era, photography is one that is called upon to render the greatest services to art. Its influence will be immensely far-reaching; for, all the while keeping the painter informed of the difficulties of his art, it cleanses public taste by accustoming it to look at nature reproduced as faithfully as possible, often moreover with effects exquisite in both taste and sentiment.

One might already have become convinced of this influence at some recent picture exhibitions. Bad portraits are becoming rarer and compositional effects generally better handled.

The canvases that attracted most public attention were precisely those that most closely approximated to the sentiment conveyed by the finest photographs.

Obviously, I do not in the least mean by this that a good painting must necessarily be possessed of the meticulous, microscopic execution of a daguerreotype plate.

From my point of view, the beauty of a photograph almost always consists, on the contrary, in the sacrifice of certain details, so as to attain an arrangement of effects that sometimes verges on the artistic sublime.

So, it is solely in the hands of artists that Daguerre's instrument can accomplish worthwhile results. In the process of copying one and the same site or model—by varying the focus and exposure time, an artist can bring out or dispose of such and such an element; he can produce powerful effects of light and shade or instead a sense of extreme gentleness and tranquility.

Thus in truth only an artist or a man of taste is sure to obtain a perfect work using an instrument capable of capturing the same object in an infinite variety of interpretations, since only he can intuit the effect most appropriate for the subject he reproduces.

Since its origin, photography has made rapid and immense strides with regard to its mechanical procedures: those remaining before it will only be achieved when the taste of its practitioners is purified.

It is a task incumbent, in my opinion, upon the museums' administration alone.

It is by admitting the better photographs to the Salon to stand among the work of artists that it will encourage the exponents of this novel art to persevere in their efforts.

To fail to take this measure is to remove an opportunity and a means of recognition from serious photographists [*sic*]; it is to abandon them to a public taste that is not yet formed and which prefers illuminated initials to genuinely artistic achievements; it would be to instill repulsion in their soul, to smother photography in its cradle.

The fine arts administration owes encouragement to photography, as it does to all branches of art. The best manner of achieving this goal is undoubtedly to stimulate emulation among those who deal with it by expunging the eminently false preconception that there is no art in taking a beautiful photograph and that all the merit belongs to the contraption. Each and everyone is astonished and finds it regrettable that the administration has so far refused to move in this direction; but it is no less generally hoped that things will not be the same in the future, and that the museums' directorship, more enlightened as to the impact and likely services of photography, will next year grant it its rightful place.

(Pages 70–71)
Perhaps the thought will be entertained that these manipulations will increase the cost price of a photograph, due to both the care lavished on it and the cost of the expensive chemicals involved.

I would like to point out that such considerations should not prevail.

Progress in photography depends, not on its cheapness, but in the quality of a print.

If a photograph is beautiful, accomplished, and long-lasting, it will acquire an intrinsic value before which its price can be virtually discounted.

For my part, I express the wish that photography, rather than joining the ranks of industry or trade, will join those of the arts. There is its sole, its true place, and it is in this direction that I will ever seek to steer its progress.

It is this principle that all men committed to its improvement ought to adopt. To seek to lower the price of prints before finding out how to create accomplished works would be to risk compromising forever the future of our extremely interesting art.

I have put these processes into practice in my studios on the covered way at the Barrière de Clichy, where a well-oiled organization enables me to supply daily to the trade one hundred positive prints more than adequately resistant to the assault of time.

I have neglected no pains, no expenditure in order to attain perfection in my products. I would thus prevail upon publishers eager for their productions to be both attractive and durable to come and visit my firm.

GEORGES NIEL
LE PAYSAGE AU SALON DE 1857
(THE LANDSCAPE AT THE SALON OF 1857)
1857

The critics and the jury were rather unjust on the landscapists. . . .

The esteem accorded landscapists, even those with talent, does not appear to us to be what it should. Their works charm: everyone agrees on that point; but if there is a prize, a commendation to be awarded, it is routinely attributed to some mediocre piece by a history or genre painter. It has been long agreed that landscape occupies a rank below the historical genre, and this has become an article of faith. . . .

Landscape is a facile genre! Thus is the word out—and the error already enshrined. The grand manner, with its deployment of colors, forms, of fabrics, by its subjects even, attracts the eye more than some tiny corner of nature, however imbued by poetry it may be. . . . To halt before a Ruysdael, to spend an hour breathing in the fresh air coming off one of his admirable pages: this, for me, is the touchstone of art.

I say this loud and clear: one needs a heart as sensitive to appreciate a Claude Lorrain or a Ruysdael, as a Rubens. And a painter of landscape has as many difficulties to overcome as a history painter. God took as much care over the violet as over most beautiful flowers. . . .

The landscape painter has to be sublime in a canvas one foot wide, with a cloud, a tree! He must needs be endowed with the most sensitive qualities of spirit, the rarest gifts of art. He must possess the key to the secrets of nature and poetry, as well as to his *trade* of color. . . .

And people maintain that copying nature, even slavishly, does not improve the mind of man, that it does not attain the topmost summits of the ideal!

The beautiful is simply the ideal as it is dreamed by the finest imaginations; the ideal is truth, and truth is never the work of man, but of God.

We can have no greater master.

Daubigny
Daubigny's masters are J.-J. Rousseau and Bernardin de Saint-Pierre; like them he is a lover of nature and it is the writings of these great men that he illustrates. . . .

Cast your eyes over *The Valley of Aptevoz*. I see in it nothing but genius, even in the smallest blade of grass. I admit that language fails me to comprehensibly convey the charm one feels standing before these unmoving, crystal-clear waters, bordered by reeds and silence, and where the water lily stretches out her broad leaves. Their surroundings—on which nature has lavished all her style—are full of grandeur; this is the valley of rest.

In all Daubigny's canvases one senses the solitary walker; long must he have dreamed in the places he depicts. He imparts its impressions to us in the manner of a poet; every brushstroke is a hemistich, imparting a sound to the spirit like a harmonious cadence.

He is, above all else, a great poet.

MM. Français, Achard, Lambinet, Blin, Marcel, De Penne, Chaigneau, De Cock, Brendel, Desjobert
The Exhibition will close and only a few people will have seen the landscape painters. All file past them without even a second look; the least Pompadour silliness attracted them more. . . .

All [the landscape painters] are driven by the same will: to rehabilitate Nature. If it is not the same hand that painted it, it is the same guiding spirit. Each chooses the effect, the moment, the site that speaks most to his instinct. Some paint with the mind, Lambinet, Desjobert; the others with the soul, Blin, Achard, but none ever takes his eyes off the model.

Sometimes they walk us though landscapes steep and wild; sometimes they offer us a tranquil avenue or brushwood that invites us to reverie or repose.

This one revels in vast horizons; this other turns our eye on the edge of a forest, the quiet edges of a river. Here the imagination of the Touraine and the Loire, the fruitfulness of the Dauphiné; there, Breton melancholy or the morbid sadness of the Sologne.

This is, finally, no conventional nature: I see real water, real skies, trees full of air and light; this is truly the Nature of the Good Lord. Green, that tender color of springtime, is here resolutely tackled: the great leap has been made.

Not one of these landscapists leaves one unimpressed; it would be bad grace to compare their delicious poems to the products of photography.

Photography has all the dryness of a plan, it reeks of death; the hand of man, creativity is lacking. Harmony is destroyed, the light is broken up by the instrument . . . there exist a thousand little effects that photography cannot capture. Air will never be photographed.

Nature is simple in its effects, she indicates with light touches, her hues melt into one another harmoniously; even in her most audacious moments, she never scandalizes the eye, always enchanting it. It is to the great merit of our landscapists that they have understood this.

Millet, Breton, Hédouin, Courbet
The ridiculous word "realism" frightens off many people; by it, they understand the painting of the ugly or the vulgar. M. Courbet and realism are seen as one and the same, and the painter from the Franche-Comté has not been afraid of taking on the title of its pontiff.

This represents a usurpation; because nobody is less realistic than he is, since realism is the painting of truth (no one will object that the beautiful and the ideal have nothing to do with the true). A history painter has to be as realistic as a painter of genre or landscape.

Artists who deserving of the title "realist" have names like Millet, Lebreton, Troyon, de Clock, etc. They have understood that art went off-track in the byways of *manner*, of tawdriness, and pastiche: they followed the example of the masters and strive to turn their steps once again to the wellspring of truth. This is a self-confessed French school that has irretrievably broken with the past and that seeks inspiration in its scenery.

LOUIS FIGUIER
LA PHOTOGRAPHIE AU SALON 1859
(PHOTOGRAPHY AT THE SALON, 1859)
Paris, October 15, 1859

In 1859, for the first time, photography has been permitted to approach, if not actually to enter, the exhibition of fine arts, and this date will be forever a landmark in the history of a marvelous invention hitherto all too often disparaged, which has fought long and hard for the recognition of its significance and artistic value.

For amateur readers and critics today, the Salons of Diderot have become a mine of information. Without being foolhardy enough to set up any kind of comparison, we venture to advance that, from the historical point of view, the few chapters that follow are intended to form a kind of abbreviated complement to the work of the great critic of the last century.

We may add, and with less fear of contradiction, that the following chapters will provide an accurate picture of the current state of photography, of its many applications, and of the expedients available to it today. . . .

If the quarrel between the ancients and the moderns did not occur in our century, we have had the quarrel *between the engravers and photographists* [*sic* et passim]. Hardly had photography appeared on the horizon of science that engraving and lithography, and not without reason alas! sounded the alarm at the unwelcome eruption of this rival, ardent like everything young and strong. . . .

Yet nothing has yet managed to tarnish this new art in the eyes of the public. On the occasion of the Universal Exhibition of 1855, photography, in spite of the vociferous claims made on its behalf, was excluded from the sanctuary on the Palais de l'avenue Montaigne; it was instead condemned to seek asylum in the immense bazaar of products of every stripe that filled the Palais de l'Industrie. Under still greater insistence, in 1859 the museums committee adopted a middle way: it granted a place to the display of photography just next to the exhibition of painting and engraving in the Palais de l'Industrie, but with a different entrance—by the back door, so to speak. Resolving the quandary in this manner is to be applauded since it sets out the respective situations of the two litigating parties and heralds the complete and permanent access of photography into the inner sanctum of the fine arts one day in the near future. . . .

For a few years now, photography has acquired the artistic character it had to work so doggedly to attain. To be convinced of the truth of this statement it is enough to study the splendid collection of French and foreign photographs that the Société de Photographie displayed with such taste in the Palais de l'Industrie, thanks to the intelligent and enlightened zeal of its secretary and agent, M. Martin-Laulerie. . . .

At a time when photography remains, one might say, so close to its birth, it is already high time that it departed the well-trodden paths of commercialism and trade; it must now elevate itself onto a higher plane and, without claiming to evince engraving, to strive to attain a par with that manifestation of art. . . .

Until now, the artist had at his disposal the brush, the pencil, the burin, and the surface of the lithographic stone; henceforth, he has at his disposal the lens of the camera [*chambre obscure*]. The lens is an instrument just like the pencil and the brush; photography is a process that resembles drawing and engraving, because what makes an artist is his sensibility, and not a process. Any man fortunate enough to be suitably gifted can thus obtain the same effect with any means of representation.

In answer to those whom this assimilation surprises, we can only beg to observe that a skillful photographist always possesses his own manner, no less than a draftsman or a painter, to the point that, with a bit of practice, one can always identify at first glance a work by such and such operator; and still more, the particular character of the artistic spirit of each nation is to be discerned with singular and striking evidence in works from the countries concerned. . . .

We would like to add that the individuality of each photographist ever remains recognizable in his work. . . .

Thus if the lens is just one more instrument at our disposal for translating the appearance of nature, if the photographist preserves in his works his individuality, personal manner, and sensibility that distinguishes and animates him, one is forced to acknowledge that photography does indeed form part of the domain of the fine arts. Rather than seeing it as a simple mechanism that can be used by the generality, it is incumbent upon us to urge it still further in the artistic direction; one should applaud the efforts of all those who work with this exalted aim in mind and hope their example be widely imitated. The exhibition jury in its selection and rejection of the photographs subjected to its examination seems to have been animated by this thought, and they should be congratulated for it. It [the jury] has driven the merchants from the temple; thus we enter it certain to find works solely by artists.

Charles Baudelaire
LE PUBLIC MODERNE ET LA PHOTOGRAPHIE (THE MODERN PUBLIC AND PHOTOGRAPHY)
1859

In these deplorable times, a new industry has developed, which has helped in no small way to confirm fools in their faith, and to ruin what vestige of the divine might still have remained in the French mind. Naturally, this idolatrous multitude was calling for an ideal worthy of itself and in keeping with its own nature. In the domain of painting and statuary, the present-day credo of the worldly wise, especially in France (and I do not believe that anyone whosoever would dare to maintain the contrary), is this: 'I believe in nature, and I believe only in nature.' (There are good reasons for that.) 'I believe that art is, and can only be, the exact reproduction of nature.' (One timid and dissenting sect wants naturally unpleasing objects, a chamber pot, for example, or a skeleton, to be excluded.) 'Thus if an industrial process could give us a result identical to nature, that would be absolute art.' An avenging God has heard the prayers of this multitude; Daguerre was his messiah. And then they said to themselves: 'Since photography provides us with every desirable guarantee of exactitude' (they believe that, poor madmen!) 'art is photography.' From that moment onwards, our loathsome society rushed, like Narcissus, to contemplate its trivial image on the metallic plate. A form of lunacy, an extraordinary fanaticism, took hold of these new sun-worshippers. Strange abominations manifested themselves. By bringing together and posing a pack of rascals, male and female, dressed up like carnival-time butchers and washerwomen, and in persuading these 'heroes' to 'hold' their improvised grimaces for as long as photographic process required, people really believed they could represent the tragic and the charming scenes of ancient history. . . .

As the photographic industry became the refuge of all failed painters with too little talent, or too lazy to complete their studies, this universal craze not only assumed the air of blind and imbecile infatuation, but took on the aspect of revenge. I do not believe, or at least I cannot bring myself to believe, that any such stupid conspiracy, in which, as in every other, wicked men and dupes are to be found, could ever achieve a total victory; but I am convinced that the badly applied advances of photography, like all purely material progress for that matter, have greatly contributed to the impoverishment of French artistic genius, rare enough in all conscience. Modern fatuity may roar to its heart's content, eruct all the borborygmi of its pot-bellied person, vomit all the indigestible sophistries stuffed down its greedy gullter by recent philosophy; it is simple common-sense that, when industry erupts into the sphere of art, it becomes the latter's mortal enemy, and in the resulting confusion of functions none is well carried out. Poetry and progress are two ambitious men that hate each other, with an instinctive hatred, and when they meet along a pathway one or other must give way. If photography is allowed to deputize for art in some of art's activities, it will not be long before it has supplanted or corrupted art altogether, thanks to the stupidity of the masses, its natural ally. Photography must, therefore, return to its true duty, which is that of handmaid of the arts and sciences, but their very humble handmaid, like painting and shorthand, which have neither created nor supplemented literature. Let photography quickly enrich the traveller's album, and restore to his eyes the precision his memory may lack; let it adorn the library f the naturalist, magnify microscopic insects, even strengthen, with a few facts, the hypotheses of the astronomer; let it, in short, be the secretary and record-keeper of whomsoever needs absolute material accuracy for professional reasons. So far so good. Let it save crumbling ruins from oblivion, books, engravings, and manuscripts, the prey of time, all those precious things, vowed to dissolution, which crave a place in the archives of our memories; in all these things, photography will deserve our thanks and applause. But if once it be allowed to impinge on the sphere of the intangible and the imaginary, on anything that has value solely because man adds something to it from his soul, then woe betide us!

I know perfectly well I shall be told: 'The disease you have just described is a disease of boneheads. What man worthy of the name of artist, and what true art-lover has ever confused art and industry?' I know that, but let me, in my turn, ask them if they believe in the contagion of good and evil, in the pressure of society on the individual, and the involuntary, inevitable obedience of the individual to society. It is an indisputable and irresistible law that the artist acts upon the public, that the public reacts on the artist; besides, the facts, those damning witnesses, are easy to study; we can measure the full extent of the disaster. More and more, as each day goes by, art is losing in self-respect, is prostrating itself before external reality, and the painter is becoming more and more inclined to paint, not what he dreams, but what he sees. And yet *it is a happiness to dream*, and it used to be an honour to express what one dreamed; but can one believe that the painter still knows that happiness?

Will the honest observer declare that the invasion of photography and the great industrial madness of today are wholly innocent of this deplorable result? Can it legitimately be supposed that a people whose eyes get used to accepting the results of a material science as products of the beautiful will not, within a given time, have singularly diminished its capacity for judging and feeling those things that are most ethereal and immaterial?

LOUIS JOURDAN
ÉTUDES PHOTOGRAPHIQUES
(PHOTOGRAPHIC STUDIES)
Préface (Foreword)
1865

We sincerely believe that we have the solution of a problem widely debated since the day when the invention of Niépce, as improved by Daguerre and perfected by Talbot, made possible photographic images all over the world.

Photography, as some saw it, stood at the antipodes of art; it could certainly fix on a glass or metal plate, and subsequently reproduce on paper, lines, and contours, monuments, landscapes, the material features of the human visage; but these reproductions would always lack life, life!, which art alone can imprint on its immortal works.

Others, on the other hand, while conceding that photography could still be greatly improved, ascribed artistic value to it in the belief that its productions, because they are able to attain a notable degree of truth, are worthy of being classified as works of art—art being, after all, none other than the most elevated and most ideal expression of truth.

This latter theory wanted one thing, only one—but it is essential. And this was a practical demonstration—and God knows the courageous and unstinting efforts made by wealthy amateurs and by a number of professional photographers alike to provide one. We would be unjust and ungrateful we were not to seize this opportunity to offer public tribute to creditable endeavors in this direction that the Société Française de Photographie has encouraged with zeal and an intelligence above all praise. . . .

To paint is not to pile up colors and lines with a certain harmony; it is not to invent random combinations of light and shade, or to imagine picturesque sites and improbable trees. To paint is to imitate nature the most perfectly, or the least imperfectly, as possible. It is her, immortal nature, ever varied and yet always the same; it is this bounteous mother, *alma parens*!, who is the great mistress of art, the fertile inspiration of all the forms human genius creates. We can do nothing without her, nor separated from her. Imperishable works that our museums preserve provoke admiration only because they reproduce the ideal aspect of some of the beauties that every day strike our eye.

If then, one of these men whose artistic instincts place them in more intimate communication with nature—one of these men who sense their splendors more forcefully, who halt, dreamily and enthused, before a site that unites all the conditions of a beautiful picture; if one of these men, I say, were to arm himself with a photographic apparatus and make it his mission to fix on glass plates the landscapes, the scenes that move him, we would have no longer vulgar photographs, but true artistic works bearing the double stamp of a love of art and a feeling for nature.

One finds truth solely on the condition that one seeks it both with diligence and with passion. I mean to say only that, in this regard, much still remains to be done. . . .

The finest of these compositions is one representing an old man reading a newspaper. In the smoke-filled room, attentive listeners stand grouped around him and do not conceal their impressions; in the corner a young woman nurses her infant with a gentle smile. The groups are well ordered, all the figures are infused with life; and I note the fact with all the more satisfaction since this, it behooves me to state, is precisely the stumbling block. Man does not lend himself as easily as trees, water, the arches of a bridge, etc., etc., to the ruses of the photographer. To produce a beautiful landscape, he has only to look for one and to seize it at its most favorable aspect and time of day. To execute a genre painting, one needs many other conditions; each character needs to imbue himself with the thought of the artist—that is to say, so to speak, that he needs to become an artist himself, and to pose with a naturalness seemingly unmindful of the photographic apparatus. Just try to make some goodly peasants, children, women remain oblivious at the moment the photographer utters the fateful words: "Look out! No one move!" Life, which is nothing else than movement, is certainly at odds with orders of this kind. To live is to be on the move and you tell life to be still! How can you hope then to capture life and truth?

So, I regard this picture of villagers listening to a man reading the newspaper as a stroke of genius; it is as successful as it could possibly be in the current state of the photographic process, whose operations demand an artificiality that almost invariably excludes naturalness.

ANTOINE FRANÇOIS JEAN CLAUDET
January 15, 1866
La Lumière

M. Claudet has recently addressed the following letter to *La Gazette des beaux-arts* [for October of the preceding year], in response to what he sees as unpleasant remarks made on the present state and the future of photography.

We are forced to admit that *there are arts that are dying off* and that it is photography that has killed them. Why are there no more painters in miniature today? For the excellent reason that those wanting a miniature find photographs superior and that instead of more or less incorrect portraits in terms of drawing and appearance, photography renders a perfect resemblance which delights the heart and charms the memory, at the very least.

Why has the number of engravers and lithographers diminished? Because photography provides us with more faithful representations of every creation of genius, in less time and with less expense than by means of any other process.

Nevertheless, these expiring arts were after all neither *stupid* nor *base* [as photography was described in the critique]; and so, ought we to apply these expressions to an art—mechanical, if you like—that has replaced them for the simple reason that its products signal an improvement on theirs?

Printing too did away with more than one art, the most regrettable being calligraphy.

Printing is even more mechanical than photography; despite that, however, who would dream of calling it *base* or *stupid*, although, like a machine speeding along the road of progress, it crushed an excellent art that will never recover?

Photography possesses several points of resemblance with printing, and, like its elder, it is sure to be called upon to exert considerable influence on all that touches the arts and the sciences, and also to contribute to the development of taste, the intellect, and education.

Would we say that the invention of the railroad was *stupid* and *base* because it occasioned the demise of the stagecoach, which, if admittedly it transported us in most poetical fashion, was painfully slow?

We traversed mountains and valleys in the midst of picturesque ruins, with ample time to admire the most varied scenery. What diverse sensations we experienced as we passed before the thatched cottages of hamlets and peaceful villages or when in the breaking dawn we crossed a drawbridge or through a massive gate of a fortified city surrounded by dilapidated ramparts and waterless moats? All this now exists solely in the memory—but that hardly justifies stigmatizing the present, more practical state of affairs as *stupid* and *base*.

And what of the courier, that nimble and intriguing being who long ago would convey our most urgent messages, should we, to please him, apply a rude-sounding epithet to the [telegraph] wire which made his occupation disappear, and which, by the invisible waves running through its rigid substance, transmits thought over any distance and at lightning speed?

All that civilization has achieved with such toil, all that the labor of man has so arduously drawn from the core of science—in a word, everything that constitutes a triumph of genius, is deserving of admiration and respect, especially on the part of writers who have embraced the mission of enlightening the judgment of the public on every issue concerning art and progress, and of spreading knowledge, educating our minds today with a view to life tomorrow.

Why, then, in our society, are we always so inclined to disparage all that is popular and take such pleasure in depreciating what the multitude admires? It is a defect in our national character that I am pained to encounter in cultured, well-educated classes.

But perhaps I have already said too much and I should have limited myself to expressing the unease I feel at such a churlish sally.

I cherish the hope that you will publish the present letter in the next number of *La Gazette des beaux-arts*. You owe reparation to the numerous class of photographers who are to be found in every station of society and who would have preferred instead to find in *La Gazette des beaux-arts* a protector willing to conduct photography along the path to the fine arts.

I hope that you will not refuse me this redress—or rather that you will demonstrate, as you have already done, that the spirit of *La Gazette des beaux-arts* can only be favorable to the interests and progress of photography.

I remain, Sir, your most humble servant,

SELECTED BIBLIOGRAPHY

Adam, Hans-Christian. *Die erotische Daguerreotypie: eine mediengeschichtliche Bestandsaufnahme*. Prague: Odefil, 1998.

Adhémar, Jean. *Un siècle de vision nouvelle*. Paris: Bibliothèque Nationale de France, 1985.

Adhémar, Jean, and Beaumont Newhall. *Daguerre et les premiers daguerréotypistes français, 1787-1851*. Paris: Bibliothèque Nationale de France, 1961.

Allard, Sébastien. *Le Louvre à l'époque romantique, les décors du Palais 1815-1835*. Paris: Fage éditions, 2006.

——, ed. *Delacroix 1798-1863, de l'idée à l'expression*. Madrid: Ediciones El Viso, 2011.

Allard, Sébastien, and Marie-Claude Chaudonneret. *Le Suicide de Gros, les peintres de l'Empire et la génération romantique*. Paris: Gourcuff Gradenigo, 2011.

Allard, Sébastien, and Guilhem Scherf. *Portraits publics, portraits privés*. Exh. cat. Paris: Réunion des musées nationaux, 2006.

Allemand-Cosneau, Claude. *Paul Delaroche, un peintre dans l'histoire*. Paris: Réunion des musées nationaux, 1999.

Alloa, Emmanuel, ed. *Penser l'image*. Paris: Presses du Réel, 2010.

Arago, François. *Rapport de M. Arago sur le daguerréotype lu à la Chambre des députés le 3 juillet 1839 et à l'Académie des Sciences, séance du 19 août*. Paris: Bachelier imprimeur, 1839.

Arasse, Daniel. *On n'y voit rien, descriptions*. Paris: Gallimard, 2003.

——. *Le détail, pour une histoire rapprochée de la peinture*. Paris: Flammarion, 2009 (repr.).

Aubenas, Sylvie. *Le Concours du duc de Luynes*. Paris: Bibliothèque nationale de France, 1994.

Aubenas, Sylvie, ed. *Gustave Le Gray (1820-1884)*. London: Phaidon, 2003.

——. "Henri Le Secq et la nature morte." *48/14, La Revue du Musée d'Orsay* 16, (Spring 2003).

——. *Des albums pour l'Empereur*. Paris: Bibliothèque Nationale de France, 2004.

Aubenas, Sylvie et al. *L'art du nu au XIXe siècle, le photographe et son modèle*. Paris: Bibliothèque Nationale de France/Hazan, 1997.

Aubenas Sylvie, and Anne Biroleau. *Portraits/Visages*. Exh. cat. Paris: Bibliothèque nationale de France/Gallimard, 2003.

Aubenas, Sylvie, and André Gunthert. *La révolution de la photographie instantanée, 1880–1900*. Paris: André Gunthert, 1996.

Aubenas, Sylvie, and Jacques Lacarrière. *Voyage en Orient*. Paris: Bibliothèque Nationale de France/Hazan, 1999.

Aubenas, Sylvie, and Paul-Louis Roubert, eds. *Primitifs de la photographie, le calotype en France*. Paris: Bibliothèque Nationale de France/Gallimard, 2010.

Aubenas, Sylvie and Dominique Versavel. *Objets dans l'objectif*. Paris: Bibliothèque Nationale de France/Sceren/Ishtmes Edition, 2005.

Aumont, Jacques. *L'Attrait de la lumière*. Paris: Editions Yellow Now–Côté Cinéma/Motifs, 2010.

Auvray, Louis. *Exposition des beaux-arts, Salon de 1869*. Paris, Veuve Renouard, 1869.

Bajac, Quentin. *Tableaux vivants, fantaisies victoriennes (1840-1880)*. Paris: Réunion des Musées Nationaux, 1999.

——. *The Invention of Photography*. London: Thames and Hudson, 2008.

——. *La photographie, du daguerréotype au numérique*. Paris: Gallimard, 2010.

Bajac, Quentin, and Dominique de Font-Réaulx, eds. *Le daguerréotype français, un objet photographique*. Paris: Réunion des Musées Nationaux, 2003.

Baldassari, Anne. *Le Miroir noir, Picasso, sources photographiques, 1900-1928*. Paris: Réunion des Musées Nationaux, 1997.

Baldwin, Gordon, Malcolm Daniel, and Sarah Greenough, eds. *All the Mighty World: The Photographs of Roger Fenton, 1852–1860*. New York: The Metropolitan Museum of Art, 2004.

Baldwin, Gordon. *Pasha and Bayadere*. Los Angeles: The Getty Museum of Art, 1996.

Balzac, Honoré de. *"Pierre Grassou," Le Chef-d'œuvre inconnu et autres nouvelles*. Annotated by Adrien Goetz. Paris: Gallimard-Folio, 1994.

Bann, Stephen. *Parallel Lines: Printmakers, Painters, and Photographers in Nineteenth Century France*. New Haven/London: Yale University Press, 2001.

Barilli, Renato et al. *L'ultimo Michetti, Pittura et Fotografia*. Florence: Fratelli Alinari, 1994.

Barthes, Roland. *La Chambre claire*. Paris: Gallimard, 1979. Translated as *Camera Lucida: Reflections on Photography*. New York: Hill & Wang, 1981.

Bataille, Georges. *Les Larmes d'Éros*. Paris: Jean-Jacques Pauvert, 1961; new ed. 2001.

Batchen, Geoffrey. *Burning with Desire: The Conception of Photography*. Cambridge, Massachusetts: MIT Press, 1999.

Baudelaire, Charles. *Critique d'art*. Paris: Gallimard, 1992 (repr.).

——. *Selected Writings on Art and Artists*. Translated by P. E. Charver. Cambridge: Cambridge University Press, 1981.

Belting, Hans. *La vraie image, croire aux images*. Paris: Gallimard, 2007.

——. *The Anthropology of Images, Picture, Medium, Body*. Princeton: Princeton University Press, 2011.

Berlière, Jean-Marc, and Pierre Fournier, eds. *Tous fichés*. Exh. cat. Paris: Archives Nationales, 2011.

Billeter, Erika. *Malerei und Photographie im Dialog, von 1840 bis heute*. Zurich: Zurich Kunsthaus, 1977.

Blanquart-Evrard, Louis-Désiré. *Intervention de l'art dans la photographie*. Lille: Imprimerie L. Danel, 1863.

Bonfand, Alain. *Le Cinéma saturé, essais sur les relations entre la peinture et les images en mouvement*. Paris: PUF, 2007.

Bonnet, Manuel, and Jean-Louis Marignier, eds. *Niépce, correspondance et papiers*. 2 vols. Saint-Loup-de-Varennes: Maison Nicéphore Niépce, 2003.

Bouillo Eva. *Le Salon de 1827, classique ou romantique?* Rennes: Presses universitaires de Rennes, 2010.

Bouillon, Jean-Paul, ed. *La Promenade du critique influent, anthologie de la critique d'art en France, 1855-1900*. Paris: Hazan, 1990.

Brême, Dominique, ed. *Le Dessin français de paysage aux XVIIe et XVIIIe siècles*. Paris: Somogy, 2011. Catalog published in conjunction with the exhibition at the Domaine de Sceaux.

Brunet, François. *La naissance de l'idée de photographie*. Paris: Presses Universitaires de France, 2000; new ed. 2012.

Cars, Laurence des, and Dominique de Font-Réaulx, eds. *Gustave Courbet, 1819-1877*. Paris: Réunion des Musées Nationaux, 2007.

Cars, Laurence des, Dominique de Font-Réaulx, and Édouard Papet, eds. *The Spectacular Art of Jean-Léon Gérôme*. Paris: Musée d'Orsay/Skira-Flammarion, 2010.

Cartier-Bresson, Anne, ed. *Éloge du négatif, les débuts de la photographie sur papier en Italie, 1846-1862*. Paris: Paris-Musées, 2009.

——. *Le vocabulaire technique de la photographie*. Paris: Marval, 2010.

Challe, Daniel, Ulrike Gauss, and Henning Weidemann. *Eugène Cuvelier*. Stuttgart: Cantz, 1996.

Challe, Daniel, and Bernard Marbot. *Les Photographes de Barbizon*. Paris: Hoëbeke/Bibliothèque nationale, 1991.

Chateaubriand, François-René de. *Lettre sur le paysage en peinture*. La Rochelle: Rumeur des Âges, 1993; 1st edition 1830 in *Les Oeuvres complètes*, vol. 3.

Chaudonneret Marie-Claude. *L'État et les artistes, de la Restauration à la monarchie de Juillet, 1815-1833*. Paris: Flammarion, 1999.

Chazal, Gilles, ed. *José-Maria Sert, Le Titan à l'oeuvre (1874-1945)*. Paris : Éditions Paris Musées, 2012. Catalog published in conjunction with the exhibition at the Petit Palais, Musée des Beaux-Arts de la Ville de Paris, Paris.

Chéroux, Clément, and Angela Lampe. *Edvard Munch, l'oeil moderne*. Exh. cat. Paris: Centre Pompidou, 2011.

Childs, Elizabeth C. *In Search of Paradise Painting and Photography in Fin de Siècle Tahiti*. Berkeley and Los Angeles: University of California Press, 2001.

Chomette, Michèle. *L'Art de la fresque de José-Maria Sert, 1874-1945: photographies inédites*. Paris: J. Damasne, 1990.
Clark, Kenneth. *Landscape into Art*. London: Murray, 1945.
Coetzee, J. M. *Paysage sud-africain*. Paris: Verdier, 2008.
Cogeval, Guy, and Ulrich Pohlmann, eds. *Voir l'Italie et mourir*. Paris: Musée d'Orsay/Flammarion, 2008.
——. *Vuillard*. Paris: Flammarion, 1991. Catalog published in conjunction with the exhibition at the Musée des Beaux-Arts, Lyon.
Cogeval, Guy, ed. *Edouard Vuillard*. New Haven: Yale University Press, 2003.
Comar, Philippe, ed. *Figures du corps, Une leçon d'anatomie à l'École des beaux-arts*. Paris: École Nationale Supérieure des Beaux-Arts, 2008.
Corbin, Alain. *Le Territoire du vide, le désir de ravage*. Paris: Aubier, 1998; new ed. Paris: Flammarion, 1990.
Crary, Jonathan. *Techniques of the Observer: On Vision and Modernity in the 19th Century*. Cambridge, MA: MIT Press, 1992.
Daguerre, Louis Jacques Mandé. *Historique et description des procédés du daguerréotype et du diorama*. Paris: Susse Frères, 1839.
Daniel, Malcolm. *Édouard Baldus*. Paris: Réunion des Musées Nationaux, 1994.
Daniel, Malcolm, and Sylvie Aubenas, eds. *Degas, Photographer*. New York: The Metropolitan Museum of Art, 1998.
Daston, Lorraine, and Peter Galison. *Objectivité*. Paris: Presses du Réel, 2012.
Eugène Delacroix. *Journal*. Paris: José Corti, 2009.
——. *The Journal of Eugène Delacroix*. Translated by Lucy Norton. Oxford: Phaidon, 1995.
Delécluze, Étienne. *David, son école et son temps*. Paris: Macula, 1983.
Deschamps, Stéphanie, ed. *Gravure ou photographie? Une curiosité artistique: le cliché-verre*. Arras: Musée des Beaux-Arts, 2007.
Desroy-Hamouda, Laurence. *Eclats d'histoire, les photographies dans les collections de l'Institut de France*. Paris: Actes Sud/Institut de France, 2003.
Diderot, Denis. *"no. 154, Van Spaendonck, Tableau représentant un vase sculpté en bas relief, rempli de fleurs et de fruits, se détachant sur un fond d'architecture," Salon de 1767*. New ed. Paris: Hermann, 1995.
Didi-Huberman, Georges. *Invention de l'hystérie, Charcot et l'iconographie photographique de la Salpêtrière*. Paris: Macula, 1984.
——. *Ce que nous voyons, ce qui nous regarde*. Paris: Editions de Minuit, 1999.
——. *Confronting Images*. University Park, PA: Penn State University Press, 2009.
Easton, Elizabeth, ed. *Snapshot: Painters and Photography, Bonnard to Vuillard*. New Haven: Yale University Press, 2011.
Edwards, Paul. *Soleil noir*. Rennes: Presses Universitaires de Rennes, 2008.
Eitner, Lorenz. *La peinture en Europe au XIXème siècle*. Paris: Hazan, 2007.
Faroult, Guillaume, ed. *La Collection La Caze*. Paris: Musée du Louvre/Hazan, 2007.
Font-Réaulx, Dominique de, ed. *L'Oeuvre d'art et sa reproduction photographique*. Paris: Musée d'Orsay/5 Continents, 2008.
Figuier, Louis. *La Photographie au Salon de 1859*. Paris: Imprimerie C. Lahure, 1859.
Ford, Colin. *Julia Margaret Cameron: 19th Century Photographer of Genius*. London: National Portrait Gallery, 2003.
Fossier, François. *La Nébuleuse nabie*. Paris: Réunion des musées nationaux/Bibliothèque Nationale de France, 1992.
Frizot, Michel, ed. *Une nouvelle histoire de la photographie*. Paris: Bordas, 1994. New ed. Paris: Larousse, 2002. Translated as *A New History of Photography*. Cologne: Konemann, 1998.
Gaillemin, Jean-Louis, ed. *Alfons Mucha*. Paris: Somogy, 2009.
Galassi, Peter. *Before Photography: Painting and the Invention of Photography*. New York: The Museum of Modern Art, 1980.
Garnier Marie D., ed. *Jardins d'hiver, littérature et photographie*. Paris: Presses ENS, 1999.
Gautier, Théophile. *Histoire du romantisme, suivi de Quarante Portraits romantiques*. With foreword by Adrien Goetz. Paris: Gallimard, 2011.
Georgel, Chantal. *La Forêt de Fontainebleau, un atelier grandeur nature*. Paris: Musée d'Orsay/Réunion des Musées Nationaux, 2007.
Gernsheim, Helmut, and Alison Gernsheim. *The History of Photography*. Oxford: Oxford University Press, 1955.
——. *L. J. M Daguerre, the History of Diorama and Daguerreotype*. London: Secker and Warburg, 1956.
Gervais, Thierry, and Dominique de Font-Réaulx. *Léon Gimpel, les audaces d'un photographe*. Paris: Musée d'Orsay/Cinq Continents, 2008.
Ginzburg, Carlo. *Mythes Emblèmes Traces, Morphologie et histoire*. New ed. Paris: Verdier, "Verdier Poches," 2010.
Grunchec, Philippe. *Les Concours des prix de Rome, 1797-1863*. Paris: École Nationale Supérieure des Beaux-Arts, 1989.
Hamber, Anthony. *A Higher Branch of the Art: Photographing the Fine Arts in England, 1839-1880*. London: Gordon and Breach Publishers, 1996.
Hamilton, Peter, and Roger Hargreaves. *The Beautiful and the Damned*. London: National Portrait Gallery, 2001.
Hamon, Philippe. *Imageries: Littérature et image au XIXème siècle*. Paris: Corti, 2001.
Hamy, E. T., ed. *Correspondance d'Alexandre de Humboldt avec François Arago*. Paris: Bibliothèque d'Histoire Scientifique, 1908.
Hannavy, John, ed. *Encyclopedia of Nineteenth-Century Photography*. New York: John Hannavy, 2007.
Haskell, Francis. *La Norme et le caprice*. Paris: Champs Flammarion, 1986; new ed. 1993.
Heilbrun, Françoise et al. *A History of Photography: Photography at the Musée d'Orsay 1839-1925*. Paris: Musée d'Orsay/Flammarion, 2009.
Heilbrun, Françoise. *Bonnard: Photographs and Paintings*. New York: Aperture, 1988.
Heilbrun, Françoise, Philippe Néagu, and Bernard Marbot, eds. *L'invention d'un art*. Paris: Réunion des Musées Nationaux, 1989.
Heilbrun, Françoise, and Philippe Néagu. *Bonnard photographe*. Paris: Réunion des Musées Nationaux, 1987.
Heilbrun, Françoise, Philippe Néagu, and Maria Morris Hambourg, eds. *Nadar, les années créatrices (1854-1860)*. Paris: Réunion des musées nationaux, 1994.
——. *Nadar*. New York: Harry N. Abrams, 1995.
Héran, Emmanuelle, ed. *Le Dernier Portrait*. Paris: Réunion des Musées Nationaux, 2002.
Hoogue, Alain d', ed. *Autour du symbolisme, photographie et peinture au XIXème siècle*. Brussels: Palais des Beaux-Arts, 2004.
Hugo, Victor. *Cromwell*. Paris: Garnier-Flammarion, 1965 (first published in 1827).
Jacobson, Ken, and Jenny Jacobson. *Études d'après nature: 19th Century Photographs in relation to Art*. London: Petches Bridge, 1996.
Jammes, André, and Eugenia Parry-Janis. *The Art of French Calotype, 1845-1870*. Princeton: Princeton University Press, 1983.
Jammes, Isabelle. *Louis-Désiré Blanquart-Evrard et les origines de l'édition photographique française*. Paris: Droz, 1981.
Jobert, Barthélemy, ed. *Delacroix, le trait romantique*. Paris: Bibliothèque Nationale de France, 1998.
Kaenel, Philippe. *Eugène Burnand, la peinture d'après nature, 1850-1921*. Lausanne: Editions Cabedita, 2006.
Kahng, Eikh. *The Repeating Image: Multiples in French Painting from David to Matisse*. Baltimore: The Walters Art Museum, 2007.
Kendall, Richard, and Jill DeVonyar. *Degas and the Ballet: Picturing Movement*. London: The Royal Academy, 2010.
Kennel, Sarah, and Kimberly Jones, eds. *In the Forest of Fontainebleau: Painters and Photographers, from Corot to Monet*. Washington: The National Gallery of Art, 2008.
Kopp Robert, and Daniel Couty, eds. *Romantisme et révolution(s)*. 3 vols. Paris: Gallimard, 2008–10.

Kosinski, Dorothy. *The Artist and the Camera*. Dallas: Dallas Museum of Art, 1999.
Kravets, Toritchan Pavlovitch, ed. *Documentii po istorii izobretenia fotografii*. Moscow/Leningrad, 1949.
Laclotte, Michel, ed. *Mucha, 1860-1939, peintures, illustrations, affiches, arts décoratifs*. Paris: Réunion des Musées Nationaux, 1980.
Lafont-Couturier, Hélène, and Pierre-Lin Renié, eds. *Gérôme et Goupil, art et entreprise*. Paris: Réunion des Musées nationaux, 2000.
Le Gray, Gustave. *Photographie, traité nouveau, théorique et pratique*. Paris: Lerebours et Secrétan, 1852.
Le Pelley Fonteny, Monique. *Adolphe et Georges Giraudon, une bibliothèque photographique*. Paris: Somogy/Archives départementales du Cher, 2005.
Leribault, Christophe, ed. *Delacroix et la photographie*. Paris: Louvre/Le Passage, 2008
Los Llanos, José de. *Tivoli, variations sur un paysage au XVIII*e *siècle*. Exh. cat. Paris: Paris-Musées, 2010.
Loyrette, Henri. *Degas*. Paris: Fayard, 1991.
Loyrette, Henri, and Gary Tinterow. *Les Origines de l'Impressionnisme*. Paris: Réunion des Musées Nationaux, 1994.
Loyrette, Henri, Sébastien Allard, and Laurence des Cars. *Nineteenth-Century French Art: From Romanticism to Impressionism, Post-Impressionism, and Art Nouveau*. Paris, Flammarion, 2007.
Mahler-Lechner, Astrid. *Martin Gerlachs "Formenwelt aus dem Naturreiche," Fotografien als Vorlage für Künstler um 1900*. Vienna: Albertina, 2005.
Mannoni, Laurent. *Trois siècles de cinéma*. Paris: Réunion des Musées Nationaux, 1995.
——. *Le Grand Art de la lumière et de l'ombre, le cinéma*. Paris: Nathan, 1995.
——. *Étienne-Jules Marey, la mémoire de l'oeil*. Paris: La cinémathèque française, 2000.
Marquet, Françoise. *Derain et la photographie*. Neuchâtel: Ides et Calendes, 1997.
Mathon, Catherine, ed. *Duchenne de Boulogne*. Paris: École Nationale Supérieure des Beaux-Arts, 1999.
McCauley, Ann. *A. A. E. Disdéri and the Carte de Visite Portrait Photograph*. New Haven: Yale University Press, 1985.
——. *Industrial Madness: Commercial Photography in Paris, 1848–1871*. New Haven/London: Yale University Press, 1994.
——. *Charles Aubry, photographe*. Exh. cat. Translated by Sylvie Aubenas. Paris: Bibliothèque Nationale de France, 1996.
McNamara, Carol, ed. *The Lens of Impressionism: Photography and Painting along the Normandy Coast, 1850–1874*. Ann Arbor, MI: University of Michigan Press, 2010.
McWilliam, Neil. *Dreams of Happiness: Social Art and the French Left, 1830–1850*. Princeton, NJ: Princeton University Press, 1993.
Mérot, Alain. *Les Conférences de l'Académie royale de peinture et de sculpture au XVIIe siècle*. Paris: École Nationale Supérieure des Beaux-Arts, 1996.
Michel, Régis. *Le Beau idéal*. Exh. cat. Paris: Réunion des Musées Nationaux, 1989.
Naugrette, Florence. *Le théâtre romantique: histoire, écriture, mise en scène*. Paris: Le Seuil, Points, 2001.
Nazarieff, Serge. *Early Erotic Photography*. Cologne: Taschen, 1993.
Newhall, Beaumont. "The Photographic Revolution in the Visual Arts." *Photographic Journal*, September 1963.
——. *Photography, Essays and Images: Illustrated Readings in the History of Photography*. New York: The Museum of Modern Art, 1980.
——. *The History of Photography: from 1839 to the Present*. 5th ed. New York: The Museum of Modern Art, 1982.
Niel, Georges. *Le paysage au Salon de 1857*. Paris: Librairie d'Alphonse Taride, 1857.
Nochlin, Linda. *The Politics of Vision: Essays on Nineteenth-Century Art and Society*. Boulder, CO: Westview Press, 1995.
Ortel, Philippe. *La littérature à l'ère de la photographie, enquête sur une révolution invisible*. Nîmes: Éditions Jacqueline Chambon, 2002.
Pinson, Stephen. *Speculating Daguerre: Art and Enterprise in the Work of L.J.M. Daguerre*. Chicago: University of Chicago Press, 2012.
Plantureux, Serge. *Joseph Hamel chez Talbot, Niépce et Daguerre*. Paris: Academi dei Venti, 2003.
Pline l'Ancien (Pliny the Elder). *Histoire naturelle*. Paris: Gallimard, "Folio," 1999 (reissued).
Pliny the Elder. *The Natural History*. Translated by. J. Bostock. London: H. T. Riley, 1855.
Pohlmann, Ulrich. *Eine andere Kunst? Eine andere Natur! Photographie und Malerei im 19. Jahrhundert*. Munich: Kunsthall der Hypo-Kulturstiftung, 2006.
Poivert, Michel, ed. *Le Pictorialisme en France*. Paris: Hoebeke/Bibliothèque Nationale de France, 1992.
——. *La Photographie pictorialiste en Europe, 1888-1918*. Rennes/Cherbourg: Musée des Beaux-Arts/Le Point du Jour, 2006.
Poivert, Michel, and André Gunthert, eds. *Une utopie photographique, Regards sur la collection de la Société française de photographie*. Paris/Cherbourg: Le Point du Jour, 2004.
——. *L'Art de la photographie des origines à nos jours*. Paris: Citadelles/Mazenod, 2007.
Pomarède, Vincent, Alexander D. Grishin, and Denis Canguilhem. *André Giroux (1801–1879)*. London: Wertheimer Foundation, 2005.
Pomarède, Vincent, Stéphane Guégan, and Louis-Antoine Prat, eds. *Ingres*. Paris: Louvre/Gallimard, 2006.
Pommier, Édouard. *Théories du portrait, de la Renaissance aux Lumières*. Paris: Gallimard, 1998.
Rapetti, Rodolphe. *Le Symbolisme*. Paris: Flammarion, 2005. Translated as *Symbolism*, Paris: Flammarion, 2005.
Recht, Roland. *La Lettre de Humboldt, du jardin paysager au daguerréotype*. Paris: Christian Bourgois, 1990; new ed. 2006.
Robinson, Henry Peach. *The Studio, and What to Do in It*. London: Piper & Carter, 1891 (2nd ed.).
Roseboom, Hans. *George Hendrik Breitner, pionnier de la photographie de rue*. Paris: Institut Néerlandais, 2011.
Rosen, Charles, and Henri Zerner. *Romanticism and Realism: The Mythology of Nineteenth-Century Art*. New York: Viking, 1984.
Rosenthal, Léon. *Du romantisme au réalisme, la peinture en France de 1830 à 1848*. Paris: Macula, 1987 (repr.).
Roubert, Paul-Louis. *L'image sans qualités, les beaux-arts et la critique à l'épreuve de la photographie, 1839-1859*. Paris: Monum, 2006.
Rouillé, André. *La photographie en France, textes et controverses: une anthologie, 1816-1871*. Paris: Macula, 1989.
Rousset, Ildefonse. *Études photographiques*. Paris: Maison Giroux, 1866.
Schaaf, Larry J. *The Photographic Art of William Henry Fox Talbot*. Princeton/Oxford: Oxford University Press, 2001.
Schaeffer, Jean-Marie. *L'image précaire, du dispositif photographique*. Paris: Le Seuil, 1987.
——. *Pourquoi la fiction?* Paris: Le Seuil, 1999.
Schama, Simon. *Landscape and Memory*. New York: Vintage, 1996.
Scharf, Aaron. *Art and Photography*. London: Allen Lane, 1968.
Sexton, Sean, Robert Flynn Johnson, and Alice Waters. *The Plant Kingdom of Charles Jones*. London: Thames and Hudson, 1998.
Société Française de Photographie. *Etudes photographiques*, nos. 1–28.
Staley, Allen, and Christopher Newall, eds. *Pre-Rapahelite Vision: Truth to Nature*. London: Tate Publishing, 2004.
Stendhal. *Salons*. Compiled and commentated by Stéphane Guégan and Martine Reid. Paris: Le Promeneur, 2002.
Sterling, Charles. *La Nature morte de l'Antiquité à nos jours*. Exh. cat. Paris: Macula, 1952; reissued as *Still Life Painting from Antiquity to the Twentieth-Century*. New York: Harper & Row, 1981.

Taylor, Roger. *Impressed by Light: British Photographs from Paper Negatives, 1840–1860*. Exh. cat. New York: The Metropolitan Museum of Art, 2007.

Ten-Doesschate Chu, Petra, ed. *Correspondance de Courbet*. Paris: Flammarion, 1996; new ed. 2007.

Thiers, Adolphe. *Adolphe Thiers, critique d'art, Salons de 1822 et 1824*. With annotations by Marie-Claude Chaudonneret. Paris: Honoré Champion, 2005.

Töpffer, Rodolphe. *Réflexions et menus propos d'un peintre genevois ou essai sur le beau dans les arts*. Paris: École Nationale Supérieure des Beaux-Arts, 1998.

Vancheri, Luc. *Cinéma et peinture*. Paris: Armand Colin, 2007.

Van Tuyll, Carel. *Claude Gellée dit Le Lorrain, le dessinateur face à la nature*. Paris: Éditions du Louvre/Somogy, 2011.

Vouilloux Bernard. *Le Tableau vivant, Phryné, l'orateur et le peintre*. Paris: Flammarion, 2002.

Waggoner, Diane, ed. *The Pre-Raphaelite Lens: British Photography and Painting, 1848–1875*. Washington: The National Gallery, 2010.

Wat, Pierre. *Constable, entre ciel et terre*. Paris: Herscher, 1995.

——. *Naissance de l'art romantique : peinture et théorie de l'imitation en Allemagne et en Angleterre*. Paris: Flammarion, 1998.

Weisberg, Gabriel. *The Realist Tradition: French Painting and Drawing, 1830–1900*. Cleveland: The Cleveland Museum of Art, 1980.

——. *The Popularization of Images: Visual Culture and the July Monarchy*. Princeton: Princeton University Press, 1994.

——. *Illusions of Reality: Naturalist Painting, Photography, Theater and Cinema, 1875–1921*. Amsterdam: Van Gogh Museum, 2010.

Wild, Nicole. *Décors et costumes du XIXème siècle : Opéra de Paris*. Paris: Bibliothèque Nationale de France, 1987.

Yon, Jean-Claude, ed. *Les spectacles sous le Second Empire*. Paris: Armand Colin, 2010.

Yon, Jean-Claude, Jean-Yves Mollier, and Martine Reid. *Repenser la Restauration*. Paris: Nouveau Monde, 2005.

Zola, Émile. *Écrits sur l'art*. Paris: Gallimard, 1991.

INDEX OF PROPER NAMES

Page numbers in **bold** refer to illustrations

PHOTOGRAPHIC CREDITS

(l = left, r = right, b = bottom, t = top, c = center)

© ADAGP, Paris, 2012 for the works by Pierre Bonnard, André Derain, Paul Haviland, Auguste and Louis Lumière, and José Maria Sert.
© Georgia O'Keeffe Museum/ADAGP, Paris, 2012 for the works by Alfred Stieglitz.

© akg-images/André Held: 232 r
© Alinari/Roger-Viollet: 274
© All rights reserved: 49
© Archives de l'Art contemporain en Belgique/Musées royaux des Beaux-arts de Belgique, Brussels: 285 l, 285 r
© Archives Flammarion: 120, 169, 176, 185, 203 l, 246
© Archives Nationales, Paris: 97
© Archives Vuillard, Paris: 287 l, 287: r, 288 l, 288 r, 289
© Bibliothèque littéraire Jacques Doucet: 278
© Bibliothèque municipale de Lille (call number S2–6, plate 332): 84
© Bibliothèque nationale de France: 16, 17 l, 22, 26, 34, 54, 55, 56, 57, 58 l, 58 r, 73, 76 l, 76 r, 77, 88, 92 t, 100 l, 100 r, 101 r, 124, 164, 229 r, 230, 232 l, 233 l, 293
© BPK, Berlin, Dist. RMN-GP/Elke Walford: 235
© BPK, Berlin, Dist. RMN-GP/Hermann Buresch: 23
© Bridgeman Giraudon: 135
© Christie's Images: 131
© Collection Alain & Audrey Flamand: 90 b
© Collection J.-G. Bouchaud/Béatrice Hatala: 153 l, 153 r
© Collection Roger Thérond: 220, 221
© Comité Derain/All rights reserved: 276, 277 c, 277 l
© École nationale supérieure des Beaux-arts, Paris: 25, 224, 237, 239, 260
© École nationale supérieure des Beaux-arts, Paris, photograph Jean-Michel Lapelerie 159 r
© Francesco Paolo Michetti/Alinari/Roger-Viollet: 275
© Courtesy of George Eastman House, International Museum of Photography and Film: 52
© Harry Ransom Humanities Research Center Gershein Collection. The University of Texas at Austin: 35
© Institut Catholique de Paris, Bibliothèque de Fels: 132 b
© The J. Paul Getty Museum, Los Angeles: 115, 121, 208 r, 283
© Luisa Ricciarini/Leemage: 213
© Mairie de Bordeaux, photograph B. Fontanel: 102 b
© Mairie de Bordeaux, photograph Lysiane Gauthier: 102 t
© Maison de Balzac/Roger-Viollet: 148
© MBA, Rennes, Dist. RMN-GP/Adélaïde Beaudoin: 27; Alexis Bran dt: 67; Jean-Jacques Sauciat: 261; Patrick Schmidt: 4, 69, 92 b, 93, 95, 101 l, 107, 113 r, 141, 150, 152 r, 190 l, 193, 194, 203 r, 204 r, 207, 253, 264, 292; René-Gabriel Ojéda: 151.
© The Metropolitan Museum of Art, Dist. RMN-GP/image of the MMA: 37, 140, 162, 172, 180, 216, 234, 282
© Montauban, Musée Ingres: 99
© Mucha Trust, 2012: 268, 269, 270 l, 270 r, 271
© Musée Baron Martin, 70100 Gray: 43
© Musée Bartholdi-Colmar. Reproduction Chr. Kempf: 244
© Musée de Semur-en-Auxois (Côte d'Or): 199
© Musée Fabre de Montpellier Agglomération/photograph Frédéric Jaulmes: 229 l
© Musée Gatien-Bonnet, Lagny-sur-Marne: 91, 198, 200
© Musée Rodin, Paris: 103
© Musées de la Ville de Rouen/C. Lancien, C. Loisel: 45
© Musées du Mans/Conservation: Le Mans, Musée de Tessé: 145
© The Museum of Modern Art, New York/Scala, Florence, 2011: 119
© The National Gallery, London, Dist. RMN-GP/National Gallery Photographic Department: 18, 171
© National Media Museum/Science & Society Picture Library/All rights reserved: 40 l, 40 r
© National Media Museum/SSPL:170, 187, 211, 212, 214 t, 214 b, 215
© Patrice Schmidt: 105
© Petit Palais/Roger-Viollet: 202
© The Philadelphia Museum of Art/Art Resource/Scala, Florence: 42
© Préfecture de Police/All rights reserved: 167
© Rheinisches Bildarchiv Köln: 64, 78, 81
© RMN-GP/All rights reserved: 111
© RMN-GP/Daniel Arnaudet: 13, 163, 223, 225
© RMN-GP (Domaine de Chantilly)/Harry Bréjat: 21
© RMN-GP/Franck Raux: 160
© RMN-GP/Gérard Blot: 146, 186, 222, 245, 249
© RMN-GP/Hervé Lewandowski: 10, 15
© RMN-GP/Michèle Bellot: 208 l
© RMN-GP (Musée d'Orsay)/All rights reserved: 63, 168, 231, 291; Béatrice Hatala: 238; Gérard Blot: 243; Gérard Blot/Hervé Lewandowski: 61; Hervé Lewandowski: 72, 94, 117, 127, 128, 129, 132 t, 136, 137, 139, 142, 147, 183, 189, 190 r, 205, 210, 240, 255, 262, 279, 280 l, 281 r, 284, 295; Jean-Gilles Berizzi: 209; Michel Urtado: 252; Michèle Bellot: 134; Patrice Schmidt: 112, 157; René-Gabriel Ojéda: 82, 83, 114, 174, 175, 306; Thierry Le Mage: 247.
© RMN-GP (Musée du Louvre)/Gérard Blot: 159 l; Hervé Lewandowski: 44, 152 l, 154; Stéphane Maréchalle: 179; Thierry Le Mage: 219.
© RMN-GP/Patrice Schmidt: 206
© RMN-GP/Philippe Bernard: 17 r, 118
© RMN-GP/René-Gabriel Ojéda: 182, 248
© RMN-GP/Thierry Le Mage: 113 l, 233 r
© The Royal Collection 2012, Her Majesty Queen Elizabeth II: 161
© Ruskin Foundation (Ruskin Library, Lancaster University): 138
© Saint Louis Art Museum, Museum Purchase: 277 r
© Service photographique de la ville de Boulogne sur mer: 125
© Société française de photographie /All rights reserved: 36, 39, 130, 155, 156, 181, 204 l
© STC, Ville de Toulouse: 90 t
© Teylers Museum Haarlem, The Netherlands: 108
© The Trustees of the British Museum: 53
© Ville de Chalon-sur-Saône, France, Musée Nicéphore Niépce: 32
© Ville de Nantes/Musée des Beaux-Arts/photograph A. Guillard: 204 c
© The Wallace Collection, London, Dist. RMN-GP/The Trustees of the Wallace Collection: 31